IFIP Advances in Information and Communication Technology 642

IFIP – The International Federation for Information Processing

IFIP was founded in 1960 under the auspices of UNESCO, following the first World Computer Congress held in Paris the previous year. A federation for societies working in information processing, IFIP's aim is two-fold: to support information processing in the countries of its members and to encourage technology transfer to developing nations. As its mission statement clearly states:

> *IFIP is the global non-profit federation of societies of ICT professionals that aims at achieving a worldwide professional and socially responsible development and application of information and communication technologies.*

IFIP is a non-profit-making organization, run almost solely by 2500 volunteers. It operates through a number of technical committees and working groups, which organize events and publications. IFIP's events range from large international open conferences to working conferences and local seminars.

The flagship event is the IFIP World Computer Congress, at which both invited and contributed papers are presented. Contributed papers are rigorously refereed and the rejection rate is high.

As with the Congress, participation in the open conferences is open to all and papers may be invited or submitted. Again, submitted papers are stringently refereed.

The working conferences are structured differently. They are usually run by a working group and attendance is generally smaller and occasionally by invitation only. Their purpose is to create an atmosphere conducive to innovation and development. Refereeing is also rigorous and papers are subjected to extensive group discussion.

Publications arising from IFIP events vary. The papers presented at the IFIP World Computer Congress and at open conferences are published as conference proceedings, while the results of the working conferences are often published as collections of selected and edited papers.

IFIP distinguishes three types of institutional membership: Country Representative Members, Members at Large, and Associate Members. The type of organization that can apply for membership is a wide variety and includes national or international societies of individual computer scientists/ICT professionals, associations or federations of such societies, government institutions/government related organizations, national or international research institutes or consortia, universities, academies of sciences, companies, national or international associations or federations of companies.

More information about this series at https://link.springer.com/bookseries/6102

Don Passey · Denise Leahy ·
Lawrence Williams · Jaana Holvikivi ·
Mikko Ruohonen (Eds.)

Digital Transformation of Education and Learning - Past, Present and Future

IFIP TC 3 Open Conference on Computers in Education, OCCE 2021
Tampere, Finland, August 17–20, 2021
Proceedings

Springer

Editors
Don Passey
Lancaster University
Lancaster, UK

Lawrence Williams
Technology, Pedagogy and Education Association
London, UK

Mikko Ruohonen
University of Tampere
Tampere, Finland

Denise Leahy
Trinity College Dublin
Dublin, Ireland

Jaana Holvikivi
Samtaim Ltd.
Helsinki, Finland

ISSN 1868-4238 ISSN 1868-422X (electronic)
IFIP Advances in Information and Communication Technology
ISBN 978-3-030-97985-0 ISBN 978-3-030-97986-7 (eBook)
https://doi.org/10.1007/978-3-030-97986-7

This Springer imprint is published by the registered company Springer Nature Switzerland AG
The registered company address is: Gewerbestrasse 11, 6330 Cham, Switzerland

Preface

This volume contains selected papers from the Open Conference on Computers in Education (OCCE 2021), organized by Working Group (WG) 3.4 of the IFIP Technical Committee 3: Education (TC3) and supported by its other working groups. The conference was run as a hybrid conference, and this event pioneered this form of practice for IFIP and TC3. The online facilities were all run from the host organization, and the onsite element was held in Tampere, Finland, from August 17–20, 2021, hosted and supported by the University of Tampere. The conference was open to researchers, policy makers, educators, and practitioners worldwide. The conference title, which was also selected as the book title, Digital Transformation of Education and Learning – Past, Present and Future, reflects the ongoing commitment to (and current interests in) research and practice in learning and technology that members of TC3 and its working groups have fostered over many years, and continue to nurture today. Submissions to the conference were invited to address the following key themes:

- Digital education in schools, universities, and other educational institutions
- National policies and plans for digital competence
- Learning with digital technologies
- Learning about digital technologies and computing

Altogether, 42 submissions of full and short papers, symposia, and system presentations were received and reviewed by an International Program Committee and additional reviewers in a double-blind peer review process. Among these submissions were 30 full and short papers, from which 24 were accepted for publication in the volume at hand. The overall acceptance rate was 80%. Each of these papers was reviewed by at least three reviewers. The papers in this book arise from contributions from (in alphabetical order) Australia, Austria, the Czech Republic, Denmark, Estonia, Finland, Germany, Ghana, India, Italy, Japan, Latvia, Lithuania, Portugal, Serbia, Slovakia, Spain, Sweden, and the UK, which reflects the conference's success in bringing together and networking experts from many countries worldwide.

The book is structured into four topical sections. There are nine papers in section 1 (Digital education across educational institutions). These cover aspects of teacher education, primary and secondary education, and then further and higher education. They are ordered in that sequence and offer new findings relating to the conference theme of "Digital Transformation of Education and Learning - Past, Present and Future". The first paper by Borukhovich-Weis et al. presents a model of digitalization-related competencies for teacher education, developed by a working group on digitalization in teacher education (WG DidL) at the University of Duisburg-Essen. Next, Černochová and Selcuk present an interesting investigation into primary education student teachers' perceptions of computational thinking using Bebras tasks. Kalaš and Horvathova then present the latest developments in their Emil school coding project and identify a set of related operations that primary pupils should learn in any particular year. Following this, the paper by Williams and Mead outlines a creative approach to the teaching of Python in secondary schools, giving worked examples of coding practice. The next two papers look at social disadvantage and inclusion. Saito contends that educational support to develop socially disadvantaged young people's digital skills and competencies has a positive impact on digital citizenship, while Cranmer and Lewin report on early findings from a research project carried out in North West England that identifies challenges in relation to the development and implementation of inclusive digital pedagogies. Batur and Brinda's paper follows, which reports on a study about students' difficulties and misconceptions in introductory programming, in the context of game design, while Corinna Mößlacher et al. look at ways to understand, and to encourage, school students' interest in computer science, through workshops and contests. A final paper on practical teaching projects, using Python, follows, in which Weigend outlines some starter projects in Python programming classes at university level.

There are seven papers in section 2 (National policies and plans for digital competence). These are also ordered and report on new insights relating to past, present, and future policy and practice in computing and digital competence in a number of different countries, reflecting the wide international scope of the book. Tatnall begins by presenting a history of the development of computing in Australia over the past fifty years. The next paper by Niemelä et al. summarizes the current situation regarding the introduction of computational thinking concepts and competencies into compulsory education in two Nordic and two Baltic countries. Following this, Fluck and Girgla provide an Australian perspective on the changing computing curricula in eight states and territories, while Kakeshita et al. from the Information Processing Society of Japan (IPSJ) present a report on their curriculum standards strategy, from the standpoint of both the academic and professional communities of computing in Japan. Castro et al. next present an analysis of contemporary, structured, and connected pedagogical approaches to the teaching of digital proficiency/fluency in 21st-century digital literacy. Following this paper, Akayuure describes Vclass, an online project for mathematics delivery at a university in Ghana, assessing the strengths and weaknesses, and ultimately validating it as a means to enhance future students' learning. Finally, Chetti et al. outline the development of digital technology to advance the teaching of smart agriculture in India.

There are five papers in section 3 (Learning with digital technologies). Initially, Andresen looks at vocational education in Denmark during school shutdown, focussing on emergency remote teaching and its implications. Then Aoki et al. analyze practical examples of a real-time online class on 'agriculture in space', using the collaborative learning tool "Digital Diamond Mandala Matrix". Opel and Netzer next describe AsTRA, a project to develop a comprehensive system to acknowledge the prior knowledge of computer science students. One of the goals is to promote permeability between vocational and higher education in computer science. Following this paper, Rötkönen et al. report on a trial of a tele-immersive platform (TIP) with elementary school 6th grade learners (12–13-year-olds) working on an environmental study lesson. They show that the 3D TIP technology has the critical potential to overcome psychological strains due to physical distance in online education. Finally, Pasterk et al. report on DigiFit4All, a project to develop a platform for POOCs (Personalized Open

Online Courses), including open teaching and learning resources, for both pre-higher and higher education.

There are three papers in the last section, section 4 (Management issues). These offer views on educational management, including a history of the significant role of IFIP TC3. Kadijevich et al. provide results of an initial study of what kinds of e-assessment feedback is important to students at university level, with suggestions for further research. Vartiainen suggests new understandings for management on how organizations may learn and fare under uncertainty, volatility, and transitioning to digital collaboration. Finally, Osorio and Banzato analyze the contribution of IFIP TC3 WG 3.7 to the development of the field of 'Information Technology in Educational Management'.

We are pleased to offer leading-edge work through this choice of papers that we hope will be of interest to further inspire your own work.

January 2022

Don Passey
Denise Leahy
Lawrence Williams
Jaana Holvikivi
Mikko Ruohonen

Organization

Program Committee Chairs

Jaana Holvikivi	Samtaim Ltd., Finland
Mikko Ruohonen	University of Tampere, Finland

Program Committee

Denise Leahy	Trinity College Dublin, Ireland
Margaret Leahy	Dublin City University, Ireland
Peter Micheuz	University of Klagenfurt, Austria
Javier Osorio	University of Las Palmas de Gran Canaria, Spain
Don Passey	Lancaster University, UK
Lawrence Williams	Technology, Pedagogy and Education Association, UK

Local Organizing Committee Chair

Mikko Ruohonen	Tampere University, Finland

Local Organizing Committee

Petteri Aaltonen	Tampere University, Finland
Mari Ainasoja	Tampere University, Finland
Erkki Brotkin	Tampere University, Finland
Maija Ekosaari	Tampere University, Finland
Tomas Front	Justin Case Productions Ltd., Finland
Kaisa Kurki	Tampere University, Finland
Harri Laitinen	Tampere University, Finland
Pia Niemelä	Tampere University, Finland
Eero Nukari	Howspace Ltd., Finland
Anneli Östman	Tampere University, Finland
Manu Pärssinen	Alasinmedia Ltd., Finland
Isabella Presnal	Tampere University of Applied Sciences, Finland
Elina Tiainen	Tampere University, Finland
Katriina Vartiainen	Tampere University, Finland
Wilma Wibom	Funzi Ltd., Finland

Additional Reviewers

Bent Andresen	Aarhus University, Denmark
Rosa Bottino	Italian National Research Council, Italy
Miroslava Černochová	Charles University in Prague, Czech Republic

Sue Cranmer	Lancaster University, UK
Keiji Emi	Kyoto College of Graduate Studies for Informatics, Japan
Gerald Futschek	Vienna University of Technology, Austria
David Gibson	Curtin University, Australia
Monique Grandbastien	University of Lorraine, France
Djordje Kadijevich	Institute for Educational Research, Serbia
Tetsuro Kakeshita	Saga University, Japan
Ivan Kalaš	Comenius University, Slovakia
Anton Knierzinger	Pädagogische Hochschule der Diözese Linz, Austria
Mart Laanpere	Tallinn University, Estonia
Angela Siew Hoong Lee	Sunway University, Malaysia
Cathy Lewin	Manchester Metropolitan University, UK
Wolfgang Müller	University of Education Weingarten, Germany
Simone Opel	FernUniversität in Hagen, Germany
Arnold Pears	KTH Royal Institute of Technology, Sweden
Christophe Reffay	University of Franche-Comté, France
Sindre Røsvik	Giske Kommune, Norway
Toshinori Saito	Seisa University, Japan
Eric Sanchez	University of Geneva, Switzerland
Hasan Selcuk	University of Latvia, Latvia
Riana Steyn	University of Pretoria, South Africa
Alan Strickley	CRIA Technologies, UK
Arthur Tatnall	Victoria University, Australia
Katriina Vartiainen	Tampere University, Finland
Maina Wagíokò	Aga Khan Academies, Kenya
Mary Webb	King's College London, UK
Michael Weigend	University of Muenster, Germany

Contents

National Policies and Plans for Digital Competence

Learning with Digital Technologies

Digital Education Across Educational Institutions

An Integrated Model of Digitalisation-Related Competencies in Teacher Education

Swantje Borukhovich-Weis(✉), Torsten Brinda,
Veronika Burovikhina, Michael Beißwenger, Björn Bulizek,
Katharina Cyra, Inga Gryl, David Tobinski, and Mike Barkmin

University of Duisburg-Essen, Essen, Germany
swantje.borukhovich-weis@uni-due.de

Abstract. This paper presents a model of digitalisation-related competencies for teacher education, developed by a working group on digitalisation in teacher education (WG DidL) at the University of Duisburg-Essen. Currently, there are various models available that outline the competencies teachers should develop for being equipped to work in a digital world. These approaches often mention various, widely applicable digitalisation-related competences that teachers are meant to acquire, or they are based on a limited or only implicit understanding of digitalisation. The aim of the presented model is to contribute to the discussion of how to best integrate existing models. It is based on an integrated understanding of digitalisation-related competencies that encompass teaching and learning with digital media, as well as learning about digitalisation as a subject matter in its own right. At the center of the model are generally formulated competency goals for teaching and learning, for professional engagement, and for reflective, critical-constructive teaching practice. The potential for achieving these goals is then illustrated by means of interdisciplinary and/or subject-specific examples. In this way, the model can also be applied to specific subject areas and to their teaching methodologies.

Keywords: Digitalisation-related competencies · Teacher education · Frameworks of digital competence · Reference models

1 Introduction: Background and Objectives

In order to systematically promote the implementation of digitalisation-related[1] competencies[2] in teacher education programmes at the University of Duisburg-Essen (UDE), there are numerous initiatives at the university, faculty, and institute levels. The working

[1] "Digital competencies" is the standard term used in most publications. Since competencies describe abilities and skills, which are not digital per se, the authors use "digitalisation-related competencies" instead.

[2] Competencies refer to the cognitive abilities and skills that individuals can learn in order to solve problems, as well as to the associated motivational, volitional, and social readiness to use such solutions successfully and responsibly in various situations [1].

Published by Springer Nature Switzerland AG 2022
D. Passey et al. (Eds.): OCCE 2021, IFIP AICT 642, pp. 3–14, 2022.
https://doi.org/10.1007/978-3-030-97986-7_1

group on digitalisation in teacher education (WG DidL)[3] supports these initiatives and at the same time develops them further for teacher education courses and for interdisciplinary cooperation between all subject methodologies at the UDE. The WG was initiated in 2017 with the participation of representatives of several school types (primary, lower and upper secondary), subjects (Computer Science, German and *Sachunterricht*[4]), Educational Sciences, and the Center for Teacher Education (ZLB). The WG works in close cooperation with representatives of other school subjects and Educational Sciences, for example through Think Tanks. The aim of the WG is to prepare student teachers adequately for their future careers by fostering their media methodology, digitalisation and computer science-related competencies across all subjects and school types and implementing them in their respective curricula. As a first step, the WG developed an Integrated Model of Digitalisation-Related Competencies for Teacher Education (hereinafter referred to as the Integrated Model). This paper is based on the German publication of the model [2] and aims at making the ideas and concepts available to a wider audience and thereby to contribute to a larger international discussion.

Currently, in Germany, there are various models and descriptive matrixes available that outline the vision for the development of digitalisation-related competencies among teachers. An analysis of existing models has led to the identification of specific focus areas and, as a result, to the need to work on further developments with regard to an integrated model:
(1) Existing models for describing digitalisation-related competencies of teachers address various aspects:

a. The much-cited Technological Pedagogical Content Knowledge (TPACK) Model [3], for example, emphasises the need for teachers to acquire and appropriately link subject-specific competencies for their respective subjects (content), pedagogical competencies, and technological or digitalisation-related competencies in order to teach in an environment shaped by technology or digitalisation.
b. The Digital Competence Framework for Educators (DigCompEdu) [4] is a European framework model for describing digitalisation-related competencies of teachers. It refers to the Digital Competence Framework for Citizens (DigComp) [5], which defines general digitalisation-related competencies of citizens. The DigCompEdu [4] as well as the German framework for North Rhine-Westphalia (NRW) called "Teachers in the Digitalized World – Orientational Framework for Teacher Education and Teacher Training in North Rhine-Westphalia"[5] [6], focus more specifically on teaching in an environment characterised by digital media as well as on the professional commitment in this regard (own professional development, school development, etc.).

[3] For more information about the working group, see http://udue.de/didlag.

[4] *Sachunterricht* (Primary Social and Physical Science) is s subject taught in primary school that combines social science and natural (physical) science education.

[5] Hereafter abbreviated as Orientational Framework NRW. Given the federal structure in Germany, the Orientational Framework NRW [6] forms a relevant basis in the German state North Rhine-Westphalia.

A model specifically tailored to the requirements of teacher education should integrate the aforementioned aspects in a suitable manner, and at the same time establish explicit, exemplary links to the content of the various subjects and their competency requirements, as well as outline associated classroom practices, pedagogies and appropriate teaching approaches. The authors consider this to be indispensable for the presentation of the subject-specific aspects of digitalisation-related competencies in teacher education programmes. They also view this to be necessary for the coordination between the different subject areas, for implementing these competencies in the respective curricula, and for communicating them within the framework of the subject-specific content and subject teaching methodology areas of teacher education programmes.

(2) Existing models for describing digitalisation-related competencies of teachers are often based on a limited or implicit understanding of these competencies: Some of the existing models, such as DigComp [5] and the German *KMK* strategy called "Educational in the Digital World" [7][6], outline digitalisation-related competencies of learners and put a special emphasis on teaching and learning with digital media. These models neglect to address digitalisation as a subject matter in its own right: analysis, design, reflection on technological and media structures and digital systems as well as their socio-cultural impact. When specifying the digitalisation-related competencies to be acquired by teachers, reference is made to the competencies to be acquired by learners. DigCompEdu [4], for example, refers to DigComp [5]. In some cases, for example, in the Orientational Framework NRW [6], the relevant competencies are not specified in any detail. This means that – as with the learner-related competencies – the understanding of digitalisation-related competencies has a one-sided emphasis, or it is not clear which aspects of digitalisation are to be used as a basis for acquiring teaching-related or other professional competencies.

The Integrated Model presented in this paper therefore integrates selected aspects of various models and descriptive matrixes into one model (see Sects. 2, 3, 4) and is explicitly based on an integrated understanding of digitalisation-related competencies.

The models considered were integrated in terms of their structural elements and explicit competency goals. In Sect. 2 the structural elements of the existing models under consideration for the integration are specified; in Sect. 3 their integration and the resulting structural model are described. Section 4 presents the result of the integration of the competency goals, which also includes their implementation and instantiation in practice from a transdisciplinary, interdisciplinary and subject-specific perspective. Section 5 gives an insight into the implementation of the model in university teacher training at the UDE.

[6] The competency descriptions contained in the KMK strategy [7] are based on the ones defined in the DigComp [5]. KMK stands for *Kultusministerkonferenz*. It is the "Standing Conference of the Ministers of Education and Cultural Affairs". The KMK strategy [7] serves as a reference framework for the development of national concepts for teacher education in various states in Germany.

2 Theoretical Basis of the Integrated Model

The core concern of the model is to bring together existing models and related discourses into an integrated model. The components of the integration are explained in the next section.

The Revised TPACK Model [8] was chosen as the structural basis, which is a further development of the original TPACK Model [3]. It describes content, pedagogy and technology as overlapping core knowledge areas for teaching in a technology-driven environment. Relevant knowledge categories for teachers are derived from the respective intersections. In the Revised TPACK Model [8] the knowledge that learners bring into the classroom is also specified, as well as the context of classroom practice and teaching methods, which, although already identified as relevant in TPACK [3], is now more nuanced (interpersonal/intrapersonal, cultural/institutional as well as physical/technological contexts are specified).

The aim of the Integrated Model is not to re-describe content-specific or teaching methodology knowledge as applicable to teacher education without a closer reference to digitalisation, because these areas of knowledge can already be found in the original TPACK Model [3]. To see how these are implemented, reference is made, for example, to the common requirements of the federal states for the subject-specific and educational requirements in teacher education programmes [9, 10].

Since the concern of the Integrated Model is to specify digitalisation-related competencies of teachers, some basic decisions are outlined below:

1. The area of technological knowledge, including its internal structuring, is taken as a basis from the TPACK Model [3], since digitalisation is assigned to this area. Due to the intersections of the technological knowledge domain with the content knowledge and the pedagogical knowledge domains in the original TPACK Model [3], the following four subdomains of teachers' technological knowledge can be identified, all of which are relevant for a model of digitalisation-related competency of teachers:

   a. Technological Knowledge, (TK) in the TPACK Model [3],
   b. Technological Content Knowledge (TCK),
   c. Technological Pedagogical Knowledge (TPK),
   d. Technological Pedagogical Content Knowledge (TPACK).
2. The knowledge areas in the TPACK Model [3] are interpreted as competency areas by the authors following the current competency orientation. The re-interpretation of the knowledge areas as competency areas is done on the basis of the TPACK structural model. The authors do not want to equate competencies with knowledge. Rather, this re-interpretation implies the transfer of knowledge elements into matching competency goals.
3. Since this article is about teachers' digitalisation-related and not technological competencies, the above-mentioned subdivision of technological knowledge in the TPACK Model [3] into sub-areas (see point 1.) including the re-interpretation of knowledge areas as competency areas (see point 2.) is taken as a basis. However, as a further step, the term "technological" is replaced with "digitalisation-related". This is in no way intended to imply that these terms should be used synonymously, only that all of the knowledge or – as interpreted here as – competency areas

defined by the TPACK Model [3] can be applied analogously to the digitalisation discussion. This idea is inspired by the DPaCK Model [11] (Fig. 1).

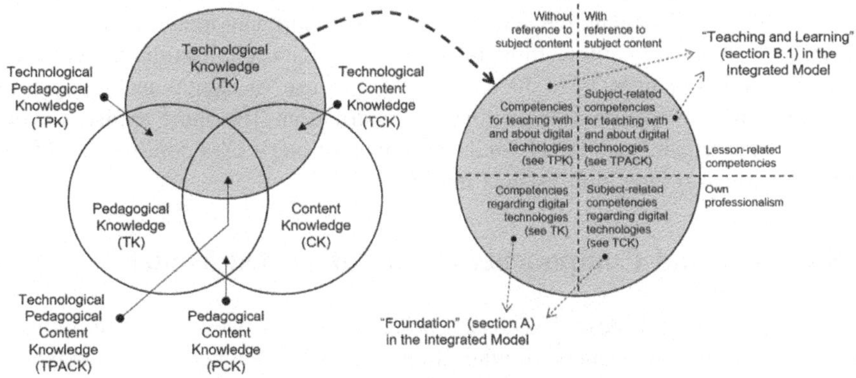

Fig. 1. Excerpt from the development of the integrated model of digitalisation-related competencies for teacher education (own representation[7] including [3])

4. Since the context categories defined in the Revised TPACK Model [8] can also be applied analogously to the digitalisation discussion, they are included in the integrated model

In addition, the Integrated Model uses relevant components from other models already mentioned (see Sect. 1):

5. DigCompEdu [4], the *KMK* strategy [7] as well as the Orientational Framework NRW [5] essentially specify teaching and learning with digital media in a subject area and beyond (included in the TPACK Model [3] as TPK and TPACK, see above). They are reified for these areas in the Integrated Model. However, an integrated understanding of digitalisation-related competencies requires an expansion of this competency area to include teaching about digitalisation as a subject (see Fig. 2, subsection B.1).
6. Furthermore, both the DigCompEdu [4] and the Orientational Framework NRW [6] describe the professional engagement of teachers with regard to digitalisation, e.g. in the areas of school development, cooperation, or professional development. This aspect is integrated as a separate area of competency (see Fig. 2, subsection B.2).
7. In order to reify the digitalisation-related basis for teaching processes and professional engagement, the Frankfurt Triangle on "Education in the Digitally Networked World" [12] is used. This model integrates perspectives from information technology, computer science education, media studies and media education. It differentiates between technological and media structures and functions, social and cultural impacts, and interaction (user options, social practices, identity construction), each of which is to be developed through analysis, reflection, and design (see Fig. 2, competency are A). The Frankfurt Triangle [12] is interpreted here as a

[7] This is a translation of a figure used in the German paper, see [2], p. 47.

meta-model over various existing models with the intention of integrating the competencies and concepts of, for example, computer science education (e.g. [13]) contained in the *KMK* strategy [7]. In this respect, it is considered by the authors to be suitable for addressing the need for further development identified in Sect. 1. By leaning on this model, the authors intent to stress that digitalisation-related teaching and learning practices must focus on both the use of digital technologies as a medium and digitalisation as a subject of instruction. The same applies to professional engagement, such as school development or one's own continuing education, which must also take both aspects into account.

3 Structure and Components of the Integrated Model

The Integrated Model describes basic prerequisites as well as institutional and instructional aspects of teachers' digitalisation-related competencies. The metaphor of a house was used for the presentation of the model in order to express, on the one hand, that all considerations of digitalisation-related teaching and learning (B.1) and professional engagement (B.2) of teachers must be based on one common foundation (an integrated understanding of digitalisation (A)). On the other hand, the metaphor is meant to illustrate that any critical-constructive reflection (C) on the overall process is to be placed over and above the aforementioned components, like a roof would be placed over a house. The inner core of the house is represented by the promotion of subject-specific and digitalisation-related competencies of learners – all surrounding aspects are aligned with these (see Fig. 2).

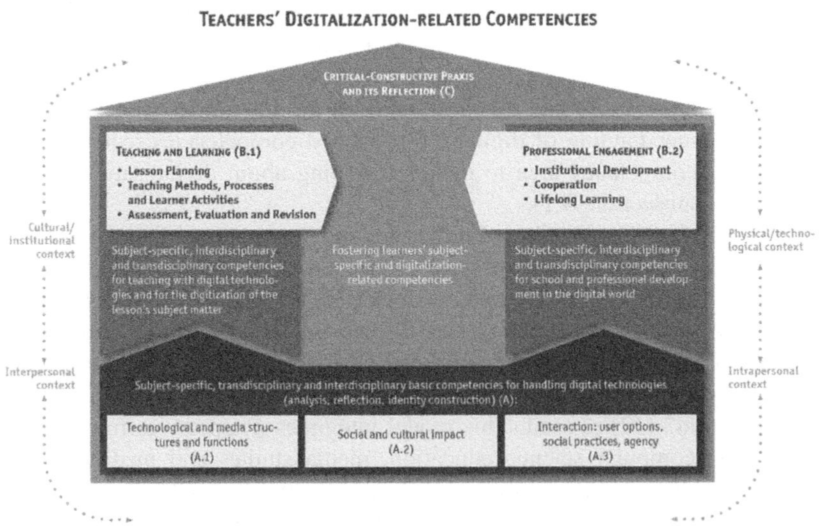

Fig. 2. Integrated Model of Digitalisation-Related Competencies for Teacher Education (own representation[8] including elements from [3, 4, 8, 12])

[8] This is a translation of the German model, see [2], p. 49.

The foundation of the house, **competency area (A)**, comprises the knowledge areas TK and TCK of the Revised TPACK Model [8] (see above). The interdisciplinary and transdisciplinary basic competencies are specified in subsections A.1, A.2 and A.3 of the Frankfurt Triangle [12]. **Subsection A.1** combines information technology and media structures and functions and thus focuses on a fundamental understanding of digital technologies and specific digital artifacts as well as the ability to participate in shaping them. **Subsection A.2** focuses on how objects of the digitalised world interact with and impact social and cultural aspects (and vice versa) and thus addresses diverse phenomena and change processes that occur in connection with digitalisation. Finally, **subsection A.3** focuses on aspects of the functional application of digital systems and media, their integration into social practices (such as teaching processes), and related aspects of identity formation. According to the subsections A1, A2 and A3 of the model, teachers and other professionals have digitalisation-related competency when they are able to analyse, reflect on, and to a certain extent help create or shape objects or phenomena of the digitalised world (e.g., data privacy, social media, virtual labs, smart home systems, self-driving vehicles) or when they are able to reconstruct them as relevant in school settings. Since the aforementioned explanations are closely connected with related subject-specific aspects (knowledge area TCK in the TPACK Model [3]), the areas TK and TCK have been combined here to form a common foundation (A).

Competency area B is subdivided into **Teaching and Learning (B.1)** and **Professional Engagement (B.2).** Competency area B is based on the DigCompEdu [4]. Since within teacher education the DigCompEdu [4] forms the counterpart of the DigComp [5], the authors consider it appropriate to lean on this model. In the DigCompEdu [4], the area of teaching and learning is divided into several separate subareas of competency: the corresponding areas are referred to as digital resources, evaluation, learner orientation, and the fostering of learners' digital competencies. In the model presented here, redundancies were identified, removed, and related competency goals combined. In the process, greater emphasis was placed on digitalisation-related subject-specific teaching and learning.

Subsection B.1 specifies the areas TPK and TPACK in the Revised-TPACK-Model [8]. Included here are competencies that relate to teaching with and about digital technologies in the respective subjects (TPACK). In addition, related interdisciplinary and transdisciplinary competencies (TPK) are also included. The area TPK includes transdisciplinary media and computer technology education aspects, for example when subject-integrated teaching and learning questions are addressed, such as algorithms or data processing, according to the *KMK* strategy [7] or the Media Competence Framework NRW [14]. In accordance with the understanding of digitalisation outlined in area A, area B.1 explicitly integrates teaching and learning with digital media and establishes the examination of digitalisation as a subject of instruction.

Subsection B.2, which includes aspects of institutional development, cooperation with colleagues and persons beyond school, and one's own lifelong learning, is outlined in the DigCompEdu [4] and in the NRW Orientational Framework [6]. In the Revised TPACK Model [8], this area is specified only in the surrounding context, which focuses on framework conditions for digitalisation-related teacher practice. Due to the practical relevance of such a framework, the context from the Revised TPACK Model [8] was included in the Integrated Model.

The institutional and cultural context as well as the network of actors involved in the process of teaching and learning (interpersonal context) influence teachers' practice. However, this scope of influence is not to be regarded as fundamentally unchangeable. Therefore, the competency areas of development (such as institutional development or collaboration) are specified. This also applies to the intrapersonal context, which includes teachers' own digitalisation-related attitudes, beliefs and competencies, which should be continuously developed through ongoing training. The physical/technological context, which refers to the systems and types of equipment available for teaching, can also be improved and adapted through appropriate media pedagogical and IT competencies, with the responsible persons ensuring that such equipment is improved and adapted in appropriate ways for the respective schools. As such, the various context categories describe relevant framework conditions for digitalisation-related teacher practice. The subsection B.2 focuses on the development of teachers' skills within these context categories as well as on their ability to co-shape them.

In **competency area C** (in the overarching roof of the model), practice is particularly emphasised once again: Within the framework of critical-constructive practice, the view should be directed not only to the overall system, which means in particular teaching-related and other professional practice of teachers at the respective school and its environment as well as the network of actors working in it. Personal involvement in and commitment to the overall system should be emphasised as well. Due to the importance of reflexivity (e.g. [15, 16]), the roof of the model expresses those competency goals that are aimed at reflection and the readiness to appreciate digitalisation for teaching and learning, school development, and one's own professionalisation.

Competency areas B and **C** are explained in detail in Sect. 4. For **competency area A**, it was decided not to specify it further here. Instead, the authors refer to the Frankfurt Triangle [12] as an interdisciplinary coordination basis. Since the Frankfurt Triangle [12] as a meta-model aims to encompass aspects of teaching and learning with and via digital technology as well as ITC education for all, reference is made to existing models for more detail, such as the *KMK* strategy [7], the NRW Media Competency Framework [14] and models of Computer Science education for all (e.g. [13]).

4 The Competency Areas and Competency Goals in Detail

The **competency areas B** and **C**, which form **the core of the Integrated Model**, are specified in the form of generally formulated competency goals. The basis for the specification of these general competency goals was an analysis of goals stipulated in already published models for education in the digitalised world, with an explicit focus on teachers' competencies: DigCompEdu [4], Orientational Framework NRW [6], the position paper "Fachliche Bildung in der digitalen Welt" [Professional education in the digital world] [17]. In addition, the *KMK* strategy [7] was used as a reference point for defining the competencies to be developed by learners that teachers, in turn, must have at a minimum. The considerations underlying the structure of the Integrated Model outlined above (see Sects. 2 and 3) thus formed a parallel, closely associated step for defining competency goals, the result of which is exemplified by some extracts from the appendix of the workshop paper [2], as shown below (see Fig. 3).

The final formulation in the Integrated Model is based on the work done by the WG DidL on various preliminary models (e.g. [18]) as well as on feedback that the WG received in exchanges with colleagues representing various other subjects and disciplines at the UDE.

The **general competency goals** are differentiated on a case-by-case basis from an interdisciplinary, transdisciplinary and/or subject-specific perspective.[9] The **interdisciplinary and transdisciplinary formulations** are based on Educational Science (especially Media Education) and, in part, on Computer Science, while the **subject-specific formulations** (initially) cover the subjects Computer Science, German and *Sachunterricht* (the three subjects represented in the WG DidL) in the German version of the model [2]; the planning of expansion through the inclusion of other subject methodologies is under way.

The formulations are not to be understood as subordinate competency goals. They are rather examples that illustrate how the general competency goals can be interpreted from a transdisciplinary, interdisciplinary, and/or subject-specific perspective. Figure 3 shows how the three competency areas, namely **Teaching and Learning (B.1)**, **Professional Engagement (B.2)** and **Critical-Constructive Praxis and its Reflection (C)**, could be operationalised from a transdisciplinary, interdisciplinary and/or subject-specific perspective.

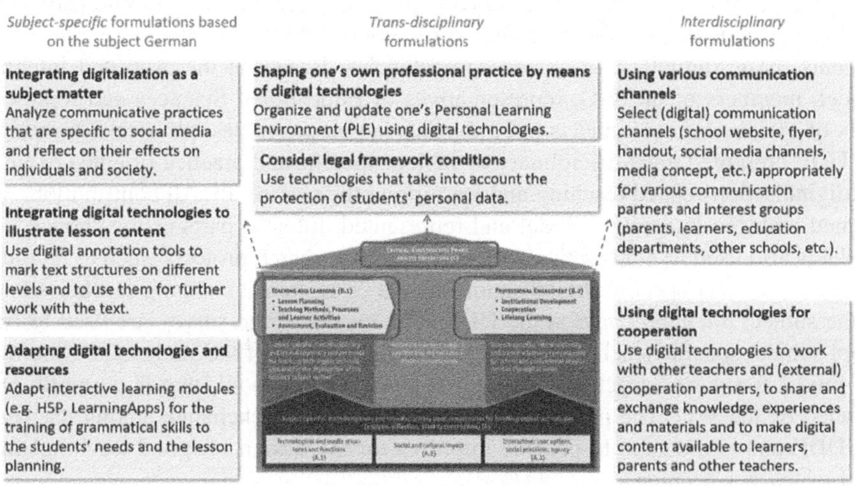

Fig. 3. Examples of how the Integrated Model could be operationalised in selected competency areas (own representation including elements from [2–4, 8, 12])

[9] Subject-specific formulations refer to observable and definable characteristics of teaching and learning in a specific subject. Interdisciplinary formulations refer analogously to a group of subjects or to teaching and learning in all subjects. Trans-disciplinary formulations go beyond teaching and refer, for example, to school development, communication or exchange with colleagues or parents, and the development of one's own digitalisation-related competencies.

The transdisciplinary, interdisciplinary and/or subject-specific formulations represent a distinction from, and at the same time a further development of the models and description matrixes mentioned in Sect. 1. The group of authors sees this as an important building block for the implementation of the fostering of digitalisation-related competencies in teacher education, as the examples serve as a guide for the practical implementation of the listed competency goals. In addition, this takes into account the fact that digitalisation-related teaching and learning should, above all, be formulated from a subject-specific perspective [17]. The examples are to be read on a case-by-case basis either as suggestions for possible implementation in university teacher training, in the classroom or as formulation sketches for the competencies to be taught.

5 Implementation and Conclusion

In this paper existing models and descriptive frameworks of teachers' digitalisation-related competencies were analysed. By focusing on specific parts of these approaches, the need for further development with regard to a model specifically tailored to the requirements of teacher education was identified. On this basis, an Integrated Model of digitalisation-related competencies for teacher education was developed.

The model can be used as a basis for research projects and teacher education. At the UDE, the model served as framework for an "Interdisciplinary Lecture on 'Education in the Digital World'". The lecture was designed and organised by the WG DidL for all teacher students at the UDE and piloted in summer 2021. The lecture aims to foster students' basic digitalisation-related competencies. Based on the proposed Integrated Model, members of the WG, representatives of Educational Sciences and representatives of various school subjects (e.g. physics, language studies, physical education) at the UDE presented trans-disciplinary or subject-specific and practice-oriented examples for digitalisation-related teaching and learning in the classroom. All contributions were aligned with the Integrated Model and represented different parts of the "house". The model is also used as a theoretical basis for several research projects, such as an online-survey on subject-specific digitalisation-related competencies among teacher students in the subject *Sachunterricht* at the UDE. The results of the survey are used to better adapt subject-specific teacher training to the requirements of the students. Furthermore, the model forms the structural basis for a good practice pool, that is currently being planned by the WG. The pool opens up opportunities for exchange among teachers at the UDE and is intended to provide impulses for the design of 'good teaching' in the field of teacher training.

In conclusion, the model synthesises existing models and is intended to contribute towards the discussion about the definition and curricular anchoring of digitalisation-related competency goals.

References

1. Weinert, F.: Leistungsmessungen in Schulen – eine umstrittene Selbstverständlichkeit. In: Weinert, F., (ed.) Leistungsmessungen in Schulen, pp. 17–32, Beltz, Weinheim, Germany (2021)
2. Beißwenger, M., et al.: Ein integratives Modell digitalisierungsbezogener Kompetenzen für die Lehramtsausbildung. In: Beißwenger, M., Bulizek, B., Gryl, I., Schacht, F. (eds.) Digitale Innovationen und Kompetenzen in der Lehramtsausbildung, pp. 45–76. Universitätsverband Rhein-Ruhr, Duisburg (2020)
3. Koehler, M., Mishra, P.: What is technological pedagogical content knowledge (TPACK)? Contemp. Issues Technol. Teach. Educ. **9**(1), 60–70 (2009)
4. Redecker, C.: European Framework for the Digital Competence of Educators: DigCompEdu. Publications Office of the European Union, Luxembourg (2017). https://bit.ly/2PKiCYL. Accessed 22 Mar 2021
5. Ferrari, A.: DIGCOMP: A Framework for Developing and Understanding Digital Competence in Europe. European Commission, Luxembourg (2013). https://bit.ly/3uqUDMS. Accessed 22 Mar 2021
6. Eickelmann, B.: Lehrkräfte in der digitalisierten Welt. Orientierungsrahmen für die Lehrerausbildung und Lehrerfortbildung in NRW. Medienberatung NRW, Düsseldorf (2020). https://bit.ly/3dLDt64. Accessed 22 Mar 2021
7. KMK: Strategie der Kultusministerkonferenz "Bildung in der digitalen Welt", KMK, Berlin, Germany (2016). https://bit.ly/2Q3xUb0. Accessed 22 Mar 2021
8. Chai, C.S., Koh, J.H.L., Tsai, C.-C.: A review of technological pedagogical content knowledge. J. Educ. Technol. Soc. **16**(2), 31–51 (2013)
9. KMK: Ländergemeinsame inhaltliche Anforderungen für die Fachwissenschaften und Fachdidaktiken in der Lehrerbildung (Resolution of the KMK of 16/10/2008, in the version of 16/05/2019) (2019). https://bit.ly/2OtmPPS. Accessed 22 Mar 2021
10. KMK: Standards für die Lehrerbildung: Bildungswissenschaften. (Resolution of the KMK of 16/12/2004 in the version of 16/05/2019) (2019). https://bit.ly/2PJlftS. Accessed 22 Mar 2021
11. Huwer, J., Irion, T., Kuntze, S., Schaal, S., Thyssen, C.: Von TPaCK zu DPaCK–Digitalisierung des Unterrichts erfordert mehr als technisches Wissen. MNU **5**, 358–364 (2019)
12. Brinda, T., et al.: Frankfurt-Dreieck zur Bildung in der digital vernetzten Welt - Ein interdisziplinäres Modell. merz - Medien + Erziehung. Zeitschrift für Medienpädagogik **63** (4), 69–75 (2019)
13. Röhner, G. (Leitung), et al.: Gemeinsamer Referenzrahmen Informatik (GeRRI). Mindeststandards für die auf Informatik bezogene Bildung. Empfehlung des MNU-Verbands zur Förderung des MINT-Unterrichts und der Gesellschaft für Informatik e.V. (GI) (2020). https://bit.ly/2Q3y4z8. Accessed 22 Mar 2021
14. Medienberatung NRW: Medienkompetenzrahmen NRW. Münster/Düsseldorf, Germany (2018). https://medienkompetenzrahmen.nrw. Accessed 22 Mar 2021
15. Hermann, H.: Lehrer: Professional—Experte—Autodidakt. In: Apel, H.J., Horn, K.-P., Lundgreen, P., Sandfuchs, U. (eds.) Professionalisierung pädagogischer Berufe im historischen Prozeß, pp. 408–428. Julius Klinkhardt, Bad Heilbrunn (1999)
16. Terhart, E.: Standards für die Lehrerbildung. Eine Expertise für die Kultusministerkonferenz. Universität Münster: Zentrale Koordination Lehrerbildung (ZKL-Texte Nr. 23), Münster (2002)

17. GFD (Gesellschaft für Fachdidaktik): Fachliche Bildung in der digitalen Welt. Positionspapier der Gesellschaft für Fachdidaktik, Hannover/Berlin, Germany (2018). https://bit.ly/3fPYO0P. Accessed 22 Mar 2021
18. Barkmin, M., et al.: Vermittlung digitalisierungsbezogener Kompetenzen an Lehramtsstudierende. Werkstattbericht einer interdisziplinären Arbeitsgruppe. In: Kaspar, K., Becker-Mrotzek, M., Hofhues, S., König, J., Schmeinck, D. (eds.) Bildung, Schule und Digitalisierung, pp. 139–144. Waxmann, Münster (2020)

Primary Education Student Teachers' Perceptions of Computational Thinking Through Bebras Tasks

Miroslava Černochová[1(✉)] and Hasan Selcuk[2]

[1] Faculty of Education, Charles University, Prague, Czech Republic
miroslava.cernochova@pedf.cuni.cz
[2] Faculty of Education, Psychology and Art, University of Latvia, Riga, Latvia

Abstract. This paper describes an investigation of primary education student teachers' perceptions of computational thinking (CT) who participated in a course 'Digital Technologies in Primary Education', and explores what these students consider difficult when developing primary school pupils' CT. In the academic year 2021/22, a revised curriculum will be introduced into Czech primary school education. Instead of 'ICT', 'Informatics' is to be introduced into the curriculum as a new subject at all school levels. Pupils' digital literacy will be formed and developed across all subjects, so all faculties of education in the Czech Republic have paid great attention to the development of primary education student teachers, to prepare them for the planned changes in school practice. Using qualitative methods, the study findings of 66 primary education student teachers (who analysed the Bebras contest for primary school pupils) were that (1) for better understanding of CT, student teachers are required to have sufficient Informatics' knowledge to be able to think computationally, (2) student teachers reported CT is close to mathematical thinking, but these two concepts are not the same, and (3) CT development in primary education requires logical thinking, reading literacy and counting abilities.

Keywords: Primary school student teacher · Computational thinking · Informatics in education · Bebras contest

1 Introduction

Since 2005, the Czech Republic's curriculum for primary and secondary school education has included 'ICT' as a compulsory subject, intending to develop pupils' ICT skills using a computer, working with basic software applications, and searching for information on the Internet. Until now, in most schools, the teaching of 'ICT' is still governed by the curricular document. Many Czech schools have, however, realised the need to prepare pupils for more advanced IT skills, and have thus included topics in informatics (programming, robotics, etc.) into 'ICT'. Such schools understand that the future of society will depend heavily on digitisation and artificial intelligence applications in most areas of the economy, industry, services, health, education, and citizenship. Therefore, for these developments, the young generation can no longer be educated according to the 2007 curriculum.

Published by Springer Nature Switzerland AG 2022
D. Passey et al. (Eds.): OCCE 2021, IFIP AICT 642, pp. 15–27, 2022.
https://doi.org/10.1007/978-3-030-97986-7_2

Under the Government's Digital Education Strategy [12], the Ministry of Education, Youth and Sport of the Czech Republic (MoEYS) decided to revise the curriculum content for ICT. In co-operation with the faculties of education over three years, textbooks and teaching guidelines were developed to introduce the new subject of informatics, and the development of digital literacy across all subjects at all levels of education. In January 2021, the MoEYS published a revised curricular document with two major changes: (1) improving pupils' digital literacy development at all educational stages, and (2) the subject of 'ICT' is replaced by 'Informatics' with new educational content aimed at computational thinking (CT) development. Both changes are radical and are to be put into practice in pre-school, primary and secondary schools by 2021/22, and no later than 1.9.2023 [13].

For faculties preparing teachers, the task is to prepare student teachers for these changes within undergraduate education; especially, to prepare primary education student teachers to develop pupils' CT in the 'new' subject of 'Informatics'. The key topics of this subject are (1) data, information and modelling, (2) algorithmization and programming, (3) information systems, and (4) digital technology.

At Charles University's Faculty of Education, two consecutive obligatory courses, 'Digital Technologies in Primary Education' and 'Didactics of Digital Technology', were included in the second year of the full- and part-time five-year MA study in Primary Education. The first is organised as a set of interactive lectures focused on Papert's constructionist theory, a concept of algorithmisation (searching algorithms, code pictures, the principle of recursion, etc.) and examples of how to develop CT (CSUnplugged activities, Bebras tasks, etc.). The second is organised as a set of practical exercises in robotics (LegoWeDo kit), and programming in Scratch.

This paper reports how primary education student teachers who participated in the course 'Digital Technologies in Primary Education' perceive CT through the Bebras contest tasks' analysis, and what these students identified as difficult, when developing primary school pupils' CT using Bebras tasks, is presented.

Based on the above aims the following research question was formulated:

RQ: How does the analysis of Bebras tasks contribute to better student teachers' understanding of computing and computational thinking in primary school education?

2 Literature Review

Seymour Papert originated the idea of CT when he stated that "certain uses of very powerful computational technology and computational ideas can provide children with new possibilities for learning, thinking, and growing emotionally as well as cognitively" [14, pp. 17–18]. Wing [20, p. 33] followed up on his idea when she introduced the concept of CT as an educational approach that "builds on the power and limits of computing processes, whether they are executed by a human or by machine". Wing [21] states the most important elements are abstraction (the "mental" tool of computing) and automation (using a computer, the "metal" tool of computer scientists) and that "computing is the automation of our abstractions".

Considering that CT has become a prerequisite skill of 21st century learners, Hemmendinger [6, p. 6] argued that the goal of teaching CT to students "to teach them how to think like an economist, a physicist, an artist, and to understand how to use computation to solve their problems, to create, and to discover new questions that can fruitfully be explored". On the other hand, Lu and Fletcher [9] highlighted the importance of teaching CT as in early school education with an emphasis on understanding "computational processes, and not on their manifestations in particular programming languages" and "skills for abstracting and representing information" [9, p. 24]. Wing [20] also stressed that "to reading, writing and arithmetic, we should add computational thinking to every child's analytical ability" [20, p. 33].

Developed countries, such as the USA, Italy, Slovakia, Ireland, UK and including the Czech Republic, have integrated computing in primary school education. There is an increasing need not only for teachers, but also for student teachers to be prepared to integrate CT into their classroom practices. For example, Switzerland recently introduced a national curriculum, "Lehrplan 21", mandating Computer Science Education, the new common curriculum for compulsory education in the 21 German-speaking cantons. To discover how practical the CS Education course organised for student-teachers was, Lamprou and Repenning [8] conducted a study collecting data from more than 600 students who took the course. The research showed that even though pre-service teachers can quickly learn basic programming, the question about learning CT remains open.

With regard to studies focusing on developing primary school student teachers' competence in CT, Jaipal-Jamani and Angeli [5] investigated the effect of robotics on the learning of 21 primary school student teachers' CT in a semester-long course on science education methods. Findings from that study revealed that student teachers showed increased interest and knowledge in robots, and in self-efficacy for teaching robotics. Sadik et al. [15] investigated 12 student teachers' understanding of CT when planning and implementing a fifth-grade activity focusing on CT, robotics, and coding. The findings of the study were that student teachers showed increased awareness of CT. Some misconceptions, such as defining CT as equal to algorithm design and suggesting a trial-and-error approach to computational problem-solving did, however, persist. Similarly, Chang and Peterson [2] examined 59 primary school student teachers' perceptions and CT conceptualisations in their teaching practices. In line with Sadik et al. [15], the findings of Chang and Peterson [2] were that student teachers increased their understanding of CT and teaching applications. Moreover, student teachers improved their attitudes to including CT in their course and workshops. A study by Ma et al. [10] focused on exploring student teachers' field experience in a pedagogical laboratory designed to challenge teacher candidates' beliefs of teaching and learning in the context of CT. After 12-h' training in programming activities on robotics and practice facilitating those activities with children, student teachers reflected that they increased knowledge and skills to facilitate learning CT. Another study focusing on primary school education student teachers by Kim et al. [7] investigated STEM engagement and learning and teaching via robotics. The authors suggested that robotics can be used as a technology in activities designed to enhance student teachers' STEM engagement and teaching through improved STEM attitudes.

3 The Study

In autumn 2020, primary school student teachers at the Faculty of Education attended a 12-h compulsory course, 'Digital Technologies in Primary Education', to understand CT. The course aimed to introduce student teachers to teaching Informatics in primary school education. It was designed as a set of six interactive lectures. At the end of this course, the student teachers were allowed to choose one of the following four activities (see Table 1) to complete the course:

Table 1. List of final activities for completing the course 'Digital Technologies in Primary Education'

Activity 1	Activity 2	Activity 3	Activity 4
Code.org	Bebras contest tasks (MINI category)	Informatics Textbooks for Primary Education	Hello Ruby (books)

3.1 Participants

The course was attended by 138 second year student teachers on the 5-year MA study for Primary Education (71,7% full-time and 28,3% part-time). During their study at lower or upper secondary school, they did not have a computer science (CS) or computing subject, only the 'ICT' subject (which, in schools, was unfortunately called 'Informatics'). Among them, a few students had participated in the Informatics Bebras contest while pupils at lower or upper secondary schools. Several of them, mainly the part-time student teachers, work in primary schools and teach the subject 'ICT' to children. In the course, 'Digital Technologies in Primary Education', which introduced them to the topics and requirements for the new school subject 'Informatics', they found many interesting examples and ideas for working with pupils in primary education.

The majority of student teachers 116 chose Activity 2 in which they had to analyse Bebras tasks [1] saved in the archive (https://www.ibobr.cz/test/archiv) of Bebras contest tasks (Informatický bobřík) since 2008 for pupils from the Czech Republic.

For the Bebras task analysis, the student teachers could choose any year for the MINI category, established in 2012. Some student teachers decided to analyse tasks from different years of the Bebras contest (MIX).

The study focused on n = 66 participants (female = 97,0%) who analysed the Activity 2 related to 2019 Bebras tasks. In this study, we therefore looked at the results reported for 2019. The student teachers were allowed to do the Activity 2 individually or to collaborate in groups (Table 2).

Table 2. How student teachers worked and collaborated in Activity 2 Bebras contest 2019.

Number of student teachers (Activity 2)	Working individually	Working in pairs	Working in threes
66	29 (43,9%)	34 (51,5%)	3 (4,5%)

3.2 Bebras Tasks' Analysis

The student teachers had to decide which Bebras tasks they consider are simple or difficult and the reason why. The following scheme (see Table 3) illustrates the key steps in how to complete the given task:

Table 3. Partial steps in solving Activity 2.

Step 1	Step 2	Step 3	Step 4
To choose a year of Bebras contest	To assess Bebras tasks and to decide which of them are easy/difficult	To justify the opinion as to why the Bebras task is easy/difficult	To design a teaching situation for three selected Bebras tasks as CSUnplugged activities (didactics approach, teaching aid, worksheet, etc.)

"Predicting the difficulty level of a task on the concepts of computer science or computational thinking, like in the Bebras contest, proves to be really hard" [18, p. 145]. Each year, data obtained from Bebras contest competitors are analysed to understand better why competitors are more successful in some tasks, or why in some cases they were not able to solve the task, which could help Bebras task authors to better estimate the difficulty of the tasks next time. "The actual difficulty of the Bebras tasks will only become apparent after the competition and will often differ from the expected difficulty" [16, p. 125]. Sometimes "estimating the difficulty level of a Bebras task is done merely by intuition" [17, p. 138].

Some student teachers not only assessed the difficulty for selected Bebras tasks, but also assigned these tasks to their primary school pupils and found out which tasks were difficult for them. In this manner, some of them verified their understanding or expectations.

Some tasks from the Bebras contest were presented to student teachers at the lecture of the course 'Digital Technologies in Primary Education', some student teachers started to show interest in these tasks: in some cases they even implemented Bebras tasks to teach their pupils in schools or to activities with their children at home.

3.3 Method

In the present study, data were collected through student teachers' reflective texts (n = 66) in which they assessed the Bebras tasks for the year 2019 and explained why they assumed the difficulty level of particular tasks. The researchers utilised also the information resulting from the design of the teaching process for the three selected Bebras tasks (see Step 4 in Table 3).

In the case of student teachers, it is not a matter of agreeing on the difficulties with the Bebras tasks' authors. Their view of the task level difficulty reflects student teachers' subjective feelings, which is mixed with their own experience, as they struggled with solving the task. The Bebras task analysis is a way how to teach student teachers to think about pupil's thinking computationally.

3.4 Findings

Unlike the authors of the Bebras contest tasks who use a three-level scale to assess difficulty (*easy - moderately difficult - very difficult*), student teachers used only a two-level scale: *easy – difficult*. The two-level scale was deliberately given to student teachers since these students have practically no experience with informatics tasks and teaching computing. They are not yet able to be sufficiently clear about the thinking process about the problem nor appreciate how pupils can analyse the task, or what strategy to choose to solve it. Thus, it is not appropriate for beginners to apply *a finer scale* (see Figs. 1 and 2).

In general, student teachers reported that they very much enjoyed solving the Bebras tasks. Some of them have already participated in the Bebras contest as lower secondary school pupils. Nevertheless, for many student teachers the Bebras contest was something completely new.

In some cases, student primary school teachers' opinions on the difficulty of specific Bebras tasks diverged from the Bebras task authors' views; while, in others, the vast majority of student teachers agreed with authors of Bebras tasks.

Practically all student teachers and task authors agreed that the task ***"Text editing"*** is an easy task (Fig. 3). The student's common view was based on their belief that everyone can work with a text editor, but does this also apply to primary school pupils? Student teachers' view of difficulty level of the task, ***"Magic with coins"***, coincides with expectations of the task authors, describing it as difficult (Fig. 1).

In some tasks, student teachers' opinions on the level of difficulty of the Bebras tasks differed, so it is not entirely clear whether, in general, for most student teachers the task is difficult or easy. Among them there are opinions both that the task is difficult, and opinions that the task is simple (see Fig. 1 and 2).

a) Bebras tasks considered very difficult according to their authors:

Student teachers evaluate these following Bebras tasks differently (Fig. 1). Like the authors of Bebras, the majority of students consider the ***"Magic with coins"*** task to be an extremely difficult. Nevertheless, some tasks that authors find very difficult, student teachers considered easy. That is the case with the logic task, ***"Entrance to the swimming pool"***, and the task, ***"Shields and swords"***, (see Appendix 2, Fig. 5).

According to the authors, the difficulty of the task ***"Entrance to the swimming pool"*** lies in the fact that pupils work with logical conditions, while the student teachers saw its difficulty only in pupils′ ability to focus on reading comprehension, associating the success of solving this task mainly with reading literacy. Only very rarely did a few student teachers comment that "in this task, pupils are required to realise what exactly the rules for entering the swimming pool say (what are the conditions for entry to the swimming pool: if - then - else) and realise what conditions are fulfilled in the given case (how old is who to whom, and who can go to the swimming pool with whom)" (Student teacher 59).

The task, ***"Shields and Swords"***, has been described by some student teachers as easy. It is enough to carefully select individual swordsmen and realise what equipment swordsmen should have at the beginning and at the end of the row. Some student teachers also reflected their views in their teaching design for working with this task with pupils in a classroom: groups of five pupils equipped the same way as in the picture (see Appendix 2, Fig. 5) and solved this task through a drama performance.

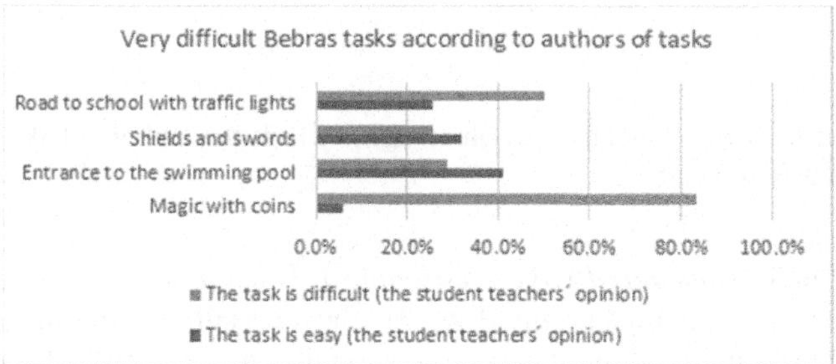

Fig. 1. Student teachers' opinions on Bebras tasks, which the authors of the Bebras contest consider very difficult.

b) Bebras tasks considered moderately difficult according to their authors:

In the case of moderately difficult tasks, the views of student teachers and authors of tasks on the task difficulty also vary (Fig. 2). Differences in the perception of difficulty were manifested mainly in the evaluation of tasks, ***"Candy vending machine"*** (see Appendix 1, Fig. 4) or ***"Cloudy weather forecast"***.

One student teacher justified the difficulty of the task ***"Candy vending machine"*** as follows: "I think that pupils will apply a "trial and error" method. They will try to apply this method until the required number (for 44 candies) appears on the display. Pupils will not understand why this happened or how to look for a more general strategy to solve this task" (Student teacher 45). The student teachers' comments showed that none of them related this task to the triple system. "In my opinion, it is difficult for children to find their way in the machine itself. Working with numbers, in my opinion, is quite a challenging task for children" (Student teacher 12).

In the case of the task, ***"Cloudy weather forecast"***, as anticipated, most student teachers described this task as easy. Problem tasks of this kind based on visual analysis are included quite a lot in the learning of primary school pupils.

A completely different type of task is ***"Little worm"***. According to some students, the task is simple; according to others, the task is difficult (Fig. 2) "because there are several solutions to the paths and pupils have to find the shortest one. On twigs, the little worm can proceed in different directions" (Student teacher 47).

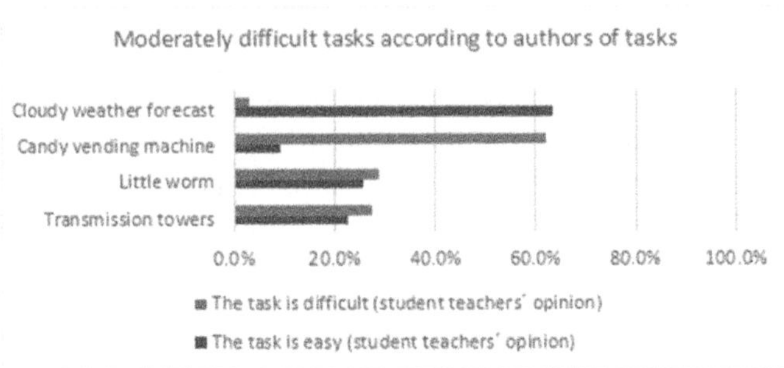

Fig. 2. Student teachers' opinions on Bebras tasks, which the authors of the Bebras contest consider moderately difficult.

c) Bebras tasks considered easy according to their authors:

For all the tasks in this group (Fig. 3), the prevailing opinion among student teachers is that these are simple tasks, corresponding to the views of the task author.

Only in case of the task, ***"Park cleaning"*** (see Appendix 3, Fig. 6), according to some student teachers the task can be difficult (Fig. 3) because the pupils will not be able to visually compare distances between objects placed in the park and "to decide which of a pair of objects is closer to the cleaning robot, and the robot then cleans it up." (Student teacher 32).

Some student teachers compared the Bebras tasks with mathematical ones used in other challenges for primary school pupils (Kangaroo, Mathematical Olympiad, etc.); they found the Bebras tasks more interesting and engaging. They appreciated the fact that the Bebras tasks usually include a picture or an interactive function, so the control of the task could be user-friendly. Student teachers also valued a theme or story of Bebras tasks –reflecting pupils' lives, interests and experiences which can be fun.

The student teachers pointed out that a significant condition for the successful solution of each task is the ability to read the assignment carefully and to concentrate on its reading with understanding. From a didactical point of view, reading and visual literacy, logical thinking and numeracy are very important for solving Bebras tasks.

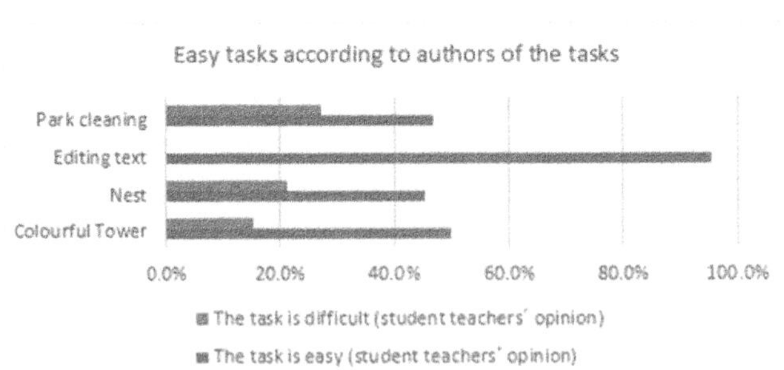

Fig. 3. Student teachers' opinions on Bebras tasks, which the authors of the Bebras contest consider easy.

The student teachers appreciated very much the opportunity they had about how a pupil could think over, and whether pupils are, indeed, capable of solving each Bebras task. They considered that to be a great contest in their initial professional development to become a primary school teacher.

As already mentioned, primary education student teachers not only assessed the difficulty of Bebras tasks, but also proposed teaching methods or approaches aimed to help pupils think about solving tasks (Step 4 in Table 3). Some student teachers created teaching aids (made of paper, wood etc.). Other teaching methods were based on pupils envisioning and enacting the whole situation as a story (something like CSUnplugged). Some examples:

Teaching Aids

Cloudy Weather Forecast: "Together with pupils, we would first number the lines in both pictures (including the weather forecast report). Then we compare step by step in which rows and columns the data from the weather report match" (Student teacher 17).

Little Worm: A teacher would explain this task to children with the use of toothpicks. "Pupils would be given a redrawn assignment on paper. The pupils' task would be to place one toothpick on each part of the branch that the little worm travels to the apple (which is bordered by a black dot for greater understanding). If the worm returns to the branch, the pupil will lay two toothpicks. Then pupils will count the toothpicks" (Student teacher 2).

Drama Teaching

Park Cleaning: "Various objects are placed around the class (garbage). One pupil will represent a robot, whose task is step-by-step to collect scattered objects according to the rules given in the Bebras task. Gradually, other pupils take on the role of a robot" (Student teacher 51).

4 Discussion and Conclusion

This study set out to explore primary education student teachers' perceptions of CT who participated in a course 'Digital Technologies in Primary Education' and explored what these students consider difficult when developing primary school pupils' CT. The finding of this study revealed that most of these student teachers completed this course successfully, analysing the required activities, especially the informatics Bebras tasks on which the study concentrated.

Based on the analysis of reflective texts of the Bebras tasks elaborated by 66 primary education student teachers, it was found that for better understanding of CT, student teachers are required to have sufficient Informatics' knowledge to be able to think computationally and to understand the informatics contexts of Bebras tasks.

During their studies at primary and secondary school, these student teachers did not have any opportunity to become introduced to computer science, as no such subject was part of the compulsory curriculum. Nor, after completing the 12-h compulsory course 'Digital Technologies in Primary Education', did the primary school student teachers show convincingly that they know what computing and computational thinking are. They did not have sufficient foreknowledge of (i) what Informatics are, (ii) how computers work, (iii) algorithms, (iv) programming, and knowledge in mathematics, but (and at the same time) they would be required to develop pupil CT.

The study's findings indicate that due to their lack of fundamental knowledge in informatics, student teachers did not differentiate greatly between CT and mathematical thinking. This conclusion concurs with Millwood et al. [11] that "mathematical concepts are clearly linked, but Computational Thinking defined as the problem solving & design to create useful solutions demands a much broader, creative and playful approach engaging children's imagination" [11, p. 8].

Informatics in primary education, including CT development, requires not only logical thinking, reading literacy and counting abilities, but also a good level of abstract thinking, which - like mathematical thinking - is still developing in primary school pupils. Teaching using puzzles, quizzes and games can support and develop understanding and learning of algorithms. Such teaching has been successful in the study of other computing disciplines [4]. Most Bebras tasks are so designed.

The study showed that primary education student teachers do not yet have an idea of what it means to think computationally. It will be necessary to focus first on this in the subject, 'Digital Technologies in Primary Education', and only then to address teaching issues of how to teach computational thinking to pupils. This finding fully corresponds to the recommendations of Yadav et al. [19], that "teacher educators need first to develop pre-service teachers' knowledge and skills on how to think computationally and then how to teach their students to think computationally. It is thus imperative for pre-service teachers to understand computational thinking in the context of the subject area which they will be teaching. This requires them to have deep understanding of their own discipline and knowledge of how computational thinking concepts relate to what students are learning in the classroom."

In primary school teacher education, it is necessary to pay great attention to the evaluation of informatics tasks for pupils, so they can "grasp" the informatics content of an assessed task. The student teachers in this study evaluated the Bebras tasks as interesting tasks (such as quizzes or games); they did not have enough insight from CS to notice what and why it may be difficult for pupils working on Beaver tasks. They assessed difficulty mainly according to their ability to solve the task. They applied a certain "automated" (stereotypical) thinking procedure for solving problematic tasks which could be a barrier to gain insight into completing the task.

For primary education student teachers to really develop CT, they need a grounding in CS, otherwise "there is a real danger that Computational Thinking becomes a label for a set of enjoyable time-filling activities with little coherence and a lack of continuity and progression" [11, p. 14]. To ensure primary school development of CT, initial teacher education cannot concentrate only on pedagogical issues of pupils' CT development but must also include informatics. We agree with Cutts, Connor and Robertson [3, p. 26] who argue that "efforts to make computer science entirely about "computational thinking" in the absence of "computers" are mistaken".

Acknowledgement. This study is a result of the research funded by the PROGRES Q17 Příprava učitele a učitelská profese v kontextu vědy a výzkumu.

Appendix 1 Candy Vending Machine

Set the candy machine to dispense 44 candies. Use red sliders to change the setting.

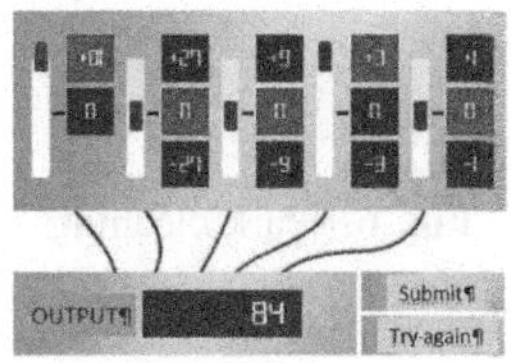

Fig. 4. Candy vending machine. (Color figure online)

Appendix 2 Shields and Swords

Drag to place masters of historical fencing (swordsmen) to apply:

- Each sword points to one of the masters (swordsmen).
- The master (swordsman) must defend himself with a shield against each sword.

Fig. 5. Shields and swords.

Appendix 3 Park Cleaning

After the concert, a lot of garbage remained in the park and the robotic waste bin has the task of collecting it. The robot works according to the following program:

As long as there is an object on the lawn, drive to the nearest object, pick it up and load it. Which of the objects will the robot load last?

Your answers: a) , b) , c) , d) 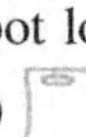, e) I do not want to answer.

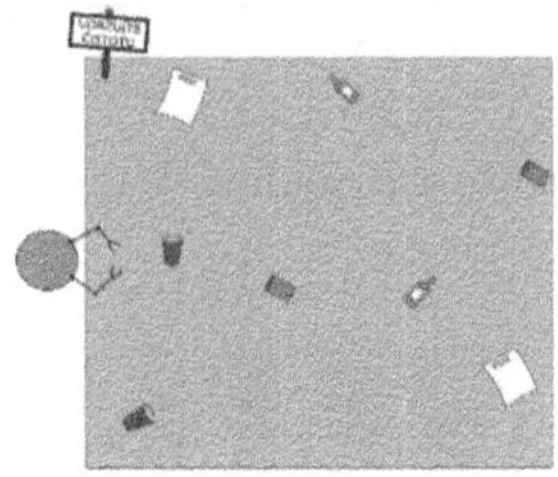

Fig. 6. Park cleaning.

References

1. Bebras. https://www.bebras.org/
2. Chang, Y.-H., Peterson, L.: Pre-service teachers' perceptions of computational thinking. J. Technol. Teach. Educ. **26**, 353–374 (2018)
3. Cutts, Q., Robertson, J., Connor, R.: Keeping the machinery in computing education. Incorporating intellectual and developmental frameworks into a scottish school curriculum. Commun. ACM **60**(11), 26–28 (2017)
4. Gibson, J.P.: Teaching graph algorithms to children of all ages. In: Proceedings of the 17th ACM annual conference on Innovation and technology in Computer Science education, pp. 34–39. ACM (2012)
5. Jaipal-Jamani, K., Angeli, C.: Effect of robotics on elementary preservice teachers' self-efficacy, science learning, and computational thinking. J. Sci. Educ. Technol. **26**, 175–192 (2017). https://doi.org/10.1007/s10956-016-9663-z
6. Hemmendinger, D.: A plea for modesty. ACM Inroads **1**(2), 4 (2010)
7. Kim, C., Kim, D., Yuan, J., Hill, R.B., Doshi, P., Thai, C.N.: Robotics to promote elementary education preservice teachers' STEM engagement, learning, and teaching. Comput. Educ. **91**, 14–31 (2015)
8. Lamprou, A., Repenning, A.: Teaching how to teach computational thinking. In: Proceedings of 23rd Annual ACM Conference on Innovation and Technology in Computer Science Education (ITiCSE 2018), pp. 69–74. ACM, New York (2018)
9. Lu, J.J., Fletcher, G.H.: Thinking about computational thinking. In: Proceedings of the 40th ACM Technical Symposium on Computer Science Education, pp. 260–264 (2009)
10. Ma, Y., Lai, G., Williams, D., Prejean, L., Ford, M.J.: Exploring the effectiveness of a field experience program in a pedagogical laboratory: the experience of teacher candidates. J. Technol. Teach. Educ. **16**, 411–432 (2008)
11. Millwood, R., Bresnihan, N., Walsh, D., Hooper, J.: Review of literature on computational thinking (2018). https://www.ncca.ie/media/3557/primary-coding_review-of-literature-on-computational-thinking.pdf
12. MoEYS: Strategie digitálního vzdělávání do roku 2020 (2014). http://www.msmt.cz/uploads/DigiStrategie.pdf
13. MoEYS: Opatření ministra školství, mládeže a tělovýchovy, kterým se mění Rámcový vzdělávací program pro základní vzdělávání od 1 Sept 2021 (2021). https://www.msmt.cz/vzdelavani/zakladni-vzdelavani/opatreni-ministra-skolstvi-mladeze-a-telovychovy-informatika
14. Papert, S.: Mindstorms: Children, Computers, and Powerful Ideas. Basic Books, Inc., New York (1980)

15. Sadik, O., Leftwich, A.-O., Nadiruzzaman, H.: Computational thinking conceptions and misconceptions: progression of preservice teacher thinking during computer science lesson planning. In: Rich, P.J., Hodges, C.B. (eds.) Emerging research, practice, and policy on computational thinking. ECTII, pp. 221–238. Springer, Cham (2017). https://doi.org/10.1007/978-3-319-52691-1_14
16. Tomcsányiová, M., Tomcsányi, P.: Analysis of tasks in the Slovakian Bebras challenge 2013/14. J. Technol. Inf. Educ. **6**(1), 122–136 (2014)
17. van der Vegt, W.: Predicting the difficulty level of a Bebras task. Olympiads Inf. **7**, 132–139 (2013)
18. van der Vegt, W., Schrijvers, E.: Analysing task difficulty in a Bebras challenge using Cuttle. Olympiads Inf. **13**, 145–156 (2019)
19. Yadav, A., Stephenson, C., Hong, H.: Computational thinking for teacher education. Commun. ACM **60**(4), 55–62 (2017)
20. Wing, J.: Computational thinking. Commun. ACM **49**, 33–35 (2006)
21. Wing, J.: Computational thinking and thinking about computing. Philos. Trans. Roy. Soc. Math. Phys. Eng. Sci. **366**(1881), 3717–3725 (2008)

Programming Concepts in Lower Primary Years and Their Cognitive Demands

Ivan Kalaš(✉) and Klara Horvathova

Comenius University, Bratislava, Slovakia
{ivan.kalas,klara.horvathova}@fmph.uniba.sk

Abstract. In our Computing with Emil project, currently in its 4th year, we are engaged in the design and research focused on productive constructionist learning of programming at the primary level, as a continuum from year to year. We are exclusively concerned with *computing for all learners* approach, being implemented by generalist primary teachers in their own classes. For similar purposes, national curricula usually list computational concepts, which pupils should learn and, in general agreement among educational experts, are considered developmentally appropriate for the primary school. However, in our work, we feel the vocabulary being normally used for this is too coarse-grained to clearly specify the learning goals, especially in the area of programming. Therefore, for each computational concept, we try to identify a set of related operations that primary pupils should learn in any particular year. In this research, we tried to verify whether our approach is comprehensible for teachers and prolific in outcomes for their pupils. We wanted to find out whether they realise that (a) different operations performed with each concept have different cognitive demands, and (b) these demands determine the arrangement of activities in an intervention. We addressed a large group of teachers who had already participated in our professional development sessions on the intervention for Year 3. We chose repetition as one of the concepts and designed six assessment tasks focused on various operations that pupils perform with it. We did not inform them of how we rank the tasks; we asked them to solve them and rank from the simplest to the most difficult, and explain their decision. We analysed the collected data by various methods, and in the paper, we discuss our findings. Teachers correctly distinguished different operations and helped us better understand challenges of projecting and assessing conceptual understanding.

Keywords: Programming in lower primary · Concepts and their cognitive demands · Generalist primary teachers' perspective

1 Introduction

In our research, we strive to better understand learning process of the primary level pupils (aged 5 or 6 to 10 or 11) in the area of computing and its programming. This arena is meagrely explored, especially if we are primarily interested in *computing for all* approach [1], i.e., in computing implemented in a regular class with all learners, possibly as a mandatory subject or integrated in mathematics. Additionally, in our case,

Published by Springer Nature Switzerland AG 2022
D. Passey et al. (Eds.): OCCE 2021, IFIP AICT 642, pp. 28–40, 2022.
https://doi.org/10.1007/978-3-030-97986-7_3

we are to build the educational content such that the generalist primary teachers feel confident to teach it themselves and consider it prolific for their pupils.

In this project, we focused on the assessment of cognitive demands [2] of the programming concepts which, according to the research literature and our own experience, we consider to be developmentally appropriate for primary school. Such concepts are often only briefly listed in policy documents, curricula or research reports, as e.g., in the current English programme of study at KS2 [3]: … *use sequence, selection, and repetition in programs; work with variables and various forms of input and output.* In our approach, however (see [4] or [5]), we prefer to use more detailed vocabulary when setting educational goals and projecting learning progression for individual years in KS1 and 2. Specifically, for each concept whose understanding we want to develop, we identify operations which we consider appropriate to perform with that concept. Subsequently, in the design research process [6], we transform the operations into gradation of activities and iteratively evaluate them in our partner primary classes.

Although such design requires a long period of time and is being evaluated in numerous iterations, here we present how we additionally tried to validate whether our *concepts and related operations* strategy is productive, i.e., whether primary pupils (and teachers) are aware of the differences between individual operations related with the concepts, perceiving them as different also in terms of their cognitive demands.

2 Programming Concepts at Primary Level and Their Difficulty

Although not always used with identical meaning and scope, several curricular documents exploit the strategy of identifying programming concepts which pupils are meant to learn (see e.g. [7, 8]). Similarly, many authors in their research and development reports take comparable approaches while presenting their area of interest and formulating their research problems. The concrete lists of concepts sometimes reflect selected programming environment. Bers [9] refers to *children learning basic concepts and powerful ideas of coding* in ScratchJr as they use programming blocks spanning *concepts from simple sequencing… to control structures*, and addresses *sequencing, repeat loop, sensors, and conditional statements* when they use KIBO.

To assess development of pupils' computational thinking in Scratch, Brennan and Resnick [10] uses three key dimensions: computational concepts (namely *sequences*, *loops*, *parallelism*, *events*, *conditionals*, *operators*, and *data*), computational practices (*being incremental and iterative*, *testing and debugging*, *reusing and remixing*, and *abstracting and modularising*), and computational perspectives (*expressing*, *connecting*, and *questioning*). When Meerbaum-Salan et al. [11] investigate whether Scratch can be used to teach concepts of computer science, they studied pupils' understanding of *initialisation* (of position, direction, costume etc. up to variables), *bounded, conditional, and unbounded repeated execution*, *variables*, *conditional execution*, *message passing*, *events*, and *concurrency*.

In K-12 Computer Science Standards [12] the authors name the concepts for ages 8–11 in chapter Algorithms and Programming by stating: *Create programs that use variables to store and modify data* and *Create programs that include sequences, events, loops, and conditionals* (p. 10) and also provide more specific justifications plus several developmentally appropriate examples of those concepts in use.

When designing their informatics curriculum, Dagiene et al. [13] specify each concept together with one or two related operations, situating them into recommended age group. For instance, *loops without parameters* (age group 7+) are presented as *First pupils recognise repetition of patterns in programs and can shorten the program description by applying repeat-loop. Secondly pupils recognise possible repetitions in task descriptions... and design programs with loops* (p. 350). Some authors specify the need to study cognitive demands of programming, such as Blackwell [2] in his discussion about why programming is deemed difficult. In 1976, Perlman [14, 15] also suggested considering *cognitive difficulties* while developing interventions for children.

Although the researchers and content designers usually have a clear idea of a certain appropriate order of the studied programming concepts, deeper understanding and systematic research in this direction is still in its early stage. Therefore, we aim to try to verify if the strategy of identifying different operations related to each programming concept and sorting them by their different cognitive demands is productive to design structure and learning progressions in curricula.

2.1 Computing with Emil: Project Background

The reason why we consider the combination of parallel research and development to be exceptionally fruitful is that we research to ensure that we can develop competently. Moreover, we develop so that we can study corresponding learning processes. These intertwined activities signify the essence of a research strategy named design research (DR for short) [6], which we employ. At the initiation of our Computing with Emil project in 2017, we wished to not only systematically support learning in informatics through all primary years, but also equip ourselves with powerful research instruments. Exploiting them already [16], we explore one of our key design principles – distinguishing between *direct manipulation*, *direct control*, and *programming*.

At the level of content development, we strive to support programming as a continuum in all primary years. We want pupils to experience it as an opportunity to encounter powerful ideas of computing, as an instrument for their computational curiosity, a way of thinking about and solving problems from different areas. So far, we have deployed Emil for Years 3 and 4 and Robotics with Ema for Years 1 to 4. All of these interventions complement each other and support a holistic learning progression, together with the ScratchMaths interventions for Years 5 and 6 [17].

Concepts, Operations, and Tasks. In Emil Y3, we focused on the following powerful ideas of computing: *experiencing order and structure* (in data and commands), *learning to control and plan*, *coping with constraints*, *considering state and tools*, *learning to aggregate and abstract*, and *thinking about programs*. From the perspective of the programming concepts, we decided to concentrate on *sequence*, *repetition* (continued in Y4), and pre-concept of *procedure* (as a preparation for Y4). As with other interventions, in the DR process of Emil Y3, we proceeded by identifying different operations related to each concept, and implemented them in small activities that constructed the whole gradation (systematic progression) of tasks. In Emil Y3, the overall gradation consists of 150^{+} tasks. Some of them have multiple solutions, a few do not have any solution (and teachers invite pupils to explain why), while other tasks are partially 'unclear'. In this case, the teachers suggest that the group discuss the task, complete its wording and solve it. Thus, pupils become co-designers of the activities. Discussions and collaboration in the group are the most important part of our pedagogy.

As an example, let us present how the operations related to *repetition* were identified in Emil Y3, here listed according to their increasing demands (as validated in the DR process). Here we refer to Fig. 1, which shows growing expressive power of the language along with the interface support for the way in which commands are displayed as small blue cards on the record/programming panel above Emil's stage:

- Directly control Emil using the *basic commands*. An *external record* of the steps taken is built in parallel on the panel (see an example on Fig. 1(i)).
- Experience the limitation of the panel's extent, which sometimes only possess 4 or 5 positions. This may affect or even preclude the solution of a problem.
- Read a given record (a simple sequence of *basic commands*) and recognise whether any command in the record is repeated more than once in a row. In Fig. 1(i) there are three such groups: two *baskets* to pick a mushroom, three *watering cans* to water a cherry tree to (1) grow, (2) bloom, and (3) ripen, and two *arrows down*.
- In direct control, discover a mechanism that any *basic command* repeated more than once in a row is automatically and immediately gathered in a *stack of commands* (see Fig. 1(ii)). This gathering is highlighted by an animation on the panel. In the example we can see three such stacks.
- Program a solution of a problem, making use of the fact that identical cards in a row are gathered in stacks. This saves positions on the panel considerably.
- When programming a solution, discover a procedure on how two consecutive *basic commands* can be merged on the panel into one 'double card', representing a pair of commands. Identical double cards in a row are then automatically gathered in *stacks of double cards* (see Fig. 1(iii) and (iv)).
- Build, read, analyse, explore, explain, simplify and compare different programs using *basic commands*, *stacks of basic commands* and *stacks of double commands*.
- When programming a solution, generalise the merging and stacking mechanism to three *basic commands*, which can later be changed to four (see Fig. 1(v)). Build, read, analyse, explore, explain, simplify and compare such programs.

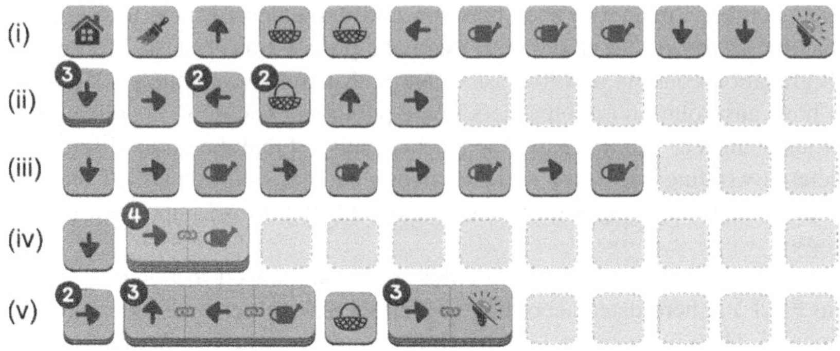

Fig. 1. Different levels of the ways in which commands are displayed on the panel.

Our intervention for Y3 began to be implemented in primary schools in Slovakia, Czech Republic, and in smaller pilot hubs of schools in Norway and England a year before the pandemic. At that time, we also finalised the evaluation of intervention for Y4 and started running professional development (PD) sessions for teachers. Admirably, many schools continued using the interventions with their pupils in one way or another through the pandemic. The actual situation of 2020/21 school year, however, did not allow us to work directly with the pupils. Therefore, at this stage of the research, we focused our effort on the teachers, as we set out to study whether they realise the difference between varying operations which pupils perform with the same computational concept and how they characterise these operations. Therefore, we formulated our first research question as: *Are the teachers aware of different operations which pupils perform with each computational concept and how would they characterise them?* (RQ1) We decided to focus on repetition as one of the central concepts of the intervention in Y3 and designed a set of six paper-based assessment tasks. They represent six different operations and were intended to examine whether teachers are aware of the different cognitive demands of the operations. Therefore, this aspect was reflected in our second research question: *How do teachers perceive cognitive demands of different operations pupils do with the same concept?* (RQ2)

3 Method

Firstly, the participants of our research are characterised. We focused on all teachers who had already participated in our PD sessions[1] aimed at Emil Y3. This comprised (as of 30 April 2021) of 1079 teachers, 823 Slovak and 265 Czech. Out of these teachers, 302 agreed to proceed with our research assignment. As the final *volunteer sampling*, 62 teachers (21%) responded and undertook the challenge, as presented in Sect. 3.1.

[1] That is, one day session of face to face or two afternoons in the online model.

We will be referring to them as our *teacher sample*. These 62 teachers represent 49 schools, 37 Slovak and 12 Czech. More details of the same are presented in Fig. 2: in (a) it shows that 36 of the sample are primary teachers, 23 are lower secondary teachers who teach both primary and lower secondary pupils, one currently teaches lower secondary pupils only but is interested to know our intervention, and two are 'other'. In (b), we see that 27 teachers have already used the intervention in their class(es) and 35 have worked with it only in the PD session(s). In (c), we see the breakdown of the sample with respect to when the teachers participated in the PD session, grouped into six half-years, starting by the second half-year of 2018.

In parallel, we also identified 13 Slovak and Czech expert informatics researchers[2] and educators in the academic population with the same request. We received eight responses, therefore deciding to use them as another validation of our method (see below). In this paper, we will be referring to this purposive sample as our *expert*.

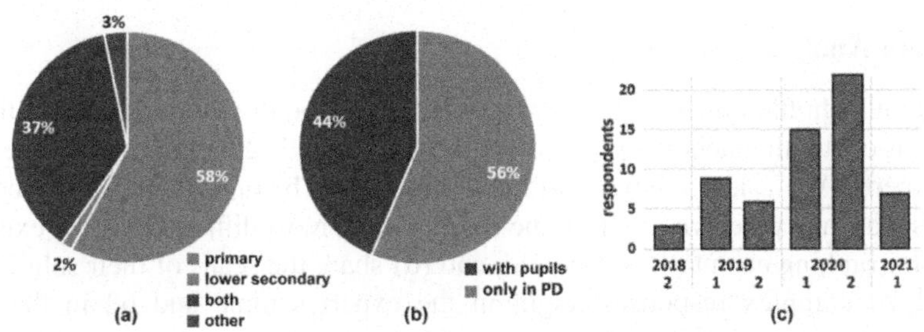

Fig. 2. Breakdown of the teacher sample.

3.1 Designing the Assessment Tasks

For this research, we designed six assessment tasks similar to activities performed by pupils (and the teachers) with repetition in Y3 intervention. Yet, the assessment tasks are dissimilar to the activities of the intervention as they are not open-ended and can be unambiguously assessed (although tasks 3 and 4 have multiple solutions). We ordered the tasks in the way corresponding to the increasing cognitive demands as implemented in the intervention. For the needs of the data analysis and the presentation of the findings, we numbered and colour-coded the data. Table 1 briefly characterises the essence of each task, while Fig. 3 illustrates one of the tasks.

[2] Familiar with our approach and our interventions.

Table 1. Cognitive characterisation of the assessment tasks focused on repetition in Y3.

Task 1	analyse a given record (program) of the single *basic commands*, recognise and mark each group of single commands repeated in the record next to each other
Task 2	read a given record of the *basic commands* and *the stacks of basic commands* and execute it; draw a resulting path of Emil through the stage
Task 3	plan a solution, i.e., program a path using *basic commands* and *stacks of basic commands* (single cards), with limited number of steps
Task 4	plan a solution, i.e., build a program that uses *basic commands* and a given 'double command', with limited number of steps
Task 5	read a given program with *stacks of cards* and *double cards* of the basic commands, and indicate the *basic command* Emil will run first, second, third etc.
Task 6	read a given program with *stacks of cards, double cards and triple cards*, and indicate the *basic command* Emil will run first, second, third etc.

3.2 Data Analysis

We randomly shuffled the set of our assessment tasks and distributed them (in the same random order) to all teachers of the volunteer sample of 302 and our purposive sample of 13 experts. We asked them to (a) solve the tasks, (b) rank them by the cognitive demands – as they perceive it – from the easiest to the most difficult one, (c) explain the reasons for ranking each task as they did, and (d) share the scans of their solutions. We obtained 70 complex responses (eight in the expert sample and 62 in the teacher sample) and analysed the data using various descriptive and analytical statistical methods, along with analyses of the explanations and the solutions. Although we applied various methods to collected rankings, we consider this research endeavour as qualitative and harness all results as a means to:

- Validate the approach of *refining granularity* of the programming concepts specifications in school informatics by identifying gradations of operations connected with each concept. Thus, we wish to learn more about how to design structure of the content and support the learning trajectory of the pupils in informatics.
- Inform our effort to better understand cognitive demands of the operations, thus improving the understanding of the programming/algorithmic thinking development at the primary stage.

To achieve this, we formulated research questions RQ1 and RQ2 (see above). As discussed in the final section of the paper, in the second period, we plan to extend this research by addressing the pupils of the teachers involved.

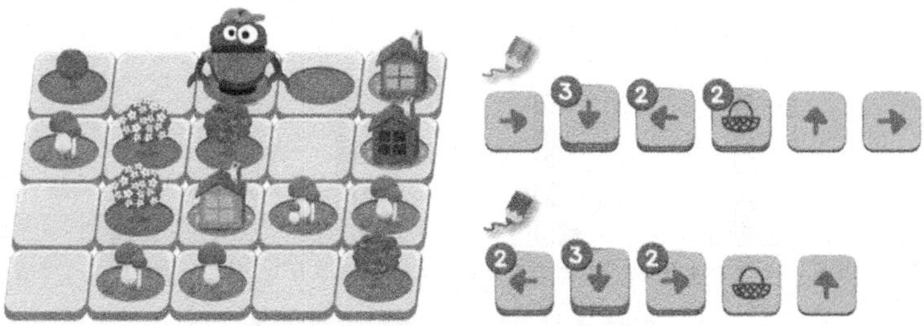

Fig. 3. Task 2, as presented to the teachers, with the following assignment: *This is Emil's stage and two records of the paths that he could take.* ***Draw both paths through the stage.***

For brevity, we present here only one method out of several which we used to analyse the collected data. Namely, we wanted to consider the degree of similarity between our understanding of the cognitive demands of the different operations' pupils in Y3 perform in the context of repetition represented as a tuple (1, 2, 3, 4, 5, 6), and collected rankings of the tasks' demands as perceived by the teachers represented as permutations of the initial tuple. To measure the ordinal association between two tuples, we used the Kendall rank correlation coefficient [18]. The value of the coefficient lies between the interval of −1 (a perfect disagreement, in this case for (6, 5, 4, 3, 2, 1)) and 1 (a perfect agreement). The correlation is high when an assessment of the perceived cognitive demands of the tasks is similar to the intended one.

Kendall's correlation coefficient, referred to as *Kendall's tau*, is calculated as the difference between the number of *concordant* and *discordant* pairs within the tuple, divided by the binomial coefficient of the tuple's length. From the CS perspective, the Kendall's tau can be easily derived[3] from the minimal number of necessary swaps between the items of a tuple when sorted by bubble sort. For example, if the perceived ranking is (2, 3, 4, 1, 6, 5), four swaps are needed to sort the tuple and the similarity between the tuple and (1, 2, 3, 4, 5, 6) is 0.467 when represented as the Kendall's tau.

4 Results

To investigate whether teachers are aware of the differences between various operations performed by the pupils with repetition in Y3, we asked them to solve our six assessment tasks and rank the task they considered the easiest to the most demanding. The resulting rankings can be analysed from two (closely related) alternative perspectives: we can review, which of our tasks was ranked by the participants as the easiest, which was ranked as the 2nd etc., while the other possible view would consider which rankings were assigned to our task 1, which rankings were assigned to our task 2 etc. Both perspectives proved to be interesting and instructive.

[3] More precisely, tau = (n – 2 * m) / n, where n is the minimal number of swaps needed in the worst case and m is the minimal number of necessary swaps for this particular tuple.

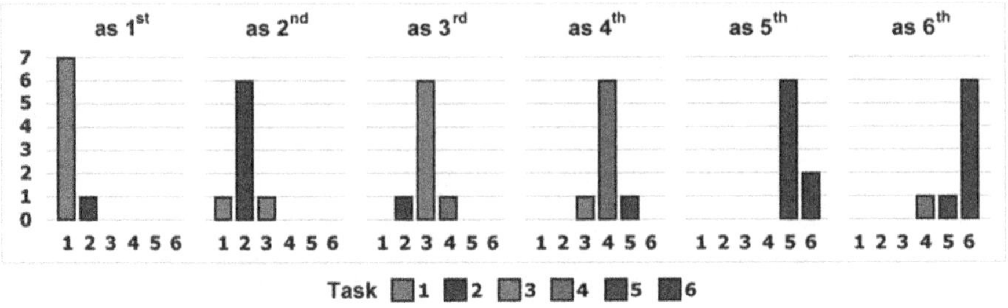

Fig. 4. Expert sample (n = 8) rankings of the tasks. (Color figure online)

In Fig. 4, the rankings of the experts are analysed (n = 8). For example, our task 1 (yellow) was assessed seven times as the simplest one and once as the 2nd. Task 2 was once assessed as the easiest, six times as the 2nd and once as the 3rd. In general, we see that experts significantly validated our understanding of the increasing cognitive demands of the different operations, although the variance in their rankings slightly increases towards more demanding tasks. As we noticed similar trend in the teacher sample, we will provide our interpretation of this in the discussion.

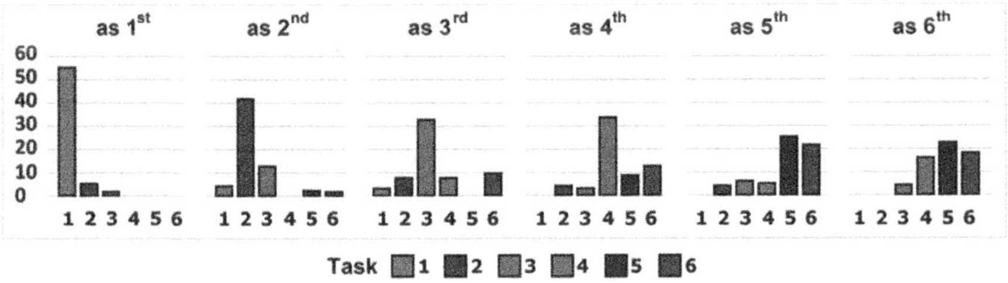

Fig. 5. Teacher sample (n = 62) rankings of the tasks. (Color figure online)

In Fig. 5, we see corresponding visualisation of the teacher sample (n = 62) rankings. In general, it shows that teachers perceive the differences between the operations related to repetition in Y3 and classify their cognitive demands in accordance with the experts and the authors. However, the variance in their rankings is significantly higher and considerably increases towards the harder tasks, with our tasks 5 and 6 being undistinguished in their cognitive demands. This is clearer when we use the alternative perspective on the rankings (see Fig. 6), showing the variability of the tasks which experts and teachers assessed as the 1st (the easiest), as the 2nd, and so on.

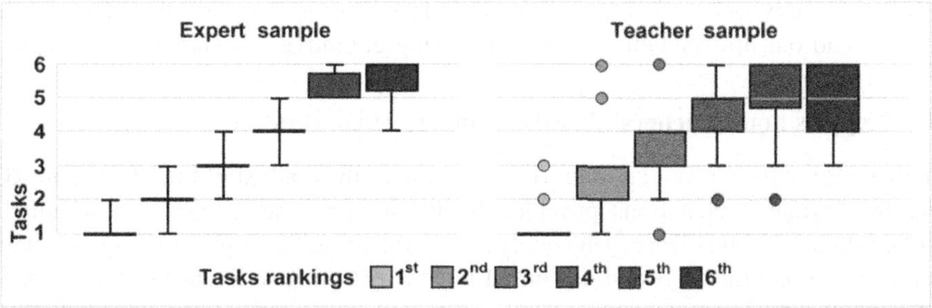

Fig. 6. Variation of the rankings in the expert and teacher samples.

Single points located *distant* from either the lower or upper quartiles (i.e., outliers) are depicted here as small circles. Note that in the expert rankings, only the last two tasks show non-zero interquartile range (Q_1, Q_2 and Q_3 being identical), with medians still being 5 in the 5th place and 6 in the 6th place. The variability in the teacher rankings is significantly higher, with the medians being 1, 2, 3, 4, 5, and 5. Clearly, while all operations are being recognised by the teachers as different, the interquartile range grows considerably from left to right and the cognitive demands of our tasks 4, 5 and 6 become blurred, especially in the last place of the rankings.

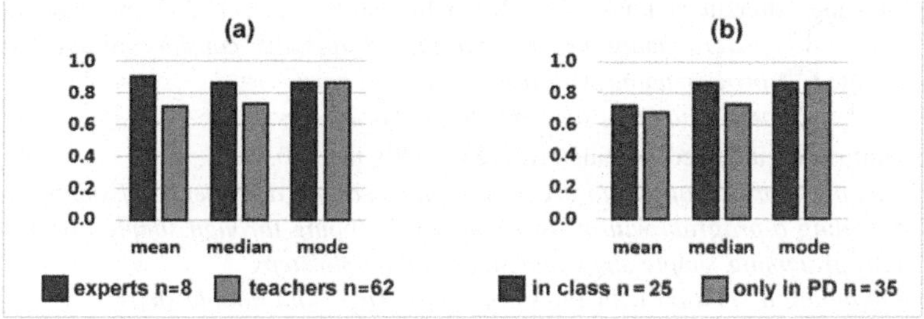

Fig. 7. Kendall's tau correlations (a) in expert and teacher samples, and (b) in the breakdown of the teacher sample into those who have used the intervention in the class and who have not yet.

To analyse the data from another perspective, we measured the ordinal association between collected rankings (cognitive demands of the tasks as perceived by the experts and by the teachers) and our implemented ranking, deriving the Kendall rank correlation coefficient (Kendall's tau) for each. Figure 7 demonstrates a few basic statistics descriptors of the results, after excluding one outlier with negative tau (based on the related textual comments). In (a) certain differences in the expert and teacher samples can be seen, most significantly in the mean and median. Diagram (b) describes the rankings of the teachers ($n = 62$) breakdown into those who have already used the intervention in their classes and those who have so far taken part only in the PD session. Any significant difference in those two data sets was not observed, except that the *in-class* data set has higher median and its upper 50% scores are between 1 and

0.8667, i.e., only one or less necessary bubble sort swap between the items of their rankings and our understanding of the increasing cognitive demands (1, 2, 3, 4, 5, 6).

4.1 Experts and Teachers' Justifications of Their Rankings

Another source for our research effort, interesting in the context of both RQ1 and RQ2, were the textual explanations provided by the experts and teachers, in which they justified their rankings. During the analysis, we relied on the corresponding correlation coefficients of the rankings and our initial intended ranking of the tasks' demands. The first important finding achieved in this manner is that all participants are clearly aware of the differences between operations with the same concept and can characterise them properly. Furthermore, we obtained better insight into why the variance in the rankings increases towards more demanding tasks (Table 2).

Table 2. Selected justifications of the experts' and teachers' rankings.

Experts confirming intended ranking (with Kendall's tau between 0.8667 and 1) • (Task 1) *simple representation, simple reading of a sequence of commands* • (Task 2) *stepping through a program with simple stacks of single basic commands* • (Task 3) *understanding basic commands, their repetition, the rules of moving Emil* • (Task 4) *looking for a solution which uses given double card repeatedly* • (Task 5) *understanding what double card represents, how to step through a program* • (Task 6) *same as 5, but containing triple cards*
Experts justifying different rankings (with Kendall's tau between 0.7333 and 0.8667) • (Task 3 as the 4th) *programming with limited number of steps, considering alternatives* • (Task 4 as the 6th) *programming with a given double card* • (Task 5 as the 6th) *understanding how repetition works*
Teachers confirming intended ranking (with Kendall's tau > 0.5) • (Task 1) *simple representation, no algorithm, only reading a sequence of simple steps* • (Task 2) *reading a program with known notation, stepping through simple program* • (Task 3) *programming simple steps and stacks of simple steps* • (Task 4) *planning a solution with stacks of simple steps and double steps* • (Task 5) *understanding the repetition of double cards* • (Task 6) *harder than 5 because it requires reading a program with triple cards*
Teachers justifying different rankings (with Kendall's tau $\leq$ 0.5) • (Task 3 as the 1st) *simple programming with commands gathered in stacks* • (Task 5 as the 2nd) *simple counting the commands* • (Task 6 as the 3rd) *understanding the order of the steps, understanding the notation* • (Task 6 as the 4th) *understanding the order of the steps when double cards and triple cards are used in the program* • (Task 3 as the 5th) *programming with limited number of steps, understanding the number of repetitions* • (Task 3 as the 6th) *programming (planning a solution) is required*

5 Discussion

In this research, our aim was to investigate whether our *granularity refinement strategy* (as we put it in [19]) is productive in setting learning goals. We tried to not only better understand which concepts are developmentally appropriate for the primary stage, but to assess this adequacy in more detail, in the context of the various operations that pupils have to perform with each concept in different KS2 years.

We contacted more than 300 teachers and computing education experts, who had already attended PD session(s) on our intervention for Y3 and asked them to solve a set of six assessment tasks, ranking them from the easiest to the most difficult and comment on their choice. We gathered 62 + 8 responses and applied various statistical methods to the data obtained in this way. For instance, we studied the degree of similarity between our understanding of the cognitive demands of the different operations implemented in the tasks and participants' own rankings.

Both expert and teacher samples clearly confirmed our assessment of different cognitive demands of the operations and their proper gradation. However, especially in the teacher sample, the variance in the rankings increased towards more demanding tasks, with tasks 5 and 6 becoming almost equal in their demands. Hence, when planning or analysing the suitability of activities gradation for certain age group and expectations, at least two factors must be considered: one stems from the inherent cognitive demands of different operations pupils must perform with a concept, the other represents the pedagogy applied. Naturally, there are several ways depicting how the intervention can implement specific progression (still respecting the inherent gradation of the cognitive demands). Our pedagogy is based on the constructionist epistemology, which always starts with concrete experience and *direct control* [16] to acquire an opportunity to discover new operation (in close collaboration in the pairs and regular whole class discussions), new mechanism or new reaction, such as the one that repeats *commands* automatically gather in a *stack of commands*, Fig. 1(ii to v). Only then the gradation proceeds to *programming control* [ibid] and practising a new piece of knowledge. This, however, has the consequence that if pupils or teachers have already made a discovery, new operation or mechanism becomes known and as such 'simple': in the assessment tasks they see well known notation and its meaning they already know.

In spite of this, all experts and teachers in general agreed on our perception of growing difficulty of the operations, with tasks 1, 2, 3 always preceding 4, 5 and 6, with 4 easier than 5 and 5 easier than 6 for most of the experts. Most importantly, all experts and teachers were aware of the differences between the operations related to repetition, correctly naming and distinguishing between them.

We also noticed other interesting details, which, however, need to be followed in more detail, such as whether the rankings are influenced by the time span since attending the PD session, whether they already have real experience from the class (Fig. 7b) etc.

Acknowledgments. This work has been funded in part by VEGA Slovak Agency under project *Productive gradation of computational concepts in programming in primary school* 1/0602/20.

References

1. Sentence, S.: Moving to mainstream: developing computing for all. In: Proceedings of the WiPSCE 2019 (2019). https://doi.org/10.1145/3361721.3362117
2. Blackwell, A.F.: What is programming? In: 14th Annual Workshop of Psychology of Programming Interest Group, pp. 204–218 (2002)
3. Department for Education: National curriculum in England: computing programmes of study (2013). www.gov.uk/government/publications
4. Gujberova, M., Kalas, I.: Designing productive gradations of tasks in primary programming education. In: Proceedings of the WiPSCE 2013, pp. 109–118. ACM, Aarhus (2013)
5. Kalas, I., Benton, L.: Defining procedures in early computing education. In: Tatnall, A., Webb, M. (eds.) WCCE 2017. IAICT, vol. 515, pp. 567–578. Springer, Cham (2017). https://doi.org/10.1007/978-3-319-74310-3_57
6. Plomp, T., Nieveen, N. (eds.): Educational Design Research. Part A: An Introduction. SLO, Enschede (2013)
7. CSTA and ACM: Computer Science K-8: Building a Strong Foundation (2012)
8. MŠMT: Rámcový vzdělávací program pro základní vzdělávání, Praha (2021)
9. Bers, M.U.: Coding, playgrounds and literacy in early childhood education: the development of KIBO robotics and ScratchJr. In: Proceedings of the 2018 IEEE Global Engineering Education Conference (EDUCAN), pp. 2094–2102 (2018)
10. Brennan, K., Resnick, M.: New frameworks for studying and assessing the development of computational thinking. In: Proceedings of the 2012 Annual Meeting of the American Edu Research Association, Vancouver (2012)
11. Meerbaum-Salant, O., Armoni, M., Ben-Ari, M.: Learning computer science concepts with Scratch. Comput. Sci. Educ. **23**(3), 239–264 (2013)
12. CSTA: K-12 Computer Science Standards, Revised 2017 (2017). www.csteachers.org/page/standards
13. Dagiene, V., Hromkovic, J., Lacher, R.: Designing informatics curriculum for K-12 education: from concepts to implementations. Inf. Educ. **20**(3), 333–360 (2021)
14. Perlman, R.: Using Computer Technology to Provide a Creative Learning Environment for Preschool Children. AI Memo 360. MIT, Cambridge (1976)
15. Morgado, L., Cruz, M., Kahn, K.: Radia Perlman: a pioneer of young children computer programming. In: Current Developments in Technology-Assisted Education, pp. 1903–1908. Formatex, Badajos (2006)
16. Kalas, I., Blaho, A., Moravcik, M.: Exploring control in early computing education. In: Pozdniakov, S.N., Dagienė, V. (eds.) ISSEP 2018. LNCS, vol. 11169, pp. 3–16. Springer, Cham (2018). https://doi.org/10.1007/978-3-030-02750-6_1
17. Benton, L., Hoyles, C., Kalas, I., Noss, R.: Bridging primary programming and mathematics: some findings of design research in England. Digit. Experiences in Math. Educ. **3**(2), 115–138 (2017). https://doi.org/10.1007/s40751-017-0028-x
18. Cohen, L., Manion, L., Morrison, K.: Research Methods in Education. Routledge, London (2017)
19. Webb, M., et al.: Moving on with informatics/computer science curricula – challenges and opportunities. In: Symposium Presented at IFIP TC3 OCCE 2021 DTEL (2021)

"Literacy from Python"

Using Python for a Proposed Cross-curricular Teaching and Learning Model

Lawrence Williams[1](✉) and Beth Mead[2]

[1] TPEA Specialist Leader in EdTech Education, London, UK
[2] Safeguarded School Student, Wimbledon, London, UK

Abstract. This pilot case study, which outlines an introductory computer programming project, using Python, builds on the international success of the "Literacy from Scratch" teaching model [1–3]. Its aim is to contextualise the teaching of Python through a cross-curricular teaching and learning model, rather than through teaching Python elements separately. It therefore recommends the development of elementary coding skills by pupils, aged from 10 to 14 years, through the creation of very short stories or scripts, using Python strings. Each story chapter of the project further introduces worked examples of additional Python programming elements such as Turtle graphics and times-tables, within the constructionist framework of a creative writing project [4]. The project is supported by a free website for teachers. Our hope is that this creative approach to coding may encourage the enthusiastic adoption of such a cross-curricular method for teaching and learning computer coding with Python in our schools.

Keywords: Python · Scratch · Story-telling · Cross-curricular teaching and learning · Creativity · Constructionism · Contextualisation

1 Introduction

Teachers in England state schools are required to teach two computer programming languages to their students, from age 5 years. One of these languages can be a visual or "block coding" program, such as Scratch, but the other must be text-based, such as Python. In practice, the programs most commonly used in England's schools, because they are free, are Scratch, frequently for pupils aged 5 to 11 years, followed by Python for ages 11 years upwards. Some schools purchase computer programming packages because they come with prepared lesson plans, and teaching strategies. To support the development of Scratch in our UK schools, Brunel University London, and Charles University in Prague, Czech Republic, with Torino University, Italy, developed the free website, "Literacy from Scratch". Devised by Lawrence Williams (at Brunel's Education Department), and quickly shared with other teacher training teams abroad, it proved to be very popular, and an accompanying text book was subsequently commissioned, and published, by Routledge [5]. The learning model for Python, presented here, is founded on the same constructionist and psychological principles [6].

Published by Springer Nature Switzerland AG 2022
D. Passey et al. (Eds.): OCCE 2021, IFIP AICT 642, pp. 41–53, 2022.
https://doi.org/10.1007/978-3-030-97986-7_4

My previous work in "Literacy from Scratch" at Brunel's partner schools in west London, resulted in pupil projects being fully completed by an entire Year 8 group (160 students, aged 12–13 years) at Bishop Ramsey School, and later by a Year 1 class (aged 5 years) and a Year 2 class (aged 6 years) at the Swaminarayan Primary School. All of the pupils involved met all the assessment criteria for the project, including story-telling, use of dialogue, animation, and simple art work for creating backgrounds and story characters. The success of this earlier project rested partly on the contextualisation of the learning of coding: secondary school pupils wanted to tell their stories, and the only way to do this was through using accurate Scratch coding, a powerful incentive to learning. At Primary school level (5 years to 11), the teachers already knew how to develop creative writing skills, and, once again, Scratch became the new means by which to deliver creative and animated narrative work. Contextualised learning, in our view, clearly helps students to make connections between the content of their studies and the context in which it is developed. Vygotsky [6] refers to this as the "gap between what is known and what is being learned". Students draw from their previous experience (in this case, of writing narratives, creating characters and dialogue) to give new meaning to what they are now learning i.e. Scratch and Python computer coding [7].

The second requirement of using a text-based computer language, however, is more difficult for UK teachers, currently still largely untrained in programming. Following the classroom success of the "Literacy from Scratch" teaching and learning project, we (the paper authors) are starting to develop "Literacy from Python", based on this earlier curriculum model. It aims to support the following elements of the Programmes of Study, Key Stage 3, England National Curriculum[1]:

"Pupils should be taught to:

- "use 2 or more programming languages, **at least one of which is textual, to solve a variety of computational problems; make appropriate use of data structures [for example, lists, tables or arrays];** design and develop modular programs that use procedures or functions
- "understand how instructions are stored and executed within a computer system; **understand how data of various types (including text, sounds and pictures) can be represented and manipulated digitally, in the form of binary digits**
- **"undertake creative projects that involve selecting, using, and combining multiple applications, preferably across a range of devices, to achieve challenging goals, including collecting and analysing data and meeting the needs of known users**
- **"create, reuse, revise and repurpose digital artefacts for a given audience**, with attention to trustworthiness, design and usability"[2].

---

[1] Statutory Guidance, announced in February 2012, National Curriculum in England, Computing Programmes of Study, Key Stage 3, for implementation (2013).

[2] The UK National Curriculum in Computing elements, highlighted in bold, are fulfilled by the "Literacy from Python" project.

The first steps taken (called Chapter 1 on the website) were originally, however, simply an experimental exploration of what might be done to contextualise the learning of Python, as we had done earlier for Scratch. Once the model had been conceptualised by the paper's authors as a possible cross-curricular working model, however, Beth (Beth Mead, a primary school pupil, then aged 11 years) and I set about developing further narrative scripts. The model was developed based specifically on the "Literacy from Scratch" model, and all of the Python coding was written by Beth. Largely self-taught, she used coding books [8], and online resources, such as the modified Turtle graphics example given in Chapter 3, shown later. Each Chapter added more Python elements as part of Beth's narrative scripts, and we created a website to share these thoughts (and the coding elements) with teachers. This thinking crystalised into the following set of project aims for the "Literacy from Python" project:

- To develop a cross-curricular project including simple story-writing skills and computer coding
- To develop elementary computer programming skills, using Python elements, such as strings and lists
- To provide support for UK Key Stage Computing courses (for ages 11 to 14 years) and GCSE Computer Science (for ages 15 to 16 years), and possibly for post-graduate teacher training courses
- To develop contextualised learning as a framework for teaching Python
- To create an educational support site, where teachers can download suitable, free classroom resources based on this teaching and learning model

The "Literacy from Python" project evolved, then, from an experiment with story-telling, which started in early 2018. Beth wrote the first short story using Python strings, set in a classroom, and involving her real-life pet dog, Maisy, and her Aunt Justine's cat, Malika. This project was itself the development of a series of short stories, "Stories for Children 2" that she had already written and published on the web, using Microsoft (MS) PowerPoint, to exemplify some basic computer coding concepts such as Algorithms, Abstraction, Decomposition, Generalisation, Logical Thinking, and If, Then, Else. These MS PowerPoint coding stories are posted on the "World Ecitizens" website as a free resource for teachers. There was then a delay, throughout 2018, while Beth and I worked together on some new projects using Scratch 2 and then Scratch 3, incorporating Sibelius music files with Lloyd Mead, at Lambeth College [9]. We returned to look at Python in 2019, to develop this storytelling idea further. Frustratingly, while positive discussions are currently underway with local schools and colleges, the classroom development of this work has, owing to severely restricted access to schools, been slowed by Covid[3].

While there is a useful (single) introductory lesson on the MIT Scratch website, showing how to download Python, there is, as yet, no material for developing story-telling using Python in the cross-curricular way suggested in this paper. The Python websites have methods for generating storytelling with Pandas ('The library called **pandas'** is a

[3] This teaching model was first accepted for presentation at ICET 2020 (Vancouver), but was later withdrawn because of health concerns caused by the Covid pandemic. Presentation of the paper was postponed, and later delivered by remote video link, at OCCE-IFIP 2021, for the TPEA.

Python package that provides data structures and is useful for structured and time-series data), but, once again, this is quite different from the creative, cross-curricular, constructionist, contextualised method of teaching and learning that we are advocating.

The accompanying Python website[4], developed to support this curriculum initiative, outlines several Python coding skills developed through creative narrative work, divided into very short Chapters or scripts. More elements are planned (see Fig. 10).

2 Method

In English lessons, or as an after-school homework, students aged 10 years and upward, will (post-Covid) be encouraged to create characters, and write a very short story which includes some dialogue - the "literacy" aspect of the project. This story can then be taken to the computer room, where, using Python, it can be reworked in the IDLE programming window, and printed out in the Shell window as an elementary Python program. This model therefore adds creative and cross-curricular elements to the computer coding process. In Fig. 1, the programming example can be seen, faintly, on the right of the illustration, with the instruction to print (in pink in Python – and on the website), with blank lines added as brackets () and the "table" imported, so that when the story is saved and "Run" as a program, the reader can choose a times-table which prints out within the story (in blue text in Python) in the left, shell, window. The "Literacy from Python" website provides a clearer, more colourful view.

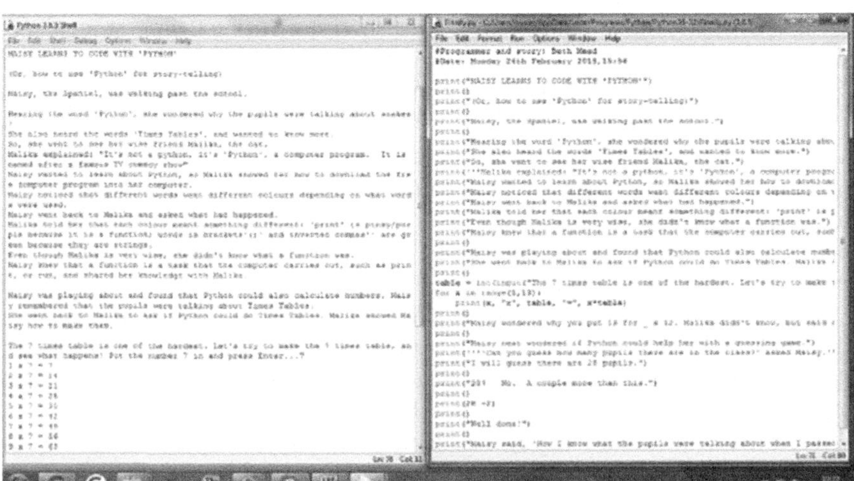

Fig. 1. Simple Python programming for storytelling and times tables. (Color figure online)

[4] The websites referenced in this paper can all be found using Google searches.

This process therefore combines storytelling, simple arithmetic (addition and times-tables), as well as computer programming. It is explained in fuller detail on the "Literacy from Python" website, together with the downloadable Python story files, for students and teachers to explore and develop in their own classrooms.

Fig. 2. Maisy, a real-life Spaniel

Maisy (Fig. 2) is one of the characters in the Python stories. She also appears in the 2017 storybook series that accompanies this ongoing project. Each story, originally in MS PowerPoint format, and free for use in the classroom, looks at a different element of computational thinking ("World Ecitizens" website). Some of these concepts are detailed below.

Computational Thinking

There is no single, agreed definition of computational thinking. It depends upon whom you ask - programmer, logician, or mathematician. There are, however, several generally agreed elements, and these are explored in these stories for children. For information on the choice of computational thinking concepts, these are shown in the resources developed by computing at school, and include:

- Algorithmic thinking (following a set of rules; sequencing skills)
- Debugging (detecting and correcting errors)
- Decomposition (breaking a complex problem down into simpler parts)
- Logical thinking (reasoning skills)
- Generalisation (recognising patterns, and using them to find solutions)
- Abstraction (sorting relevant information from unnecessary detail)

These concepts [8] are presented individually through these Maisy stories, and can be shown to pupils on an interactive whiteboard, or printed out for use in the classroom (see Fig. 3). They can then be discussed in class and incorporated into the narrative work before embarking on Python coding.

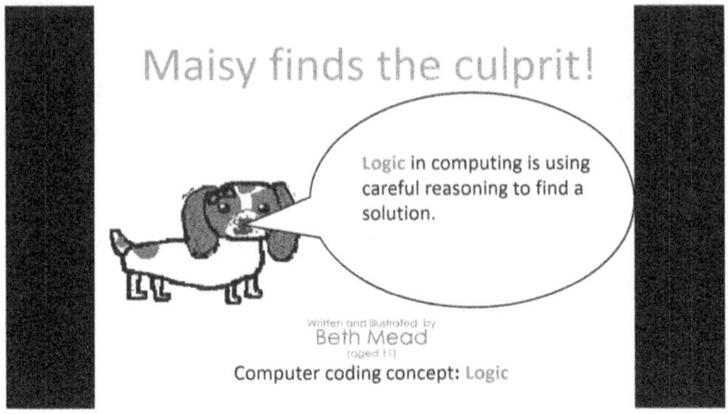

Fig. 3. A sample title page (one of six stories) exemplifying a coding concept

This teaching method has inspired us (Beth and myself) to develop the idea further, in addition to the MS PowerPoint method, above, incorporating more and more Python programming elements, as well as developing the storybook characters along the way [7]. "Literacy from Python" can be seen, therefore, as the latest development of a series of storytelling projects, which can be found set out in historical sequence, on the "World. Ecitizens" web site (see the homepage and scroll down: http://www.worldecitizens.net/).

The five-chapter story series, together with the Python elements is given below.

Chapter 1: Addition and Times Tables
Python Elements: Text Entry plus Importation of Times-tables

Using Python 3.6.5 originally (see the small text in the top bar of the Fig. 4 file), Beth created a children's story which introduced her animal characters, Maisy and Malika, to Addition and Time Tables within an imaginary classroom scenario. This teaching and learning process is further explained on the website, with practical hints for teachers (see Introduction and Teachers' Notes).

It is a creative, cross-curricular project that so far involves:

- English (writing short stories, including very careful punctuation)
- Mathematics (addition, times-tables, geometry – and we hope to add graphs later)
- Geography
- Art
- Computing (using Python coding, as a second coding language after Scratch)
- ICT (file management as part of computing)

Beth used the print text facility in Python to make the following short story chapters. It shows how Python sub-routines (a table, table = int) can be imported and used within a story-telling context. The text appears within the brackets in green, and "prints out" as blue:

table = int(input("The 7 times table is one of the hardest. Let's try to make the 7 times table, and see what happens! Put the number 7 in and press Enter..."))

for x in range(1,13):

print(x, "x", table, "=", x*table)

This is found to be much easier than it looks.

So, she wrote the following story, called "Finally" on the website (Finally.Py) while still in primary school, Year 6, aged 11 years. This later became "Chapter 1" of the current larger computer coding project, "Literacy from Python", i.e. writing short stories created by using Python.

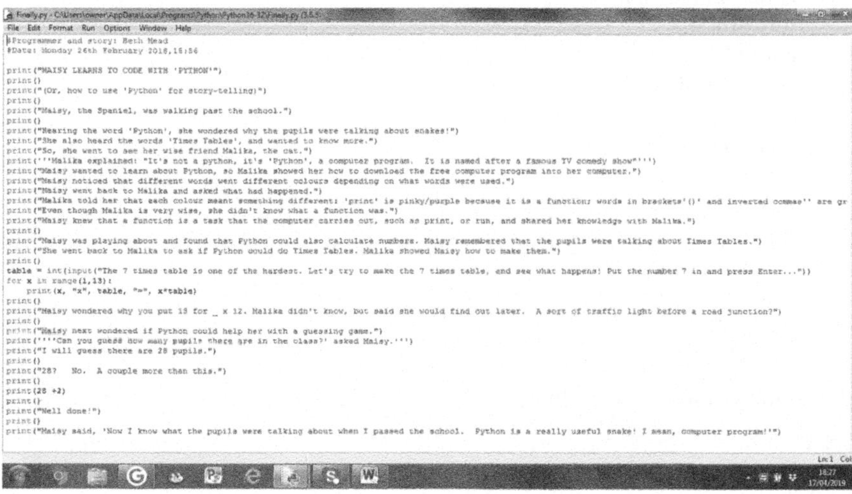

Fig. 4. With table included. (Color figure online)

Chapter 2: A Geometry Lesson
Python Elements: Text Entry plus Turtle Module

This Chapter looks at python for making geometrical shapes. (A year on from Chapter 1, we are now using version 3.7.2.) In the story, the animal characters learn to make a circle and a square, by importing turtle graphics (Fig. 5).

Here is an excerpt from the story:

```
    print('''Malika said, "My friend Maisy and I have been working on Python.
We have been learning how to draw geometrical shapes.
    Maisy, would you like to remind everyone how these look? How about a
circle and a square?"''')
    print()
    import turtle
    window = turtle.Screen()
    turtle.bgcolor("mintcream") #background colour of the window
    turtle.color("olive") #stroke colour
    turtle. begin_fill()
    turtle. circle(80)
    turtle.end_fill
    from turtle import*
    color("mintcream")
    forward(50)
    color("skyblue")
    shape("turtle")
    pensize(4)
    forward(50)
    right(90)
    forward(50)
    right(90)
    forward(50)
    right(90)
    forward(50)
    right(90)
```

The result of the above coding:

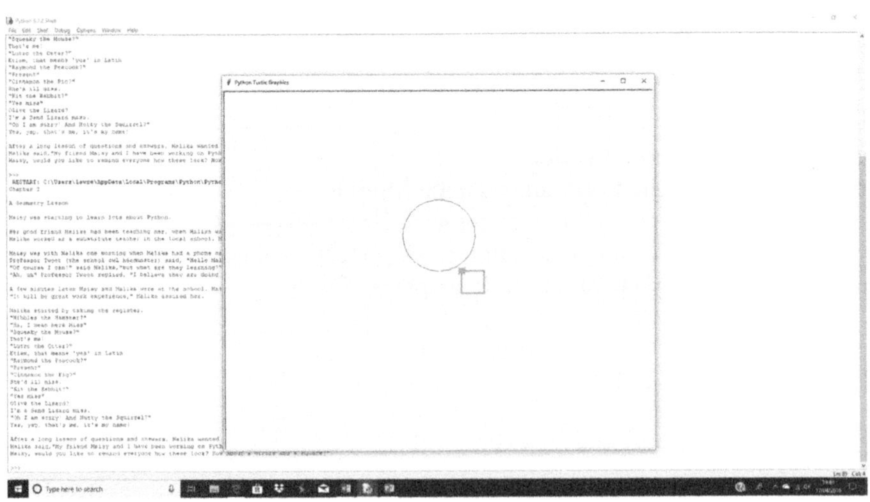

Fig. 5. Drawing a circle and square in Python, with the story and dialogue on the left

Chapter 3: A Biology Lesson
Python Elements: Text Entry plus Turtle Graphics
This Chapter was demanding. It is a biology lesson, with graphics. The story has a decorative flower at the end, thanks to inspiration from Aibek Toroev (a software engineer from Kyrgyzstan). There is a useful YouTube video created by Aibek Toroev, and with his coding later adapted by Beth, at: https://www.youtube.com/watch?v=ZsnKkyRCWR4.

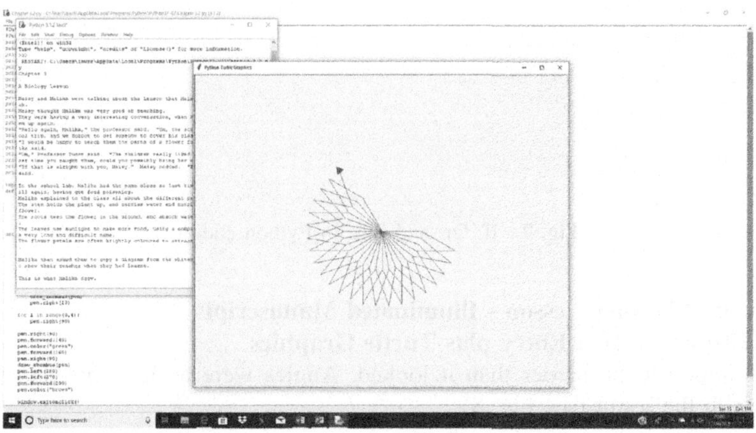

Fig. 6. The flower in progress (see the website file for the finished bloom)

As noted above, the England National Curriculum in Computing requires pupils to "**create, re-use, revise and re-purpose**" digital information, and Fig. 6 is an example of this requirement.

Chapter 4: A Geography Lesson (Quiz)
Python Elements: Text Entry plus If, Or, Else
The curriculum focus of this Chapter is geography, with a classroom quiz based on If, Or, and Else in Python coding (see Fig. 7).

```
#Monday 1st April 2019
#Programmer Beth Mead
#Thanks to Ethan and Nate (testers)
print("A Geography Lesson")
print()
print("Malika is a very kind cat. She has always liked helping others in need, and so she is friendly with almost all of the teachers at the school.")
print("One morning the phone rang.  It was Miss Bindi, the Koala teacher of Geography, who came from Australia.")
print('''"G'day Malika," Miss Bindi said.  "Would ya mind coverin' my lesson t'day? It's the last day of school, and I'm goin' back t' Oz for the hol'days."''')
print('Malika, of course, said she would. She then called Maisy, who said she wanted to come, too.')
print('Maisy and Malika met outside the school gates.')
print('"So, what are we teaching today?" Maisy asked.')
print('"We are teaching the same class as usual, but we are teaching them Geography."')
print('''Maisy and Malika knew the class so well now they didn't even need to call the register. They just did it themselves.''')
print('They taught the class some general geographical knowledge. The class enjoyed the lesson very much.')
print('At the end of the lesson, Malika spoke to the class.')
print('"This is a quiz on what we have learnt." Malika said, "Remember you must NOT put Full Stops at the end, as the computer will mark it as wrong."')
print()
print()
print('"What is the capital city of France?"')
ans=input()
if ans=="Paris" or ans=="paris":
    print("You are correct!")
else:
    print("It's called Paris.")
print()
print('"What is the longest river in the UK?"')
ans= input()
if ans=="Severn" or ans=="severn":
    print("Well done!")
if ans=="Seven" or ans=="seven":
    print("Close, but it is spelt Severn.")
else:
    print("It's called The River Severn.")
print()
print("What are the four MAIN compass points?(Remember capital letters!)")
print("CLUE: put it in NOEW order.")
ans=input()
if ans=="North South East West" or ans=="North South East and West" or ans=="North, South, East and West":
    print("Correct!")
else:
    print("North, South, East and West are known as compass points.")
print()
print("Is the North or South pole colder?")
ans=input()
if ans=="north" or ans=="North" or ans=="north pole" or ans=="North pole" or ans=="North Pole":
    print("It's the south that is colder.")
if ans=="south" or ans=="South" or ans=="south pole" or ans=="South pole" or ans=="South Pole":
    print("Well done! Not many people know that.")
print()
print('Well done!  You have completed the quiz!')
```

Fig. 7. If, Or, and Else in Python coding

Chapter 5: A History Lesson - Illuminated Manuscripts

Python Elements: Text Entry plus Turtle Graphics

This was found to be harder than it looked. Angles were a challenge, but we were pleased with the result (see Fig. 8).

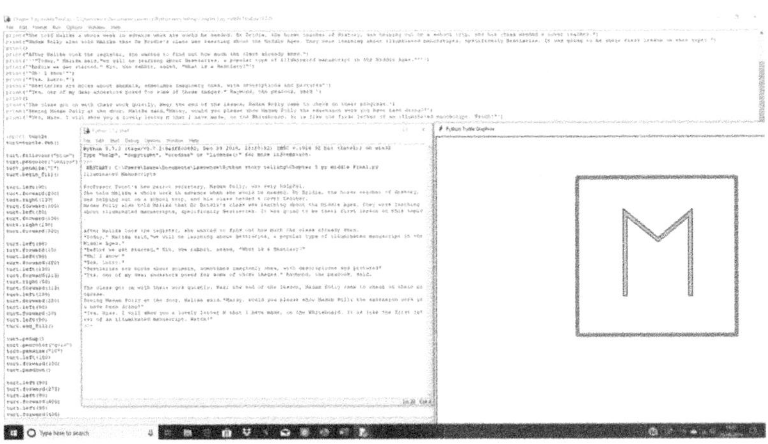

Fig. 8. Coding input with story output, and an "illuminated" letter M

This ended up as a Chapter about a history lesson. However, Beth and I had some discussion about it possibly being part of an English punctuation lesson (on capital letters) or possibly an art lesson (on calligraphy), or Mathematics (on angles).

3 Outcomes

The "Literacy from Python" project is steadily meeting its objectives. The teachers' website (see Fig. 9) now has a series of five completed exemplar stories in short "Chapters" in which the animal characters, using Python, explore simple arithmetical concepts such as addition, and times-tables; a lesson in geometry; a lesson in biology; a lesson with a geography quiz (if, or, else); and using Python to create lettering (graphics). There are background and introductory notes for teachers, a MS PowerPoint file indicating the general teaching method, and links to related websites, including one on constructionism, on which the project is based. The project also supports the Programmes of Study for the England National Curriculum in Computing for Key Stage 3. So far (October 2021), the Python website has had over 1,000 visitors. How far the ideas posted there have been applied in schools remains to be seen: we have added a Contact Form to the website to support this evidence gathering.

Fig. 9. Literacy from Python website

This constructionist project therefore brings together many elements of the England school computing curriculum (including ICT skills, computer programming, and computational thinking), together with creative writing, elements of simple mathematics, geography, biology, and other curriculum subjects, all presented through storytelling (see Fig. 10).

	Literacy elements	Curriculum focus	Python coding elements
Chapter 1	Narrative, description, dialogue	Mathematics	Text entry; times tables
Chapter 2	Narrative, description, dialogue	Geometry	Text entry; Turtle graphics
Chapter 3	Narrative, description, dialogue	Biology	Text entry; Turtle graphics
Chapter 4	Narrative, description, dialogue	Geography	Text entry; If, Or, Else
Chapter 5	Narrative, description, dialogue	History	Text entry; Turtle graphics
Chapter 6 (pending)	Narrative, description, dialogue	TBC	Lists, loops, libraries, iteration

Fig. 10. Project elements and future plans

4 Future Plans

Further work is currently under discussion with local schools and colleges, with a view, post-Covid, to widening the number of students participating in the project, and to developing the number of computer coding concepts, such as loops or lists, within it. The initial project aims and objectives have, however, all been met: the constructionist/contextualised method is now clearly established through the exemplar stories; the supporting website has been started; and the dissemination of these ideas (through IFIP TC3 OCCE 2021Tampere) has begun. We need, next, to ascertain how many, and how easily, pupils can develop their own narrative script; create lists, loops, iteration and so on; and then integrate these elements successfully into their narrative scripts, thus contextualising their learning [8]. There are two curriculum levels possible for this development in England schools: at Key Stage 3 (ages 11 to 14 years), and within Key Stage 4 GCSE Computer Studies courses (ages 14 to 16 years), where a coursework element in coding is a requirement. It may also be a useful model for postgraduate teacher training courses in computer science. In this way, local school and college feedback can, in the future, be incorporated into the project and its website, and greater quantitative data about uptake of the model will thereby be generated to assist in evaluating the success, in wider practice, of the teaching approach suggested in this paper.

The international success of the cross-curricular coding project "Literacy from Scratch", encourages our development of "Literacy from Python", despite current progress being severely slowed by the Covid pandemic.

We hope that the free teaching materials on the now-integrated websites ("World Ecitizens", "Literacy from Scratch" and "Literacy from Python") may be of practical use in the classroom.

References

1. Passey, D., Mavengere, N. (Eds.): Literacy from Scratch. In: Proceedings of the 10th IFIP World Conference on Computers in Education, Torun, Poland, 2–5 July 2013, pp. 17–27. Springer, Heidelberg, Germany (2013)
2. Demo, G.B., Williams, L.: A working model for teacher training in computing through the "literacy from scratch project - the many facets of scratch". In: Proceedings of the ISSEP Conference 2014, September, Istanbul, Turkey. Springer, Heidelberg, Germany(2014)
3. Passey, D., Tatnall., A. (Eds.): An international working model for teacher training in computing: key competencies for educating ICT professionals. In: Proceedings of the 10th IFIP World Conference on Computers in Education, Potsdam, Germany, pp 25-33.Springer, Heidelberg, Germany (2014)
4. Kalaš, I., Mikolajová, K., Tomcsány, K.: "Konštrukcionizmus. Od Piageta po školu v digitálnom. DidInfo 2011, Slovakia (2011)
5. Williams, L. (ed.): Introducing Computing: A Guide for Teachers. Routledge, London (2014)
6. Vygotsky, L.S.: Mind in Society: The Development of Higher Psychological Processes. Harvard University Press, Cambridge (1978)

7. Williams, L., Černochová, M., Dorling, M.: Developing computational thinking skills through the literacy from scratch project: an international collaboration. In: 11th IFIP Conference, July 2015, Vilnius, Lithuania (2015). (unpublished paper)
8. Stowell, L.: Coding for Beginners: Using Python. Usborne, Tulsa, TX (2018)
9. Luckin, R. (ed.): Enhancing Teaching and Learning with Technology - What the Research Says. UCL Press, London (2018)
10. Younie, S., Bradshaw, P. (eds.): Debates in Computing and ICT Education, pp. 97–114. Routledge, London (2017). https://doi.org/10.4324/9781315709505

Advocating for Educational Support to Develop Socially Disadvantaged Young People's Digital Skills and Competencies: Can Support Encourage Their Human Development as Digital Citizens?

Toshinori Saito(✉)

Seisa University, Yokohama, Kanagawa, Japan
t-saito@gred.seisa.ac.jp

Abstract. Digital skills and competencies, and civic participation based on such skills and competencies (i.e. digital citizenship), are recognised as a challenge for the coming digital society. This paper contends that educational support to develop socially disadvantaged young people's digital skills and competencies has a positive impact on digital citizenship. Accordingly, findings based on four years of action research among a support group for socially disadvantaged youths in a provincial city in Japan and a discussion of the support's impact are presented. Our results suggest that such educational support can expand one's freedom to explore digital technology's potential, self-determination as an active learner in a digital environment, and space to participate in a digital society as a digital citizen.

Keywords: Digital skills · Digital competency · Digital citizenship · Computational thinking · Human development · ICT4D

1 Introduction

Common understandings of the significance of citizens' knowledge, skills, competence, and attitudes in relation to digital technology are reflected in frameworks and concepts developed over the past decade. Such frameworks provide a perspective on both simple digital technology use, and complex activities such as "communication and collaboration" or "problem-solving". Typical of these frameworks are the European Commission's Digital Competence Framework for Citizens (DigComp 2.0) [1] and UNESCO's Digital Literacy Global Framework (DLGF) [2], the latter based on a review of DigComp 2.0 and further investigation into global examples of digital skill frameworks. Both refer specifically to offering a comprehensive and synthesised competence model for digital technology use and for activities emerging from its use by defining several competence areas as targets for citizens' digital competence improvement. Digital citizenship is also a concept that focuses on citizens' knowledge, skills, competence, and attitude in relation to digital technology, but it stresses achieving and protecting citizens' rights of democratic participation in digital

Published by Springer Nature Switzerland AG 2022
D. Passey et al. (Eds.): OCCE 2021, IFIP AICT 642, pp. 54–66, 2022.
https://doi.org/10.1007/978-3-030-97986-7_5

environments. The Digital Citizenship Education Handbook by the Council of Europe [3] introduces a conceptual model for digital citizenship based on the Council's 20 competences for democratic culture (CDCs). A UNESCO report [4] explains that a core competency of digital citizenship should address how to use digital technology in an ethical, safe, and responsible way, without restricting users' full participation in and contribution to the knowledge society.

Nevertheless, there are few empirical studies on whether and how the establishment of digital citizenship through digital skills acquisition might function to ensure citizens' rights and dignity, especially among socially disadvantaged people in developed countries with advanced digital environments. Among such studies, Kafai, Peppler, and Chiu [5] and Fields, Kafai, and Giang [6] suggest that: the acquisition of digital skills and competencies by citizens is the very social participation that digital citizenship is concerned with; gaps in social participation are strongly reflected in the encounter with programming in particular; educational support within schools and beyond can reduce participation gaps in digital skills and competencies. However, these studies do not highlight the changes that such skills and competencies can bring about in citizens' participation in society, particularly by expanding their freedom.

This paper's purpose is to discuss the actual impact of educational support on developing socially disadvantaged young people's digital skills and competencies (ESDC) in view of establishing digital citizenship. Accordingly, we address this subject using the human development approach (HDA), initially presented by Amartya Sen, which provides a holistic view in terms of fulfillment, well-being, and quality of life. One example of the HDA's practical use is the United Nations' Human Development Index, a composite index of achievements in human development [7, 8]. Uniquely, the HDA centers on expanding human capabilities [8]. In the context of HDA, capabilities represent the freedoms available to every individual, such as social, political, and economic participation, which equal full citizenship and the capacity to lead the kind of life she/he values [9–11]. Deprivation of these capabilities is considered equivalent to poverty [12, 13]. From an HDA perspective, we ought to understand an individual's educational attempts in terms of the development of capabilities, i.e., the expansion of the freedoms that an individual with full citizenship can enjoy to realise a life worth living.

Hence, this paper presents a research study into the human developmental meaning of ESDC for socially disadvantaged youths living in a mid-sized provincial city in a developed country. For this purpose, the author both engaged in a support group activity to aid the social participation of young people experiencing social withdrawal or school absenteeism and conducted a participatory study to help such young people with their learning about computing. The study addressed the research question: How could ESDC encourage disadvantaged young people's human development as digital citizens?

2 Relevant Literature

This research was motivated by an ethical concern to promote social participation equity through the development of digital skills and competencies. Promoting equity in social participation has been a topic of debate in digital divide studies [14]. Early discussions based on techno-optimism insisted on digital technology's potential for social equalisation [15]. However, at the beginning of the 2000s, sociological arguments pointed out the limitations of technological determinism (see [14]). For instance, Norris [16] asserted that computer access, cultural background, ethnicity, and literacy would become critical elements in the digital divide, i.e., inequality produced by a social gap that determined who successfully benefited from digital technology and who did not. "Digital equity" was derived from these digital divide arguments, which stressed an ethical viewpoint that problematised social inequities in involvement with digital environments (see [17, 18]). Gorski described digital equity as a "social justice goal," focusing on the environment that causes the gap between advantaged groups and others, [11] based on comparative research into young children's computer use among schools with different socioeconomic status and cultural backgrounds.

In pursuit of digital equity, this study focuses on the potential of ESDC to empower young people in a supported group. We focus especially on computing skills as the underpinning of digital skills and competency, which we define as the ability to use computing functions actively for self-defined purposes such as problem-solving and play. This definition is strongly related to "3. Digital content creation" and "5. Problem-solving" in DigComp 2.0 [1]. We also refer to the thinking skills underlying such computing skills as computational thinking. The definition of the latter for our purposes follows competence 5.5 of the DLGF [2]: "To process a computable problem into sequential and logical steps as a solution for human and computer systems." Previous literature deemed lack of skills in the use of digital technology as a possible factor broadening divides in social and political participation [19, 20]. This suggests the significance of educational approaches to close the divide. However, literature debating the digital divide in a sociological context has focused on gaps in the availability of information among different social classes, and thus, considers Internet access and information acquisition skills the main issues. By contrast, we focus on the contribution of productive digital skills and competencies to civic participation in digital environments, such as the aforementioned computing skills and computational thinking.

This study also highlights the expansion of "freedom of choice" to reflect human development. "Freedom of choice" represents what a person can choose in each real-life context. The exercise of this freedom corresponds to Kleine's choice framework [21, 22], developed to assess ICT4D (ICT for Development) outcomes. Previous literature on ICT4D (see [23, 24]) has shown ICT's benefit to improve the living conditions of disadvantaged people in rural communities. ICT, including legacy information systems, such as analog telecommunications and the digital network of the Internet, has been observed and conceptualised as a critical factor for community development that improves residents' poor life conditions by expanding their freedom of choice for living.

From the perspective of Kleine's framework, ESDC should be recognised as a means of expanding digital technology's impact on local community members' circumstances. During the development of the ICT4D study, the focus both in research and actual development moved from technology-centered "passive diffusion" toward resident-centered "active innovation" [25]. In response to this shift, assessment frameworks for ICT4D, which incorporated Sen's HDA view, emerged to describe the development of residents' living conditions [22, 26]. Kleine's choice framework [21] was among those that attempted to identify ICT's contribution toward specific development goals by observing individuals' freedom of choice. The choice framework featured the "enormous potential" of digital technology represented by ICT to facilitate individuals' freedom of choice. Then, to address the actual conversion of this potential into a freedom, it highlighted the comprehensive and plural relationships among several factors such as social structure, agency, dimension of choice, and development outcomes [21]. Our study's focus was thus on active innovation concerning freedom of choice among the supported young people and other support group members, stimulated by ESDC. In particular, we attempted to observe the promotion of young people's freedom as demonstrated by their attitudes as digital technology learners and users, which Shonfeld et al. [27] conceptualised as digital agency acquisition. Our study also aimed to provide an otherwise rare example of ICT4D in a developed country.

3 Methodologies

The study chose action research (AR) as a participatory research methodology. This approach enables participants to find effective solutions to problems they confront in their lives [28] and seeks positive social changes based on democratic values [29]. In AR, researchers and other participants need a shared vision for the process and goal of problem-solving, and learning through shared reflection is most critical in this process [30]. The AR process was implemented in a support group for disadvantaged young people in a rural city in Japan, a developed country. With the cooperation of group members, we worked together to establish ESDC as a new option for supporting young people's social participation. This paper focuses particularly on the findings of a reflective exercise conducted from an HDA perspective on the significance of ESDC.

The author engaged in the group's activity, aiding the rehabilitation and social participation of youths who had experienced social withdrawal or school absenteeism, to conduct a participatory study. The group met in a mid-sized provincial city, and varied in size during the study period from five to ten young people with two to five staff members, either full-time or part-time. The author acted as a part-time supporter, assisting youths in learning various things about computing and informatics. The author collected data in the form of field notes, a series of text descriptions with some pictures and movies, noting events and occurrences, dialogues with the participants, findings and interpretations, and reflections on every session during the study period.

The study commenced in May 2015, following a similar pilot study from December 2013 to January 2014, and finished in March 2020. Findings are based on analysis of field notes from May 2015 to February 2018. During this period, the author and the youths in the group were involved in introductory computing and informatics learning through practices such as making games, teaching older adults programming with Scratch, constructing a programmable robot called MugBot[1], and practising introductory programming with the C and Ruby languages.

[1] MugBot is a nonproprietary, open-source social robot originally designed by the Koike Laboratory in Tokyo Metropolitan University. http://www.mugbot.com.

Data were coded by thematic analysis [31, 32] to highlight the research question's essential factors. The coded data contains field notes for 66 days taken from May 2015 to February 2018. For this coding, the author scrutinised the field notes to identify themes capturing important facets of the data related to the research question [32] and concepts relevant to explaining the themes. The author then reinterpreted the coding results to determine themes and issues essential to the research question. This process was supplemented by further observations and dialogues in the field. Full ethics approval was obtained from the Research Ethics Committee of Seisa University (No. 1613).

4 Findings

Based on the data analysis, the author identified four thematic topics as those that gave insight into the research question: (1) ESDC stimulated the youths' motivation to learn computing skills and knowledge autonomously; (2) Computer programming led the youths to the joy of thinking computationally; (3) The youths learned more actively when the author behaved as a co-learner rather than a teacher; (4) The youths' computing capacities augmented their expected roles in the group.

4.1 Autonomous Participation in Learning Computing Skills and Knowledge

Participation in ESDC by youths in the support group should be characterised as a sign of "autonomy"—an autonomous attitude toward learning computing skills and knowledge. For example, one youth, who was late 20s and had experienced school drop-out and social withdrawal ("Y1" for anonymisation), attended the computing workshop, organised by the author at the group's office almost every Thursday afternoon, alone every week. Attendance at the workshop was left optional for every group member. Although it was rare for Y1 to express motivation to participate in the workshop, Y1 did occasionally show a will to continue learning about computing and to practice independently whatever interested them in the workshop. The author found this "autonomy in learning" during the workshop to be valuable in human development because most participating youths had been more or less deprived of this autonomy by their drop-out experiences. Below are excerpts from the field notes (originally written in Japanese) suggesting Y1's autonomous participation in learning computer programming (Tables 1 and 2).

Table 1. Excerpt from field notes, June 15, 2017

*(This is the answer Y1 gave to a question from a group staff member asking the motivation to learn computing. ** signifies the author's name.) "Maybe if ** cannot visit here, I think I will open the PC by myself and do something with it." (June 15, 2017)*

Table 2. Excerpt from field notes, July 13, 2017

By the way, from Y1, the decision to learn Ruby language after C language was clearly stated. C and Java, according to Y1's examination, are the languages that "learning cost" is high and should be avoided as a learning object, and learning Java after learning C seems complicated for Y1. (July 13, 2017)

Y2, who was also late 20's and had experienced school drop-out and social withdrawal, had been a supported member of the group and participated in the author's workshop to learn computer programming for one year. Y2 then stopped attending the group (for reasons that included getting a part-time job and starting a high school correspondence course). Subsequently, Y2 suddenly visited the group's office and described their decision to learn programming again, in response to the author's invitation (Table 3).

Table 3. Excerpt from field notes, February 15, 2018

*Today, Y2 will join the workshop again. I received a message about that from S1 (the chairman of the group) this morning. Y2 visited ** last week. At that time, ** invited Y2 to learn computer programming again. Y2 seems to have captured it positively. (February 15, 2018)*

4.2 Computer Programming Leading to the Joy of Computational Thinking

The experience of computer programming in the workshop seemed to lead youths to feel the joy of thinking computationally. The author featured computer programming as the workshop's main content as it would allow learners to use active and creative thinking. In particular, they go back and forth between their imagination and sequential and logical ideas to solve their problems, which might correspond to computational thinking as defined by competence 5.5 of the DLGF. This happened in the workshop, and the youths seemed to be motivated mainly by the joy of writing and executing the programs they made. Programming especially appeared to give youths room to reasoning about a problem, express their ideas, obtain immediate feedback through executions, and to debug if errors occurred. This process seemed valuable from a human development viewpoint as, through computer programming, youths regained the joy of active thinking they had previously lost. The excerpt below describes this (Table 4).

Table 4. Excerpt from field notes, May 11, 2017

When Y1 tried to give a hint about the execution result of the program S2 (one of the supporting members and also one of the participants in the workshop) made, S2 said, "Don't say that, don't say that, please!" However, it seemed that S2 had heard the hint after all. S2 said "boring (with a laugh)" after hearing it. S2 seemed to have enjoyed thinking alone (that is, S2 loved to solve problems without help). (May 11, 2017)

Typically, in Y1's case, computer programming encouraged a more profound interest in computing and thinking computationally. When the excerpts below were written, Y1 had experienced programming for more than one and a half years with Scratch, Ruby, JavaScript, and C languages. Y1's programming skill level was not extremely high (though it seemed better than that of the average freshman undergraduate). By creating and debugging small pieces of programs, however, Y1 could enjoy reasoning about the cause-and-effect relationship within an algorithm and applying their understanding of the algorithm to new situations (Table 5).

Table 5. Excerpt from field notes, December 7, 2017

*Y1 used the program they created just now to calculate the difference from 0:0:0 AM to 23:59:59 PM and told me that "the number of seconds in a day is ...." Y1's use of imagination to get interesting results by creating and running programs made me feel Y1's computing affinity. Probably, such imagination came out because Y1 had developed ideas of computing while programming to some extent. ** thinks the thought that produces such computing ideas may well be called computational thinking. (December 7, 2017)*

4.3 Supporting the Youths as a Co-learner Rather Than a Teacher

Providing support as a co-learner was key to the supporter's attitude when helping youths to learn digital technology. Youths seemed to learn more actively when the author behaved as a co-learner rather than a teacher. When the workshop started, the author acted as a teacher rather than a co-learner because the youths who were interested in or joined the workshop were all complete computing beginners. The author thus had to teach many things about computing and computational thinking, which resulted in the author adopting the attitude of a teacher. This attitude, however, sometimes led workshop participants to adopt a passive learning role. Y1 in particular expressed apparently negative responses, typified by the excerpt below, toward something the author recommended that Y1 should learn next (Table 6).

Table 6. Excerpt from field notes, March 9, 2017

*** explained the outline of the HCP Chart[a] and said, " I think that this is a big learning point, isn't it?" In contrast, Y1 muttered in a small voice, "I do not want to do it." Then, as an outline, ** explained, "The most important thing is that it enables us to show the purpose and means firmly, in the flowchart you will only write means." Y1 put down a book and said, "I do not understand." (March 9, 2017)*

[a]An HCP Chart (Hierarchical ComPact description chart) is a notation system for designing program structures developed by Yokosuka Electrical Communication Laboratory Nippon Telegraph and Telephone Corporation (currently NTT). See [33]

Conversely, when the author behaved as a co-learner who was tackling the same problem as the youths participating in the workshop, their attitudes to learning computing skills and knowledge seemed to become more active and even autonomous.

Learning over time, the author tried to express a manifestly "co-learner attitude," sitting beside the learners in what the author regarded as a "co-learner position." The excerpt below describes the author's reflections on practicing programming alongside the youths in the workshop (Table 7).

Table 7. Excerpt from field notes, February 1, 2018

*As soon as Y1 saw the state that ** got an error saying "Hmm...," Y1 immediately looked into **'s PC monitor. As ** expected, sitting in the co-learner position seemed to make it easy to create a cooperative (?) learning space. Then Y1 began to tell their progress of the same problem spontaneously. (February 1, 2018)*

4.4 Computing Capacities Augmenting the Expected Roles

As youths' computing capacities grew, their expected roles in the group expanded accordingly. This amplification of roles accounts for human development in terms of expanding the capacity to participate in real society. S1 expected Y1 and Y2 to contribute to organising elementary computing workshops for children as facilitators. In practice, such workshops were not realised. However, the author saw several times that Y1 personally undertook the role of introducing programming to the group's newcomers, as the excerpt below describes (Table 8).

Table 8. Excerpt from field notes, December 21, 2017

*Currently, in front of **, Y1 introduces Scratch programming for the visitor. [...] Y1 is doing it for the visitor just by their own decision. (December 21, 2017)*

Y1 also helped the author several times when the author faced problems in coding during the workshop. Judged by performance, Y1 became more knowledgeable about C language functions after several months' learning. It was therefore natural for the author to sometimes ask for their help during the workshop as a co-learner, which granted Y1 a new role in addition that of learner in the workshop. Below is the excerpt, which reveals the author's recognition of this pattern (Table 9).

Table 9. Excerpt from the field notes, November 9, 2017

*Today's workshop saw more scenes that ** asked for help that ** would like to be taught by Y1 (and actually taught) than the scene ** taught something to Y1. [...] Y1 was obviously more enthusiastic regarding searching for C language system functions, and as a result, Y1 came to acquire more knowledge of C language than ** which could be utilized for problem-solving. [...] In other words, the relationship between Y1 and ** at this workshop became clearly closer to the relationship that supports each other in learning just as "co-runners with learning." (November 9, 2017)*

During the study period, the group began to consider undertaking a website development project for a local shopping mall association with which the group had a close relationship. The author was asked to advise about utilising the project for Y1's job training and agreed to supervise it. Y1 was invited to join the project as the primary coder and accepted this role. Below is an excerpt of a discussion log involving S1, Y1, and other group staff (Table 10).

Table 10. Excerpt from field notes, September 14, 2017

S1 wants to use Y1's skills to create a chance for him to participate in society since Y1 is studying a lot at the workshop. S1 thinks it desirable if such a chance is created not purely inside the group's daily activities but within the relationship between the group and the surrounding societies. […] *What is the structure (of the website development project)?* *· S3 (another staff member) is likely to be in charge of management […]* *·Y1 will be in charge of the production, and S1 also wants to be involved in the production with Y1 if possible. (September 14, 2017)*

5 Discussion

What bearing do the above observations have on the question of ESDC's capacity to encourage the development of digital citizens? In terms of human development, ESDC could encourage the human development of disadvantaged youths as digital citizens by, for example: (a) expanding their freedom to explore the potential of digital technology by themselves; (b) stimulating their self-determination as active learners in a digital environment; (c) expanding their space to participate into a digital society.

Concerning point (a), ESDC could help disadvantaged youths to expand their freedom, described by Sen as the opportunity and process of choice [34], to explore the potential of digital technology by themselves. This argument reflects findings (1) on autonomous participation in learning computing skills and knowledge and (2) on the joy of computational thinking. In the author's eyes, this argument implies that such educational support may act as a potential liberator for participants from imposed uses of digital technology. Participants may then expand their computing capacity, regain their freedom of choice in learning about digital technology, and create new technology uses for their own interest. During the workshop, the author took care not to give firm recommendations to participants concerning pragmatic uses of their computing skills and knowledge, such as acquiring job-related skills or qualifications. For the participants, learning computing in the workshop seemed to involve just a spontaneous enjoyment of the freedom of exploring the potential of computing. They seemed to become creative thinkers as they tackled programming problems or made open source robots. The youths' achieved what should be regarded as an expansion of Sen's capability, representing a person's enjoyment of the opportunity to do or be what she/he values [9].

While point (a) focuses on the learning opportunities of digital technology, point (b) illuminates a broader perspective on learning activity itself. Findings (1) and (3), the latter of which relates to the supporter's attitude as a co-learner, suggests that such educational support could assist disadvantaged youths to gain self-determination as active learners in a digital environment. The learner's shift toward self-determination may have multiple causes, however, the expanded freedom of exploring digital technology, shown in point (a), is undoubtedly a significant trigger. Self-determination as a learner in a digital environment signifies readiness to become a digital citizen possessing sense and use of choice, especially the choice to participate in a digital society that Kleine argued is an essential part of the dimensions of choice [21]. Moreover, the shift also indicates that such educational support corresponds to problem-posing education, which Paulo Freire [35] conceptualised as a liberating education model for oppressed people to become self-determining learners in a digital society.

Point (c) is derived from finding (4) on the expansion of youths' expected roles in the group. As (4) shows, ESDC could encourage disadvantaged youths to acquire new roles in their community as a result of their enlarged capacity to utilise digital technology. During the research period, the supported youths, who were initially novice computing learners, came to acquire new roles, such as workshop facilitator, co-learner in computing, and coder in a website development project. The acquisition of digital skills and competencies by youths expanded the choices available to them both within the group and in the surrounding community. This sort of role expansion inevitably occurs in a contemporary society that is filled with the need to utilise digital skills and competencies in problem-solving and is crucial in strengthening the individual's ability to live as an independent citizen in a digital society.

Role expansion among the youths in the support group was essentially an achievement of ESDC's development goal to contribute to the supported youths' social participation. Judged by the choice framework [21], this achievement was a result of input from the following individual agency-based capability factors: education resources (e.g., the computing workshop); information (e.g., textbooks, web resources, the author's suggestions, etc.); material resources (e.g., computers and other devices the group offered); and social resources (e.g., the group's membership). The achievement was also affected by structure-based capability inputs such as institutions and organisations (e.g., the support group, the local shopping mall association), formal and informal laws (e.g., the NPO law to support non-profit organisations, daily rules held by the group's members), and access to ICT. In the ICT4D context, skill enhancement in ICT use is considered to expand residents' choices and opportunities to live in society [36].

6 Conclusion and Limitations

The findings of this paper reaffirm that ESDC has the potential to solve social problems pertaining to digital equity. Furthermore, this study has revealed a need for inclusive educational support for socially disadvantaged people in local communities. This is the third area, after schools and families, in terms of skills and knowledge of digital technology and the capability to learn digital technology independently. In this context, pedagogical studies of the relationship between computer programming and learner's self-determination in learning, as Seymour Papert argued in his chapter "Computers and Computer cultures" [37], are a focal point for considering the learning content of such support. Moreover, the author argues that the ICT4D research approach is valid even in developed countries and that it should be pursued more actively, focusing not only on the diffusion of ICT infrastructure but also on the provision of educational support. The author believes that this study is a leading example of addressing this issue.

It must nonetheless be emphasised that this research is a qualitative study based on a small sample. One should therefore be cautious about generalising the research outcome. The results must be read critically, especially in light of different socio-cultural factors, diffusion of digital technologies, and educational circumstances surrounding digital skills and competencies.

Acknowledgments. The author would like to thank all of the members of the support group who kindly offered the opportunity to conduct the study. This study was supported by JSPS KAKENHI Grant Number 16K01136.

References

1. Vuorikari, R., Punie, Y., Carretero, S., Van Den Brande, L.: DigComp 2.0: The Digital Competence Framework for Citizens. Update Phase 1: the Conceptual Reference Model. Publications Office of the European Union (2016)
2. Law, N., Woo, D., Torre, J. de la, Wong, G.: A Global Framework of Reference on Digital Literacy Skills for Indicator 4.4.2. UNESCO Institute for Statistics (2018)
3. Richardson, J., Milovidov, E.: Digital Citizenship Education Handbook: Being Online, Well-Being Online, and Rights Online. Council of Europe Publishing, Strasbourg (2019)
4. UNESCO: Fostering Digital Citizenship through Safe and Responsible Use of ICT: A Review of Current Status in Asia and the Pacific as of December 2014. UNESCO Bangkok (2015)
5. Kafai, Y.B., Peppler, K.A., Chiu, G.M.: High tech programmers in low-income communities: Creating a computer culture in a community technology center. In: Steinfield, C., Pentland, B.T., Ackerman, M., Contractor, N. (eds.) Communities and Technologies 2007, pp. 545–563. Springer, London (2007). https://doi.org/10.1007/978-1-84628-905-7_27
6. Fields, D.A., Kafai, Y.B., Giang, M.T.: Youth computational participation in the wild: understanding experience and equity in participating and programming in the online scratch community. ACM Trans. Comput. Educ. **17**(3), 1–22 (2017). https://doi.org/10.1145/3123815
7. Sen, A.: Development as Freedom, vol. 144. Anchor Books, New York (1999)
8. Fukuda-Parr, S.: The human development paradigm: operationalizing Sen's ideas on capabilities. Fem. Econ. **9**, 301–317 (2003). https://doi.org/10.1080/1354570022000077980
9. Sen, A.: Development as Freedom, vol. 18, p. 18. Anchor Books, New York (1999)
10. Hart, C.S., Brando, N.: A capability approach to children's well-being, agency and participatory rights in education. Eur. J. Educ. **53**, 293–309 (2018). https://doi.org/10.1111/ejed.12284
11. Agboli, A., Botbol, M., O'Neill, S., Richard, F., Aujoulat, I.: Transforming vulnerability into power: exploring empowerment among women with female genital mutilation/cutting (FGM/C) in the context of migration in Belgium. J. Hum. Dev. Capab. **21**, 49–62 (2020). https://doi.org/10.1080/19452829.2019.1661981

12. Sen, A.: Social exclusion: Concept, application, and scrutiny. Asian Development Bank (2000)
13. Zheng, Y., Walsham, G.: Inequality of what? Social exclusion in the e-society as capability deprivation. Inf. Technol. People. **21**, 222–243 (2008). https://doi.org/10.1108/09593840810896000
14. Revenaugh, M.: Beyond the Digital Divide: Pathways to Equity (2000). http://eric.ed.gov/?id=EJ615183
15. Russell, D.L., Schneiderheinze, A.: Understanding innovation in education using activity theory. Educ. Technol. Soc. **8**, 38–53 (2005)
16 Norris, D.T., Conceição, S.: Narrowing the digital divide in low-income, urban communities: narrowing the digital divide in low-income, urban communities. New Direct. Adult Continuing Educ. **2004**(101), 69–81 (2004). https://doi.org/10.1002/ace.129
17. Becker, J.: Digital equity in education: a multilevel examination of differences in and relationships between computer access, computer use and state-level technology policies. Educ. Policy Anal. Arch. **15**, 1–36 (2007)
18. Gorski, P.C.: Insisting on digital equity: reframing the dominant discourse on multicultural education and technology. Urban Educ. **44**, 348–364 (2008). https://doi.org/10.1177/0042085908318712
19. Hargittai, E.: Second-level digital divide: differences in people's online skills. First monday. **7**, 1–16 (2002)
20. Min, S.-J.: From the digital divide to the democratic divide: internet skills, political interest, and the second-level digital divide in political internet use. J. Inf. Technol. Polit. **7**, 22–35 (2010). https://doi.org/10.1080/19331680903109402
21. Kleine, D.: ICT4WHAT?—using the choice framework to operationalise the capability approach to development. J. Int. Dev. **22**, 674–692 (2010). https://doi.org/10.1002/jid.1719
22. Kleine, D.: The capability approach and the "medium of choice": steps towards conceptualising information and communication technologies for development. Ethics Inf. Technol. **13**, 119–130 (2011). https://doi.org/10.1007/s10676-010-9251-5
23. Abraham, R.: Mobile phones and economic development: evidence from the fishing industry in India. Inf. Technol. Int. Dev. **4**, 5–17 (2007)
24. Vaughan, D.: Using information and communications technology to build capabilities for well-being in post-conflict communities. In: Panzironi, F. (eds.) The Capability Approach: Development Practice and Public Policy in the Asia-Pacific Region, vol. 18, pp. 186–206 (2012)
25 Heeks, R.: ICT4D 2.0: The next phase of applying ICT for international development. Computer **41**(6), 26–33 (2008). https://doi.org/10.1109/MC.2008.192
26 Loh, Y.A.C.: Approaches to ICT for development (ICT4D): vulnerabilities vs. capabilities. Inf. Dev. **31**(3), 229–238 (2015). https://doi.org/10.1177/0266666913513198
27. Passey, D., Shonfeld, M., Appleby, L., Judge, M., Saito, T., Smits, A.: Digital agency: empowering equity in and through education. Technol. Knowl. Learn. **23**(3), 425–439 (2018). https://doi.org/10.1007/s10758-018-9384-x
28. Stringer, E.T.: Action Research. Sage Publications, Thousand Oaks (2013)
29. Brydon-Miller, M., Greenwood, D., Maguire, P.: Why action research? Action Res. **1**(1), 9–28 (2003). https://doi.org/10.1177/14767503030011002
30. Järvinen, P.: Improving Guidelines and Developing a Taxonomy of Methodologies for Research in Information Systems. JYU dissertations (2021)
31. Braun, V., Clarke, V.: Using thematic analysis in psychology. Qual. Res. Psychol. **3**(2), 77–101 (2006). https://doi.org/10.1191/1478088706qp063oa
32. Braun, V., Clarke, V.: Using thematic analysis in psychology. Qual. Res. Psychol. **3**, 77–101 (2006). https://doi.org/10.1191/1478088706qp063oa

33. Aoyama, M., Miyamoto, K., Murakami, N., Nagano, H., Oki, Y.: Design specification in Japan: tree-structured charts. IEEE Softw. **6**(2), 31–37 (1989)
34. Sen, A.: The Idea of Justice, pp. 228–230. Penguin Books, London (2010)
35. Freire, P.: Pedagogy of the Oppressed, pp. 1–181. Penguin Books, London (1996)
36. Gigler, B.-S.: Informational capabilities-the missing link for the impact of ICT on development. In: World Bank ICT Sector Week. E-Transformation Working Paper Series: World Bank Working Paper Series, 1 (2011). https://ssrn.com/abstract=2191594
37. Papert, S.: Mindstorms: Children, Computers, and Powerful Ideas, Basic Books, Chapter 1. Basic Books, New York (1993)

Developing Inclusive Digital Pedagogies: Reflections on the Past, the Present and Future Directions

Sue Cranmer[1(✉)] and Cathy Lewin[2]

[1] Department of Educational Research, Lancaster University, Lancaster, UK
s.cranmer@lancaster.ac.uk
[2] Education and Social Research Institute, Manchester Metropolitan University, Manchester, UK
c.lewin@mmu.ac.uk

Abstract. Disabled children's experiences of using digital technologies in mainstream classrooms are very mixed. On the one hand, children's rights and digital rights legislation and inclusive education policies have promoted inclusive and equitable pedagogical practices for decades. Digital technologies are becoming increasingly prevalent in homes and schools, a phenomenon rapidly accelerated by the global Covid-19 pandemic. Despite this positive rhetoric, the reality on the ground is that inclusive digital pedagogies – that prevent disabled children experiencing exclusionary educational practices in mainstream classrooms – are underdeveloped and require significant research and development. Current uses of digital technologies by disabled children, harnessing accessibility features in mobile technologies, can focus attention on their differences. Digital technologies in classrooms generally are often used in mundane ways which do not make the most of opportunities for creativity, collaboration and student-centred learning. This paper reflects on the situation in the past and present in relation to the impact of disability studies, children's rights, policies on inclusive education and, digital technology developments and educational practices, on the development of inclusive digital pedagogies. It concludes by outlining early findings from a research project carried out in North West England that identifies challenges in relation to the development and implementation of inclusive digital pedagogies.

1 Introduction

Inclusive education and digital use practices have a great deal in common in their lack of realisable promise. Inclusive education has a disappointing legacy in mainstream schools. Typically, disabled children and young people are integrated but then experience ongoing exclusionary practices. These compromise the positive values of inclusion within the very environments expected to welcome and support them. Likewise, digital use practices - children's uses of digital technologies to support formal learning - have frequently been integrated into schools but not well embedded into pedagogy, often replicating learning practices in mundane, uncreative ways. This situation has formed a stark comparison to the more exciting and innovative uses and

Published by Springer Nature Switzerland AG 2022
D. Passey et al. (Eds.): OCCE 2021, IFIP AICT 642, pp. 67–78, 2022.
https://doi.org/10.1007/978-3-030-97986-7_6

experiences outside of school including at home. The implications of the impact of the pandemic on digital practices and inclusion in the longer-term remain to be seen following the shift to emergency remote learning then subsequent re-entry into schools. This means that we are at a fulcrum, a critical and potentially transformational moment in time, for reflecting on and learning from the past; taking stock of the current; and making recommendations to build more innovative, effective and inclusive digital pedagogies in future. Keeping this in mind, this paper will introduce disabled children's childhood studies perspectives to situate this paper at the intersection of disability studies and digital education. It will reflect on the past via the development of disabled children's practices in mainstream schools in the context of children's rights and inclusive education over the last four decades alongside development of inclusive (digital) pedagogies. Secondly, it will explore the current situation in the context of the newly introduced children's digital rights amendment; the apparent emerging trends towards the development of inclusive (digital) pedagogies; the opportunities provided by mobile technologies; and the potential opportunities triggered by the pandemic. Third, it will consider future directions and conclude that more research and development is needed. In light of this, it will introduce early findings from a current project with teachers to develop effective inclusive digital pedagogies to support disabled children and young people's digital use practices to learn post-pandemic in inclusive education settings. By bringing these perspectives together, we will be able to provide a platform to consider how best to support disabled children with digital technologies within inclusive educational environments in the future.

2 Disabled Children's Childhood Studies and Digital Education

This paper is written from a disabled children's childhood studies perspective drawn from disability studies and founded on three main principles: a) disabled children should not be automatically conflated with impairment and vulnerability; b) disabled children's voices should be placed at the centre of research designs; c) an agenda for change is essential given the need to challenge the authority of the 'norm' [1]. The first author has adapted the principles in relation to disabled children's digital use practices [2] as follows: i) digital activities should enable all children in the class to learn; ii) disabled children should have the same opportunities to benefit from digital use practices as their non-disabled peers; (iii) digital use practices should be inclusive, not intensifying differences between children or creating stigma; (d) class teachers should be supported to develop inclusive digital pedagogies; (e) research should explore and develop disabled children's digital use practices to enhance their learning and their lives more generally. Reluctantly, the term 'SEND,' to describe children with special educational needs and disabilities is used in the paper to reflect its dominant currency in policy and schools while recognising that associations with being 'special' and having 'need' [3] are more aligned to the medical than the social model.

3 Reflecting on the Past: Developing Inclusive (Digital) Pedagogies

3.1 Children and Human Rights Legislation

Human rights legislation underpinned the shift to inclusive education. In particular, the UN Convention on the Rights of the Child (UN CRC) [4] was instrumental in supporting children's rights. Article [2] of the (UN CRC) stated that all children have the right 'to receive education without discrimination on any grounds' [4, p. 14]. This was reinforced by the UN Convention on the Rights of Persons with Disabilities (UN CRPD) [5], emphasised within Goal 4 of the United Nations "Sustainable Development Goals" with the intention being to "Ensure inclusive and equitable quality education and promote lifelong learning opportunities for all" [6].

3.2 Inclusive Education

The driver for global inclusive education since the 1990s has been the Salamanca statement [7]. It sought to distil human rights legislation into practice by urging each country to develop a comprehensive educational strategy that emphasised 'special needs education.' It was argued that 'ordinary' schools needed to be reformed given their importance to include: 'everybody, celebrate differences, support learning, and respond to individual needs. As such, they [schools] constitute an important contribution to the agenda for achieving Education for All and for making schools educationally more effective' (p. iii). The Salamanca statement was integrated into many countries' educational policy, oft seen as a mechanism for promoting social justice and improving society as a whole via access to education in high-income countries within Europe, Australasia and North America.

In practice, the impact of inclusive education has been disappointing. Taking the UK as an illustration, policy introduced in 1978 specified that disabled children should be educated 'wherever possible' within mainstream settings [8, 9]. This was followed by the SEN [Special educational needs] Code of Practice [10]; the Social Exclusion Task Force [11]; the Children and Families Bill [12]. Yet, successive governments, researchers and activists have consistently identified failures in implementation. Inclusion in schools remains underdeveloped reflecting integration rather than inclusion [13]. Schools have been unable to develop an inclusive ethos whereby inclusion is recognised and embedded in all aspects of activity. The role of the teacher is key to this but instead of planning inclusive lessons, many class teachers do not design lessons from the outset that take 'primary responsibility' for the disabled children and young people in their classes [14]. Instead, disabled children are frequently stigmatised and marginalised, denying their independent access to the curriculum. Teaching assistants and other support staff are relied on to "'bridg[e]' the learning in the moment" [15]. When this happens, staff responsibilities can be unclear or overlapping; teaching assistants can be called on to mediate the teacher's pedagogical approach.

Evidence has shown that the limited uptake of inclusive pedagogies results from a range of difficulties. This includes a lack of useful guidance underpinned by research that can be introduced to teachers during initial teacher education programmes and via in-service professional courses, to enable teachers to develop the skills and knowledge they need. Moreover, heavy teacher workloads and related time constraints limit both the opportunity for teachers to access this training or to incorporate inclusive pedagogies into their lessons even when they are able to see the potential for this approach.

3.3 Digital Education

The introduction of digital technologies into schools has also been somewhat disappointing (up until the point of the pandemic where longer-term changes to digital use practices and implications are not yet knowable). There has been much promised about the potential of digital technologies to support disabled children, offering them incomparable opportunities to facilitate independent access to the curriculum and learn alongside their peers [16]. This is particularly evident when inclusive digital pedagogies are adopted that enable 'teaching and learning activities whereby class teachers have designed lessons for all children from the outset using digital technologies, thereby facilitating independent access to the curriculum for disabled children' [2, p. 11]. Yet, successive studies have shown that digital practices in schools by children are often uncreative and dull. While some pockets of innovative and creative uses of technologies clearly exist, many reflect traditional teaching practices rather than enabling the development of more innovative digital pedagogies that could enhance and revive the curriculum. For example, limited digital practices such as Excel for tables and graphs, PowerPoint and word processors for writing have often been reported [17]. These typical 'office' uses are in contrast to the potentially more collaborative and student-centred learning approaches that digital technologies can afford. In the last decade, possible opportunities that are more exciting have arrived with the increased use of mobile devices in schools. These are potentially really useful for disabled children due to in-built accessibility functions. Researchers quickly observed that the use of well-chosen apps were received positively by young people [18]. Yet, since then mobile devices have been criticised and banned [19]. The continuation of mostly mundane digital use practices undermines the opportunities for disabled children to take part in expansive, engaging and innovative activities alongside their peers. Instead, mobile devices have been used mainly as assistive technologies by disabled children thereby potentially stigmatising them and highlighting individual differences between children [20].

3.4 Developing Inclusive (Digital) Pedagogies

A key issue within debates in the past has been that teachers are rarely introduced to disability studies in education to support positive change [21]. Alongside this, there has been an accompanying lack in guidance available to teachers about how to develop pedagogies that reflect the underlying beliefs, values and attitudes of inclusive education [22]. Important exceptions are, for example, the 'Index of Inclusion', a set of resources for schools to develop inclusive practices [23]. Florian and Spratt also developed a model for use in teacher education [22]. This was a holistic model built on themes of learning, social justice and every teacher's role as an 'active professional'. They argued the need for a set of underlying principles that enable teachers to develop the knowledge and skills they need to provide meaningful learning with the same opportunities available to all children.

In relation to the development of inclusive digital pedagogies, this area has been underdeveloped with little attention given to digital use practices in situ in the context of inclusive education policy. There have been studies and evaluations of particular software or hardware; or interventions aimed at improving specific learning outcomes such as learning and independence [24]; communication, organisation and social skills [25]. Some providers and educators have also generated useful lists of accessible apps for disabled children to use. But in general, there has been very little research about how disabled children use technologies for learning in situ in ways that embed the underpinning beliefs and values of inclusive education with associated guidance for teachers about how to implement this.

4 Exploring the Current Context

We are now at a critical moment in time. To take stock of this key moment, a review is presented of the current state of play of each of the key categories of children's and human rights, inclusive education, digital education and stage of development of inclusive digital pedagogies. This will provide the foundations to make recommendations to build more innovative, effective and inclusive digital pedagogies for the future.

4.1 Children's and Human Rights Legislation

The United Nations Convention on the Rights of the Child General Comment No. 25 [26] recommends four general principles. Firstly, children should not be discriminated against and should not be excluded digitally. Secondly, the best interests of the child should guide the development of any online provision. Thirdly, children should be protected from risks to their 'life, survival and development'. Finally, digital technologies should be harnessed so that children can express their opinions and give their views on matters that relate to them. The importance of digital technologies in supporting children's learning is highlighted including access to educational resources, teachers and peers, and opportunities to continue learning outside classrooms. The General Comment also notes that digital technologies can address barriers that disabled children face and that attention should be paid in schools to ensuring that new barriers are not introduced by offering them assistive technologies, multiple formats of digital resources and meeting the principles of universal design.

4.2 Inclusive Education

Despite policies in all four UK nations that promote inclusive education, in reality progress has remained slow [27] as it has been internationally [28]. Since the introduction of the Children and Families Act in 2014 in the UK, disabled children can access support through an education, health and care (EHC) plan if they are assessed to need more 'special educational needs' support than can be routinely provided by the school. However, despite this provision, a House of Commons government Education Committee report in 2019 stated that current policy, the Children and Families Bill (2014), had ‘let down’ a generation of children and young people [29]. Implementation had resulted in buck-passing, lack of general accountability, shortage of the resources available and a bureaucratic nightmare. More recently, a parliamentary report [30] concluded that ‘Mainstream schools have little financial incentive to be inclusive of pupils with SEND [Children with special educational needs and disabilities] (p. 6). This suggests that inclusion in the UK at least currently remains problematic.

4.3 Digital Education

Many schools across the globe were generally unprepared to meet the challenges posed by the pandemic and in particular the necessity to support their students’ remote learning. Teachers, both experienced and inexperienced with digital pedagogies, were forced to move teaching online with little time for planning and developing best practice [31]. Initially, there was little synchronous interaction (e.g. ‘live’ lessons) as schools investigated safeguarding issues and were cautious not to exclude students due to lack of technology access [31]. The pandemic compelled parents and carers to become more involved in supporting their children’s learning. This obligation came with great upheaval and anxiety for all citizens with the societal move to a lockdown situation, with parents and carers facing competing demands on their time and feeling that they lacked the knowledge to undertake this new role [31].

The shift to emergency remote online learning has provided unique opportunities for effective, innovative solutions to be identified, created and scaled, albeit over a period of many months as schools rushed to develop remote learning strategies, invest in new technologies and provide professional development for their staff. As noted earlier, research carried out pre-pandemic has shown how digital practices outside of school settings are often more expansive and engaging than the typical, passive uses of technology in schools [32]. Yet in school, mobiles devices, for example, have often been criticised and banned [19]. Therefore, it is essential that we know how emerging effective remote learning strategies can be sustained and scaled to mitigate educational disadvantage both as pupils go back into school and during further disruption caused by future lockdowns. Not only is this a necessity but teachers and parents are desperate for evidence-based guidelines and strategies to support effective practices in the current crisis and for post-pandemic schooling.

The rapid pivot to remote learning in March 2020 created particular problems for teachers trying to support SEND students in mainstream schools. 73% of SENDCos reported that they experienced challenges including supporting SEND students remotely and supporting teachers to provide differentiated learning [33]. However, there is some evidence that SEND students found remote learning to be beneficial. For example, school leaders reported that students with autism and hearing impairments found it easier to study at home without so many distractions [34]. Furthermore, SEND students benefited from working at their own pace and being able to revisit and review learning activities [35].

4.4 Developing Inclusive (Digital) Pedagogies and Future Directions

Recent searches of the literature suggest an emerging trend towards encouraging and supporting teachers to develop inclusive pedagogies. These include examples by Moriña [36] who carried out a systematic review of approaches to inclusive pedagogies; Pozo-Armentia et al. [37] who explored pedagogical limitations to inclusive education and books aimed at teachers such as the recent edition, 'Inclusive Teaching in a Nutshell. A visual guide for busy teachers' [38].

In addition, a growing number of resources are available, such as the principles of Universal Design for Learning (UDL) (http://www.cast.org/our-work/about-udl.html#.XIZNwqbnW6k); Universal Instructional Design (UID); and resources provided by organisations such as CALL Scotland to enable disabled children to be supported by inclusive digital pedagogies (https://www.callscotland.org.uk/home/).

Universal Design for Learning is a design framework that is intended to ensure that teaching and learning is flexible and accommodates the needs of a diverse range of learners [39]. It does this through guiding teachers to develop inclusive pedagogy that represents knowledge in multiple ways, enables learners to express what they know in multiple ways, and maximises student engagement (e.g. through offering choice) [39]. Very little high quality empirical research has been conducted to date but there is a growing body of work that highlights its promise for making teaching and learning more inclusive and accessible [40–42]. The framework has not always been studied holistically with more studies focused on multiple representation of knowledge than multiple ways of students evidencing their learning [40]. Technology is often used to support a UDL approach as it lends itself to multimodal presentation, flexibility and adaptability [42, 43]. Evidence of the impact on attainment to date is mixed but some suggest that UDL can have a positive impact [41] whilst others claim there is, as yet, insufficient evidence [44]. Irrespective of this, of course teachers require professional development and time to develop new skills [40–43], whilst collaborative approaches to developing UDL resources and approaches can be beneficial [41].

In terms of inclusive education policy, enactment has been impeded in the past due to the inability to incorporate inclusion in competing political agendas [45]. Thus, more joining up is required to ensure that inclusive education is addressed consistently across all relevant policies. Future policies for inclusive education need to focus on funding, teacher education, establishing a repository of supporting information for practitioners and unlocking the potential of UDL-informed digital pedagogy to support inclusive education [28, 30]. This includes future policies that should pay attention to technology-enabled assessment which currently is often not informed by UDL principles and requires more research to ensure that access is equitable [30, 46]. To summarise, research and development in the coming years needs to enable disabled children to realise digital practices in inclusive ways within every aspect of learning and assessment within and outside of schools. In addition, on the ground, research is urgently needed to understand, capitalise on and maintain pandemic related benefits for teachers and for all children including disabled children in terms of knowledge and skills that have developed via the shift to emergency online learning.

5 Developing Fully Inclusive Digital Pedagogies

With this in mind, we report here on early findings from a participatory pilot project carried out in the North West of England, designed to engage class teachers and other key personnel who support disabled children in mainstream education to identify, assess and develop inclusive digital pedagogies. The project aims to identify the key factors at different levels that support class teachers to develop inclusive digital pedagogies; collect exemplars of good practice (4–5); and understand the current success factors and challenges faced by classroom teachers in developing inclusive digital pedagogies. Participants will identify exemplary inclusive digital use practices alongside those that require further development. Stages planned are: a summary review of previous studies drafted in relation to the principles of Universal Design for Learning; a workshop held with practitioners in each school to co-construct a framework for shaping understanding of how inclusive digital pedagogies can be recognised; a two-day visit to each school to identify and document practices at different levels of maturity in the use of inclusive digital pedagogies; thematical analysis [47] drawing on the framework developed in stage 2; a final workshop at each school to review the analysed data with experienced practitioners to ensure the participatory approach is integrated throughout the project. Draft reports will also be shared with the schools and final feedback from participants in the project incorporated before finalising. Ethical approval will be obtained through Lancaster University's rigorous and mandatory ethical approval process.

The project was originally planned for 2020, delayed until Summer term 2021, because of COVID-19. This meant that results; and the guidance the project will provide will take account of the re-entry point of teachers and children in England into schools. Two schools were recruited on the basis of externally recognised reputations for supporting disabled children. However, the ongoing impact of the pandemic on schools during Summer term 2021, including further lockdowns, resulted in data collection in one school only. Two group interviews were carried out using MS Teams with 2 teachers (a Mathematics teacher, also a digital learning leader; and a Science Teacher) and 2 support personnel for disabled children who work in the same school and described themselves as the 'Physical and sensory lead for children'; and a 'teacher of deaf children'). Questions focused on support for disabled children provided by the school pre-pandemic, during the lockdowns, with re-entry into schools, both generally and using digital technologies. Interviews lasted one hour. We have drawn on the data to provide examples of key challenges faced by teachers and support personnel during the pandemic and what this highlights in relation to inclusive digital pedagogies.

Providing student access to appropriate technology was a major challenge in this school. It took some time (beyond the first lockdown period) to provide laptops or iPads to SEND students. The school initially gave some students old laptops from in-house stock but they had a number of technical issues that needed to be resolved and the IT support staff were unable to respond quickly due to increased workload. In addition, not all students could access the live lessons. One of the main challenges that teachers reported were the difficulties of working with accessibility features in the standard software (e.g. Microsoft Teams, PowerPoint) adopted for remote teaching. Using live captions in Microsoft Teams to support hearing impaired students meant that teachers had to talk more slowly and annunciate carefully. Even then 100% accuracy was not achieved. Teachers partially addressed this by typing in further instructions through the chat facility, adding to their workload. Accuracy issues were also noted with the use of captions when pre-recording PowerPoint presentations. Standard software used to present curriculum content was also noted to be challenging to access for some students due to the lack of contrast and the colours used. The teachers pointed out that it was difficult for them to adapt their teaching resources due to the need to have a greater level of technical skill and confidence in using educational technology. Teaching assistants would have liked to provide simultaneous interpreting in Microsoft Teams for hearing impaired students but were unable to set this up, for example, as laptop cameras had been turned off. The teaching assistants also noted that some staff lacked understanding about some of their students' needs and were therefore unaware of pedagogic changes that could improve accessibility for some of these students. They also commented that sometimes teachers presented too much information simultaneously.

These early findings suggest the lack of readiness of teachers and schools to support disabled young people in the shift to remote learning in relation to students' access to laptops and tablet computers. This was amplified by time constraints for teachers combined with challenges to their pre-existing technical and accessibility skills. Moreover, teachers lacked the pedagogical knowledge needed to support these students' learning once teaching assistants were unable to provide their usual backup.

6 Conclusions

This paper has considered the different policies and perspectives that aim to ensure that disabled children's right to inclusive learning with digital technologies becomes a certainty. As noted earlier, we are at a fulcrum where teachers' and children's digital knowledge and skills have developed during the pandemic. We need to ensure that these shifts are maintained in order that the opportunities that they can provide are realised. On the other hand, historically, and as our early project findings show, the situation for disabled children's digital learning is not secure. Our project will continue working with teachers to identify, assess and develop inclusive digital pedagogies. However, we conclude by emphasising the urgent need for further research in this field to ensure that disabled children's rights to use digital technologies to support their learning in inclusive ways is recognised and supported.

References

1. Curran, T., Runswick-Cole, K.: Disabled children's childhood studies: a distinct approach? Disabil. Soc. **29**(10), 1617–1630 (2014)
2. Cranmer, S.: Disabled Children and Digital Technologies: Learning in the Context of Inclusive Education. Bloomsbury Academic, London (2020)
3. Benson, D.: Education (School). In: Cameron, C. (ed.) Disability Studies: A Student's Guide, pp. 50–53. Sage, London (2014)

4. United Nations (UN): Convention on the rights of the child. Geneva: Office of the United Nations High Commissioner for Human Rights (1989). https://www.ohchr.org/en/professionalinterest/pages/crc.aspx. Accessed 14 Oct 2021
5. United Nations (UN): Convention on the rights of persons with disabilities. UN, New York (2016). https://www.un.org/development/desa/disabilities/convention-on-the-rights-of-persons-with-disabilities.html. Accessed 14 Oct 2021
6. United Nations: Committee on the Rights of Persons with Disabilities (2016) General comment No. 4. Article 24: Right to inclusive education (2016). https://www.right-to-education.org/resource/general-comment-4-article-24-right-inclusive-education. Accessed 14 Oct 2021
7. UNESCO: The Salamanca Statement and framework for action on special needs. Salamanca, Spain, UNESCO (1994). https://www.european-agency.org/sites/default/files/salamanca-statement-and-framework.pdf. Accessed 14 Oct 2021
8. Department for Education and Skills (DfES): Removing the barriers to achievement: The Government's strategy for SEN. DfES (2004). https://dera.ioe.ac.uk/4955/13/8b56f1b2944d88f593e89ae3009fa5c3_Redacted.pdf. Accessed 14 Oct 2021
9. Mallett, R., Runswick-Cole, K.: Approaching Disability: Critical Issues and Perspectives. Routledge, Abingdon (2014)
10. Department for Education and Skills (DfES): Special educational needs code of practice, London (2001). https://assets.publishing.service.gov.uk/government/uploads/system/uploads/attachment_data/file/273877/special_educational_needs_code_of_practice.pdf. Accessed 14 Oct 2021
11. Social exclusion task force: Reaching Out: An Action Plan on Social Exclusion. Cabinet Office, London (2006). https://webarchive.nationalarchives.gov.uk/ukgwa/20070402100533/http://www.cabinetoffice.gov.uk/social_exclusion_task_force/publications/reaching_out/progress_report.asp. Accessed 14 Oct 2021
12. Department for Education, Department of Health: Children and Families Act, London (2014). https://services.parliament.uk/bills/2012-13/childrenandfamilies.html. Accessed 14 Oct 2021
13. Luccio, F.: Inclusion. In: Cameron, C. (ed.) An Introduction to the Theory of Automata. ICMS, vol. 88, pp. 37–51. Springer, Vienna (1971). https://doi.org/10.1007/978-3-7091-2816-9_6
14. Jordan, A., Schwartz, E., McGhie-Richmond, D.: Preparing teachers for inclusive classrooms. Teach. Teach. Educ. **25**(4), 535–542 (2009)
15. Webster, R., Blatchford, P.: Making sense of 'teaching', 'support' and 'differentiation': the educational experiences of pupils with education, health and care plans and statements in mainstream secondary schools. Eur. J. Spec. Needs Educ. **34**(1), 98–113 (2019)
16. European Schoolnet: Tablet computers and learners with special educational needs. SENnet project thematic report no. 3. Brussels, European Schoolnet (2014). http://sennet.eun.org/studies-and-evidence-wp2. Accessed 14 Oct 2021
17. Davies, C., Eynon, R.: Teenagers and Technology (Adolescence and Society). Routledge, London (2013)
18. Blikstad-Balas, M., Davies, C.: Assessing the educational value of one-to-one devices: have we been asking the right questions? Oxf. Rev. Educ. **43**(3), 311–331 (2017)
19. Burden, K., Kearney, M., Schuck, S., Hall, T.: Investigating the use of innovative mobile pedagogies for school-aged students: a systematic literature review. Comput. Educ. **138**, 83–100 (2019)
20. Cranmer, S.: Disabled children and young people's uses and experiences of digital technologies for learning. Lancaster University, Lancaster (2017). https://eprints.lancs.ac.uk/id/eprint/88991/4/Disabled_children_final_report_30.11.17.pdf. Accessed 14 Oct 2021

21. Moore, M., Slee, R.: Disability studies, inclusive education and exclusion. In: Watson, N., Roulstone, A., Thomas, C. (eds.) Routledge Handbook of Disability Studies. Routledge, Abingdon (2012)
22. Florian, L., Spratt, J.: Enacting inclusion: a framework for interrogating inclusive practice. Eur. J. Spec. Needs Educ. **28**(2), 119–135 (2013)
23. Booth, T., Ainscow, M.: Index for Inclusion: Developing learning and participation in schools. Centre for Studies on Inclusive Education, Bristol (2011). http://www.csie.org.uk/resources/inclusion-index-explained.shtml. Accessed 14 Oct 2021
24. O'Malley, P., Lewis, M., Donehower, C.: Using tablet computers as instructional tools to increase task completion by students with autism, San Francisco (2013). https://files.eric.ed.gov/fulltext/ED541157.pdf. Accessed 14 Oct 2021
25. Sultana, N., Hayhoe, S.: Assistive technology for students with special needs. In: Dowling, S., Gunn, C., Raven, J., Hayhoe, S. (eds.) Learning in Action: Redefining Learning. HCT Press, Abu Dhabi (2013)
26. United Nations Convention on the Rights of the Child: General comment No. 25 (2021) on children's rights in relation to the digital environment (2021). https://5rightsfoundation.com/our-work/childrens-rights/uncrc-general-comment.html. Accessed 14 Oct 2021
27. Robertson, C.: Policy for SEND and Inclusion: examining UK national and some European differences. Section 2: a comparative account of England, Scotland, Wales and Northern Ireland. J. Res. Spec. Educ. Needs **19**(3), 245–250 (2019)
28. UNESCO: Inclusion and education. Technology for inclusion. Paper commissioned for the 2020 Global Education Monitoring Report, Inclusion and education (2020). https://unesdoc.unesco.org/ark:/48223/pf0000373655. Accessed 14 Oct 2021
29. House of Commons Education Committee: Special educational needs and disabilities. First Report of Session 2019. London, House of Commons (2019). https://publications.parliament.uk/pa/cm201919/cmselect/cmeduc/20/20.pdf. Accessed 14 Oct 2021
30. House of Commons Committee of Public Accounts: Support for children with special educational needs and disabilities. First Report of Session 2019–21. HC85. London: House of Commons (2020). https://committees.parliament.uk/download/file/?url=%2Fpublications%2F941%2Fdocuments%2F7292&slug=85pdf. Accessed 14 Oct 2021
31. Greenhow, C., Lewin, C., Staudt Willet, K.B.: The educational response to COVID-19 across two countries: a critical examination of initial digital pedagogy adoption. Technol. Pedagog. Educ. **30**(1), 7–25 (2021)
32. Selwyn, N., Nemorin, S., Bulfin, S., Johnson, N.F.: Left to their own devices: the everyday realities of one-to-one classrooms. Oxf. Rev. Educ. **43**(3), 289–310 (2017)
33. Curran, H., Boddison, A., Maloney, H.: National SENCO Workforce Survey 2020. Supporting children and young people with special educational needs and their families during the coronavirus (COVID-19) pandemic: A national survey of SENCOs (2021). https://nasen.org.uk/news/senco-workforce-survey. Accessed 14 Oct 2021
34. Education Policy Institute: Addressing the digital divide in education. Enabling a blended learning approach for all pupils and teachers. Virtual roundtable Tuesday 21st July. Summary paper (2020). https://epi.org.uk/wp-content/uploads/2020/08/EPI-Digital-Divide_summary-paper.pdf. Accessed 14 Oct 2021
35. Heavey, A.: Whole School SEND - The future of schools (2020). https://www.sendgateway.org.uk/blog/whole-school-send-future-schools. Accessed 14 Oct 2021
36. Moriña, A.: Approaches to inclusive pedagogy: a systematic literature review. Pedagogika **140**(4), 134–154 (2021)
37. Pozo-Armentia, A., Reyero, D., Cantero, F.G.: The pedagogical limitations of inclusive education. Educ. Philos. Theory **52**(10), 1064–1076 (2020)

38. Cosgrove, R.: Inclusive Teaching in a Nutshell. A Visual Guide for Busy Teachers. Routledge, London (2020)
39. Hall, T.E., Meyer, A., Rose, D.H.: Universal Design for Learning in the Classroom: Practical Applications. The Guildford Press, London (2012)
40. Capp, M.J.: The effectiveness of universal design for learning: a meta-analysis of literature between 2013 and 2016. Int. J. Incl. Educ. **21**(8), 791–807 (2017)
41. Ok, M.W., Rao, K., Bryant, B.R., McDougall, D.: Universal design for learning in Pre-K to Grade 12 classrooms: a systematic review of research. Except. Spec. Educ. J. **25**(2), 116–138 (2017)
42. Smith-Canter, L.L.S., King, L.H., Williams, J.B., Metcalf, D., Potts, K.R.M.: Evaluating pedagogy and practice of universal design for learning in public schools. Except. Educ. Int. **27**(1), 1–16 (2017)
43. Evmenova, A.: Preparing teachers to use universal design for learning to support diverse learners. J. Online Learn. Res. **4**(2), 147–171 (2018)
44. Murphy, M.P.A.: Belief without evidence? A policy research note on universal design for learning. Policy Futures Educ. **19**(1), 7–12 (2021)
45. Williams-Brown, Z., Hodkinson, A.: Development of inclusive education in England: impact on children with special educational needs and disabilities. In: Papa, R. (ed.) Handbook on Promoting Social Justice in Education, pp. 1561–1583. Springer, Cham (2020). https://doi.org/10.1007/978-3-030-14625-2_151
46. Hoogerwerf, J.-E., et al.: Digital Inclusion. A White Paper. European Network for Technology Enhanced Learning in an Inclusive Society (2016). https://www.entelis.net/white-paper-with-roadmaps-entelis-deliverable-5-6/
47. Braun, V., Clarke, V.: Using thematic analysis in psychology. Qual. Res. Psychol. **3**(2), 77–101 (2006)

Students' Conceptions of Programming in the Context of Game Design

Fatma Batur(✉) and Torsten Brinda

Computing Education Research Group, University of Duisburg-Essen, 45127 Essen, Germany
{fatma.batur, torsten.brinda}@uni-due.de

Abstract. Several attempts have been made to understand novice programmers' difficulties and misconceptions in introductory programming. Most studies in the field of students' conceptions of (object-oriented) programming have only focused on identifying (mis-)conceptions without including popular contexts like game design. Since digital games are an important part of students' everyday life, exploring students' conceptions of digital games and their programming may give some recognisable patterns which might be helpful for teaching. This paper presents a brief overview of an empirical qualitative pilot study with the aim to investigate undergraduate students' conceptions of (object-oriented) programming in the context of the game Tetris®. For this study, we interviewed four students who were 19 to 21 years old, and analysed the transcripts using qualitative text analysis. Moreover, an online survey provided qualitative data from 25 participants. The first findings show that students' conceptions are based on the rules of the game, and first indications about influence factors could be found. As a result of these investigations, implications were made for the future main study.

Keywords: Conceptions · Computer science · Game design · Digital games · Programming · OOP · Qualitative text analysis

1 Introduction

Programming, especially object-oriented programming (OOP), is challenging for many students. Besides, many teenagers play digital games in their free time. Therefore, designing digital games in a computer science (CS) class could be a useful context in introductory programming. Unsurprisingly, designing and creating games is a common context to teach OOP or programming in general. By exploring students' conceptions of digital games and their programming with a long-term study, we want to get some insights into the development of conceptions in the introductory class and about possible influencing factors such as teaching materials, teacher instructions, or integrated development environments (IDEs). It has previously been observed that students especially develop misconceptions of object-oriented concepts [1]. CS teachers should be able to: identify and address students (mis-)conceptions for creating adequate learning arrangements. What is known about the investigation of students' perspectives is largely based on studies conducted in natural sciences [2]. Diethelm et al. [3] adapted

Published by Springer Nature Switzerland AG 2022
D. Passey et al. (Eds.): OCCE 2021, IFIP AICT 642, pp. 79–90, 2022.
https://doi.org/10.1007/978-3-030-97986-7_7

the model of "Educational Reconstruction" for computer science education which emphasises that students' conceptions should be considered for course design and arrangement.

2 Theoretical Background and Related Work

2.1 Educational Reconstruction

Figure 1 provides the summary for the model of *Educational Reconstruction* adapted to computer science education (CSE) [3]. Nowadays, children are sur rounded by digital technologies (which can be defined as CS phenomena), "and at an early age, children start to form conceptions of how these technologies work and their basic capabilities" [4]. Therefore, students' perspectives have to be taken into account for designing courses equally to statements by the scientific community. Particularly, this model can be used for research in order to support CS teaching by exploring students' conceptions of various topics of CS. It is important to clarify that this model focuses on students' (pre-) conceptions rather than "mis"-conceptions, as this term already conveys that ideas might be wrong or invaluable.

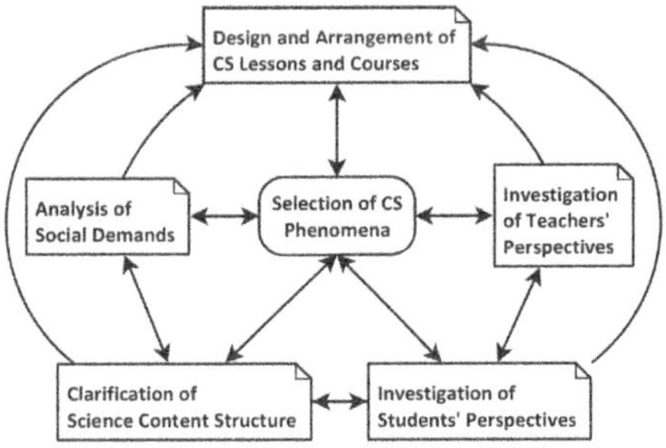

Fig. 1. Educational reconstruction for computer science education [3]

2.2 Students' Conceptions of Programming and OOP

Previous studies focused on different aspects of OOP concepts when investigating students' conceptions and mental models. For instance, Eckerdal et al. [4] describe a study of investigating students' conceptions of the OOP concepts *object and class* with a phenomenographic research approach. Other specific OOP topics were for example *objects* [5], *this operator* [6, 7], *storing objects* [8], *program state visualisations* [9], *primitive and object variables* [10]. In a literature review, Qian and Lehman [1] summarised "that students exhibit various misconceptions and other difficulties in syntactic knowledge, conceptual knowledge, and strategic knowledge." [1]. They have identified several impact factors on students' conceptions: "unfamiliarity of syntax, natural language, math knowledge, inaccurate mental models, lack of strategies, programming environments, and teachers' knowledge and instruction." [1]. Besides, Xinogalos, [11] lists numerous studies on novice programmers investigated, partially contradictory, conceptions of OOP [11]. In his study he found similar conceptions as in the study of Eckerdal et al. [4]. Most of the students had the conception of "'objects' as models/entities of some real-world phenomenon and 'classes' as models describing kinds of objects." [11]. A longitudinal study of the comprehension of OOP concepts by novices by Ragonis et al. [12] report that their results can be "divided into four primary categories: class vs. object, instantiation and constructors, simple vs. composed classes, and program flow" [12].

A much-debated question is how to survey students' conceptions properly [2]. Many studies used qualitative data as interviews and/or questionnaires with open-ended questions. Concept maps [13] and diagnostic tools [6] were also used to identify misconceptions. A literature analysis revealed few studies which surveyed high school students [7, 12, 14]. Most studies in the field have only focused on novice programmers in introductory courses at colleges or universities.

Up to now, no research has been found that surveyed students' conceptions of (object-oriented) programming in the context of digital games.

2.3 Game-Design in Computer Science Education

Thinking about creating games means thinking about objects and how they react to one another and to the player's input. So the game creator naturally thinks in an object-oriented way [15].

It has been demonstrated that various reasons such as motivation, interest or reference to students' everyday life are given for using a game-based approach in teaching. For instance, Rais et al. [16] say that a game-based approach supports students' understanding of object-oriented concepts. Even games (e.g. in [17]) with the content of object-oriented concepts were developed for an introductory CS course. Xinogalos et al. [18] emphasise the importance of engaging students in introductory programming by connecting the contexts to "their interest, such as games and mobile apps" [18]. In "Does Computer Game Design and Programming Benefit Children?" Denner et al. [19] analysed over 400 articles with the result that "computer game design and programming can lead to changes in programming knowledge, problem solving, and computer science attitudes and confidence." [19]. In another study conducted by Troiano et al. [20], it was shown that the game genre supports students' development of computational thinking skills. Besides, it helps students to focus on game design. Moreover, the researchers indicate to consider the impact of game genre while teaching programming with a game-based approach. To conclude this section, the literature identifies the lack of research in students' conceptions of designing and programming games.

2.4 Research Questions

The model of Educational Reconstruction suggests that successful CS courses should be designed by considering students' perspectives, and that game-based approaches in CSE are relevant for teaching introductory programming. Therefore, the research questions in this study focus on programming (OOP) conceptions of novice programmers in the context of digital games. Interviews will be conducted at several different points during a programming introductory course. The long-term investigation of students' developed conceptions may will also give insight into possible influencing factors. In particular, this study will examine the following main research question:

Which conceptions do students develop in different phases of introductory programming when learning OOP in the context of game design? The research question is divided into:

- Which conceptions do learners have about digital games and their functions?
- Which programming-related conceptions do learners develop about digital games and their functions and about (relevant) object-oriented concepts?
- How do programming environments/teacher instructions/materials influence students' conceptions of OOP?
- How does previous knowledge of programming/algorithms influence students' conceptions of OOP?

3 Study Design

The use of qualitative case studies is a well-established approach to investigate students' conceptions [2] and is a main part of the Educational Reconstruction for CSE (see Sect. 2.1). This investigation uses longitudinal data from semi-structured interviews to explore possible influence factors on students' conceptions. The semi-structured approach was chosen in order to compare the data of each individual and among each other. Furthermore, a questionnaire with open-ended questions generates qualitative data in addition to the interviews. The study uses qualitative analysis by using the method of Kuckartz [21] in order to gain insights into categorised conceptions.

3.1 Pilot Study

The pilot study was conducted in order to test the method and the developed instruments for investigation of students' perspectives. Particularly, it was important to check if the questions were chosen adequately. For the pilot study, the game Tetris® was chosen because it is well-known[1], has simple rules and a 2D game structure. Therefore, programming Tetris® could be a suitable task for undergraduate students. By surveying in two phases at the beginning and at the end of a course, the development of students' conceptions was conducted. This paper presents the results of the first surveys. The research questions were specified for the pilot study as follows:

- Which associations of the term "programming" do novice programmers have?
- Which conceptions of Tetris® do novice programmers have?
- Which conceptions of (object-oriented) programming do novice programmers have about Tetris® as an example for a digital game?

[1] "one of the best-selling video game franchises of all time" [https://en.wikipedia.org/wiki/Tetris].

Data Collection. The data was gathered via an online questionnaire, and interviews using an online video conference tool. It was carried out with an introductory course of Media Informatics at a college in Germany, in November 2020.[2] In total, four interviews and 25 questionnaires (19 filled-in completely) were used for the analysis. 49% (14) of the students were male, 41% (12) female, and 10% (3) made no indication of gender. Almost half of the participants had no previous school experience in the field of computer science. Several limitations to this pilot study need to be acknowledged. The sample size is small, probably due to excessive demand in the first semester and COVID-19 pandemic. Only online observations of exercises were possible due to the pandemic and distance teaching. The interviews were conducted with a video conference tool, where social interactions were limited.

4 Evaluation

The structured **questionnaire** has four parts: (1) general personal questions (age, gender, prior experience in computer science education), (2) open-ended questions "What do you associate with the term 'programming'?", (3) open- ended questions "How would you program this game? Please describe a possible approach by drawing or writing your ideas." and (4) questions about gaming in everyday life, and self-evaluation in programming skills and digital media usage. The **interviews** were semi-structured with a prepared guideline[3]. For the evaluation of the four interviews, we used the qualitative text analysis of Kuckartz [21]. By applying the first two steps, the interviews have the following main logical categories:

1. Concept of the term "programming"
2. Explanation of the game Tetris®
3. Explanation of elements in the game Tetris®
4. How to program Tetris®
5. Main game situations in Tetris®
6. Add-ons for Tetris®
7. References to the course contents
8. General personal information

Within the questionnaire and the interview, the students had the option to play[4] Tetris® for several minutes.

The following evaluation shows selected results of the qualitative text analysis. All the analyses were carried out using the software MAXQDA 2020. It is important to mention that some sections were coded twice.

[2] The course OOP 1 (based on *objects-later*) has started in October 2020, so the students have attended the course already for 3–4 weeks.

[3] See Appendix A.

[4] https://save-society.org/browser-game/tetris/.

4.1 Associations of the Term *Programming*

In Fig. 2, to the question "What do you associate with 'programming'?" overall 26 [4 interviewed and 22 surveyed students] responses are grouped into 82 categories. This means that the responses were very diverse. About a third of the respondents stated "to code", "programs" and/or "programming languages". Generally, the responses may be divided into following four aspects: **close to everyday life** (e.g. "games, smart home, robots, future"), **application-oriented** (e.g. "websites, apps, server, systems"), **technical view** (e.g. "loops, variables, functions, Java, C#") and **focus on planning—processes** (e.g. "pair programming, planning, testing, functional specifications, requirement specifications"). Interestingly, in only four answers we could find the term "object-oriented programming". All of them, can be classified with **technical view**. No more analyses are feasible due to incomplete details of prior experiences in computer science education.

4.2 Conceptions of Game Design

The overall response to the online questionnaire was poor. There were 18 responses to the question, "How would you program this game? Please describe a possible approach by drawing or writing your ideas." In contrast, the four interviewees responded their ideas extensively.

Table 1 illustrates the proportion of categories found. Almost 30% of those surveyed indicated that they do not have any idea. The themes of the **process** of designing Tetris and **implementing** of Tetris® recurred throughout the dataset. Some subcategories could be found in **implementing**: statements related to programming (**programming oriented**), the **bricks** and other **elements** of Tetris®. Several responses indicate conditionals, while explaining the design of the game execution. Just two participants used terms of OOP for their explanation. Furthermore, most of the statements were made from a *user's view* rather than *developer's view*. Overall, these results indicate that the majority of the students explained Tetris® by using their gaming experiences. It is therefore possible that the participants had almost no ideas of designing and/or programming a game before asking them. This result may be explained by the fact that at least 60% of those who were surveyed indicated not having any CS experience.

Fig. 2. Tag cloud of found categories of the term "programming" [N = 26]

4.3 Conceptions of the Game Tetris®

For the following analyses, we used the four interviews. Table 2 lists some details of interviewees, such as age, gender and former CS experience[5]. Altogether, three identified categories *bricks*, *game execution* and *anthropomorphism of computers* are presented.

Bricks. First of all, three interviewees (A, B & D) stated that the *appearance* of the bricks should have been defined. For example, a brick is formed by smaller parts like *pixels* or *squares*. One participant commented: "How are the pixels arranged for the specific brick?" [A]. Other responses included: "One brick is built with small squares. So, I would first define a square." [D]. These two conceptions show the idea of composition and may reveal an implicit object-oriented way of thinking. A common view amongst interviewees was that the following features of a brick can be changed: its *orientation* by turning it, the *position* (motion to left or right) or the *speed* while moving top-down. As one interviewee put it: ". . . a brick moves constantly in the same speed except the user speeds it up with the arrow keys. . . " [D]. Interestingly, the same participant stated that as soon as a brick does not move any more, it has reached the bottom and no more changes of that specific brick are possible. This statement may indicate the object-oriented concepts of *object* and/or *message passing* [22]. In one case, the participant B said that the game should also know "how many bricks to use and that bricks do not overlap" [B]. This may indicate the conception of a *defined number* of bricks and the characterisation of a brick with *constraints*.

[5] In the following text the quoted person is written in square brackets after the quotation.

Table 1. Conceptions of designing the game Tetris®: categories and examples (loosely translated from German) [N = 22]

Cat.		Subcategory	Example	Total
process		design	"…set the UI and the constructionby drawing up a mock-up…" [P21]	13
		planning	"…thinking about the elements and the requirements…" [P7]	9
		investigation	"…to get information about tools online…" [C]	5
		cooperation	"…by asking others for help…" [P19]	3
implementing	programming oriented	conditionals	"…delete a row, when its full…" [P13]	9
		algorithm	"calculating the score" [P13]	8
		testing	"generating automated tests" [P21]	3
		language	"… it depends on the selected programming language and its library…" [A]	2
		OOP	"… in a class diagram… required methodsand variables…" [P7]	2
		complexity	"…easy to run by the computer because no complex 3D models…" [A]	2
	bricks	creating bricks	"…defining shapes for the bricks…" [P24]	9
		navigation	"…process player inputs (cursor keys) to move the bricks." [P24]	9
		random generator	"Select next object randomly…" [P8]	5
		speed	"define the speed of the bricks while moving" [P24]	3
		bricks in motion	"…the bricks should move from top to bottom…" [D]	5
	elements	grid	"some kind of a table to use as the game field" [P23]	6
		scores	"… high score should be saved…" [P7]	6
		scoreline	"… scoreline increases when getting more scores" [P1]	3

Table 2. Details of interviewees

	Age	Gender	CS experience
A	19	m	5 years CS at school
B	21	f	1 year CS at school and some YouTube learning videos
C	20	f	no CS at school, but tried to learn coding with an online course
D	21	f	no CS at school, no experience

Game Execution. A variety of perspectives were expressed to describe different game situations. For example, one interviewee said: "… every pixel needs to be diminished with a specific value as it moves down on the y-axis." [A]. This view reveals the idea of the game field corresponding with bricks. Talking about this issue, another interviewee said: "... control if a row is occupied with bricks, then you can disappear [delete the bricks]." [D] Furthermore, the same participant thought that the bricks move nonstop top-down "without the opportunity of stopping them because otherwise the game would never end" [D]. In a similar way, another student said: "... there is a 'main-loop' for execution of everything ... or for checking the user inputs... " [A]. In all cases, the students reported different game procedures by using *conditionals* which indicates concepts of *imperative programming*. As one interviewee said: "... *if* the bricks are outside the field, *then* the game is over." [C]. Another interviewee, when asked about the end of the game, explained: "... the game recognises, that the border is reached, so it does not run anymore" [B].

Anthropomorphism of Computers. In all cases, the students assigned human characterisations to the computer: "the computer needs to record" [A], "the game identifies" [B], "the program should know" [C], "the program sees" [D] or "the computer needs to know" [D]. In one case, phrasing the questions with personification of the computer "Do you have an idea, which information the computer needs to move [the bricks] to the left or right?" helped to evoke the student's conceptions: "He definitely would need the number of the fields and if they are unoccupied... " [D].

5 Discussion

While surveying the students about programming Tetris®, we recognised that the responses have been shallow. By asking the interviewees about specific game situations, e.g. "What is happening while a brick is falling down?", conceptions of game execution could be revealed in more detail. To summarise, these results show that students' conceptions are based on the rules of the game. One interesting finding is, when asked about possible add-ons for Tetris®, all of the students thought about *special bricks* which act as a *bomb* like in *Candy Crush Saga*. Overall, these results indicate that the investigated conceptions are very specific to the game Tetris®. Therefore, these findings are rather difficult to interpret as general conceptions for digital games, even though some of them could be adapted, e.g. "main loop" [A], to other digital games. Unsurprisingly, student A with prior knowledge in programming showed more concrete conceptions. Perhaps, the students will develop more conceptions about digital games by gaining more programming experience.

6 Conclusion and Further Work

First results of the pilot study show insights into students' conceptions of game design in the example of Tetris®. Furthermore, the current study found that students possess implicit imperative programming and object-oriented concepts. However, the exploration of students' conceptions of programming by using a game-based approach showed some weak points, e.g. conceptions based on specific characteristics of Tetris®.

The use of the open-ended questionnaire was not meaningful for our research goal. Therefore, we will focus on interviews in the main study.

After interviewing the students at the end of the introductory class, the evaluation will be consolidated. It is expected that object-oriented concepts will have a stronger influence. By finalising the evaluation of the pilot study, the interview guidelines will be optimised for the main study. In particular, we will add explicit questions about digital games in general, and will use Tetris® as an example and not as the focus of the interviews. In the main study, high school students will be interviewed at least three times (at the start, in the middle and at the end of the course) during the introductory class with the aim of getting more detailed conceptions related to object-oriented programming in the context of game design.

A Interview Guideline

The questions of part I will be asked on the different survey dates recurrently, whereas part II will be asked just the first time.

Part I - Game Design:

1. What do you associate with the term “programming”?
2. Play the game *Tetris®*.
3. Do you know this game? How would you explain it to a friend? What is the goal of the game?
4. How would you describe the different parts of the game? Which function could they have?
5. How would you program this game? Please describe a possible approach by drawing or writing your ideas.
   - Which function could have the playing field?
   - How could the controls work?
   - How does the game start or end? Can you describe it in detail?
6. Additional: Which expansion could you imagine for this game? How could you implement it/them?
7. Later on: Which topics of the class have caused the change of your conception(s)/ idea(s)? Was there anything in particular that helped you construct this new understanding?
8. What features and content of the learning materials presented in the class did you find beneficial to your understandings of programming concepts? How did it (they) help your learning experience?
9. So far, how would you evaluate your programming skills? Choose a number between 0 for very low and 10 for very high.

Part II - Individual Background:

1. Do you play digital games in your free time? If yes, how often and with which devices?
2. Do you have any experience in programming? Have you ever had any CS classes or programming courses?

References

1. Qian, Y., Lehman, J.: Students' misconceptions and other difficulties in introductory programming. ACM Trans. Comput. Educ. **18**(1), 1–24 (2017)
2. Duit, R., Gropengießer, H., Kattmann, U., Komorek, M., Parchmann, I.: The model of educational reconstruction – a framework for improving teaching and learning science1. In: Jorde, D., Dillon, J. (eds.) Science Education Research and Practice in Europe, pp. 13–37. SensePublishers, Rotterdam, Netherlands, Cultural Perpectives in Science Education (2012)
3. Diethelm, I., Hubwieser, P., Klaus, R.: Students, teachers and phenomena: Educational reconstruction for computer science education. In: Laakso, M.J., McCartney, R. (eds.) Proceedings of the 12th Koli Calling International Conference on Computing Education Research - Koli Calling 2012, pp. 164–173. ACM Press, New York, NY (2012)
4. Eckerdal, A., Thunè, M., Berglund, A.: What does it take to learn 'programming thinking'? In: Anderson, R., Fincher, S.A., Guzdial, M. (eds.) Proceedings of the 1st International Computing Education Research Workshop, pp. 135–142. ACM Press, New York, NY (2005)
5. Holland, S., Griffiths, R., Woodman, M.: Avoiding object misconceptions. SIGCSE Bull. **29** (1), 131–134 (1997)
6. Noa, R., Ronit, S.: A diagnostic tool for assessing students' perceptions and misconceptions regards the current object "this." In: Pozdniakov, S.N., Dagienė, V. (eds.) ISSEP 2018. LNCS, vol. 11169, pp. 84–100. Springer, Cham (2018). https://doi.org/10.1007/978-3-030-02750-6_7
7. Shmallo, R., Ragonis, N.: Understanding the "this" reference in object oriented programming: misconceptions, conceptions, and teaching recommendations. Educ. Inf. Technol. **26** (1), 733–762 (2020). https://doi.org/10.1007/s10639-020-10265-6
8. Sorva, J.: Students' understandings of storing objects. In: Proceedings of the Seventh Baltic Sea Conference on Computing Education Research, Koli Calling 2007, vol. 88, pp. 127–135. Australian Computer Society, Melbourne, VIC (2007)
9. Sajaniemi, J., Kuittinen, M., Tikansalo, T.: A study of the development of students' visualizations of program state during an elementary object-oriented programming course. J. Educ. Resour. Comput. **7**(4), 1–31 (2008). https://doi.org/10.1145/1316450.1316453
10. Sorva, J.: The same but different students' understandings of primitive and ob ject variables. In: Proceedings of the 8th International Conference on Computing Education Research, Koli 2008, pp. 5–15. ACM, New York, NY (2008)
11. Xinogalos, S.: Object-oriented design and programming: an investigation of novices' conceptions on objects and classes. Trans. Comput. Educ. **15**(3), 13:1-13:21 (2015)
12. Ragonis, N., Ben-Ari, M.: A long-term investigation of the comprehension of OOP concepts by novices. Comput. Sci. Educ. **15**(3), 203–221 (2005)

13. Sanders, K., et al.: Student understanding of object-oriented programming as expressed in concept maps. In: Dougherty, J.D., Rodger, S. (eds.) Proceedings of the 39th SIGCSE Technical Symposium on Computer Science Education. p. 332. ACM Press, New York, NY (2008)
14. Teif, M., Hazzan, O.: Partonomy and taxonomy in object-oriented thinking. In: Unknown (ed.) Working Group Reports on ITICSE on Innovation and Technology in Computer Science Education, p. 55. ACM, New York, NY (2006)
15. Overmars, M.: Teaching computer science through game design. Computer **37**(4), 81–83 (2004)
16. Rais, A.E., Sulaiman, S., Syed-Mohamad, S.M.: Game-based approach and its feasibility to support the learning of object-oriented concepts and programming. In: Harun, M.F. (ed.) 5th Malaysian Conference in Software Engineering (MySEC), 2011, pp. 307–312. IEEE, Piscataway, NJ (2011)
17. Wong, Y.S., Yatim, M.H.M., Tan, W.H.: Use computer game to learn object- oriented programming in computer science courses. In: IEEE Global Engineering Education Conference (EDUCON), 2014, pp. 9–16. IEEE, 3–5 April 2014
18. Xinogalos, S., Satratzemi, M., Malliarakis, C.: Microworlds, games, animations, mobile apps, puzzle editors and more: what is important for an introductory programming environment? Educ. Inf. Technol. **22**(1), 145–176 (2015). https://doi.org/10.1007/s10639-015-9433-1
19. Denner, J., Campe, S., Werner, L.: Does computer game design and programming benefit children? A meta-synthesis of research. Trans. Comput. Educ. **19**(3), 1–35 (2019)
20. Troiano, G.M., et al.: Exploring how game genre in student- designed games influences computational thinking development. In: Bernhaupt, R., et al. (eds.) Proceedings of the 2020 CHI Conference on Human Factors in Computing Systems, pp. 1–17. ACM, New York, NY (2020)
21. Kuckartz, U., Radiker, S.: Analyzing Qualitative Data with MAXQDA: Text, Audio, and Video. Springer, Cham, Switzerland (2019)
22. Armstrong, D.J.: The quarks of object-oriented development. Commun. ACM **49**(2), 123–128 (2006)

A Closer Look at and Confirmation of the General and Study Interests of Future Computer Science Students

Corinna Mößlacher(✉), Max Kesselbacher, and Andreas Bollin

Department of Informatics Didactics, University of Klagenfurt, Carinthia, Austria
{corinna.moesslacher,max.kesselbacher,
andreas.bollin}@aau.at

Abstract. Many factors can indicate pupils' tendencies to be interested in specific fields of study in the future. Examples of such measures are personal interests, which can also evaluate and develop institutional programmes and interventions that can support pupils' education in computer science. In this work, we report on a study to document characteristic profiles in general interests and study interests, surveying pupil cohorts that attend different activities related to computer science: workshops (compulsory and non-compulsory) and contests related to computer science. We match these interest profiles with the interests of first-semester students of computer science. Pupils attending computer science activities in their leisure time show similar or higher interests in study fields related to studying computer science than the students, differentiating them from pupils attending compulsory workshops. We also show that the relations between general interests and study interests are uniform for pupils and students, helping teachers and syllabus builders promote encouragement towards the interest in computer science.

Keywords: Interests · K-12 education · STEM · Student acquisition

1 Introduction

At the beginning of 2018, the European Union (EU) Commission presented the Digital Education Action Plan [1] and outlined how the EU intends to support educational institutions and education systems regarding digital transformation. According to the EU, the development of relevant digital competences is urgently needed in the age of rapid digital change, both professionally and privately. The Digital Education Action Plan focuses on the use of digital and innovative education practices and has three priorities: (a) making better use of digital technologies for teaching and learning, (b) developing relevant digital competences and skills for the digital transformation, and (c) improving education through better data analysis and foresight. The plan is also linked to the hope of getting more young people interested in technology and, ideally, inspiring them with a degree in, for example, computer science.

A lot of initiatives were started world-wide, by the EU and the European Countries. Also, at our university and department, we are trying to improve the situation at schools and universities by improving teaching quality [2, 3] and by providing motivating

Published by Springer Nature Switzerland AG 2022
D. Passey et al. (Eds.): OCCE 2021, IFIP AICT 642, pp. 91–103, 2022.
https://doi.org/10.1007/978-3-030-97986-7_8

(gamely, inspiring) units of computer science and digital competencies [4] to pupils of different age groups. However, the critical question always remains: how sustainable are our interventions and programmes, and can we thereby create enthusiasm for technology and computer science among our young learners? Our long-term goal is to survey the sustainability to improve the quality and effects of our interventions.

To achieve that it is essential to know what characteristics are present in the pupils' target group, if and how these characteristics can be influenced, and what the 'ideal' characteristic for our goal is. This paper focuses on surveying specific interests that are present in pupil and student cohorts[1] to be used as a basis for further research.

The data that is collected in schools is often limited to the pupils' achievement in certain subjects or topics (mapped to grades). This is continued at university. But achievement (experienced success and failure) is not the only factor that is relevant to pupil's interests and motivation, and we can observe that (a) the achievement may be influenced by the academic self-concept of the pupils or vice versa [5], (b) high achievement does not indicate high interest in the subject, and (c) the personality influences the interest (also in certain kinds of tasks and therefore certain subjects) [6]. Therefore, when trying to motivate students, we should consider additional variables like self-concept, interest and personality, and not only their achievements. When measuring these variables, we can gain more information about the students we want to motivate, to see what differs pupils that claim to be interested in computer science or not, and, in the best case, we are also equipped with a way to measure the effect of our classroom interventions to show that they are working as they should. With the help of a survey tool for long-term studies (that is also compliant with the basic data protection regulations of the EU), we can learn more about the characteristic traits of pupils. Results on the gender differences in *personality*, *interests* and *self-concept* in the pupils' results have already been shown [7].

The objective of this paper is now to describe the interest profiles of pupil cohorts attending different CS-related activities (compulsory and recreational CS workshops, CS-related contests) and to compare these profiles to first-semester CS students' interests to confirm findings in literature and present (site-specific) new findings. So, this paper focuses on pupils with (and without) a high interest in CS and CS students. Future work will also compare students with (and without) interest in CS.

2 Related Work

There are many factors that influence the personal achievement and the success in school, at university and the working environment. PISA studies show that pupils are interested in science and technology until the age of 10 [8] but education in school is not able to convey a positive image of technology [9].

[1] In this paper we refer to school students as "pupils" and to university students as "students" to clearly distinguish the cohorts.

Curricula, school activities and school material could be designed in a way to strengthen (or raise) interest of pupils during their schooldays and encourage them to choose a STEM study. There are many (local) initiatives that try to fill this gap but they are often not surveyed scientifically [10]. Our framework can be used to survey the effects of interventions long-term and determine which interventions cause which effects on the interests.

Vocational interests (as defined by Holland [11]) are a known characteristic for many future life predictions, for instance educational choices and choice of work fields. Holland describes six areas of interest: *Realistic*, *Investigative*, *Artistic*, *Social*, *Enterprising* and *Conventional* (RIASEC). The fitting of the interest profile and the type of the (work) environment are important for the work satisfaction. These interests should not only be taken into account when evaluating work satisfaction: they can also be used in advance when choosing the field of study. In this work, we denote the vocational interests with the term **general interests**.

Some interests tend to be more stable than others over time: A three-cohort study with pupils of grades 7 to 12 indicates a more stable specification on interests in the areas denoted as *Investigative*, *Artistic*, *Enterprise* and *Prestige*. Older students have a higher interest in the areas *Realistic*, *Artistic*, *Enterprise* and *Conventional*. But the profile pattern of the interest showed stability over time [12]. A study of university students showed that increased scores in the interest *Investigative* increases the likelihood of the selection of a STEM study. Higher interests in *Artistic* and *Enterprising* decreased the likelihood. Males are generally more likely to choose a STEM study, especially if they have low scores in Social personality [13].

A study of pupils showed that high results on *Investigative*, *Artistic*, or *Enterprising* interests result in higher educational tracks than students that have high results in *Realistic*, *Social*, or *Conventional* interests. An explanation might be that pupils with a high interest in *Investigative* choose jobs in a higher social status because there they can pursue their interests [14].

When observing gender differences in the interests, girls have more interest in *Artistic* and *Social*: boys have more interest in *Realistic*. Regarding the STEM fields, the greatest difference in interests can be found in technology and engineering where boys are more interested. The same study observed the correlations between RIASEC interests and STEM interests, that were all positive [15].

Literature shows that there are interest profiles that advantage or disadvantage the future choice of a STEM study. We want to observe similarities and differences in these profiles of pupils and computer science students. So, we can identify if pupils currently interested in STEM activities have certain profiles, and if these profiles fit the profiles of computer science students. In this work, we chose to divide the cohorts only by age (pupils and students). The cohort of pupils is additionally divided by their STEM-related activity. We chose not to divide the cohorts by gender, which is a study focus in the future. Results for pupils divided by gender can already be found in [7].

3 Methodology

3.1 Research Objective

Our long-term objective is to learn more about key characteristics of pupils with (and without) a high interest in computer science. By using a test instrument supporting long-term studies, we set ourselves two goals, namely:

1. to demonstrate that (with our measuring framework) there are assessable differences between different pupil cohorts (pupils attending compulsory school workshops, non-compulsory recreational workshops and contests), and
2. compare these pupils' profiles with the results of first semester computer science students.

In this work, we report on differences in **general interests** [11, 16] and future **study interests**. We will use these results to investigate if and how relevant characteristics can be fostered and developed by classroom interventions in further studies.

To address the first goal, we investigate three questions. First, we investigate differences in the characteristics of different cohorts of pupils, to form a baseline of pupils' profiles regarding general interests and study interests. For this, we look closer at the following question:

- Q1: What are the differences between pupils who attend compulsory computer science workshops in their daily school life, and pupils who attend recreational workshops or contests related to computer science?

Second, we investigate if there are differences between the pupil cohorts and first semester students of computer science, with the assumption that interests of computer science students could be target interests when fostering pupils. Thus, our next question is:

- Q2: Are there measurable differences between the pupil cohorts' interests and interests of computer science students?

Third, aside from differences between cohorts, we investigate the relation between **general interests** and **study interests** in all cohorts. This way, we shed light on the cohorts from an inter-cohort and intra-cohort perspective. Our final question is:

- Q3: What is the relation between **general interests** and **study interests** in all cohorts?

We answer these questions by comparing responses to a long-term survey of personality, interests, and self-concept (Sect. 3.2) of different cohorts (Sect. 3.3). We compare mean values and confidence intervals and report correlations between **general interests** and **study interests** to detect differences and form profiles.

3.2 KAUA – Data Collection Framework

In this section, we briefly introduce the data collection framework used to survey the cohorts. KAUA (Košice and Alpen-Adria University Assessment) is an online survey system that was designed and implemented with the General Data Protection Regulation of the European Union[2] in mind. The framework contains a hashing service which converts personal data to unique ids, enabling anonymous longitudinal studies.

Table 1. Dimensions and items collected by KAUA [7]

Dimension	Items	Scale
General interests [11, 16]	Realistic, investigative, artistic, social, enterprising, conventional	9-level Likert [−4, 4]
Personality [6, 17]	Dominant/easygoing formal/informal	13-level Likert [−6, 6]
Self-concept [18]	3x verbal self-concept 3x mathematical self-concept	4-level [1, 4]
CS interest [7]	Computer science interest	6-level [1, 6]
Study interests [7]	History, art, music, literature, language, economy, law, social fields, health, natural sciences, informatics (CS), math, engineering, none	Yes/no [0, 1]

The data collection framework has already been used in studies [7, 19], and is explained in detail in [7]. In this work, we report on the first study that includes (undergraduate) students. Table 1 summarises the items included in the surveys:

- **General Interests**: Six dimensions of general interests following Holland (RIASEC) [11, 16]
- **Personality**: Two dimensions (Dominant/Easygoing, Formal/Informal) of the Five-Factor and Stress Theory [6, 17]
- **Self-Concept**: Verbal and mathematical self-concept, with formulations used in PISA surveys [18]
- **CS Interest**: Interest in Computer Science specifically [7]
- **Study Interests**: Interest in specific fields of study (now or in future) [7]

The purpose of the framework is to accompany pupils and students in their education. This includes specifically set activities and interventions that are great opportunities for informal learning. Such activities are popular but often not adequately accompanied scientifically [10].

3.3 Pupil and Student Cohorts

We have collected the following cohorts with the KAUA data collection framework:

- Participants of compulsory computer science workshops of years 2018–2020, organised by the Department of Informatics Didactics of the University of

[2] http://data.europa.eu/eli/reg/2016/679/2016-05-04.

Klagenfurt and attended by whole school classes, comprise the cohort School (n = 855, mean age = 13.97 ± 0.34).

- Participants of recreational computer science workshops of years 2018–2020, organised by the Department of Informatics Didactics of the University of Klagenfurt in Austria and attended by interested individual pupils, comprise the cohort Recreational (n = 104, age = 13.05 ± 0.53).
- Participants of computer science related contests: winners of the Austrian Bebras contest 2018 and participants of the School *Contest Catalysts Coding Contest* 2018 and 2019 comprise the cohort Contest (n = 90, age = 15.30 ± 0.73).

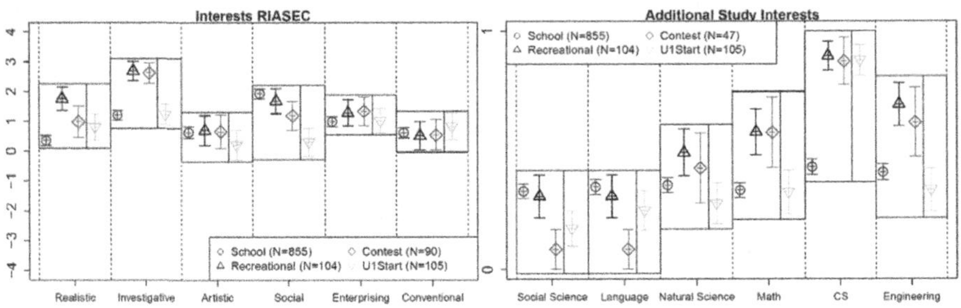

Fig. 1. Mean values and 95% confidence intervals of RIASEC and study interests of the cohorts

- First semester students of years 2018 and 2019, studying computer science at the University of Klagenfurt in Austria, comprise the cohort U1Start (n = 105, age = 24.54 ± 1.61).

All participants have attended a university or school in Austria. Note that a part of the cohort Contest, the investigated winners of the Austrian Bebras contest 2018 (n = 43), have been administered a former version of the survey, and have not been surveyed regarding their study interests. This leaves 47 participants in the cohort for those items.

4 Data Analysis

In this section we descriptively analyse and compare the responses of the described cohorts to the survey, focusing on general and study interests. We show mean values and 95% confidence intervals of the cohorts' survey responses in Fig. 1 and significant differences in Table 2.

4.1 Differences Between Pupil Cohorts [Q1]

First, we report on differences between the three cohorts School, Recreational and Contest regarding their **general interests** and **study interests**. Regarding the **general interests**, School pupils have a significantly lower *Investigative* interest than the other cohorts, and a significantly lower *Realistic* interest than Recreational pupils, but have a significantly higher *Social* interest compared to `Contest` pupils. There are no significant differences between the `Recreational` and `Contest` cohorts, although the latter features a lower mean in *Realistic* and *Social* interests. There are no significant differences for *Artistic*, *Enterprising* and *Conventional.*

For **study interests**, `School` pupils have a significantly lower interest in *Math*, *CS* and *Engineering* compared to both other cohorts. `School` pupils have a significantly lower interest in *Natural Science* compared to `Recreational` pupils, but have a significantly higher interest in *Social Science* and *Language* compared to `Contest` pupils. `Recreational` pupils have a higher interest in *Social Science* and *Language* compared to `Contest` pupils, but this difference is not significant.

Table 2. Significant differences, compared by mean values and 95% confidence intervals, between the cohorts regarding the collected items. The dimensions include, in order: general interests (gi), study interests (si). Superscript signs denote direction of the difference: lower (-) or higher (+) mean value for the row-cohort, compared to the column-cohort.

Q1	***Recreational (n=104)***	***Contest (n=90, n=47*)***
School (n=855)	(gi) Realistic$^-$, Investigative$^-$ (si) Natural Science$^-$, Math$^-$, CS$^-$, Engineering$^-$	(gi) Investigative$^-$, Social$^+$ (si*) Social Science$^+$, Language$^+$, Math$^-$, CS$^-$, Engineering$^-$
Recreational (n=104)		(si*) Social Science$^+$, Language$^+$

Q2	***U1Start (n=105)***
School (n=855)	(gi) Social$^+$, (si) Social Science$^+$, CS$^-$
Recreational (n=104)	(gi) Realistic$^+$, Investigative$^+$, Social$^+$ (si) Natural Science$^+$, Math$^+$, Engineering$^+$
Contest (n=90, n=47*)	(gi) Investigative$^+$, (si*) Math$^+$, Engineering$^+$

4.2 Differences Between Pupil Cohorts and AAU Students [Q2]

We next report differences between the pupil cohorts and first-semester computer science students at the University of Klagenfurt (`U1Start`). Regarding their **general interests**, `U1Start` students have a significantly lower interest in *Social* than both `School` and `Recreational` pupils, a significantly lower interest in *Realistic* than `Recreational` pupils, and also a significantly lower interest in *Investigative* than both `Recreational` and `Contest` pupils. Again, there are no significant differences for *Artistic*, *Enterprising* and *Conventional* interests.

Looking at the **study interests**, `U1Start` students have a significantly lower interest in *Social Sciences*, but a significantly higher interest in *CS* compared to `School` pupils. `U1Start` students have a similarly high interest in *CS* compared to both `Recreational` and `Contest` pupils, but have a significantly lower interest in *Natural Science* compared to `Recreational` pupils, and a significantly lower interest in *Math* and *Engineering* compared to both `Recreational` and `Contest` pupils. There are no significant differences for *Language* interests.

The students show a more differentiated interest in STEM fields: They have the highest interest in *Computer Science* (their field of study) and lower interest in *Natural Science*, *Math* and *Engineering*.

4.3 Correlations Between Interests [Q3]

We only report significant Spearman correlations ($p < .05$) with an absolute correlation value $\sigma \geq .20$ (indicating at least a weak correlation). We mark correlations with sufficient power with an asterisk, following a power test with $p < .05$, a power of $.95$, and the respective cohort size.

The correlations between **general interests** and **study interests** yield a uniform picture across the cohorts. There are no significant correlations for `Contest` pupils.

For non-technical **study interests** of the `School` cohort, the **general interest** *Artistic* is weak positively correlated to interest in *Social Science* ($\sigma = 0.21$*) and *Language* ($\sigma = 0.27$*). The **general interest** *Social* is weak positively correlated to interest in *Social Science* ($\sigma = 0.34$*).

In the `Recreational` cohort, *Language* is weak positively correlated to *Investigative*, *Artistic* and *Social* ($\sigma = \{0.21, 0.21, 0.22\}$), and *Social Science* is weak positively correlated to *Social* ($\sigma = 0.28$). The `U1Start` cohort shows positive correlations of *Social Science* to *Social* and *Enterprising* ($\sigma = \{0.44$*, $0.20\}$), and of *Language* to *Artistic* ($\sigma = 0.37$*).

Regarding technical **study interests**, the **general interest** *Realistic* is positively correlated to the interest in *Natural Science* (`Recreational`: $\sigma = 0.22$, `U1Start`: $\sigma = 0.31$), *CS* (`School`: $\sigma = 0.24$*) and *Engineering* (`School`: $\sigma = 0.40$*, `Recreational`: $\sigma = 0.27$, `U1Start`: $\sigma = 0.42$*). The **general interest** in *Artistic* is positively correlated to the **study interest** in *Natural Science* (`Recreational`: $\sigma = 0.26$), but negatively correlated to *Math* (`Recreational`: $\sigma = -0.31$) and *Engineering* (`Recreational`: $\sigma = -0.32$, `School`: $\sigma = -0.21$*).

The **general interest** in *Social* is weak negatively correlated to the **study interest** of *Natural Science* in the `U1Start` cohort ($\sigma = -0.23$), but weak positively correlated in the `School` cohort ($\sigma = 0.16$*). *Social* is weak negatively correlated to the interest in *Engineering* (`U1Start`: $\sigma = -0.20$). The **general interest** in *Enterprising* is weak negatively correlated to *Natural Science* (`U1Start`: $\sigma = -0.23$). The **general interest** in *Conventional* is weak positively correlated (only in the `Recreational` cohort) to **study interests** in *Math* ($\sigma = 0.25$) and *CS* ($\sigma = 0.21$), and (only in the `U1Start` cohort) weak negatively correlated to the interest in *Engineering* ($\sigma = -0.21$).

5 Discussion

In this section, we present a discussion and possible explanations for the differences of **general interests** and **study interests** of our cohorts. Many factors, such as socio-cultural ones, have an influence on these interests and can be assessed in studies. But educators can hardly change them in their classroom settings. We therefore only assess factors that we believe to be *malleable*, such as **general interests** and **study interests**. Pupils' learning can also be influenced by their peer group (e.g., see [20]) but in our study we see learners as individuals and aim to provide a baseline of interest measures, assessing the effects of classroom interventions in the future.

5.1 Differences Between Pupil Cohorts [Q1]

With our first question (Q1) we were looking for the differences between pupils who only attend compulsory CS workshops (`School`), and pupils who attend recreational workshops (`Recreational`) or contests (`Contest`) related to CS.

`Recreational` pupils and `Contest` pupils show similarities in their interests. But these two cohorts show significant differences compared to the `School` pupils. So, pupils who attend computer science activities have a specific profile of interests. They can be distinguished from `School` pupils by these traits.

`Recreational` pupils and `Contest` pupils have a high **general interest** in the *Investigative* domain (a factor that is important for their choice of fields of study [13]). This is confirmed by their higher **study interests** in *Math*, *Computer Science*, and *Engineering*, compared to `School` pupils. This factor can also be seen as an essential factor for choosing to attend a computer science activity.

Given these differences in traits between pupils of compulsory computer science workshops and pupils who attend computer science activities, as a next step we plan to design workshops intended to influence the *Investigative* interest (and other traits) of pupils. With our framework, we can also survey changes of traits over time that will show us the effects of our interventions in the future.

5.2 Differences Between Pupil Cohorts and AAU Students [Q2]

With our second question (Q2) we wanted to know if there are measurable differences between pupils' characteristics and students' characteristics.

Pupils of recreational workshops and contests show higher **general interest** in the *Investigative* area, which plays an important role for the choice of fields of study and is thus in line with current research [13]. Surprisingly, the students do not show such a high *Investigative* interest. We assume that the study specialisation offered at this university has an influence on that factor.

`Recreational` pupils and `Contest` pupils as well as `U1Start` students show higher **study interest** in *Computer Science* compared to `School` pupils. The pupils attend these activities because of their interest in the subject, whereas pupils in school workshops have to attend them regardless of their interest. The higher interest is thus expected. The other two pupil cohorts have a similar interest in *Computer Science* compared to the students.

The `Recreational` pupils and `Contest` pupils show a higher interest in *Natural Science*, *Math*, and *Engineering* than the students. Possible explanations are that the students already chose their field of study and therefore rate their interest in this field (CS) highest, or that they have more insight into different fields of study and their respective characteristics which allows them to give a more differentiated rating.

5.3 Correlations Between Interests [Q3]

The *Artistic* interest is negatively correlated to some STEM studies (which is expected, see [13]), but not to *Natural Science*. It is possible that pupils have a different understanding of the fields of study of *Natural Science* compared to students (although the corresponding survey items account for different age groups). This could also be an explanation for the discrepancy observed between the pupils and students in the correlation of *Social* interest and *Natural Science*. The pupil cohorts show a positive correlation, the student cohort shows a negative correlation. There is no discrepancy on the correlations of the *Social* interest and the study interest *Engineering*: the correlation is negative in all cohorts.

The *Investigative* interest is positively correlated to all study interests of `School` pupils ([0.07, 0.16]). Although this interest is seen as a predictive factor for STEM studies, our data shows that this factor has a (small) effect on different fields of study. The *Realistic* interest shows only positive correlations to STEM interests.

The correlations between **general interest** and **study interest** confirm results presented in literature. But it also shows differences between the cohorts. The (future) study interests of pupils are always dependent on their current knowledge of the field. Pupils may have a different imagination of a certain field of study, compared to students who actively chose a study.

6 Threats to Validity

When comparing vocational and study interests of pupils and students, social and cultural backgrounds could have uncontrolled effects on the investigated characteristics. In this study, all participants originate from Austria, mitigating this threat.

Potential threats to validity arise from the survey that was used to collect the data. Although the pupils and students participated in the same survey, the wording of the survey items are different to fit them to the age group. This may have an influence on the results. Moreover, answers of self-assessments are dependent on the personal perception of the question - this may be different for pupils and students. Pupils may have a different preconception of specific fields of study due to their level of knowledge about the field.

Another source of threats to validity arises from the division of pupils into cohorts. The pupil cohorts are divided by the kind of computer science activity they participated in. Our assumption is that the pupils attending recreational workshops are specifically interested in STEM activities. This may not be true: they may be registered as their parents want them to attend. However, the results support our assumption. Also, the cohort of pupils attending compulsory workshops is a heterogeneous group, with pupils that are interested in a wide variety of additional activities. The correlation analysis reveals that all relations between the interests are uniform between the pupil cohorts. Therefore, the cohort of pupils attending compulsory workshops forms a control group of all pupils, while still containing pupils with specific characteristics.

Regarding internal validity, we report significant findings with $p < .05$, and report correlations following a power test with $p < .05$ and a power of $.95$.

7 Conclusion

In this paper, we show the use of a survey tool for gathering specific characteristics (general interests and study interests) of pupils that indicate future interest in computer science. We compare pupil cohorts attending compulsory CS workshops, recreational CS workshops, and CS contests, and first semester students of computer science. We demonstrate that there are differences in the profiles of interests between pupils attending compulsory and non-compulsory activities and student cohorts, and that there are uniform correlations between general interests and study interests.

It turned out that pupils of compulsory computer science workshops are significantly less investigative, and significantly less interested in numerous fields of study (Natural Science, Math, CS, Engineering) compared to pupils attending non-compulsory activities. This confirms the assumption that an Investigative interest is a possible influence on the choice of a STEM study.

Concerning the characteristics of first semester students, we learned that the study interest in CS was high, but the study interest in all other STEM fields (Natural Science, Math, Engineering) was lower than expected. Moreover, the interests in these STEM fields are lower compared to the pupil cohorts of non-compulsory activities. A possible explanation is that the pupils may have a broad interest in STEM and do not (or cannot) differentiate the characteristics of STEM fields, in contrast to the student cohort that already chose a study of their specific interest (and rejected the other choices).

Correlations between general interests and study interests show that the Investigative interest is very weak, but positively, correlated to all study interests, not only CS. An Artistic interest is negatively correlated to an interest in Engineering, making it a possible target of interventions to improve interest in STEM-related fields of study. Observed discrepancies between pupil and student cohorts (Social interest is positively correlated to Natural Science in the pupil cohort, but negatively correlated in the student cohort) can be attributed to different states of knowledge.

We demonstrate that it is possible to collect interest profiles of pupils' cohorts with our KAUA framework, and we confirm findings in literature that there are certain interests that influence the (future) choice of study in STEM-related fields (Artistic, Social, Enterprising). To improve enrollment in computer science and STEM-related fields, an avenue of future research is the design of interventions to convey holistic notions of those fields, attracting students who previously saw themselves as a bad fit.

References

1. European Commission, Brussels, 17 January 2018: Digital Education Action Plan (2018). https://eur-lex.europa.eu/legal-content/EN/TXT/?uri=CELEX:52018DC0022
2. Kesselbacher, M., Bollin, A.: Discriminating programming strategies in scratch– making the difference between novice and experienced programmers. In: 14th Workshop in Primary and Secondary Computing Education (WiPSCE 19), 23–25 October 2019, p. 10. ACM, New York (2019)

3. Reci, E., Bollin, A.: Managing the Quality of Teaching in Computer Science Education. In: 6th Computer Science Education Research Conference (CSERC 17), Helsinki, Finland, p. 10 (2017)
4. Pasterk, S., Sabitzer, B., Demarle-Meusel, H., Bollin, A.: Informatics-Lab: attracting primary school pupils for computer science. In: Proceedings of the 14th LAC-CEI International Multi-Conference for Engineering, Education, and Technology: Engineering Innovations for Global Sustainability, p. 7 (2016)
5. Marsh, H.W., Martin, A.J.: Academic self-concept and academic achievement: relations and causal ordering. Br. J. Educ. Psychol. **81**(1), 59–77 (2011)
6. Mujkanovic, A., Bollin, A.: Improving learning outcomes through systematic group reformation - the role of skills and personality in software engineering education. In: 2016 IEEE First International Conference on Connected Health: Applications, Systems and Engineering Technologies (CHASE), pp. 97–103 (2016)
7. Bollin, A., Kesselbacher, M., Mößlacher, C.: Ready for computing science? A closer look at personality, interests and self-concept of girls and boys at secondary level. In: Kori, K., Laanpere, M. (eds.) ISSEP 2020. LNCS, vol. 12518, pp. 107–118. Springer, Cham (2020). https://doi.org/10.1007/978-3-030-63212-0_9
8. OECD: Organisation For Economic Co-Operation and Development. PISA 2006: Naturwissenschaftliche Kompetenzen für die Welt von morgen. OECD Publishing, Paris; Bielefeld, W. Bertelsmann Verlag, Germany (2008)
9. de Vries, M.J.: The 'I' in MINT: a tale of two translations. In: Proceedings of the 11th Workshop in Primary and Secondary Computing Education, WiPSCE 2016, p. 1–4. Association for Computing Machinery, New York (2016)
10. Begel, A., Ko, A.J.: Learning outside the classroom. In: Fincher, S.A., Robins, A.V. (eds.) The Cambridge Handbook of Computing Education Research. Cambridge University Press, Cambridge (2019)
11. Holland, J.: Exploring careers with a typology - what we have learned and some new directions; am psychol. Am. Psych **51**(4), 397–406 (1996)
12. Xu, H., Tracey, T.: Stability and change in interests: a longitudinal examination of grades 7 through college. J. Vocat. Behav. **93**, 129–138 (2016)
13. Chen, P.S.D., Simpson, P.: Does personality matter? Applying Holland's typology to analyze students' self-selection into science, technology, engineering, and mathematics majors. J. High. Educ. **86**, 725–750 (2015)
14. Usslepp, N., Hübner, N., Stoll, G., Spengler, M., Trautwein, U., Nagengast, B.: Riasec interests and the big five personality traits matter for life success—but do they already matter for educational track choices? J. Pers. **88**(5), 1007–1024 (2020)
15. Babarović, T., Devic, I., Burusic, J.: Fitting the STEM interests of middle schoolchildren into RIASEC structural space. Int. J. Educ. Vocat. Guidance **19**, 111–128 (2018)
16. Bergmann, C., Eder, F.: AIST-R. Allgemeiner Interessen-Struktur-Test mit Umwelt-Struktur-Test (UST-R) – Revision, Manual, 1 edn. Hogrefe (2005)
17. Yamada, Y., et al.: The impacts of personal characteristic on educational effectiveness in controlled-project based learning on software intensive systems development. In: 2014 IEEE 27th Conference on Software Engineering Education and Training (CSEE&T), pp. 119–128. IEEE (2014)
18. Kunter, M., et al.: PISA2000: Dokumentation der Erhebungsinstrumente. Materialien aus der Bildungsforschung. General and Study Interests of future CS Students 13, vol. 72 (2002).

19. Bollin, A., Demarle-Meusel, H., Kesselbacher, M., Mößlacher, C., Rohrer, M., Sylle, J.: The Bebras contest in Austria – do personality, self-concept and general interests play an influential role? In: Pozdniakov, S.N., Dagienė, V. (eds.) ISSEP 2018. LNCS, vol. 11169, pp. 283–294. Springer, Cham (2018). https://doi.org/10.1007/978-3-030-02750-6_22
20. Schellens, T., Van Keer, H., De Wever, B., Valcke, M.: Student elaborations and knowledge construction in asynchronous discussion groups in secondary education. In: Proceedings of the 8th International Conference for the Learning Sciences, (ICLS 2008), vol. 3, pp. 413–415. International Society of the Learning Sciences (2008)

Starter Projects in Python Programming Classes

Michael Weigend(✉)

Westfälische Wilhelms-Universität, Corrensstr 80, 48149 Münster, Germany
mw@creative-informatics.de

Abstract. Starter projects are part of constructionist learning arrangements (1, 2). The term was mainly coined by the Scratch community and describes a simple, executable program that is designed to encourage copying, exploring and further development. This contribution first discusses three types: test programs, examples that illustrate programming techniques and algorithms, and architectural prototypes. It then presents self-observations of university students, describing how they use starter projects for learning.

Keywords: Starter project · Programming · Constructionism · Python

1 Introduction

1.1 Starter Projects

A starter project is an executable computer program that has been designed as learning material. Beginners copy, test and change the starter project, and develop it further according to their interests. The term starter project was coined and cultivated by the scratch community. There are collections of starter projects on various topics on the Scratch website. A well-known example is a minimal version of the video game Pong. The concept of the starter projects is based on the fundamental idea of constructionism [1, 2]: People learn best when they construct relevant (digital) artifacts and share them with others. The term "starter" expresses that a development process is being started. This can be seen both as an individual and as a collective process. From the individual perspective, the starter project is the starting point for a series of iterations in which the software is refined, expanded and improved. This roughly corresponds to the procedure for agile programming (e.g. Extreme Programming [3]). A collective development process happens, when remixing Scratch projects takes place: Somebody picks a Scratch project that she or he likes from the Scratch website and develops it further in the online editor. In this way, a tree of derived projects (remix tree) is created from a starter project. For example, there were more than 26,000 remixes of the just mentioned starter project Pong (February 2021).

1.2 Starter Projects and Tinkering

A constructionist concept connected to starter projects is tinkering. "The tinkering approach is characterised by a playful, experimental, iterative style of engagement, in

Published by Springer Nature Switzerland AG 2022
D. Passey et al. (Eds.): OCCE 2021, IFIP AICT 642, pp. 104–115, 2022.
https://doi.org/10.1007/978-3-030-97986-7_9

which makers are continually reassessing their goals, exploring new paths, and imagining new possibilities." [4, p. 164]. Resnick and Rosenbaum see spontaneous trying out and tinkering in contrast to instructional guidance in tutorials and detailed task descriptions that hinder an independent and self-controlled approach. They [5] point out that trying out also includes making mistakes and requires a "Failure-friendly way of thinking". However, failure is only helpful for learning if there is an opportunity to improve. The time frame of lessons is strict and children from socially disadvantaged backgrounds often do not have the opportunity to finish their projects at home [5]. A starter project makes it easier to start a tinkering process, and guarantees success because it already works. From the starter project, students can carefully find their (individual) ways into new areas, and try out unfamiliar programming concepts. The number and scope of the iterations can be determined by themselves. Which working environment do programming exercises with starter projects require? They [6] describe the general conditions for (physical) tinkering activities. Among other things, a seed, a playground (physical and organisational environment), tools and materials are needed.

Seed. The seed is the reason for starting the tinkering. This can be anything which arouses interest and motivates students to start. By definition, a starter project can be the seed of a software project.

Playground. The ambience of the room should support a playful attitude, cooperation and sharing results [7]. Terms such as Makerspace, Incubation Space or Fab Lab have been established for the architectural concept. Regarding the organisation, it is important that there is enough time for creating presentable products at every pace of work, and that there is opportunity to share results.

Tools. In programming projects, the primary tool is the development environment. In the case of Python programming, these are e.g. IDLE (Integrated Development and Learning Environment), which is included in the standard distribution, or other educational development environments such as Thonny and Geany.

Material. In a physical maker project, the materials that can be used are typically spread on a table. They invite participants to touch and try out. At the same time, they also represent a limitation or channeling, because the project can only be completed with the material offered, and with nothing else. In a programming exercise, the materials to create a digital artifact are the programming concepts used. A starter project can be a material in several ways. It explains and illustrates certain programming techniques, and it is also a model for good programming style (structuring, meaningful names, comments etc.). Sometimes, a collection of starter projects, each one illustrating a different technique, may be of help. Further materials that are brought in are language references, sheets with overviews ("cheat sheets"), skill cards, or posters on the walls.

2 Starter Projects and Examples

2.1 Types of Starter Projects

Principally, every computer program can be the starting point of a development, and can therefore be a starter project. However, in this paper it is assumed that a Starter Project has been designed specifically to encourage and facilitate learning. Regarding the intended learning activities one can roughly distinguish three types of starter projects: Test program, example, and architectural prototype.

Test Program. A test program is a small program with the primary function of demonstrating that the mechanics of program execution work. The classic example of a test program is a "Hello World program" that displays a short text like "Hello world" on the screen, and does nothing else. Probably the first Hello World program was published by Brian Kernighan in 1974 in a tutorial for the C programming language. The much-quoted original text reads.

```
main() {
        printf("hello,world");
}
```

Although the program text is very short, it contains some abstract concepts and is not easy to comprehend. In Python syntax the code is much simpler:

```
print("Hello world")
```

However, if this is the very first program that a person writes and runs on the computer, it is not expected that they understand the program constructs. When a student just writes the program in the editor, starts it, and looks at the output, he or she has not understood the print() function better. But this person, who has never done this before, gets confident that he or she can do it. Exploration and trying out is not targeting the program text itself but its digital environment: The integrated development environment (IDE) (write a program text, understand the syntax highlighting) the operating system (create a project folder, store, load and run a program) and the interpreter or compiler of the programming language (understand system messages).

Test programs may be more complex than a "Hello World" program. Figure 1 shows a screenshot from the run of a simple Python program showing the live image from a public webcam (webcam viewer). When you click the button, the image is updated. You can see the changes. The source code is truly short (17 lines of code). However, to understand it requires specific programming knowledge (e.g., about GUI programming and image processing). The program is not suitable for introducing new programming concepts, such as the definition of button widgets. That would be done with different (more specific) examples. The program is a test program if the purpose of running it is to get certainty that it works in the current environment.

Fig. 1. Webcam-viewer

A test program like the webcam viewer can be used to initiate a creative task. Example: "Describe the idea for a Python project that evaluates live images from web cams and extracts meaningful information". In case of the web cam image shown in Fig. 1, a possible project idea is: The program checks whether someone tries to climb over the site fence. (The program checks changes in colour from the pixels on the site fence.)

The advantage of a test program over simple verbal or visual descriptions is that it proves to beginners that an implementation of a project idea in this topic is within reach. They may not understand the program completely, but they see that a few lines of code suffice to implement a certain functionality.

Example Program. An example program illustrates a programming technique and thus combines a topic and programming concepts into a holistic unit. In contrast to a test program, the focus is on the program text – in terms of functionality and style. This Python project illustrates the Python string-method format() and how to use it in a storytelling project.

```
STORY = """ One Saturday morning {she} was walking down
the street with her {thing}. She thought, "How good that
I have the {thing} with me. " """
name = input("Female first name: ")
thing = input("A thing to carry around: ")
text = STORY.format(she=name, thing=thing)
print(text)
```

Example programs can initiate specific *learning* activities like experimenting with the code. Additionally, they can be designed to provoke different *creating* activities, including extending, improving, and transferring.

Extend: The starter project is a very basic program, which must be extended by adding functions. Example: The starter project manages a dictionary and allows nothing more than to look up the translation of a word. Possible extensions are to add new items and to store the updated dictionary.

Improve: The starter program has an extremely low performance. The challenge is to improve the quality of the output and/or the time complexity. E.g., consider a path-finding Python program with a dictionary representing a graph (mapping nodes to lists of adjacent nodes) and a simple recursive function:

```
from random import choice
G = {1: [2, 4], 2: [1, 3, 5], 3: [2, 5],
     4: [1, 5], 5: [4, 2, 3, 6], 6: [5]}

def search_path(node, goal):
    if node == goal:
        return [node]
    else:
        path = []
        while not goal in path:
            path = search_path(choice(G[node), goal)
        return [node] + path
```

The function works fine and returns a path from node to goal, if such exists. But the path may be not the shortest and may even contain loops. This is a sub-optimal result, and the program spends considerable unnecessary time.

Transfer: The starter project can represent functional pattern, which can be applied broadly. The Python program illustrating how to use string methods in a storytelling project can easily be transferred to different projects in a large variety of domains. Another widely applicable pattern is an interactive program, which first reads some data, then processes the data, and finally outputs the results. The creating process does not necessarily imply learning according to the teacher's goals. Sometimes students invest much time for developing a project just by creating beautiful graphics, or adding data without changing the program's structure. For example, in a grade 10 programming class students got a Python starter project, illustrating how to pick a random item from a list. When the user hits the ENTER key, the program prints a "motivating motto" on screen.

```
import random
mottos = ["You look great today!",
          "Never give up.",
          "Yes, you can do it!"]
while True:
    text = random.choice(mottos)
    print(text)
    input()
```

One group loved this project and developed a version, printing random "fun facts". For several hours, they searched fun facts on the internet and created a very long list with dozens of items. This way they transferred the example program to a new domain and extended it, without learning much about programming.

Architectural Prototype. An architectural prototype is a program that is syntactically correct, but is functionally incomplete. The source text provides the architecture of a more complex project. An example is a graphical user interface with widgets for input and output and buttons that trigger actions when clicked. The function definitions are dummies that have no effect; e.g., in Python syntax:

```
def action():
    pass
```

Another example is a program with incomplete class definitions (attributes and dummy methods) illustrating an aggregate of classes modelling some real structure. An architectural prototype can help to cope with complexity by providing cognitive offload and channeling. When it is the starting point of an iterative development process, the students could start with filling the gaps, for instance by writing function definitions based on verbal specifications (pre- and post-conditions or test requirements). On the one hand, the architectural prototype – since it is already running – offers a test environment. You can start the program, and see from the output whether the self-defined function is working properly. On the other hand, the programming challenge (focusing on mere technical programming concepts) becomes part of a "real" project. Architectural prototypes are sometimes used for written exams because both analytical skills (explaining the program text) and constructive skills (formulating the program text) are tested.

2.2 Starter Projects and Worked Examples

Starter projects are comparable to worked examples in problem centred science education. A worked example is a prototype solution that guides the student through solving the problem, step by step [8]. Worked examples (in science, as well as in mathematics and informatics) are presented in different forms: e.g. in the classroom by a teacher, in explaining videos, in textbooks or animated tutorials [9]. When students solve science problems on their own, they tend to look for work they had recently elaborated in class, and try to adapt these for solving the new task [10]. The advantage of worked examples (compared to problem solving) is the reduction of cognitive load resulting from processes that do not contribute to learning (ineffective load). Like worked examples, starter projects are prototype solutions, and help to reduce cognitive load. They prevent learners from being overwhelmed by the number of information elements that need to be processed simultaneously, when they start a programming project from scratch. However, one can point out three major differences:

1. A starter project is processed actively and self-controlled, whereas a worked example includes guidance. Instead of following a given path, students explore the code in their own way and change it.
2. A starter project is designed to initiate learning activities and to challenge creativity. It encourages the students to apply certain programming techniques (covering the curriculum) by the given material. But the students can decide, themselves, about design goals. Tinkering with the code may lead to new design ideas, and consequently to research and implement activities that go beyond the scope of the original code of the starter project.
3. A starter project is supposed to be used immediately (and not eventually later like a worked example). It reduces cognitive load (that might act like a barrier) and motivates to start a development and learning process.

These three attributes of starter projects lead to the research questions of a survey, which is presented in the following section.

3 Self-observations on Learning with Starter Projects

This section presents self-observations of university students who have attended an introductory Python course. Two questionnaires were used at two different days covering these research questions:

1. How do students process the code of a starter project?
2. What kind of learning activities do students choose during the development initiated by a starter project?
3. What kind of creative design activities (improving, extending, transferring to a new context) students are interested in?

The University of Münster (Germany) has offered introductory Python programming courses for students of all faculties. The participants can achieve two different types of certificates: everyone who has attended the course regularly receives a certificate of participation without any grade. Students who have successfully passed a written exam at the end of the semester will receive a higher-ranked certificate with a grade. One can assume that at least the exam writers were – additionally to intrinsic motivation – extrinsically motivated to accomplish programming competence during the exercises. The lectures usually have taken place in a computer lab. Each lecture has lasted 180 min plus one 30-min-break. Beside presentations and discussions, a main part has been hands-on programming exercises based on different types of starter projects. In each hands-on session, the students could pick from a small repertoire of two or three tasks. In the winter semester 2020/21, this course took place in a digital form (Zoom meetings with breakout sessions for programming exercises). The students were asked to fill questionnaires related to these exercises. One question was whether they intended to take part in the written exam, but no further questions about the person (like age or gender) were asked. Primarily, the questionnaires should encourage students to reflect on their style of work, which was not seen as a part of a scientific study, but a regular part of the learning process.

3.1 Processing Starter Projects

The first questionnaire was filled by 29 students (group "all"), 12 of them intended to do the written examination (group "exam") 8 did not (group "no exam") and the remaining were still undecided. The exercises that day contained 5 tasks with starter projects (type "Example") the students should try out and change at will. On average, each student worked on 55% of the tasks. The students were asked to reflect on how they handled starter projects, and to check all statements that applied. Table 1 shows the results.

Table 1. Processing starter projects

Statement	All (N = 29)	Exam (N = 11)	No Exam (N = 8)
1: I typed program text and did not just copy it with drag and drop	15 (52%)	9 (82%)	2 (25%)
2: I have not copied program text literally but changed it immediately	11 (38%)	4 (36%)	4 (50%)
3: I have copied program text with drag and drop	9 (31%)	1 (9%)	4 (50%)
4: I have modified program text in order to explore the effects of instructions	19 (66%)	8 (73%)	7 (88%)
5: Only after I fully understood the program, I tried to implement my own ideas	10 (34%)	5 (45%)	1 (12%)

It is remarkable that many students (15 out of 29), and especially exam writers (9 out of 11), typed the program texts of the starter projects instead of copying them into the editor with drag and drop. Most students reported that they actively explored code by modifying it.

3.2 Initiated Learning Activities and Effects

Beside tinkering tasks, the exercises on that day included four problem-oriented tasks in the style of exam tasks. In these tasks, the challenge was to write a Python program according to a given verbal specification. Example: "Write an interactive program that calculates the volume of a pyramid." On average, each student worked on 53% of these tasks. The students were asked to reflect on their work, related to these problem-oriented tasks, and to check statements that applied. The same statements (partly with slightly different wording) were also given for the tinkering tasks with starter projects before. Table 2 compares the results regarding the two types of tasks. The results show that both problem-oriented tasks and tinkering tasks with starter projects initiated a considerable amount of learning activities, and a feeling of learning success (no significant differences with chi-square statistic on $p < .05$).

Table 2. Initiated learning activities and effects

Statement	Tinkering (N = 29)	Problem (N = 29)
6: I have made experiments in the Python Shell to explore the effects of instructions	22 (76%)	17 (59%)
7: I felt inspired to develop my own programming project	9 (31%)	9 (31%)
8: I looked in the course material or other sources for Python commands that I might need	17 (59%)	21 (72%)
9: I feel like I have learned something new while working on the task	23 (79%)	24 (83%)
10: I was proud of my result	6 (21%)	11 (38%)

3.3 Tinkering Versus Problem Solving

The students were asked to make an overall assessment of which type of task they preferred. The majority preferred solving problems over free tinkering (Table 3).

3.4 Motivation for Creative Development

On another day, the students got three different types of tasks with starter projects (type: example). They differed in their expectations about what way the given code should be developed. The students were asked to rate their motivation, to extend, improve or transfer starter projects. They had experienced examples of these three types, but they were asked to rate the task type and not the concrete example. The 18 respondents reported to be motivated by all three types of challenges with a median of 4 on a 1-5-Likert scale (1: not motivated, 5: highly motivated).

Table 3. Overall assessment of task types

Statement	All (N = 29)	Exam (N = 11)	No Exam (N = 8)
11: I prefer to tinker with a starter project	9 (31%)	3 (27%)	2 (25%)
12: I prefer to solve tasks with a problem specification	15 (52%)	7 (64%)	4 (50%)

4 Discussion

4.1 Active Writing

A perhaps surprising result of the first questionnaire is that students see writing (typing) rather than copying from the digital hand-out by drag and drop as an appropriate way to elaborate starter projects. Since they created individual versions of the code by changing and adding words, this can be seen as a special type of "writing to learn" like journal learning [11]. According to [11] the positive effect of journal writing can be increased by appropriate learning strategy prompts. Some successful prompts from journal learning could be adapted to exercises with starter project. An example of an elaborative prompt would be, "Add explaining comments to the program code." A metacognitive monitoring prompt is, "Indicate (by comments) the lines of code, you have problems to understand."

4.2 Desire for Challenge

The results of the survey suggest that many students are attracted by the challenge of problem-based tasks (including the risk of failure). To make exercises with starter projects more challenging, teachers could add specific prompts articulating expected goals of development (improve, extend, transfer). Examples for improve-prompts, "Make the program faster.", or "Improve the user interface."

4.3 Creativity

31% of the respondents of the first questionnaire reported to be inspired to create their own project. In the revised version of Bloom's taxonomy of educational objectives, "Create" is the top category [12] in the cognitive process dimension. Accordingly, one might say, that these 31% have high learning ambitions. Constructionism assumes that the wish to create something relevant is a strong motive for learning. However, in this specific context (at the beginning of a programming course), tinkering and exploring code (mainly corresponding to the process categories understand, apply and analyse) seem to be more important than implementing own ideas. According to Csikszentmihalyi, creativity is a social phenomenon and requires a "field" of experts who decide whether an artifact is a novelty within the domain. Learning arrangements with starter projects can get more challenging, if the students are explicitly asked to create something new and unexpected. To make the development a creative process according to Csikszentmihalyi's model [13], students must present their work to the "local field" of classmates who decide about its novelty in some way, for example by rating and commenting. To foster self-efficacy and creative confidence [14], the students should be made aware that there are many ways to add something to a starter project and that at least some of the possibilities are within their reach.

5 Conclusion

Starter projects are digital artifacts that are carefully designed by teachers and textbook authors. In contrast to worked examples (which have a long tradition in math and science education), students and book reader process these code examples in order to learn programming. Starter projects may explain concepts, but they also initiate further exploring activities. Participants of an introductory programming course at a university report, that they, at least at the beginning, prefer a "learning by writing" approach. Typing code beats copying it by drag and drop. It seems to be important to embed starter projects in an "educational environment" that supports tinkering (by offering additional material and support) and is challenging. Starter projects could be enriched by learning strategy prompts, and creativity challenging prompts.

References

1. Harel, I.E., Papert, S.E.: Constructionism. Ablex Publishing, Norwood (1991)
2. Resnick, M.: Give P's a chance: projects, peers, passion, play. In: Constructionism and Creativity: Proceedings of the Third International Constructionism Conference, pp. 13–20. Austrian Computer Society, Vienna (2014)
3. Beck, K.: Extreme Programming Explained. Addison-Wesley, Reading (2000)
4. Resnick, M., Rosenbaum, E.: Designing for tinkerability. In: Honey, M., Kanter, D.E. (eds.) Design, Make, Play: Growing the Next Generation of STEM Innovators, pp. 163–181. Routledge (2013)
5. Ryoo, J.J., Bulalacao, N., Kekelis, L., McLeod, E., Henriquez, B. Tinkering with "failure": Equity, learning, and the iterative design process. In: FabLearn 2015 Conference at Stanford University, September 2015
6. Mader, A., Dertien, E.: Tinkering as method in academic teaching. In: DS 83: Proceedings of the 18th International Conference on Engineering and Product Design Education (E&PDE16), Design Education: Collaboration and Cross-Disciplinarity, Aalborg, Denmark, 8–9 September 2016, pp. 240–245 (2016)
7. McKay, C., Banks, T., Wallace, S.: Makerspace classrooms: where technology intersects with problem, project, and place-based design in classroom curriculum. Int. J. Des. Learn. **7** (2) (2016)
8. Zhi, R., Price, T. W., Marwan, S., Milliken, A., Barnes, T., Chi, M.: Exploring the impact of worked examples in a novice programming environment. In: Proceedings of the 50th ACM Technical Symposium on Computer Science Education, pp. 98–104 (2019)
9. Van Gog, T., Paas, F., Sweller, J.: Cognitive load theory: advances in research on worked examples, animations, and cognitive load measurement. Educ. Psychol. Rev. **22**(4), 375–378 (2010). https://doi.org/10.1007/s10648-010-9145-4

10. Chi, M.T., Bassok, M., Lewis, M.W., Reimann, P., Glaser, R.: Self-explanations: how students study and use examples in learning to solve problems. Cogn. Sci. **13**(2), 145–182 (1989)
11. Nückles, M., Roelle, J., Glogger-Frey, I., Waldeyer, J., Renkl, A.: The selfregulation-view in writing-to-learn: using journal writing to optimize cognitive load in self-regulated learning. Educ. Psychol. Rev. **32**, 1–38 (2020)
12. Krathwohl, D.R.: A revision of Bloom's taxonomy: an overview. Theory Pract. **41**(4), 212–218 (2002)
13. Fritz, J.M., Fritz, J.M.: Creativity. In: Fritz, J.M. (ed.) Moving Toward a Just Peace. CSRP, pp. 35–47. Springer, Dordrecht (2014). https://doi.org/10.1007/978-94-007-2885-1_3
14. Jobst, B., Köppen, E., Lindberg, T., Moritz, J., Rhinow, H., Meinel, C.: The faith-factor in design thinking: creative confidence through education at the design thinking schools Potsdam and Stanford? In: Plattner, H., Meinel, C., Leifer, L., (eds.) Design Thinking Research. Understanding Innovation. Springer, Heidelberg (2012). https://doi.org/10.1007/978-3-642-31991-4_3

National Policies and Plans for Digital Competence

Computer Education in Australia Fifty Years Ago

Arthur Tatnall(✉)

Victoria University, Melbourne, Australia
Arthur.Tatnall@vu.edu.au

Abstract. This paper is about computer education in Australia fifty years ago when it was just at its beginning. It makes particular reference to the State of Victoria. The paper covers the period of the 1950s–1980s. It looks at how, after the first mainframe computers appeared, university courses in programming began in the 1950s and 1960s. In 1960 the Australian Commonwealth Government began looking for ways in which government departments could make use of computers and in 1963 set up the Programmers-in-Training scheme. This was later taken over by the Colleges of Advanced Education and became the template for many future business computing tertiary courses. Computing in schools made a minor start in the early 1970s with a few schools teaching programming in Maths classes using punch cards that were run at a local university. Arrival of the low-priced microcomputer in the late 1970s changed the situation dramatically with many schools quickly making use of them in education. Initially this involved teaching about information technology, but in the later 1980s computers began to be used in other subject areas.

Keywords: Information technology · Education · Curriculum history · Australia

1 Introduction

It is fifty years since IFIP WG3.4 (Professional and Vocational Education) – Professional and Vocational Education in ICT was formed. Fifty years ago in Australia, like many other countries, teaching about and use of computers in education was just at its beginning. Computer Science had appeared in universities, followed by various forms of Business Computing (which relates closely to WG3.4), but very little was happening in schools. The Australian Computer Society (ACS), founded in 1966, was offering some professional education in computing. The first major change was when the Australian government set up its Programmer in Training scheme in 1963.

There are two aspects to information technology in education: teaching about computers and information technology and using computers in other subject areas. This paper deals primarily with teaching about information technology as, in this period, very little else was done with computers as few academics or teachers had much idea of how they could be used, and there were also not enough available computers.

Published by Springer Nature Switzerland AG 2022
D. Passey et al. (Eds.): OCCE 2021, IFIP AICT 642, pp. 119–130, 2022.
https://doi.org/10.1007/978-3-030-97986-7_10

2 Computer Education Pre-history

CSIRAC[1], Australia's First 'internally Stored-Program Computer', and One of the world's First, Commenced Operations in 1948 [1, 2].

CSIRAC was located at the University of Sydney until 1956 when it moved to the University of Melbourne. CSIRAC continued in use at the University of Melbourne until 1964 when it was offered to the Museum of Melbourne. It is now on display in Melbourne's Scienceworks museum[2] [1].

Fig. 1. CSIRAC on display at the Museum of Melbourne

University computing education in Australia began at the Department of Mathematics in the University of Sydney in 1947, before CSIRAC was operational, with a course on *The Theory of Computation, Computing Practices and the Theory of Programming*. In 1959 the university offered a *Post-graduate Diploma in Numerical Analysis and Automatic Computing*, followed in 1961 by other computing courses at undergraduate, masters, and doctoral levels. In the University of Melbourne, programming courses were given from 1956 as part of a Bachelor of Science degree, and in 1959 a formal subject in *Numerical Methods and Computing* was developed as part of the undergraduate Bachelor of Arts degree in Pure Mathematics [3]. Various computer courses evolved in the 1960s, but in most cases were still based in schools of mathematics or electrical engineering. It was not until the mid-1960s that computing began to be seen as a separate discipline, and university computer science and information science departments started to appear [4].

In 1968 in the US the ACM published "Curriculum 68: Recommendations for the undergraduate program in computer science" [5], and later its 1978 curriculum recommendations [6] which was widely used throughout the world.

3 Research Methodology – Curriculum History

In the broadest sense, this paper could be seen as a study of how the computing curriculum at both tertiary and school levels developed over the last fifty or so years. It was thus appropriate in this study to make use of the lens of Curriculum History. Goodson [7, 8] who worked mainly with secondary school subjects and how they appeared, evolved, and sometimes disappeared, asserts that "*curriculum history is primarily a study in curriculum rather than a study in history*" [9]. Curriculum history is not a new lens with which to view educational change, dating from at least 1909:

[1] CSIRAC – Commonwealth Scientific and Industrial Research Automatic Computer.

[2] It is believed that CSIRAC is the only remaining first generation computing still intact and on display in the world.

"If a history of any educational subject encourages and deepens with us the habit of looking with a keener interest for educational provision to the full social, economic, political and religious needs of a community in a past period, from the point of view of the contemporary aims and scope of knowledge of that period, then the study justifies itself." (10: vii-viii)

The methods applied in Curriculum History involve documents analysis, oral narratives and life-story interviews of those involved. Two important documents here are *A History of Australian Computing*, a book by Trevor Pearcey [1] creator of CSIRAC, and *The Last of the First - CSIRAC: Australia's First Computer* [2], but neither has much to say about education. The main source of data for this study was thus life history interviews with those involved in computers and education at this time, covering the parts they played. They included Gerry Maynard (O&M Inspector with the PMG and PBS Inspector), Geoff Dober (trainee from a Programmer in Training course), Peter Juliff (academic from a College of Advanced Education), Tony Montgomery (University academic), Bill Davey (secondary school teacher) and Tony Salvas (secondary school teacher). The interviews were informal, but opportunity was given for the interviewees to tell of the part they played in this, and how it was important.

4 The Commonwealth Defence and PMG Computing Projects

In 1957, no computers were in use in business in Australia [1]. The only computers outside universities were at the Bureau of Census and Statistics and the Weapons Research Establishment. In 1960, the Australian Commonwealth Government directed the Commonwealth Public Service Board (PSB) to look at ways computers could be used in administration of the Department of Defence and the Postmaster General's Department (PMG). There was, however, a problem with the severe shortage of people having a good knowledge of computing. Added to this was that after fulfilling the needs of these projects, very few knowledgeable people were left to undertake other computing work (11). Clearly more training was needed, but the universities were then unable to deliver business-related training. It was not possible to get these needed people from overseas as many other countries were experiencing the same problem.

In 1960 the PSB began the needed training by running a twelve-week course in '*Analysis and Design of Mechanised Systems*' [12]. Although this was seen as successful in providing a 'crash course' in computing (11), the Commonwealth Public Service Board saw a need for a complete and more detailed course and so, in 1963, set up the twelve-month Programmer in Training Scheme (PIT). Its 1966 PIT Automatic Data Processing (ADP) Course Outline and Syllabus indicated that:

The Public Service Board has been conducting courses in A.D.P. Systems Analysis and Design since 1960. These courses have provided essential training not only to a large number of practitioners in the Commonwealth Service but also to personnel engaged in A.D.P activities in Commonwealth Instrumentalities, State Government Departments and in Departments and Authorities of Malaysia and Singapore. Technical Colleges in Victoria and a number of State and overseas organisations have adopted the course as a basis for their A.D.P. training [13].

4.1 The Programmer in Training Scheme

These twelve-month courses trained staff in establishing and operating commercial and administrative applications, and involved twenty hours per week of formal class time for one year. They were open only to graduates. The curriculum of the Programmer in Training (PIT) courses had four phases [1, 11]:

- Phase 1 (10 weeks): Introduction to the Course and to the Service (1 week), Computer Equipment and Techniques (1 week), Computer Mathematics (1 week), Programming (5 weeks), Systems Analysis and Design (1 week), Examinations (1 week).
- Phase 2 (12 weeks): Departmental training.
- Phase 3 (12 weeks): Computer Equipment and Techniques (1 week), Programming (4 weeks), Systems Analysis and Design (4 weeks), Statistics (2 weeks), Examinations (1 week).
- Phase 4 (12 weeks): Departmental training.

Maynard [11] points out that:

> *The programming part of the early PIT courses started off with a study of machine code then moved to assembly language before finally getting down to Business FORTRAN, which was a very powerful language developed by Control Data. Later, studies of COBOL and PL1 were also introduced* [11].

The Commonwealth Public Service Board continued to run the PIT courses until 1970 when it handed over their operation to four tertiary institutions: Caulfield Institute of Technology, Bendigo Institute of Technology, Canberra College of Advanced Education and New South Wales Institute of Technology [11]. In many ways the PIT courses could be seen as laying the foundations of later business computing diplomas and degrees offered in Colleges of Advanced Education (CAEs) and Institutes of Technology. The importance of the PIT courses on the developments in business computing and information systems degrees was significant [14].

5 Information Technology Hardware in This Period

5.1 Non-computer Information Technology

Information Technology does not just involve computers, and Oxford University Press [15] defines it this way: "*The study or use of computers, telecommunication systems, and other devices for storing, retrieving, and transmitting information*". Several non-computer technologies that were available at this time and had a use in education included Cassette tape (1963), Videotape – VHS (1976) and CD (1982).

5.2 Early Mini and Micro Computer Technology

It was not until development of the minicomputer that educational computing became easily accessible to universities and CAEs. Significant machines were the Digital Equipment Corporation PDP 11/70 (1975) and the DEC VAX which was introduced in

1977. These were readily accessible to tertiary institutions because of their lower cost than mainframes.

At this time also, a number of computer technologies appeared, leading the way towards affordable microcomputers, and perhaps the most significant was the Intel 4004 Microprocessor (1971). Floppy disks became available in the 1970s and 1980s: 8-inch disk (1972), 5.25-inch disk (1976) and 3.5-inch disk (1981).

5.3 Development of the Internet and Email

Beginning with the ARPANET (1969), after several intermediaries the Internet appeared widely in Australian universities and elsewhere in the world in 1989. It wasn't until 1991 that the World Wide Web became available. Although some forms of email had been available since the 1960s, it was not until the 1990s that it came into popular use with Microsoft Mail, Gmail, Hotmail and Yahoo.

6 Tertiary Courses in Computing

As mentioned earlier, university computing began in mathematics and later also in engineering departments. Computer Science did not appear as a separate discipline until the mid-1960s but held an important place from that time on. From then on 'academic' computer science courses were taught in Melbourne and Monash Universities in Victoria, and later in other universities.

At that time tertiary education in Australia was undertaken in two different types of institutions: Universities and Technical Colleges. University courses were mainly in Computer Science. The universities typically made use of mainframe computers to perform their major processing needs, but Mathematics, Engineering and Computer Science departments more often had minicomputers like the PDP-11.

Peter Juliff [16] points out that in the 1960s, 'computing subjects' in the Technical Colleges taught about punch-card machines, accounting machines and computers. The Technical Colleges were later to become Colleges of Advanced Education (CAE) and by the 1970s were all offering some type of computing course, usually based on the use of minicomputers. Although some courses in Computer Science were offered, most courses were Business Computing related, aimed at: "*developing computer professionals for employment in government and industry*" [17: 8] as what was important in business was not so much the computer itself as using one to perform business functions well.

In the 1970s, CAE computing degrees of a Computer Science nature were offered in Applied Science Faculties, and Business Computing degrees in Business Faculties. Business computing courses in the CAEs did not evolve from university Computer Science courses, but instead their foundation can be seen to have come from the PIT courses, which were "*oriented towards training staff for the establishment and running of commercial and administrative applications of computing*" [11]. This was particularly the case after their operation moved to the Caulfield, Bendigo, Canberra, and New South Wales Technical Colleges. By the late 1980s, Business Computing had come to be known as Information Systems.

Montgomery [18] remarked that it was unfortunate that often Department of Computer Science and Department of Business Information Systems at the CAEs did not work together closely. He argued that "*What should be taught to a Business Information Systems person is in many respects what we are teaching to our Computer Science students: information processing techniques. There should be one decent systems analysis course…*" [18]. This made communication between teaching staff and students in these separate areas quite difficult.

7 Computer Education in Australian Schools

Early in the 1970s a few Secondary Schools had managed to acquire access to minicomputers and made use of these in Maths classes. This was the beginning of the use of computers in Australian schools, but in the later 1970s things began to take off.

In the 1970s and 1980s each state set up its own Computer Education Centre, beginning in 1968 with the Angle Park Computing Centre in South Australia [19]. In the mid-1970s Tasmania set up the Elizabeth Computer Centre and a state-wide timesharing network (TASNET).

To assist schools in coming to grips with this technology, in the early 1980s Victoria set up a system of Computer Education Consultants who were seconded teachers who travelled around schools to illustrate this technology and assist teachers with its use. I was a Computer Education Consultant for Northern Region in Melbourne. In Victoria, the State Computer Education Centre (SCEC) commenced operations in 1985 [20]. At SCEC I held the appointment of Educational Computer Systems Analyst.

Following Seymour Papert's use of a turtle in conjunction with Logo programming, in 1979 a Tasmanian company produced the Tasman Turtle, designed for use with Logo and an Apple II computer [21, 22]. This proved popular both in making programming in Logo more concrete and as a demonstration of the power of robotics [23]. Later a connection was established between Lego and Logo [24, 25].

As a result of the rapidly growing number of microcomputers in schools in the late 1970s and early 1980s, in 1983 the Commonwealth Schools Commission set up the National Advisory Committee on Computers in Schools (NACCS) to provide funding and co-ordination of computers in education nationally [26]. The NACCS report: *Teaching, Learning and Computers* pointed out that *"The widespread availability of a variety of hardware has opened up opportunities for school use of computing that have not previously existed"* [27]. These included:

- Computer Awareness (Computer Literacy) courses in upper primary and lower secondary schools,
- Computer Science/Computer Studies/Information Processing,
- Using computers across the curriculum,
- Curriculum Support including preparation of teaching materials and student records,
- Communications with other teachers, students, and remote databases, and

- Administrative applications for database management and financial management [27].

The most popular machine in Secondary Schools in the late 1970s and early 1980s was the Apple II, while some Primary Schools started to venture into computing with the Commodore Pet. In Victoria in the late 1970s the Technical Schools Division recommended that its schools use the Micromation computer – a multi-user CP/M machine. It then tried to convince the Secondary Schools Division to standardise on CP/M, rather than using the Apple II, Commodore or Tandy. This caused some dispute, but the Secondary Schools decided not to adopt CP/M.

7.1 Educational Software

In the 1970s South Australia, Tasmania and Western Australia had support for developing software and set up the TASAWA consortium for its exchange. Three examples of educational software from overseas at the time were 'Oregon Trail' (MECC), 'Lemonade' (Apple //) and 'Suburban Fox' (Acorn BBC computer). Although having much in its favour, this software had a very foreign outlook – lemonade stalls and fox hunting are unknown in Australia. This highlighted the need for locally produced software, and this soon began to appear, the most well-known and popular being the First Fleet Database from the Elizabeth Computing Centre in Tasmania.

8 Educational Computers Specially Built for Schools

The first 'Personal Computers' appeared in the late 1970s and early 1980s with the most significant for education in Australia being Apple II (1977), Radio Shack TRS-80 (1977), Commodore PET (1977) and Atari (1979). Many others appeared later into the 1980s including Commodore VIC-20 (1980), Acorn BBC (1981), IBM PC (1981), Microbee (1982), Apple Macintosh (1984) and IBM JX (1984). These were, however, incompatible with each other, and in the early to mid-1980s, before the PC and Macintosh became dominant, many countries around the world worked to develop their own educational computers. These included: Poly Computer (New Zealand, 1980), Acorn BBC Computer (UK, 1981), Compis (Sweden, 1981), ICON Computer (Canada, 1983) known locally as the 'Bionic Beaver', Piccoline (Denmark, 1984) and Tiki (Norway, 1984).

In 1985, the Australian Government decided that, like these other countries, Australia should develop its own educational computer, mainly to provide an opportunity for the Australian computer industry to manufacture it and provide software for this new machine. Another reason was that, as mentioned earlier, much of the available software at the time had a very foreign outlook – American or British, and little things like the Apple Macintosh's 'Trash Can' were annoying as in Australia we use a 'Rubbish Bin' (Fig. 2).

Fig. 2. Bunyip stamp

The Government set up Educational User Requirement and Educational Technical Requirement working groups to develop the computer [28]. These groups met and worked in Canberra and came up with a design for the Australian Educational Computer. When all the design work was done, however, the Australian Government decided not to proceed, and the computer was never built. Like Frankenstein's monster [29], the Australian Educational Computer was never sufficiently 'real' [30] to be given a name of its own, but I will call it the Bunyip[3]. Those of us involved in this project had assumed that the computer would be manufactured by an Australian company such as Microbee, but in retrospect, after the PC and Apple Macintosh came to dominate the market in the late 1980s, the decision not to proceed was probably correct [31].

9 Computers in Secondary Schools

Early in the 1970s a small number of Victorian Secondary Schools began to make some use of minicomputers purchased through innovation grants from the Commonwealth Government. Burwood High School obtained a PDP-8 (initially loaned from DEC), McKinnon High School purchased a Wang computer, but because of the high maintenance cost shared it with Box Hill High School, and Maribyrnong High School also used a Wang computer. These computers were expensive, not very powerful, and quite difficult to use. They were typically based in Maths departments to teach programming. In most cases this was the result of their teachers' own experiences in Computer Science at university [32].

In 1974, Monash University introduced MONECS (Monash Educational Computer System) that made use of mark-sense cards to teach programming in FORTRAN or BASIC to school students [33]. This provided a big computer education impact on schools at this time, as before the advent of the microcomputer it was impossible for an average school to offer students hands-on access to a computer [33]. With MONECS, students would mark the cards in class and their teachers would take a batch of cards to a local university to run on its PDP-8 computer. This allowed a class of 30 students to each get two program runs in a one-hour period [34]. Unfortunately, in most cases the initially results were disappointing for the students as they involved finding many syntax errors. At this stage, like the universities, schools saw computing as a branch of mathematics concerned with algorithm design, and most teachers involved came from a Maths/science background.

In 1978, the Victorian Education Department's Secondary Mathematics Committee, recognising the potential of computers in mathematics education, set up a Computer Education Subcommittee. They then formed the 'Computer Travelling Road Show' which visited schools around the state and performed demonstrations to teachers of computer applications in mathematics, commerce, word processing and graphics. They normally showed these on an Apple II computer [35].

9.1 Computer Awareness Courses

By the end of the 1970s, microcomputer like the Apple II, Tandy TRS-80 and Commodore PET, being much cheaper than minicomputers and less difficult to use than arranging for the use of mark sense cards on a university minicomputer, changed things considerably in schools. Costing about A$2,000 a 16 KB Apple II[3] was affordable by most schools, but expensive enough that most schools could only afford one or two machines. This placed restrictions on how they could be used. But the question was, apart from teaching programming, what could you do with a computer?

In Australia, like most countries in the late 1970s and early 1980s, few teachers had any knowledge or experience in using computers. A report by Anne McDougall, commissioned by the Victorian education department, noted that:

> *Computers have been called electronic 'brains' and there is no doubt that in the popular view, they are surrounded by an aura of mystery and are credited with powers they do not possess. The result is that most people outside the computing profession have attitudes of awe and fear towards computers and feel helpless and powerless in a highly computerised society* [36].

It was thus seen that students needed to be made *aware* of computers and what they could and could not do, and so *Computer Awareness* courses[4] began to be offered in Secondary Schools when the situation was quite different to what it is today. A typical Computer Awareness might have the following three components:

1. What a computer is and how it works, computer programming (probably in BASIC), history of computer technologies.
2. Uses of information technology in science, engineering, and business.
3. The implications on society of increased use of computers [33].

9.2 Secondary School Computer Science Courses

In 1981, Computer Science was first offered as a Higher School Certificate (Year 12) subject in Victoria. Year 12 subjects are important for university entrance and so it was disappointing when both Melbourne University and Monash University did not allow it for admission for their courses. They said that they did not see the 35% external examination as sufficient. The subject assessment also comprised option work with 35% school-based consensus moderation and 30% practical work. The universities consider the subject to have insufficient serious academic worth, and not appropriate at a secondary school level. The other Victorian universities and the CAEs however did accept Year 12 Computer Science as a valid subject [37].

9.3 Use of Computers in Other Subject Areas

Probably the first use of computers in different subject areas began in 1982 with the release of the First Fleet Database software by the Elizabeth Computing Centre in Tasmania. This attracted immediate interest as students were keen to see if they had a convict relative who arrived from England in 1778. The software was available for Apple II computers and required no background knowledge of computers to use [38].

[3] The Apple II used a cassette tape recorder as storage and a television set as a monitor.

[4] In some countries these courses were called Computer Literacy.

Use of computers in accounting, science and other subject areas followed, but discussion of this is beyond the scope of this paper.

10 Conclusion

Fifty years ago in Australia, Computer Science was underway in universities, and the government and business were just starting to make use of computers. The Programmer in Training scheme had run successfully and was just transferring to the CAEs. Courses in Business Computing were beginning. Only a few schools were then using computers, and these for programming in Maths classes. It is difficult now to look back at this period in education as it is so different to today when almost every student has an iPad, and computers are used for many functions in schools. But why is it worthwhile to look at computer education in the 1970s and 1980s? Will this help us to understand things today or to plan how to deal with future educational technologies? As George Santayana [39] once said: "*Those who cannot remember the past are condemned to repeat it.*"

References

1. Pearcey, T.A.: History of Australian Computing. Chisholm Institute of Technology, Melbourne (1988)
2. McCann, D., Thorne, P.: The Last of the First - CSIRAC: Australia's First Computer. The University of Melbourne, Melbourne (2000)
3. Philipson, G.A.: Vision Splendid - The History of Australian Computing. Australian Computer Society, Sydney (2017)
4. Tatnall, A.: A Curriculum History of Business Computing in Victorian Tertiary Institutions from 1960–1985. Deakin University, Geelong (1993)
5. Atchison, W.F. et al.: Curriculum 68: recommendations for academic programs in computer science: a report of the ACM curriculum committee on computer science. Commun. ACM **11**(3), 151–197 (1968)
6. Austing, R.H., Barnes, B.H., Bonnette, D.T., Engel, G.L., Stokes, G.: Curriculum'78: recommendations for the undergraduate program in computer science— A report of the ACM curriculum committee on computer science. Commun. ACM **22**(3), 147–166 (1979)
7. Goodson, I.: The Making of Curriculum, Collected Essays. The Falmer Press, London (1988)
8. Goodson, I.: Subjects for study: towards a social history of curriculum. In: Goodson, I.F., Ball, S.J. (eds.) Defining the Curriculum, pp. 25–44. The Falmer Press, UK (1984)
9. Goodson, I.: School Subjects and Curriculum Change: Studies in Curriculum History -, a revised and extended The Falmer Press, UK (1983)
10. Watson, F.: The Beginnings of the Teaching of Modern Subjects in England. Pitman, London (1909)
11. Maynard, G.: Interview on the History of Business Computing. Melbourne (1990)
12. Philcox, R.: The Commonwealth Public Service Board and the Introduction of Computer Technology, Early Australian Computer Systems [MA Thesis]. University of Melbourne, Melbourne (1978)

13. Grainger, K.E.: A.D.P. Training: Automatic Data Processing, A.D.P Systems Course: Course Outline and Syllabus. Commonwealth Public Service Board, Melbourne (1966)
14. Dober, G.: Personal Communication. Melbourne (1992)
15. Oxford University Press: Oxford Reference - Information Technology On line: Oxford University Press (2021). https://www.oxfordreference.com/view/https://doi.org/10.1093/oi/authority.20110803100003879
16. Juliff, P.: Interview on Business Computing Curriculum. Melbourne (1990)
17. Greig, J., Levin, P.: Computing at Chisholm: The First Twenty Five Years, 1965–1989. Chisholm Institute of Technology, Melbourne (1989)
18. Montgomery, A.Y.: Interview on Business Computing Curriculum. Melbourne (1992)
19. Shears, L.W., Dale, E.C.: Computers in Education. A report to The Honourable Robert Fordham M.P. Minister of Education, Victoria, Melbourne (1983)
20. Tatnall, A.: The Role of the State Computer Education Centre of Victoria [MA (preliminary) thesis]. Deakin University, Geelong (1985)
21. Powerhouse Museum: Powerhouse Museum Collection Search - Tasman Turtle. Powerhouse Museum, Sydney (2012). http://www.powerhousemuseum.com/collection/database/?irn=262955
22. Denning Branch International: The Old Robots Web Site - the First Wave of Robotics: Denning Branch International (2009). http://www.theoldrobots.com/turtle1.html
23. Tatnall, A., Tatnall, B. (eds.): Logo in control: control technology in education. In: Australian Computer Education Conference – Tomorrow's Technology Today. CEGV, Adelaide (1987)
24. Carter, P. (ed.): Lego and logo: the bits between. In: Australian Computer Education Conference - Golden Opportunities. CEGV, Adelaide (1988)
25. Tatnall, A., Davey, B.: Reflections on the history of computer education in schools in victoria. In: Tatnall, A. (ed.) Reflections on the History of Computing. IAICT, vol. 387, pp. 243–264. Springer, Heidelberg (2012). https://doi.org/10.1007/978-3-642-33899-1_16
26. Tatnall, A., Davey, B.: Computer education support structures in victorian schools in the 1980s. In: Impagliazzo, J. (ed.) History of Computing and Education 3 (HCE3). IAICT, vol. 269, pp. 1–22. Springer, New York (2008). https://doi.org/10.1007/978-0-387-09657-5_1
27. Commonwealth Schools Commission: Teaching, Learning and Computers. Report of the National Advisory Committee on Computers in Schools. Commonwealth Schools Commission, Canberra (1983)
28. Tatnall, A.: The australian educational computer that never was. IEEE Ann. Hist. Comput. **35**(1), 35–47 (2013)
29. Shelley, M.: Frankenstein, or the Modern Prometheus, 261 p. Penguin Classics, London (1818). Edition published by Penguin Classics in 1992
30. Latour, B.: Aramis or the Love of Technology. Harvard University Press, Cambridge (1996)
31. Tatnall, A., Leonard, R.: Purpose-built educational computers in the 1980s: the australian experience. In: Tatnall, A. (ed.): History of Computing: Learning from the Past, pp. 101–111. Springer, Heidelberg (2010)
32. Salvas, A.D.: Personal Communication. Melbourne (1985)
33. Tatnall, A., Davey, W.: Early computer awareness courses in Australian secondary schools: curricula from the late 1970s and early 1980s. In: Impagliazzo, J. (ed.) History of Computing and Education 2, pp. 107–116. Springer, New York (2006)
34. Monash Computing Museum: MONECS Deamon Educational Computer system. CSSE Computer Museum, Melbourne (2003). http://www.csse.monash.edu.au/museum/
35. Davey, W.: Personal Communication (1985)
36. McDougall, A.: Computers and Post-Primary Education in Victoria: A Study of Needs. Education Department of Victoria CPC, Melbourne (1980)

37. Tatnall, A. (ed.): Computing and education: the business connection. In: Tenth Annual Australian Computing in Education Conference, 5–8 Jul 1992. Computing in Education Group of Victoria, Melbourne (1992)
38. Tatnall, A.: The growth of educational computing in Australia. In: Goodson, I.F., Mangan, J. M. (eds.). History, Context, and Qualitative Methods in the Study of Education, vol. 3, pp. 207–248. University of Western Ontario, London, Canada (1992)
39. Santayana, G.: The Life of Reason: C. Scribner's Sons (1905)

Computational Thinking – Forces Shaping Curriculum and Policy in Finland, Sweden and the Baltic Countries

Pia Niemelä[1(✉)], Arnold Pears[2], Valentina Dagienė[3], and Mart Laanpere[4]

[1] Tampere University, Tampere, Finland
pia.niemela@tuni.fi
[2] KTH Royal Institute of Technology, Stockholm, Sweden
pears@kth.se
[3] Vilnius University Institute of Educational Sciences, Vilnius, Lithuania
valentina.dagiene@mif.vu.lt
[4] Tallinn University, Tallinn, Estonia
mart.laanpere@tlu.ee

Abstract. Through an increased focus on computing and computational concepts in the school curriculum the Nordic and Baltic countries are preparing to equip themselves to explore the opportunities that Industry 4.0 and beyond can offer. Realising this vision has inevitable consequences for the curriculum in compulsory schooling (preschool to year 9) as new scaffolding for the development of new competencies is needed, and adapting to technological change involves also integrating Computational Thinking topics and skills, as well as elements of programming and digital literacy into existing curricula. The Nordic countries (Finland and Sweden) have chosen not to create a new school subject, advocating the integration of these skills and competencies into existing subjects such as Arts and Crafts, Language, Mathematics and Technology. In contrast, the Baltic countries emphasise introduction of a subject called Informatics in which programming and Computational Thinking skills and competencies are intended to be developed. This paper provides an analysis of approaches taken to scaffolding access to Computational Thinking in the Nordic and Baltic countries.

Keywords: Computational thinking · Digital skills · Technological fluency

1 Introduction

Programming and Computational Thinking (CT) have emerged as a hot topic in the redesign of national school curricula over the last decade. Driving this debate is a belief that the increasing presence of digital computing systems in all sectors places demands on compulsory education to respond by adjusting curricula to equip citizens to both understand and contribute to this new world.

The Nordic and Baltic countries responded rapidly in terms of the integration of computing in their school curriculum, however, they have adopted rather different

Published by Springer Nature Switzerland AG 2022
D. Passey et al. (Eds.): OCCE 2021, IFIP AICT 642, pp. 131–143, 2022.
https://doi.org/10.1007/978-3-030-97986-7_11

approaches. This paper contributes to the debate by exploring the power factors and positioning of CT in the national educational political debate in Estonia, Finland, Lithuania and Sweden.

In the European context, the Nordic and Baltic countries have spearheaded the integration of computing in their school curriculum. The vision has been to realise competitive benefit from small size, unified culture, advanced infrastructure, digitalisation, and well-established, centralised national curricula. These benefits result in three driving forces acting to produce nation-wide changes to the curriculum, and in consequence the development of computing and digital literature addressing the sector. The refinement of the computing syllabus is necessary to ensure a consistent learning trajectory, as well as the establishment of this new subject among other subjects with a longer history. Similarly to mathematics, computing would fit as an entry criteria for Computer Science (CS) studies, and to a lesser extent also for natural sciences. This adds to the relevance of the subject, and makes it a reasoned choice for intentional students orienting toward these domains.

The main contribution of the current paper is to chart and analyse curricular developments in the Nordic and Baltic region with a focus on how curricular pressure can be understood and traced over time. This study benchmarks the current situation of CT in curricula of Nordic and Baltic countries, and targets the following questions:

- RQ1: What is the current status of Computational Thinking in K-9 education in Nordic and Baltic countries?
- RQ2: What factors influence national priorities in digital skills curricula for all citizens?

2 Computational Thinking in Compulsory Education

Curricula are one of the central instruments through which policy makers set strategic direction and establish common goals at the national level in the context of compulsory schooling. By "compulsory schooling" we mean education provided by the state to all citizens in the school years from preschool to year 9, thus comprising the first 10 years of a citizen's engagement with formal education.

The concept of compulsory schooling as a means to equip people for a productive life in human society can be traced back to educational policy makers in the early 19th century [1]. By examining existing and past curricula, it is possible to deduce the values, ideals, and how these are shaped by the societal and political agenda. We argue that the evolution of technology places civilisation on the cusp, and that radical change in education, especially in regard to reforming the curriculum is underway.

An example of a similar situation can be found in the Soviet technological accomplishments resulting in Sputnik I and II in 1957, which prompted much of the Western world to examine their technological capabilities, research programmes and education systems [2]. In a similar vein international comparisons, such as PISA and TIMMS, have provoked both reflection and redesign of curricula in multiple countries [3]. A common theme is the desire to ensure technological competitiveness, which is also one of the aspects behind the move to address computing topics in national curricula [4]. Other aspects of the debate include promoting democracy and gender equality, using the argument that every child has a right and opportunity to learn digital skills, and that these are comparable to the more established civic skills to which we have become used. In Nordic and Baltic countries, curricula are state-run and centralised to ensure the equality of students and schools regardless of their resources or location, whether in rural or urban environments.

The first traces of discourse of CT date back to the late 60's - early 70's. Seymour Papert was a significant influence in the international discourse. His Logo programming language made its debut in 1967 with an apt pedagogical rationale derived from the theory of constructivism [5]. The CT idea was popularised by Jeannette Wing in her 2006 paper [6] and the definition of the concept and what is included has been hotly debated over the last decade [7–9]. During the ensuing decades, digitalisation has accelerated and brought digital devices within the reach of nearly every citizen, and transformed a significant segment of the workplace, further strengthening the ideas behind the goal to equip all citizens for future agency in society through the teaching of digital skills. In 2014, Mannila [10] summarised the situation of CT in education of multiple European countries and USA Mannila's study pinpoints the lack of qualified teachers as a crucial bottleneck, the impact of which cannot be underestimated in terms of the importance of the teaching of computing to a broader segment of the population.

However, it is clear that at primary school, teaching the basics of CT via unplugged activities is not particularly demanding on either teacher or pupil, thus, achieving low level goals in relation to CT should be achievable without an extensive CS education. In terms of enhancing teachers' knowledge to achieve higher levels of computing education, we observe that universities and teacher associations provide courses, material and even certificates to support this process in the Nordic and Baltic regions, however more needs to be done [11]. In-service teacher training is provided by a range of organisations. In Finland the Association of mathematics teachers - MAOL, offers a variety of courses, and in Sweden similar courses are offered by universities through the government agency Skolverket [12]. In Lithuania, a variety of courses is offered by Vilnius University [13], while in Estonia similar initiatives are provided through the Lifelong Learning Strategy (2014–2020) that also targets the provision of open material for school use [14]. In addition, there are a number of European funded projects, for instance, the TeaEdu4CT ERASMUS+initiative[1] that provide extensive teaching resources for teacher education programmes, and practising teachers.

At secondary school, CS/CT is provided either as a separate subject, or integrated within other subjects, mainly mathematics. For instance, Baltic countries have been swinging between separation and integration since late 60's, see Fig. 2. In PISA, mathematics is the closest counterpart to CS/CT if not the very subject where the CT has been integrated.

[1] https://www.fsf.vu.lt/mokslas/projektai/tarptautiniai-projektai/erasmus?layout=edit&id=2720=future-teachers-education-computational-thinking-and-steam.

2.1 Nordic Countries

Computational Thinking education in the Finnish and Swedish systems have a common ground based on the idea that CT should be integrated into subjects such as Language, Mathematics, Arts and Crafts, and Technology, rather than introduced as a separate subject. This approach differs from that adopted in the UK, USA, Germany, New Zealand and Australia, where computing and informatics were introduced into the curriculum as a new subject to address these educational challenges. The Nordic approach has assumed that courses in languages will be able to handle the relevant aspects of digital literacy, in particular those that aim to develop critical thinking and reflective learning capabilities. This content is increasingly emphasised in the national curricula for Swedish language and literature over the past couple of decades, culminating in the current version [15]. The language curriculum emphasises the influence of digitalisation on the curation of information, including internet media, and a focus on large scale systems operating on big data to derive modern data-driven platforms, primarily Google and Facebook, which have significant impact on information provision.

The political discourse underlying this strategy is that it will be necessary to enhance awareness of the data these systems collect about users, and the impact of algorithms and machine learning on social media experience. Examples include social bubbles of like-minded people, emotion engineering [16], targeted advertising based on our preferences, and even manipulating users' political views, which has been reported in the much debated Brexit process [17] and the 2016 USA presidential election [18].

Computational Thinking in Finland through Language, Craft and Mathematics. After introducing programming as an elective course in 1984, the 2014 Finnish National Curriculum (FNC-2014) established general goals for teaching programming in compulsory education [19]. FNC-2014 introduces hands-on experimentation (e.g., programmable robots) as a precursor to CT, emphasising using robots, and following stepwise commands. At the secondary level, CT is integrated into mathematics, the motivation for this approach is that aspects of mathematical thinking applied in problem solving are analogous with CT. There are also expected benefits for mathematics education, in particular in the area of algebra where CT is expected to improve outcomes due to transfer effect [20].

However, the FNC-2014 programming content is painted with a broad brush: logical and algorithmic thinking are mentioned, as well as problem-solving through decomposition. These goals are the integral parts of "computational thinking" yet the CT term does not appear in the FNC-2014 text. Concrete guidance for teachers is largely lacking, and the targeted computer science concepts and skills are left undefined. Indeed, the clarification of the learning goals for CT has largely been delegated to book publishers in Finland. The biggest publishers (SanomaPro, Otava and Edita) seem to have reached consensus to publish texts promoting Scratch at primary and Python at secondary level [21].

Finnish PISA results have been falling since 2006, especially in mathematics. Male students and minorities are over-represented at the lower end of the results [22, 23] see Fig. 1, and the gap between native and immigrant students is the largest [24]. Too open and unstructured learning environments provide no support. Instead of the anticipated empowerment, students may be left overwhelmed and clueless about how to study. [25] also points to a correlation between increased online and digital learning and deteriorating learning outcomes, e.g., in PISA-2015 [26]. To counter this trend the Ministry of Education provides new support through the "Right to Learn" initiative [27], in particular the New Literacies [28] sub-programme. New Literacies highlights source criticism, critical thinking and a thread of programming and CT as an integral part of new literacies. During the next few years, New Literacy pilots are scheduled in 100 schools to gather evidence, and create CC-licensed material for other schools, including material for CT.

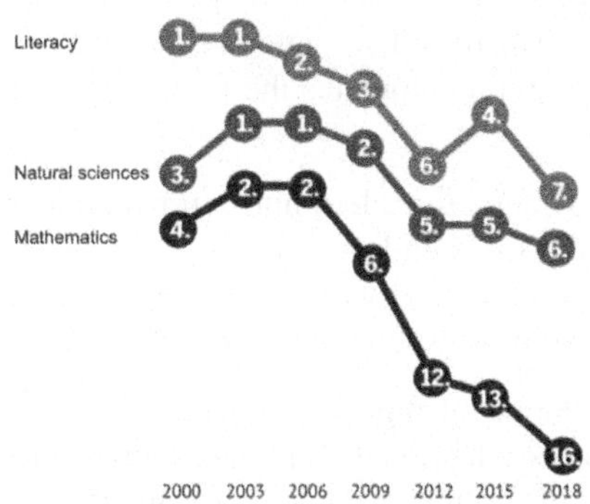

Fig. 1. The drop of PISA results in Finland, retrieved from the Ministry of Education

Computational Thinking in Sweden, Integration with Mathematics and Technology. Despite early forays into computing in schools in the 1980's[2], the subsequent Swedish education policy has emerged as more conservative than the Finnish model. Programming was ensconced in the national curriculum for the second time in 2016. However, the educational act for compulsory education (SWEA) [29] did not include computing or programming prior to 2017 [30]. The subject of Technology and the corresponding upper secondary school programme, an elective programme, (teknik programmet) provided access to similar content, also including courses covering various aspects of computing.

In 2012, the Swedish government established a committee with the task of giving recommendations and guidelines for how Sweden can, and should, benefit from digitalisation. In a report published in March 2014 [31], the committee emphasises the need for an additional focus on digital competences in national curricula. One concrete recommendation is for programming to be introduced as a cross-curricular element in already existing subjects. This ultimately resulted in programming being included into the compulsory school subjects Mathematics and Technology. The associated political discourse also emphasised the need to enhance technological fluency. The assumption

[2] https://undervisningshistoria.se/programmering-i-skolan.

is that technology is a transverse skill, can be applied to all subjects, and that the necessary computing skill set can be partially addressed in the digital literature curriculum.

In 2015, the government commissioned the Swedish National Agency for Education to propose content in the national strategy for digitalisation. As a result, the curriculum for compulsory school was revised and digital competence was added. The revised curriculum has been in operation since 2018 and describes digital competence as follows: a) to understand the impact of digitalisation on human society; b) to be able to use and comprehend digital tools and media; c) to adopt a critical and responsible attitude to change; d) to be able to solve problems/challenges and implement theoretical solutions in practice. After considerable consultation with the academic and industry sectors the revised compulsory curriculum was released in 2017, and became mandatory from August 2018 for all schools in Sweden.

The revised 2018 curriculum stipulates the following four main goals for students' digital competence:

- to learn to put one's own creative ideas into action and learn how to solve problems,
- to be able to use digital tools and media,
- to understand the digital transformation of society and how it affects us,
- to be critical and develop a responsible approach to digital technology.

The Swedish interpretation of digital competence includes aspects of digital literacy, such as the importance of critical thinking, source criticism, fact checking, and safe use of the internet by being aware of security threats, as well as attempts at information manipulation. The key areas are considered as critical components of the strategy to establish Sweden as a strong democracy in alignment with Swedish policy in the 21st century.

2.2 The Baltic Countries

The Baltic countries started to reform informatics education, and ever since it was introduced, it has been swinging between integrated and separated subjects, as illustrated in the Fig. 2. The swing started from an independent optional subject and currently, in 2021, has almost returned to the starting point.

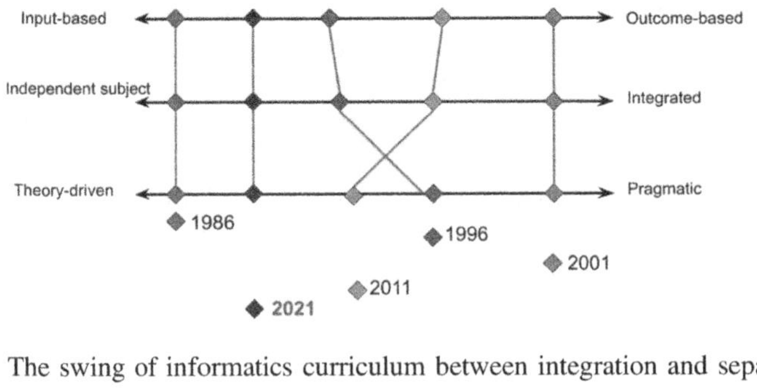

Fig. 2. The swing of informatics curriculum between integration and separation.

Computational Thinking in Lithuania Focuses on Informatics. Lithuania has taught informatics at schools for almost 40 years [32]. In 1986, informatics was first introduced as a school subject, and it focused on logical principles of computers, information transmission, storage and processing, and algorithms, particularly data types and basic control structures of programming (based on Logo and Pascal). Before that, Lithuania had already established the Young Programmers' School, a Correspondence school, and one of the first programming schools for pupils in the world. The School triggered a number of research articles, books, contests and competitions [33]. In 1981–83, lessons in programming for beginners were even published in one of the biggest daily newspapers in Lithuania.

The most significant influence on the status of informatics education was the introduction of the informatics maturity exam in 1995. Those who pass the informatics exam have enhanced opportunities to enter CS-related studies in higher education. The test also provides a reliable indication as to whether a student has the aptitude to study informatics. The informatics exam consists of two parts: one part (over 50% of the full exam) is allocated to programming, while the rest concerns computer literacy and applications.

A revision of the informatics core curriculum was initiated in 2005, expanding the scope from two to four years' teaching time (in total 136 h) with more focus on developing algorithmic thinking and applications. The teachers were formally qualified, usually with a bachelor's or master's degree in informatics, combined with mathematics. 5th and 6th grade pupils are introduced to the basics of informatics based on Logo or Scratch. In grades 9 to 10, more advanced students are recommended to enrol in the optional module of algorithm design and coding.

In 2019, the Lithuanian Ministry of Education, Science and Sport developed new guidelines for pre-school, primary, basic and secondary education[3]. The general curriculum framework is a document governing the content of national level education, which helps teachers to scaffold performance in relation to learning goals, and the levels required to attain them.

The Ministry and the National Agency of Education manage all update efforts within the framework, documents under consideration and planned events are published online (www.mokykla2030.lt). In 2020, one hundred primary schools started to pilot the proposed informatics curriculum. The pilot targets the development of learning resources and textbooks, as well as teacher training. The full-scale implementation commences in 2022.

The revised curriculum includes fundamental CS topics such as programming, problem solving and algorithms, data mining, data representation and information, networks and communication, digital technology and human computer interaction, security, and privacy and ethical considerations. Attention is given to the key concepts in the field, and the constructive aspect of the discipline. Figure 3 illustrates six areas of informatics education with main focus on four core areas: 1) Data mining and information, 2) Algorithms and programming, 3) Technological problem solving, and 4) Digital content creation.

[3] https://www.e-tar.lt/portal/lt/legalAct/e3e9269009e511ea9d279ea27696ab7b.

The most pressing current challenge is to redesign an existing informatics course in upper secondary school (grades 11–12) so that it would also introduce some new technologies such as artificial intelligence, machine learning, and big data. The renewed informatics curriculum at upper secondary school is expected to be ready for incorporation into the new national curriculum in 2023.

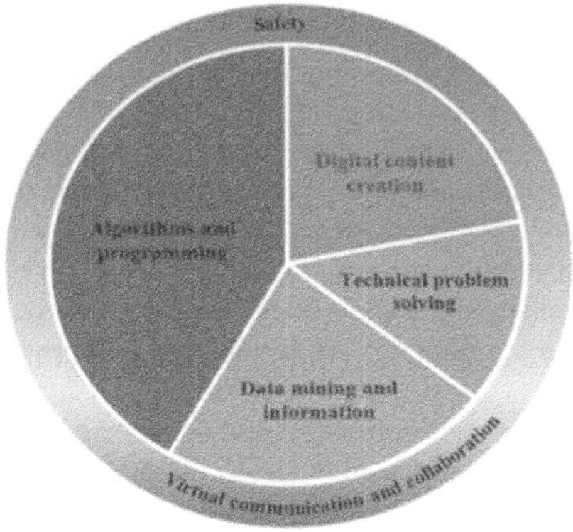

Fig. 3. The areas of informatics curriculum

Computational Thinking and Estonia's Commitment to Digitalisation. The national curriculum for a newly independent Estonia was introduced in 1996. In this process, a new elective school subject called informatics was introduced that comprised four 35-h modules for grades 10–12. The new informatics curriculum contained no coding, algorithms or other abstract elements of CT, as opposed to the theoretical CS course that was forcibly introduced into the curricula of all Soviet Union's republics in 1986. Instead, the focus was on everyday use of computers: word processing, spreadsheets, computer graphics, and internet. The next version, National Curriculum 2001, dismissed informatics completely, which resulted in a sharp decline in teaching popularity. While removing informatics, the 2001 curriculum introduced instead a set of compulsory ICT skills that were assessed by the National Exam Centre at the end of basic school, in the ninth grade.

The current renewed national curriculum came into force in 2011. One of the four prioritised elective subjects is informatics, and it is recommended by the policy makers. This informatics curriculum outlines syllabi for two 35-h courses in basic school:

- Y5/6 working with computer: word processing, file management, digital presentations, spreadsheets, internet search, citations, plagiarism, evaluation of online information, cyber-threats, digital identity;
- Y8/9 information society technologies: online communities, blog and wiki usage for digital content creation, metadata and annotations (tags, bookmarks), online content aggregation (e.g., RSS), collaborative digital project, digital safety.

The high school curriculum (grades 10–12) does not mention informatics as a subject, but describes a set of new technological elective courses under Natural Sciences domain, each accompanied by a textbook, e-course in Moodle, tests and educational videos. Elective courses are: 1) inquiry-based learning (data collection, data analysis and visualisation in Excel, presenting the research results); 2) introduction to programming and software development; 3) robotics and mechatronics; 4) 3D-modelling; 5) Geoinformatics.

As in the Nordic system, there is a tension in the Estonian national curriculum and educational practice between the content of informatics and generic digital competence. Are these the same subject, partly overlapping, or completely different things? In 2014, a minor update to the national curriculum introduced digital competence as one of the eight compulsory key competences (e.g. the DigComp model). An online test of digital competence has been conducted in grades 9 and 12 since 2017 by HARNO, an agency responsible for exams. In some schools, teaching digital competence is the responsibility of the informatics teacher, whereas schools without informatics teachers have integrated the teaching of digital competence into other subjects. The third group of schools tries to offer both: informatics as a separate subject focusing on development of CT and digital competence nurtured by other subject teachers.

The development of a radically changed informatics curriculum for primary and upper secondary schools was led by the HITSA agency 2016–2019. This curriculum is still classified as an "unofficial document", but the majority of primary schools already apply it to some extent in grades 1–6, thanks to the corresponding online textbook for informatics (digiopik.it.ee). The new informatics curriculum for high schools was introduced in 2019, but its uptake is significantly poorer compared to primary school, with less than 10% of high schools offering it. The Fig. 4 illustrates the new elective courses for grades 1–6 and 10–12. The most complicated stage is grades 7–9, due to no "free space" in the national curriculum.

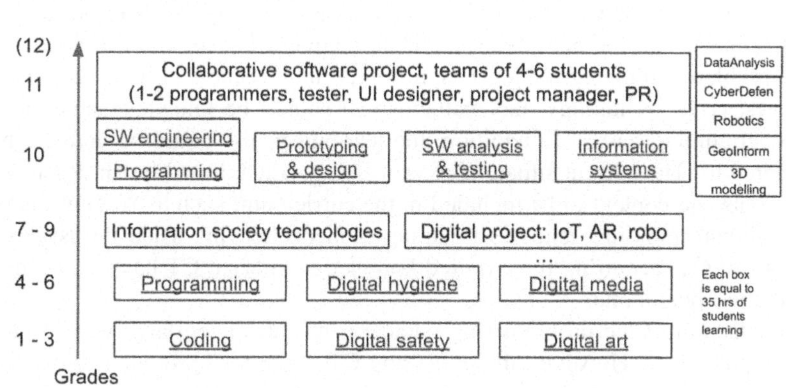

Fig. 4. The proposed K-12 informatics curriculum

The new task force group has been formed to design a solution for this grade level by 2022. The key idea is to redesign an existing informatics course "Information Society Technologies" to introduce new technologies such as artificial intelligence, augmented reality and big data analytics in grade 7. The school renewal has been successful, which manifests in international comparisons, such as PISA, see Table 1. The new additions to informatics curricula, such as artificial intelligence and machine learning, are intended to be incorporated into the new national curriculum in 2024.

3 Discussion

As Fig. 2 illustrates, the Baltic countries have acted in a more synchronised manner. Estonia has taken the lead, for instance in open e-textbooks that are prepared together with academia, and its advancements are well disseminated within other Baltic countries. Adoption among policy makers is promoted by the results reached in Estonia, such as a constant improvement in national PISA results of mathematics (Table 1) [34].

Table 1. Math PISA results of 2006–2018

	2006	2009	2012	2015	2018
Finland	548 (1)	541 (2)	519 (12)	511 (13)	507 (16)
Sweden	502	494	478	494	502
Lithuania	486	477	479	478	481
Estonia	-	512 (11)	521 (11)	520 (10)	523 (8)

Finland and Sweden have adopted integrative approaches to the introduction of CT to an already full curriculum, through the subjects mathematics, craft and (in Sweden) technology. Efforts in the Nordic countries are not as coordinated as the Baltic approach, but they have considerable similarities, and face common challenges. Educators and policy makers are faced with the necessity to establish priorities between existing subjects and the new demands of the digital transformation of society.

The problem with integrating CT is, however, that teachers of the target disciplines (languages, craft, technology and mathematics) should be knowledgeable enough to teach programming basics. In addition, the learning goals should be defined in detail and adhered to. The current situation of vaguely specified, broad brush descriptions of the CT goals and content to be included in the curriculum; such as "digital fluency" or "computational thinking" tends to frustrate teachers. Leaving aside the issue of poor definitions of CT, acquiring the required knowledge to teach CT has also been largely left to the teachers alone.

The selection of the programming paradigm has also been largely left to teachers and book publishers. However, the prevailing CT definitions provide a strong impetus towards the imperative programming paradigm represented by languages such as Python and Scratch. While some arguments have been advanced for adopting a functional approach, this is a marginalised area [35, 36]. The rationale for adopting a functional paradigm is the close conceptual correspondence with mathematics, and the absence of contradicting concepts, such as mutable data. However, this argument has gained little traction among policy makers. To establish its position, CT/CS should consider following the lead of mathematics. A more concise definition for CT should be developed, and that definition should be linked to a consistent learning trajectory. Ideally elements of the CT learning outcomes would be added to the matriculation exam.

4 Conclusions

This paper summarises the state of play in the introduction of CT concepts and competencies into compulsory education in two Nordic and two Baltic countries. We conclude that while much progress has been made into incorporating CT into the Nordic and Baltic school curricula, there is still a considerable way to go. The major dilemma facing policy makers and curriculum designers is whether computational thinking and digital skills should be integrated into other subjects, or provided as a separate subject. Since then, various CT teaching experiments have ranged from optional to compulsory, and from a separate subject to wholly integrated into one or more existing subjects.

The trend we see from our analysis is that this integration has focused most often on mathematics or handicrafts in Finland, with Sweden also making efforts to include some content in language and technology subjects. Our observation is that integrating CT into other subjects makes the coordination of content and learning outcomes considerably more complex, while offering the advantage of enhancing the relevance of CT in familiar contexts.

References

1. Soysal, Y.N., Strang, D.: Construction of the first mass education systems in nineteenth-century Europe. Sociol. Educ. **62**(4), 277–288 (1989)
2. Krige, J.: NATO and the strengthening of Western science in the post-Sputnik era. Minerva **38**(1), 81–108 (2000)
3. Haugsbakk, G.: From Sputnik to PISA shock–New technology and educational reform in Norway and Sweden. Educ. Inquiry **4**(4), 1–23 (2013). 23222
4. Kjällander, S., Åkerfeldt, A., Petersen, P.: Översikt avseende forskning och erfarenheter kring programmering i förskola och grundskola (2016)
5. Papert, S.: What is Logo? Who needs it. Logo philosophy and implementation (1999)
6. Wing, J.M.: Computational thinking. Commun. ACM **49**(3), 33–35 (2006)
7. Tedre, M., Denning, P.J.: The long quest for computational thinking. In: Proceedings of the 16th Koli Calling International Conference on Computing Education Research, pp. 120–129. ACM (2016)
8. Denning, P.J., Tedre, M.: Computational thinking: a disciplinary perspective. Inf. Educ. **20** (3), 361–390 (2021)
9. Pears, A.: Developing computational thinking, "fad" or "fundamental"? Constructivist Found. **14**(3), 410–412 (2019)

10. Mannila, L., Dagiene, V., Demo, B., Grgurina, N., Mirolo, C., Rolandsson, L., Settle, A.: Computational thinking in K-9 education. In: Proceedings of the Working Group Reports of the 2014 on Innovation & Technology in Computer Science Education Conference, pp. 1–29 (2014)
11. Mannila, L., Nordén, L., Pears, A.: Digital competence, teacher self-efficacy and training needs. In: Proceedings of the 2018 ACM Conference on International Computing Education Research, pp. 78–85. ACM (2018). https://doi.org/10.1145/3230977.3230993
12. Heintz, F., Mannila, L., Nordén, L.Å., Parnes, P., Regnell, B.: Introducing programming and digital competence in Swedish K-9 education. In: International Conference on Informatics in Schools: Situation, Evolution, and Perspectives, pp. 117–128. Springer (2017)
13. Dagienė, V., Jevsikova, T., Stupurienė, G., Juškevičienė, A.: Teaching computational thinking in primary schools: worldwide trends and teachers' attitudes. Comput. Sci. Inf. Sys. **19**, 1–24 (2021). https://doi.org/10.2298/CSIS201215033D
14. Põldoja, H., Laanpere, M.: Open educational resources in Estonia. In: Current State of Open Educational Resources in the Belt and Road Countries (Lecture Notes in Educational Technology), pp. 35–47 (2020)
15. Skolverket: Läroplan för grundskolan, förskoleklassen och fritidshemmet (2019)
16. Del Vicario, M., et al.: Echo chambers: emotional contagion and group polarization on Facebook. Sci. Rep. **6**(1), 1–12 (2016)
17. Bastos, M., Mercea, D.: The public accountability of social platforms: lessons from a study on bots and trolls in the Brexit campaign. Philos. Trans. R. Soc. A Math. Phys. Eng. Sci. **376** (2128) (2018). 20180003
18. Golovchenko, Y., Buntain, C., Eady, G., Brown, M.A., Tucker, J.A.: Cross-platform state propaganda: Russian trolls on Twitter and Youtube during the 2016 US presidential election. Int. J. Press/Polit. **25**(3), 357–389 (2020)
19. Finnish National Board of Education: Finnish National Curriculum (2014)
20. Schanzer, E.T.: Algebraic Functions, Computer Programming, and the Challenge of Transfer (2015)
21. Haapakangas, E., et al.: Yläkoulun ohjelmoinnin opetuksen kehittäminen oppimateriaalin keinoin (2020)
22. Välijärvi, J., et al.: Milläeväillä osaaminen uuteen nousuun? PISA 2012-tutkimustuloksia (2015)
23. Leino, K., et al.: PISA 18: ensituloksia. Suomi parhaiden joukossa. Opetus-ja kulttuurim-inisteriön julkaisuja (2019)
24. Salmela-Aro, K., Chmielewski, A.K.: Socioeconomic inequality and student outcomes in Finnish schools. In: Socioeconomic Inequality and Student Outcomes (2019)
25. Saarinen, A.: The relationships of temperament, character, and depressive symptoms with paranoid ideation. Ph.D. thesis, University of Helsinki (2018)
26. OECD (2015). https://www.oecd.org/finland/pisa-2015-finland.htm
27. Ministry of Education: Oikeus oppia - tasa-arvoinen alku opinpolulle; varhaiskasvatuksen laadun ja tasa-arvon kehittämisohjelma 2020–2022 (2019)
28. Kulju, P., Kupiainen, R., Pienimäki, M.: Raportti luokanopettajien käsityksistä moniluku-taidosta 2019 (2020)
29. Skolverket: Curriculum for the compulsory school, preschool class and school-age educare (2010)
30. Heintz F., Mannila L., Nygårds K., Parnes P., Regnell B.: Computing at school in Sweden – Experiences from introducing computer science within existing subjects. In: Brodnik A., Vahrenhold J. (eds) Informatics in Schools. Curricula, Competences, and Competitions. ISSEP 2015. LNCS, vol 9378. Springer, Cham (2015). https://doi.org/10.1007/978-3-319-25396-1_11

31. Gulliksen, J. (ed.): En digital agenda i människans tjänst: en ljusnande framtid kan bli vår: delbetänkande. No. 2014:13 in Statens offentliga utredningar. Fritze, Stockholm (2014)
32. Dagienė, V.: Resurgence of informatics education in schools. In: Adventures Between Lower Bounds and Higher Altitudes, pp. 522–537. Springer (2018)
33. Dagienė, V.: The road of informatics (2006)
34. Tire, G.: Estonia: a positive PISA experience. In: Crato, N. (ed.) Improving a Country's Education, pp. 101–120. Springer, Cham (2021). https://doi.org/10.1007/978-3-030-59031-4_5
35. Partanen, T.: Coder's Handbook (in Finnish). http://racket.koodiaapinen.fi/manuaali/ (2016)
36. Niemelä, P.: From legos and logos to lambda: A hypothetical learning trajectory for computational thinking (2018)

Changing Computer Curricula in Australia

Andrew E. Fluck[1(✉)] and Anit Girgla[2]

[1] Independent Educator, TAS Launceston, Australia
Andrew.Fluck@utas.edu.au
[2] University of Tasmania, TAS Launceston, Australia
Anit.Girgla@utas.edu.au

Abstract. This paper was developed from a symposium entitled 'Moving on with informatics/computer science curricula – challenges and opportunities.' It provides an Australian perspective for that debate. From 1901, the eight Australian States and Territories accepted constitutional authority for school education. Hence, a nationally developed curriculum only arose in 2014, for optional adoption. Computers were initially included as a general capability to enhance learning in all subjects. This focused on Office-suite applications. In 2016, the new Digital Technologies subject was added to the curriculum. This paper looks at the adoption of the new subject and changes proposed in the 2021 public consultation draft Review. We reveal the answers to the following questions about the proposed update for Digital Technologies: 1. Will Australia abandon the general ICT capability (as in the UK) to provide greater focus on Digital Technologies? 2. Will Australia put a greater emphasis on coding/programming than the current meagre mention? 3. What does a tutor of pre-service teachers think about the proposed changes?

Keywords: Digital technologies curriculum · Coding proportion · Pre-service teachers

1 Introduction and Context

1.1 A Nationally Developed Curriculum

Curriculum responsibility in schools was vested with the states of Australia by the constitution of 1901. A nationally developed curriculum for school subjects was only made available from 2014 and was incrementally adopted or appropriated by the states, in various ways.

At that time, computers were written into the nationally developed curriculum as a general capability to enhance learning in all subjects. This was designated as the Information and Communication Technologies (ICT) general capability. The core ICT capability was conceived as comprising Investigation, Communication and Creation. These elements are underpinned by 'managing and operating ICT' and 'applying social and ethical protocols and practices.'

Because different learning areas of the curriculum were developed along a staggered timeline, the Technologies learning area curriculum did not become available

D. Passey et al. (Eds.): OCCE 2021, IFIP AICT 642, pp. 144–155, 2022.
https://doi.org/10.1007/978-3-030-97986-7_12

until 2016. This contains the Digital Technologies subject. At its core is the concept of creating digital solutions, approached by processes and production skills. Underpinning these are Digital Systems and Representation of data.

Therefore, the Digital Technologies subject is quite separate from the ICT general capability. Very few teachers had computer education in their own schooling, or have encountered it in their pre-service training. While ‘creating digital solutions’ is core to the subject, coding or programming are mentioned very sparsely in the document. The design-time for this subject is 30 min per week in Years Foundation-2, 40 min for Years 3–4, an hour per week in Years 5–6, and 80 min per week in Years 7–8.

In 2020, the Australian Government agency responsible for the nationally developed curriculum announced the commencement of a Review. This review produced a public consultation draft of a new version of the curriculum in late April 2021.

The Review had the key task of simplifying the curriculum. Partly due to the staggered implementation, teachers initially focused on core subjects, and had felt overloaded as additional subjects such as Digital Technologies were released.

Recent indications are that principals and teachers confound the current ICT capability and the Digital Technologies subject. 30% of tools and websites used in Digital Technologies were seen to be content management systems, office suites and other generic tools rather than subject content specific software applications.

There are some key issues to be examined. First of all, there is tension between the two ways in which computers are used in Australian classrooms (general ICT capability and discrete Digital Technologies subject). It remains to be seen how these tensions will be addressed by the curriculum revision. Second, programming or coding is a key component in computing curricula in other countries – we will examine this aspect in the proposed revision of the Digital Technologies curriculum. Finally, it is useful to understand how teachers respond to the proposed revision. One of the authors had worked as a Digital Technologies Education tutor, and informally discussed the topic with some pre-service teachers. This article is now framed in such a way to find the answers to these three questions: 1. Will Australia abandon the general ICT capability (as per the UK) to provide greater focus on Digital Technologies? 2. Will Australia put a greater emphasis on coding/programming than before? 3. What does a tutor of pre-service teachers think about the proposed Digital Technologies curriculum changes?

After consideration of these research questions, we show how they illuminate the four focus points of the symposium on “Moving on with informatics/computer science curricula – challenges and opportunities”. These were:

1. What is driving the emphasis of specifications for informatics/computer science curricula in different countries?
2. What do we know about how students learn some of the core concepts and processes of informatics/computer science that will enable us to design structure and progressions in curricula?
3. How should we incorporate new challenges associated with rapid developments in artificial intelligence and machine learning into informatics/computer science curricula?
4. What is the relationship between an informatics/computer science curriculum and other academic disciplines?

The responses to the three questions will shed light on the focus points of the symposium, as shown below.

1.2 The Proposals of the Review

The Public Consultation draft release in late April 2021 contained two main changes in the curriculum concerning student computer use:

1. The ICT general capability will be renamed as the 'Digital Literacy' learning continuum.
2. The Digital Technologies subject will grow from 43 to 71 Content Descriptors.

The Digital Literacy learning continuum [1] differs from its predecessor (ICT) in several ways. Digital safety and wellbeing replace social and ethical practices. Thus, there is a greater emphasis on cyber-safety and management of personal digital authentication tokens. Recognition of intellectual property, referencing and copyright is now balanced with exploration of creative commons, collaboration and information exchange. Figure 1 shows the proposed new structure and the new nomenclature.

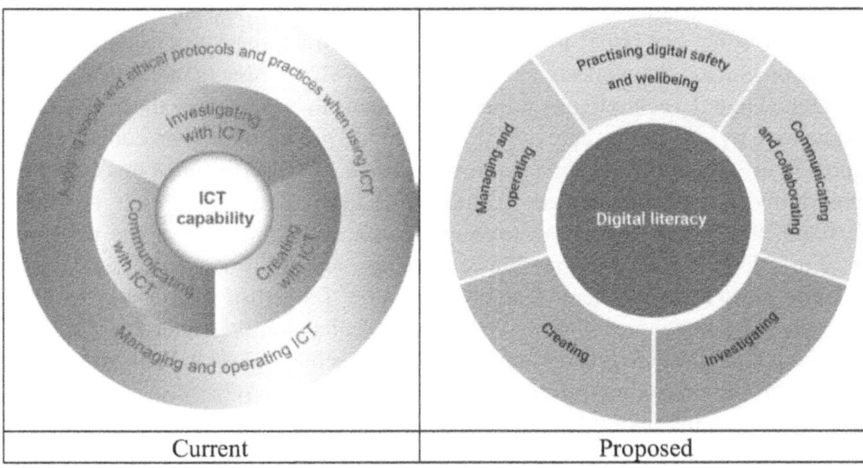

Fig. 1. The organising elements for the ICT general capability and the proposed Digital Literacy replacement (ACARA, 2016, 2021)

The Digital Technologies curriculum is due for a massive shakeup if the review proposal proceeds [2]. The current and proposed structures for this subject are shown in Fig. 2, with minor rearrangements of the elements.

The biggest change is a massive increase in Content Descriptors from 43 to 71. This appears designed to make them more understandable to teachers. More complex ideas have been broken into smaller components. For example, in Years 5–6 (student ages 10–12 years): "*Examine how whole numbers are used to represent all data in digital systems*" has been replaced by: "*Explain how digital systems represent all data*

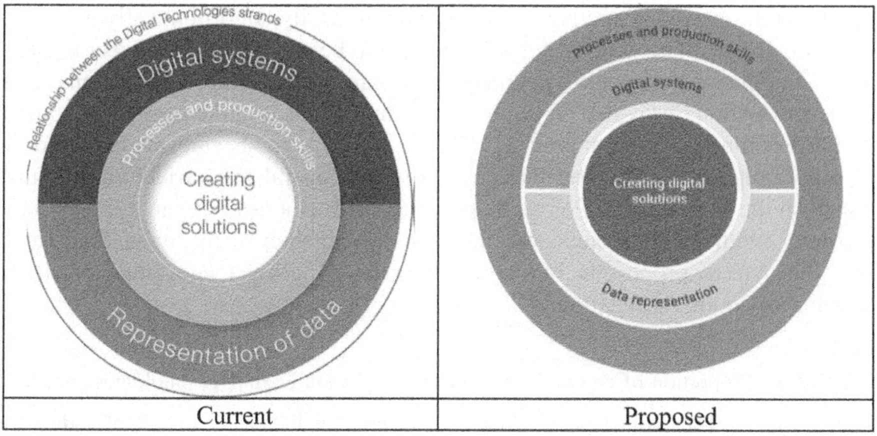

Fig. 2. The organising elements for the Digital Technologies subject (ACARA, 2017, 2021)

using numbers" and *"Explore how data can be represented by off and on states (zeros and ones in binary)"*.

This kind of simplification can help teachers by using simpler language while introducing otherwise hidden concepts (such as binary). The increase in more explicit language throughout the new proposal is likely to be well accepted by teachers.

Another noticeable change is the recognition that early childhood students (referred to as Foundation students, aged 5–6 years) have quite distinct learning needs from Years 1 & 2 (6–8 years old). These Foundation students are asked to engage with fewer concepts and use play-based learning. One content descriptor requires them to be taught to *identify some data that are personal and owned by them*. This is quite complex, but indicates a perception that cyber-safety awareness begins at a very young age.

2 The Issue of Coding

Having described the current status of computers in the Australian curriculum, and the impending changes, we now look at the issue of coding and compare this with the situation in other countries.

2.1 The Current Place of Coding

One of the consequences of the proposed increase in content descriptors for Digital Technologies is a proportionate reduction in coding-relevant teaching activities. The key concept in the subject is 'creating digital solutions'. The language used in the original curriculum does not ask students to code or program, but instead asks for them to *implement simple digital solutions* (Years 3–4).

In the overall Technologies learning area, computational thinking is fundamental to the subject. Computational thinking is defined as a "process of recognising aspects of computation in the world and being able to think logically, algorithmically, recursively and abstractly" [3]. The way digital solutions are to be created in the subject is through "using combinations of readily available hardware and software applications, and/or specific instructions provided through programming". It is quite clear from this language that coding or programming is just one of the methods students can employ.

To put programming/coding into context in the Australian Curriculum, it is useful to establish the format used. For each age range there is a description, a list of content descriptors (with elaborations), and the assessable achievement standards. Table 1 shows the current proportion of content descriptors in each age range where programming or coding is mentioned.

Table 1. Proportion of coding in the current Australian Digital Technologies subject

Student years	Total content descriptors	Content descriptors including programming or coding	% of coding in the subject
F - Year 2	6	0	0%
Years 3–4	7	1	14%
Years 5–6	9	2	22%
Years 7–8	10	1.5	15%
Years 9–10 (optional)	11	1.5	14%

Programming/coding is first mentioned with respect to visual programming in a content descriptor ("implement simple algorithms as visual programs involving control structures, variables and user input"), in the elaborations for Years 3 and 4 and in the achievement standards. Visual programming is a way of coding using coloured shapes on the screen. This recurs in Years 5 and 6.

In the current Australian curriculum, by Years 7 and 8, general-purpose programming/coding languages are mentioned in the description, and this occurs for the first time in content descriptors ("implement algorithms and modify and debug programs involving control structures and functions in a general-purpose programming language") at this level. "Use of a programming language" is also mentioned in the current Achievement Standards, so students are to be assessed on their programming skills for the first time once they reach this age (high school). In Years 9 and 10 (where Digital Technologies becomes an optional subject), we now see object-oriented programming/coding in the description, in two content descriptors ("implement, modify and debug modular programs, applying selected algorithms and data structures, including in an object-oriented programming language"), and in the achievement standards.

Overall, the current curriculum design has students progressing through the core F-8 Digital Technologies subject with visual coding in Years 3–6 and only undertaking general purpose programming/coding in Years 7 and 8.

2.2 Coding in Other Countries

In other countries, we see a different perspective on computer education in schools. In Singapore, for example, coding classes for primary school students were mandatory from the start of 2020 [4]. The initiative aims to develop an early appreciation of computational thinking and coding concepts—through simple visual programming.

While the number of content descriptors for the Digital Technologies subject in Australia is proposed to grow by 65%, coding/programming will decline from 14% to 8% of these. This proportional decline is in contrast to curricula in competing countries. For example, 27% of England's Computing attainment targets relate to coding, and 28% of progress outcome sentences in New Zealand involve programming.

In the New Zealand curriculum [5], coding is referred to as creating a 'Digital Outcome'. Reading through the supporting documentation to understand what this is, we find these kinds of explanations:

- Data management software like Filemaker Pro, Access or MySQL would be appropriate for this standard.
- Students iteratively develop, trial, and improve components in order to develop an increasingly refined outcome. During the development process, students are expected to describe and address relevant implications.
- The digital outcome must have been developed by the student.

It is not clear that creating a digital outcome necessarily implies writing code: however, it is also clear that doing so is one such method. The proportion of direct coding content in various national curricula can be seen in Table 2. It is clear there is no commonality in respect of the age at which coding should begin to be learned. There is also a range of coding proportions, even given the non-congruent age ranges.

Table 2. Proportions of direct coding in informatics/computing/digital technologies curricula

Country	Curriculum subject	Proportion of direct coding content
Australia (proposed)	Digital Technologies [F-8]	8%
Australia (current)	Digital Technologies [F-8]	14%
Singapore [6]	Computer Applications [Secondary 1–4]	17%
India [7]	ICT [Years 6–8]	18%
England [8]	Computing [Years 1–11]	27%
New Zealand	Technology – Digital Technologies [Years 1–13]	28%

For Australia, we believe there is an increased need for a foundation on computational thinking and coding at all levels, especially the upper junior, middle, and senior school curriculum. The current Digital Technologies subject shows a greater emphasis on teaching computational and programming/coding concepts in the higher junior school years. However, this decreases in the middle and senior school. We believe it should be similar across all ages of learning.

The Australian Digital Technologies curriculum also highlights, via the content descriptors for each stage, a significant mismatch. Teachers in the junior school who are not trained in programming, have more to deliver in this aspect compared to the specialist Digital Technologies teachers in the senior school, yet are required to be highly trained in this coding skill.

3 Views of Pre-service Teachers

Here are some considered opinions from a tutor of pre-service teachers who had nearly completed a unit on Digital Technologies when the public consultation draft for the reviewed curriculum was released. As previously mentioned, one of the authors was a Digital Technologies Education tutor. In the tutorial group, one pre-service teacher aimed to become a specialist computing teacher; half had a teacher parent or worked in a school; but none had attended a school placement because of Covid-19.

The tutor felt these pre-service teachers were ambivalent about ICT because priority had previously been given to the teaching of literacy, numeracy and science/inquiry. Although inquiry, deep and critical thinking could be promoted by teaching coding, Digital Technologies was not taught to them in school, and so was foreign to their thinking.

Through the informal discussions, the tutor formed three clear ideas about the proposed new curriculum for Digital Technologies. These concerned granularity – number & complexity of content descriptors; language – tension between clarity/specificity and abstraction/ambiguity; and year-on-year progression.

3.1 Granularity

When comparing the original curriculum with the proposed update, some content descriptors have been replaced by two. This change multiplies the total number of content descriptors, but generally splits complex learning activities into separate, more clearly defined activities. An example is shown in Table 3.

Table 3. Split content descriptor example, with distinction between pre-school and Years 1–2

Original	Recognise and explore digital systems (hardware and software components) for a purpose [Foundation to Year 2]
Proposed	Recognise and explore digital systems (hardware and software) and how they can be used to solve simple problems [Foundation/pre-school]
	Identify and explore digital systems and their components for a purpose [Years 1–2]

The original content descriptor has been segregated into two sub-components (see Table 4). While the split retained the essence of the original content descriptor, the distinction between Foundation and years 1 and 2 is an improvement because younger children need to have more specific content descriptors.

Table 4. Another split content descriptor – using more specific language

Original	Examine how whole numbers are used to represent all data in digital systems [Years 5–6]
Proposed	Explain how digital systems represent all data using numbers
	Explore how data can be represented by off and on states (zeros and ones in binary)

The proposed changes to the curriculum appeared to have reduced ambiguity, but not removed it entirely. Splitting an original content descriptor added clarity by breaking the topic into easy digestible parts. Table 5 shows use of specific language such as 'off and on – zeroes and ones in binary' made more sense than using the phrase 'whole numbers.' This leads onto a consideration of the language used in the proposed curriculum revision.

3.2 Language

In some cases, content descriptors in the revision have been re-written using different language (for example, shown in Table 5).

Table 5. A re-written content descriptor, to provide assistance for early career teachers

Original	Recognise different types of data and explore how the same data can be represented in different ways [Years 3–4]
Proposed	Recognise different types of data and explore how the same data can be represented differently depending upon the purpose

With a small change in the language, the revised content descriptor provides greater clarity. The proposed descriptor is more specific and would assist the teacher. Young teachers about to begin their careers would face a lot of uncertainties. If the curriculum was made more specific like this, they would have one less thing to worry about.

In other parts of the proposal, some new terms are introduced. 'User stories' occur in several content descriptors, but are not defined, which is a difficulty. In a couple more, students 'co-construct' products, which is a positive aspect of the proposal, leading to greater learner engagement.

3.3 Year-On-Year Progression

In some ways, the curriculum change had a mixed level of applicability. While some strands such as Collaborating and Managing had increased clarity for the lower years, the content descriptors had become less clear and briefer. Some sub-strands would not be applicable to science and maths teachers as they focused too much on programming, requiring dedicated lessons.

In respect of increased granularity, it was the tutor's opinion that some pre-service teachers perceived scope to build the digital curriculum around a spiral – giving children the advantage of linking back into foundational learning as they progressed towards deeper learning on the same topic.

To conclude, the tutor felt pre-service teachers who were going to teach lower grades felt better about the revised curriculum as it gave them more guidance. Pre-service teachers who were preparing to teach senior grades found the revised curriculum vague. While this is not a comprehensive approach to gauging the value of the revised curriculum, it nonetheless gives us a brief glimpse into the minds of pre-service teachers.

4 Discussion

4.1 Responding to the Research Questions

This discussion is framed around the three research questions posed at the start of this article. The first question addresses the tension between the general ICT capability and the discrete Digital Technologies subject. The proposed curriculum revision perpetuates both aspects but renames the former as Digital Literacy. There are some changes, such as the increased focus on cyber-safety in this general capability, but there is still some overlap in the areas of intellectual property and digital ethics. Unlike other countries which have abandoned the general IT skills aspects, Australia will continue to run both curriculum components. The renaming could accentuate pre-existing confusion between them, which could become a problem. Overall, there is hope that the new Digital Literacies capability and Digital Technologies subject will be more useful than their predecessors. However, the similar names are expected to exacerbate continuing confusion of these different aspects of student computer use.

Other countries have solved this issue by writing appropriate software tools into each subject curriculum and eliminating the ICT/Digital Literacy capability. This is beginning to happen in Australia, for example, dynamic geometric software is required in Mathematics at several Year levels. Another approach is to see that digital technology fundamentally changes the curriculum (for instance, there are no positive online translation skills embedded in the Languages subjects). However, it seems Australia is not yet at this point of curriculum transformation.

The second question looks at the place of programming or coding in the Australian Digital Technologies subject. Whereas other countries have over a quarter of their subject devoted to this topic, Australia proposes to diminish this from 14% to less than 10% of the subject. Curriculum designers appear to fear the explicit mention of programming/coding in the antipodes, masking this skill with terms such as 'create a digital solution' or 'digital outcome'. These very nebulous phrases may resonate with a teaching workforce largely untrained in coding, but also generate diverse alternatives which may not generate the meta-cognition implicit in programming. While the current authors shy away from multitudes of coding languages in schools, some diversity, clarity and logically conceptualised problem-solving culminating in coding can be seen as good preparation for active citizens.

Finally, our tutor discussions with pre-service teachers have highlighted tensions between granularity, language and progression. Teachers will feel comfortable in delivering good education if these issues can be resolved.

4.2 Responding to the Symposium Focus Points

This analysis from Australia sheds some useful light onto the four focus points of the symposium. The first focus point was on the impetus for informatics/computer science curricula specifications. As we have shown, the Review in Australia has led to greater granularity and clarity of language in the curriculum. Looking deeper, the reasons for actually having a Digital Technologies subject in the school curriculum is more complex. Day-to-day computer consumption/use by students was encapsulated by the ICT/Digital Literacies general capability at an early stage of the nationally developed curriculum. The more specialised and creative teaching of digital solutions resonates with economic rationales. While ICT/Digital Literacy contribute to greater gross domestic product, knowledge economies depend far more on digital innovation. The stated rationale for the Digital Technologies subject opens with: "*In a world that is increasingly digitised and automated, it is critical to the strength and sustainability of the economy, the environment and society that digital solutions are purposefully designed to include user empowerment, autonomy and accountability*".

This rationale accords with OECD economic imperatives [9] to prepare citizens for participation in the knowledge society, and to become innovative creators for it. The rationale however goes further, incorporating environmental and social benefits. Finally, the rationale exhorts student personal achievement and responsibility.

The second question in the symposium enquires about student learning in this Informatics/Computer Science/Digital Technologies subject. Two observations can be made in the light of the Australian experience. At this stage, direct focus on programming is deprecated compared to curricula in other countries, with less than 8% of curriculum content descriptors related to coding. Instead, students use computer-based tools to create digital solutions. This is rather vague, but a lot of computer science skills and understandings are woven into the curriculum. The other observation that can be made is that coding instruction commences at age 9 (Years 3–4) with visual coding, and progresses to a general-purpose language at age 13 (Years 7–8). Object-oriented languages are optionally taught at age 15 (Years 9–10).

The third question asks about the incorporation of innovations such as artificial intelligence and machine learning into the curriculum. Many of these fall into the realm of non-deterministic computing. There are two issues to be considered: learning resources and teacher professional development. International companies have made some excellent learning resources for machine learning [10] and quantum computing freely available [11]. The Australian curriculum provides about 7 examples where students can engage with the use of artificial intelligence systems, but only one where they would work directly with such a system: "*...exploring artificial intelligence data* *analysis where an algorithm is trained by a structured dataset, for example, engaging with online machine learning examples (AC9TDI10P02_E2) [Year 10]".*

The final symposium question about the relationship between the Digital Technologies subject and the use of computers across the curriculum has already been answered. In brief, the relationship is one in tension, and fraught with misunderstandings by teachers, schools, students and parents.

5 Conclusion

The revised curriculum is due to be implemented from the start of 2022. Given the scope of changes to the use of computers in class, a great deal of communication and teacher training will be required.

The proposed revision to the Australian Digital Technologies subject appears to embed the rapidly changing nature of Information Technology. However, there is little mention of non-deterministic programming. Given recent government funding initiatives, artificial intelligence/machine learning and quantum computing might well be included in the Year 9–10 curriculum. The three take-home messages from this analysis are:

a) To what extent should the Informatics/Computing/Digital Technologies curriculum specification in each country be atomised? Greater detail can assist teachers with weaker content knowledge in the subject. Fewer specifications are inevitably phrased using more general language, which may facilitate innovation adoption.
b) The extent to which coding/programming is addressed in the subject is contested. Australia proposes to have a relatively small proportion of learning explicitly focused on coding (8%), which contrasts with the 25% or more in other countries. Perhaps an intermediate level is more appropriate?
c) Countries appear to differ in the framing of general ICT capabilities and dedicated Informatics/Computing/Digital Technologies subjects. Having both aspects in the Australian Curriculum seems to be confusing to teachers, but apparently will be a feature for the next five years.

As a final note of personal opinion, some pre-service teachers in our careers have submitted draft lesson plans for assessment, expecting school students to code with up to three languages in a single session. Understandably, these trainees are keen to demonstrate their capacity, knowledge and agility, but it does put a focus on how much coding is enough. The authors consider a maximum of four computer languages over the ages 5–16 should be sufficient, with only one taught in any year. This would provide practical experience to consolidate the other computational thinking skills acquired. Also, bearing in mind the Sapir-Whorf linguistic relativity hypothesis [12] that your language determines your thinking, these coding languages should have varied characteristics. Current curricula often portray computers as von Neuman uniprocessors or Turing machines programmed procedurally within an algorithmic paradigm. Machine learning, object-orientation and quantum scoring illustrate more parallel problem-solving processes which we believe should be part of each citizen's understanding of information technology.

References

1. ACARA (Australian Curriculum Assessment and Reporting Authority): Review of the Australian curriculum F–10: General capabilities - Information and Communication Technology (ICT) capability (Digital Literacy) (2021). www.australiancurriculum.edu.au/media/7024/gc_digital_literacy_ict_capability_consultation_curriculum.pdf
2. ACARA (Australian Curriculum Assessment and Reporting Authority): Technologies consultation curriculum – Digital Technologies – comparative information F-10 (2021). www.australiancurriculum.edu.au/media/7054/technologies_digital_technologies_comparative_information_f-10.pdf
3. ACARA (Australian Curriculum Assessment and Reporting Authority): The Australian Curriculum: Technologies, p.109 (2016). https://www.australiancurriculum.edu.au/download?view=f10. [select Digital Technologies > all year levels > all curriculum elements >Download PDF]
4. Tan, Z.: Singapore makes coding classes mandatory for primary school students, starting 2020. KrASIA (2019). https://kr-asia.com/singapore-makes-coding-classes-mandatory-for-primary-school-students-starting-2020
5. Ministry of Education (NZ): Technology in the New Zealand Curriculum (2019). https://nzcurriculum.tki.org.nz/content/download/168478/1244184/file/NZC-Technology%20in%20the%20New%20Zealand%20Curriculum-Insert%20Web.pdf
6. Ministry of Education (SG): Computer applications syllabus: Secondary One to Four (2020)
7. Central Institute of Educational Technology: Information and Communication Technology for the School System: Curricula for ICT in Education (2017)
8. Department for Education: Statutory guidance: National curriculum in England: computing programmes of study (2013). https://www.gov.uk/government/publications/national-curriculum-in-england-computing-programmes-of-study/national-curriculum-in-england-computing-programmes-of-study
9. OECD (Organisation for Economic Co-operation and Development): ICT resources in school education: What do we know from OECD work? (2020). https://www.google.com/url?sa=t&rct=j&q=&esrc=s&source=web&cd=&cad=rja&uact=8&ved=2ahUKEwjSnsvX3JjyAhWG73MBHUCdAXQQFnoECAYQAw&url=http%3A%2F%2Fwww.oecd.org%2Fofficialdocuments%2Fpublicdisplaydocumentpdf%2F%3Fcote%3DEDU%2FEDPC%2FSR%2FRD(2020)2%26docLanguage%3DEn&usg=AOvVaw26MIEcWfGbQiS8qWburPu_
10. IBM & Dale Lane: Machine Learning for Kids (2017). https://machinelearningforkids.co.uk
11. IBM: Quantum Experience & Composer (2016). https://quantum-computing.ibm.com
12. Hojier, H. (ed.): Language in culture. In: Proceedings of a Conference on the Interrelations of Language and Other Aspects of Culture. Am. Anthropol. **56**(6) (1954). Part 2, Memoir No. 79

Development of IPSJ Data Science Curriculum Standard

Tetsuro Kakeshita[1(✉)], Kazuo Ishii[2], Yoshiharu Ishikawa[3], Hitoshi Matsubara[4], Yutaka Matsuo[4], Tsuyoshi Murata[5], Miyuki Nakano[6], Takako Nakatani[7], Haruhiko Okumura[8], Naoko Takahashi[9], Norimitsu Takahashi[10], Gyo Uchida[4], Eriko Uematsu[11], Satoshi Saeki[12], and Hiroshi Kato[7]

[1] Saga University, Saga, Japan
kake@is.saga-u.ac.jp
[2] Suwa University of Science, Nagano, Japan
[3] Nagoya University, Aichi, Japan
[4] University of Tokyo, Tokyo, Japan
[5] Tokyo Institute of Technology, Tokyo, Japan
[6] Tsuda University, Tokyo, Japan
[7] The Open University of Japan, Chiba, Japan
[8] Mie University, Mie, Japan
[9] Kokugakuin University, Tokyo, Japan
[10] Digital Growth Academia, Inc., Tokyo, Japan
[11] Musashino Gakuin University, Saitama, Japan
[12] The Japan Data Scientist Society, Tokyo, Japan

Abstract. The Information Processing Society of Japan (IPSJ) published a curriculum standard for university-level education majoring in data science (DS) (An English translation of the IPSJ Data Science Curriculum Standard is available at: https://www.ipthree.org/wp-content/uploads/IPSJ-DS-Curriculum_202104_en.pdf). In this paper, we shall report strategy and development of the DS curriculum standards. Data science education and the development of data scientists are recognised to be quite important in both social and business contexts. The IPSJ DS curriculum standard is developed by integrating various related initiatives and has the following unique features. (1) The DS curriculum standard covers a wide range of related fields to ensure international compatibility through mapping to the ACM Data Science curriculum and the European EDISON Data Science Framework. (2) It collaborates with the IPSJ Data Scientist certification (under development) by referring to the Data Scientist skill checklist (assistant level) developed by the Data Scientist Society of Japan. (3) It clarifies the knowledge and skills required of students majoring in data science. (4) It assigns a time to each educational content so that the curriculum size becomes approximately 675 class hours (60 credits in the Japanese credit system). (5) It collaborates with the Model Curriculum for Mathematics, Data Science and AI Education (literacy level) developed by the Japan Inter-University Consortium for Mathematics and Data Science, supported by the Japanese government.

Published by Springer Nature Switzerland AG 2022
D. Passey et al. (Eds.): OCCE 2021, IFIP AICT 642, pp. 156–167, 2022.
https://doi.org/10.1007/978-3-030-97986-7_13

Keywords: Data science · Curriculum development · Statistics · Artificial intelligence · Computer science · Data management · Software engineering · Data scientist certification

1 Introduction

Various initiatives, such as [1] in Japan, are promoted around the world to develop curriculum standards and professional certification schemes in the field of data science (DS). In this context, the Information Processing Society of Japan (IPSJ) intends to contribute to the development of systematic data science education from the standpoint of both the academic and professional community of computing discipline in Japan.

IPSJ has developed curriculum standards for computing education at the university level for nearly 30 years and has promoted a variety of activities related to computing education at the primary, secondary, high school, and university levels. The J17 curriculum standard [2] was supported by the Ministry of Education of Japan (MEXT). But as of FY2017, IPSJ could not publish a curriculum standard for the DS domain.

However, as of the end of FY2019, various efforts are in progress on curriculum standards in the DS domain in the United States, Japan, and Europe so that standardisation to ensure international compatibility is coming into view. Furthermore, IPSJ is working on the development of a data scientist (DS) certification scheme. IPSJ recently published its strategy for data science and intends to create collaboration between the DS certification and the DS curriculum [3].

Observing the above situation, IPSJ developed a curriculum standard for college students majoring in data science from the viewpoint of computing discipline. Although the Japan Inter-University Consortium for Mathematics & Data Science [4] published two model curriculums [5] in the data science field, the model curriculums do not cover expert level. Compared with other efforts in DS curriculum development, there are significant differences between the IPSJ DS curriculum and other DS curriculums. The major differences are listed below.

(1) IPSJ DS curriculum covers a wide range of related fields to ensure international compatibility by integrating the ACM Data Science curriculum [6] and the European EDISON Data Science Framework [7].
(2) IPSJ DS curriculum is in collaboration with the IPSJ Data Scientist certification (under development) by referring to the Data Scientist (DS) skill checklist [8] (assistant level) developed by the Japan Data Scientist Society.
(3) IPSJ DS curriculum assigns time to the educational contents so that the curriculum size becomes approximately 675 class hours (60 credits in the Japanese credit system).
(4) IPSJ DS curriculum regards the model curriculum as a prerequisite since the model curriculum is designed to teach data science literacy to all college students and its size is much smaller than the IPSJ DS curriculum.

IPSJ DS curriculum is intended to be used as a reference by universities and undergraduate level professional education programmes majoring in data science.

This paper is organised as follows. We shall overview the representative work related to our DS curriculum standard in Sect. 2. EDISON Data Science Framework, ACM Data Science Curricula, and Data Scientist Skill Checklist will be introduced. The development policy of the IPSJ DS curriculum will be explained in Sect. 3. We have three major policies. The first one is the integration of classification criteria of the related BOK and skill set. The second one is the assignment of time to each educational topic. The third one is the adjustment of the contents considering the allocated time restriction. Our effort related to these policies will be explained in Sects. 4 to 6 respectively. In the last section, we shall conclude the paper with an explanation of our vision to implement systematic development and evaluation system of the data scientists of various levels.

2 Related Works

Many efforts are in progress in the DS field. Many DS programmes and seminars are provided by many universities and companies. Target students/engineers and levels are quite diverse among these programmes and seminars. Development of curriculum and body of knowledge (BOK) is essential in the DS field to provide systematic education programmes and seminars for recurrent education. We shall introduce three major works which we refer to develop the IPSJ DS curriculum standard.

2.1 EDISON Data Science Framework [7]

The EDISON Data Science Framework defines DS-BoK as a set of DS knowledge areas (KA) through the analysis of various BOKs related to data science. The EDISON DS Framework also contains DS Model Curriculum and assigns ECTS (European Credit Transfer and Accumulation System) to each KA as represented in Table 1.

Although the EDISON Framework does not provide further detail of the topics at each KA, it covers a wide area of the related fields. Thus, we shall utilise the KAs and the assigned ECTS in developing the IPSJ DS curriculum since DS has an interdisciplinary nature.

2.2 ACM Data Science Curriculum [6]

ACM Data Science Task Force announced the final report of "Computing Competencies for Undergraduate Data Science Curricula" in January 2021. Different from the EDISON DS-BoK, the educational contents are described in detail. Furthermore, the curriculum defines the priority of each content using T1, T2, and E. T1 stands for mandatory content, while T2 represents semi-mandatory content with 80% of the enrollment. E stands for elective content with 50% of the expected enrollment. This information is utilised to develop the IPSJ DS curriculum standard.

On the other hand, the ACM DS curriculum does not contain certain important KAs such as mathematics, statistics, modeling and simulation, and business fundamentals. Thus, we shall add these KAs to our DS curriculum.

Table 1. Organisation of EDISON DS-BoK and assigned ECTS.

KA groups	KA#	DS knowledge areas	ECTS
Data Science Analysis	KA01.01	Statistical methods for data analysis	13.2
	KA01.02	Machine Learning	19.4
	KA01.03	Data Mining	9.7
	KA01.04	Text Data Mining	7.9
	KA01.05	Predictive Analysis	14.6
	KA01.06	Computational modeling, simulation and optimisation	9.4
Data Science Engineering	KA02.01	Big Data Infrastructure and Technologies	8.4
	KA02.02	Infrastructure and platforms for Data Science applications	14.0
	KA02.03	Cloud Computing technologies for Big Data and Data Analytics	12.5
	KA02.04	Data and Applications security	4.6
	KA02.05	Big Data systems organisation and engineering	15.5
	KA02.06	Data Science (Big Data) applications design	15.5
	KA02.07	Information systems (to support data driven decision making)	11.3

We assign a sequence number (SEQ#) to each topic to define the mapping between the ACM DS curriculum and our DS curriculum. The prefix of the SEQ# corresponds to each KA defined in the ACM DS curriculum.

2.3 Data Scientist Skill Checklist [8]

The Japan Data Scientists Society first published the Data Scientist Skill Checklist (DS Skill Checklist) in November 2015, which defines the set of skills required for three levels of the data scientists. In June 2017, the DS Skill Checklist was fully adopted in the ITSS+ (DS domain) developed by the Information-Technology Promotion Agency (IPA), which is a governmental agency governed by the Ministry of Trade and Industry (METI) of Japan. The DS skill checklist is revised every two years and the latest version was published in October 2019.

The DS skill checklist classifies data scientists into three levels: Assistant, Full, and Senior Data Scientist Levels. Each level roughly corresponds to ITSS (IT Skill Standards [9]) levels 3 to 5, which corresponds to SFIA levels 4 to 6 [10] respectively.

The DS skill checklist defines essential skills and other skills at each level. A data scientist is evaluated at a certain level by satisfying all essential skills and a specific percentage of all skills (assistant level 70%, full level 60%, senior level 50%). Table 2 illustrates the organisation of the checklist.

The DS Skill Checklist is developed from the viewpoint of business and covers detailed skills of the KA's which are missing in the ACM DS curriculum. Thus, we shall integrate the DS Skill Checklist and the ACM DS curriculum to fully cover the EDISON DS-BoK.

Table 2. Organisation of the Data Scientist Skill Checklist.

Category	Subcategories
Data Engineering	IT Security, Data Processing, Data Sharing, Data Structure, Data collection, Data storage, Programming, Environment construction
Data Science	Graphical Models, Grouping, Sampling, Simulation, Data assimilation, Data understanding/validation, Data processing, Data visualisation, Pattern discovery, Connotation extraction & insight, Speech/music processing, Image/video processing, Basic mathematics, Machine learning techniques, Testing/decision making, Language Processing, Optimisation, Time series analysis, Understanding properties/relationships, Analysis process, Prediction(<-Forecasting)
Business Fundamentals	Data Acquisition, Understanding data from a business perspective, Problem definition, Activity Management, Contracts and Rights Protection, Code of Conduct, Business Implementation, Conception and Design, Analysis and evaluation, Logical thinking

3 Curriculum Development Policy

The development policy of the IPSJ DS curriculum is defined in this section. Each of the previous works introduced in Sect. 2 has its limitations explained in the section. We shall overcome these problems by integrating these three works. We shall mainly discuss the intention of each policy in this section. Implementation of the major policies will be explained in the succeeding sections.

A) Covers a Wide Area of Data Science to Ensure International Compatibility
DS is considered multidisciplinary since various existing areas are related to DS. Some of them are statistics, artificial intelligence, machine learning, data engineering, business analysis, and security and privacy as can be observed in EDISON DS-BoK. ACM DS curriculum and DS Skill checklist cover only a part of DS-BoK so that both are required to cover DS-BoK.

Furthermore, different KAs are used in the ACM DS curriculum and DS Skill checklist due to their different viewpoints so that integration of the classification criteria is necessary. Thus, IPSJ utilises the organisation of DS-BoK with some modification to reduce the hierarchy of the KAs. The detail will be explained in Sect. 4.

B) Collaboration with IPSJ Data Scientist Certification (Under Development)
IPSJ is currently developing a certification scheme to recognise the ability of data scientists. The certification scheme is based on the DS Skill Checklist since it is approved by a governmental agency (IPA) and is widely accepted among Japanese IT companies. The DS Skill Checklist defines three levels of the data scientist. IPSJ is planning to provide two, assistant and full, levels of the data scientist among them.

When we developed our DS curriculum, we selected the DS Skill Checklist of the assistant level since the DS curriculum is prepared for undergraduate students. There are also many DS seminars in the Japanese industry that reference the DS Skill Checklist of the assistant or the full levels. Utilisation of the topics at the assistant level from the DS Skills Checklist will be useful to develop a unified system to develop and evaluate data scientists in academia and industry in Japan.

C) Specify the Knowledge and Skills Required of the Students Majoring in DS
Although EDISON DS-BoK covers a wide range of data science areas, it only specifies the required knowledge and skills abstractly. Thus, we shall utilise the ACM Data Science curriculum and the DS Skills Checklist to specify them concretely. The topics derived from the ACM DS curriculum are assigned serial numbers beginning with "ACM" in the IPSJ DS curriculum standard, while the topics originated from the DS Skills Checklist are numbered with a serial number beginning with "DS". All other topics are assigned serial numbers beginning with "IPSJ".

D) The Size of the IPSJ DS Curriculum is Approximately 675 Class Hours (60 Credits in the Japanese Credit System
More than 124 credits are required to graduate from university in Japan. A student can typically earn 2 credits by taking 90-min class 15 times (22.5 class hours). IPSJ commonly assigns 60 credits to develop a curriculum standard for undergraduate majored in some computing disciplines such as CS, CE, SE, IS, and IT. We shall also adopt this policy in developing our DS curriculum standard.

At a typical Japanese university, 20–30 credits are assigned to general education for all undergraduate students regardless of their major subject. Approximately 10 credits are assigned for the graduation research project. Thus 85–95 credits can be assigned to the education for the major subject. Considering the diversity of the education programme, it is realistic to leave a certain amount of room to utilise the characteristics of each educational programme.

We shall explain the details of the time assigned to the topics contained in the IPSJ DS curriculum in Sect. 5. When we assign a specific time to each topic, we need to adjust the contents of the topic so that we can teach the topic within the assigned time constraints. The detail of the adjustment will be described in Sect. 6.

E) Students are Assumed to Have Studied the Model Curriculum in Mathematics, Data Science, and AI (Literacy Level)
The Model Curriculum for Mathematics, Data Science and AI Education (Literacy) [5] is developed by the Japan Consortium for Strengthening Bases for Mathematics and Data Science education and is authorised by the Ministry of Education (MEXT) of Japan. Since all university students are expected to learn the model curriculum, the model curriculum is considered a prerequisite of the IPSJ DS curriculum standard.

Thus, no time will be assigned for the topics included in the model curriculum.

4 Integrating Classification Criteria

We shall integrate classification criteria of the ACM DS curriculum and DS skill checklist utilising EDISON DS-BoK in this section since EDISON DS-BoK covers the broadest areas.

4.1 General Principle

The integrated KA has two levels represented in Table 3. The integrated KA also utilises the classification of the ACM DS curriculum as well as EDISON DS-BoK to balance the number of topics at each subcategory.

We define a mapping between the IPSJ DS KA's and the three KA's defined in Sect. 2. We also assign SEQ# to each topic of the IPSJ DS curriculum standard. A SEQ# beginning "ACM" and "DS" respectively represents a topic originated from the ACM DS curriculum or DS Skill Checklist, while a SEQ# beginning "IPSJ" represents a topic added by IPSJ. We also confirm that the IPSJ DS KA system covers the ACM DS curriculum and DS Skill Checklist by assigning the SEQ#.

4.2 Individual Considerations

38 topics are assigned to category A, which are related to the mathematical basis for data science and AI. It is assumed that students have taken Mathematics I, which is a compulsory course in the Japanese high school curriculum guidelines, and the model curriculum (literacy level) established by the Japan Inter-University Consortium for Mathematics and Data Science Education, but is not assumed that students have taken Mathematics II, III, A, B or more, In other words, students are not supposed to have learned exponential and logarithmic functions, differential and integral calculus, vectors, and matrices. Therefore, each school needs to discard related topics according to its admission policy.

Regarding Category B2, Artificial Intelligence, we put topics in that category based on the ACM Data Science Curricula, though some may suggest Artificial Intelligence should entail a wider/narrower range of topics.

Category C contains 44 topics, including two DS Knowledge Areas of EDISON DS-BoK: "Predictive Analytics (KA01.05: 11 topics)" and "Computational modeling, simulation and optimisation (KA01.06: 33 topics)". And it contains subcategories of the "Data Science" category in the Data Scientist Skill Checklist, such as Prediction, Understanding properties/relationships, Sampling, Data visualisation, Analysis process, Data understanding/validation, Connotation extraction & insight, Time series analysis, Language Processing, and Image/video processing. However, there are no corresponding topics in the ACM DS curriculum.

Categories G1 to G3 cover the following topics:

1. Identification of business challenges; gathering, storing, processing, and sharing data; understanding data from a business perspective
2. Building operating environments, planning systems
3. Codes of conduct (data ethics, compliance), activity management, contracts, protection of rights
4. Logical thinking, application in business

The ACM curriculum focuses mainly on teaching technical aspects, whereas the Japan Data Scientist Society's skills checklist focuses more on displaying the skills required in business. The differences between the two are particularly conspicuous.

Table 3. Organisation of the IPSJ data science knowledge areas.

Top level category	Subcategories
A: Basic Mathematics and Mathematical Statistics	1. Basic Linear Algebra, 2. Differential and Integral Calculus, 3. Mathematical Statistics
B1: Data Mining	1. Similarity Measures, 2. Data Preparation, 3. Information Extraction, 4. Cluster Analysis, 5. Classification and Regression, 6. Pattern Mining, 7. Outlier Detection, 8. Time Series Data, 9. Web Data Mining
B2: Artificial Intelligence	1. General, 2. Knowledge Representation and Reasoning (Logic-Based Models), 3. Knowledge Representation and Reasoning (Probability-Based Models), 4. Planning and Search Strategy
B3: Machine Learning	1. General, 2. Supervised Learning, 3. Unsupervised Learning, 4. Mixed Methods, 5. Deep Learning
C: Modeling and Simulation	1. Sampling, 2. Data Visualisation, 3. Analysis Process, 4. Data Understanding and Verification, 5. Language Processing, 6. Image and Video Processing
D1: Fundamental Computer Science	1. Basic Computer Architecture, 2. Storage System Basics, 3. Operating System Basics, 4. File System, 5. Network, 6. Web and Web Programming, 7. Compilers and Interpreters, 8. Algorithmic Thinking and Problem Solving, 9. Algorithms, 10. Data Structures, 11. Programming, 12. Numerical Computation
D2: Big Data System	1. Challenges Associated with Scale, 2. Computer Architecture to Handle Big Data, 3. Parallel Computing Framework, 4. Distributed Data Storage, 5. Parallel Programming, 6. Big Data Application Development Technology, 7. Cloud Computing, 8. Complexity Theory, 9. Software Support for Big Data Applications
E1: Security and Privacy	1. Security Basics, 2. Privacy Protection, 3. Data Security, 4. Data Consistency, 5. Security Analysis
E2: Human-Computer Interaction	1. General
F: Software Engineering	1. Software Design and Development, 2. Software Testing, 3. Collaboration with Related Domains
G1: Data Collection, Management, and Governance	1. Database Basics, 2. Data Collection, 3. Data Processing, 4. Data Sharing, 5. Data Storage, 6. System Operation, 7. Data Management, 8. Information Retrieval
G2: Professionalism	1. Continuing Professional Development, 2. Communication, 3. Teamwork, 4. Economic Issues, 5. Privacy and Confidentiality, 6. Ethical Issues, 7. Legal Issues, 8. Intellectual Property, 9. Automation
G3: Business Fundamentals	1. Logical Thinking, 2. Project Management, 3. Business Implementation

By integrating the two curriculums into our curriculum, we have been able to show how the knowledge, skills, and dispositions in the ACM curriculum are applied in business. If students can learn, through education, to bridge the gap between theory and practice, we will have succeeded in achieving the goals of this category. In terms of educational methods, we recommend providing business case studies alongside theory, using practical exercises as opportunities to discuss ways of applying knowledge, and evaluating the ethical aspects of handling data from a business perspective. Such education should also motivate students to study DS.

5 Assigning Education Time

We assign education time to each topic in the IPSJ DS curriculum standard. The general principle and the individual effort are explained in this section.

5.1 General Principle

The EDISON Data Science Model Curriculum (MC-DS) contains the assignment of ECTS credit points for the BSc programme for major DS-BoK knowledge areas as represented in Table 1. We assign the education time to each IPSJ KA so that the assigned time is proportional to the ECTS points to the corresponding KA of the DS-BoK. The assigned education time is represented in Table 4. Since MC-DS does not provide assignments to the three categories G1, G2 and G3, we assign 112.5 h to these categories considering the balance to the other categories.

The hours for each KA are divided into three categories: T1, T2, and E. The definitions of T1, T2 and E are the same as the ACM DS Curriculum.

The IPSJ DS curriculum is designed so that the effective teaching time is approximately 675 h (60 credits $\times$ 11.25 h/credit), where the effective teaching time is the sum of the number of hours allocated to each teaching topic multiplied by the completion rate defined for the three categories.

The Japan Data Scientist Society assigns the education time for the topics belonging to the DS Skill Checklist. They assigned a time based on their experience at data science seminars for business persons. A total of 180 h is assigned to the topics derived from the DS Skill Checklist, which is 26.7% of the education time of the IPSJ DS curriculum.

When allocating education time for ACM education topics, the time allocated for skill topics should be approximately two to three times the time allocated for knowledge topics. The time allocated for attitude topics will be decided by the team in charge after considering the time allocated for knowledge and skills.

5.2 Individual Considerations

The three categories B1, B2 and B3 are assigned 135, 72, and 117 topics respectively. As the numbers of topics are big, we simply divided the allocated time of each top-level category by the number of topics of the corresponding category. Since the allocated time for some of the topics is very small for its content, we recommend that any

Table 4. Top-level categories and assigned time.

Top level category	Assigned time (h)				Effective time (h)
	T1	T2	E	Total	
A: Mathematical Fundamentals and Statistics	18.25		19.00	37.25	27.75
B1: Data Mining	28.00	36.00	78.00	142.00	95.80
B2: Artificial Intelligence	3.25	17.00	12.50	32.75	23.10
B3: Machine Learning	13.75	19.50	13.50	46.75	36.10
C: Modeling and Simulation	11.80	18.38	47.00	77.18	50.00
D1: Fundamental Computer Science	81.16	22.50	26.25	129.91	112.28
D2: Big Data System	7.00	59.50	47.00	113.50	78.10
E1: Security and Privacy	41.93		4.00	45.93	43.93
E2: Human-Computer Interaction	16.83			16.83	16.83
F: Software Engineering	50.50	25.00	38.00	113.50	89.50
G1: Data Collection, Management and Governance	27.01	25.67	17.00	69.68	56.04
G2: Professionalism	16.14	12.01	7.99	36.14	29.74
G3: Business Fundamentals	10.50		8.33	18.83	14.67
Total	326.12	235.55	318.57	880.24	673.85

potential lecturer or course organiser may want to integrate multiple topics so that they can have a reasonable amount of time to cover them, as it would be usually the case that covering multiple relevant topics would make the lecture more efficient.

Category C was assigned 50 h of effective time (Assigned Time (h) T1: 11.8, T2: 18.38, E: 47.0, Total: 77.18; as shown in Table 4). It was assigned based on "Hours required for education" of corresponding topics in the Data Scientist Skill Checklist. Because, indeed, "Hours required for education" in the Data Scientist Skill Checklist of corresponding topics in Category C was quite shorter than the assigned time proportional to the ECTS points, the assigning education time was adjusted and elongated based on the ECTS points.

The topics initially assigned to Security and Privacy (category E1) come from the ACM DS curriculum and are rather rich and of high level, while the time assigned to information security is limited to 4.6 ECTS in DS-BoK. Thus, we decided to assign 45 h to this area, which corresponds to two classes at a Japanese university.

Although the number of topics belonging to Software Engineering (category F) is not many, the granularity of the topics varies. Some of the topics are simple knowledge, while some topics require extensive software development projects. Thus, we assign 0.5 to 6 h to each topic, taking into account the educational content.

6 Adjusting Educational Contents

The educational contents of each topic depend on the time assigned to the topic so that there is a strong relationship between the decision made in Sects. 5 and 6. We shall summarise the decision to adjust educational contents in this section. We shall mainly explain the differences by focusing on the changes made to the educational content of the original curriculum.

Due to the limitation of assigned time for Security and Privacy (category E1), we assign time only to the topics with T1 priority. Although a data scientist should have sufficient knowledge of security and privacy, a data scientist is not an expert on computer security. The Japanese government provides a certification scheme [11] for computer security professionals based on ISO/IEC 27000 series. A data scientist is expected to collaborate with such security professionals.

There are many descriptions such as "can practice something in all fields" in Software Engineering (category F) of the ACM DS curriculum. We have changed the wording to "can practise something in multiple fields" because it is considered unrealistic considering the assigned time constraints.

We also added the following topics based on the revision plan of SWEBOK 2021: Design patterns for AI and IoT applications, Value creation and proposition, Agile software development practice, and DevOps. However, since the contents of the revision of SWEBOK have not yet been finalised, changes may be made in the future.

7 Conclusion and Future Direction

IPSJ has made the draft DS Curriculum Standards available for public comment and published the DS Curriculum Standard on April 2021 after a minor revision considering the submitted comments and the updates of the ACM DS curriculum.

The educational content of this data science curriculum standard is quite rich, and not many universities can cover all these contents by themselves. However, with the Corona disaster, online education has become popular in universities. The Japanese Standards for the Establishment of Universities have recently been revised to allow multiple universities to collaborate to run a single educational programme. We believe that a combination of online education and university collaboration is quite effective to realise quality assurance of specialised education in data science.

IPSJ is also working to develop a collaboration of college-level education majoring in data science and certification scheme for data scientists in industries. A seamless development and evaluation system are essential for the effective development of data scientists expected to contribute to many aspects of society and business.

Acknowledgement. This research is supported by JSPS Kakenhi #20K03232.

References

1. Integrated Innovation Strategy Promotion Council of Japan: AI Strategy (2019). https://www.kantei.go.jp/jp/singi/ai_senryaku/pdf/aistratagy2019en.pdf
2. Information Processing Society of Japan: J17 Computing Curriculum Standard (in Japanese) (2017). https://www.ipsj.or.jp/annai/committee/education/j07/curriculum_j17.html
3. Information Processing Society of Japan: Data Scientist Strategy (in Japanese) (2021). https://www.ipsj.or.jp/release/20210413_DSstrategy.html
4. Japan Inter-University Consortium for Mathematics & Data Science. http://www.mi.u-tokyo.ac.jp/consortium/en/
5. Japan Inter-University Consortium for Mathematics & Data Science: Model Curriculum for Mathematics, Data Science and AI Education (Literacy) - Learning Data-Thinking (in Japanese) (2020). http://www.mi.u-tokyo.ac.jp/consortium/model_literacy.html
6. ACM Data Science Task Force: Computing Competencies for Undergraduate Data Science Curricula (2021). http://dstf.acm.org/
7. EDISON Data Science Framework. https://edisoncommunity.github.io/EDSF/
8. The Japan Data Scientist Society: Data Scientist Skill Checklist (in Japanese) (2019). https://www.datascientist.or.jp/common/docs/skillcheck.xlsx
9. IPA: IT Skill Standard. https://www.ipa.go.jp/english/humandev/forth_download.html
10. SFIA Foundation: Skills Framework for the Information Age, Version 8. https://sfia-online.org/en
11. IPA: Registered Information Security Specialist Examination. https://www.ipa.go.jp/files/000009645.pdf

Proof of Concept Teaching for 21st Century Digital Literacy in Portugal: A Pedagogical Approach Towards a New Educational Model

António Castro[1], Rui Trindade[1], and Teresa Pereira[2](✉)

[1] Centre for Research and Intervention in Education (CIIE), University of Porto, Porto, Portugal
antonio.castro@aefontespmelo.pt, trindade@fpce.up.pt
[2] Institute of Mechanical Engineering and Industrial Management (INEGI), Porto School of Engineering, Polytechnic of Porto, Porto, Portugal
mtp@isep.ipp.pt

Abstract. This paper addresses an analysis of contemporary, structured, and connected pedagogical approaches to the teaching of digital proficiency/fluency in 21st-century digital literacy. We present a proof of concept and epistemological valorisation of digital literacy previously underestimated. This epistemological valorisation focuses on teaching digital literacy through understanding how teachers work - pedagogical planning, teacher training, syllabus design, practical work - enabling us to train technology producers instead of passive technology consumers, to enable agents instead of clients. The term "digital" will refer to 21st-century digital literacy. To "think digital" will refer to the mental process carried out by digital natives when conducting operations involving ICT - as their native language and framework. The pedagogical background is paramount to the structures underlying teaching of 21st-century digital literacy, characterised by its disruptive building process achieved through the acknowledgement of epistemological foundations. High school teaching of 21st century digital literacy is by no means at ground zero. The fundamental concepts to be conveyed remain the same: electric coding, input and output devices, memories, processors and transistors – the process/system is just faster and smaller. The development of a proof of concept was built according to a DSR framework, in an iterative way, giving evidence of architecture configuration, an asset of information, of tools, procedures, and attitudes.

Keywords: Pedagogical architecture · Digital teaching · Digital · Pedagogical communication paradigm

1 Context

The former pedagogical approach to the digital society provided high school students with 3 separate stages: electricity, electronics, and coding. Our pedagogical architecture proposal seeks to realign the pedagogical approach to 21st century digital literacy [1] in high school. Learning should be contemporary, structured, and integrate pedagogical structures that introduce concepts, technologies, coding languages, etc. The teaching of

Published by Springer Nature Switzerland AG 2022
D. Passey et al. (Eds.): OCCE 2021, IFIP AICT 642, pp. 168–178, 2022.
https://doi.org/10.1007/978-3-030-97986-7_14

digital fluency ought to intervene in three different domains: learning spaces, what to teach and how to teach it, and feedback structures. To teach how to be "digital" would be to teach digital fluency – beyond digital usage or digital literacy. Teaching digital fluency in the 21st century requires understanding how technological components work, where they can work and why - not only what they are, or how to use them as mere tools.

This new alignment assumes a heuristic knowledge of the technology and its impact, over mechanical repetitive processes. These might be productive, but will hardly generate knowledge or digital literacy, let alone fluency. The simple development of mechanical skills falls short of the ambitions set for 21st century education. The tacit assumption that the intense/repetitive use of a tool or a method could be a valid pedagogical approach to ICT has proven not to result in digital empowerment. Hence, new strategies and pedagogical approaches are necessary to maintain a connection between users and their perception of how it works, steering them towards real life problem-solving skills. Students must be immersed in experimentation, in construction, and to be able to build their own knowledge using previous stages of acquired knowledge. This pedagogical approach addresses a conceptual redefinition of the learning context and the learning environment - this early stage of the iterative methodology will be described later. This first stage provides proof of concept for the original project [2]. The proposal is originally based on the perception of how 21st century digital skills are taught in high school – the distance between using and functioning is increasingly high.

A computational device can automate processes, but it does not and will not automatise learning. Pedagogy lies not in the computational device nor in its use. Despite an abundant proliferation of various computer support technologies in education, Portugal faces a lack of pedagogical reflection to sustain such proliferation. Despite the introduction of technology in the national education system, and despite the internet being available since the 1980s, most school crystallised in a unidirectional pattern of education: instructions are directed to students lined up in traditional spaces, facing a lecturer-style teacher who replicates concepts, teaching the same to everyone. The introduction of technology did not bring a much-needed disruption to this instructional pattern. Nor did the introduction of psychology techniques or of active methodologies that were only a panoply of platforms or 'apps'. We should point out that the proliferation of computer platforms in education that resulted from the general demand for access to digital communications, for any and all purposes, burdened the schools' administrations in such a way that it reallocated financial resources due to investigation and innovative work, to "feed" administrative requirements. Both focus and educational "energy" steered away from innovation towards administration.

The existence/acquisition of technology is not, contrary to common knowledge, tantamount to innovation or modernisation in secondary education levels. Nor does it lead to a quality education, or a more sustainable organisation. Misguided use of digital hardware and software can be damaging to an organisation should the volume of technological investment not generate knowledge, innovation, or disruption – the lack of epistemological values will be detrimental. Thus, we seek to contribute to an educational enterprise that is reflexive and set on epistemological values, and on contemporary pedagogical approaches that will incorporate the grounds, structures, and development of the conditions to the adequate teaching of 21st century digital literacy.

This pedagogical approach results from identifying the need to reduce the gap between the use of digital tools and the awareness of how they work. This led to the questioning of how to empower students for digital fluency. Should it be through digital skills, or through the improvement of digital proficiency and awareness?

For clarification, when using the term "digital" we refer to the pedagogical architecture being proposed. Terms such as 'electronic platform', 'computers', 'robotics', 'ICT', 'digital application', 'digital tools', 'platforms', 'learning platforms', 'new technologies', Internet, informatics, etc., are often indistinctly used, though they are not interchangeable. Thus, the term "digital" as a noun rather than as an adjective, refers to and includes this entire value chain. "Digital" is assumed as a concept including the spectrum of hardware devices, software, 'machine learning', IoT (Internet of Things), Industry 4.0 or even 'Artificial Intelligence'. It includes, in addition to 'System and Communications Hardware and Software', applications of the educational processes it supports, as well as the representation of its relationships with humans. Taking "digital" as a noun in education is also the recognition that more discussion is needed amongst educational experts regarding the ambiguity of the lexicon. "Digital" refers to digital literacy/fluency - the ability to function in the digital world as a native, fluent in the language, capable of using the tools, sufficiently skilled to function with hardware, software, languages, and technologies, and able to create innovation and knowledge.

1.1 Literature

The democratisation of ICT in Portuguese education was always based on national government programmes, consistently introduced in public schools. That first programme – *Minerva* (1985–1995) – was introduced by the Ministry of Education (ME) and overseen by the Planning and Studies Office and the Department of Programming and Financial Management. *Minerva* was developed in articulation with higher education institutions. Programme *Nónio Século XXI* (1996–2002) sought not only to integrate ICT, but also to enforce a series of measures to redesign the national educational system, stimulating new pedagogical practices. The *UARTE* (1997–2003) project, supervised by the Ministry of Science and Technology, sought to provide Internet access to all national primary and secondary, equipping school libraries with a computer and Internet connections. In 2005, the ME created EDUTIC unit as part of the Information and Evaluation Office for the Education System. That same year, all the competences exercised by EDUTIC were transferred to the Computers, Networks, and Internet at School Mission Team. The purpose was to install computers, networks, and *School Internet* – access to the internet in school facilities. The unit designed, developed, implemented, and evaluated mobilising and integrating initiatives in the use computers in the teaching and learning processes. The latest governmental programme for ICT and digital literacy - *Technological Plan for Education (PTE)* began in 2007, and sought school modernisation to create *in situ* spaces of interactivity and knowledge transfer. This was the first programme that focused on the certification of the digital skills of education agents, and on preparing children and young people for the knowledge society. This programme is still active in Portuguese public schools, focusing on the upkeeping and updating of technological assets (Fig. 1).

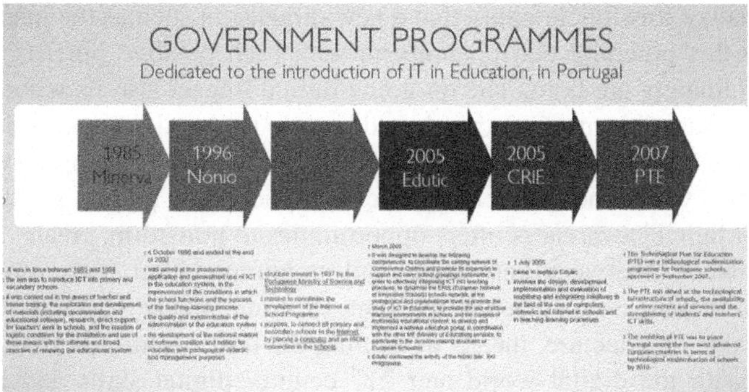

Fig. 1. Temporal introduction of Portuguese digital governmental programmes or education [3]

Since 1985, we can identify three differentiating moments of intervention: Introducing computers at the school (*Minerva* and *Nónio*); Bringing schools on-line – internet connectivity at school facilities (*UARTE*); Hardware maintenance (*PTE*). None of the aforementioned government programmes presented a pedagogical axis, a vision, or a structuring pedagogical design for a true systemic, global and transformational model. Thus, it is necessary to revisit the pedagogical context of continuity and adaptability – how did schools keep up with the EU digital transformation Agenda? [4]. Thus, it is an opportunity to implement the concept of the digital literacy instead of technological skills (an upgrade), and digital literacy instead of mechanical digital skills. Should literacy be set as an educational objective, the particularities of the "digital" should be analysed: how it appeared; how it was built; why was it built; what difficulties were overcome; what successes, failures, challenges, and evolution stages were overcome. Challenges set for students should encourage reflection on their relationship with the digital world and digital knowledge. The inclusion of the relationship between students and the digital world acknowledges the value of a cultural asset common to the communication paradigm [5], information assets, tangible pedagogical assets, and culturally accepted procedures and attitudes [6]. Our pedagogical architecture proposal recommends a feedback structure, following the concepts of John Hattie [7], Paul Black and Dylan William [8], that, deprived of judgement or assessment, seeks to provide support and guidance to students and to the community. These support and guidance functions have a signalling function to support the capture of meanings, so that the action of exploring can make sense within such an architecture. The feedback structure, though sometimes not explicit in its action, is set to underpin verification and improvement.

The digital society influenced everyday life from the 1980s when the computer evolved into its domestic form as the 'Personal Computer' (PC). The computational devices' epistemological foundations led to the need for automated support of human operations (initially only for calculus), and led to a use of automation in the information processing, with concerns about integration and recording of the operations properties considered relevant, to extract valuable information, to extract knowledge. In this evolution the need to put these machines 'talking' with each other also arises. It is through the use of this functionality that a new dimension such as the internet emerges. It is through this potential that phenomena with both positive impacts and negative impacts for humanity are born. The on-going digital impact also increases the demand for digitally literate citizens. Citizens should be able to use digital tools in a wide range of circumstances, and above all, able to adapt flexibly to ever-changing environments and ecosystems, where there are clearly social implications. From a social and cultural perspective, "digital" awareness offers opportunities to transform, create, and innovate. It is in this balance, between knowledge and its interpretation, its questioning and its construction, that it is considered relevant to contemplate teaching digital skills. "Digital", in this architecture, means deepening the dimension of digital literacy – the relationship with the digital world and 21st century digital skills and its awareness begins in the cradle.

2 Research Plan and Methods

The project that originated this architecture involves the construction of an artefact – a construction for a certain purpose. The purpose of the construction of this artefact is to develop a pedagogical process for teaching 21st century digital literacy – by intervening in the pedagogical components, the teaching/learning environment of teachers' relationship with the praxis, and the learners' relationship with knowledge.

The methodology includes the following points: the creation of a new artefact – development and implementation to redesign practice to achieve the goal – to redesign the traditional pedagogical approach to digital training, shaped towards a true process of creating digital actors – digitally fluent and proficient. The artefact results from inputs from literature and field work. Thus, we believe it stands before a typical 'DSR' research scenario [9]. The construction was developed iteratively, and each iteration was evaluated. The re-evaluation of the problem should refine the quality of the design process, each iteration and so on. This building and evaluating cycle is also typical, and happens several times before the final artefact design is considered completed [10]. DSR can be seen as a realisation of three cycles closely related to research activities [11]. A relevance cycle initiates the DSR, in an iterative process with the application context, which not only provides the requirements for the research but also its 'inputs'. The rigor cycle iterates between the artifact design and the block that provides the knowledge for the project. This was the path followed by this project.

Figure 2 embodies the definitive representation of the methodological framework adopted in this research project. The three constituent blocks of the 'framework' stand out, and their adaptation to the reality of this project to the tasks that are part of its construction, as well as the iterative cycles that, along with the moments of evaluation, mark the whole dynamics of the project and promote its relevance and rigor. In a summary of the framework, the cycles represent the dynamics of the research that takes place in the context identified in the 'Environment' Block and receives the 'inputs' with contribution to innovation from the 'Knowledge Base' Block.

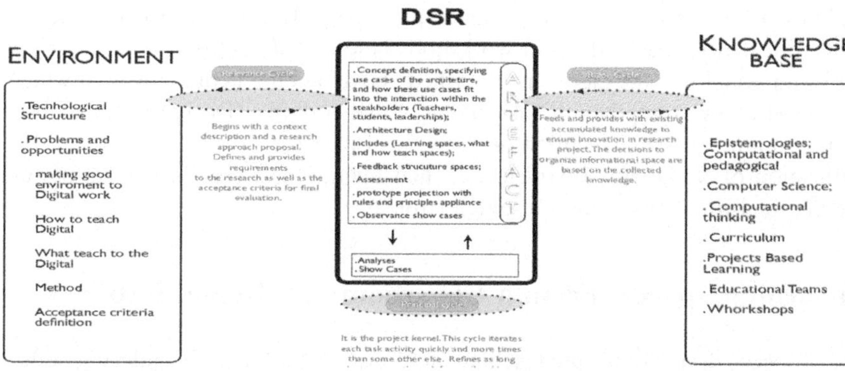

Fig. 2. Methodological framework applied (adapted from Hevner & Chatterjee [11])

The ‘environment’ Block – clearly and precisely characterises the environmental element of this project, represented in this specific sector. It includes the needs and requirements of the project, identifying in the educational environment the relevance in the following areas of application: i) Structure and culture of the organic units or schools, in relation to what is in the focus of the research project – the technological infrastructure made available to the community, as well as the way of teaching and learning digital literacy, and with the digital technologies; ii) Creation of favourable conditions for the smooth running of the implementation. It focuses on the process and on people, and on the conditions available; iii) The characterisation of the acceptance criteria will be revisited in the evaluation phase of the project to dictate or not its success. In an initial phase, from the teaching side, these criteria relate to the functional success of the implementation of the pilot demonstration case. The same happens on the learners’ side, where it is relevant that they go further, autonomously.

The ‘Design Science Research’ Block – the activities of creating, designing, and recording the representation of the implementation proposed in this project. In this block, two groups of tasks are worked on: i) The production of a viable artefact – understood in our project in the form of ‘construction’ and identifying the constituent components for prescriptive implementation, as well as the new ideas sought that serve the intentional purpose of aligning the educational activity in and with digital technologies; ii) Justification and validation of the artefact – The demonstration activity is exercised through demonstration cases and seeks to affirm the viability of the prescription in its usefulness and in its explanation. These cases are produced in real environments – on a school floor and with information produced in the laboratory preparation.

The ‘Knowledge Base’ Block – stores the concepts on which the research is based. These concepts are obtained by collecting information from already developed, evaluated, and mature scientific work (theories, axioms, taxonomies, methods, etc.). It is composed of epistemological foundational work, from which more mature, substantiated and applied knowledge is derived. Some examples are the body of theoretical grounding of algorithmic thinking, the epistemological foundations of pedagogical paradigms or even from computer science principals. This block also includes information collected in the field, from workshops held at different times.

It is important that the elements described above and the iterative way in which the project progresses, strengthen the placement of the work in a 'Design Science' research paradigm. In the faithful execution of this way of research, it is also important that the identification of the iterative work cycles that operate between the blocks presented, make the final implementation presented stronger.

3 Learning Spaces: From a Classroom to a Digital Lab

Physical spaces designed for the teaching and learning of ICT in secondary school have been the subject of study since the year 2000. There is a trend towards studying the transition from the classroom to what are called learning spaces. Some examples: "Learning spaces" [12], "Learning spaces: involving teaching staff to improve pedagogy" [13] and the work "Designing learning spaces" [14]. These works highlight concerns in the interconnection between the physical design of spaces and how it may or may not have impact on the organisation of individuals, on their relationships, and on how teaching and learning take place. The proposal is to upgrade from a mere space to a learning environment.

Our proposal resorts to a teaching and learning space based on the organisational architecture of the inviting classroom project of the 'Future Classroom Lab' [15] - a work resulting from the iTEC project [16]. The configuration in AP_PDF is adapted, with the resources organised to ensure "digital" inception via the teaching and learning process and not to use digital tools as a means to an end – but as an end in itself.

This configuration adds resources that facilitate the connection to the particularities of the "digital", that allows us to deconstruct how they were built, why they were built, and that allows us to present students with the challenges for the construction of new digital solutions. It goes further: it addresses how challenges are being developed step by step, in a pedagogical analysis. Thus, we ensure that inputs on the construction of the space are aligned with educational literacy goals. We suggest the inclusion of some technological and computational equipment to support the afore-mentioned goals applied to the "digital" teaching. The following equipment should include: the 5 components of a PC (Power supply, Motherboard, processor, memories and disks - both Hard & SSD); PCs assembled exposed in their components; Soldering irons, solder, dupont connectors and resistors; Set of Sensors dedicated to educational objectives; Multimeter; SBC (Single Board Computers) with 4-core processors; SDCards of at least 32 GB; LCD monitors, with multiple video inputs (HDMI, DVI and VGA); Wired and wireless keyboards; Wired and wireless mouse.

A way was found to provide the student with equipment and accountability using that equipment that includes kits with the last five items. Each student or group of students take responsibility for, unpack, check, use and pack up again after work. Although digital items are often designated as 'smart' ('smart watches'; 'smart phones'; 'smart cities'), it does not grant these digital technologies with "magical" powers nor does it make them entities, let alone thinking beings. In the learning space we advocate, it is also relevant to understand the value of each item that will support the pedagogical practice - how and when to place them and with which technology (hardware, software and settings) to pair it. These actions should be aligned with the transversal curriculum and have a yearly update. This will allow us to ensure that the classroom is a space of discovery, passion, and joy, see Fig. 3a and b. The technology supports the action, but the planning, the development, the questioning, and the execution of the educational act must also take part – likely a most significant one - in the pedagogical architecture AP_PDF. Only when such premises are fulfilled and students are allowed to enter a space that complies with the patterns set to achieve digital and values students' relationship with knowledge can we grant due value to information, tangible, procedures, and behavioural assets.

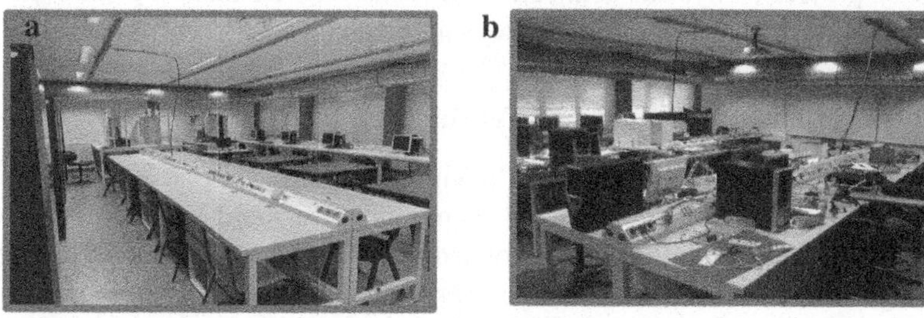

Fig. 3. a) Digital skills classroom and b): Digital immersion space displaying evidence of digital literacy challenges (Fontes Pereira de Melo high school in Porto, Portugal)

4 Educational Structure

4.1 What to Teach and How to Teach It

The disruptive architectural space proposed above for the teaching of digital literacy, values conceptual particularities for student challenges, and combines epistemological justification in the design of the pedagogical innovation plan, in the learning spaces, in relationship with knowledge, and in the feedback iterations for improvement. The proposal we advocate identifies with the movements that propose to grant the "power" of computing and digital production to all those interested (digital democracy) [16]. Syllabus and digital base contents should be designed for contemporary teaching and learning spaces, according to AP_PDF, respecting differentiation, and the singular identity of students. The contents and intellectual challenges are aimed at establishing a relationship with knowledge in ten broad, in-depth points, considered structuring in the relationship with Digital knowledge, namely: (AL) Algorithm; (CS) Computational systems; (MLT) Multimedia; (DIK) Data, information, and knowledge; (DD) Design and Development; (EUT) Effective Use of Tools; (CN) Computer Networks; (P) Programming; (SP) Safety and Protection; (IT) Impact of Technology.

This element of the architecture referring to the relationship with knowledge is designed and adapted to 12 years of compulsory education in Portugal. The first years focus mainly on development of dexterity in digital skills, which helps students to understand how those digital devices, such as a keyboard, work, and what happens when a key is pressed and a letter or a symbol appears on the screen. As students advance in their schooling it will be necessary to introduce the concepts mentioned above. These paths through the pedagogical space of architecture, about what to teach include work in the dimensions of physical devices, in the dimensions of the logical and abstract components, and in the dimensions of their relationships with humans.

Regarding teaching methodologies, we propose conceptual adaptable spaces. Considering that digital literacy is a relatively recent subject in the curriculum, there is little specific scientific-pedagogical work able to illustrate teaching approaches. Given that lack of in-depth pedagogical studies in the area, we propose ten pedagogical principles for teaching digital literacy: Leading with concepts; Leading with error; Real-world activities; Collaborative work; Priority in reading and code exploration; Creation of projects; Physical connections (Hands on); Dismantling misconceptions; Writing texts; Adding variety to activities and challenges.

4.2 The Equipment - Designed to Teach

In this space of architecture, we should mention that a recent piece of equipment has been made available to the educational community - a trend for those who want to develop the relationship with digital knowledge [17]. This equipment is referred to as SBC (Single Board Computer), and is very similar to regular computers. It has, however, a significant physical difference, as this computer has the physical dimensions of a credit card. This equipment allows internet navigation, sending an email, or using any MS Office tool such as a word processor. It is possible to go further as the equipment allows establishing a physical link to electrical or electronic devices, via forty metallic pins included on the SBC board. The device can be programmed to provide or receive electrical impulses. This opens a universe of computational and construction possibilities not available on other desktop, laptop, or tablet computational devices. The low cost (around 70€) device was designed from scratch to teach digital production to youngsters. The SBC works as desktop or laptop, runs on a free and open operating system, and uses a memory card like those in digital cameras or mobile phones. A 'USB' charger of a mobile phone can power the SBC, it can be connected to a 'USB' mouse and keyboard and to a TV or monitor desktop. At school, this equipment can be an asset to teaching and learning, coding, and can help in dozens of other multi-disciplinary activities like science and music, for example.

To validate the viability of the digital literacy pedagogical architecture proposed, we designed and implemented a workshop for teacher training at the Porto Polytechnic Faculty of Education. The workshop design included: the reasons behind the relevance of the workshop (disruption); the target-audience; goals; contents; methods; and assessment. The workshop produced meaningful results – a multitude of strategies to the discovery and implementation of pedagogical approaches.

5 Conclusions

The paper begins with a clarification of the term "digital" to seek broad-acceptance terminology and to dismiss ambiguity. The proposed pedagogical architecture uses dedicated equipment designed for teaching, pedagogical strategies in syntony with prior epistemological assertions, empirical classroom experience in the creation of activities, curriculums mapping, plans, and support materials for teaching digital literacy.

The new ICT classroom proposed is now designed for teaching digital literacy. The current agenda for teaching digital literacy is embodied in a digital transformation policy that seeks greater digital empowerment. This digital empowerment should be achievable by combining digital skills with digital literacy to create a conscious relationship with the digital world. The AP_PDF addresses digital literacy by trying to deepen digital proficiency and awareness by teaching how technology works and not simply how to make use of it.

A disruptive pedagogical architecture might be the solution to achieve the goals set for 21st century digital literacy and break the patterns of traditional secondary education in Portugal. Our approach analysed current pedagogical trends and the contemporary pedagogical paradigm on digital literacy teaching tools and methods. The former paradigm is based on prior learning digital skills as instruments, procedures and attitudes culturally and contextually accepted. We have also analysed how digital literacy training follows a different path as it respects the relationship between form and function of the digital skills, in the teaching and learning process. Disruption of the paradigm emerged on the first stage of the design framework, which revealed that intensive repeated usage does not create knowledge, nor new digital assets, regardless of how new forms of training are adopted, or even how correct they are. Thus, we can assume this as an opportunity to propose the use of the term "digital" as a replacement to ICT, training for digital literacies instead of for digital skills. This opportunity is relevant in primary and secondary education. Considering literacy as an educational objective, the particularities of digital literacy must be considered - how digital reality appeared and how it was built, why was it built, what difficulties it had to assert itself, its successes and failure, challenges and evolution that have taken place. The paradigm disruption for digital literacy can be conveyed from early education by designing adequate learning environments for digital awareness, pedagogical methodologies, and 'feedback' structures that ensure that trial and error are developed in the process.

This pedagogical architecture was designed to generate disruption in the Portuguese ITC teaching culture and induce the migration to the teaching of digital literacy. Digital empowerment requires training students to become digital entrepreneurs instead of digital consumers. By providing disruption in the teaching and learning environments, inducing diversity, nurturing experimentation within the respect for epistemology, our pedagogical architecture proposal for digital literacy education can foster meaningful relationships with the digital society, to enable awareness of both concepts and tools, and a conscious relationship with digital knowledge. Though disruptive indeed, this is a path likely to aggregate digital awareness, technological awareness, and combine both with digital skills to achieve digital literacy.

References

1. Rubach, C., Lazarides, R.: Addressing 21st-century digital skills in schools – Development and validation of an instrument to measure teachers' basic ICT competence beliefs. Comput. Hum. Behav. **118**, 106636 (2021)
2. Castro, A., Miranda, J.C.: The PDF (Pensar Digital E Fazer) project. In: A Proof of Concept in Progress (T16) Scientix Conference (2016). http://files.eun.org/Scientix3conf/Scientix_3rd_Conf_Programme_Full-small.pdf
3. Castro, A.: SI2ME: Um Serviço de Informação para o trabalho no binómio monitorização-melhoria, no setor educativo não superior em Portugal. Universidade do Minho, Tese de Doutoramento (2016)
4. UE, Ministerial meeting during the German Presidency of the Council of 2020: Berlin Declaration on Digital Society and Value-Based Digital Government. Berlin. eu2020.de
5. Trindade, R., Cosme, A.: Educar E Aprender Na Escola. Vila Nova de Gaia: Fundação Manuel Leão (2010)
6. Cosme, A., Trindade, R.: Organização E Gestão Do Trabalho Pedagógico: Perspetivas, Questões, Desafios E Respostas. Mais Leitura (2013)
7. Hattie, J., Timperley, H.: The power of feedback. Rev. Educ. Res. **77**(1), 81–112 (2008)
8. Black, P., Wiliam, D.: Inside the black box: raising standards through classroom assessment. Phi delta kappan **92**(1), 81–90 (2010)
9. Vaishnavi, V.K., Kuechler, W.: Design Science Research Methods and Patterns: Innovating Information and Communication Technology. Taylor & Francis (2008)
10. Hevner: A three cycle view of design science research. Scand. J. Inf. Syst. **19**, 87 (2007)
11. Hevner, A., Chatterjee, S.: Design Science Research in Information Systems. Springer (2010)
12. Oblinger, D., Lippincott, J.K.: Learning Spaces, Boulder, Colo, EDUCAUSE, llustrations (2006)
13. Lippincott, J.K.: Learning spaces: involving faculty to improve pedagogy. Educause Rev. **44**(2), 16–25 (2009)
14. Woolner, P.: The Design of Learning Spaces. A&C Black (2010)
15. FCL.: Future Classroom Lab (2012). https://fcl.eun.org/about. 20 Jan 2001
16. Lewin, C., McNicol, S.: Creating the Future Classroom: Evidence from the iTEC Project: Summary Report (2014)
17. https://www.raspberrypi.org/app/uploads/2021/05/Understanding-computing-education-Volume-1-%E2%80%93-Raspberry-Pi-Foundation-Research-Seminars.pdf. Accessed 31 May 21

Use of *Vclass* in Mathematics Education Delivery: The UEW Experience

Peter Akayuure(✉)

Department of Mathematics Education, University of Education, Winneba, Ghana
pakayuure@uew.edu.gh

Abstract. The onset of Covid-19 pandemic has compelled institutions of higher learning to experiment with various online learning management modes, in lieu of the traditional face-to-face mode of instruction. However, conclusions about the effectiveness and sustainability of these new learning modes are not well-established. This study explored experiences of mathematics education lecturers and students who were first time users of an online learning management system referred to as *UEW vclass*. The sample comprised 10 students pursuing the degree of Bachelor of Mathematics Education and four lecturers who taught them five different courses at the University of Education Winneba (UEW), Ghana. Data were collected via interviews, and a survey item created on Google forms and administered through WhatsApp pages of respondents. The results of SWOT analysis show that lecturers found the *UEW vclass* useful and amenable to their teaching and assessment practices. As first-time users, the lecturers found the course creation, online delivery and e-assessment practices exciting, though challenging in terms of their digital and pedagogical skillset. Internet connectivity and system errors affected lecturers' real-time lesson delivery sessions while the trustworthiness of e-assessment scores was a serious concern. Students found the *UEW vclass* suitable, convenient, interesting, and user friendly. However, students' challenges were login, network, timing, real-time feedback and typing mathematical symbols. The paper therefore recommends an upgrade of network bandwidth to improve access, a built-in math symbols app, training and orientation of lecturers and students. The hybrid mode of learning is also recommended to enhance learning outcomes.

Keywords: Mathematics · Online experiences · LMS · UEW *vclass*

1 Introduction

The advent of the Covid-19 pandemic has rapidly influenced every domain of human existence and drifted human undertakings to a *new normal* in which social distancing becomes the norm. With the emergence of the new normal, educational institutions worldwide are beset with teaching, assessment and learning sustainability crises [1]. These crises compelled many educational managers and lecturers to rethink mathematics educational access and delivery, while students strive to adjust to new learning

Published by Springer Nature Switzerland AG 2022
D. Passey et al. (Eds.): OCCE 2021, IFIP AICT 642, pp. 179–191, 2022.
https://doi.org/10.1007/978-3-030-97986-7_15

systems external to the orthodox face-to-face mode. The quest to determine *which* and *how* learning platforms can be used for mathematics educational delivery remains unsettled.

Institutions of higher learning are quickly adapting to the crises. Universities across the world were obliged, after March 2020 lockdowns, to quickly migrate into purely online modes [2]. The people's Republic of China where the Covid-19 first hit, for example, moved fully into online platforms and implemented the "School's Out, But Class's On" policy to promote broad-based online teaching and learning to sustain academic work [3]. Universities in developing countries like Ghana, though unprepared, were also coerced to experiment with various online learning management systems in a bid to continue educational delivery [1, 4]. For example, new and emerging digital learning platforms such as Moodle, Sakai, Zoom, Edmodo, Quipper, Google meet, have been experimented in schools without prior evidences of their effectiveness, successes and shortfalls. For the past one and half years, there has been unprecedented push in Ghana towards online teaching, learning and assessment. Providers of commercial digital learning platforms also rushed to provide support and solutions to educational delivery, sometimes for free. Government of Ghana directives and regular updates of tensions and increasing spread of Covid-19 also obliged universities to sustain the drive towards online learning [1].

The University of Education Winneba (UEW) trains competent professional mathematics teachers for all levels of education in Ghana and the West African sub-region. Prior to March 2020, the move to online mathematics instructional delivery was met with resistance due to faculty deficiency in digital pedagogy, low ICT infrastructure and resources, as well as a lack of student support systems. When Ghana recorded its first case of the Covid-19 in March 12, 2020, culminating in lockdowns and closure of all institutions on 16th of March, 2020, the academic calendar was disrupted [4]. UEW was therefore compelled to devise innovative ways of using Learning Management Systems (LMS) to enable students to learn at home amidst the pandemic, to bring the 2019/2020 academic year to a successful close. After some few weeks of experimenting various low cost and open learning sources such as Zoom, WhatsApp, Google class and Telegram, UEW management finally mandated its faculty and students to use the LMS called *vclass* as an official platform for online learning [5].

The UEW *vclass* is a Moodle based platform enhanced with BigBlueButton for live video lecturing which can be recorded, saved and played back online or offline. In the *vclass*, lecturers are given privileges to create and develop courses, upload course materials onto the online platform and subsequently engage students in learning using e-resources such as chats, forum discussions, assignments, quizzes and downloadable materials. All lectures, live videos, study materials and assessment data are stored in UEW server for retrieval. To facilitate its use, UEW ICT directorate provided short time training and hotline support system for faculty to create courses, teach in front of a computer screen and implement e-assessment. Students were also given virtual orientation on how to login to the vclass, enroll for courses, access study materials and participate in lesson delivery and assessment online, while at home. A diagrammatically representation of the UEW *vclass* is shown in Fig. 1.

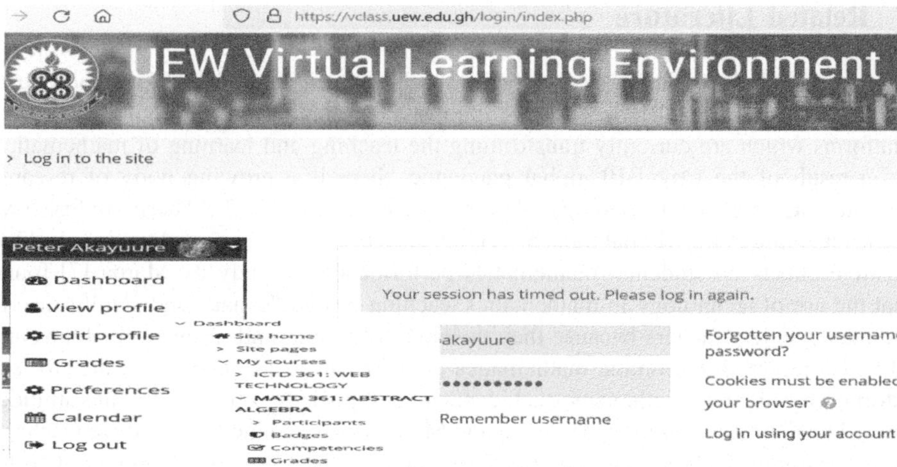

Fig. 1. The interface of the UEW vclass

As a result of the Covid-19 pandemic and digital experiences, UEW plans to emphasise, consolidate and serve as a pace setter of online instructional delivery for its regular, sandwich, and distance modes beyond the Covid-19 era. However, due to the swift and abrupt nature of moving courses online, and as first-time users of the *vclass*, lecturers and students are likely to encounter challenges or discover some potential of the *vclass* [4]. In other words, attempts to sustain this new innovation of using the *UEW vclass* for mathematics education delivery in UEW require an understanding of the new dilemmas and contextual issues regarding ICT infrastructures, faculty capacity, and students' support and welfare. Around the world, researchers and educators are trying to research into the paradigm shift from the face-to-face learning to online education and users' experiences [6]. This is because understanding users' experiences in online learning platforms is crucial to its success and sustainability. This study therefore mirrors students' and their lecturers' experiences in the use of the *UEW vclass* platform to learn various courses in mathematics education in UEW.

The study was guided by the following research questions:

1. How do lecturers and students experience the use of *vclass* to teach and learn mathematics courses?
2. What are the challenges faced by lecturers and their students in using the *vclass* in the teaching and learning of mathematics courses?

It is hoped that this empirical data on how lecturers and their students experience and adjust to the new learning system to meet curriculum requirements would help in decision-making towards improvement and sustainability of *vclass* in UEW. Evidence from this study would also provide first-hand information that would shed light on the strengths, weaknesses, opportunities and threats (SWOT) regarding deployment of emerging digital platforms in mathematics instructional delivery in the Covid-19 pandemic era and beyond, in developing countries such as Ghana.

2 Related Literature

Advances in digital technology have given birth to a new era referred to as the Fourth Industrial Revolution (4IR). The 4IR comprises technology-based tools and digital platforms which are currently transforming the teaching and learning of mathematics. As a result of the Covid-19 global pandemic, there is a growing body of research currently focusing on technology platforms in education [2, 7]. These studies have shown that integrating digital tools in mathematics pedagogy supports learning, and has positive effects on students' mathematics performance. A study by Marpa [7] found that the use of technology in mathematics teaching bears relevance and significance to the mathematics teachers because they develop positive attitudes toward it. Johns and Mills [2] reported that online mathematics tutoring can be as effective as face-to-face tutoring on students' mathematics achievement and positive self-concept, and attitudes toward mathematics learning. Mulenga and Marbán [6] examined prospective teachers' online learning mathematics activities in the age of the Covid-19 pandemic. Cluster analysis revealed that students engaged in the online learning of mathematics activities exhibited excellent online learning skills for mathematics in technology-rich environments. Ricker [8] utilised Hrastinski's theory of online learning as online participation and Moore's 3 types of interactions model of online student behaviour to determine whether 2 types of student LMS interactions could predict mathematics course performance. The study concluded that student clicks navigating the course content pages, and the number of times a student accessed resources, predicted student mathematics performance after allowing for the effects of student demographic covariates. Finally, according to a study [6], online learning in mathematics maximises personalised education of every student, and promotes sense of freedom during the Covid-19 isolation period. The study proposes a comprehensive and advanced pedagogic design to render lessons through virtual classrooms during and beyond the Covid-19 age.

While there are evidences in the literature about the advantages of online mathematics instruction, other studies have reported various challenges and barriers that users of technology encountered in the learning process [6]. In terms of challenges Agormedah, et al. [4] in a descriptive phenomenology study, found that poor internet connectivity and high cost of data were challenges faced by students. Owusu-Fordjour, et al. [9], said the high cost of internet data is one of the major challenges hindering students' online learning in Ghana. Tsitsia, et al. [10] revealed that students are also distracted mostly by home related factors. They recommended a blended teaching to manage cost and internet data usage, and prepare students in physical and virtual classrooms experiences.

In terms of barriers, Mailizar, et al. [11] categorised online learning barriers into student, teacher, curriculum and school levels. Student level barriers include skill and knowledge, motivation and e-learning infrastructure. Teacher level barriers comprise confidence, knowledge, belief and experience. Curriculum level barriers include structure of contents, assessment and e-learning resources that are aligned to the curriculum while at school level these consist of availability of software and hardware, internet, textbooks, school policy, time and technical support. These evidences suggest that the use of online learning platforms come with various challenges. Naidoo [12] found that most mathematics teachers are hesitant in using technology in their classroom, even though there are many digital applications and websites that can support learning and improve mathematics achievement. In the case of *vclass*, little is documented about users' experiences and challenges in learning mathematics, particularly in developing countries such as Ghana. This study seeks to fill the gap and to provide information about its sustainability. Due to the Covid-19 pandemic, Mulenga and Marbán [6] posited that "we are being challenged to think in different ways, to solve problems together, to collaborate and to communicate in different ways, to educate and be educated in a different way" (p. 3). In view of this, evidence from this study may serve as a lesson for the mathematics education community of learning regarding the prospects of deploying online learning management systems.

2.1 Conceptual Framework

The study focused on first time users' experiences of the LMS referred to as *vclass*. The users' experiences are conceptualised and framed as Strengths, Weakness, Opportunities and Threats (SWOT). These are constructs adopted from SWOT analysis conducted by Businessmen to identify viability of business setups. The strength of vclass refers to its ability to replace face-to-face instruction and facilitate effective online teaching, learning and assessment of mathematics. To support the use of the *vclass*, it is expedient to determine from the users' perspective if this strength was met, and to identify the weakness encountered by users in terms of challenges and barriers. As a new mode of instructional delivery, it would also be apposite to understand the opportunities that exist with deployment of *vclass* in teaching and learning mathematics as well as the threats resulting from refusal or complete abandonment of the system at student, lecturer or school levels.

3 Methodology

This qualitative study relies on the interpretive paradigm, and views experiences of people as ontologically internal and epistemologically subjective in nature. Therefore, the study views lecturers and students' *vclass* experiences as personal constructions which are subjectively and qualitatively interpreted. Collecting and analysing qualitative data provides better opportunity to understand practicality/usability issues as well as challenges of lecturers and students in the use of the *vclass*.

3.1 Participants

Participants for the study comprised ten students (3 in 4th year, 3 in 3rd year and 4 in 2nd year), and four of their lecturers. The students were pursuing the Bachelor of Mathematics Education programme, UEW. These students were contacted randomly, and they voluntarily shared their experiences in the use of the *vclass*. By the structure of UEW mathematics education courses, the students were exposed to ICT courses including Introduction to use of ICT tools, Basic programming techniques and Courseware design using multimedia tools. All of them disclosed they were intermediate users of ICT tools. Five of the participants reside on the university campus. The other five also reside outside campus, and did not have access to the university Wi-Fi network at their place of residence, except when on campus.

The four lecturers engaged the students in different courses using the *vclass*. One lecturer taught Ordinary differential equations and Partial differential equations. The other three lecturers taught Mechanics, Vector algebra and Methods of teaching senior high school mathematics respectively. Two were male lecturers who described their ICT proficiency as basic, while one male lecturer was at advanced proficiency level in ICT. The only female lecturer described her ICT proficiency level as intermediate. To assure the participants of their anonymity, only pseudonyms were used in this study.

3.2 Data Collection and Analysis

Data were collected through an open-ended item survey, and interviews. The open-ended item was constructed in Google forms to gather data on challenges encountered in using the *vclass*. Accompanying the Google forms was an informed consent message outlining the study purpose, the use of the data for publications, and participants' right not to respond to the item. Unstructured interview sessions were also conducted online with the ten students and four lecturers to share their experiences and challenges of *vclass* usage.

The interview data were transcribed and analysed by coding and categorising into themes and subthemes based on the SWOT constructs described earlier in this study. Open coding was first done to familiarise with the data, scrutinise and organise codes. This was followed by processing of codes, creating connections, and the grouping of excerpts of data into themes reflecting SWOT constructs in using the *vclass*. As recommended by Fusch and Ness [13], the principle of data saturation was applied to end further codes when it became obvious that responses produced were similar, or no new information or further coding were feasible. To ensure trustworthiness, clarity and accuracy of results, member checking was undertaken with participants. The data file on challenges in the use of *vclass* was download from Google forms. The file was then imported into INVIVO 12.0 software and run to obtain word cloud and reference codes of words that demonstrate the frequency of challenges encountered by students and lecturers.

4 Results

This section presents the experiences and challenges of the lecturers and students who used *vclass* as a teaching and learning platform. The interviews revealed that lecturers relied more on their personal computers, while smartphones were the main devices used by students in most of the interactions in the *vclass*. All the students interviewed admitted they mainly used the mobile phones, but occasionally used personal computers or tablets. This means that the students relied more on their own devices and data to access the *vclass* since they could not access the university Wi-Fi at home. When students rely on their own data to connect online, it is likely that they may not visit the *vclass* frequently for interactions, downloads or uploads of study materials [8].

4.1 Mathematics Lecturers' Experience in the Use of *Vclass*

The interview responses of the lecturers who shared their *vclass* experiences are presented in the following subthemes.

A. *Vclass* as a Course Creation Platform
The lecturers had different expressions regarding the user friendliness of the *vclass*. They said that the *vclass* was quite convenient, exciting and flexible to use in creating courses online in one's own time and space. The lecturers, however, pointed out that they had limited digital expertise to create courses on *vclass* but were able to learn new digital skills in content generation and course development, as articulated in the following excerpts:

> *Akos: the vclass has provided flexibility in terms of creating the course and course delivery. Of course you can be at the comfort of your home, create the course and upload online... Again, in term of course creation . . . , it has helped to learn new technical skills . . . learning how to create the course and upload them online.*
>
> *Aliu: We don't have even the expertise of creating the course online. So we were experimenting, try and error kind of...*

These responses support previous findings [11, 12] that first time course creators are often threatened by limited digital skills. However, they also tend to develop new digital pedagogies when they engage in developing courses online.

B. *Vclass* as a Platform for Delivery of Lectures
In *vclass*, all instructions are delivered to students online by text, audio and/or video with BigBlueButton. Expressing their experience of *vclass* lectures, the lecturers claimed the *vclass* was a suitable platform for virtual communication, collaboration and interaction with students, and for monitoring attendance. They admitted, however, that they had limited skills in presenting mathematics content on *vclass,* and felt it might be impossible to demonstrate mathematical concepts, show procedures and write mathematical symbols on the *vclass* as revealed in the following excerpts:

> *Akos: It has helped to improve virtual communication and collaboration . . . I think the vclass has made me a more effective communicator. I will have to be more efficient in relaying information to the students. You have ample time to spend on the vclass interacting with the students.*
>
> *Atua You'll be able to see those that are able to login . . . like checking attendance . . . [But] there is that inability to communicate effectively with the students online . . . it is very difficult [with] video conferencing.*
>
> *Aliu: I was teaching ordinary differential equations [with] symbols . . . all these symbols were not found in Vclass.*

These responses reveal the opportunities and threats which come with the deployment of emerging technology in teaching mathematics. Indeed, in the fourth industrial revolution led by technology [12], digital communication, collaboration, and interaction skills are undoubtedly key skills needed for active instructional delivery and workplace interactions. However, acquiring these skills depends on one's exposure or experience.

C. *Vclass* as E-assessment Platform

Regarding activities and resources for implementing e-assessment such as online quizzes, assignments and examinations, the lecturers shared their experiences in the interviews as follows.

Atua: when you give a quiz which is objectives you don't have to worry. The thing [vclass] will do the arrangement for you, mark for you, then you download the spreadsheet.

Akos: And another exciting thing is . . . how to create a question bank . . . it was exciting to do those things.

Adua: I downloaded all . . . the soft copies . . . marked as hard copies . . . I was having problem with the screen marking.

Aliu: . . . not sure if the actual student answered the assignment.

These responses illustrate the usefulness of the *vclass* in assisting lecturers to mark and store assessment results for future retrieval. Particularly, the development of a question bank was a new and exciting aspect expressed by the lecturers. There were, however, some frustrations as lecturers attempted to transfer the usual face-to-face assessment practices onto online assessment practices. While the frustrations might threaten the sustenance of *vclass*, research [2] suggests that they can also lead to new learning curve and opportunity for lecturers to devise novel ways to conduct valid and reliable e-assessment.

D. *Vclass* as an Innovative Way of Supplementary Face-to-face Teaching

The interview responses revealed that the lecturers valued the use of the *vclass* as innovation to the face-to-face interactions despite systems errors as highlighted below.

Akos: It is innovative way of teaching. . . . [that] should not be abandoned.

Adua: . . . I think . . . this vclass . . . we can upload things for students to get access to it first hand before . . . [But] it was impossible for 100 students to be enrolled.

Atua: [Vclass] is a record keeper like a database.

Aliu: The shared screen was a terrible one . . . [the] screen doesn't work.

The lecturers' responses suggest that *vclass* could serve as a database of students and lecturers' activities and interactions. The lecturers, however, lamented the video streaming errors with the BigBlueButton, system login errors and download/upload errors resulting from large enrolment, large videos, or mathematical symbols.

4.2 Mathematics Students' Experience in the Use of *Vclass*

Students' responses during the interviews are presented in subthemes as follows.

A. *Vclass* as Positive Intervention in the Era of Covid-19
All ten students expressed the view that it was the right intervention by the university to have introduced the *vclass* in the era of Covid-19 as exemplified here:

> *Sama: [I]t is something good . . . as we all know to help in terms of this crisis so that they can help finish our course outline on time.*
> *Ssala: it was big intervention management took . . . myself it helped me to put into practice my ICT.*

Students' comments reflect their feeling that the *vclass* can be a potential platform for addressing the mathematics learning crisis.

B. *Vclass* as a Platform for Uploading and Downloading Study Materials
The following excerpts show how three students responded to the issue of study materials.

> *Ssala: . . . some of the lecturers upload a video in a form of teaching and then you will listen.*
> *Sadu: they only put slides on the LMS, some courses you will only go and see slides on the LMS, no explanation.*
> *Saku: Is not that interactive . . . sometimes they only put slides on the LMS . . . and that doesn't help.*

These comments reveal that students view the vclass as a platform where lecturers produce mathematical content in the form of video, audio and text and upload it for them to download and learn at their own pace and time. It also reveals that the materials presented to students were not quite interactive for self-study, and did not meet their learning needs.

C. *Vclass* as a Favourable and Useful Instructional Platform
In terms of instructional delivery, students responded that the *vclass* was useful as illustrated in the following excerpts:

Sadu: It helps in finishing the course outline on time . . . the number of weeks in a semester and the workload meeting face-to-face for 2 hours every week would not help. So the LMS has come to help . . . so much in exploring much in internet.
Satia . . . lecturers upload a video in . . . you will listen and . . . involve almost all your senses like your ears, your eyes, everything is very attentive just like how you do it in the lecture room . . . you are relaxed.
Ssala: the LMS was able to make lessons to go fast. We are able to complete most of the topics compared to the face to face.

These comments illustrate that students view the *vclass* as comparable to face-to-face teaching and as an opportunity to explore the internet anytime and anywhere. Thus, through the *vclass*, students gained skills by taking the courses and conducted research online to develop their own learning.

D. *Vclass* as an E-assessment Platform
In terms of assessment, students expressed views that reflect both the opportunities and weaknesses of using *vclass* for e-assessment, as exemplified in the following two excerpts.

Sama: . . . the assignment and exams were marked by the LMS, especially the multiple-choice.
Ssule: we were not getting much feedback from the lecturers anyway, so if the LMS will also be improved in such a way that there can be some prompt feedback from the lecturers.

Students' responses suggest that even though the *vclass* supports e-assessment and eases the workload of lecturers, they did not receive prompt feedback from their lecturers.

4.3 Challenges Experienced by Lecturers and Students in Using *Vclass*

Word Cloud using INVIVO 12.0 software was used to categorise the data according to the most occurring challenges in terms of system functioning, course creation, lesson delivery, and assessment and support services experienced by both lecturers and students. The results are presented in Figs. 2 and 3.

Fig. 2. Lecturers' most frequent challenges in vclass

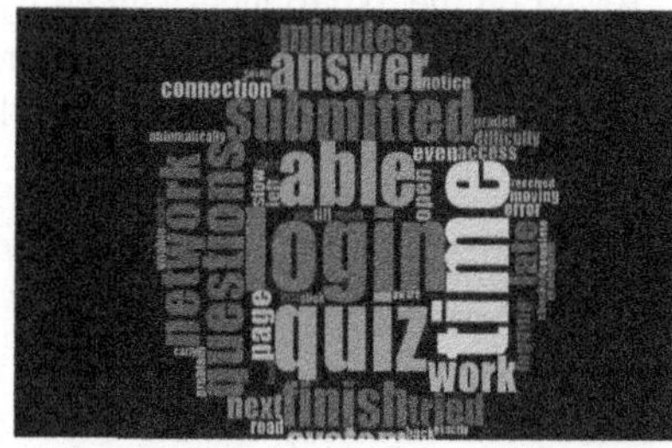

Fig. 3. Students' most frequent challenges in vclass

Figure 2 shows that the most frequent or pronounced challenge encountered by lecturers was *time* i.e. *time* to create course and questions bank, *time* for students to answer questions, and *time* to give marks online. This was followed by *questions* to set, and *login* to do quizzes and submit online. Issues concerning system network, answers and mathematics symbols were other frequently occurring challenges faced by lecturers in the use of the *vclass* (Fig. 2). Also, Fig. 3 shows that the most frequent or pronounced challenge encountered by students was *login*, followed by *time* and *quiz* submission on vclass. These issues were mentioned 42, 42 and 40 times by the students. These challenges demonstrate the level of students' frustrations and anxieties in the use of *vclass*.

5 Conclusion

The study shows that *vclass* experiences of lecturers and students can be summarised into strengths, weaknesses, opportunities and threats. The strengths were internal positive attributes of *vclass* that allowed users to operate efficiently to achieve their learning goals. The study found that the *vclass* platform was easy to create courses, deliver live video lessons using BigBlueButton, create question bank and e-assessment including system marking, quiz, assignment, chat, forums, etc. The weaknesses included aspects that affected lecturers' and students' effective use of the *vclass* platform. In this study, these were lack of quick feedback, low digital literacy levels, lack of mathematical symbols, and inability to conduct practical lessons. The opportunities were experiences that could be leveraged to gain advantage in the use of the *vclass* in learning mathematics. These included improvement in the digital skillset of students, and the digital pedagogy of lecturers, transformation of e-assessment skills of lecturers, promotion of the reuse of existing courses, use of assessment data in research/decision making, and the adoption of a hybrid mode of mathematics instructions. The threats were activities that negatively impacted on the effective use of the *vclass*. In this study, these comprised assessment security, registration challenges, and login and network problems.

Based on the experiences shared by lecturers and students, the study concludes that there are more strengths and opportunities than weakness and threats when *vclass* is used for mathematics instructional delivery. Hence, the *vclass* should be encouraged and sustained.

6 Recommendations

The study recommends that the UEW should improve the bandwidth and connectivity, and include a Maths built-in app to facilitate effective online interaction among mathematics lecturers and their students. There is also the need for the university to organise training and professional development sessions for lecturers on the principles and theories of instructional design, course creation, digital pedagogy and e-assessment. Lecturers should be trained on how to use data in the *vclass* for research, SWOT analysis and decision-making regarding performance, assessment and online interactions. Students should also be provided with regular orientation and support services at departmental levels, to enable them to adjust to the new learning platform. Finally, the study recommends a hybrid mode of mathematics teaching and learning to enable both lecturers and students to make amends for the weaknesses and threats associated with the *vclass*.

References

1. Murugesa, S., Chidambaram, N.: Success of online teaching and learning in higher education-covid 19 pandemic: a case study valley view university Ghana. Int. J. Appl. Eng. Res. **15**(7), 735–738 (2020). http://www.ripublication.com
2. Johns, C., Mills, M.: Online mathematics tutoring during the covid-19 pandemic: recommendations for best practices. Primus **31**(1), 99–117 (2021). https://doi.org/10.1080/10511970.2020.1818336
3. Zhou, L., Li, F., Wu, S., Zhou, M.: "School's Out, But Class's On", the largest online education in the world today: taking China's practical exploration during the covid-19 epidemic prevention and control as an example. Best Evid. China Educ. **4**(2), 501–519 (2020). https://doi.org/10.15354/bece.20.ar023
4. Agormedah, E.K., Henaku, E.A., Ayite, D.M.K., Ansah, E.A.: Online learning in higher education during Covid-19 pandemic: a case of Ghana. J. Educ. Technol. Online Learn. **3**(3), 183–210 (2020)
5. University of Education Winneba Learning Management System (UEW LMS). https://vclass.uew.edu.gh/login/index.php
6. Mulenga, E.M., Marbán, J.M.: Prospective teachers' online learning mathematics activities in the age of Covid-19: a cluster analysis approach. EURASIA J. Math. Sci. Technol. Educ. **16**(9), em1872 (2020)
7. Marpa, E.P.: Technology in the teaching of mathematics: an analysis of teachers' attitudes during the Covid-19 pandemic. Int. J. Stud. Educ. **3**(2), 92–102 (2021)
8. Ricker, G.M.: Student Learning Management System Interactions and Performance via a Learning Analytics Perspective. Walden Dissertations and Doctoral Studies. 6656 (2019)

9. Owusu-Fordjour, C., Koomson, C., Hanson, D.: The impact of Covid-19 on learning - the perspective of the Ghanaian student. Eur. J. Educ. Stud. **7**, 88–101 (2020). https://doi.org/10.5281/zenodo.3753586
10. Tsitsia, B.Y., Kabbah, S.K., Doyi, V., Kabe, S.K., Safo, P.: Colleges of education student-teachers' perceptions on the e-learning in the era of covid-19 pandemic. Eur. J. Educ. Stud. **7** (12), 561–571 (2020)
11. Mailizar, M., Almanthari, A., Maulina, S., Bruce, S.: Secondary school mathematics teachers' views on e-learning implementation barriers during the Covid-19 pandemic: the case of Indonesia. Eurasia J. Math. Sci. Technol. Educ. **16**(7), 1–7 (2020)
12. Naidoo, J.: Postgraduate mathematics education students' experiences of using digital platforms for learning within the Covid-19 pandemic era. Pythagoras **41**(1), 568 (2020)
13. Fusch, P., Ness, L.: Are we there yet? Data saturation in qualitative research. Qual. Rep. **20** (9), 1408–1416 (2015). http://www.nova.edu/ssss/QR/QR20/9/fusch1.pdf

Needs and Challenges of Smart Agriculture and Entrepreneurship Education – A Case Study by the University of Agricultural Sciences, Dharwad, Karnataka, India

M. B. Chetti, K. V. Ashalatha, and S. S. Dolli(✉)

University of Agricultural Sciences, Dharwad, Karnataka, India
{vc, dolliss}@uasd.in

Abstract. India has a history of more than 100 years of organised teaching, research and development of agriculture, and has grown from few teaching and research institutes at the beginning of 20th century to one of the most productive, vibrant and advanced agricultural systems in the world. Agriculture plays a vital role in the Indian economy and contributes 17.4% to the country's GDP. Government of India has launched several programmes for sustainable development and the state of Karnataka now aspires to be the national hub for smart agriculture. The University of Agricultural Sciences, Dharwad (UASD) has been exploring the possibility of establishing the Centre of Excellence in smart agriculture with the objective of skilling, re-skilling and up-skilling agriculture graduates, and to provide industry-ready man power and to educate farmers through the use of ICT. The university has been a pioneer in imparting quality agriculture education, and has introduced digital technology in several domains. A thrust has been given to areas such as agri-informatics in precision agriculture, conservation agriculture, mechanisation, use of robotics, drone technology, artificial intelligence, machine learning, cloud computing, trade and market intelligence, weather forecast and developing suitable agri-web-portals. The role of agri-business and agricultural entrepreneurship is critical in the overall economy of many developing countries. UASD is implementing a World Bank funded Institution Development Plan (IDP) under National Agriculture Higher Education Project (NAHEP) which has a prime objective of developing entrepreneurship and promoting start-ups. The UASD is utilising digital technology in order to empower students, staff and farmers in future digital agriculture and allied sectors.

Keywords: Smart agriculture · Entrepreneurship · Start-up · Higher education · Digital transformation

1 Introduction

India has a history of more than 100 years of organised teaching, research and development of agriculture and has grown from few teaching and research institutes at the beginning of 20th century to one of the most productive, vibrant and advanced agricultural systems in the world. Starting with only 17 Agricultural, three Veterinary

Published by Springer Nature Switzerland AG 2022
D. Passey et al. (Eds.): OCCE 2021, IFIP AICT 642, pp. 192–201, 2022.
https://doi.org/10.1007/978-3-030-97986-7_16

and one Agri. Engineering colleges in 1950, now the country has 63 State Agricultural Universities (SAU), four Deemed Universities (DU), three Central Agricultural Universities (CAU) and four Central Universities with more than 400 constituent colleges, and intake capacity has risen from less than 5,000 to more than 50,000. The Indian Council of Agricultural Research (ICAR) - SAU Model has been quite successful and adopted in many Asian and African countries. The Government has made substantial investment for development of research capacity within the ICAR and SAUs. ICAR has provided leadership, resources and environment for development of a pluralistic system, and also facilitated partnership with international organisations which paid rich dividends in terms of making the country self-sufficient in food production, diversifying production and reducing rural poverty.

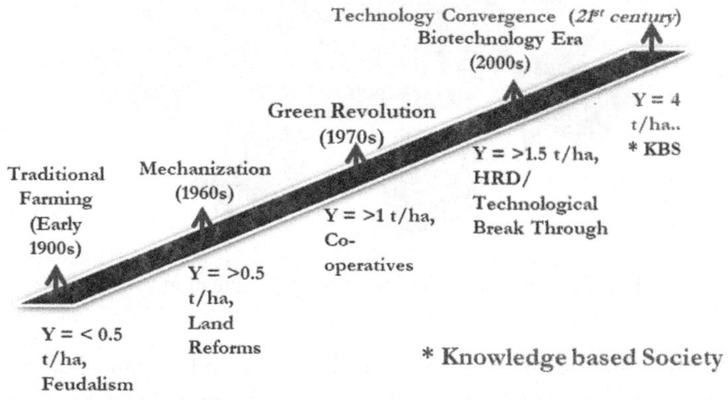

Fig. 1. Distinct transitions: history of agriculture.

India has achieved a significant improvement in the productivity of food grains from the level of 0.5 t/ha in 1900 to 4 tones/ha in 2021.This was made possible due to several interventions such as mechanisation in the 1960s, followed by a green revolution (1970s) and biotechnology in 2000 (Fig. 1). The Indian Council of Agricultural Research (ICAR) - SAU Model has been quite successful, and was adopted in many Asian and African countries. The Government has made substantial investment for development of research capacity within the ICAR and SAUs. ICAR has provided leadership, resources and environment for the development of a pluralistic system, and also facilitated partnership with international organisations which paid rich dividends in terms of making the country self-sufficient in food production, diversifying production and reducing rural poverty.

ICAR is the nodal agency for Research and Development and the Agriculture Minister of Government of India is the President. The Director General and Secretary DARE (Directorate of Agricultural Research and Education is the executive head. It has seven divisions, namely natural resource management, crop science, horticulture science, animal science, fisheries science, agriculture education, agricultural engineering and agricultural extension. It has research centers on different crops located in different agro climatic zones of India.

National Agriculture Research Education System (NARS) is one of the largest in the World. In addition to universities and colleges, it has 101 ICAR institutes, 79 All India coordinated research projects (AICRP) and 721 Krishi Vignan Kendras (Farm Science centers) (Fig. 2). The widely spread and specific NARS system established strong linkage with research, extension and the education systems in India. AICRP and KVK are part of State Agriculture Universities, ICAR closely linked with all State Agricultural Universities (SAU).

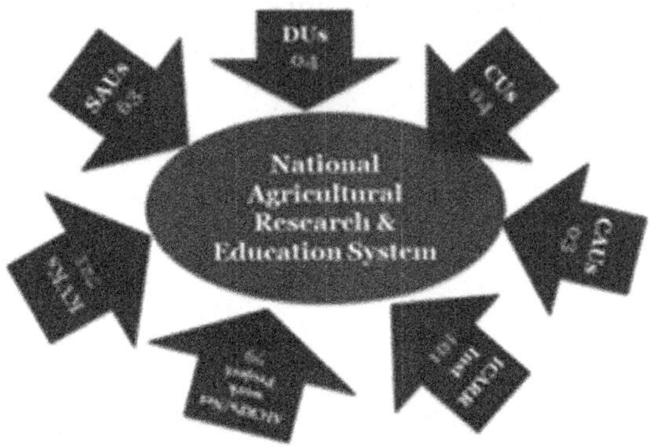

Fig. 2. National agriculture research education system.

Several new initiatives have been introduced in the education system in India that includes, implementation of fifth Deans Committee Recommendations with a focus on Experiential Learning and student READY (Rural Entrepreneurship Awareness and Development Yojana) programmes, apart from including several new courses in emerging areas of Science and Technology. This has brought a major qualitative and quantitative impact in the teaching and learning process.

Some consider entrepreneurship as a very specific occupation, related to Schumpeter's creative as a key driver of economic growth and job creation [2]. This is also the most common reason [3] why researchers and experts promote entrepreneurship education. Lingelbach [4] suggested that, "Yet, entrepreneurship in developing countries is arguably the least studied significant economic and social phenomenon in the world today."

Higher education in India is well established, and caters to the needs of a growing population. Some of the facts about higher education in India include, 993 Universities, and under these universities there are 39,931 colleges affiliated to them. In addition, there are 10,725 standalone institutions. Total enrolment of students in higher education is 37.4 million (19.2 million male & 18.2 million female), out of which 79.8% study in undergraduate degree programmes (maximum in B.A., B.Sc., B.Com.). There are only 0.5% (1,69,710) in doctoral programmes (PhD) mostly in science, followed by engineering and technology.

2 Key Challenges and Policies for Higher Agricultural Education

There are needs to balance elements in the higher agricultural education, that includes balancing tradition and change, building universities as innovation hubs, improving leadership in universities – learning lessons of strategic management from the best in business, and the role of online learning in reforming India's education system.

The present strategy is to align the agricultural education system in tune with the National Education Policy (NEP) – 2020 of Govt. of India [1]. The national education policy 2020 is distinct and broad-based and gives choices to the students to pursue their interest, and to excel in the area of their interest apart from giving a thrust to skill acquisition. The NEP 2020 vision is to enhance the Gross Enrolment Ratio (GER) of higher education to reach at least 50% by 2035. The present GER is 26.8% as compared to USA (86.7%), Germany (65.5%), and China (39.4%).

NEP 2020 includes many features listed below:

1) It emphasises large, multidisciplinary universities and colleges.
2) Liberal and flexible undergraduate programmes.
3) Faculty and institutional autonomy.
4) National Research Foundation.
5) Better regulatory system.
6) Expansion and improvement of new architecture, research universities, teaching.
7) Universities and colleges; degree by granting powers to them.
8) Overall changes from school level to faculty upgradation.

Several policy initiatives are taken in enhancing industry-academia linkage, Alumni network, dual degree programmes, and specialised courses for entrepreneurship, skill and personality development. The visibility of Indian universities is enhanced through attracting international students mainly from African and Asian countries. To enhance faculty competence, both ICAR and State Governments are encouraging training programmes both at national and international level in cutting-edge technologies. UASD is in the forefront in establishing entrepreneurial and start up eco systems. Important ones are listed below:

1) Encouraging startup culture through funding from RKVY-RAFTAAR of the Government of India, ICAR-NAHEP of the World Bank.
2) Biotechnology Industry Research Assistance Council (BIRAC) of the Department of Biotechnology, the Government of India.
3) Karnataka Innovation and Technology Society (KITS) from the Government of Karnataka.

With the implementation of new policies, there is likely to be enhancement in Gross Enrollment Ratio (GER) in higher education, which eventually may lead to India becoming a USD 5 trillion economy by 2025. apart from sustaining Gross Domestic Product (GDP) growth rate.

The development and usage of a Smart Agriculture system based on artificial intelligence and machine learning is changing the agriculture sector by not only improving the crop production, but also making it cost effective. Recognising the importance of artificial intelligence (AI), the National Institution for Transforming India (NITI) Aayog initiated a National Programme on AI, with a view to guiding research and development in new and emerging technologies. Considering the growing acceptance of farmers for the internet and mobile based services, the Indian Council of Agriculture Research (ICAR) made an attempt to provide valuable agro-met information to the users through web portal (Crop Weather Outlook) which provides 'Value Added Agro-advisory Reports'. University of Agricultural Sciences (UAS) Dharwad has excelled in the area of smart agriculture and entrepreneurship development. The University stands in the 9th rank at national level and first in the state.

3 Agriculture Education and Careers

The role of agricultural education is to provide improved, relevant and effective teaching [5]. Nawaz, [6] referred to the lack of business education in agriculture, and Knudson [7] confirmed that agricultural entrepreneurship is at an early stage of development. Inadequate education and training as well as technological know-how make small businesses less competitive and more vulnerable to the economic downturn [8]. Agricultural education as under-graduation and post-graduation is available to the students in State Agricultural Universities (SAU) as well as Central Universities (CU). The students seeking admission for under-graduation programmes must have studied two years of pre-university course (PUC). There are total of 71 Agricultural Universities in India spread in different states. The respective state conducts a Combined Entrance Test (CET) for the students, and selects the students based on the merit of both their regular exam and the marks obtained in the CET. Universities follow guidelines of the state government with respect to the quota/reservation of seats for different categories such as a Scheduled Caste (SC), Scheduled Tribes (ST) and otherclasses. The Undergraduate course of BSc. Agriculture, Horticulture, Sericulture etc., are for the period of four years. During the last decade, the competition for admission to agricultural courses has increased due to more job opportunities in government and private sectors.

Students join the course with different aspirations and aspire for a job such as an appointment in government organisations, universities, and jobs in banks.

Table 1. Placements of graduates of UAS Dharwad, during 2008 to 2018.

Sl. No	Career working field	Number	Percentage
1	Government jobs	300	37
2	Private	393	49
3	Bank	33	4
4	Entrepreneurs	60	8
5	Farming	20	2

The analysis of the data of the passed-out students from 2008 to 2018 reveal that, 49% of the students secured job in private sector followed by government jobs (37%), banks (4%). Only 8% choose to become entrepreneurs, and 2% opted for farming (Table 1 and Fig. 3).

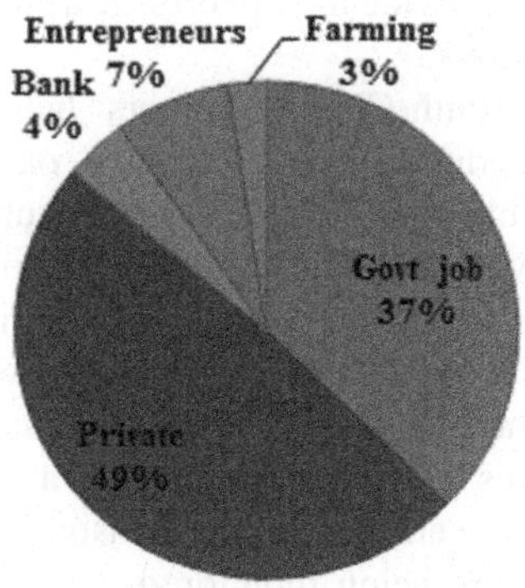

Fig. 3. Placements of graduates of UAS Dharwad during last 10 years.

It clearly indicates that students are more oriented towards the Government or a private job, rather than starting their own enterprise.

4 Smart Agriculture Initiatives at UAS Dharwad

Agriculture plays a vital role in the Indian economy and contributes 17.4% to the country's GDP. The Government of India has launched several programmes for sustainable development and state of Karnataka now aspires to be the national hub for smart agriculture. The University of Agricultural Sciences, Dharwad, has been exploring the possibility of establishing the Centre of Excellence in smart agriculture, with the objectives of skilling, re-skilling and up-skilling agriculture graduates, thus providing industry with ready manpower, to educate farmers through the use of ICT. The university has been a pioneer in imparting quality agriculture education, and has introduced digital technology in several domains. The thrust has been given to agri-informatics in precision agriculture, conservation agriculture, mechanisation, use of robotics, drone technology, artificial intelligence, machine learning, cloud computing, trade and market intelligence, weather forecasting. And developing suitable agri-web-portals. Efforts have been made in implementing an Academic Management System (AMS), a Human Resource Management System (HRMS), a Public Finance Management System (PFMS), and other web portals in daily activities of the university. Farmers are educated through university-owned FM radio, sending updated information on weather, outbreak of pest and diseases, and timely management practices through mobile apps and SMS.

In view of the COVID-19 pandemic during 2020, on line classes and on-line examinations have become regular phenomena. To facilitate the students in better learning, all the course contents are digitised and uploaded on the university website. The proposed Centre of Excellence in Smart Agriculture will have training modules for agriculture informatics, simulations, agriculture equipment design and modifications, machine learning and imaging. It is also proposed to create the digital assets, develop Virtual Learning (VR) ready contents, and develop 3-D contents on advanced/smart agri-technologies. Which will provide a wonderful learning experience not only for the students, but also for the farmers.

An agri-war-room called Raith Chetan (farmers' helpline) has been established to help the farmers not only by educating them, on-line, on cultivation practices but also on marketing of the produce like the e-National Agriculture Market (e-NAM) by which several thousand farmers have benefited during the lockdown period. GIS technology has been profusely utilised in soil resource mapping, nutrient mapping, land suitability evaluation for different crops, crop coverage, identifying water-logged and saline areas, watershed characterisation and planning, land and land capability classification. UAS, Dharwad has taken initiatives in the setting up of a GIS lab and remote sensing facilities through which early warnings and forecasting of weather, pest and disease incidence and crop coverage are being monitored.

Facilities are also created for an Automatic Smart Irrigation Decision Support System (SIDSS) to educate the farmers in effective water management. Watershed delineation, mapping soil resources, land capability and crop suitability, identification of water logged and saline prone areas, flood-mapping, land use and land cover, nutrient mapping for precision agriculture are being done at UAS, Dharwad. Algorithms are being developed for disease-forecasting, nutrient management, precision water management and sensor-based irrigation scheduling in association with Indian Institute of Technology (IIT), Dharwad and Fourth Paradigm Institute, Bengaluru.

Farmers are being trained to use the National Agriculture Market (e-NAM), an online trading platform for agricultural commodities set up by the Government of India. The market linkage is a must for agriculture, and to realise these, models on price forecasting for different commodities are developed by the University. Efforts are being made to develop drones for the spraying of chemicals and also to monitor crop health status. Efforts are also being made in establishing a Centre of Excellence in Smart Agriculture with a view to skill, reskill and upskill agriculture graduates, providing industry-ready manpower and information to educate farmers in smart agricultural technologies at UAS, Dharwad.

5 Entrepreneurship Development Initiatives at UAS Dharwad

5.1 Course on Entrepreneurship Development in Undergraduate (UG)

The fifth Dean's Committee of Indian Council of Agricultural Research (ICAR) has introduced entrepreneurship development related courses as a mandatory course with two credits in all degree programmes. This was one of the important changes brought by the orientation of the education system with the introduction of exclusive courses in Entrepreneurship development, with 2 credit hours for undergraduate students.

The course curriculum includes topics, for example the concept of entrepreneurship, project identification, management, supporting institutions and Government schemes. Students visit different institutes, and entrepreneurship is a part of their practical classes. During the final year, Student READY (Rural Entrepreneurship Awareness and Development Yojana) is offered, which includes placement of students at the grass-roots level unit of the Agriculture Department called by name Raita Samparka Kendra (farmers' contact centre) for eight weeks, to understand the agricultural ecosystem in rural areas and the practices adopted by the farmers.

After eight weeks, they would undergo two weeks of internship in the Agri-Clinic, where they conduct diagnosis of soil/plants followed by five weeks of institutional attachment and two weeks of Industrial attachment. The institutional attachment includes placement in Krishi Vignana Kendra (KVK), Agricultural Research Stations (ARS), horticulture or seed farm and processing plants.

Thus, the programme of 20 credit hours provides an opportunity to learn in the field, and develop feasible enterprises, and the programme is called student READY. During the second semester, students undergo experiential learning modules in five different subject-matter areas (Fig. 4).

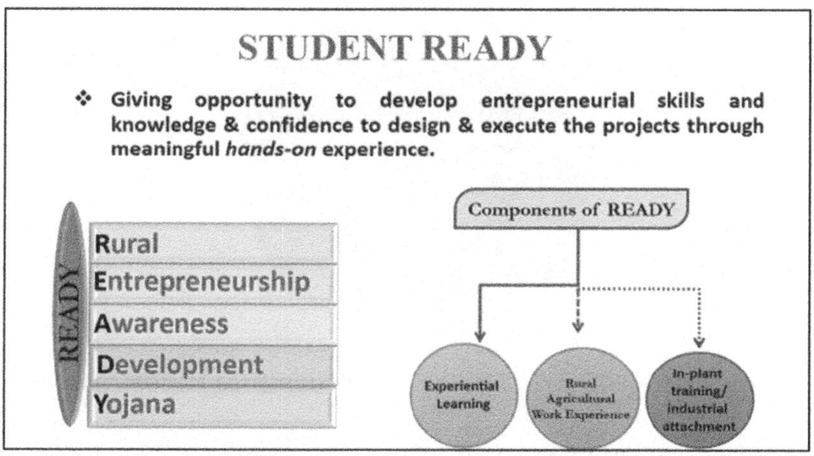

Fig. 4. Curriculum transition with the thrust on hands-on experience and entrepreneurship.

5.2 EDP and Ideation (Ideathon) Workshops

The role of agri-business and agricultural entrepreneurship is critical in the overall economy of many developing countries. Agri-business represents perhaps half of the Gross Domestic Product (GDP) in many countries and over 2.5 billion people in these countries depend on agriculture for their survival [9].

UASD is implementing the World Bank funded Institution Development Plan (IDP) under National Agriculture Higher Education Project (NAHEP) which has a prime objective of developing entrepreneurship and promoting start-ups. Under the

Table 2. EDP conducted under NAHEP-IDP during 2020–21.

Particulars	Training or workshop	Percentage
Total programmes	6	-
Total participants	1,688	-
SC and ST participants	292	17
SC and ST girls	122	7
General girls	644	38

project, six EDP programmes covering 1688 students have been conducted during 2019–21.

It was observed that the participation of girls was on a par with boys, and care was taken to ensure participation of special category students namely schedule caste and schedule tribes (Table 2 and Fig. 5). In addition, sixteen webinars on opportunities in entrepreneurship development was conducted and benefitted 2,593 students.

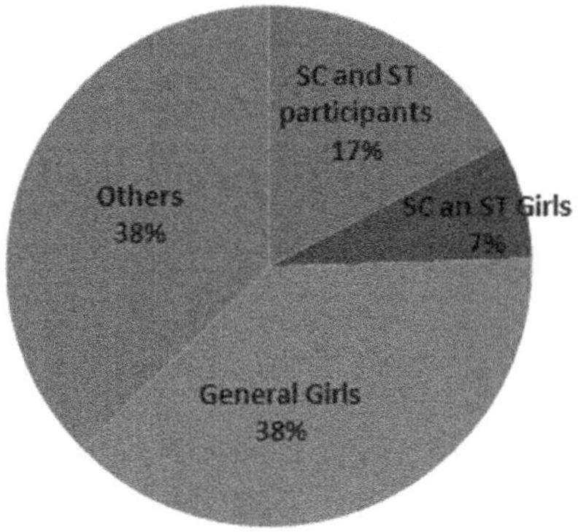

Fig. 5. Representation of different category participants in Ideathon workshop.

Another project called RAFTAAR (Remunerative Approaches for Agriculture and Allied Sector Rejuvenation) promotes Agribusiness incubator. It has promoted over 20 startups in agriculture and allied areas. A Section 8 Company, ASTRA (Association for Startup and Technology Refinement in Agriculture) has been established to support entrepreneurship and start-ups by students. Efforts are being made to establish close linkage with industries, as well as alumni entrepreneurs, to strengthen the endeavor of entrepreneurship development in agriculture.

5.3 Incubation Centre

Under the flagship programme of Karnataka Innovation and Technology Society (KITS), Department of Information Technology (IT), Biotechnology (BT) and Science and Technology (ST), Government of Karnataka, the incubation centre with common instrumentation facility was established at the University of Agricultural Sciences, Dharwad for promoting the innovation in agriculture and biotechnology, with a grant of 60 million rupees (approximately 716,000 Euro). Since the inception of the project, several workshops/conferences were organised to develop skill enhancement.

The state government's novel initiative, New Agriculture Incubation Network (NAIN), was established under the Karnataka Start-up Policy for 2015–20 by the Department of Information Technology, Bio-Technology, Science and Technology to encourage students, research scholars and alumni to share their ideas, to solve chosen local problems, and to validate, refine and nurture ideas, provide an ecosystem to convert ideas into proofs of concept, and convert them into minimum viable products/services, and encourage and lead the teams towards setting up a business enterprise.

6 Conclusion

The University of Agricultural Sciences, Dharwad has been exploring the possibility of establishing the Centre of Excellence in smart agriculture with the objectives of skilling, re-skilling and up-skilling agriculture graduates, thus providing industry-ready manpower, educating farmers through the use of ICT. The UAS Dharwad has been a pioneer in imparting quality agriculture education, and has introduced digital technology in several domains in order to digitally empower students, staff and farmers for digitally-enabled future agriculture, and allied sectors.

References

1. Anonymous: Ministry of Human Resource Development Government of India, New Delhi, India (2020)
2. Reynolds, P., et al.: Global entrepreneurship monitor: data collection design and implementation, 1998–2003. Small Bus. Econ. **24**(3), 205–231 (2005)
3. Wong, K.Y.: Critical success factors for implementing knowledge management in small and medium enterprises. Ind. Manag. Data Syst. **105**(3), 261–279 (2005)
4. Lingelbach, D.C., De La Vina, L., Asel, P.: What's distinctive about growth-oriented entrepreneurship in developing countries? UTSA College of Business Center for Global Entrepreneurship Working Paper No. 1. (2005). https://doi.org/10.2139/ssrn.742605
5. Ajayi, M., Fapojuwo, O.: Agricultural education and training as panacea for sustainable food security in the developing countries. Int. Conf. Sustain. Environ. Agric. **57**(12), 62–66 (2013)
6. Nawaz, F.: Critical factors of women entrepreneurship development in rural Bangladesh. In: Bangladesh Development Research Working Paper Series (BDRWPS), No.5 (2009)
7. Knudson, W., Wysocki, A., Joseph Champagne, H., Peterson, C.: Entrepreneurship and innovation in the agri-food system. Am. J. Agric. Econ. **86**(5), 1330–1336 (2004). https://doi.org/10.1111/j.0002-9092.2004.00685.x
8. Hussain, J., Scott, J., Matlay, H.: Access to entrepreneurial finance: an international perspective. J. Small Bus. Enterp. Dev. **13**(4), 584–599 (2006)
9. World Bank: Growing Africa: Unlocking the Potential of Agribusiness (2013). http://siteresources.worldbank.org/INTAFRICA/Resources/africa-agribusiness-report-2013.pdf

Learning with Digital Technologies

Vocational Education During School Shutdown - A Danish Case on Emergency Remote Teaching

Bent B. Andresen(✉)

Danish School of Education (DPU), Aarhus University, Tuborgvej 164, 2400 Copenhagen, NV, Denmark
bba@edu.au.dk

Abstract. This paper focuses on the emergency remote teaching during the temporary shutdown of physical learning environments in the spring of 2020. It presents findings from a survey among about 14,000 Danish teachers and students at vocational colleges and upper secondary schools regarding their experiences with online education. The analysis and interpretations of the survey data provide evidence suggesting that the teachers generally need professional development regarding online education and blended learning events. Most often, they did not succeed in their attempts to realise the potentials of online education: First, they did not manage to coordinate their expectations regarding the students' daily workload and meet their individual need for teacher support. Second, they did not provide clear announcements and formative feedback. Third, they had difficulty supporting students experiencing learning difficulties and they did not support students with motivational challenges due to social isolation.

To overcome these challenges, teachers need to be more informed by data and research than they were during the emergency remote teaching. This includes information derived from analysis of local data on students' independent and collaborative work, learning challenges, and perceived self-efficacy. Moreover, it includes information about the main findings in research about the benefits of blended learning compared to online teaching and f2f teaching.

Keywords: Blended learning · Online education · Vocational education · Emergency remote teaching · Case study

1 Introduction

The Danish vocational colleges and upper-secondary schools, like many schools around the world, had to introduce emergency remote teaching in the spring of 2020. Faced with the risk of spreading COVID-19 virus, the purpose was to maintain ongoing education during the school shutdown. The teachers at all the schools made an extraordinary effort to reorganise teaching and learning activities. The paper analyses the main experiences of the teachers and students in the spring of 2020.

Teachers usually obtain knowledge about teaching methods by reflecting on their experiences in previous teaching situations. Their individual reflections often begin

Published by Springer Nature Switzerland AG 2022
D. Passey et al. (Eds.): OCCE 2021, IFIP AICT 642, pp. 205–214, 2022.
https://doi.org/10.1007/978-3-030-97986-7_17

while the teaching is in progress and continue afterwards [1]. These reflections regarding previous teaching and learning events may increase their ability to choose effective teaching methods. However, these reflections relate to previous experiences, so they are less useful when teachers need to carry out their work in completely new ways. Faced with an immediate need to reorganise educational events, most teachers lacked experience of and routines for carrying out online education.

Over recent years, all vocational colleges and upper-secondary schools implemented 1:1 environments where each student has a laptop or tablet with internet access and all students are digitally literate. The Danish schools were among the first in the world to implement such 1:1 learning environments [2]. For years, the level of digital literacy among students in Denmark has been among the highest in the world [3]. Moreover, the need of Danish teachers for professional development regarding ICT skills for teaching has been among the lowest in the world. Before the shutdown of classrooms, just 8% of upper-secondary teachers reported a high level of need for professional development in this area [4, Table 1.5.23]. However, they had no experience with emergency remote teaching and it was a challenge for them to adjust to it.

Accordingly, the paper addresses these two research questions:

1. What were the main challenges regarding emergency remote teaching at vocational colleges and upper-secondary schools in the spring of 2020, and
2. How can teachers overcome these challenges in future?

The paper addresses these questions by analysing data from a survey conducted shortly after the closure of the physical learning environments in the spring of 2020. The respondents included about 14,000 Danish teachers and students. Based on an analysis of data about their challenges and experiences, the paper examines how the teachers organised their online teaching by adopting a trial-and-error strategy.

Furthermore, it explores an alternative approach in which the teachers adopt a research-informed strategy. In particular, it explores how teachers can handle future disruptive events if they are informed by research findings on technology-enhanced teaching and learning activities.

2 Theoretical Framework

The theoretical framework includes theory on basic forms of teaching. This notion refers to constructions suitable for analysing and understanding different types of teaching [5]. The paper explores two basic forms of teaching in digital learning environments: 1) teacher-centered and 2) student-centered teaching respectively. There is research evidence suggesting that a synthesis of these forms of teaching generally has a greater impact on student learning outcomes than traditional f2f education [6].

Essentially, the former involves communication between a teacher and students (oral teaching, guidance, written dialogue and oral and written feedback). In general, such teacher-centered activities influence students' learning outcomes positively [7]. When teachers and students are not allowed to meet in a classroom, teachers can either organise one-way communication via the school's digital learning platform or apply a more dialogical approach and communicate with individual students or groups of students via online media.

The second basic form of teaching and learning is defined as "teaching with a high degree of individual work or group work" [5]. When teachers organise such activities, they make a number of choices regarding for instance small-group interaction and learning content and tasks. The students work individually, in pairs or in groups, and they can adjust the time they spend on each task according to their prior knowledge and current abilities.

The teachers need to evaluate these activities with virtual attendance. In particular, the teachers need to evaluate the student-centered learning processes systematically in relation to academic and other expectations, which can be defined in terms of the students' zone of proximal development [8]. Whenever expectations fall outside this zone, students risk being demotivated by tasks that are too difficult, or, conversely, do not learn anything at all because the tasks are too easy for them. In consequence, the teachers have to:

- Identify the students' zone of proximal development
- Select appropriate student tasks
- Provide feedback on the students' work in progress
- Evaluate their final results

Sometimes, teachers use a retrospective and summative approach to determine the students' current knowledge and skills or to grade student work. This approach is less suitable than a formative approach when it comes to determining the students' developmental potentials. Additionally, the students' belief in their own ability may suffer when their assignments and other products are returned with comments regarding their flaws and shortcomings.

There is also research evidence suggesting that summative evaluations in the longer term demotivate many students [9]. Although they may learn from their shortcomings and mistakes in the short term, the use of summative evaluation may decrease their motivation and momentum in the end.

Frequently used complementary approaches include formative feedback and process-oriented evaluation. About twenty years ago, researchers provided evidence suggesting that formative feedback has a relatively large influence on students' motivation and learning outcomes [10]. I addition, there is research evidence suggesting that formative evaluation fosters these factors a great deal [7]. When reflecting on their formative feedback, the students are encouraged to complete and present the results of their self-directed activities. In general, the benefits of such approaches are twofold: strengthening the teachers' insight into the students' learning processes, and fostering these processes.

In general, the teachers use various approaches to provide feedback on the students' work, but there has been a shift in focus from result-oriented to process-oriented evaluation in the Danish educational system. More and more frequently, teachers provide feedback on work in progress tailored to the students' educational needs and challenges and applied to strengthen their continued learning processes.

3 Methodology

As mentioned above, the paper analyses data from a survey among teachers and students at vocational colleges and upper-secondary schools. This survey was conducted in close collaboration between a Danish knowledge center and a Danish think-tank [11]. The author of this paper provided research guidance.

The survey was conducted in 2020 from April 27 to May 8 at schools offering upper-secondary education after the compulsory ten years of education at primary and lower-secondary schools. The total number of schools was 55. The forms of upper-secondary education involved are shown in Table 1.

Table 1. Overview of schools and forms of education involved in the survey (some schools offer more than one form of education)

Form of education	Explanation	Number of schools
VET	Vocational Training	25
EUX	Vocational Student Exam	22
HF	Higher Preparatory Exam	20
STX	General Student Exam	25
HHX	Mercantile Student Exam	9
HTX	Technical Student Exam	8

1,886 teachers and 12,352 students responded to the survey. The main theme in the teachers' questionnaire is their work experiences. The questionnaire focuses on the teachers' experiences when organising teaching and learning activities in which physical attendance was not possible. They were asked to relate to statements about their work experiences with online teaching in the last two full teaching weeks in April 2020. The main theme of the students' questionnaire was their experiences of online teacher-centered and student-centered activities during the same weeks.

4 Results

In the spring of 2020, the majority of teachers obtained insight into online teaching, which they expect to make use of in the future to develop and improve online teaching [11]. In particular, teachers who already had some experience in this area obtained insight that they plan to use in the future.

The transition to pure online teaching due to the closure of the physical learning environments was a top-down decision. When this decision was announced, there were no clear guidelines for the necessary reorganisation of teaching at the vocational schools and colleges [11]. Although some school leaders inspired the teachers and provided feedback on their online teaching, a number of teachers were given inadequate guidelines:

- One in every eight teachers "received useful and sufficient guidelines for distance learning from the school" either very little or not at all.
- One in every four teachers "received useful and sufficient support and guidance from the school in relation to the choice and use of digital technologies" either very little or not at all.
- One in every four teachers said that their school "organised sharing of knowledge about and experience with distance learning between colleagues" either very little or not at all.
- About half of the teachers said that their school "organised sharing of materials and/or teaching courses between colleagues" either very little or not at all.

In this situation, the teachers increased their knowledge sharing about: 1) the use of digital technology and materials, and 2) the reorganisation of teacher-centered and student-centered learning events.

Teachers primarily shared knowledge about and reorganised their oral communication using interactive video methods. In general, the influence of interactive video methods is above the average for all the methods used (Table 2).

Table 2. The effect of using digital technology [12]

Type of method	Influence (effect size)
Interactive video methods	0.54
Average of all types of methods	0.40
Programmed instruction	0.23
Web-based learning activities	0.18

The teachers often scheduled lessons on the screen for an audience of students lying in their beds with their cameras and microphones turned off. The teachers could easily be seen and heard, but it was obviously much more difficult to ensure that the students were paying attention. Some students were distracted by, for example, social media updates [11].

When they perceive academic instruction and web-based learning as homework, their industriousness and self-discipline varies as with other types of homework. Consequently, not all students managed to prepare for scheduled lessons by watching video-based homework.

The influence of interactive video methods on student learning may also decrease if the students regard them as elements of programmed instruction or web-based learning activities. This is in line with general research findings. As indicated in Table 2, programmed or web-based instructional activities have relatively little influence on students' learning outcomes.

Although the online teaching was never referred to as 'programmed instruction', it did resemble programmed instruction to some extent. For example, this form of instruction is often monotonous because it involves sequences of repeated activities such as introduction of new material, assignments, tests, repetitions and additional tests. In the spring of 2020, the teachers and students experienced increased uniformity: "Both teachers and students felt that the teaching became more monotonous in the way it was approached during the COVID-19 virus shutdown" [13, p. 7].

Due to inadequate coordination between the teachers, they provided plenty of assignments: "The first period of teaching was characterised by the students being given tasks that they had to perform individually or in groups and hand in for assessment. In other words, the teachers provided plenty of tasks to ensure that the students had enough to do during the allocated teaching time" [13, p. 5]. The increased amount of homework affected the students' motivation and learning outcomes negatively. Students were generally less motivated and learned less [13, p. 5].

Moreover, many students called for clear announcements regarding their self-directed learning activities. The teachers generally: "Had difficulty expressing their expectations to the students. Teachers are used to expressing and explaining their expectations during face-to-face contact with students. When this possibility disappears, it is much more difficult to ensure that individual students understand the presentation" [13, p. 6].

In addition, many students wanted formative feedback and guidance when working independently or in pairs or small groups. As previously mentioned, the students may learn a lot from this kind of feedback. Ideally, they can resubmit some of their work to obtain summative feedback. However, most students wanted feedback that was more comprehensive in the spring of 2020.

Regarding the amount of feedback, the teachers were more positive than the students were [11]. However, the teachers provided so many tasks that they did not have "the opportunity to give feedback on all the tasks" [13, p. 6].

In the regular classrooms, most teachers continually consider the students' need for support related to individual tasks and collaborative work. After the school shutdown, they were not able to develop alternative methods to cater for this need. Therefore, it was more difficult to assess students' motivation, working efforts and learning outcomes during the school shutdown [11, p. 5].

During face-to-face teaching, the teachers circulate among student groups, answer questions and provide ongoing feedback to the students regarding their self-directed activities. When this is no longer possible, the teachers tend to decrease their observations. In consequence, they knew less than usual about the students' motivation and the extent to which the students actually met the given learning objectives. Many teachers failed to support their students adequately during the shutdown of the classrooms in the spring of 2020.

In other words, the teachers did not have time to develop alternative methods to observe and support the individual students. Consequently, the students found it harder to work with the educational materials. This included students who felt they were academically weak. It is significant that students at the lower end of the achievement scale felt a lack of support from their teachers more than students at the other end of the same scale did [11].

5 Discussion

In general, feedback for teachers provided by an external research-informed certifier improves technology-enhanced education and e-learning [14]. In particular, it promotes consistency between expected learning outcomes, preconditions as regards content, duration, flexibility, use of digital platform etc., and design in terms of the organisation and evaluation of learning activities. Therefore, the vocational colleges and upper-secondary schools might consider implementing a system of certification of e-learning concepts in future.

Furthermore, the teachers could apply more research-informed practice. This does not mean that they regard research findings as a recipe for action, but research does provide useful information whenever they plan educational events in 1:1 learning environments. For example, there is research evidence suggesting that clear announcements influence students' learning outcomes to a considerable extent. In the first weeks after the sudden shutdown of the classrooms, it is quite understandable that not all announcements and learning objectives were completely clear. Afterwards, however, there was a need for clearer announcements and objectives to ensure that control of the learning activities was not transferred in its entirety to the students.

In general, students' control over learning has low influence on their performance compared to actions like formative evaluation and feedback, and clear announcements and learning objectives (Table 3).

Table 3. Selected effect sizes [12]

Type of method	Influence (effect size)
Students' perceived self-efficacy	0.92
Formative evaluation	0.90
Formative feedback	0.75
Clear announcements	0.75
Clear learning objectives	0.50
Average of all types of methods	0.40
Students' control over learning	0.04

Usually, students' learning processes are assisted whenever they receive formative feedback and have sufficient time to learn from this feedback and possibly resubmit some of their work (Table 4). This includes feedback on activities requiring them to work alone or in groups, but as mentioned above, many students experienced little motivating feedback from their teachers in the spring of 2020.

The students' motivation relates to their perceived self-efficacy, which correlates with their learning outcomes [15]. When they feel that they cannot perform an increasing number of tasks on their own, their perceived self-efficacy may decrease. Consequently, the teachers need to develop methods to replace the methods they use in the classroom to identify students with relatively low self-efficacy, and provide tasks which all the students are able to master individually or in groups with proper support.

Otherwise, the dropout rate at vocational schools and colleges could increase. This may be a serious problem, since just one out of twelve Danish municipalities complies with the current requirements relating to student dropout rates [16].

This problem was intensified by the fact that students also, in their own opinion, lose motivation as time goes on [13, p. 6]. For obvious reasons, many students reported increased needs for social contact during the closure of the physical learning environments. They generally missed social interaction with other students during the period of pure online teaching and learning events [11]. From day to day, they actually became less happy with their situation, which affected their motivation and industriousness.

Under these circumstances, teachers should consider more dialogical approaches allowing the students to ask questions and present their academic understanding and major results of their self-directed learning activities. Moreover, they should consider collaborative learning activities and peer feedback. There is research evidence suggesting that collaborative learning generally leads to a greater learning outcome than individualised approaches (Table 4).

Table 4. The effect of student collaboration [12]

Type of method	Influence (effect size)
Collaborative vs. individual learning	0.59
Average of all types of methods	0.40
Individualised teaching	0.22

In some situations, it is most appropriate for students to develop specific skills individually, but in many other cases, students may benefit from working together for three major reasons. First, collaborative learning can help reduce feelings of social isolation. Second, it can cause subject terms to become part of students' active vocabulary. Third, it can strengthen students' commitment and serious work because they feel obligated by their agreements with other students.

Accordingly, it is crucial that the teachers foster collaboration in student-centered activities. For example, the teachers could promote co-creation, dialogue and other kinds of collaboration by allowing the students to use digital learning platforms, social media platforms, Google Docs, Skype, Zoom, etc. Additionally, the students could prepare for lessons, perform tasks, and receive feedback in pairs or in larger groups. Moreover, they could exchange and comment on each other's draft assignments and the like.

6 Conclusion and Perspectives

The paper addresses two research questions: What were the main challenges of emergency remote teaching after the closure of classrooms at vocational colleges and upper-secondary schools in the spring of 2020, and how can teachers overcome these challenges in future?

The research findings provide evidence suggesting that the schools did not succeed in utilising the potentials of online learning during these circumstances. From a student perspective, there were shortcomings regarding announcements of learning activities, feedback, professional support, differentiation in teaching, and social contact.

Consequently, both teachers and students experienced reduced student motivation and increased monotony in their teaching and learning experiences. In particular, the students became mentally distracted and demotivated, or lost their sense of self-efficacy, due to an increased number of assignments, which they generally regard as more difficult than before the emergency remote teaching was introduced.

Therefore, the teachers need to coordinate their expectations regarding the students' daily workload and individual need for teacher support. In addition, the teachers need to provide clearer announcements and more formative feedback and support. This includes supporting students who experience learning difficulties and social isolation during emergency remote teaching.

Generally, the teachers need to be informed by data generated by their formative evaluation of students' perceived self-efficacy, learning challenges, collaborative work and social isolation if they wish to practice blended learning in future. Additionally, they need to be informed by important findings in school research. This includes information about the strengths of blended learning synthesising teacher-centered and student-centered activities, which has a greater positive influence on students' learning processes than pure online and pure classroom education.

References

1. Schön, D.A.: Den reflekterende praktiker. Hvordan professionelle tænker, når de arbejder. Klim, Aarhus (2001)
2. Søby, M.: Editorial: Synergies for better learning – where are we now? Nord. J. Digit. Lit. (01–02) (2013)
3. Bundsgaard, J., Pettersson, M., Puck, M.R.: Digitale kompetencer. Aarhus Universitetsforlag, Aarhus (2014)
4. OECD: TALIS 2018 Results (Volume II). Teachers and School Leaders as Lifelong Learners. OECD, Paris, France (2019)
5. Meyer, H.: Hvad er god undervisning? Gyldendals Lærerbibliotek, København, Denmark (2014)
6. Means, B., Toyama, Y., Murphy, R., Bakia, M.: The effectiveness of online and blended learning: a meta-analysis of the empirical literature. Teach. Coll. Rec. **115** (2013). https://archive.sri.com/sites/default/files/publications/effectiveness_of_online_and_blended_learning.pdf
7. Hattie, J.A.C.: Visible Learning. A Synthesis of Over 800 Meta-Analyses Relating to Achievement. Routledge, Abingdon (2009)
8. Vygotsky, L.: Læringen. In: Lindqvist, G. (ed.) Vygotskij om læring som udviklingsvilkår. Kapitler af Lev Vygoskijs 'Pædagogisk Psykologi'. Klim, Aarhus (2014)
9. Nordenbo, S.: Pædagogisk brug af test – et systematisk review. Danmarks Pædagogiske Universitetsforlag & Dansk Clearinghouse for Uddannelsesforskning, København, Denmark (2009)

10. Black, P., Wiliam, D.: Inside the black box: raising standards through classroom assessment. Phi Delta Kappan **80** (1998)
11. eVidencenter, DEA: Fjernundervisningstemperatur.dk. En rundspørge blandt elever og lærere på ungdomsuddannelser om erfaringer med fjernundervisning under Coronanedlukningen. eVidencenter and DEA, Viby, Denmark (2020)
12. Hattie, J.A.C.: Visible Learning for Teachers Maximizing Impact on Learning. Routledge, Oxford (2012)
13. eVidencenter, DEA: Sammenfatning af Fjernundervisningstemperatur.dk. En rundspørge blandt elever og lærere på ungdomsuddannelser om erfaringer med fjernundervisning under Coronanedlukningen. eVidencenter and DEA, Viby, Denmark (2020)
14. Andresen, B.B.: Formative research on e-learning certification. The National Danish Knowledge Centre of e-Learning, Aarhus, Denmark (2019). https://epale.ec.europa.eu/sites/default/files/formative_research_on_e-learning_certification.pdf
15. Bandura, A.: Self-Efficacy: The Exercise of Control. Freeman, New York (1997)
16. Jakobsen, K.T., Holm, K.H.: Optag og frafald på EUD blandt de yngste elever. DEA, København (2020). www.datocms-assets.com/22590/1594196716-optag-og-frafald-pa-eud.pdf

Analysis of Practical Examples of a Real-Time Online Class on Agriculture in Space, Using the Collaborative Learning Tool "Digital Diamond Mandala Matrix"

Seiichiro Aoki[1,2(✉)], Shinzo Kobayashi[1], Takahiko Naraki[1], and Toshio Okamoto[1]

[1] The Kyoto College of Graduate Studies for Informatics, Kyoto 6068225, Japan
s_aoki@kcg.ac.jp
[2] Kyoto University, Kyoto 6078471, Japan

Abstract. The effectiveness of our "digital Diamond Mandala Matrix (dDMM)" application on a real-time online class is shown based on the results of analysis of output by students. The dDMM application which is something like a mind map limiting words to nine plus a description field for explaining the whole of the dDMM data. We can easily view several dDMMs at a glance for comparing them with each other, so it is highly suitable for an online class where only one screen can be shared. In order to improve the effect on students' learning, the class was offered in an active learning style, so that it consists of pre-learning, a real-time online class with a lecture, and discussions based on the pre-learning using Zoom Meeting, and students' re-thinking based on the online class as post-learning. Students input data into the dDMM application as pre-learning dDMMs before participating in the online class, and then join the class consisting of a lecture and discussions based on the pre-learning dDMMs. They input data into the dDMM application as post-learning dDMMs after the online class. In order to investigate the efficacy of the dDMM application on real-time online class, we compared them statistically using the text data analysing tool KH Coder pre-learning and post-learning dDMMs, which are outputs by students. From the results, we found that post-learning dDMMs are improved from post-learning dDMMs due to the lecture and discussions in the online class. Therefore, the dDMM application is an effective tool in real-time online courses. We will improve the application by adding functions such as automatic grouping for supporting collaborative learning, with multilingual support.

Keywords: Online class · Diamond Mandala Matrix · Text analysis · KH coder

1 Introduction

The results and its analysis of a real-time online class using our collaborative tool "digital Diamond Mandala Matrix (dDMM)" are shown. The class was part of the course "Agricultural Informatics in Next Generation" (instructor: Takahiko Naraki, lecturer: Seiichiro Aoki, director: Shinzo Kobayashi, number of students: 50) offered in

Published by Springer Nature Switzerland AG 2022
D. Passey et al. (Eds.): OCCE 2021, IFIP AICT 642, pp. 215–221, 2022.
https://doi.org/10.1007/978-3-030-97986-7_18

Japanese at The Kyoto College of Graduate Studies for Informatics (KCGI) in the Autumn semester of 2020. In order to improve the effectivity on students' learning, the class was offered in an active learning style. The class consists of pre-learning, a real-time online class with lectures and discussions based on the pre-learning, and students' rethinking based on the online class as post-learning.

In Japan, Diamond Mandala Matrix is sometimes used as a framework to realise "total optimisation of business and systems" in Enterprise Architecture (EA), which has been mainly worked on by the Ministry of Economy, Trade and Industry (METI). The advantage of DMMs is that cells are limited to up to nine [1] (comparable to a dotted line rectangle in Fig. 1a), so we can see all of the cells in a DMM at a glance. We thought DMM is highly suitable for online classes, so we have been developing a dDMM application inspired by DMM. In the class, we used the dDMM application for pre-learning and post-learning of students. In order to investigate the effectiveness of the dDMM application on a real-time online class, we compared and analysed the statistical output by students such as pre-learning dDMMs and post-learning dDMMs. dDMM data are text type data, so the analysis was performed using the free text analysing tool "KH coder" [2] as the first step of analysis. A similar analysis using KH Coder was performed by Aoki et al. (2020) for the answers to the questionnaire taken in astronomy lectures [3].

The dDMM application has been developed as a collaborative learning tool inspired by DMM. The dDMM application is used before a real-time online class consisting of lecture and discussion as pre-learning dDMM, and after the class as post-learning dDMM. The structure of dDMM can be seen in Fig. 1a. In the nine cells at the top (dotted line rectangle in Fig. 1a), a student input words in the surrounding eight cells and representative phrase in the central cell. In the three middle cells (dashed line rectangle in Fig. 1a), SDGs (Sustainable Development Goals) related to words in dDMM are selected. The bottom field (single dashed line rectangle in Fig. 1a) is a descriptive field for explaining the whole of the dDMM using words in the top nine cells. So, dDMM is something like a mind map that limits the number of words up to

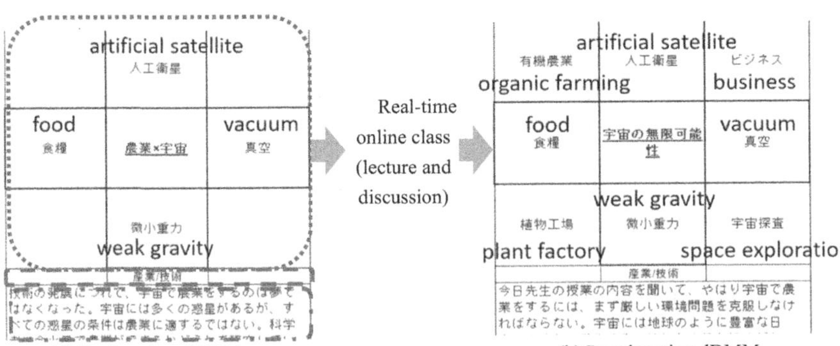

(a) Pre-learning dDMM (b) Post-learning dDMM

Fig. 1. Examples of dDMMs created by a student. (a) Pre-learning dDMM. (b) Post-learning dDMM. A student creates a pre-learning dDMM before real-time online class and post-learning dDMM after the class.

nine, extended with SDGs labels and descriptive fields. SDGs labels were setup because the course was related to sustainable society. And the dDMM application is highly suitable for an online class, where a single screen only is shared using an online conference system. We can easily compare several DMMs through discussion, whenever only one screen can be shared using an online conference tool such as "Zoom Meetings".

In this paper, we show the effectiveness of the dDMM application on a real-time online class, by comparing pre-learning and post-learning dDMMs statistically.

2 Structure of Online Class

The main theme of the course was "Thinking about Sustainable Agriculture and Community". In the course, "Agriculture × Something = Sustainable Society" was set as the common theme (target scope) for all classes. Based on the target scope, we set up a subdivided scope (topics related to the target scope) in each class session. The scope of the class for analysis was "Agriculture × Space = Sustainable Society".

The classes consist of pre-learning, real-time online classes (lecture and discussion) and post-learning (see Fig. 1).

1) (Pre-learning) Each student found words related to agriculture in space by referencing websites, books or papers supplied by the lecturer, and input them in eight cells surrounding the central cell at the top of dDMM (see Fig. 1a). The phrase in the central cell was set to "Agriculture x Space," which was common to all students. In the bottom field, students input sentences explaining whole of the dDMM. Here, the pre-learning dDMM was completed. These tasks were done by each student before attending the real-time online class.
2) (Real-time online class) The real-time online class was offered using a Zoom Meeting. The first half of the class was a lecture, explaining the Sun, Mars, Europa, Enceladus, and other satellites and exoplanets, especially from the perspective of agriculture in space. In the second half, discussions were held on the subject of pre-learning dDMMs (lecturer: Aoki, facilitator: Naraki, director: Kobayashi).
3) (Post-learning) On the basis of the real-time online lecture and discussions, each student created a post-learning dDMM by investigating words related to agriculture in space one more time. In the central cell at the top, each student thought up a phrase that represents the words in the surrounding cells. The results of the analysis of the central cell will be shown in another paper.

In order to offer the classes, we used the following tools.

(a) digital DMM (dDMM) application: It can be used on a browser, so students can use it with either a PC or a smartphone.
(b) Online conference system: Zoom Meeting is used for real-time online classes.
(c) Learning Management System (LMS): dotCampus of KCGI was used to share course materials.

3 Results of Analysis Applied to dDMMs

dDMM data for pre-learning and post-learning created by a student are shown in Fig. 1. At the bottom field of the post-learning dDMM, we can see that "after hearing the lecture today, I understood that we must first overcome the harsh environment in order to farm in space" (see Fig. 1b). The overall difference between the pre-learning and the post-learning dDMMs is shown in the correspondence analysis diagram of words in the surrounding eight cells at the top (see Fig. 2). In the pre-learning dDMM,

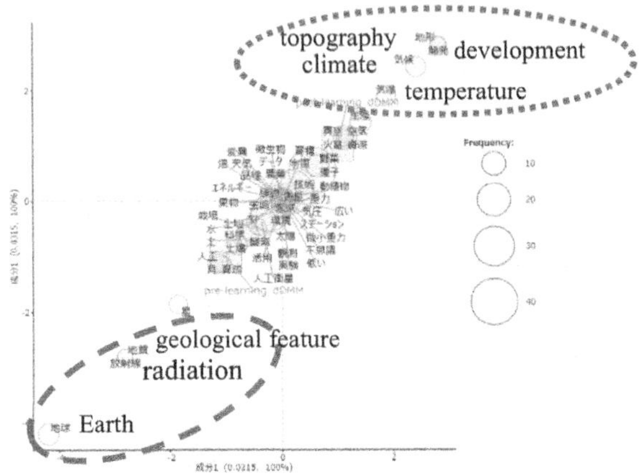

Fig. 2. Correspondence analysis diagram of the words in the surrounding eight cells of the central cell at the top in the dDMMs. Words that appeared four or more times are used. The words in the lower left (dashed line ellipse) are those appeared more times in the pre-learning dDMM relative to post-learning dDMM. The words in the upper right (dotted line ellipse) are those that ap-peared more times in the post-learning dDMM relative to pre-learning dDMM.

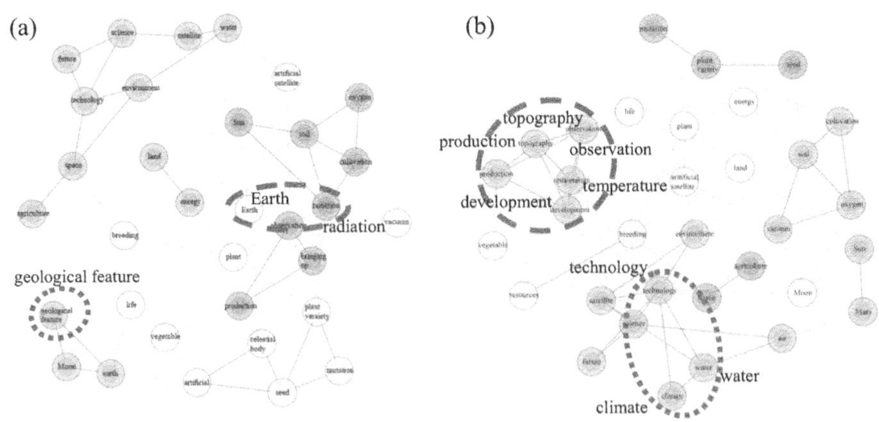

Fig. 3. (a) The co-occurrence network diagram of words in the surrounding eight cells at the top of the pre-learning dDMM and (b) that of the post-learning dDMM. The minimum number of appear-ances of a word is set to three. The darker the connecting line, the more students entered the words into the cells at the sametime.

"Earth," "radiation," and "geological feature" are more common, while in the post-learning dDMM, "topography," "development," "climate," and "temperature" are more common. From these characteristics, the perspectives of students about agriculture in space before attending the online class were with a point of view of an Earth-centered mind and the effects of radiation and geological feature, whereas after the class students got a broader perspective such as "climate," "temperature," "topography," and "development".

The co-occurrence network diagrams of words in the surrounding eight cells around the central cell at the top of the pre-learning dDMM and post-learning dDMM are shown in Fig. 3a and b, respectively. The connected words with lines are those which students put into the surrounding cells at the same time. Comparing Fig. 3a and Fig. 3b, we can see that the number of students who entered "Earth" and "radiation" (see dashed line ellipse in Fig. 3a) and "geological feature" (see dotted line ellipse in Fig. 3a) at the same time in the post-learning dDMM is decreased, because they are not appeared in the post-learning dDMM. On the other hand, the number of students who entered "topography" and "observation," "temperature," "development," or "production" (see dashed line ellipse in Fig. 3b) at the same time is increased. And the number of students who entered "climate" and "water" or "technology" (see dotted line ellipse in Fig. 3b) at the same time is also increased.

The overall trend of differences between the pre-learning and the post-learning dDMMs also can be seen in the correspondence analysis diagram of word in sentences in the bottom field of dDMMs (see Fig. 4). In the pre-learning dDMMs, "other" (other stars, other planets), "vegetable," "mutation," "growing," "science," etc. are more common, while in the post-learning dDMMs, "outside" (outside stars, outside planets, etc.), "growth," "water," "breeding," "necessary," etc. are more common. From these characteristics, it can be seen that before the online class, the students were aware of the

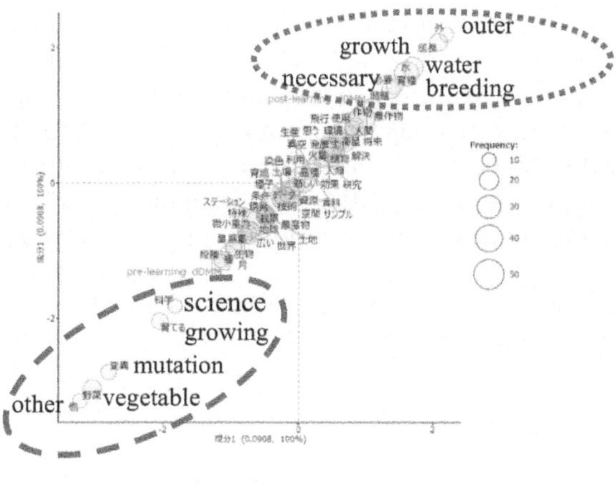

Fig. 4. Correspondence analysis diagram of the words entered in the bottom cell of the dDMMs. Words that appeared ten or more times are used. The words in the lower left (dashed line ellipse) are those that appeared more times in the pre-learning dDMM relative to post-learning dDMM. The words in the upper right (dotted line ellipse) are those that appeared more times in the post-learning dDMM relative to pre-learning dDMM.

genetic "mutation" of organisms due to the effects of radiation, and the use of "science" to "grow" crops such as "vegetables", while after the class students became to be aware of the active use of "breeding" and the "necessity" of "water" for "growth".

The differences are probably due to the fact that the lecturer took Mars as an example in the real-time online class, showing the low temperature and severe climatic conditions, the difficulty in getting water, and the topography line a desert. In addition, "breeding" was discussed between the students and the lecturer during the online class for active use of genetic mutations, which possibly led to the differences.

4 Summary and Future Work

It was shown that each student came to think more realistically about agriculture in space due to the real-time online class, because dDMMs were influenced by the topic of lecture and discussions, which was seen in the statical text analysis of pre-learning and post-learning dDMMs with the KH Coder. So, the dDMM application is an effective tool in a real-time online class, and its advantage is that several dDMM data can be easily compared on one screen. Here, the practical examples on online class were shown, but it is not an online-only tool, so it can also be used effectively on offline courses. The dDMM application can be also useful for writing a learning portfolio. In a course of computer networks, we assigned students to compile portfolios comparing pre-learning and post-learning dDMMs as evidence, in order to indicate what they learned in the course.

We have been developing the dDMM application as a collaborative tool, but we have not yet used it in online multiple groups, which is assumed in typical collaborative learning. We are considering implementing the dDMM application the function such as automatic grouping, based on pre-learning dDMMs to support collaborative learning. Then, we will apply it on a class with multiple groups to investigate its effects in collaborative learning. We have used the dDMM application in a paper-based style for group work in an offline class in a high school. But we did not undertake analysis because of insufficient data. We will also implement multilingual support using Google Translate for users whose native language is not Japanese. In addition, we have been improving the dDMM application adding a function to input images for symbolising the words in the top nine cells of dDMM. This function is very useful for elementary and junior high school students, who may not be good at verbalising their ideas.

Acknowledgements. This work was supported by JSPS KAKENHI (Grants-in-Aid for Scientific Research) Grant Numbers 16H03087 and 19H01724.

References

1. Kobayashi, S., Emi, K., Yushita, H., Onishi, K., Tsuchimochi, G.H., Okamoto, T.: Development practice of multi-lingual flipped learning materials by instructional design using diamond Mandala Matrix. In: IPSJ Symposium Series 2019, pp. 283–286 (2019)

2. Higuchi, K., Komoda, N., Tamura, S., Ikkai, Y.: A support tool for composing social survey questionnaires by automatically summarizing questionnaires stored in data archives. WSEAS Trans. Inf. Sci. Appl. **4**(2), 280–287 (2007)
3. Aoki, S., Sakka, K., Emi, K., Kobayashi, S., Okamoto, T.: Text data analysis on answers written in Japanese to free text questions obtained at astronomy lectures. In: Brinda, T., Passey, D., Keane, T. (eds.) OCCE 2020. IAICT, vol. 595, pp. 139–143. Springer, Cham (2020). https://doi.org/10.1007/978-3-030-59847-1_15

AsTRA – An Assessment Tool for Recognition and Adaptation of Prior Professional Experience and Vocational Training

Simone Opel[1(✉)], Cajus Marian Netzer[2], and Jörg Desel[2]

[1] FernUniversität in Hagen, Universitätsstraße 27, 58097 Hagen, Germany
simone.opel@fernuni-hagen.de
[2] FernUniversität in Hagen, Universitätsstraße 11, 58097 Hagen, Germany
{cajus-marian.netzerl,joerg.desel}@fernuni-hagen.de

Abstract. Educational systems in most countries are differentiated by level and entail transitions between different school types. The different school types do not always support a transition without gaps or repetitions. For students, this can be very frustrating, demotivating and time-consuming. For example, many graduated IT specialists bring work experience, a number of relevant competencies and previous knowledge from their vocational education and training into a degree programme in computer science – yet they still have to take the associated courses and pass examinations. To improve this situation and value the competencies brought along, we implemented a project to develop a comprehensive system to honour the prior knowledge of these students in various ways. One of our goals is to promote permeability between vocational and higher education, not only in computer science. The core element of this System is AsTRA, a comprehensive assessment tool which we developed to evaluate the common learning content and its difficult level. This system is designed to credit previous knowledge and to adapt the students' learning paths, based on reliable decisions. In this paper, we present our tool AsTRA that supports these decisions as well as a brief overview of our resulting recognition system.

Keywords: Higher education · Vocational education · Adaptation · Permeability · Assessment · Assessment tool · Educational systems · IT specialist · Competence · Recognition · Recognition of prior learning · Study programme · Bachelor computer science

1 Introduction

All differentiated education systems have one challenge in common: Ensuring a smooth transition of students between the different parts of the system. In Germany, the education system is very diverse. Students can switch between different pathways in secondary education as well as in vocational and higher education. The latter two fields tend to compete rather than interact in many professional fields such as computer science. Therefore, students with general university entrance qualifications how have

D. Passey et al. (Eds.): OCCE 2021, IFIP AICT 642, pp. 222–233, 2022.
https://doi.org/10.1007/978-3-030-97986-7_19

completed dual vocational training[1], e.g., as IT specialists (generally recognised apprenticeship), can take up higher education studies, but the competencies they have acquired during their apprenticeship are only partly recognised by the universities. This means that students like these IT specialists bring work experience, personal and professional competencies, and previous knowledge from their vocational education and training into a degree programme, for example in computer science; yet they still have to take all the associated courses and pass examinations.

Apprenticeships in computer science, such as IT specialists, are widely considered to be of high professional quality, and many IT specialists work hand in hand with academically educated computer scientists [1]. Furthermore, in a study addressing multiple training in terms of vocational education and university studies, Jacob [2] concluded that for many high school graduates, vocational education before university studies is not considered a detour but has a value of its own. In the students' perceptions, university studies subjectively build upon vocational training in their specific field of study [2, p. 156].

Nevertheless, the universities hardly recognise competencies acquired in vocational education or during a professional activity. Crediting more than a few modules fails due to knowledge about the extent of overlap between vocational and higher education [3]. Universities argue that vocational training is located at level four of the DQR ("Deutscher Qualifikationsrahmen für lebenslanges Lernen")[2] [4] – the national implementation of the EQF (European Qualifications Framework)[3] [5, pp. 82–83] – whereas bachelor modules (duration: 6 semesters) are classified at level six. This difference in levels, as well as the different focus (professional vs. academic education), makes the implementation of permeability concepts between vocational training and university studies challenging. On the other hand, increasing permeability between these vocational education and training and academic education has been on the agenda in education politics for some time now (cf. [6]).

For this reason, we started a project that introduces and systematises the *formal recognition of professionally gained competencies of IT specialists in computer science as a prototype* and thus, promotes comprehensive permeability between vocational and academic education as a first example for such a general recognition system. Our tool AsTRA is an essential part of this project. It is an important result as well as an important tool for further use.

2 Foundations of the Project

2.1 Formal Recognition of Former Competencies in Higher Education

At later stages of their career, some of the professionally trained individuals go on to professional further training or study at university to gain additional competence and to

---

1 *Completed dual vocational training*: students attend vocational school for their profession and are paid apprentices of their training companies for 3 years. The dual vocational training ends with a final examination approved by the state.

2 https://www.dqr.de/content_en/home.php.

3 https://europa.eu/europass/en/european-qualifications-framework-eqf.

achieve a degree. They do so for better progression and promotion in their professional development. Some of these students continue to work in their company and take up part-time studies, often at distance learning universities such as FernUniversität in Hagen.

This professional development path is relatively common for IT specialists who bring several competencies as well as professional experience and previous knowledge into their studies. But their competencies are usually only credited and recognised with credit points (CP) selectively by the universities (cf. for example in the context of the NEXUS[4] or the ANCOM project[5] [7]). However, crediting previously acquired competencies, qualifications, and skills is a key element in the transition from a vocational training path to university studies. Hence, in 2002 the "standing conference of the ministers of education and cultural affairs" (KMK) put a resolution into effect to promote a smooth transition by *formal recognition of previous gained competencies* [8, 9]. The various projects (e.g., [10] or [11]) of this initiative have not yet achieved a broad impact. One factor is the academic self-image of the universities, which want to maintain the academic nature of the studies. Another reason for the missing impact could be that universities and other higher education institutions rely on the elaborate judgement of experts (such as professors) when it comes to questions of recognition (cf. [12]). These experts then decide according to their respective expertise. The sole assessment by one person can bias the recognition decision since it is influenced by the individual attitude towards recognition in general and other conscious or unconscious factors. That means that existing recognition systems lack a decision-making process based on transparent, reliable, and binding criteria [13, pp. 60–61] that can be understood by others (cf. [14]). This situation is unsatisfactory because transparency and reliability are quality criteria in the context of recognition [15, p. 238] and will therefore be addressed explicitly.

In our project, we base the recognition system on existing recommendations for higher education in computer science [16] as well as on facets of existing competence models for IT specialists [17, 18] and computer science education. For example, the MoKoM project group (e.g., [19, 20, pp. 77–96]) developed a comprehensive competence model for computer science. For this competence model, the researchers implemented competency level tests with several facets. They defined different knowledge dimensions, the level of connectedness, combinatorial complexity, and the level of the necessary understanding of systems of computer science [21, pp. 199–216]. Although this model was developed to measure individual competencies, some of the different parameters could be used to generally evaluate the levels of competencies gained in vocational education. Other competence models focus on general education – such as the KUI model [22] – or address only certain aspects of computer science like OOP [23] or privacy [24] and are thus not suitable for direct use in our project.

Therefore, an important part of our project is to develop a reliable, transparent, and comprehensible tool to evaluate and assess prior skills and competencies – to become more or less independent from expert ratings.

---

[4] https://www.hrk-nexus.de/projekt-nexus/information-in-english/.

[5] http://ankom.dzhw.eu/know_how/anrechnung.

2.2 Research Questions

Although the project aims to develop and evaluate an exemplary recognition system to promote permeability for IT specialists at FernUniversität in Hagen, the aim of the project part presented in this paper is to develop a tool for assessing the equivalence between the prior knowledge and the competencies to be acquired at higher education. The tool will initially be used for the transition from IT specialist to the bachelor programme in computer science. After successful evaluation, it will gradually be used for other professions and degree programmes.

Considering the current situation of formal recognition for vocational education, the following questions arise:

1. How can competence descriptions from vocational education and training be systematically and comprehensibly compared with those from higher education?
2. What would a system or a tool look like that would support this comparison?
3. How must an assessment tool be designed so that it can make statements about the equivalence of competencies without in-depth expert knowledge?

To answer the research questions, we implemented the interdisciplinary research project called "Permeability"[6], which we describe in Sect. 4. Within the framework of this research project, we developed the tool AsTRA as an answer to these questions.

2.3 General Approach

We use methods from design science (cf. i.e. [25]) and develop the planned recognition system by a cyclical approach. In this approach, we develop several process flows that will be used to implement and later to manage a comprehensive recognition system. These process flows will also be evaluated, further developed, and validated in several cycles while implementing them into a functioning system at FernUniversität in Hagen to support our students.

As previously described, one of our aims is to reduce the influence of expert assessments on the recognition decision by developing clear guidelines and decision-making aids. Our solution, a comprehensive system to assess and compare competencies from different education systems will be presented in the next section.

3 *AsTRA* – *As*sessment *T*ool for *R*ecognition and *A*daptation

Our guiding questions are how to recognise the right competencies and how to support the students by enabling them to study more efficiently. To recognise the right things, we needed a tool to assess and compare competencies described in the official documents from vocational education with our bachelor programme. To master this challenge, we required a system to translate and compare the difficulty and complexity of both education systems within the DQR (IT specialist: DQR level 4, bachelor programmes in higher education: DQR level 6). Although the level description verbs of

[6] https://e.feu.de/permeability (in German).

both DQR levels are based on the taxonomy of Anderson & Krathwohl (AKT) [26], it must be examined to what extent the actual DQR level descriptions correspond to each other.

Furthermore, the German vocational education system's regulatory documents are based on a work process and competence-oriented description (e.g., "Apprentices develop and extend software components"). Competence has been defined as "vocational action competence" which includes the facets of professional and personal competence [27]. In contrast, similar documents for higher education have a subject logical structure (e.g., "Introduction to theoretical computer science" or "advanced aspects of operating systems"). For this reason, we assume that "*competence in the field*" (work experience, ability to contextualise theoretical knowledge and skills) is a fundamental differentiation criterion between an IT specialist and a computer scientist from university. This means, that questions arise whether, e.g., "they *implement* programmes in a high-level programming language" (competence model for IT specialists [17]) has an equivalent meaning both in vocational and academic education. Or – more abstract – what conclusions can be drawn from a possible equivalence in the *learning contents* as well as in the *level of the educational programmes*.

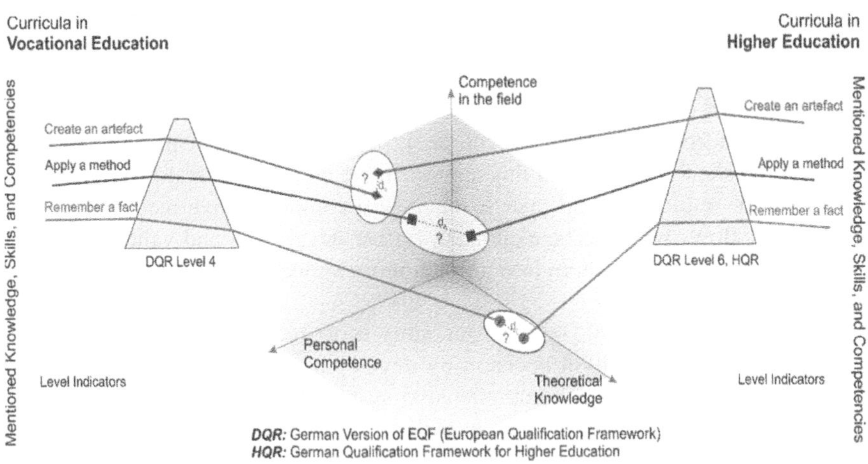

Fig. 1. AsTRA development approach: conceptual idea of matching knowledge, skills, and competencies from vocational to higher education in computer science.

3.1 Development of AsTRA

In the context of recognition "equivalence" does not mean "equal". However, a general definition of this equivalence does not exist. Therefore, we developed such a definition by including several aspects and dimensions:

The DQR proposes *professional knowledge and competency* as a key aspect. Another facet that should be included is *personal competence* (e.g. the competence to organise oneself, to work independently, to work and communicate in teams). As we see "*competence in the field*" as a differentiation criterion, this should be the third aspect. The latter is a combination of experience, professional knowledge, and personal competence. Hence, this aspect is orthogonal to the other two. This results in our 3-dimensional model to assess the inherent equivalence of both educational systems, which can be seen in Fig. 1.

Based on this first model concept, we discussed the possible implementation. We assume that a typical task on a certain level has typical characteristics in both vocational and higher education contexts. These characteristics can be seen each as a triple of values which defines a point in the 3-dimensional model. The open question at this stage is, what is the decision criterion? Is it enough to evaluate the distance d between the points, or does the mutual position of the points in relation to each other also have to be evaluated? This question is a fundamental part of the development of our tool named AsTRA.

As depicted in Fig. 1, we decided to develop a system that translates the AKT level indicators between the two education systems. It became apparent soon that in the first step, we should develop this transfer system based on a specific module. As the module "*Introduction into Imperative Programming*" is a promising module for recognition, we decided to use it as the prototype. Thus, we analysed several documents and sources of information:

The formal documents from vocational education such as *curricula* and *formal training regulations* have a low granularity. Therefore, we used an existing competence model for the profession of IT specialist [17] which we improved by analysing further information gained of previous final examinations. Furthermore, we took a close look at the *module descriptions* and *exercises*. Especially the module descriptions are not always detailed and precise. For this reason, we also analysed the course texts and the several exercises and quizzes which have to be mastered by the students.

As a result, we obtained a comprehensive and structured list of learning outcomes – represented by a level description verb and a learning content noun – with different granularity from both education systems. These statements allow the mapping to the AKT levels and therefore a more precise comparison of competencies. The list contains statements such as "IT specialists *extend* existing software with customer-specific functions or interfaces" or "IT specialists *implement* source code for small problems" from vocational education as well as "students *master* small programming tasks" or "students *complete* a given programme according to specification" from university level. The challenge here is that the content areas are similar, but sometimes very different level indicators are used. For example, in vocational training, the statement "IT specialists *develop* algorithms and functions for processing given lists" can be found, while in the bachelor programme the competence "they *use* simple dynamic data structures such as linear lists" has been described. Although these two competencies are different in terms of level, they refer to the same area (data structures/lists). The question of equivalence can therefore not be decided by looking at individual characteristics and statements alone, but the entirety of the contents of the training and the modules under assessment, and their level must be considered.

Therefore, we postulate that equivalence can only be achieved if there is first equivalence in terms of content (necessary but not sufficient criterion). Only then can equivalence be assessed by evaluating the level in the second step. Hence, we developed AsTRA in a way that each assessment consists of two stages:

First Stage: Content Analysis. To assess whether the content and level of vocational education and training as IT specialist is equivalent to the module "Introduction into imperative programming", we first used AsTRA for a content analysis. We grouped the statements of both education systems by content areas such as "testing", "modelling", or "implementing and programming" (see Table 1). We found that all content areas from university studies are also part of the apprenticeship as an IT specialist. Moreover, the content priorities are similar in both programmes. Areas such as software ergonomics, documentation, data security and data protection are not addressed in the module but are part of the training. Only one single aspect from the module is not part of the vocational training, namely recursion, which is not a core aspect of the module. Therefore, we assume equivalence in terms of content.

Table 1. Content analysis: content areas in the module "Introduction into imperative programming". The numbers show the ratio of statements in each area. Total: 40 statements for IT specialists, 45 statements for the university module.

Content area	IT specialist	University module
Modelling concept development	10.0% knowl., 20.0% skills	4.4% knowl., 0.0% skills
Software ergonomics	2.5% knowl., 2.5% skills	–
Implementing and Programming	0.0% knowl., 45.0% skills	4.4% knowl., 73.3% skills
Testing	2.5% knowl., 5.0% skills	2.2% knowl., 15.6% skills
Documentation	2.5% knowl., 5.0% skills	–
Data security and Privacy	2.5% knowl., 2.5% skills	–

Second Stage: Level Analysis. The DQR classifies a finished bachelor programme at level 6. Students reach this level step by step. For this reason, we first introduced a *level translation* for modules. We assume that students start their studies at level 4 on average, because the vocational baccalaureate diploma as university entrance is also located on this level. By acquiring credit points and gaining competencies, they reach level 6 at the end of their bachelor studies. Our exemplary module is located in the study entry phase, and we assume that students reach a maximum of DQR level 4.5 in the first year of study. We further assume that after second year of study, students reach level 5, and after the third year, they finally reach level 6. We define this value as *relative module complexity* (cf. Fig. 2).

Vocational Training

DQR 4	Complexity Adjustment Factor: Theoretical Experise	Complexity Adjustment Factor: Personal Competence	Complexity Adjustment Factor: Competence in the Field	Absolute Complexity: Theoretical Experise	Absolute Complexity: Personal Competence	Absolute Complexity: Competence in the Field	Overall Indicator (2:1:2)
Creating	0	0	1	4	4	5	6,00
Evaluating	1	1	1	5	5	5	6,71
Analyzing	1	0	1	5	4	5	6,57
Applying	0	0	1	4	4	5	6,00
Understanding	0	-1	-2	4	3	2	4,22
Remembering	-1	-2	-2	3	2	2	3,35
							5,475

Weighted vector length for each level

Relative Module Complexity: 4,5

Bachelor Programme

Overall Indicator (2:1:2)	Absolute Complexity: Theoretical Experise	Absolute Complexity: Personal Competence	Absolute Complexity: Competence in the Field	Complexity Adjustment Factor: Theoretical Experise	Complexity Adjustment Factor: Personal Competence	Complexity Adjustment Factor: Competence in the Field	DQR 6
5,33	4,5	3,5	3,5	0	-1	-1	Creating
5,33	4,5	3,5	3,5	0	-1	-1	Evaluating
5,33	4,5	3,5	3,5	0	-1	-1	Analyzing
5,33	4,5	3,5	3,5	0	-1	-1	Applying
4,86	4,5	3,5	2,5	0	-1	-2	Understanding
4,01	3,5	2,5	2,5	-1	-2	-2	Remembering
5,03							

Unweighted mean of level vector lengths

Fig. 2. AsTRA – Level translation of the module "Introduction into Imperative Programming". The overall indicators for each AKT level on both sides are weighted to give more weight to professional than to personal competencies. The overall mean was calculated unweighted over all AKT levels.

The next step was to estimate a *complexity adjustment factor* to consider both the individual difficulty and requirements of the module and the working field in apprenticeship. This is the only step that only depends on the inherent knowledge and experience of the assessing person. In our example, to master the basic programming module, students need only little personal competence or competence in the field – so the adjustment factors lower the absolute complexities of each AKT level for these factors. The resulting triples of absolute complexities describe 3-dimensional position vectors in the coordinate system of Fig. 1. Calculating the (weighted) lengths of the vectors provides an *overall indicator* for each AKT level (see Fig. 2). Comparing only the length seems sufficient in the first development cycle, as the position vectors are very close to each other and therefore the absolute length is sufficient as a criterion. A refinement including the position is planned for the next development steps.

The learning content from vocational education is rated as more complex and on a higher DQR-related level in this case. To improve this first result, we evaluated the statements of the content analysis again. We subsequently calculated the (relative) complexity of each AKT level (see Fig. 3), which also takes the relative frequency of the different level statements into account. As a result, we obtained a complexity level, based on the weighted number of statements from the content analysis and the overall indicator of the module respectively the professional working field. In our first application, we defined equivalence if the deviation between the scores is not more than 20%, referred to the complexity of the university module.

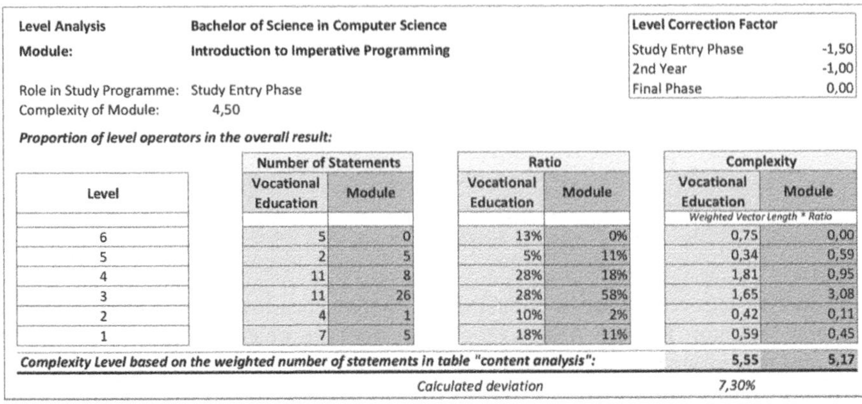

Level Analysis	**Bachelor of Science in Computer Science**
Module:	**Introduction to Imperative Programming**
Role in Study Programme:	Study Entry Phase
Complexity of Module:	4,50

Level Correction Factor	
Study Entry Phase	-1,50
2nd Year	-1,00
Final Phase	0,00

Proportion of level operators in the overall result:

Level	Number of Statements: Vocational Education	Number of Statements: Module	Ratio: Vocational Education	Ratio: Module	Complexity (*Weighted Vector Length * Ratio*): Vocational Education	Complexity: Module
6	5	0	13%	0%	0,75	0,00
5	2	5	5%	11%	0,34	0,59
4	11	8	28%	18%	1,81	0,95
3	11	26	28%	58%	1,65	3,08
2	4	1	10%	2%	0,42	0,11
1	7	5	18%	11%	0,59	0,45
Complexity Level based on the weighted number of statements in table "content analysis":					5,55	5,17
				Calculated deviation	*7,30%*	

Fig. 3. AsTRA – Level analysis of the module "Introduction into Imperative Programming". The complexity of the contents from vocational education in this field is higher than of the resp. module. The calculated deviation has been based on the (relative) complexity of the module.

3.2 How Can AsTRA Support Recognition?

We used AsTRA in this version for all modules that have been promising due to expert judgement to analyse for our project. We compared the results with several expert ratings and found only little need for change in our model at this stage. This tool allows us to evaluate whether or not a module could be credited by recognition. It also helps to support the development of adapted teaching material and to identify gaps in competencies reported by our students for individual recognition. Currently, we use AsTRA to evaluate courses and modules, and as a further step we plan to apply it also for the analysis of study programmes. Furthermore, AsTRA helps us to ask the relevant questions, such as 'is it appropriate to adapt this teaching material for all students of a cohort (like IT specialists), because we can assume that most students already have certain competence?', 'does it make more sense to adapt the courses for the individuals?' or 'are there key aspects for individual recognition of a module we should take care of?'. In the next section we show how the implementation of the tool moves the project forward by using and evaluating it.

4 Structure of the "Permeability Project"

In our project, we defined *three pillars of recognition* to promote reaching our goal to create a comprehensive recognition system.

First Pillar – Blanket Recognition: For this recognition, students have only to submit their training certificate from their completed vocational training as IT specialist to the examination office. Assessing our course modules with AsTRA, we identified "*Introduction into Imperative Programming*" (5 CP) to be recognised on-demand for all these students, and "*Basic Training in Programming*" (10 CP) from the second study year for IT specialists in application development.

Second Pillar – Individual Recognition: This can be applied to all modules whose learning content is not or only partially part of the vocational training. The procedure of individual recognition is an assessment of individual cases to acknowledge and recognise non-formally and informally acquired competencies with up to 20 CP by assessing a portfolio written by the students.

Third Pillar – Adaptation of Learning Pathways: Using AsTRA, we found several modules (e.g., "*Databases*", "*Operating Systems & Computer Networks*" or "*OOP*") which have an overlap in learning content and level with vocational education. This overlap is not enough to recognise the whole course. Therefore, we offer the opportunity to use adapted (digital) course material that allows the students to design their learning pathways by getting recommendations for their next steps based on their prior knowledge. In this way, students can thus study more effectively by only working on the content that is new to them.

5 Conclusion

The tool named AsTRA that we presented in this paper is an essential part of the "Permeability Project" which scrutinises the permeability between vocational and academic education systems. We found that competence descriptions from vocational education and training, and those from higher education, can be systematically and comprehensibly compared by mapping them to a metric space and then calculating the distance. This has been implemented into our tool AsTRA that allows us to assess the previous competencies of students based on transparent, reliable, and binding criteria and formulae. It therefore provides the possibility to create a transparent, reliable, and comprehensive recognition system that has been practically implemented in Winter 20/21. Further work will show how we can deal with students who bring lots of competencies into their studies – but competencies that do not match our modules, for example because the students are physicists, or engineers, or something completely different.

So how can we value and recognise these competencies? To do that we need an approach that goes beyond our three-pillar model and AsTRA. Our intention is to formally value further competencies. For this reason, our future question is, what constitutes a degree programme and what role do individual modules play in the various degree programmes?

References

1. Opel, S., Desel, J., Magenheim, J.: Aspekte horizontaler und vertikaler beruflicher Informatikausbildung. In: Dreher R., Jenewein, K., Neustock, U., Schwenger, U. (eds.) Wandel der technischen Berufsbildung: Ansätze und Zukunftsperspektiven, W. Bertelsmann Verlag, Bielefeld, Germany, Berufsbildung, Arbeit und Innovation, vol. 41, pp. 67–76 (2016)
2. Jacob, M.: Mehrfachausbildungen in Deutschland – Karriere, Collage, Kompensation? Springer, Berlin, Germany (2013). https://doi.org/10.1007/978-3-322-80553-9

3. Bednarz, S.: Gestaltung von Übergängen. Durchlässigkeit zwischen beruflicher und hochschulischer Bildung, pp. 365–384 (2019)
4. European Centre for the Development of Vocational Education (CEDEFOP): GERMANY – European Inventory on NQF 2018. European Centre for the Development of Vocational Education (CEDEFOP), Brussels, Belgium (2018)
5. Børnåvold, J.: The potential impact of the European qualifications framework (EQF) on systems for validation of non-formal and informal learning. In: Managing European Diversity in Lifelong Learning, p. 79 (2007)
6. Powell, J.J., Graf, L., Bernhard, N., Coutrot, L., Kieffer, A.: The shifting relationship between vocational and higher education in France and Germany: towards convergence? Eur. J. Educ. **47**(3), 405–423 (2012)
7. Stamm-Riemer, I.: Accreditation of prior certificated learning – learning pathways from vocational education and training to higher education. In: 6th International Colloquium of the UNIversity in the Society (2007)
8. Freitag, W.K., Buhr, R., Danzeglocke, E.M., Schröder, S., Völk, D.: Übergänge gestalten: Durchlässigkeit zwischen beruflicher und hochschulischer Bildung erhöhen. Waxmann Verlag, Münster, Germany (2015)
9. Kultusministerkonferenz (KMK): Anrechnung von außerhalb des Hochschulwesens erworbenen Kenntnissen und Fähigkeiten auf ein Hochschulstudium (Beschluss der Kultusministerkonferenz, 28 June 2002) (2002)
10. Schermutzki, M.: Learning Outcomes – Lernergebnisse: Begriffe, Zusammenhänge, Umsetzung und Erfolgsermittlung. Lernergebnisse und Kompetenzvermittlung als elementare Orientierungen des Bologna-Prozesses (2008)
11. Müskens, W., Müskens, I., Hanft, A.: Application and impact of learning outcomes on institutional cooperation, accreditation and assessment. In: Prager, K., Schabauer, E., Winkler, E. (eds.) Implementing Competence Orientation and Learning Outcomes in Higher Education – Processes and Practises in Five Countries, pp. 82–109. Danube University, Krems (2008)
12. Müskens, W., Wittig, W., Tutschner, R., Eilers-Schoof, A.: Module level indicator. MLI User Guide Assessment of the Level of Competence Orientation (2013)
13. Desel, J.: Modellieren lehren – Lehren modellieren (Extended abstract of invited lecture). In: Joint Proceedings of Modellierung 2020: Short, Workshop and Tools and Demo Papers, Workhop zur Modellierung in der Hochschullehre, pp 58–62 (2020)
14. Hartmann, E.A., Knust, M., Loroff, C., Stamm-Riemer, I.: Towards permeability between vocational and academic education. Eur. J. Educ. **44**(3), 351–368 (2009)
15. Seger, M.S., Waldeyer, C.: Qualitätssicherung im Kontext der Anrechnung und Anerkennung von Lernergebnissen an Hochschulen. Shaker, Herzogenrath, Germany (2014)
16. Desel, J., et al.: Empfehlungen für Bachelor- und Masterprogramme im Studienfach Informatik an Hochschulen (Juli 2016). Gesellschaft für Informatik e.V., Bonn, Germany (2016)
17. Opel S.: Entwicklung eines arbeitsprozessorientierten Kompetenzstrukturmodells für die Ausbildung zum Fachinformatiker/zur Fachinformatikerin. University of Duisburg-Essen (2020). https://doi.org/10.17185/duepublico/72913
18. Opel, S., Brinda, T.: What do I have to know and to do? Development of a theory-based, normative competence description for the profession of computer specialists. In: Proceedings of the Workshop in Primary and Secondary Computing Education, WiPSCE 2015, pp. 96–101. ACM (2015)
19. Linck, B., et al.: Competence model for informatics modelling and system comprehension. In: 2013 IEEE Global Engineering Education Conference (EDUCON), pp. 85–93 (2013)

20. Bröker, K., Kastens, U., Magenheim, J.: Competences of undergraduate computer science students. In: KEYCIT 2014: Key Competencies in Informatics and ICT, vol. 7, pp. 77 (2015)
21. Magenheim, J., Nelles, W., Neugebauer, J., Ohrndorf, L., Schaper, N., Schubert, S.: Expert rating of competence levels in upper secondary CS education. In: KEYCIT 2014: Key Competencies in Informatics and ICT, vol. 7, pp. 199 (2015)
22. Margaritis, M., Magenheim, J., Hubwieser, P., Berges, M., Ohrndorf, L., Schubert, S.: Development of a competency model for computer science teachers at secondary school level. In: 2015 IEEE Global Engineering Education Conference (EDUCON), pp. 211–220 (2015)
23. Kramer, M., Tobinski, D., Brinda, T.: Modelling competency in the field of OOP: from investigating computer science curricula to developing test items. In: Brinda, T., Mavengere, N., Haukijärvi, I., Lewin, C., Passey, D. (eds.) SaITE. IAICT, vol. 493, pp. 37–46. Springer, Cham (2016). https://doi.org/10.1007/978-3-319-54687-2_4
24. Hug, A., Grimm, R.: Extension of a didactic media competence model by privacy risk. In: Proceedings of the 11th Workshop in Primary and Secondary Computing Education, pp.104–105 (2016)
25. Reimann, P.: Design-based research. In: Markauskaite, L., Freebody, P., Irwin, J. (eds.) Methodological Choice and Design. Methodos Series (Methodological Prospects in the Social Sciences), vol 9, pp. 37–50. Springer, Dordrecht (2011). https://doi.org/10.1007/978-90-481-8933-5_3
26. Anderson, L.W., Krathwohl, D.R. (eds.): A Taxonomy for Learning, Teaching, and Assessing: a Revision of Bloom's Taxonomy of Educational Objectives. Longman, New York (2001)
27. Kultusministerkonferenz (KMK): Handreichung für die Erarbeitung von Rahmenlehrplänen für den berufsbezogenen Unterricht in der Berufsschule. KMK Referat für berufliche Bildung, Bonn, Germany (2011)

Is It Real? – Learners' Perceptions on Tele-Immersive 3D Video Technology and Its Further Use in K-12 Education

Erkki Rötkönen[1], Calkin Suero Montero[2(✉)], Nicolas Pope[1], and Erkki Sutinen[1]

[1] Department of Computing, University of Turku, 20014 Turku, Finland
{erkki.rotkonen,nicolas.pope,erkki.sutinen}@utu.fi
[2] School of Educational Sciences and Psychology, University of Eastern Finland, 80101 Joensuu, Finland
calkins@uef.fi

Abstract. Current immersive technology applications, such as virtual and augmented reality (VR/AR), are still limited in providing an immersive experience in which a user is perceived in 3 dimensions (3D) as their real self. Furthermore, research on such immersive environments applied to educational contexts is scarce. To investigate the unexplored opportunities of immersive technologies in education, we carried out a trial of our tele-immersive platform (TIP) with elementary school 6th grade learners (12–13-year-olds) working on an environmental study lesson. During our investigations, we applied qualitative analysis of the learners' focus group interview, researchers' field notes, and recordings of test sessions, alongside descriptive statistics of questionnaires. Learners expressed feelings of positive surprise and excitement, and felt the technology enabled their participation throughout the lesson. Learners recounted feelings of 'being there' inside the environment, and in the company of the teacher. Learners agreed that their sense of physical proximity and presence inside the immersive environment is similar to that of face-to-face interaction with the teacher. With our investigations, the opportunities of this emerging technology towards boosting online educational activities for learners to develop their 21C skills are highlighted. Our findings indicate that the introduced 3D TIP technology has the critical potential to overcome psychological strains due to physical distance in online education.

Keywords: Sense of presence · Immersive learning environments · 21C skills

1 Introduction

The outbreak of the Covid-19 pandemic since 2020 has rapidly increased the demand for online communication in education. We see the use of online platforms ranging from asynchronous email, online discussion boards, and blogs, to synchronous video conferencing, text messaging and Voice-over-IP services (in which the learners and instructor are together online at the same time) as well as hybrid formats combining different forms of media (e.g., text, audio, video) and different timescales (e.g.,

Published by Springer Nature Switzerland AG 2022
D. Passey et al. (Eds.): OCCE 2021, IFIP AICT 642, pp. 234–246, 2022.
https://doi.org/10.1007/978-3-030-97986-7_20

asynchronous, synchronous) within the same meeting [1]. Technologies such as virtual (VR), augmented (AR) or extended reality (XR), might be used to create more realistic group encounters for distance learning and online collaborative activities, for instance. In this vein, immersive learning environments expanding traditional VR or telepresence are emerging as a suitable solution for supporting novel forms of online collaboration and practices [2, 3]. Nevertheless, the fast demand for the development of immersive technologies in educational practices is ridden with limitations that can be addressed at the design stage, through the involvement of students and teachers throughout the design process, as advocated by co-design [4]. Still, there remains insufficient evidence about the effect of immersive 3D video technology on an overall sense of presence or on key factors related to learning [3].

In previous work, in which primary school children collaborate across national, regional, political and cultural boundaries in the same immersive virtual learning space, Rötkönen et al. (2019) [5] reported concrete suggestions that the learners provided for improvements, including the use of real faces rather than drawn avatars, and their wish to meet, get to know each other, talk, shake hands, play and be together in the virtual environment as normally as they act in real life.

To further investigate this matter, we have designed and implemented a live 3D tele-immersive platform (TIP) - an environment for K-12 education providing an immersive three-dimensional alternative to video. TIP integrates novel 3D video technologies, within which the teacher can be perceived in 3 dimensions, generating a sense of being with a real-life person, instead of an avatar. In our prototype, rather than using immersive virtual environments, real environments are digitally captured live to form a high-fidelity model of a physical space and its occupants.

Extending the work of Rötkönen et al. (2019), our study is, therefore, a preliminary investigation of the experiences and sense of presence that TIP technologies can generate. We are seeking for signs of the potential positive effects of the TIP technology, as well as identifying the main challenges the technology presents in online educational contexts. Hence, this paper investigates further the opportunities and challenges in relation to the *sense of presence*, *technology* and *education* that is perceived within our TIP prototype during an online learning activity for elementary school children. We believe this kind of technology is very promising for creating and supporting novel forms of collaboration and practices for students and teachers during distance, as well as hybrid, learning activities. Our research questions, therefore, are:

RQ 1) *What are the perceptions of the learners towards the new 3D telepresence technology for education?*
RQ 2) *What impact does the new 3D telepresence technology currently have on the learners' sense of presence?*

2 Related Work

Information and communication technology (ICT) tools are now mainly used in schools in traditional ways to communicate, create, disseminate, store, and manage information, for instance, which has been reported to undermine the potential by which technology can reform the education realm [6]. However, as new pedagogical approaches emerge, aided by ICT tools, there is a change in education from the traditional teacher-centred classroom to a collaborative learner-centred classroom where learners can be actively engaged in the educational process, and knowledge, skills and attitudes are constructed and distributed in a collaborative way. Furthermore, the trend of the 21C towards a globally connected world, facilitated by the access to online technologies, has also had a profound impact on developing online collaborative learning as a new paradigm, connecting learners globally beyond the classroom. When learners are geographically dispersed, online technologies can be used to create connections and communication for sharing ideas and to co-create new understandings with others, making the local connect with the global, and learning happens in interconnected situations, utilising online technologies [7]. The utilisation of ICT is a way for learners to develop 21C skills [8], to prepare them as global citizens. Thus, under the collaborative learning paradigm, a future school needs to be equipped with people, tools and partnerships that allow the school to support its learners and local communities to act in the world, to set problems and solve them, extend their curiosity and to act upon it from a global perspective [9].

In order to support online collaborative learning and connect globally, emerging immersive technologies may provide functional solutions, since they can support the user to perceive each other in a natural way inside an otherwise virtual, or digitally generated, environment. For instance, VR applications can enhance learning and advance social and creative skills, and the use of them in learning situations seems to improve digital-age interactive literacy, creative thinking, communication, collaboration and problem-solving ability, which constitute 21C skills [10]. However, currently available educational technologies, such as e-learning tools, or traditional VR platforms, such as Second Life and Active Worlds, do not offer realistic learning experience environments, as these technologies are not able to replicate the perception of presence, a sense of "being there" with another person as in real life, which is vital for providing close-to-real-life experience and interactions. Social interactions are particularly important in K-12 educational contexts [11], as peer learning and socially constructed knowledge have been demonstrated to be fundamental for the socio-cognitive development of the learners in that age.

However, the concept of *presence* is very broad and has a variety of definitions and meanings. In our study, we look at the *sense of presence* in three dimensions: *presence* can offer insights into the medium's ability to provide the feeling that the user is "there" inside the media (*telepresence*), as well as in the "company of others" (*copresence*). At the same time, *presence* can measure the extent to which people feel that the interface is able to provide some sense of access to another's mind and connect people (*social presence*) [12]. Presence has been recognised as a key performance goal for many systems e.g., social presence as direct contributor to the success of the educational experience [13]. However, it is still a complex task to evaluate presence in an objective way [14]. To our knowledge, there is yet no known work on measuring a sense of presence of 3D video technologies with children. Moreover, there is a challenge that the questions of existing data collection mechanisms are difficult for children to answer, due to them being targeted at adults (and in our case, also language translation being required).

In the research area of technology use to support computer mediated collaboration, there is now an increasing, but still limited, amount of work towards synchronous telepresence technologies in education. Asynchronous collaboration tools have been receiving more attention [15]. In terms of applications of live 3D capture technology in education, there has been little if any progress since a few early trials [16, 17]. There is an abundance of work on immersive virtual learning environments or Collaborative Virtual Environments (CVEs), but not on 3D tele-immersive capture technology [15]. To our knowledge, there are currently three broad approaches being taken in industry and academia to achieve real time hyper-realistic 3D representation of people and spaces: a) Microsoft "Holoportation" or similar depth map fusion technologies [18]; b) Facebook "Codec Avatars" generated using machine learning; and c) dynamic reconstruction using only a single camera [19, 20]. Our own solutions at the University of Turku fit within category (a) currently.

The focus in the literature remains technical in nature, with little pedagogical evaluation and a very narrow view of the future potential. Moreover, there is little research on the pedagogy needed to make full use of the technology in K-12 education, and there is limited understanding of the affordances it may offer [3]. Our 3D TIP technology can be considered as a strong candidate to meliorate the shortcomings found in online technologies when applied to K-12 connective learning and education. In this paper, therefore, we present opportunities and challenges of a TIP prototype, towards its relevance in fostering a sense of presence among the learners that participated in our study.

3 3D Tele-Immersive Platform Prototype

In our study we use an in-house developed live 3D tele-immersive video platform (TIP). Our prototype setup consists of 6 stereo pairs of cameras, each pair connected to a desktop computer with a GPU (NVIDIA GeForce RTX 2080) for depth processing. The cameras are arranged around the edges of the room or group to passively capture the scene without intrusion. Once the depth data is captured from each camera, the camera views are merged together using camera pose information gained through a calibration step, to achieve a high-quality fusion with reduced noise distortion and errors in the different individual depth estimates from each camera.

Following fusion, the data are compressed as regular videos, using hardware for real-time performance. After transmission, the multiple video feeds for colour and depth are decoded, compression artefacts are filtered, and then arbitrary 3D views can be rendered locally using a straightforward point-cloud or mesh rendering combined with reprojection to the colour video feeds to add texture. Additionally, virtual objects, including live screen captures placed on walls or tables, can be mixed into the final scene. The overall latency of our prototype is around 200 ms, allowing a two-way experience where each physical space is captured and transmitted to the same web server. A viewing client can then obtain the data of multiple spaces and merge them together during the render step. The rendering is then viewed via a computer 2D display (using a web browser or an Open GL renderer), via an AR/VR headset or via a mobile phone.

4 Study Methodology

Our work is framed within a pragmatic research paradigm and is using research through design as a methodology [21]. This methodology states that research may develop not only through increasing agreement, but also through discursiveness and elaboration. Thus, rather than making statements about what is, the design aspect of the research is concerned with creating what might be [22]. In order to understand the applicability of 3D immersive video technology in real educational settings, we carried out testing sessions of an in-house prototype system together with learners, teachers and researchers. The prototype testing was designed to allow measuring the sense of presence that the technology fostered in the learners. As such, this study is framed within the following hypotheses:

H1: *The perceptions of the learners on the use of 3D immersive video in education will be positive (RQ1).*
H2: *Immersive 3D video technology will foster a high sense of presence in the learners (RQ2).*

4.1 Participants

Fourteen learners (6th grade, 12–13-year-olds) at one elementary school in Finland were chosen via random selection and given the opportunity to participate in testing our 3D tele-immersive video technology prototype. The elementary school involved is governed and financed by the municipality. Written permission was obtained from the parents or guardians of all participating learners, and the learners were also informed at the beginning about the nature of the research. Some learners had previously participated in research studies on unrelated VR technologies with our university. A single teacher at the same school was involved in the prototype testing and the learners knew the teacher well.

4.2 Experimental Setup and Testing Sessions

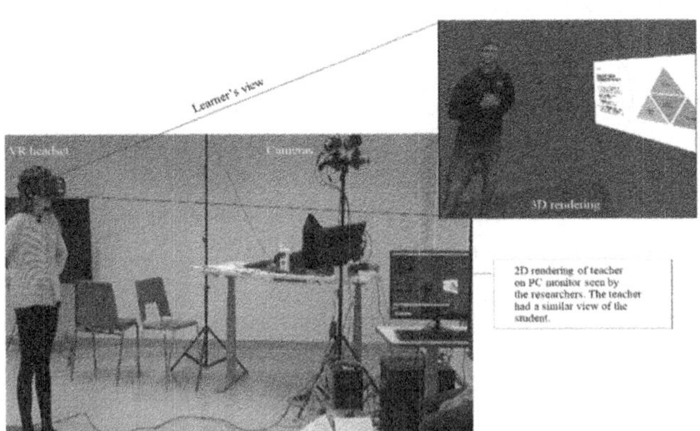

Fig. 1. Experimental setup, learner's view, and 3D rendering (Calkin Suero Montero 2021©, reprinted with permission)

During testing, the learners were in the school whilst the teacher was in another physically separate space off site, at our university facilities. The system was set one-way so that the digital view of the captured physical space where the teacher was located was received by the learners using an AR/VR headset (see Fig. 1). The teacher viewed the learners via a 2D display of a client computer using GeForce 1050+ and OpenGL renderer. This implementation was used in order to test a suitable trade-off between the system affordances, the costs of implementation, and the beneficial outcome of using this type of emerging technology in education from the learner's perspective (the learners are the ones that observe the teacher in 3 dimensions inside the immersive environment). Two researchers and a single video camera were located with the children to record the activity. The digital view of the VR headset viewpoint was recorded also for analysis. The 3D data was also recorded in addition to the video view of the participant. Between each participant, the equipment was disinfected due in part to the ongoing pandemic.

Each session with each learner lasted for approximately 20 min of which 10 min was the activity using the technology. After entering the testing room, the learner filled in a pre-questionnaire on the computer. The learner was then given brief instructions how to use the immersive 3D video prototype. After this, the learner was set to work on an educational activity together with the teacher within the virtual environment. The educational activity was a typical environmental study lesson related to the different kinds of fire, a subject that they had covered in their previous academic year and the instruction by the teacher was done by exploring the topic with the learner synchronously using a whiteboard. Each learner was assigned a random number which they then used to identify themselves to the observers and in their survey responses. Immediately following the learning activity, the learner answered the presence questionnaire using an online survey tool.

4.3 Data Collection

A presence questionnaire, researchers' observation, video analysis, and focus group interview were used to investigate the hypotheses. The questions in the questionnaire were translated into Finnish by an experienced teacher to ensure they were phrased appropriately for the learners in their native Finnish language. The measures used included *the Temple Presence Inventory* [23] *the Networked Minds Questionnaire* [24] *and the MEC Spatial Presence Questionnaire* [25]. The sessions as well as the digital view of the VR headset viewpoint, the 3D data and the video view of each participant were recorded for analysis. Two researchers were located with the learners to record the activity by taking field notes. The observations helped the researchers notice, identify, and understand different types of practical challenges that are faced during the sessions. After all the sessions were conducted a focus group interview was arranged with the learners. The purpose of the focus group interview was to deepen our understanding on the issues that were found from the observations. The interview protocol consisted of inquiring about the learners' feelings and experiences, feedback, and evaluation, as well as suggested improvements.

5 Results and Analysis

The recordings and observation notes thereof from the sessions, together with the interview transcript were content analysed. We used an inductive approach to thematic analysis [26] which resulted in three themes: *sense of presence perceptions*, *technology perceptions* and *educational applications perceptions*. Here, we present these three key themes and discuss opportunities offered and further challenges to address in relation to the use and development of 3D tele-immersive video in educational contexts, also answering the hypothesis set in the study.

5.1 Sense of Presence Perceptions

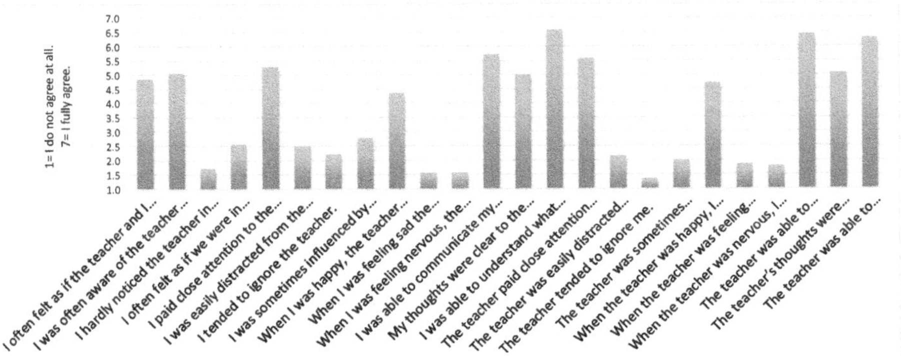

Fig. 2. Social presence questionnaire (descriptive statistics)

In relation to a sense of presence, from the social presence perspective, the learners reported that they highly perceived the teacher being immersed in the environment together with them (telepresence) also being easy to understand the teacher's expressions and ideas as if they were physically close (copresence), (see Fig. 2). For instance, item 2 (Q2), *(I often felt that the teacher was in the same space as me)* had an average response of over 5 on a 7-points Likert scale (1 = completely disagree | 7 = completely agree), while questions 3 (*I hardly notice the teacher in the space*) and 4 (*I felt as if we were in different places*) had an average score of 2.5 or below. Similarly, items 14, 22 and 24 related to the perception of understanding between the teacher and the learners had a high average response of 6 and above, indicating that it was easy for the students to understand the teacher's expressions and meanings within the virtual environment. This validates our H2 (also providing answers to RQ2).

The learners said in the focus group interview they had a feeling of being in the actual environment themselves and in the same space as the teacher, as indicted by the following quote: "*... and it felt as if* [I was] *in the same place with the teacher. I didn't* *even notice that I was wearing the glasses.*" (Girl2). Furthermore, the learners reported that it was not really important for them whether the environment contained errors or contradictions in order to work on the lesson: "*I looked around in a way so how the place looked like,..., looking.., like, where you are and all... like, What's in here?*" (Boy1 and Boy2). In general, the learners paid attention to the teacher, his voice and body expressions and gestures and they understood what the teacher meant during the lesson, which shows good potential for an educational application.

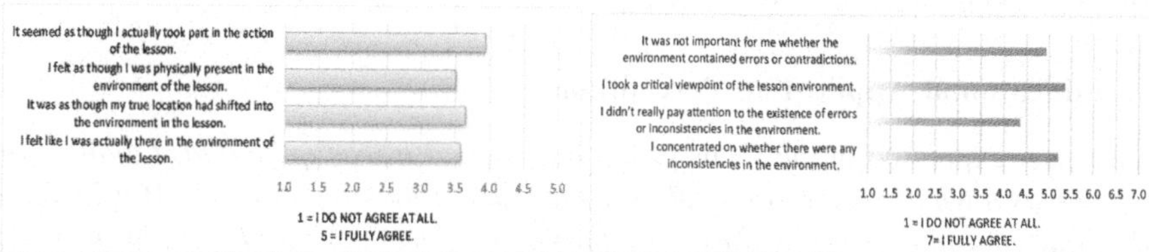

Fig. 3. (Left) sense of self-location in the immersive environment. (Right) perceived errors in the immersive environment

5.2 Technology Perceptions

We observed from the collected questionnaire that even though the learners enjoyed the immersive aspect of the technology (e.g., the feeling of 'being there') there are still several issues to address in terms of their self-location within the virtual environment. That is, for instance Fig. 3, Left, item Q4 "*I felt like I was actually there in the environment of the lesson*" had an average score of 3.6 from the respondents (Likert scale 1= not at all, 5 = completely). This indicates that the learners, perhaps, could not perceive themselves physically in the immersive environment as fully as they could perceive their teacher. Furthermore, due to the preliminary nature of the technology the environment tested was very basic, without distracting backgrounds or clues as to where the learners could be located inside of it. Also, Fig. 3, Right, item Q3 "*I didn't really pay attention to the existence of errors or inconsistencies in the environment*", had average score of 4.4 (Likert scale 1 = completely disagree, 7 = completely agree), indicating that in fact the learners did pay attention to glitches that occurred in the TIP environment.

Nevertheless, the focus group discussion revealed that the learners were comfortable enough with the technology, even at this stage, to accept it despite the limitations of self-location and errors that it presented, having strong feelings of 'being there', in the company of their teacher. During our testing, even though some of the learners had previous experiences of VR environments this novel immersive technology was totally new and different from anything else they had experienced before: the first time they could see someone else as her/himself in a virtual environment. A sample quote in the following from the focus group interview highlights the issue:

Interviewer: "*How did you feel when you went to the VR environment and you saw the teacher*...".
Girl1: "*Interesting, cool*".
Girl2*:* "*It was quite odd. I didn't expect to see him as a whole*...".
Boy1*:* "*It was kind of odd and interesting and exciting to see*...".
Boy2*:* "*It was kind of surprising, it was different than I expected.*"

These impressions of positive surprise and excitement also reveal a sense of novelty from the use of the technology, since all the students were experiencing a 3D immersive technology for the first time.

5.3 Educational Application Perceptions

The learners expressed in the focus group interview: "*It was quite odd, I didn't expect to see him as a whole, when you could see the teacher moving and all.*" (Boy2). "*It was kind of odd and interesting and exciting to see all expressions and the movements and all the little things.*" (Girl1) This indicates support for the learners to perceive each other in a more realistic way inside a virtual environment enabling observation of subtle details of objects e.g. for recognising people's faces and body language and (facial) expressions which can indicate the emotional state or level of comprehension of the others when communicating and working together.

In their answers, the learners also indicated they were able to communicate their intentions clearly to the teacher and that their thoughts were clear to the teacher, thus understanding each other meanings. The learners felt that the teacher paid close attention to them. Some of the learners mentioned they look curiously around the environment but that this did not actually disturb their concentration. They thought that when the novelty factor diminishes it would be even more like a normal learning environment for them. These reported experiences validate our H1, also offers a positive answer to RQ1.

6 Discussion

Based on results of preliminary experiments, we pose in Table 1 opportunities offered and further challenges to address use of immersive 3D video in educational contexts.

Table 1. Summary of challenges and opportunities offered by immersive 3D video

Perspective	Challenges	Opportunities
Sense of presence	HMD gadgets difficult usage. Lack of eye contact when using the headset Lack of eyes and face gestures when using the headset	Feeling of being inside the actual environment Feeling of being in the same space as the other and in his/her company Feeling of being able to understand the other's intentions and feelings
Technology	Need for technical assistance Laborious setup Cost of equipment HMD technology Environment background Technical glitches	Positive technology acceptance Technology attractiveness Support the learners to perceive each other in a more realistic way inside a virtual environment Recognising and observing people's faces and other objects in great detail High-fidelity body language and facial expression Ability to arbitrarily shift the focus of attention
Education	Dependence on adults, with pre-established power dynamics, which may result in a power imbalance Dependence on specialised technical skills	Learning and developing collaborative skills through online interaction Learning and developing digital skills for learners and teachers Learning to express and communicate ideas in an online environment Wide array of tools available for online and hybrid collaboration Non-obstructiveness enabling learners to focus on the learning process Shared interaction with real objects (e.g., using a real whiteboard, not a digital one) Unrestricted or informal positioning in the physical environment

Regarding a sense of presence, we observed from the collected questionnaire that even though learners enjoyed the immersive aspect of the technology there are still issues to address in terms of their self-location. The learners were comfortable enough with the technology, even at this stage, to accept it despite limitations of self-location that it presented, having strong feelings of 'being there', in the company of their teacher.

In terms of the technology implementation, the learners found the idea of being immersed in a 3D environment appealing, in spite of the issues reported with the use of an early prototype technology. Through the technology, the learners could perceive subtle body language and expressions that indicate the emotional state or level of their teacher's understanding of what the learner say. The technology also could offer the teacher the ability to direct their focus and look for cues on whether they and the task are being understood. A point of consideration, however, is the high costs of implementation of the technology at the present (about 30,000€ in this setup).

With regards to education, the technology could advance 21C skills in terms of collaborative online and hybrid learning. Furthermore, the technology is able to isolate or extract elements from the physical environment that could create distractions during interactive learning activities, or conversely it could augment the virtual environment with virtual elements. For online collaborative learning and connecting globally, beyond the classroom the technology could provide suitable solutions, since it can support the learners to perceive each other in a more realistic way inside a virtual environment enabling observation of subtle details of objects e.g. for recognising people's faces and body language and (facial) expressions which can indicate the emotional state or level of comprehension of the others when communicating and working together.

7 Conclusions

In this study, we investigated the experiences and sense of presence generated with a tele-immersive 3D video environment in K-12 education. We investigated what the main challenges are for the technology at the present as well as its potential positive effects. Based on the collected data, we were able to provide answers to our research questions regarding the preliminary investigation on the perceptions of the learners towards 3D telepresence technology for education and the impact the new medium currently has on the learners' sense of presence. According to our assumptions and first hypothesis, the perceptions of the learners on the use of immersive 3D video in education were positive. The learners expressed feelings of positive surprise and excitement and felt the technology enabled participation for them in the action of the lesson. Our second hypothesis was also confirmed, as immersive 3D video technology fostered a high sense of presence in the learners. The learners recounted the feeling that they were "there" inside the environment and in the company of the teacher being able to communicate their intentions and thoughts and to reciprocally understand the teacher.

Our study, however, presents limitations including the accessibility of the technology at present due to the high cost of the equipment, and persistent technical challenges, such as physical discomfort and software glitches that may hinder the system's use during regular curriculum instruction and education. Also, the number of participants was small, making it difficult to draw conclusions that are statistically relevant. Nevertheless, it is important to highlight the novel nature of our TIP technology under development. It would be useful to further investigate the effectiveness of instruction within an immersive 3D video environment in multiple iterations and lengthy implementations, in order to counter the novelty effect in the new technology, and increase the credibility of research findings, particularly under the participatory design paradigm. More research and development work are also needed to ease user access with lighter technical setups and enhanced portability to, for instance, mobile devices.

References

1. Nash, C.: Report on digital literacy in academic meetings during the 2020 COVID-19 lockdown. Challenges **11**(2), 20 (2020). https://doi.org/10.3390/challe1102002
2. Hacker, J., vom Brocke, J., Handali, J., Otto, M., Schneider, J.: Virtually in this together - how web-conferencing systems enabled a new virtual togetherness during the COVID-19 crisis. Eur. J. Inf. Syst. **29**(5), 563–584 (2020). https://doi.org/10.1080/0960085X.2020.1814680
3. Luo H., Li G., Feng Q., Yang Y., Zuo M.: Virtual reality in K-12 and higher education: a systematic review of the literature from 2000 to 2019. J. Comput. Assist. Learn. 1–15 (2021). https://doi.org/10.1111/jcal.12538
4. Johnson-Glenberg, M.C.: Immersive VR and education: embodied design principles that include gesture and hand controls. Front. Robot. AI **5**, 81 (2018). https://doi.org/10.3389/frobt.2018.00081
5. Rötkönen, E., Najmul Islam, A.K.M., Sutinen, E.: Toward pedagogy driven virtual reality learning space design. In: Tatnall, A., Mavengere, N. (eds.) SUZA 2019. IAICT, vol. 564, pp. 235–244. Springer, Cham (2019). https://doi.org/10.1007/978-3-030-28764-1_26
6. IIEP-UNESCO. https://learningportal.iiep.unesco.org/en/issue-briefs/improve-learning/curriculum-and-materials/information-and-communication-technology-ict. Accessed 4 Apr 2021
7. Lindsay, J.: Connecting beyond the classroom - move from local to global learning modes. Scan. **36**, 27–38 (2017)
8. Liesa-Orús, M., Latorre-Cosculluela, C., Vázquez-Toledo, S., Sierra-Sánchez, V.: The technological challenge facing higher education professors: perceptions of ICT tools for developing 21C skills. Sustainability **12**(13), 5339 (2020). https://doi.org/10.3390/su12135339
9. Facer, K.: Learning Futures: Education, Technology and Social Change, 1st edn. Routledge, London (2011). https://doi.org/10.4324/9780203817308
10. Papanastasiou, G., Drigas, A., Skianis, C., Lytras, M., Papanastasiou, E.: Virtual and augmented reality effects on K-12, higher and tertiary education students' twenty-first century skills. Virtual Reality **23**(4), 425–436 (2018). https://doi.org/10.1007/s10055-018-0363-2
11. Hurst, B., Wallace, R., Nixon, S.B.: The impact of social interaction on student learning. Read. Horiz. J. Lit. Lang. Arts, **52**(4), 375–398 (2013). https://scholarworks.wmich.edu/reading_horizons/vol52/iss4/5
12. Nowak, K.L., Biocca, F.: The effect of the agency and anthropomorphism on users' sense of Telepresence. Copresence, and social presence in virtual environments. Presence Teleoperators Virtual Environ. **12**(5), 481–494 (2003). https://doi.org/10.1162/105474603322761289
13. Garrison, D., Anderson, T., Archer, W.: Critical inquiry in a text-based environment: computer conferencing in higher education. Internet High Educ. **2**, 87–105 (1999). https://doi.org/10.1016/S1096-7516(00)00016-6
14. Herbelin, B., Vexo, F., Thalmann, D.: Sense of presence in virtual reality exposures therapy (2003)
15. Ens, B., et al.: Revisiting collaboration through mixed reality: the evolution of groupware. Int. J. Hum Comput. Stud. **131**, 81–98 (2019)
16. Kurillo, G., Bajcsy, R.: 3D teleimmersion for collaboration and interaction of geographically distributed users. Virtual Reality **17**, 29–43 (2013). https://doi.org/10.1007/s10055-012-0217-2

17. Economou, D., Doumanis, I., Argyriou, L., Georgalas, N.: User experience evaluation of human representation in collaborative virtual environments. Pers. Ubiquit. Comput. **21**(6), 989–1001 (2017). https://doi.org/10.1007/s00779-017-1075-4
18. Orts-Escolano, S., et al.: Virtual 3D teleportation in real-time. In: Proceedings of the 29th Annual Symposium on User Interface Software and Technology (UIST 2016), pp. 741–754. Association for Computing Machinery, New York (2016). https://doi.org/10.1145/2984511.2984517
19. Zhang, H., Xu, F.: MixedFusion: real-time reconstruction of an indoor scene with dynamic objects. IEEE Trans. Vis. Comput. Graph. **24**(12), 3137–3146 (2018). https://doi.org/10.1109/TVCG.2017.2786233
20. Marniok, N., Goldluecke, B.: Real-time variational range image fusion and visualization for large-scale scenes using GPU Hash Tables. In: 2018 IEEE Winter Conference on Applications of Computer Vision (WACV) on 2018 IEEE Winter Conference on Applications of Computer Vision (WACV), pp. 912–920, Piscataway, NJ (2018). https://doi.org/10.1109/WACV.2018.00105
21. Zimmerman, J., Forlizzi, J., Evenson, S.: Research through design as a method for interaction design research in HCI. In: Proceedings of the SIGCHI Conference on Human Factors in Computing Systems (CHI 2007), pp. 493–502. Association for Computing Machinery, New York (2007). https://doi.org/10.1145/1240624.1240704
22. Gaver, W.: What should we expect from research through design? In: Proceedings of the SIGCHI Conference on Human Factors in Computing Systems (CHI 2012), pp. 937–946. Association for Computing Machinery, New York (2012). https://doi.org/10.1145/2207676.2208538
23. Lombard, M. et al.: Measuring presence: the temple presence inventory. In: Proceeding Presence 2009, 12th International Workshop on Presence, January, pp. 1–14 (2009)
24. Biocca, F., et al.: The networked minds measure of social presence: pilot test of the factor structure and concurrent validity. In: 4th Annual International Workshop, Presence, pp. 1–9 (2001)
25. Vorderer, P., et al.: MEC Spatial Presence Questionnaire (MEC-SPQ) Short Documentation and Instructions for Application. Report to the European. Community, Project Presence MEC (2004)
26. Braun, V., Clarke, V.: Using thematic analysis in psychology. Qual. Res. Psychol. **3**, 77–101 (2006). https://doi.org/10.1191/1478088706qp063oa

DigiFit4All – Conceptualisation of a Platform to Generate Personalised Open Online Courses (POOCs)

Stefan Pasterk(✉), Lukas Pagitz, Albin Weiß, and Andreas Bollin

Department of Informatics Didactics, University of Klagenfurt, Klagenfurt, Austria
{stefan.pasterk,lukas.pagitz,albin.weiss, andreas.bollin}@aau.at

Abstract. The need for evaluated digital resources arose over the last years as blended learning applications became even more popular, and distance learning essential. Besides well-known *massive open online courses (MOOCs)*, approaches called *personalised open online courses (POOCs)*, which present individual learning resources to the users, are developed. Personalisation is, in most cases, based on different information about the users. *DigiFit4All* is a project to develop a platform for POOCs, including open teaching and learning resources for lower and higher education. In the background, a competency model is used, which enables the definition of learning outcomes for courses, the determination of learning paths, and the assignment of learning resources. With the help of pretests, competencies that are already known can be identified. The learning resources are integrated into a *learning management system (LMS)* which imports them from open repositories. This contribution gives detailed information about the concepts of the *DigiFit4All* project and compares it to other approaches.

Keywords: POOC · e-learning · Digital learning resources · Competency models

1 Introduction

In our society, the relevance of digital teaching and learning is constantly increasing. Various forms of blended learning, e-learning or even distance learning are widespread, and partly necessary due to the current pandemic. A lot of material is available online in the form of massive open online courses (MOOCs). These platforms differ in several aspects concerning technological background and usability. The presentation of the learning resources is, in most cases, the same for all participants, and heterogeneity is not considered. Further, MOOCs often follow an asynchronous form and present their content in the form of videos, quizzes or reading tasks. Approaches that offer individually prepared courses and incorporate heterogeneity are called *personalised open online courses (POOCs)*. They often base on learner profiles and an analysis of the results from prior assessments [1].

The project *DigiFit4All* started in May 2020 and has the aim to develop a platform for POOC creation. Based on competency models, which are stored as graphs, teachers

Published by Springer Nature Switzerland AG 2022
D. Passey et al. (Eds.): OCCE 2021, IFIP AICT 642, pp. 247–258, 2022.
https://doi.org/10.1007/978-3-030-97986-7_21

can create their own courses and identify learning paths to reach the goals of the course. Students can attend individual courses by participating in pre-tests to determine competency profiles. In addition to the platform, resources for computer science and digital education topics are developed during the project. A cooperation between the University of Klagenfurt[1], the Danube University Krems[2], the Johannes Kepler University Linz[3], and the Vienna University of Technology[4] ensures that the different target groups of students in lower and higher education, teachers, and administrative staff can be covered.

This contribution summarises findings from the research literature (Sect. 2) that influenced design decisions during the conceptualisation of the *DigiFit4All* project, and different approaches are compared (Sect. 3). In Sect. 4, the components of the *DigiFit4All* system are explained in more detail, and the technological background is described. Section 5 presents an overview of the user roles in the project and sample workflows for teachers and students.

2 Related Work

To get a first overview of existing systems that can generate *personal open online courses*, several approaches that have been published already are reviewed, and the most relevant are briefly described below.

In 2007, Leung et al. [2] identified students' diversity as a significant issue in terms of e-learning. To answer how course materials can be presented student-centered, they suggested an approach following the elaboration theory of instruction combined with the so-called educational ontology.

El Mawas et al. [3] discussed the personalisation of massive open online courses in the context of lifelong learning. Their architecture consists of a *content management system (CMS)* and a *learning management system (LMS)* and supports different roles such as pedagogical engineer, teacher, and learner. Subjects, topics, and concepts are stored in *domain models*, while the individual results are saved in *learner models*.

Due to the low completion rates of MOOCs, Brinton et al. [4] developed the so-called MIICs. MIIC stands for *mobile integrated and individualised course* and is an *adaptive educational system* that updates students' user models based on their interaction with the course. MIICs offer multiple learning paths, whereby one path consists of several segments. One segment represents the 'smallest unit of knowledge' offered in different versions (depending on the path selected for the learner).

Another aspect in the context of MOOCs is big data. Compared to traditional classroom learning settings, online courses allow collection and analysis of learners' behavior as all actions performed by users can be logged. Xi et al. [5] described how the collected data could be interpreted using a behavior analysis model. They described

[1] https://www.aau.at.

[2] https://www.donau-uni.ac.at.

[3] https://www.jku.at.

[4] https://www.tuwien.at.

a model consisting of six components, whereby the *predictive model* is the centerpiece of it. Students can access the course content, and based on their interaction with it, the adaption engine updates their personal model. Teachers can intervene through the so-called intervention engine, which allows manual adjustments in the otherwise automatic system.

Analysing the related work showed that many ideas in personalising MOOCs had been made already. However, unfortunately, most of the introduced prototypes are no longer available, or the work on this subject was discontinued. However, some of the concepts that were described can or will be re-used in the *DigiFit4All* project in the presented or a similar way.

3 Components for POOCs

3.1 Used Components in Existing Projects

Analysing related work showed that the models described in the papers consist of several components, which will be identified and explained in this section.

A *pre-test* is used to determine the prior knowledge of a student before they start with the course. Based on their individual result during this evaluation, the course is adjusted to their personal needs. In the approach of Leung et al. [2], a pre-test has to be performed by the students, which sets the ground for the individual study path, while El Mawas et al. [3] ask the learner to fill a so-called positioning questionnaire as a basis for the learner model, created by the platform. Additionally, statements by the user are considered for the initiation of the model. The approaches suggested by Brinton et al. [4] and Xi et al. [5] do not contain any pre-test, and the learning paths are calculated later on.

A *post-test* is a test that has to be performed by a learner, and it is used to check the knowledge once a given activity, exercise or segment was finished. An automated mechanism that adjusts the learner model based on the users' behavior is not considered a post-test. The model of Leung et al. is the only one that lets their learners submit post-tests, while the other models use different approaches of measuring the performance.

Learning paths allow the individualisation of how someone learns. A person's path is adjusted to their personal needs, either depending on post-tests or calculations in the background. In the approach of El Mawas et al., the learning path is based on the positioning questionnaire and static, while the model of Leung et al. allows changes in the path depending on the pre- and post-tests. The platform by Xi et al. allows automatic as well as manual adjustments of the learning paths, and the approach of Brinton et al. considers the users' behavior in each segment to select the next one.

User behavior can be considered to create dynamic personalised courses, depending on how a learner interacts with the platform. As just described, Brinton et al. select the segment and version of the following learning object based on the results yielded in the current one. As the approach of El Mawas et al. is static, the user's behavior is not analysed during the course. The same applies to the model of Leung et al., as it depends on the tests performed by the user. Xi et al.'s platform uses behavioral data to recommend activities to the learner.

A *repository* is a platform where learning material that can be linked to learning objects is stored. Repositories can either be open platforms where everyone is able to provide course material that can even be used outside a course, or closed platforms that do not share their contents with the public. Three of the researched papers do not describe where and how the material is stored in detail; only Brinton et al. tell that all files are stored in EPUB containers, and videos are streamed via HTTP.

MOOCs are held in *learning management systems (LMS)* that offer a variety of features for course management. The analysed approaches used different platforms for the integration of their personalised courses: Leung et al. used Moodle, El Mawas et al. used edX, and both Brinton et al. and Xi et al. did not specify the platform or used a custom-created website.

Exams are defined as actual exams that are relevant for the grade of a learner in the subject of the course. None of the four analysed approaches supports writing an exam within the personalised course.

Learning objects can be used to modularise content for learning scenarios. They represent the teaching and learning materials and are defined following the *IEEE Standard for Learning Object Metadata (LOM)* [6]. Compared to segments in the approach of Brinton [4], learning objects collect 'smallest units of knowledge' to a didactically meaningful package. This concept appears only in the work of Leung [2].

A *microservice architecture* is a method to develop software based on small services with well-defined interfaces to easily add new services. In none of the analysed approaches a comparable architecture is described.

3.2 Comparison of the Approaches

The comparison of the approaches is based on the descriptions of the methods in the respective papers. In case any information was not found for a specific component, it is considered as not existent. As presented in Table 1, all components include learning paths for course personalisation. The pre-test approach is only used by two out of four models, and only Leung et al. included post-tests as well. None of the ideas presented used an open repository which allows uploading learning material. The components of the *DigiFit4All* approach together with the technical background will be described in the following section.

4 Components of the DigiFit4All Project

4.1 Overview of the Project

During the development process of the *DigiFit4All* project, literature was reviewed and approaches from related work were analysed. Existing expertise, previous work and research results of the partner institutions had the strongest influence on the project's basic idea.

Table 1. Component comparison of personalised online course systems

Component	Approach				
	Leung [2]	El Mawas [3]	Brinton [4]	Xi [5]	DF4A
Pre-test	Yes	Yes	No	No	Yes
Post-test	Yes	No	No	No	Yes
Learning paths	Yes	Yes	Yes	Yes	Yes
User behavior	No	No	Yes	Yes	No
Repository	No	No	Yes	No	Yes
LMS integration	Yes	Yes	No	No	Yes
Exams	No	No	No	No	Yes
Learning objects	Yes	No	No	No	Yes
Microservice architecture	No	No	No	No	Yes

Based on this prior knowledge, the following components were selected to be part of this project.

- Competency models: The background calculations for the personalisation are based on competency models and learning paths within the models.
- Learning objects: The teaching and learning materials to reach competencies are developed in the form of *learning objects*.
- Assessment: Course participants are assessed before a course starts, to get information about their knowledge and which competencies they already have acquired. After finishing a course, the learners are assessed again to find out which competencies they reached during the course.
- Learning management systems (LMS): The *learning objects* are presented in form of courses in chosen LMS.

These components work together to create personalised open online courses in the *DigiFit4All* project and are described in more detail in the following sections.

4.2 Competency Models and Learning Objects

As already mentioned, the personalisation of the courses in the *DigiFit4All* project is based on competency models. For this purpose, national and international curricula, educational standards, and competency models for different target groups are collected and analysed. As a central element, the learning outcomes of the models, here called *competencies*, are part of this process. In a first step, the competencies have to be standardised because some of them contain more than one outcome. This leads to *subcomptencies* which are *part of* competencies in their original form. The models are mapped to a graph-based representation form, and stored in a graph database as Pasterk and Bollin describe it [7, 8]. Competencies represent the nodes, and dependencies between them are displayed as directed edges. Pasterk defines the two dependency types *expands* and *requires*, which show that a competency *C1* is necessary to reach another competency *C2* within the same topic (*C2 expands C1*) or from another topic

(*C2 requires C1*) [9]. Nodes and edges are sometimes given by the curricula, educational standards, or competency models, but in many cases, the dependencies have to be added by experts. As the models are in general developed for one target group, i.e., primary school children or students of an undergraduate programme, Pasterk presents a method to combine them to one overall model, here called the *main index*. This approach uses so-called *intersector nodes*, which collect a set of similar competencies from different models in one single node. *Intersector nodes* inherit all dependencies from their included competencies, thereby connecting competency models to each other [9]. In the *DigiFit4All* project, the approach from Pasterk and Bollin is applied with some adaptations concerning the *intersector nodes*. Similar competencies are not collected in sets but are connected over an *equal to* relation. If a competency *A* is similar to another already existing competency *B* their respective nodes are set to be *equal to* another. In the main index only the node of the first competency B is shown and used for calculations. Again, the existing competency inherits all dependencies from competencies which are later added and set to be *equal to* it. For the purpose of collecting, analysing and combining the models, the *Graph-based Environment for Competency and Knowledge-Item Organization (GECKO)*[5] platform presented by Pasterk and Bollin in 2017 [7, 8] and described by Pasterk 2020 in detail [9] is adapted and extended by some functionalities.

In the graph-based representation, *central competencies* of the models and the *main index* can be identified and *learning paths* can be calculated. To find *central competencies*, the centrality values of the nodes are measures. This method is used in network analysis and adds information about important competencies [9]. *Learning paths* include competencies, which are necessary to reach a selected competency, by following the direction of the edges back to a selected starting node. Especially in the *main index* more than one learning path to a given competency can exist. In the *DigiFit4All* project, the *learning paths* support teachers, and lecturers to find necessary prerequisites for targeted competencies and to include them in their courses. Additional components, which are new in the *DigiFit4All* project, are *learning objects*. The mentioned LOM [6] standard includes different forms of materials, also non-digital ones, which are excluded from the *DigiFit4All* project. It is required that the materials are tagged with metadata to record information about them. Additionally, the *learning objects* are in subject to further project-specific requirements like a time limit and the highest possible degree of independence to other learning objects. These two requirements are important for the reuse of learning objects in different courses and contexts. *Learning objects* are developed to reach given competencies and are directly linked to corresponding competencies in the GECKO system.

4.3 Self-assessment for Personalisation

At the beginning and the end of a course, assessment questions are addressed to learners and serve to evaluate individual skills and competencies acquired before and after a course. The results of these pre-tests are used to determine the competencies that

[5] https://gecko.aau.at.

the learner would still have to reach to pass the course positively. These are then highlighted in the personalised online course, while topics that have already been mastered remain accessible, but are kept in the background. Items for the post-tests are used to check whether a competency has been achieved after finishing the course. They can be part of the exam and, with that, the grading. Both types of questioning, assessment questions and test items, are carried out via the *KAUA (Košice and Alpen-Adria University Assessment)*[6] platform of the Department of Informatics Didactics at the University of Klagenfurt. For the purposes of the *DigiFit4All* project, the platform is modified and extended. The idea behind the *KAUA* platform is to use hash values to identify users instead of storing specific user data [10].

4.4 Support for Learning Management Systems

To allow teachers to create courses for their students, integrations for *learning management systems (LMS)* are being created. Once the corresponding plugin for the LMS is installed, it will allow teachers to import courses for their classes. Students are then able to perform the pre-test and use their personalised course. As a first LMS, Moodle – which was already used by Leung et al. [2] in their implementation of personalised courses – will be supported as it is open-source, therefore available for free and open for further modifications.

4.5 Technical Background

The *DigiFit4All* system is designed as a microservice architecture. Most of the services are Spring Boot applications and therefore implemented in Java. During the project, two Single Page Applications (SPA) are also developed. Among other things, the application also provides an interface to an external repository and LMS. The repository in turn provides an interface to the LMS. Figure 1 below shows a section of this architecture. The API *Gateway Services* serves as the central access point to the backend. All stateless communication runs through this gateway, so the different microservices cannot be addressed directly. In Fig. 1, the most important services of *GECKO* and *KAUA* are visible. The *Auth Service* manages all users and authentication. The *Graph Service* manages the Neo4J graph database, which is used to map the various competency models. The *Liza Service* provides various recommendations when creating a competency model. This application is implemented in Python and communicates with the rest of the Spring-based application via the *Liza Service Sidecar*. The *Library* is not a standalone service but is added by each core service as a dependency. The *Survey Service* handles the creation of questions and questionnaires. The created questions can be added to surveys, competencies or learning objects. The survey data and the results of the tests for the personalisation of the different users are stored anonymously. Each time a user logs in, a hash value is generated from the user credentials in the *UID Service*. This hash value serves as an identifier for the user.

[6] https://kaua.aau.at.

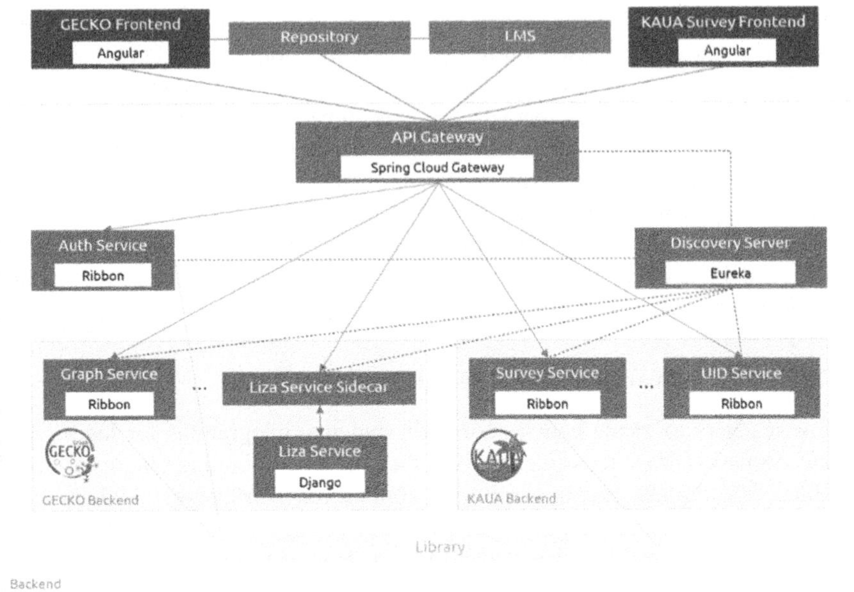

Fig. 1. Detail of the *DigiFit4All* system architecture

5 Roles and Workflows in the DigiFit4All Project

5.1 User Roles

Within the *DigiFit4All* project, different user roles exist for different functionalities in *GECKO* as well as in *KAUA*. In *GECKO*, users can register for free, but at this stage only have the possibility to view the *main index* as a list of competencies or in its graph representation. Every user can send a request to get the role of a *GECKO-author* or of a *GECKO-lecturer*. *GECKO-authors* are responsible for the competency models collected in *GECKO* and are able to upload or build their own models for their selected target group. The individual models have to be submitted and are evaluated by an expert team. In contrast to that, *GECKO-lecturers* use the given competencies in the *main index* to represent their goals for their own courses. This allows teachers or lecturers to follow the suggestions of the system, or to choose their own ways. Two of the three roles existing in *KAUA* work in a similar matter. *KAUA-authors* develop questions and question modules of different forms and for different purposes. The *KAUA-lecturers* combine given and evaluated modules to prepare their own surveys. The last role which does not require a typical registration is the *KAUA-student* role. An enrolled student can access their personal course through the LMS using their student data. After submitting the pre-test, students can start with the personalised online course. In the following section, the workflows for lecturers and learners within the project are described in more detail.

5.2 Sample Workflows

Workflow for Teachers. Based on the knowledge about the components of the project, the typical workflow for a teacher or lecturer starts with the assignment of competencies to a course in *GECKO*. They need to login to the platform with a corresponding account and define a new course, or work on an existing one. Starting to work on a new model, the first step is to select the target competencies from the *main index*. As an example, a teacher wants to introduce simple SQL statements in their databases course. For this category several competencies can be found but the following two are selected by the teacher:

1. Learners formulate SQL queries using a projection.
2. Learners formulate SQL queries with a selection.

These competencies are based on the *ACM/IEEE Computer Science Curriculum 2013*[7] but go more into detail. In the background, the system calculates necessary prerequisites for the target competency and suggests the results to the teacher. They receive a list of additional competencies including competencies from the topic's *relation schema* and *datatypes*. However, for the teacher, only competencies for SQL statements are of interest. That is why for the two selected target competencies, the following list of competencies is added to the course:

3. Learners can reproduce what is meant by a projection in SQL queries.
4. Learners understand and can explain what is meant by a projection in SQL queries.
5. Learners can reproduce what is meant by a selection in SQL queries.
6. Learners understand and can explain what is meant by a selection in SQL queries.

Competencies 3 and 4 are prerequisites for (1), and 5 and 6 for (2), as they deal with the same topics on different cognitive levels. The teacher decides whether as foreknowledge suggested competencies should be added to the course or not (step 2). In the given example, the teacher also adds the prerequisites to the course. After the competencies are selected, the teacher gets a list of teaching and learning materials that can be used to reach the corresponding competencies (step 3). Again, the teacher selects those materials that are appropriate for the course (step 4). This step includes the option to create a final exam with questions related to selected competencies and marked to be exam questions. For the competencies in the database-example, the teacher chooses interactive videos to be appropriate for the course, but chooses not to have a final exam through the system. These steps are illustrated in Fig. 2 and show the actions taken in the *GECKO* platform. Additionally, a teacher can create own surveys and tests in *KAUA*. Again, existing modules for different purposes can be chosen from the existing collection, or own questions can be defined. Once the teacher enabled the connection to *GECKO*, the course created can be selected by its title. The learning objects corresponding to the selected competencies are imported from the repository into the LMS section.

[7] https://www.acm.org/binaries/content/assets/education/cs2013_web_final.pdf.

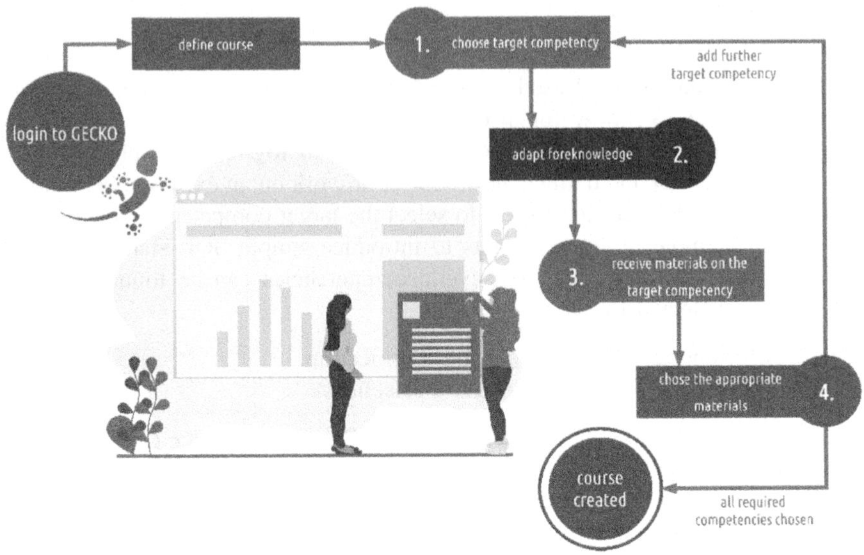

Fig. 2. The workflow for teachers and lecturers in the *DigiFit4All* project

Workflow for Learners. As mentioned above, the students do not register to the system on their own. In higher education, a student enrolls for a course in the affiliated institution's usual system. Through the student account, they get access to the used LMS and with it to the learning resources. For students in schools, the administrator or the teacher must generate a list of student accounts in the LMS system of the school. With that account, the students can enter the online course. From this point on, the workflow for all kind of students is the same. The first step is the pre-test. Depending on the LMS, the students can participate directly in the LMS or have to follow a given link to *KAUA*. Based on the results of the pre-test, a competency profile of each student is created and stored. Looking at the example for a database course with competencies in SQL statements, a section of the pre-test would include self-assessment questions in the following form and for the corresponding competencies (see the referencing numbers in the brackets):

- Have you heard about projections in the context of databases and SQL statements? (Competency 3)
- Can you explain a projection in the context of databases and SQL statements? (Competency 4)
- Have you created an own SQL query including a projection? (Competency 1)
- Have you heard about selections in the context of databases and SQL statements? (Competency 5)
- Can you explain a selection in the context of databases and SQL statements? (Competency 6)
- Have you created an own SQL query including a selection? (Competency 2)

As a next step, the student has access to the learning material of the online course. With the help of the competency profile, the course is personalised for each student. This means, the sections for already reached competencies are put into the background and the other sections are highlighted. Through this approach, the student identifies on the first glance which sections are important for them. However, they still have access to all learning resources, as they are relevant for the exam.

So, for the given example it can be assumed that a student has already read something about SQL statements and knows the difference between projection and selection, but has never created an own query. This student only replies with 'No' to the questions for competencies 1 and 2. With this profile, the course for this student includes four collapsible sections which contain the interactive videos for competencies 3 to 6. Two already opened sections present the two videos for competencies 1 and 2, which are not yet reached by the student. After a student has worked through all the materials, they participate in a post-test. This test depends on the selected competencies for the course and not on the profiles of the students. Therefore, even questions about topics, which the student already knew about before participating in the course, can be included. Results from the pre-test have no influence on the post-test.

In case of the given example about SQL statements, post-test questions can include the following questions or tasks:

- What is a projection in the context of databases?
- What is necessary to create a simple SQL query?
- What is the result of a given query over a given table?
- Create a query to get given results from a given table.

It has to be mentioned that the post-test is not the same as an exam, which has to be passed to receive a grade for the course. The post-test informally shows the progress of participating students, but does not influence the grades.

6 Conclusion

This paper presents an analysis of existing approaches for *personalised open online courses (POOC)* and discusses differences and similarities. Research in related work shows that several prototypes were created. However, most of them are no longer available as they only served as proof of concepts or were discontinued for other reasons. Several components used in the mentioned approaches could be identified and compared to each other as well as to the *DigiFit4All* project. The results show that all selected approaches use *learning paths* in the background. Three of five approaches include *pre-tests* and some kind of *LMS integration*. Considering other points like *post-tests*, *exams* or *user behavior*, the approaches differ more. A detailed description of the structure of the *DigiFit4All* project includes the use of *competency models* in the background to create courses and calculate *learning paths*, the development of independent and reusable *learning objects*, the necessity of assessment before and after the course, *learning management systems* support as well as the technical background. By explaining the roles and two sample workflows, it is shown what users (both learners and lecturers) can do on the *DigiFit4All* platform. The project started one year ago, and a first prototype of the *GECKO* platform is already online, including some first competency models. In a next step, a repository will be created and linking learning objects to competencies will be supported, as well as the import into learning management systems.

References

1. Sanchez-Gordon, S., Luján-Mora, S.: Moocs gone wild. In: INTED2014 Proceedings, 8th International Technology, Education and Development Conference, IATED, pp. 1449–1458 (2014)
2. Leung, E.W.C., Li, Q.: An experimental study of a personalized learning environment through open-source software tools. IEEE Trans. Educ. **50**(4), 331–337 (2007)
3. El Mawas, N., Gilliot, J.M., Garlatti, S., Euler, R., Pascual, S.: As one size doesn't fit all, personalized massive open online courses are required. In: McLaren, B.M., Reilly, R., Zvacek, S., Uhomoibhi, J. (eds.) CSEDU 2018. CCIS, vol. 1022, pp. 470–488. Springer, Cham (2019). https://doi.org/10.1007/978-3-030-21151-6_22
4. Brinton, C.G., Rill, R., Ha, S., Chiang, M., Smith, R., Ju, W.: Individualization for education at scale: MIIC design and preliminary evaluation. IEEE Trans. Learn. Technol. **8**(1), 136–148 (2015)
5. Xi, J., Chen, Y., Wang, G.: Design of a personalized massive open online course platform. Int. J. Emerg. Technol. Learn. (iJET) **13**(04), 58–70 (2018)
6. IEEE: Standard for learning object metadata (IEEE 1484.12.1–2020) (2020). https://standards.ieee.org/standard/1484121-2020.html
7. Pasterk, S., Bollin, A.: A graph-based approach to analyze and compare computer science curricula for primary and lower secondary education. In: Proceedings of the 2017 ACM Conference on Innovation and Technology in Computer Science Education,ITiCSE 2017, pp. 365–365. ACM, New York (2017)
8. Pasterk, S., Bollin, A.: Graph-based analysis of computer science curricula for primary education. In: 2017 IEEE Frontiers in Education Conference (FIE), pp. 1–9 (2017)
9. Pasterk, S.: Competency-Based Informatics Education in Primary and Lower Secondary Schools. Ph.D. thesis, Department of Informatics Didactics, University of Klagenfurt, Austria (2020)
10. Bollin, A., Kesselbacher, M., Mößlacher, C.: Ready for computing science? A closer look at personality, interests and self-concept of girls and boys at secondary level. In: Kori, K., Laanpere, M. (eds.) ISSEP 2020. LNCS, vol. 12518, pp. 107–118. Springer, Cham (2020). https://doi.org/10.1007/978-3-030-63212-0_9

Management Issues

What Kind of E-assessment Feedback Is Important to Students? An Empirical Study

Djordje M. Kadijevich[1(✉)], Danijela Ljubojevic[2], and Nikoleta Gutvajn[1]

[1] Institute for Educational Research, Belgrade, Serbia
djkadijevic@ipi.ac.rs
[2] Faculty of Information Technologies, Belgrade Metropolitan University, Belgrade, Serbia
danijela.ljubojevic@metropolitan.ac.rs

Abstract. E-assessment needs to provide detailed feedback that students would use. To this end, the content of feedback should include assessment information that is important to students. By using a convenient sample of twenty second-year undergraduate students, this study explored the extent to which different kinds of assessment feedback were important to students. Therefore, an online questionnaire was administered which, apart from asking values of some background variables including academic achievement, listed a number of different feedback techniques supporting activities applied in deep and strategic approaches to learning and studying. For each technique, students had to indicate the extent of the importance they assigned to it. It was found that: (1) although feedback techniques supporting a deep approach were as important to students as those supporting a strategic approach, the importance of the former was positively related to that of the latter; (2) feedback techniques supporting a deep approach were more important to females than males; (3) when the importance of all these feedback techniques together was considered in a specific way, their relevance to an increase in students' knowledge, skills and motivation could be demonstrated. Although this study used a small sample that might characterise it as preliminary research, it revealed valuable findings, which due to their considerable effect size, make the sample size less questionable. Suggestions for further research are included.

Keywords: E-assessment · Feedback · Language learning · Learning approach · Undergraduate students

1 Introduction

Feedback has one of the highest effects on learning (e.g. [1]). Concerning e-learning, research has identified some kinds of feedback that may be important to instructors (e.g. [2]). Less is known about the kinds of feedback that may be important to students (e.g. [3]), especially about those related to e-assessment. These kinds of feedback should be personalised [4] and have content that engages students in self-regulated learning [5]. Furthermore, students should have some control over learning analytics (e.g. what can

Published by Springer Nature Switzerland AG 2022
D. Passey et al. (Eds.): OCCE 2021, IFIP AICT 642, pp. 261–273, 2022.
https://doi.org/10.1007/978-3-030-97986-7_22

be seen by them, what by other students), respecting their preferences for automated alerts over those sent by teaching staff [3].

As a critical component of education, assessment can be used to improve both learning and instruction (e.g. [6, 7]). In the context of e-learning one may first focus on e-assessment feedback and later on other feedback types sent by teaching staff, which, as mentioned above, may be less preferred than feedback automatically sent by the assessment system. To improve e-learning, among other things, assessment needs to provide detailed feedback that students would actually use [8]. Accordingly, the content of feedback should include assessment information important to students (e.g. [3]). Such information may support students' activities applied in their approaches to learning and studying [9].

The concept of an approach to learning, introduced about forty years ago, made a distinction between a deep approach and a surface approach. While the former aims at understanding the material learned, relating it to previous knowledge and experience and examining evidence supporting conclusions, the latter aims at satisfying requirements of a task or a course through memorising details that would be most likely assessed. The strategic approach was added later to denote a combination of deep and surface approaches applied in order to maximise achievement [10]. The so-called SAL (Student Approaches to Learning) perspective has been mainly concerned with students' behavior that can be described using their self-reports or the questionnaires they complete [11].

Subsequent research has clarified the main features of these three categories. These features may be summarised in the following way: "deep (intention to understand, relating ideas, use of evidence, and active learning); surface (intention to reproduce, unrelated memorising, passive learning, and fear of failure); strategic (study organisation, time management, alertness to assessment demands, and intention to excel)" ([12], p. 433). Note that while deep and surface approaches are approaches to learning, the strategic approach, which combines them, may be considered more as an approach to studying than as an approach to learning [13].

Having in mind the features of the approaches summarised above, to facilitate genuine learning based upon understanding, assessment feedback may support the deep approach. This feedback may also support a strategic approach because it involves a deep approach to some extent (e.g., a good study organisation may contribute to relating ideas).

Are deep and strategic approaches related to achievement? Research suggests that there may be a positive relationship between academic achievement and a strategic approach, whereas this achievement might be unrelated to a deep approach (e.g., [12]).

To contribute to under-represented research on kinds of assessment feedback that may be important to students, this study asked its participants to assign importance to different feedback techniques supporting activities applied in deep and strategic approaches to learning and studying. Hence, they completed an online questionnaire that also collected their basic background data including academic achievement.

The study examined the following research questions:

1. Which feedback techniques were more important to students: those supporting a deep or a strategic approach?

2. Considering each approach, were there any relationships between the importance of feedback techniques supporting it and background variables used?

These questions were answered by a sample of second-year undergraduate students who studied information technologies at a private faculty.

2 Method

2.1 Sample

This study used a convenience sample comprising twenty second-year undergraduate students who studied software engineering, information technologies, information systems, and game development at the Faculty of information technologies. Students enrolled in an English course – "English for IT" were invited to participate in the online survey administered. Of those who completed this course and passed the final exam, about 40% also completed the survey, which is a good response rate, bearing in mind that the average response rate for online surveys is around 30% (e.g., [14]).

The participants' background data were the following: five students were females; eleven students completed almost all tests; course achievement of ten students was 9 or 10, i.e. they received the highest marks (a 6–10 scale was used with 6 denoting the lowest passing mark); average academic achievement (considering all courses completed) was between 8 and 10 for ten students.

2.2 English Course

Course Content. "English for IT" is an LSP (Language for Specific Purposes) course held in the fall semester in Year 2 following two General English courses in Year 1. It is an upper intermediate course at level B2+ (Strong Vantage), with some elements at level C1, but it is more demanding than the previous two courses regarding the use of specialist language. It combines General English and English for specific purposes (Information technology). The course objective is to consolidate grammar use at upper intermediate level, expand general, and particularly professional vocabulary, as well as practice its use in various language functions. The course helps students to improve and integrate all language skills: speaking, listening, reading, writing, and translation.

This course comprised 15 units regarding IT topics to be covered in 15 weeks of academic work. Each unit focused on different vocabulary, linguistic, and grammatical content. For example, Unit 4 "Networks" focused on vocabulary about computer networks and relative clauses as far as grammar is concerned. Although the content of these units might be considered unconnected at first sight, there was some overlapping content. For example, Unit 2 "ICT in Education" focused on present tenses which appeared later on throughout the course; Unit 3 "The History of ICT" revised all past tenses without which it was also impossible to deal with later grammatical areas (conditionals, etc.).

The syllabus of this course and all learning materials, including tests, were developed by the second author of this study, who taught most students engaged in the course. The remaining students at another faculty site were taught by a different teacher who followed the approach developed.

E-tests and Feedback Provided. In order to get points for effort as a pre-final exam activity, students had to complete successfully two progress tests in every unit, thirty tests in total. There were two test restrictions to choose from: Time limit and Assessment passing mark. The former was not taken into consideration in this study while the latter was set to 5 questions: each test comprised six questions to answer, and the test was passed if correct answers were given to at least five questions. If the student failed the test, he/she could take another test with similar content.

There were three types of questions in the tests: multiple choice, fill-in-the-blank/short-answer (one word only), and true or false; for example:

> Choose the correct idiom to complete the following sentence: In today's world, computers are ___________ of daily life.
> a) part and parcel
> b) first and foremost
> c) belt and braces

There were 30 questions prepared in the question base for each test to be included in a 6-question test randomly: 900 questions in total for the whole course. All the questions were meticulously created in order to check if the students had understood the lesson they had just read and interacted with. Each lesson consisted of six learning objects[1]. While Test 1 was given after presentation of the third learning object, Test 2 was given at the end of the lesson.

The tests included limited feedback to students. Some of the possibilities in the test settings allowed by the e-learning environment were the following:

- Display all questions and answers once the learner finishes;
- Allow learners to see question feedback after each question;
- Indicate choices that have been answered correctly;
- Indicate choices that have been answered incorrectly;
- Allow learners to see history of responses at the end of each attempt;
- Display overall feedback at the end of each attempt;
- Allow learners to see grades at the end of each attempt.

In this course, the e-learning system only displayed the number of correctly answered questions, and for each question, information on whether the given answer was true or false, i.e. the learners were allowed to see grades at the end of each attempt. For example, when a student answered correctly three out of 6 question, he/she got the following feedback:

[1] A learning object is a specifically designed, modular unit of a learning resource – content items, practice items, and assessment items that are combined based on a single learning objective.

Sorry, you haven't scored 5 required to pass the activity. Please, try one more time. Grade: 3 out of a maximum of 6 (50%)

This was followed by a list of questions just ticked or crossed. Although different types of automatic feedback were available, the faculty executives decided to use standard summary responses to correct and incorrect answers, as well as the test score. Additional feedback received by students during the course includes the teacher's comments about the outcomes of project work and its presentation, as well as of individual and group practice including and combining various language issues (vocabulary, grammar, pragmatics).

This study aimed to collect students' responses about feedback techniques that were important to them to have solid grounds to improve the system in months to come and to provide feedback that would be more valuable to students.

2.3 Design and Variables

This study mainly used a factorial design and a correlative design. There were four background variables: *Gender* (with values: 1-male, 2-female); *Course achievement* (1-grade 9 or 10 was received, 0-otherwise); *Academic achievement* (1-average achievement for the courses completed was between grades 8 and 10; 0-otherwise); and *E-assessment participation* (1-almost all tests were completed, 0-otherwise).

The main variables were: *Deep approach feedback techniques importance – DAFTs importance* (average value of the importance of five feedback techniques supporting a deep approach, expressed on a 0–10 scale for each technique); and *Strategic approach feedback techniques importance – SAFTs importance* (average value of the importance of five feedback techniques supporting a strategic approach, expressed on a 0–10 scale for each technique).

2.4 Instrument and Procedure

The values of the variables used in this study were collected through an online survey using a questionnaire available on the Internet. Table 1 lists items (indicators) used to measure the two importance variables. *DAFTs importance* was measured using items D1–D5, whereas *SAFTs importance* was measured using items S1–S5. These items were listed in the questionnaire in the following order: D0, S1, D1, S2, D2, S3, D3, S4, D4, S5, D5, S0; D0 and S0 denote discarded items. Although there is no clear-cut solution to ordering items, there may be a certain advantage of intermixing them when different but related constructs are measured within a particular context [15].

The students involved in the English course were invited to participate in the survey by the second author of this study via e-mail. The survey was conducted in March 2021.

2.5 Data Transformation and Statistical Analyses

To attain a more reliable measurement of DAFTs and SAFTs importance, the raw data regarding the indicators of each importance variable were transformed into Guttman's [16] image scores (e.g. [17]). (It should be noted that the means and medians of the transformed data are slightly different from those of the raw data).

Table 1. Indicators of the two importance variables

Variable/activities to support [12]	Indicators
DAFTs importance/intention to understand, relating ideas, use of evidence, and active learning	**D1** Information is obtained about areas that I have successfully mastered in the current knowledge test versus areas that require additional learning **D2** A link is given to a file whose content shows how certain questions from the test are related to the content which needed to be learned **D3** A link is given to a file whose content indicates which test contents are related to other contents that are studied in the course **D4** A link is provided to a file whose content indicates how knowledge and skills that are the subject of the test can be implemented from different point of view **D5** Information is obtained about which areas in the current knowledge test I could receive special learning assistance for, from the professor
SAFTs importance/study organisation, time management, alertness to assessment demands, and intention to excel	**S1** A link is provided to a reminder with the most important facts about the knowledge and skills assessed by the test **S2** Information is obtained about how successful I was in solving the tasks in relation to the success of other students who had already solved the test **S3** Information is given about my individual results and the average result on completion of the knowledge tests **S4** A link is given to a file that, according to the order of presentation, locates the part of the course (lesson) that is the subject of the test in relation to other parts that appeared or will appear in other tests **S5** Information is obtained about the order in which individual knowledge and skills will be assessed at tests that should be completed during the semester

This resulted in a considerably improved reliability of both importance variables: from 0.732 to 0.936 for DAFTs importance and from 0.730 to 0.942 for SAFTs importance.

Apart from determining medians of the two importance variables, this study made use of two statistical tests. Wilcoxon signed-ranks test for dependent samples was applied to answer research question 1, whereas Wilcoxon rank-sum test for independent samples were carried out to answer research question 2. These nonparametric tests were used because no assumption needs to be made about the shape of the population distribution of variable in question, which is appropriate when small samples are used and the assumption of normality is violated for some variables (e.g., [18]).

To find out effect size, Cohen's r was calculated. As usually assumed, 0.5 evidences a large effect, 0.3 a medium effect, and 0.1 a small effect (e.g., [19]).

A correlative analysis concerning the applied variables was used to signal the relationships among them, if any. To this end, Spearman's correlation coefficients were determined. Note that for dichotomous (binary) variables, these coefficients are equal to those of Kendall or Pearson.

3 Results

The medians of the two importance variables were 7.43 for feedback techniques supporting a deep approach and 7.54 for feedback techniques supporting a strategic approach. These values were not different statistically ($z = -0.747$, $p = 0.469$).

Correlations among the six variables applied and their significances are given in Table 2. Considering relationships between the importance variables and four background variables applied, only one relationship was found (0.571, $df = 18$, $p = 0.009$). This positive relationship evidenced that feedback techniques supporting activities applied in the deep approach were more important to females than males ($W = 129.0$, $z = -2.489$, $p = 0.010$; Cohen's $r = 0.56$ – a large effect).

Table 2. Spearman's correlations among the six variables applied

Variable	Correlations				
	2	3	4	5	6
1. DAFTs importance	0.825**	0.571**	0.000	0.121	−0.044
2. SAFTs importance		0.351	−0.069	0.052	0.009
3. Gender			−0.115	0.346	0.058
4. Course achievement				0.600**	0.503*
5. Academic achievement					0.503*
6. E-assessment participation					

*$p < 0.05$ **$p < 0.01$

As DAFTs and SAFTs importance were almost unrelated to the four background variables applied, these importance variables were then jointly considered using a new importance variable named *Golden middle feedback techniques importance – GMFTs importance* with values: 1–both DAFTs and SAFTs importance values were between the 25th and 75th percentiles of their values; 0–otherwise. Two significant relationships emerged: between GMFTs importance and Course achievement (0.612, $df = 18$, $p = 0.004$) and between GMFTs importance and E-assessment participation (0.533, $df = 18$, $p = 0.015$). These positive relationships evidenced that participants indicating a golden middle importance not only had a higher course achievement ($\chi 2 = 7.500$, $df = 1$, $p = 0.006$) but also participated in e-assessment more often ($\chi 2 = 5.690$, $df = 1$, $p = 0.017$).[2]

4 Discussion

The first research question asked which feedback techniques would be more important to students: those supporting a deep or a strategic approach. It was found that both sets of techniques were equally important to students, who assigned high importance to them (both medians were above 7 on a 0–10 scale). Correlation between these was also high (Spearman's rho was 0.83, $df = 18$, $p = 0.000$; 95% CI: [0.54, 0.94] – an analytic estimate versus [0.62, 0.92] – a bootstrap estimate [20]). This outcome suggests that these two sets of feedback techniques were viewed beneficial to each other as deep and strategic approaches might contribute to each other positively; measures of these approaches may positively correlate in general (e.g., [21]). This line of reasoning may be used to explain the equal importance found because the participants' responses to adjacent item-pairs (S1, D1; S2, D2; S3, D3; S4, D4; S5, D5) were not similar to one another.[3] Another possibility is that the issues in question differ for different sub-groups of students (canceling each other), which was not found in this study.

As underlined in the Introduction, knowledge about feedback that may be important to students is scarce, especially related to e-assessment. However, this feedback should be personalised [4] and have content that engages students in self-regulated learning [5]. Furthermore, students should have some control over learning analytics (what can be seen by them, what by other students; whether information is communicated by the e-learning system automatically or by teaching staff), respecting their preferences for automated alerts over those sent by teaching staff [3]. Bearing in mind these feedback requirements, learning could be improved by applying learning/studying-approaches-based feedback techniques which students find important. In doing that, students' preferences for automated alerts over those sent be teaching staff may hold true in general, as found in this study for feedback technique D5 – "Information is obtained for which areas in the current knowledge test I could receive special learning assistance

[2] GMFTs importance and Gender correlated (−0.471, $df = 18$, $p = 0.036$). Relevant partial correlations concerning GMFTs importance controlling for Gender were: 0.637, $df = 17$, $p = 0.003$ (with Course achievement); 0.444, $df = 17$, $p = 0.057$ (with Academic achievement); 0.637, $df = 17$, $p = 0.003$ (with E-assessment participation).

[3] The mean of absolute difference between the responses to these item-pairs was calculated for each participant (e.g., [15]), and the mean and standard deviation of this measure were 1.86 and 1.37, respectively. Furthermore, the measure positively correlated with Course achievement (0.574, $df = 18$, $p = 0.008$), meaning that participants with lower course achievement responded to adjacent item-pairs in a more similar way [22].

from the professor" compared to the remaining feedback techniques of not only the deep approach but also both approaches.[4]

The second research question sought to uncover relationships, if any, between the importance of feedback techniques supporting a particular approach and background variables considered. It was only found that feedback techniques supporting a deep approach were more important to females than males. Although gender differences in language learning have not followed consistent patterns, several studies have evidenced that females may be better learners than males due to their higher language proficiency, stronger vocabulary knowledge, and better use of learning strategies (e.g., [24, 25]). To attain and maintain such a status, females may in general more often apply a deep rather than a strategic approach. They thus might, compared to males, assign more importance to feedback techniques supporting a deep rather than a strategic approach.

As mentioned in the Introduction, there may be a positive relationship between academic achievement and a strategic approach, whereas this achievement might be unrelated to a deep approach (e.g., [12]). Because of that, it was expected that feedback techniques supporting a strategic approach might be more important to students who had better achievements, but this importance was not related to any achievement variable ($W \geq 98.5$, $|z| \leq 0.492$, $p \geq 0.643$). However, significant relationships in question were found when DAFTs and SAFTs results were combined using variable GMFTs importance mentioned above: there were positive relationships between GMFTs importance on one side and Course achievement and E-assessment participation on the other. These findings provide some evidence that, where considered together in a specific way, DAFTs and SAFTs importance could explain an increase in students' knowledge, skills and motivation. The findings also suggest that instead of focusing on individual relationships between the importance of particular feedback techniques and relevant learning variables, researchers may relate these variables by combining different kinds of feedback techniques.

The previous paragraphs present some educational benefits of the feedback techniques examined. Apart from discussing these benefits, the cost of producing this feedback may also be examined. As the production of quality feedback has a high development time cost (e.g., [26]), the implementation of feedback examined in this study may at first sight appear as a costly enterprise. Typical automated response in a learning management system (e.g., "Correct" or "Incorrect! The answer is bridge!") may be extended in the direction of feedback techniques D1 and S1 (e.g., D1 – "Please go back to Sect. 3 Vocabulary Building to consolidate basic terminology on Networks"; S1 – "Please refer to our mind map with the basic terminology about Networks"), but this extension requires that each question entity is coupled with different feedback techniques, which may not be supported by the assessment system at hand. Because our feedback techniques need to be connected to various assessment entities at different levels (whole course – S5; lesson – D4, D5, S1, S4; learning object – D1;

[4] The medians of D5 importance, DAFTs4 importance (the remaining four DAFTs), FTs9 importance (the remaining nine FTs) were 6.66, 7.58, and 7.42, respectively. Their differences in question were significant: D5 importance – DAFTs4 importance: $z = -3.286$, $p = 0.000$; D5 importance – FTs9 importance: $z = -2.688$, $p = 0.005$. D5 importance was of high reliability by applying correction for attenuation (e.g., [23]).

question – D2), an appropriate form-based editor supporting a field hierarchy needs to be previously implemented at the assessment system. When this editor is available, which increases (possibly not much) the overall production cost, the test developer task would only require modest extra work beyond the typical [27].

Due to different experience with tests, feedback techniques that were important to students who completed almost all tests might differ from those important to students who completed these tests (much) less often or not at all. Because such differences were not found for two importance variables as well as their individual items ($W \geq 70.5$, $|z| \leq 1.846$, $p \geq 0.073$ for all these indicators), it was possible to consider all students as being members of one homogeneous group.[5]

To summarise: this study used a small sample that might characterise it as preliminary research, especially when gender differences were considered (there were only five females). Despite these limitations, the study revealed valuable findings, which due to their considerable effect size, make the sample size less questionable. These findings may be re-examined in future research using larger samples and a number of background variables. Such elaboration may reveal additional differences among students from different sub-groups. Knowing these differences can support the implementation of e-learning feedback that is more relevant to students, which would hopefully improve their learning outcomes.

5 Conclusion

This study aimed to enhance our knowledge about the feedback techniques that are important to students. Focusing on deep and strategic approaches to learning and studying, this study explored students' opinions about the importance of feedback techniques supporting these approaches and searched for student characteristics that might relate to that importance. It was found that feedback techniques supporting a deep approach were as important to students as feedback techniques supporting a strategic approach. Furthermore, feedback techniques supporting a deep approach were more important to females than to males. Finally, when the importance of these feedback techniques were considered together, their relevance to increase in students' knowledge, skills and motivation could be demonstrated. This survey was conducted for English courses. Further research may examine whether similar conclusions might apply for other courses in different subject areas.

Despite some ambiguity regarding the notion of a learning approach (e.g., [28] often considered as a learning style), this notion can be used to define e-assessment (e-learning) feedback techniques through associating them with key features of particular learning approaches, especially those that contribute to genuine learning (e.g., [9]). Although this study did not consider students' learning approaches, further research may do so through connecting feedback techniques endorsed by students with learning approaches they apply. With such connection at hand, e-learning systems may adapt

[5] As expected, E-assessment participation was positively related to achievement (see Table 2; $\chi 2 = 5.051$, $df = 1$, $p = 0.025$ for both achievement variables).

not only learning content and sequence (path) to student's learning approach (e.g., [29, 30]), but also learning feedback to that approach (done automatically or with respect to students' preferences), aiming at, whenever possible, facilitating self-regulated learning with understanding.

Acknowledgement. The authors wish to thank all students who participated in this study. The research done by the first and third authors was funded by the Ministry of Education, Science and Technological Development of the Republic of Serbia (Contract No. 451-03-68/2022-14/200018).

References

1. Hattie, J.A.C.: Visible Learning: A Synthesis of over 800 Meta-Analyses Relating to Achievement. Routledge, Abingdon (2009). https://doi.org/10.1109/ITHET.2015.7218029
2. Vozniuk, A., Rodrguez-Triana, M.J., Holzer, A., Govaerts, S., Sandoz, D., Gillet, D.: Contextual learning analytics apps to create awareness in blended inquiry learning. In: Proceedings of 2015 International Conference on Information Technology Based Higher Education and Training (ITHET). IEEE, New York (2015). https://doi.org/10.1109/ITHET.2015.7218029
3. Roberts, L.D., Howell, J.A., Seaman, K.: Give me a customizable dashboard: personalized learning analytics dashboards in higher education. Technol. Knowl. Learn. **22**, 317–333 (2017). https://doi.org/10.1007/s10758-017-9316-1
4. Lim, L., Dawson, S., Joksimović, S., Gasevic, D.: Exploring students' sensemaking of learning analytics dashboards: does frame of reference make a difference? In: LAK19: Proceedings of the 9th International Conference on Learning Analytics & Knowledge, pp. 250–259. ACM, New York (2019). https://doi.org/10.1145/3303772.3303804
5. Howell, J.A., Roberts, L.D., Mancini,V.O.: Learning analytics messages: impact of grade, sender, comparative information and message style on student affect and academic resilience. Comput. Hum. Behav. **89**, 8–15. https://doi.org/10.1016/j.chb.2018.07.021
6. Suurtamm, C., et al. (eds.): Assessment in Mathematics Education. ITS, Springer, Cham (2016). https://doi.org/10.1007/978-3-319-32394-7
7. Hidri, S. (ed.): Revisiting the Assessment of Second Language Abilities: From Theory to Practice. SLLT, Springer, Cham (2018). https://doi.org/10.1007/978-3-319-62884-4
8. Webb, M.E., et al.: Challenges for IT-enabled formative assessment of complex 21st century skills. Technol. Knowl. Learn. **23**, 441–456 (2018). https://doi.org/10.1007/s10758-018-9379-7
9. Kadijevich, D.M., Ljubojevic, D.: E-assessment feedback: Students' opinions on what to include. In: Jovanović, S., Trebinjac, B. (eds.) Proceedings of the 11th Conference on E-learning, pp. 82–85. Metropolitan University, Belgrade (2020)
10. Entwistle, N.: Motivational factors in students approaches to learning. In: Schmeck, R.R. (ed.), Learning Strategies and Learning Styles, pp. 21–51. Prenum Press, New York (1988). https://doi.org/10.1016/0022-2836(81)90087-5
11. Richardson, J.T.E.: Approaches to studying, conceptions of learning and learning styles in higher education. Learn. Individ. Differ. **21**(3), 288–293 (2011). https://doi.org/10.1016/j.lindif.2010.11.015
12. Cassidy, S.: Learning styles: an overview of theories, models, and measures. Educ. Psychol.-UK **24**(4), 419–444 (2004). https://doi.org/10.1080/0144341042000228834

13. Lindblom-Ylnne, S., Parpala, A., Postareff, L.: What constitutes the surface approach to learning in the light of new empirical evidence? Stud. High. Educ. **44**(12), 2183–2195 (2019). https://doi.org/10.1080/03075079.2018.1482267
14. Saldivar, M.G.: A Primer on Survey Response Rate. Learning Systems Institute. Florida State University, Tallahassee (2012)
15. Gehlbach, H., Barge, S.: Anchoring and adjusting in questionnaire responses. Basic Appl. Soc. Psychol. **34**(5), 417–433 (2012). https://doi.org/10.1080/01973533.2012.711691
16. Guttman, L.: Image theory for the structure of quantitative variates. Psychometrika **21**(3), 277–296 (1953). https://doi.org/10.1007/BF02289264
17. Kadijevich, D., Odovic, G., Maslikovic, D.: Using ICT and quality of life: comparing persons with and without disabilities. In: Miesenberger, K., Bühler, C., Penaz, P. (eds.) ICCHP 2016, Part I. LNCS, vol. 9758, pp. 129–133. Springer, Cham (2016). https://doi.org/10.1007/978-3-319-41264-1_18
18. Lind, D.A., Marchal, W.G., Wathen, S.A.: Statistical Techniques in Business & Economics, 15th edn. McGraw-Hill/Irwin, New York (2013)
19. Fritz, C.O., Morris, P.E., Richler, J.J.: Effect size estimates: current use, calculations, and interpretation. J. Exp. Psychol. Gen. **141**(1), 2–18 (2012). https://doi.org/10.1037/a0024338
20. Ruscio, J.: Constructing confidence intervals for Spearman's rank correlation with ordinal data: a simulation study comparing analytic and bootstrap methods. J. Mod. Appl. Stat. Methods **7**(2), 416–434 (2008). https://doi.org/10.22237/jmasm/1225512360
21. Burton, L., Nelson, L.: The relationships between personality, approaches to learning and academic success in first-year psychology distance education students. In: Critical Visions, Proceedings of the 29th HERDSA Annual Conference, Western Australia, 10–12 July 2006, pp. 64–72. Higher Education Research and Development Society of Australasia, Milperra, Australia (2006)
22. Kadijevich, D.M., Ljubojevic, D., Gutvajn, N.: Anchoring and adjusting in students' responses to a questionnaire about the importance of given e-feedback techniques. In: Domazet, B., Raspopović Milić, M. (eds.) Proceedings of the 12th conference on e-learning, pp. 122–124. Metropolitan University, Belgrade (2021)
23. Wanous, J.P., Hudy, M.J.: Single-item reliability: a replication and extension. Organ. Res. Methods **4**(4), 361–375 (2001). https://doi.org/10.1177/109442810144003
24. Okk Saengsawang, P.P.: The use of blended learning to support vocabulary learning and knowledge retention in Thai tertiary EFL classrooms, Durham theses, Durham University, Durham, UK (2020). http://etheses.dur.ac.uk/13762/
25. Kaushanskaya, M., Marian, V., Yoo, J.: Gender differences in adult word learning. Acta Psychol. (AMST) **137**(1), 24–35 (2011). https://doi.org/10.1016/j.actpsy.2011.02.002
26. Jeria, H., Villalon, J.: Incorporating open education resources into computer supported marking tool to enhance formative feedback creation. In: 2017 IEEE 17th International Conference on Advanced Learning Technologies (ICALT), pp. 256–260. (2017). https://doi.org/10.1109/ICALT.2017.154
27. Kadijevich, D.M., Gutvajn, N.: Feedback supporting deep and strategic approaches to learning and studying: a case study on production cost. In: Domazet, B., Raspopović Milić, M. (eds.) Proceedings of the 12th Conference on E-learning, pp. 119–121. Metropolitan University, Belgrade (2021)
28. Papadatou-Pastou, M., Touloumakos, A.K., Koutouveli, C., Barrableet, A.: The learning styles neuromyth: when the same term means different things to different teachers. Eur. J. Psychol. Educ. **36**, 511–531 (2021). https://doi.org/10.1007/s10212-020-00485-2

29. Truong, H.M.: Integrating learning styles and adaptive e-learning system: current developments, problems and opportunities. Comput. Hum. Behav. **55-B**, 1185–1193 (2016). https://doi.org/10.1016/j.chb.2015.02.014
30. Kolekar, S.V., Pai, R.M., Pai, M.M.M.: Adaptive user interface for Moodle based e-learning system using learning styles. Procedia Comput. Sci. **135**, 606–615 (2018). https://doi.org/10.1016/j.procs.2018.08.226

Shifting to a Technology-Driven Work Mode: Workplace Learning and Dynamic Capability in the Case of a Public-Sector Service Organisation

Katriina Vartiainen(✉)

Tampere University, Tampere, Finland
katriina.vartiainen@tuni.fi

Abstract. Learning to operate in technology-driven working modes is topical in many organisations today due to the COVID-19 pandemic crisis. The pandemic has forced especially knowledge-work organisations to quickly shift to remote or hybrid working modes, where all or some of the staff are operating and collaborating via digital tools. The aim of this qualitative case study is to explore and explicate a learning story of an organisation within the public sector transitioning quickly to a technology-driven hybrid working mode during the crisis. As findings, the paper presents the identified immediate and evolving facilitators that point to the organisation's learning to develop capabilities for operating effectively in the enforced and volatile conditions. Additionally, the potential long-term organisational development effects stemming from the situation are considered. In the findings, social aspects of work, such as open communication, collaboration, and awareness gained emphasis, while digital technology is one of the ground enablers. We apply a frame of dynamic capabilities together with workplace learning and aim to provide new insights into their development processes with a cross-organisational approach. In terms of practical implications, we suggest new understandings for the management on how organisations may learn and fare under uncertainty, volatility, and transitioning to digital collaboration.

Keywords: Dynamic capabilities · Workplace learning · Remote working · Hybrid · Facilitators · Qualitative · Case study

1 Introduction

The COVID-19 pandemic has had significant effects around the globe since the turn of the year 2019–2020. From an organisational perspective, it has forced many organisations to suddenly move to a vast remote working mode, and, consequently, to "technology-driven" [1, p. 1] collaboration enabled by digital technologies. [1–3] To successfully manage in the new working conditions, organisations need to learn, and they need to learn fast. Topical research on the effects on workplaces and organisations has already been conducted (e.g. [2, 4, 5]). However, more understanding of organisational learning mechanisms is required, both as the current crisis unfolds and as digitally enabled operating modes keep transforming work in different ways [3, 6, 7].

Published by Springer Nature Switzerland AG 2022
D. Passey et al. (Eds.): OCCE 2021, IFIP AICT 642, pp. 274–285, 2022.
https://doi.org/10.1007/978-3-030-97986-7_23

In addressing this need, we identify a confluence of two research streams. First, dynamic capabilities research relates to organisational agility and the capability to quickly adapt to changing conditions in operational environments. The conditions may include changing markets, competition, disruptive technologies, and other factors that make organisations' environments turbulent. [7–9] Second, the workplace learning perspective and particularly learning organisations appear relevant in the contexts of increasing technology use in working life and the changing contents of work [10, p. 131]. This motivation appears yet more topical in the current conditions and future anticipated digitalisation of work [6].

Against this background, we apply dynamic capability [9, 11] and workplace learning [6, 10] as lenses for studying organisational learning and capability development in suddenly changing conditions, where digital technologies play a key role in effective operation [1]. We ask, *what facilitates organisational learning for developing the capability to operate effectively in an enforced technology-driven work mode during a volatile situation?* In addressing the question, the paper covers a qualitative case study [12] exploring organisational learning and capability development in the case company, which operates within the public sector in the Nordic region. The data were collected by twelve semi-structured interviews [12] conducted during the pandemic restrictions with professionals from the case company. The interview material was analysed by a combination of abductive [13] and inductive approaches [14].

As findings, we present a set of organisational phenomena, which we suggest facilitate learning and capability development in the case organisation. The facilitators encompass *organisational response and managerial action*; *staff readiness and commitment*; *multi-functional, continuous collaboration*; *increased awareness*; *learning new practices*; and *anticipated long-term organisational development*. The facilitators appear to progress temporally [3] from immediate and evolving to longer-term development, as the pandemic situation and the new working mode become familiar. The findings point towards interrelated cycles of dynamic capabilities of sensing, learning, integrating, and coordinating [9] manifesting across the organisation [11] as the facilitators evolve. Finally, social aspects of work [6], such as open communication, collaboration, and awareness (cf. [10]), gained emphasis in the findings, while digital technology is one of the ground enablers.

This paper aims to contribute to the understanding of organisational learning and capability development in an interdisciplinary manner [10] in the context of a suddenly enforced technology-driven work mode [1, 2]. We primarily build on information systems (IS) and management literature while reaching to the related field of workplace learning. Next, the background and theoretical underpinnings are discussed in Sect. 2, followed by the case description and methodology in Sect. 3. The qualitative findings are presented with examples in Sect. 4. The theoretical and practical discussion is carried out in Sect. 5, and the limitations, suggestions for further research, and concluding remarks are found in Sect. 6.

2 Background and Theoretical Underpinnings

The COVID-19 pandemic started to shake the world at the end of 2019 and reached Northern Europe in early 2020. In the wake of the pandemic, virtually all organisations capable of conducting their tasks in a remote working mode were suddenly forced to do so, which transformed collaboration from an on-site, face-to-face mode to a largely virtual one [1, 2]. Recent research has uncovered many effects of the situation on working and organisations, such as technology issues in different industries [5], changes in the means and affordances of knowledge-work teams' collaborations [2], the impact of the situation on IS management [4], and assessments of adopting new practices in organisations [1].

Two notable aspects emerge from the literature. First, managing in the situation seems not only to be about the technology itself (cf. [6]). Remote working practices appear to play an important role in organisations' success in these circumstances [1, 2, 5]. As the means and affordances of collaboration shift from an office environment to a home environment, both positive and negative effects on collaboration have been seen. Technologies enable continued collaboration to meet business goals, but they also introduce challenges to traditional ways of collaboration [2]. Second, time seems to be a central variable [3]. It becomes a scarce resource and organisations are under time pressure when moving to the new technology-driven ways of working [1]. The faster an organisation managed to operate as business-as-usual, the sooner it was found to recover to normal operations [4], which highlights the importance of organisational agility [7, 15].

While organisations aim to sustain their business as usual under the new circumstances (cf. [2, 4]), quick adaptation and learning on many levels are required. On the one hand, many organisations had no existing strategies, practices, or infrastructures in place to accommodate such a sudden, large-scale shift. On the other hand, not all individuals and teams were used to operating in a virtual mode [1, 2]. The situation underscores the necessity of quick, "continuous learning" in the workplace [10, p. 131]. In developing "digital workplaces," technologies and systems, and their use, have gained importance, while an understanding of work practices, creating a common goal, and a view of the whole have been found necessary from a learning perspective [6, p. 11–12]. Learning as an organisation revolves around the organisation's and its members' capacity for change and increased effectiveness. Open communication, empowerment, and collaborative culture are identified as requirements. In the context of this study, we identify learning in the workplace as an informal, emerging, and participative process of creating and learning new modes of operation, practices, and knowledge at the organisational level. [10]

Next, dynamic capabilities [9, 11] are identified as fitting lenses to explore learning and capability development in a turbulent, digital technology-intensive environment [7] where organisations operate under time pressure [1]. Dynamic capabilities have been defined in several ways [16]. A high-level core definition names three main organisational capacities, sensing opportunities and threats in the environment, seising the identified opportunities, and continually renewing, or transforming, the organisation [8]. In this paper, we utilise a somewhat more detailed model including *sensing*, as "the ability to spot, interpret, and pursue opportunities in the environment," *learning* "to revamp existing operational capabilities with new knowledge," *integrating* "to embed new knowledge into the new operational capabilities by creating a shared understanding and collective sense-making," and *coordinating* capability "to orchestrate and deploy tasks, resources, and activities in the new operational capabilities" [9, p. 247]. Following [11], and in line with learning as a participative process [10], we explore dynamic capabilities as multi-level constructs, where experts in different roles, also beyond the management, are connected by productive and interpersonal dialogue for adapting to a changing environment [11].

3 Case Description and Methodology

This study is an independent part of a longitudinal, interpretive case study [12, 17] initiated in the fall of 2018 to explore organisational capability development in the context of digital transformation [18]. The case company from the Nordic region operates within the public sector and provides professional procurement and logistics services to its customers. The company employs close to 300 people in three locations. This paper reports findings from the third and final round of the overall study. The data were collected by twelve individual qualitative semi-structured interviews [12] between November 2020 and January 2021.

At the time of the interviews, the company had operated from eight to eleven months in a working mode where most of the office staff worked remotely, while the operative staff worked on-site with special protective measures. This mode we call *hybrid*, where part of the staff collaborates in a face-to-face mode and part via digital technologies. Therefore, the overall collaboration among teams is often at least partly enabled by digital tools. Prior to the pandemic, the organisation had digitalised most of its operations, and it largely functions with the support of advanced IS and technology-driven [1] tools. The transition to vast remote working by a large part of the staff required learning in terms of the new hybrid working mode practices and the active utilisation of remote collaboration tools, such as Microsoft Teams. During the pandemic, the organisation's functioning became crucial in procuring and delivering supplies to its customers, including protective gear for health care.

3.1 Data Collection

The interviews were conducted over Microsoft Teams with interviewees from both managerial and non-managerial positions. Their tasks involved knowledge-intensive work with a mix of operative-oriented and planning and coordination-oriented responsibilities. The overall goal of the interviews was to gain an understanding of how the organisation had developed during the past year.

The interview themes included topics, such as change and developing operations, IS and their utilisation, and key competencies and capabilities. In addition to answering questions according to the interview themes, the participants were encouraged to share their views also outside the themes. Due to the COVID-19 pandemic, a new theme examining the impact of the situation was introduced. This paper reports the findings related to that theme and the new hybrid mode of working. During the interviews, it became apparent that the pandemic situation was intertwined with the organisation's activities, including the hybrid working mode and the changing emphasis of core operations, so that it reflected in many of the responses in different interview themes.

The interviews were recorded by audio and researcher notes, as permitted by the participants. The recording length varied from approximately 37 min to 57 min, with an average duration of approximately 48 min. Introducing the research, addressing questions from the participants, discussing the findings from the previous interview rounds at the end of the session, and closing the session were excluded from the recordings.

3.2 Data Analysis

For the analysis, which was conducted in March 2021, the audio recordings were listened to and freely transcribed into text. The transcription was conducted as detailed notes from the recordings aiming to capture the essential responses for prompt reporting (cf. [3]). This process amounted to approximately 65 pages and 22,000 words of transcribed interview material.

The transcribed material was coded and categorised with the support of Atlas.ti qualitative data analysis software depicting items and phenomena related to the COVID-19 situation and the resulting hybrid working mode. Challenges, strategies, facilitators, and outcomes of managing the critical, prolonged situation were identified and coded as inductively as possible. [14, 19] Next, the codes were categorised in two ways. First, following Carroll and Conboy [1], normalisation process theory (NPT, May and Finch, 2009 in [1]) was utilised, as it provided a lens to understand how the new practices may have been perceived, internalised, implemented, and evaluated in the organisation. The value of NPT was in guiding us through the nuances of the data in a structured, abductive way [13]. After this way gaining an understanding of the data by their parts and the whole [17], we commenced the second round of categorisation, extracting emerging themes from the data.

The findings presented in the next section were derived from this second categorisation. They reflect the practical life and learning of the organisation in the face of 1) a critical situation affecting the society and the organisation's operations, and 2) a hybrid working mode involving new heavily technology-driven [1] collaboration and other operational practices. Finally, during writing this paper, the findings were discussed with the organisation's representatives for validation. The findings were perceived as identifiable and relevant, while some remarks were made for deepening them.

4 Findings

In this section, we present facilitators of learning to develop capabilities for functioning effectively in the technology-driven, hybrid working mode and volatile situation. The facilitators appear to manifest as immediate and evolving phenomena, and they are further divided into five different categories. In the final section of the findings, we will anticipate some long-term effects based on the interview material.

4.1 Immediate Facilitators

The *immediate facilitators* we identify as phenomena and action that were initiated soon after the COVID-19 situation escalated and the new hybrid working mode was enforced. We further describe this as *an organisational response to the situation*, including three categories of facilitators.

First, as grounding facilitators, we suggest *prompt organisational response and continued managerial action*, which refer to organisational actors anticipating and preparing for the situation, and management providing quick input and guidance to their teams. Further, management working close to the teams also in operative questions and rewarding staff under pressure were perceived as supportive measures. Importantly, open information sharing by the management enabled team members to take adequate and timely action in tackling emerging challenges in daily operations, or to provide accurate status information.

The second grounding facilitator appears to be the *readiness and commitment of staff* in the face of a critical situation. Examples of such are commitment to handle the increased, fast-paced workload and completing tasks with a high sense of responsibility. Willingness to transfer between tasks to cover resource shortages in the organisation was perceived of as helpful, while operating according to one's best knowledge as essential.

Finally, and according to the interview material crucially, *seamless, multifunctional, and continuous collaboration* appears to enable successful operations in an atypical situation. Close collaboration and information sharing with teams and customers was emphasised. Communicating, interacting, and working toward a common goal as one team as well as helping one another across organisational borders were found as keys to managing well in the situation. Table 1 summarises these findings with examples.

Table 1. Summary of the immediate facilitators with examples.

Immediate facilitators (an organisational response to the situation)		
Facilitators	*Examples*	*Interview excerpts*
Prompt organisational response and continued managerial action	Anticipating and preparing; providing quick input and guidance; working with the team; rewarding staff under pressure; engaging and sharing information openly	"[W]e pulled such a team together really quickly –" "[M]anagers have been – very close to practice –"
Readiness and commitment of staff	Commitment of personnel in the face of a challenging situation; readiness to bear responsibility; readiness to operate according to one's best knowledge	"[P]eople have – an excellent sense of responsibility –"
Seamless, multi-functional, and continuous collaboration	Close collaboration and continuous information sharing within the organisation and with stakeholders; communication, interaction and working for a common goal as a team; mutual assistance across borders	"[T]hat close collaboration was probably key –" "[Collaboration] has, indeed, enabled it –"

4.2 Evolving Facilitators

Next, by *evolving facilitators* we mean phenomena and actions that are forming as the new situation matures. These could be seen as manifestations of *organisational learning*, as the immediate factors of prompt organisational response, continued managerial action, the readiness and commitment of staff, and close, continuous collaboration are enacted.

First, the interview material indicates *increased situational and organisational awareness* resulting from the situation and focus on collaboration. It appears as a two-way street of listening to and sharing information. On the one hand, the customers are listened to carefully to identify potential sources of disruption in the supply chain. On the other hand, colleagues are internally kept updated with special care that the message is understood. Additionally, it was perceived that the awareness of the effectiveness and expertise within and of the organisation was also heightened due to the measures taken to address the unusual situation.

Second, and closely tied to the technology-driven working practices, is *learning to operate in a new hybrid working mode and volatile situation*. It appears that forming a new remote working culture and practices takes place over time, and, in this case, mostly as an organic process. Remote working is becoming part of the normal mode in the organisation in contrast to the conditions prior to the situation. Multimodal information sharing practices are implemented, also pro-actively by teams themselves, and trust in remote working practices and tools is increasing. Finally, it appears that reliable remote working tools and connections are prerequisites. Table 2 summarises these findings with examples.

Table 2. Summary of the evolving facilitators with examples.

Evolving facilitators (organisational learning as the situation matures)		
Facilitators	*Examples*	*Interview excerpts*
Increased situational and organisational awareness	Listening to the customers carefully; keeping colleagues updated; increased understanding of the big picture and effectiveness of work; increased awareness of expertise within the organisation	"[W]e keep each other on the ball all the time of surrounding events –" "[I]t is good that you have learned – what my knowledge [base] is, or someone else's knowledge [base]"
Learning to operate in a new hybrid working mode and a volatile situation	Forming of new remote working practices; multimodal information sharing; trust on remote working practices and tools; remote working mode perceived to become part of the normal	"[We] are already used to [a hybrid work mode], and practices have become routinised, and it works better" "Somehow, [remote working] has even increased collaboration"

4.3 Anticipating Long-Term Organisational Development

As the last and the temporally most far-reaching component of the findings, we briefly anticipate the long-term opportunities that the immediate and evolving facilitators may create. As the situation still unfolds while we are writing this paper, the materialised evidence of such development remains for subsequent research.

However, already at this point, we can discuss the potential *long-term organisational development* and the expected *organisational evolution stemming from the experience gained* grounded on the interview material. For instance, it would be beneficial to consider the fruitful multifunctional collaboration and utilisation of the understanding gained from the distributed collaborative practices in the future, when the enforced hybrid working mode has ceased. Table 3 summarises these findings with examples.

Table 3. Summary of the anticipated long-term development with examples.

Long-term development (organisational evolution from the experiences gained)		
Facilitators	*Examples*	*Interview excerpts*
Organisational development of collaborative culture, practices, and new working modes?	Utilising the understanding gained for the best information sharing channels; adopting new, more flexible working modes; an increased understanding of distributed collaboration	"I believe – that the [multi-functional collaboration] will continue from here on too –"

5 Discussion

In this paper, we set out to better understand *what facilitates organisational learning for developing the capability to operate effectively in an enforced technology-driven work mode during a volatile situation.* As a response, we propose a set of immediate and evolving facilitators, as well as the anticipated long-term effects that appeared in the organisation as it navigated through the sudden move to a hybrid working mode amid the COVID-19 pandemic. It appears that in this case and in the context of events, such capability forms as a result of 1) contextual base factors, such as the advanced digitalisation of operations, digital collaboration tools, and the existing expertise in the operational domain; and 2) the facilitators described in the preceding sections. The facilitators are summarised in Fig. 1.

We propose that the learning and capability development were initiated as the interaction of prompt organisational and managerial action and continued support, and the commitment and readiness of staff to operate effectively in the situation. For example, open information sharing by the management and the readiness to act with high commitment by the employees seem to have contributed to effective operations,

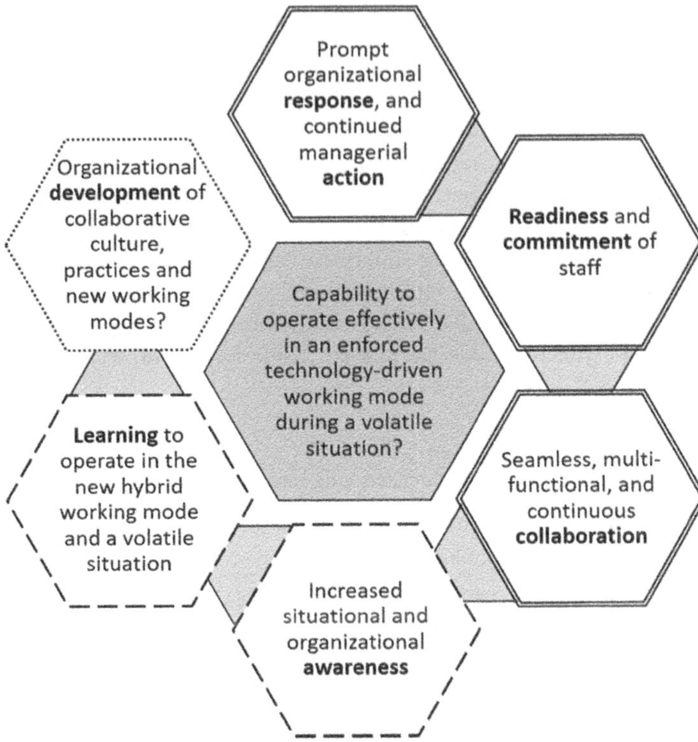

Fig. 1. Summary of the findings, including the proposed immediate and evolving facilitators and the anticipated long-term development. The first three hexagons from the top (with double lines) denote the immediate facilitators, the fourth and fifth hexagons (with dashed lines) represent the evolving facilitators, and the final hexagon (with dotted lines) marks the anticipated long-term development, as learning is accrued from the situation.

and moreover, to seamless, multifunctional, and continuous collaboration. It also appears that this combination may enable an increased situational and organisational awareness, which aligns with the learning outcomes categorised in previous research (Eraut, 2004b in [10]).

Further, it seems that as the new mode of working had been in place for some time, organisational members had learned to operate by utilising digital tools for collaboration and addressing the requirements stemming from the situation. Finally, as the long-term facilitating effect, it is anticipated that the learning gained from operating in such conditions will contribute to organisational development in terms of adopting new practices and promoting a collaborative culture. It could be asked whether, as the immediate facilitators unfold toward the evolving ones and long-term development, organisational learning could also transform from the informal toward the more structured and formal [10]. As a whole, the facilitators seem to place more emphasis on social rather than technological aspects of learning in the workplace [6].

From the dynamic capability perspective, applying the model by Pavlou and El Sawy [9], we suggest that the organisational response and managerial action stem from the capability to *sense* changes in the operating environment and act accordingly. The response and action are then translated by committed and ready staff into *integrated* and *coordinated* activity, multifunctional collaboration. As the situation was volatile with sudden changes both in the mode of collaboration and task priorities, we suggest that *learning* happens iteratively around the immediate facilitators. In terms of the evolving facilitators, as awareness of the situation and organisational expertise increases, it appears that the *sensing* capability is strengthened. We further suggest that in time, new hybrid working mode practices are *learnt*, which both feeds back into daily operations and the immediate facilitators, enabling the *integration* and *coordination* of refined practices as longer-term organisational development.

Finally, we may see these processes as two connected cycles of dynamic sensing, learning, integrating, and coordinating capabilities [9]. In the immediate facilitators, the capabilities are exploited for quick action, and in the evolving facilitators and long-term effects, they are strengthened to enable the further refined practices. This could lead to a "virtuous circle" [11, p. 1745], where through the productive and interpersonal dialogue of employees in different roles, the input of individuals accumulates into an organisational dynamic capability [11], enabling effective response to environmental change (cf. [7]).

6 Conclusions

The paper presented the findings of a qualitative case study, the immediate and evolving facilitators of organisational learning to develop capabilities for operating effectively in an enforced, technology-driven working mode and a volatile situation imposed by the COVID-19 pandemic. The paper explicated the findings theoretically from multi-level dynamic capability [9, 11] and workplace learning [6, 10] perspectives.

As limitations of the study, we wish to highlight two main aspects. First, even though we discuss how learning and capability development may have happened in this case, events have likely taken place in an interlinked, emerging [10, 11] manner. Thus, we refrain from claiming causal relationships. Second, the handling of risks and challenges was excluded from the paper due to space constraints. The risks and challenges, and their potential impact, should be addressed in subsequent work. For example, the endurance of staff, ability to drive new development activities, and induction of new team members may pose challenges if the enforced situation is prolonged.

While we can see the linkages of organisational learning and capability development, further research would be required for a more solid understanding of the antecedents of such agility and the role of digital technologies in it [15]. For example, do the antecedents lie in the previous experiences of the organisation or the existing knowledge the organisation has harnessed in a new situation? Next, what about collaboration as a facilitator; is it immediate or evolving? Here it was categorised as immediate, as it was perceived of as key, and it initiated quickly. Further, longitudinal research is required to uncover how the anticipated long-term effects grow in the aftermath of the situation. Additionally, a more elaborate analysis with learning typologies, such as discussed by Tynjälä [10], should be incorporated. Finally, while the NPT frame [1] was utilised in the early stage of the qualitative analysis, it turned out that an inductive approach provided a more practice-oriented insight into our interview material. However, NPT appears as a viable model and its utilisation should be further explored. It seems likely that it would yield more understanding on the mechanisms of adopting new practices in organisations.

By connecting the research streams of workplace learning [6, 10] and dynamic capabilities [9, 11], we explored the effects of a sudden and enforced transition to a technology-driven work mode [1, 2] in an organisation. With this, we wish to contribute to research on organisational learning and capability development processes in technology-intensive and volatile operating conditions, which require the capacity of organisations to learn and adjust rapidly [7]. As implications for practice, we propose a new understanding for management in navigating through such situations. While further work is still required, we believe this case will inspire discussion in the scientific community regarding organisational learning.

Acknowledgements. We thank the case organisation for making the research possible. We also thank Tampere University, The University of Tampere Foundation, The Foundation for Economic Education, and Jenny and Antti Wihuri Foundation for support.

References

1. Carroll, N., Conboy, K.: Normalising the "new normal": changing tech-driven work practices under pandemic time pressure. Int. J. Inf. Manage. **55**, 102186 (2020). https://doi.org/10.1016/j.ijinfomgt.2020.102186
2. Waizenegger, L., McKenna, B., Cai, W., Bendz, T.: An affordance perspective of team collaboration and enforced working from home during COVID-19. Eur. J. Inf. Syst. **29**(4), 429–442 (2020). https://doi.org/10.1080/0960085X.2020.1800417
3. Ågerfalk, P.J., Conboy, K., Myers, M.D.: Information systems in the age of pandemics: COVID-19 and beyond. Eur. J. Inf. Syst. **29**(3), 203–207 (2020). https://doi.org/10.1080/0960085X.2020.1771968
4. Conger, S.: The impact of the COVID-19 pandemic on information systems management. Inf. Syst. Manag. **37**(4), 327–331 (2020). https://doi.org/10.1080/10580530.2020.1820636
5. Herath, T., Herath, H.S.B.: Coping with the new normal imposed by the COVID-19 pandemic: lessons for technology management and governance. Inf. Syst. Manag. **37**(4), 277–283 (2020). https://doi.org/10.1080/10580530.2020.1818902
6. Vallo Hult, H., Byström, K.: Challenges to learning and leading the digital workplace. Stud. Contin. Educ. (2021). https://doi.org/10.1080/0158037X.2021.1879038
7. Teubner, R.A., Stockhinger, J.: Literature review: understanding information systems strategy in the digital age. J. Strateg. Inf. Syst. **29**(4), 101642 (2020). https://doi.org/10.1016/j.jsis.2020.101642
8. Teece, D., Peteraf, M., Leih, S.: Dynamic capabilities and organisational agility: risk, uncertainty and strategy in the innovation economy. Calif. Manage. Rev. **58**(4), 13–35 (2016). https://doi.org/10.1525/cmr.2016.58.4.13

9. Pavlou, P.A., El Sawy, O.A.: Understanding the elusive box of dynamic capabilities. Decis. Sci. **42**(1), 239–273 (2011). https://doi.org/10.1111/j.1540-5915.2010.00287.x
10. Tynjälä, P.: Perspectives into learning at the workplace. Educ. Res. Rev. **3**(2), 130–154 (2008). https://doi.org/10.1016/j.edurev.2007.12.001
11. Salvato, C., Vassolo, R.: The source of dynamism in dynamic capabilities. Strateg. Manag. J. **39**(6), 1728–1752 (2018). https://doi.org/10.1002/smj.2703
12. Yin, R.: Case Study Research and Applications: Design and Methods, 6th edn. SAGE Publications, Los Angeles (2018)
13. Kennedy, B.L.: Deduction, induction, and abduction. In: Flick, U. (ed.) The SAGE Handbook of Qualitative Data Collection, pp. 49–64. SAGE Publications Ltd. (2018). https://doi.org/10.4135/9781526416070
14. Urquhart, C.: Grounded Theory for Qualitative Research: A Practical Guide. SAGE Publications Ltd. (2013). https://doi.org/10.4135/9781526402196
15. Tallon, P.P., Queiroz, M., Coltman, T., Sharma, R.: Information technology and the search for organisational agility: a systematic review with future research possibilities. J. Strateg. Inf. Syst. **28**(2), 218–237 (2019). https://doi.org/10.1016/j.jsis.2018.12.002
16. Peteraf, M., Di Stefano, G., Verona, G.: The elephant in the room of dynamic capabilities: bringing two diverging conversations together. Strateg. Manag. J. **34**(12), 1389–1410 (2013). https://doi.org/10.1002/smj.2078
17. Klein, H.K., Myers, M.D.: A set of principles for conducting and evaluating interpretive field studies in information systems. MIS Q. **23**(1), 67–93 (1999). https://doi.org/10.2307/249410
18. Vial, G.: Understanding digital transformation: a review and a research agenda. J. Strateg. Inf. Syst. **28**(2), 118–144 (2019). https://doi.org/10.1016/j.jsis.2019.01.003
19. Corbin, J., Strauss, A.: Grounded theory research: procedures, canons and evaluative criteria. Qual. Sociol. **13**(1), 3–21 (1990). https://doi.org/10.1007/BF00988593

Digital Transformation of Education and Learning Through Information Technology in Educational Management

Javier Osorio[1(✉)] and Monica Banzato[2]

[1] Faculty of Business Management, Universidad de Las Palmas de Gran Canaria, Las Palmas, Spain
javier.osorio@ulpgc.es

[2] Research Institute for Digital and Cultural Heritage, Ca' Foscari University, Venice, Italy
banzato@unive.it

Abstract. 2021 is a year of anniversaries in the IFIP family. IFIP TC3 WG3.7 is 25 years old. Celebrating anniversaries is a good opportunity to reflect on how far we have come, and what the future holds. The incorporation of digital technology in education reflects an evolution of light and shadow, with many challenges for the future. Information technology has not only been present in the field of education as a teaching-learning tool, but has also played an important role in educational management. This paper analyses the contribution of IFIP TC3 WG3.7 to the development of the field of Information Technology in Educational Management. It contextualises its origins within the framework of the evolution of digital technology and analyses the most recent situation. The challenge for the future is to reflect on the possible contribution of contemporary educational management trends to help create a balance that facilitates the implementation of digital technologies in education while meeting the social objectives that give meaning to the educational system.

Keywords: Information technology · Educational management · WG3.7

1 Introduction

In 2021, the Working Group 3.4 (WG3.4) of the Technical Committee 3 (TC3) of the International Federation for Information Processing (IFIP) celebrates its 50th anniversary. During its years of existence, WG3.4 has successfully contributed to the creation of knowledge in the field of Professional, Higher and Vocational Education in ICT. Numerous publications attest to this, as well as a remarkable number of international conferences and events in which researchers and practitioners from all over the world have contributed. Interestingly, one of the most relevant results of WG3.4 was the birth of a new Working Group within TC3. In 1994, WG3.4 organised a conference in Jerusalem with the theme Information Technology in Educational Management (ITEM). The conference aroused a great deal of interest in the scientific community and during the conference there was a high level of agreement on the importance and timeliness of the chosen topic. This interest led to the creation, after its approval by

Published by Springer Nature Switzerland AG 2022
D. Passey et al. (Eds.): OCCE 2021, IFIP AICT 642, pp. 286–295, 2022.
https://doi.org/10.1007/978-3-030-97986-7_24

IFIP in 1996, of the Working Group 3.7 (WG3.7) focused on the discipline of Information Technology for Educational Management. The year 2021 is therefore also an important anniversary for WG3.7, namely its 25th anniversary.

The Open Conference on Computers in Education 2021 (OCCE2021 DTEL) is a good opportunity to celebrate such an important date for WG3.4, the host of the conference, and for WG3.7, both of which are linked by close ties. The conference is also a good opportunity to reflect on the contribution that WG3.7 has made to the Digital Transformation of Education and Learning over the past 25 years. Schools, high schools and universities prepare students for the world of the future, and this requires the management of educational centres for the upcoming years. The digital transformation of education and learning has necessarily been linked to a process of digital educational management, which has also had to adapt to new technologies. From the beginning of the existence of WG3.7, it was established as a premise that the focus of the research would be on the impact of information technology for educational management on the teaching-learning process. However, after 25 years, questions can be raised as to whether the use of digital technology (DT) in educational management is the same as the use of DT in business management. There are many parallels between the two types of management, although perhaps the biggest difference lies in the tempus or time lag between the implementation of new management techniques in business and education.

This paper reviews the topics of research interest in information technology in educational management in the past and present, as well as considers foreseeable future trends. Parallel to the review, the contribution of WG3.7 in this arena is described - the Annex 1 summarises the conferences organised by WG3.7 and the books published in these 25 years. Finally, a conclusion is offered on the potential role WG3.7 can play in new scenarios.

2 Information Technology for Educational Management: Origins

Educational management is a broad field that, as its name denotes, encompasses two converging disciplinary areas. The appropriate management and administration of educational institutions has been a matter of concern since the creation of the modern educational system all around the world. Independently of the profit or non-profit nature of schools, universities and other educational centres, the need to efficiently invest in certain resources with the purpose of providing an effective socio-economic education to citizens, has grown a body to manage and administrate the educational process. Educational management includes managing the internal work of educational institutions (budget, personnel, infrastructures, strategies, goals) as well as their external work (external stakeholders' demands and needs, goals coherence within a broader educational setting, policies). Another dimension to be managed in the educational arena has to do with teaching and learning aspects of the education process, i.e. the promotion of best educational practices by part of teachers and trainers to achieve the educational goals. These goals are set by the policies and strategies stated externally and internally to educational centres. The educational picture widens as societies increase their complexity.

In the educational setting, technology, to a greater or lesser extent, has always be present (buildings, papyrus, abacus, pencils, slide rules). With the development of computer technology and its popularisation because of the continuously decreasing costs and improved performance, digital technology has become an additional actor in the educational arena, accompanying the work of teachers and educational administrators and managers. Although no universal definition for information technology for educational management has been provided, the term may include the combination of computing and communication hardware and software adapted to support the administration and management of internal and external work of educational institutions. The beginnings of the use of information technology for educational management date back to the 1970s [1]. At that time, some teachers created the first amateur school administration programs for their own schools or colleges, and also in some university departments. At the end of that decade, software providers entered this market by producing software adapted to more professional standards. Some developed countries had school software applications in place in a large number of schools by the end of the 1970s. These applications were primarily for administrative purposes. In the 1980s, with the commercialisation of personal computers, there was a period of expansion in school computing. At this stage, office and administrative computer applications were used with the characteristic that they were not integrated with each other. The lack of integration limited the possibilities for management support, as managers needed to identify relationships between data. During the initiation and expansion stages, the main objective of software development was to improve the efficiency of school office activities. The next stage, the integration stage, can be characterised by information management and the integration of computer modules with administrative and teaching functions. In those years, educational authorities in technologically advanced countries became aware of the importance of information technology in the field of educational management, and invested large sums of money in the improvement of school computer systems [2, 3].

Parallel to the development of information technology for educational management, academic interest in this field was growing. In 1994, the first International Conference on Information Technology in Educational Management was held in Jerusalem, where the creation of WG3.7 was conceived. Subsequently, in 1995, at the World Conference on Computers in Education held in Birmingham, a considerable number of papers were presented on this topic. A professional group of 20 experts from ten different countries worked during the conference to produce a report addressing the development, research and implementation issues central to the continued growth of information technology for educational management. The report also proposed research methods and strategies needed to generate the desired knowledge and understanding.

In the last decade of the 20th century and the first decade of the 21st century, the use of information technology for educational management grew enormously in industrialised countries. Also, since the beginnings of the 21st century, developing countries began to utilise the potential of these systems, with very high levels of use in countries such as Botswana and Uganda [4].

Typical data processing functions in schools during the early stages of the uptake of educational management information systems included [1]:

1. Updating of the computer database with affiliation information of students, educators and support staff.
2. Retrieval of information and production of documents to obtain information on the situation of the school.
3. Support to the decisions of the educational managers based on the available information.
4. Internal communication within the educational community and external communication to stakeholders of the educational system.
5. Student monitoring systems by assessing students' progress over the long term. This function was considered as one of the most important, as it enables the management of data on student progress. Technology facilitates the production of student progress reports, which can be used by both teachers and school management.

Special mention should be made of the research carried out on information technology for educational management in the sphere of the activities organised by WG3.7. The most popular topics over their first ten years were Assimilation and integration of DT into educational management, followed by Assessment of DT support to educational management, DT applications in educational management, and National, regional and local experience in the use of DT for educational management. All together these topics represented 76.2% of all papers (117) included in the publications by WG3.7 during their first ten years of existence. The most recurrent topic was the Assessment of DT support to educational management, which was repeatedly dealt with because of the importance of analysing the results obtained after implementing new strategies, policies, techniques or tools [5]. Annex 2 describes the research topics covered primarily by WG3.7 members during the initial period of activities. Further information about research methodologies and main contributions that were put forward during this stage can be found on [5].

3 Information Technology for Educational Management: Maturity

Whilst progress is clearly marked during the origins of the field, some common elements requiring development remained. In particular, the following issues were common concern during the transition stage to maturity [6]:

1. Use of the management information systems (MIS) limited to administrative tasks.
2. Lack of MIS availability to all teaching staff.
3. Unsuitable training and support.
4. Inappropriate software interface.
5. Usability and functionality limitations.
6. Inadequate reporting and decision support facilities.
7. Lack of user-centric implementations.
8. Minimal interoperability with other systems.

A review of the literature related to the field of information technology for educational management shows that the main driving force is information technology. The vast majority of publications are related to the description of new software applications or the results obtained after applying a particular information technology in an educational context. The number of publications related to the incorporation of new management theories in the educational arena is very small compared to those dealing with educational technology. Also, many publications referring to recent trends in the field of management that have been put into practice in the educational management area have, as their background, the use of some form of information technology as a supporting tool. Information technology has been growing steadily both in terms of computing power and its incorporation into people's daily lives. The spectacular development of the Internet and the rise of social networks has also had a decisive influence on educational management. On the other hand, one of the greatest advances in information technology has been the integration of information among previously isolated systems.

The opportunities provided by information technology in recent years should not obscure the risks inherent in the massive incorporation of digital technology in education. Teachers' use of technology can be uneven. Some instructors design effective and creative learning opportunities for their students that precipitate deep thinking and reflective engagement in the development of conceptual knowledge. However, some use digital technologies as shortcuts to learning, without focusing on intended outcomes. For example, some educators do not deliberately teach effective online search and verification strategies, nor are they even aware that they should, nor do they know how to incorporate such practices into classroom work. Some teachers, especially at secondary level, struggle to see beyond the content of their subjects, looking only for content-oriented digital solutions, rather than how they might enhance students' own abilities to problem solving, critique and create knowledge with expert guidance [7].

Moreover, many technology companies have turned their attention to education, given that, because of its volume, it can be a lucrative business. Large firms with an interest in education constitute what have come to be known as big Edtechs or Lordtechs. Most of the software applications currently used as learning and educational tools are practically the same all over the world. The influence and ability of big Edtechs to reach all geographical areas has made this possible [8]. All of the above is an element of concern for those responsible for educational management, who must ensure that information technology does not become a mere commercial instrument that prevents the real objectives of the education system from being achieved. However, it is worth highlighting the information technologies that have played a leading role in recent years, given that they have influenced and, foreseeably, will continue to influence the educational process and, therefore, are and will be the object of attention from the perspective of educational management. Weller [9] identifies the most influential educational technologies developed in the last twenty years, with their lights and shadows: E-Learning, Learning Objects, Open Educational Resources, Blogs, Learning Management Systems, Video, Web 2.0, Second Life and Virtual Worlds, E-Portfolios, Twitter and Social Media, Personal Learning Environments, MOOCs, Learning Analytics, Digital Badges and Artificial intelligence. From the mentioned technologies, Learning Analytics and Artificial Intelligence are having an increasing weight in the educational management arena and, very likely, they will constitute critical tools supporting for decision making in this field [10–12].

In this period of maturity, research on information technology for educational management has followed the path of technological development. In the sphere of the conferences organised by WG3.7, the most popular topics over their second ten years of existence have been Assimilation and integration of DT into educational management, DT applications in educational management, and DT applications for teaching. Although the latter is not directly related to the scope of the WG 3.7, this theme gradually has gained importance [13]. Annex 3 describes the research topics covered primarily by WG3.7 members during the maturity period. Further information about research methodologies and main contributions can be found on [13].

4 Information Technology for Educational Management: Future Trends

The rapid development of technology and the constant innovation and application of computer and information technology make information technology change the future lifestyle of human beings and induce comprehensive changes in human learning. The promotion of information technology education policy will enable education to present a new appearance of learning [14].

Drawing on current technological developments and existing applications in digital education, such as mobile apps, learning management solutions and anti-plagiarism software, Popenici and Kerr [15] raise the critical question of who will set the educational agenda in the future, i.e. corporate companies or educational institutions. Large digital and technology-driven companies such as Netflix, Samsung, Google, Microsoft and Facebook, also referred to as Lordtechs, are seeking to develop new data-driven learning programs that enable new teaching tools in public institutions through the optics of these business-driven companies [16]. For example, the Netflix group developed the DreamBoxLearning program for mathematics in the US market, which enables personalised learning based on Artificial Intelligence (AI) technologies with an adaptive intelligent learning system. That these Lordtechs are investing heavily in the development of AI-based teaching and learning solutions inevitably raises the question of whether educational institutions are prepared to implement such data-driven technology in their teaching and learning programmes [17].

This leads one to consider the importance of the challenge facing educational institutions if they are not to become mere instruments of the decisions taken at Lordtechs' headquarters. One possible answer lies in the importance of strengthening the knowledge and skills of future educational managers through a structured training process. In this respect, it could be pointed in two research directions [18]:

1. To analyse the level of training of modern managers in accordance with the requests of the society on DT competences of managers in the educational system.
2. To analyse the problems of selection and application of professionally oriented information technologies in the educational process to meet the needs of educational stakeholders (students, educators, society).

Moreover, the importance of national responses to these challenges should be anticipated. Schools and higher education systems are continuously confronted with the growing challenges of preparing students to successfully participate in the digital age. In many countries, this is leading to multiple efforts and changes in national policies regarding the integration of DT into education systems [19]. Educators, researchers and policy makers believe that the full potential of educational technology will ultimately only be realised when educational policymakers, administrators and teachers effectively integrate and authentically incorporate technological improvements along with data science concepts into their practice and curriculum [20].

It can be expected that alongside the commercial interests of the Lordtechs, national policies align as frameworks for establishing the objectives and limits to the indiscriminate implementation of new technologies in education. The agents that can serve as a means to align both legitimate kind of interests may ultimately be the educational managers, because of their proximity to the reality of students' and educators' demands to consume the latest available technology, but also as guardians of the social interest of national education systems. It is on this latter aspect that the research activity of WG3.7 may focus part of its future activities.

5 Conclusions

Information technology for educational management offers solutions for a wide range of activities at different levels of education - primary, secondary, higher education and adult learning. The broad spectrum of needs to be covered by providers of technology solutions for educational management means that there is no single product that can cover all needs. Moreover, it could be considered that the search for such a single product is a naive and unachievable goal. However, it is necessary to assume that the need to develop multiple products to meet the different demands of the educational management field implies that these have a low level of data integration with each other, at least in their initial stages of development.

Looking back, it can be concluded that in the field of information technology for educational management the technological part of the sentence has been the most prominent. Most of the innovations in this field have been technology-driven. Sometimes they have been accompanied by strong educational frameworks, but sometimes they have only been technologies in search of an application. It is also true that, from an educational management perspective, the social impact of promoting or implementing a technology beyond its uses as an educational tool has often not been addressed. The widespread adoption of technologies such as social networks, MOOCs, learning analytics and AI have social implications that educational authorities have often been unable to appreciate. It is therefore necessary to learn from the past and anticipate the future by studying the social and educational implications of emerging technologies. A good example in this regard is the initiative carried out by IFIP's TC3, under the name of Zanzibar Declaration, which involves a large number of actors in the educational arena to reflect and expose their concerns and recommendations to identify the social and educational implications of technologies such as Big Data, Machine Learning, Autonomous Systems and Artificial Intelligence, among others. Therefore, the challenge facing the discipline of information technology for educational management, and for WG3.7, is to better balance digital technology with conceptual frameworks, both managerial and educational pedagogies, and social movements.

Annex 1 Conferences and Publications Led by WG3.7

Venue	Year	Book title	Editor
Jerusalem (Israel)	1994	Information Technology in Educational Management	Chapman & Hall
Hong-Kong (China)	1996	Information Technology in Educational Management for the Schools of the Future	Chapman & Hall
Maine (USA)	1998	The Integration of Information for Educational Management	Felicity Press
Auckland (New Zealand)	2000	Pathways to Institutional Improvement with Information Technology in Educational Management	Kluwer
Helsinki (Finland)	2002	Management of Education in the Information Age: The Role of IT	Kluwer
Gran Canaria (Spain)	2004	Information Technology and Educational Management in the Knowledge Society	Springer
Hamamatsu (Japan)	2006	Knowledge Management for Educational Innovation	Springer
Darwin (Australia)	2008	Evolution of Information Technology in Educational Management	Springer
Kasane (Botswana)	2010	Information Technology and Managing Quality Education	Springer
Bremen (Germany)	2012	Next Generation of Information Technology in Educational Management	Springer
Guimaraes (Portugal)	2016	Stakeholders and Information Technology in Education	Springer

Annex 2 Number of Papers Classified by Research Subject Published by WG3.7 (1994–2004)

Topic	Number percentage (%)
Strategies to integrate IT into educational management	9
	7.7
Assimilation and integration of IT into educational management	27
	23
ITEM state of the art. The discipline's present situation and trends	3
	2.7
Assessment of IT support to educational management	20
	17.1
National, regional and local experience in the use of IT for educational management	18
	15.4
IT applications in educational management	20
	17.1
Mathematic tools employed to make models for educational management	6
	5.1
IT applications for teaching	8
	6.8
Teacher and manager training in the use of IT for educational management	6
	5.1
Total	117
	100

Annex 3 Number of Papers Classified by Research Subject Published by WG3.7 (2006–2014)

Topic	Number percentage (%)
Strategies to integrate IT into educational management	7 7.3
Assimilation and integration of IT into educational management	26 27.1
ITEM state of the art. The discipline's present situation and trends	3 3.1
Assessment of IT support for educational management	9 9.4
National, regional and local experience in the use of IT for educational management	5 5.2
IT applications in educational management	20 20.8
Mathematical tools employed to create models for educational management	4 4.2
IT applications for teaching	16 16.7
Teacher and manager training in the use of IT for educational management	6 6.3
Total	96 100

References

1. Visscher, A.J.: Information technology in educational management as an emerging discipline. Int. J. Educ. Res. **25**, 291–296 (1996)
2. Visscher, A.J., Spuck, D.W.: Computer assisted school administration and management: the state of the art in seven nations. J. Res. Comput. Educ. **24**, 146–168 (1991)
3. Wild, P., Fung, A.: Evaluation of information technology in educational management for proactive development. Educ. Inf. Technol. **1**(3–4), 239–249 (1996). https://doi.org/10.1007/BF02350661
4. Bisaso, R., Kereteletswe, O., Selwood, I., Visscher, A.: The use of information technology for educational management in Uganda and Botswana. Int. J. Educ. Dev. **28**, 656–668 (2008)
5. Osorio, J., Bulchand, J.: Ten years of ITEM research. In: Tatnall, A., Okamoto, T., Visscher, A. (eds.) ITEM 2006. IIFIP, vol. 230, pp. 1–8. Springer, Boston (2007). https://doi.org/10.1007/978-0-387-69312-5_1

6. Baker, G., O'Mahony, C.D., Selwood, I.D., Strickley, A.: ITEM evolution. In: Tatnall, A., Visscher, A., Finegan, A., O'Mahony, C. (eds.) ITEM 2008. ITIFIP, vol. 292, pp. 189–199. Springer, Boston (2009). https://doi.org/10.1007/978-0-387-93847-9_17
7. Selwyn, N.: Minding our language: why education and technology is full of bullshit … and what might be done about it. Learn. Media Technol. **41**, 437–443 (2016)
8. Wright, N., Peters, M.: Sell, sell, sell or learn, learn, learn? The EdTech market in New Zealand's education system – privatisation by stealth? Open Rev. Educ. Res. **4**, 164–176 (2017)
9. Weller, M.: Twenty years of Edtech. Educ. Rev. Online **53**, 34–48 (2018)
10. Hannan, E., Liu, S.G.: AI: new source of competitiveness in higher education. Compet. Rev. **1**, 1–12 (2021)
11. Ismail, S.N., Hamid, S., Ahmad, M.: Exploring students engagement towards the learning management system (LMS) using learning analytics. Comput. Syst. Sci. Eng. **37**, 73–87 (2021)
12. Beerkens, M.: An evolution of performance data in higher education governance: a path towards a 'big data' era? Qual. High. Educ. **28**(1), 29–49 (2021)
13. Osorio, J., Nieves, J.: Vingt ans après: analysis of WG 3.7's published work on information technology in educational management (1994–2014). In: Brinda, T., Mavengere, N., Haukijärvi, I., Lewin, C., Passey, D. (eds.) SaITE 2016. IAICT, vol. 493, pp. 130–138. Springer, Cham (2016). https://doi.org/10.1007/978-3-319-54687-2_13
14. Chen, C.: Effects of the application of webquest to technology education on business management students' critical thinking psychology and operation capability. Contemp. Educ. Technol. **13**, 1–8 (2021)
15. Popenici, S.A.D., Kerr, S.: Exploring the impact of artificial intelligence on teaching and learning in higher education. Res. Pract. Technol. Enhanc. Learn. **12** (2017). Article number: 22. https://doi.org/10.1186/s41039-017-0062-8
16. Renz, A., Hilbig, R.: Prerequisites for artificial intelligence in further education: identification of drivers, barriers, and business models of educational technology companies. Int. J. Educ. Technol. High. Educ. **17** (2020). Article number: 14. https://doi.org/10.1186/s41239-020-00193-3
17. Ifenthaler, D., Yau, J.: Higher education stakeholders' views on learning analytics policy recommendations for supporting study success. Int. J. Learn. Anal. Artif. Intell. Educ. **1**(28) (2019)
18. Tkachenko, L.P., Dolgopol, O.O., Zhiglo, O.O.: Implementation of professionally oriented (ICT) in the process of managers training. J. Phys. Conf. Ser. **1840**, 12064 (2021)
19. Zagami, J., et al.: Creating future ready information technology policy for national education systems. Technol. Knowl. Learn. **23**(3), 495–506 (2018). https://doi.org/10.1007/s10758-018-9387-7
20. Webb, M., Gibson, D.: Technology enhanced assessment in complex collaborative settings. Educ. Inf. Technol. **20**(4), 675–695 (2015). https://doi.org/10.1007/s10639-015-9413-5

Author Index

The manufacturer's authorised representative in the EU is Springer Nature Customer Service Centre GmbH, Europaplatz 3, 69115 Heidelberg, Germany. If you have any concerns regarding our products, please contact ProductSafety@springernature.com

Printed and bound by CPI Group (UK) Ltd, Croydon, CR0 4YY
28/09/2026
02224088-0015

Blockchain Driven Supply Chains and Enterprise Information Systems

Abdelaziz Bouras • Ibrahim Khalil • Belaid Aouni
Editors

Blockchain Driven Supply Chains and Enterprise Information Systems

Springer

Editors
Abdelaziz Bouras
College of Engineering
Qatar University
Doha, Qatar

Ibrahim Khalil
School of Computing Technologies
RMIT University
Melbourne, VIC, Australia

Belaid Aouni
College of Business & Economics
Qatar University
Doha, Qatar

ISBN 978-3-030-96153-4 ISBN 978-3-030-96154-1 (eBook)
https://doi.org/10.1007/978-3-030-96154-1

This Springer imprint is published by the registered company Springer Nature Switzerland AG
The registered company address is: Gewerbestrasse 11, 6330 Cham, Switzerland

Foreword

Industrial modern supply chains are becoming very complex. Mastering their management is a key success factor for companies and enterprises wishing to grow and increase their gains.

We totally understand the huge potential impact that disruptive technologies such as fintech, artificial intelligence, and blockchain have on current and future supply chains. These technologies are demonstrating the ability to increase business performance, by helping to optimize growth, to establish trust and transparency in the business and in the financial transactions, as well as to better secure information and its infrastructure.

At Qatar Rail, we are currently closely following such progress through collaborations with research institutions and research projects, such as the SupplyLedger project which aims at enhancing traditional supply chains using digital technologies.

This book provides opportunities to industries and organizations to explore the benefit of blockchain technology for their business innovations and supply chains transparency.

I thank the authors and editors for their efforts in bridging the gap between research and industry applications.

Doha, Qatar

H.E. Dr. Abdulla Abdulaziz Turki Al Subaie
Managing Director & CEO/Qatar Rail

Preface

This book, titled *Blockchain Driven Supply Chains and Enterprise Information Systems*, aims at establishing a common ground to provide solutions and best practices around blockchain for supply chain management and enterprise information systems. This book considers the implementation of blockchain platforms in both existing traditional supply chain systems and future enterprise information solutions.

The book has 11 chapters related to important blockchain topics, addressing some of the current needs:

The first chapter provides a scientific analysis of key factors that affect the influence of the blockchain on supply chains performance. The analysis was performed using SPSS and AMOS and the study relied on literature review and surveys of Indian firms. The study is valuable for the industry as it helps decision makers assess the current standing of blockchain and assists them in making the decision for the technology adoption. The chapter proposes a research model based on literature review and surveys to identify critical determinants, namely knowledge sharing, higher authority support, and business partner pressure, to be considered when adopting blockchain technology to better increase the supply chain performance.

The second chapter discusses the role of blockchain in establishing trust in traditional supply chain systems. This trust is analyzed based on a case study involving the finance process of supply chain. It focuses on an important discussion on the notion of trust, though globally there is still lack of consensus on what constitutes trust, and there is no generally widely accepted definition. However, some attempts have been made in other domains, such as the work done by the NIST group around a standardized definition of "trustworthiness" as one of the facets of the CPS (cyber-physical systems).

The third chapter proposes a blockchain-powered digital certificate management system for supply chain systems in the context of transportation of dangerous goods. The chapter suggests a blockchain-based digital certificate platform to monitor the transport of dangerous goods as a supply chain process in terms of verification of stakeholders' identity, history of transportation, environmental data, and real-time location. It focuses on the use of Hyperledger Fabric blockchain network to implement the proof of concept which ensures digital management of transport of dangerous goods.

The fourth chapter presents the challenges of global supply chain systems from the perspective of centralized design. A blockchain-enabled ERP system is presented to mitigate the issues in the centralized global supply chain. This chapter deals with centralized and decentralized supply chains. It proposes a taxonomic analysis of challenges and highlights some solution tracks based on appropriate use of technology.

The fifth chapter seeks to show the pertinence of adopting blockchain technology in textile supply chain and the benefits of such technology in term of traceability and temper proofing. It proposes a blockchain-based solution to enhance traceability and information sharing in the textile supply chain.

The sixth chapter deals with IoT-driven food supply chain management systems, taking advantage of blockchain to improve traceability, transparency, and trustworthiness of the transactions. A complete step-by-step operational flow detailing agri-food supply chain management process would help readers understand how traceability is achieved and how the system saves tremendously with cost-effective measures. The proposed architecture highlights traceability, and software architecture details how the architecture can be realized in practice. The proposed concept, that is, from farm to fork, was implemented in Ethereum and Hyperledger Sawtooth.

The seventh chapter highlights the most known consensus algorithms–based blockchains and their application in the healthcare sector, such as proof of work, proof of stake, and proof of authority. The main objective of this chapter is to illustrate applications and implications of several consensus mechanisms in blockchain-based healthcare supply chain systems.

The eighth chapter shows how blockchain can help improve the authenticity and transparency of supply chain transactions in the automotive industry. It has identified the weakness of the existing supply chain system in the automotive industry and explained the challenges of adoption and deployment of blockchain in this area. It gives a great insight to managers and blockchain practitioners on how to overcome the difficulties that they will encounter during implementation of blockchain technology.

The ninth chapter presents a new consensus mechanism for blockchain-based supply chain management systems to provide solutions to data security and establish trust among different supply chain participants. The proposed consensus mechanism offers a less complicated implementation of the distributed ledger and ensures higher efficiency and scalability for achieving consensus. It is designed considering a consortium blockchain network involving all supply chain stakeholders.

The tenth chapter focuses on blockchain technology and its features, such as distributed ledger and smart contracts from a regulation point of view. It defines the current regulatory landscape and international initiatives. The chapter highlights some applications of the blockchain technology through regulation perspective in the finance, healthcare, logistics, and construction sectors. It emphasizes some challenges faced by blockchain technology and comes up with some recommendations to tackle those challenges.

The eleventh chapter presents a broker-based integration of blockchain smart contracts with industrial workflows. It uses Hyperledger Fabric as a permissioned blockchain platform to store the transaction data and manage the lifecycle of smart contracts. It uses as well Odoo which is an open-source framework written in Python. The chapter proposes a proof-of-concept integration with a scenario of a small-scale manufacturing supply chain involving a limited number of actors and demonstrates that the Odoo workflows can easily be adapted to be fully managed using smart contracts. Thus, increasing the security and enhancing the traceability and trust of critical business transactions.

We would like to thank the authors for their valued contributions and efforts and the reviewers for their help and support in achieving this book. We hope that this book serves as a step forward in this exciting area of blockchains for industry and businesses.

Doha, Qatar — Abdelaziz Bouras
Melbourne, VIC, Australia — Ibrahim Khalil
Doha, Qatar — Belaid Aouni

Acknowledgments

This book was made possible by NPRP grant NPRP11S-1227-170135 from the Qatar National Research Fund (a member of Qatar Foundation). The statements made herein are solely the responsibility of the authors.

About the Book

This book provides several international case studies across different domains such as healthcare, agri-food, logistics, and transportation. Those case studies are mainly related to the implementation of blockchain platforms on modern systems and the integration of such technology with existing traditional systems. The book highlights as well subjects and concerns such as efficiency of blockchain-based supply chains, blockchain consensus protocols and mechanisms, and blockchain based enterprise information systems. It concludes with some directions and recommendations with regards to the adoption of standardized blockchain frameworks. The editors' and authors' expertise across different contexts and countries has made this book a worthy contribution to both theory and practice. Through its solutions and best practices, this book constitutes an interesting source for practitioners and students interested in the domain of blockchain for supply chains management and enterprise information systems.

Contents

Impact of Blockchain Technology Adoption in Performance of Supply Chain

Manish Mohan Baral, Subhodeep Mukherjee, Venkataiah Chittipaka, and Bhaswati Jana

1 Introduction

The supply chain management (SCM) industry has gone through many disruptions recently. The development of new technologies and their implementations have a high impact on the supply chain, operations, etc. Blockchain technology (BT) allows decentralization and helps in the digitalization of business models [1]. Prior studies [2–11] stated that BT could transform the business models related to SCM, improves the SC process, and improvises SC performance. The SC performance refers to the SC's expanded activities in meeting final customer requirements, including product availability, delivery on time, and all the required inventory and capacity in the supply chain for the reactive delivery of such performance [12]. The benefits of performance measuring systems in the supply chain are overwhelmed by implementation and maintenance costs. This will most likely be applied to small companies without the resources, time, or information required to optimize supply chain activities [13]. When the characteristics or features of BT are considered, then its adoption in the field of the SC will increase for enhancing the SC performance.

BT can help in improving complicated SC issues and also enhance traceability of operations [9], regardless of segment involved: healthcare, security, wine industry, etc. [14–20]. This new technology can be utilized to solve complexities in the SC such as accountability and transparency [21], security [22], reduction in SC

M. M. Baral (✉) · S. Mukherjee
Department of Operations, GITAM School of Business, GITAM (Deemed to be University), Visakhapatnam, Andhra Pradesh, India

V. Chittipaka
School of Management Studies (SOMS), Indira Gandhi National Open University (IGNOU), Maidan Garhi, New Delhi, India

B. Jana
Department of Management, GD Goenka University, Haryana, India

A. Bouras et al. (eds.), *Blockchain Driven Supply Chains and Enterprise Information Systems*, https://doi.org/10.1007/978-3-030-96154-1_1

expense [23], resilience [24], etc. Integrating BT with SCs is a trusted approach for remodeling and supporting SC. Also, BT can be a means of achieving SC sustainability [12].

Most of the prior studies have discussed the benefits and advantages of adopting BT in various fields. To date, its application is not practical and is in its infant stage [25]. There is a lack of empirical study in this area of BT and SCM. Hence, the current study aims to contribute to the existing literature gap by identifying the value of BTA in SCM. This study identifies the antecedents of BTA and its impact on SC performance in developing country perspective. Hence, the proposed model helped get a piece of evidence that the assumed parameters affect SC performance. The study contributes not an only blockchain but also to the SCM.

The rest of the paper is as follows: Sect. 2 discusses the literature survey; Sect. 3 discusses the theoretical framework and hypothesis development; Sect. 4 discusses the research methodology, which includes sampling techniques utilized for collecting data and demographics of respondents; Sect. 5 discusses the data analysis which states the data analysis which provides for EFA, CFA, construct validity, and SEM approach for establishing the model fit; Sect. 6 contains discussion of the current research, contribution to study, and practice and managerial implications; and finally Sect. 7 contains the conclusion, scope, and future research directions.

2 Background of the Study

SC performance plays a critical role in all types of firms and due to operations complexity in the present digital era. Hence, it is essential to understand the BT relationship and SC performance to achieve better efficiency by the firms.

2.1 Application of Blockchain

Over a decade ago, in the cryptocurrency market, BT emerged (Nakamoto, 2008). BT does not require any third-party involvement; it is an individual-to-individual transaction platform. For the business reason, various entities engaged with the transaction function as nodes, and the cycle is being approved through cryptography. These transactions are stored as decentralized and shared ledgers over the participating entities [2]. BT integrates various other technologies like cryptographic technology, database technology, software development, etc. [26]. Blockchain is an encoded computerized record put away on multiple PCs of a public or private organization [3]. It consists of blocks or data records. When these individual blocks are combined in a chain form, a single player cannot change the data stored in the blocks. They can be verified by shared governance protocols and automation [27]. Blockchain is a shared network, so every member keeps a duplicate copy of the record [4]. BT helps provide a single, tamper, shared, tamper-evident ledger that records the transaction per occurrence [28]. All members ordinarily affirm transactions in a BT through an agreement instrument. Once information is recorded and validated in a blockchain, it becomes permanent. A single participant cannot change or modify the transactions [5]. This quality of blockchain differentiates it from the centralized system. This technology helps the SC players to control and share data [6]. If the blockchain becomes so large, a risk of centralization exists that just a few nodes can process a block. This might lead to two blockchain systemic problems: centralizing a public directory such as bitcoin and slowing down the network [29]. Hence, this helps in risk reduction, which exists in the centralized system.

A typical BT-based SC consists of suppliers, manufacturers, distributors, retailers, end users, logistics services, airport, port, and banks which are a provider of financial services. In general, SC firms will shape consortia as vehicles to investigate the capability of BT because joint effort just as cost/hazard sharing is, for example, BT. The implementation of BT is not without challenges. The expected difficulties could be intra- or interorganizational hindrances (like the absence of expertise and knowledge, economic imperatives and data sharing issues), administrative uncertainties, energy utilization, deceptive practices and technological interoperability, and so on [30–32]. Regardless of the expanding exertion by researchers, empirical examination exploring how firms could plan a blockchain empowered SC stays restricted, and confirmations to help the guaranteed benefits are as yet deficient [33]. This research fills the gap by providing empirical evidence for the proposed model.

2.2 Technology Adoption in SC

In the current study, we have identified the determinants of BTA and its benefits on SC performance. There is a need to consider the theories on technology adoption for the literature foundation (Warshaw and Davis, 1985; Davis, 1989). Davis (1989) identified two constructs for predicting technology adoption and its usage at a single firm level. The two constructs are perceived usefulness (PU) and perceived ease of use (PEOU). Over the last three decades, different models were proposed which are based on this theory constructs [34–36].

TAM theory has been extended by [34]. Seven more theories were included on user behavior to get an influential model called the unified theory of acceptance and use of technology (UTAUT). It consists of four constructs: social influence, performance expectancy, facilitating conditions, and effort expectancy. Other variables like age, gender, the voluntariness of use, and experience act as moderators in the model [34]. As a result, studies have utilized an advanced version of the initial UTAUT [37, 38].

TAM constructs have been used in the Indian perspective by [9] for understanding blockchain behavior. They expressed that PEOU is an indicator of PU, which accomplished a solid force of anticipating the expectation to utilize blockchain. Hence, as per the features of TAM and UTAUT, a model has been proposed in this study for BTA and its impact on SC performance. Also, [39] proposed adopting well-known TOE perspectives to examine the BTA in operations and SCM. They found that relative advantage, cost, complexity, and peer pressure significantly impact intention to BTA. Therefore, in the next section, we discuss the proposed research model and the development of the hypothesis using knowledge sharing, higher authority support, business partners' pressure, SC performance, and blockchain technology adoption (BTA) as a dependent variable.

3 Research Model and Development of Hypothesis

3.1 Knowledge Sharing (KS)

KS refers to the knowledge exchange between firms along with their SC players. With the help of BT, the players of the same SC can exchange information and improve traceability [40]. It also includes skills and best practices on the utilization of various SCM processes. KS is concerned with individual behavior while sharing information within the firms [41–43]. If the knowledge is being shared between the players, it will help make the SC more efficient and create transparency in the system. Hence, KS between the partners of firms in the same SC is a critical determinant in BTA. Hence, the proposed hypothesis is:

- H1: KS influences BTA.

3.2 Higher Authority Support (HAS)

HAS has a significant role in accepting and implementing new technologies in a firm. Suppose the higher authority individuals are aware of the benefits of BTA in SCM and support the transition to this new technology in the firm by creating a positive climate within the firm and its staff. In that case, this will help in removing the resistance and get ready to adopt the new technology [12, 15, 21, 44–47]. As BTA in a firm requires allocating human and financial resources, integrating BT with existing IT infrastructures, and BPR in client and supplier relationship management [48]. Hence, HAS is considered as a determinant in BTA. Therefore, the proposed hypothesis is:

- H2: HAS influences BTA.

3.3 Business Partner's Pressure (BPP)

BPP refers to the pressure faced by firms from its business partners [49] and has a critical impact on advanced technology adoption. There is a need to have supply chain collaboration for integrating BT in SCM systems. Suppose a business partner dominating the SC decides to adopt BT to manage SC for cooperating efficiently. In that case, other SC partners also have to adopt BT to maintain the trade relations [21, 48, 50]. A business partner's relationship is a critical element. When we consider the SC perspective, the relations tend to be more complex, and BPP can optimize a firm's capabilities. Also, BPP can impact BTA, and the pressures can come from other stakeholders and trade partners, all capable of adopting BT. BPP has been a critical factor in BTA in SCM in prior studies [14, 40]. Hence, BPP has been considered as an indicator in the current study.

- H3: BPP influences BTA.

3.4 *BT and SC Performance (SCP)*

Every day there is an exchange of data between the SC networks. With increased complexity (like asymmetry information and the amount of available technology), SC performance enhancement is enhanced. In these circumstances, BT will prove to be very fruitful for improving operations and SC performances; this will also contribute to the revenue generation of a business [51, 52]. This advanced technology will be playing a critical role in solving various challenges like trust and transparency between SC members [53, 54]. As BT improves traceability, there is a gain of transparency and accountability on all members positively. BT can also eliminate the variability of information in SC. As a result, cooperation and trust will improve SC performance. Hence, the proposed hypothesis is:

- H4: BT influences SC performance.

4 Research Methodology

The objective of this study is to examine the BTA for improving SC performance. Secondary and primary sources collected data. Secondary sources include a literature review and other reports, and the primary source has the collection of data through a structured questionnaire. The reliability test of the questionnaire was also done. The target population was SC professionals working in various industries running in India. Multinational companies and listed companies on stock exchange were set as the target population. IT service providers were excluded from the targeted population. The respondents from the selected firms were the IT workforce and officers who have IT information on their firms' present and future tasks. The stratified random sampling method has been used to choose samples from various subsets of populations [55]. After data cleaning in SPSS 20.0, the usable responses used for the analysis were 285 out of 850 targeted professionals who agreed to participate in the survey. Hence, 33.52% was the response rate.

To avoid a common method, bias on the research team has taken few fundamental precautions during the pre-data collection stage. A note was mentioned at the beginning of the questionnaire that indicated the survey is intended for academic research, and confidentiality of data will be maintained. In the gathered dataset, the first cleansing was finished by case screening, trailed by factor screening to clarify variations in the information. Information cleaning measure had been reasoned that missing information had been extraordinarily sparse, and in this way, they were not viewed as a principal supporter of any predisposition. No cases were therefore removed. However, after the data is collected, the research team applied Harman's single factor test. Exploratory factor analysis was performed, and the results show that the first factor explains maximum covariance (32.453%), which is below the recommended value of 50% [56].

SEM was adopted for data analysis. The data analysis was done in four stages: demographics of firms, reliability and validity test, exploratory factor analysis (EFA), confirmatory factor analysis (CFA), and structural equation modeling (SEM). EFA was done to check the total variance explained to identify and group the variables using a rotated component matrix table. SPSS 20.0 was utilized for reliability tests and EFA on data collected. After that, CFA was implemented for testing and approving the model. AMOS 22.0 was used for CFA on gathered data to estimate model results as CFA chooses whether a legitimacy test on an expected model is duplicated [57, 58]. At last, the model fit was determined by SEM for testing of hypothesis.

5 Results

The following section displays output obtained from the performed analysis. First, the analysis of demographics has been displayed in Table 1, followed by reliability and validity measures along with EFA. Thereafter, the model validity measures were calculated which shows the values for composite reliability, convergent and divergent validity measures for the final SEM model. Finally, the model fit measures are displayed which compares the values for model 1 (CFA) and the final model (SEM).

5.1 Demographics of Firms Surveyed

A questionnaire-based survey method was used. Table 1 shows the distribution of respondents based on different industries. The majority of respondents were male (82%), polytechnic level education (52.31%), work experience 6–10 years (40.10%), and healthcare segment (33.42%).

Table 1 Firm demographics

Gender	Percentage
Male	82%
Female	18%
Educational qualification	
Secondary	6%
Polytechnic	52.31%
Bachelor's degree	29%
PG/PhD	12.69%
Work experience	
<5 years	7.80%
6–10 years	40.10%
11–15 years	35.57%
>15 years	16.53%
Industry	
Hotel industry	21.34%
Manufacturing	20.67%
IT service	8.44%
Healthcare	33.42%
Retail	16.13%

5.2 *Reliability and Validity*

5.2.1 Cronbach's Alpha (α)

Assessment of reliability helps examine the degree of internal consistency between variable measurement items and its freedom of error at any point in time [59]. α-value was utilized to test the reliability of the data for all the constructs as it is the most common measurement method. The values for all the scales must be the above-recommended level of 0.70 [60]. Utilization of 7-point Likert scale was done in preparing the structured questionnaire. For analyzing the information collected, SPSS 20.0 and AMOS 22.0 were used. The latent variable KM has four indicators, KM1, KM2, KM3, and KM4, and its α-value is 0.849; BPP has four indicators, BPP1, BPP2, BPP3, and BPP4, and its α-value is 0.882; HAS has three indicators, HAS1, HAS2, and HAS3, and its α-value is 0.848; BTA has four indicators, BTA1, BTA2, BTA3, and BTA4. Hence, all the values are within the threshold level (Hair et al., 2014), and the 15 components are utilized in further analysis.

5.3 *Exploratory Factor Analysis*

The first step of the EFA was to evaluate the appropriateness of the sample size. SPSS 20.0 was utilized for EFA. The correlations between its items had been inspected using Bartlett's test of sphericity [61]. Principal component analysis

Table 2 KMO and Bartlett's test

KMO and Bartlett's test		
Kaiser-Meyer-Olkin measure of sampling adequacy		.778
Bartlett's test of sphericity	Approx. Chi-square	2624.257
	df	105
	Sig.	0.000

was performed to identify meaningful bias and express the same qualities. For the interpretation of initial results, the varimax rotation has been utilized; it is assumed (based on the relevant literature) that there does not exist any correlation within factors [61]. With this test, the statistic had generated that should have been significant ($p < 0.05$) for EFA has been considered as an appropriate technique [61].

As a result, Kaiser-Meyer-Olkin (KMO) test was utilized to quantify whether those items are sufficiently correlated and determine whether a factor analysis could be performed. KMO value for the current research is 0.778. The minimum level set for this statistic is 0.60 [55]. The significance value is 0.000, which is less than 0.05, i.e., the probability value level acceptable. Table 2 displays the KMO and Bartlett's test.

The extraction method used was principal component analysis. Only the eigenvalues which have values greater than one were extracted as it explains maximum variance. For the components, the percentage of total variance is explained by component 1 (20.028%), component 2 (18.502%), component 3 (18.409%), and component 4 (15.616%). The cumulative percentage of total variance explained by all three components is 72.553%. Table 3 displays the total variance explained.

The rotated component matrix is important for interpreting the results of the analysis. Rotation helps in grouping the items, and each group contains more than two items, which simplifies the structure. Hence, this is the aim of the goal of rotation. In this research, we have achieved this aim. This helps to identify the cross-loadings on more than one group, and then it can be corrected by removing those that are cross-loaded. In this research, the loadings having less than |.40| are suppressed because loadings of more than |.40| are typically high. So, in the end, we achieve a simple structure. Eleven total variables were grouped under three different components. The rotation method used was varimax rotation. BPP1, BPP2, BPP3, and BPP4 are grouped under the first component with values of 0.825, 0.832, 0.859, and 0.833. KS1, KS2, KS3, and KS4 are grouped under the second component having values 0. 0.817, 0.828, 0.783, and 0.670. SCP1, SCP2, SCP3, and SCP4 are grouped under the third component with values 0.702, 0.768, 0.813, and 0.720. HAS1, HAS2, and HAS3 are grouped under the fourth component with values 0.855, 0.891, and 0.777. Table 4 shows the rotated component matrix output.

Confirmatory factor analysis (CFA) was performed in the next stage, which constructs identified from the literature survey can be tested and how well the variables represent the constructs. Structural equation modeling (SEM) was used for testing the model fit of the proposed research model [57]. When their instrument

Table 3 Total variance explained

Component	Initial eigenvalues			Extraction sums of squared loadings			Rotation sums of squared loadings		
	Total	% of variance	Cumulative %	Total	% of variance	Cumulative %	Total	% of variance	Cumulative %
1	5.887	39.245	39.245	5.887	39.245	39.245	3.004	20.028	20.028
2	2.221	14.806	54.051	2.221	14.806	54.051	2.775	18.502	38.529
3	1.619	10.791	64.842	1.619	10.791	64.842	2.761	18.407	56.936
4	1.157	7.711	72.553	1.157	7.711	72.553	2.342	15.616	72.553

Table 4 Rotated component matrix

	Component			
	1	2	3	4
KS1		.817		
KS2		.828		
KS3		.783		
KS4		.670		
BPP1	.825			
BPP2	.832			
BPP3	.859			
BPP4	.833			
HAS1				.855
HAS2				.891
HAS3				.777
SCP1			.702	
SCP2			.768	
SCP3			.813	
SCP4			.720	

Extraction method: Principal component analysis
Rotation method: Varimax with Kaiser normalization
Rotation converged in five iterations

shows the typical structures inside, this could have been demonstrative to construct validity (CV) [62] and, explicitly, factorial validity.

5.4 *Model Validity Measures*

5.4.1 Composite Reliability

Composite reliability (CR) was also measured for all the components. It is calculated for internal consistency reliability because of its ability to provide better results [63]. The construct KS has a CR value of 0.828; BPP has a CR value of 0.828; and HAS has a CR value of 0.791. Three constructs are >0.7, which indicates that the composite reliability measures are reliable [64]. Table 4 displays the CR values.

5.4.2 Convergent Validity

It is measured with the help of the average variance extracted (AVE). As per [65], AVE is >0.5 for the convergent validity. Table 4 represents AVE values for the constructs. All the values are greater than 0.5, satisfying convergent validity for all the constructs [61].

Table 5 Master validity output

	CR	AVE	MSV	MaxR(H)	KS	BPP	HAS	BTA
KS	0.853	0.596	0.288	0.876	**0.772**			
BPP	0.877	0.643	0.145	0.908	0.327***	**0.802**		
HAS	0.85	0.654	0.24	0.859	0.412***	0.274***	**0.809**	
BTA	0.871	0.633	0.288	0.906	0.536***	0.381***	0.490***	**0.795**

Significance of Correlations:
†$p < 0.100$
$p < 0.050$; **$p < 0.010$; ***$p < 0.001$

5.4.3 Divergent Validity

To calculate this validity, [65] suggested that the AVE of the construct must be more than a square of the correlation between that construct and the other constructs [61]. Table 5 represents the values for divergent validity output (MSV < AVE), and it was obtained using the master validity plugin in AMOS 22.0.

5.5 *Structural Model and Testing of Hypothesis*

The model fit measures for model 1 (CFA), which has the latent variables, are shown in Table 6. The latent variables along with its indicators are KS, knowledge sharing, along with four indicators, KS1, KS2, KS3, and KS4; BPP, business partners' pressure, has four indicators, BPP1, BPP2, BPP3, and BPP4; and HAS, higher authority support, has three indicators, HAS1, HAS2, and HAS3. The CMIN/Df is 5.710; goodness-of-fit indices (GFI) is 0.847; comparative fit index (CFI) is 0.851; Tucker-Lewis Index (TLI) is 0.782; incremental fit index (IFI) is 0.852, parsimony comparative fit index (PCFI) is 0.608, and parsimony normed fit index (PNFI) is 0.661. All the items' loading was greater than 0.5 and SE < ± 2.5, which is acceptable.

To test the hypothesis, SEM was used [57]. AMOS 22.0 was utilized for this research because of its powerful graphic representations and user-friendly interfaces. The results of the model are shown here. Figure 1 represents the final model and the latent variables and their indicators and dependent variable. The latent variables along with its indicators are KS, knowledge sharing, along with four indicators, KS1, KS2, KS3, and KS4; BPP, business partners' pressure, has four indicators, BPP1, BPP2, BPP3, and BPP4; HAS, higher authority support, has three indicators, HAS1, HAS2, and HAS3; and BTA, blockchain technology analytics, has four indicators BTA1, BTA2, BTA3, and BTA4. The dependent variable is SCP, supply chain performance, with four indicators, SCP1, SCP2, SCP3, and SCP4.

Table 5 shows the model fit values and fit indices. For the final model, the value of chi-square is 699.971, and the degree of freedom is 145. The estimations of absolute fit indices are CMIN/Df is 4.827, CMIN represents the chi-square value, and Df

Table 6 Final goodness-of-fit indices for the CFA and structural model

Goodness-of-fit indices	Model 1	Final model	Benchmark
CMIN/Df	5.710	4.827	Lower limit:1.0; upper limit 2.0/3.0 or 5.0
GFI	0.847	0.819	>0.80
Absolute badness-of-fit measure			
RMSEA	0.129	0.08	⩽0.08
Incremental fit measure			
CFI	0.851	0.838	⩾0.80
IFI	0.852	0.839	⩾0.80
TLI	0.782	0.809	⩾0.80
Parsimony fit measure			
PCFI	0.680	0.710	⩾0.50
PNFI	0.661	0.683	⩾0.50

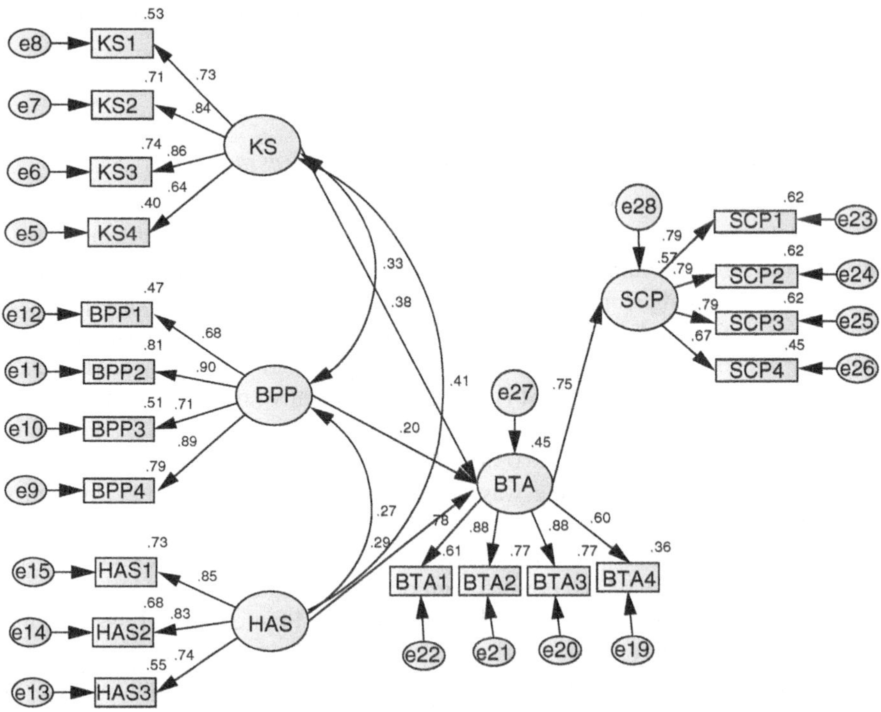

Fig. 1 Blockchain technology adoption model for improving SC performance

represents the degree of freedom, and the value is less than 5, which is the accepted threshold value [66]. The goodness-of-fit index (GFI) value is 0.819, and root mean square error of approximation (RMSEA) value is 0.08, within the threshold value of 0.08. The comparative fit index (CFI) is 0.838; incremental fit index (IFI) is 0.839;

Table 7 Structural model results

	Estimate	SE.	CR.	*P*
BTA <—HAS	0.222	0.052	4.294	***
BTA <—BPP	0.149	0.044	3.36	***
BTA <—KS	0.432	0.084	5.138	***
SCP <—BTA	0.893	0.105	8.508	***

Tucker-Lewis Index (TLI) is 0.809; parsimony comparative of fit index (PCFI) is 0.710; and parsimony normed of fit index (PNFI) is 0.683 which are having values in the threshold level and are acceptable [67]. Figure 1 shows the final structural model generated after analysis in AMOS 22.0.

Hence, we can see that the model fit values of the final model are better than model 1. The mediating variable (BTA) and dependent variable significantly contribute to the three latent variables in establishing the model fit.

Table 7 shows the path estimate analysis results. The result demonstrates the three hypotheses are supported by P-value [64]. Hence, three factors, TP, OP, and EP, have a positive impact on BTA. The square multiple correlations (R^2) help measure how well a regression line estimates the real data points between 0 and 1, which states how well one variable predicts another [64]. The more the value is closer to 1, the better is the model's ability to predict that technology [59]. The proposed model can explain 45% variance in BT adoption and 57% of the variance in SC performance. Hence, the mediating variable (BTA) plays a critical role in establishing the model fit.

6 Discussion

The current study empirically examined the role of the adoption of blockchain technology in supply chain performance. The study also contributed toward the literature of BT and SCM and increased the understanding. Further, structural equation modeling was used for testing the hypothesis. Three hypotheses were proposed for testing the model, and all were found to be significant which is in line with previous literature on adoption of innovation.

KS comprised of four indicators, and all four indicators contributed significantly toward the model fit. The first hypothesis (H1) examined the impact of knowledge sharing on blockchain technology adoption. The second hypothesis (H2) examined the impact of higher authority support on blockchain technology adoption, and the third hypothesis (H3) examined the impact of business partner's pressure on blockchain technology adoption. The validation of all the three constructs is applied in BTA. KS has been a significant contributor in electronic SCM (Lin 2017) but is not related to BT. HAS has been found as a significant contributor in cloud computing adoption studies [21, 50, 68–70] in various segments like SMEs, healthcare, manufacturing, etc. BPP has been found as a significant contributor, which is in line with previous kinds of literature [5, 6, 13, 47, 71]. Hence, in the current study, also the three latent variables contribute significantly toward the model fit. The estimate of KS ($\beta = .432$, $p = .000$), BPP ($\beta = .149$, $p = .000$), and HAS ($\beta = .222$, $p = .000$) is positive, and hence we can conclude that they have significantly positive impact on BTA.

BTA act as a mediating variable. The fourth hypothesis (H4) examined the impact of BTA in SC performance. Also, the prior studies [14, 15, 72–74] were unable to demonstrate transparency in BT on SC performance. But in the current study, BTA impacts SC performance, and the dependent variable SC performance explains 57% of the variance. Hence, the current research helped in adding value to the existing works of literature [20, 75–78].

Also, our results are providing empirical evidence to the findings of the advantages of BTA in SCs [79]. The prior literature talks about BT's adoption increases transparency, privacy and decreases the cost of the SC process. The HAS, KS, and BPP are also described in prior works of literature and discussed their benefits and roles. Hence, in the current study, we provided empirical evidence for the same.

6.1 Managerial Implications

The current study will be helping managers to decide on adopting BT for improving the SC performance. The managers should have in-depth knowledge about the new technology and also about its consequences after its adoption. The latent variables knowledge sharing, business partners' pressure, and higher authority support have significantly contributed to BTA in India. Also, BTA has acted upon as mediating variable and serves as a significant contributor toward improving SC performance and achieving the overall model fit. As per prior studies [23, 80, 81], this study also reports that knowledge is an essential resource for increasing performance. If the managers of various firms develop their knowledge and understanding of BTA in SC performance, they will play a critical role in supporting multiple firm operations.

6.2 Theoretical Contribution, Scope, and Future Research

The current study discussed the BTA and SC performance with a proposed research model. The results validated the theoretical model empirically also. From the output, it is concluded that BTA influences positively on SC performance. Also, the proposed three latent variables contributed positively toward the mediating variable (BTA) and the overall model fit. Also, theoretically, we can say that SC performance can be predicted with the help of few constructs. BT is in the infant stage, but its contribution to SC performance cannot be neglected.

Future studies can be conducted to test the proposed research model in various other developing countries and particular sectors to validate the outcomes.

7 Conclusion

This study aims to identify variables from literature review and propose a research model for BTA, which will ultimately help in SC performance. The proposed model in the present study was supported by the results, which were obtained empirically. These results are in line with the literature, which also included the improvement in SC performances. Also, this study helped us to verify the results empirically and highlighted the advantages of BTA for improving SC performance. The results also contributed toward the theoretical and managerial contributions on BTA. It further motivates the managers to understand the relation between BTA and SCM. Also, scholars can perform more research in this area in various sectors.

Appendix A. Measurement Items

Constructs	Labels	Measures	Sources
KS	KS1	The firm shares blockchain-enabled SC knowledge with its partners	
	KS2	Firm shares market and BT knowledge to SC partners	
	KS3	The firm has enough trust in sharing knowledge with its partners	
	KS4	Knowledge sharing helps in business planning	
BPP	BPP1	The partners enable BT implementation	[82]
	BPP2	Partners are interested in adopting BT	
	BPP3	Partners recommend the implementation of BT	
	BPP4	Partners encouraged the implementation of BT in SC	
HAS	HAS1	A higher authority is interested in adopting BT	[46]
	HAS2	The higher authority has enough knowledge regarding these new technologies	
	HAS3	Higher authority motivates the staff to change from traditional system to advanced technology	
BTA	BTA1	The firm is ready to invest in new advanced technologies	[83]
	BTA2	The firm requires the use of BT for efficiency	
	BTA3	BT will help in providing transparency in the SC process	[11, 12]
	BTA4	BT will enable cost reduction	
SCP	SCP1	BT can improvise the linkage of physical goods to bar codes, serial numbers, etc.	[12, 84]
	SCP2	BT adoption improves the efficiency of the SC process	
	SCP3	BT adoption helps to verify the assigned tasks	
	SCP4	SC can handle the quick introduction of new products	

References

1. Monfared, R. (2016). *Blockchain ready manufacturing supply chain using a distributed ledger*. Accessed 06 Mar 2021. [Online]. Available: http://esatjournals.net/ijret/2016v05/i09/IJRET20160509001.pdfMetadataRecord: https://dspace.lboro.ac.uk/2134/22625.
2. Dolgui, A., Ivanov, D., Potryasaev, S., Sokolov, B., Ivanova, M., & Werner, F. (2020). Blockchain-oriented dynamic modelling of smart contract design and execution in the supply chain. *International Journal of Production Research, 58*(7), 2184–2199. https://doi.org/10.1080/00207543.2019.1627439
3. Sunny, J., Undralla, N., & Madhusudanan Pillai, V. (2020). Supply chain transparency through blockchain-based traceability: An overview with demonstration. *Computers & Industrial Engineering, 150*.https://doi.org/10.1016/j.cie.2020.106895.
4. Ikeda, K., & Hamid, M. N. (2018). Applications of blockchain in the financial sector and a peer-to-peer global barter web. In *Advances in computers* (Vol. 111, pp. 99–120). Academic Press Inc..
5. Aslam, J., Saleem, A., Khan, N. T., & Kim, Y. B. (2021). Factors influencing blockchain adoption in supply chain management practices: A study based on the oil industry. *Journal of Innovation and Knowledge, 6*, 124. https://doi.org/10.1016/j.jik.2021.01.002
6. Tipmontian, Alcover, & Rajmohan. (2020). Impact of blockchain adoption for safe food supply chain management through system dynamics approach from management perspectives in Thailand. *Proceedings, 39*(1), 14. https://doi.org/10.3390/proceedings2019039014
7. Tan, B., Yan, J., Chen, S., & Liu, X. (2018). The impact of blockchain on food supply chain: The case of walmart. In *Lecture Notes in Computer Science (including subseries Lecture Notes in Artificial Intelligence and Lecture Notes in Bioinformatics)* (Vol. 11373 LNCS, pp. 167–177). https://doi.org/10.1007/978-3-030-05764-0_18.
8. Dutta, P., Choi, T. M., Somani, S., & Butala, R. (2020). Blockchain technology in supply chain operations: Applications, challenges and research opportunities. *Transportation Research Part E: Logistics and Transportation Review, 142*, 102067. https://doi.org/10.1016/j.tre.2020.102067
9. Kamble, S., Gunasekaran, A., & Arha, H. (2019). Understanding the Blockchain technology adoption in supply chains-Indian context. *International Journal of Production Research, 57*(7), 2009–2033. https://doi.org/10.1080/00207543.2018.1518610
10. Koh, L., Dolgui, A., & Sarkis, J. (2020). Blockchain in transport and logistics – Paradigms and transitions. *International Journal of Production Research, 58*(7), 2054–2062. https://doi.org/10.1080/00207543.2020.1736428
11. Alazab, M., Alhyari, S., Awajan, A., & Abdallah, A. B. (2020). Blockchain technology in supply chain management: An empirical study of the factors affecting user adoption/acceptance. *Cluster Computing, 24*(1), 83–101. https://doi.org/10.1007/s10586-020-03200-4
12. Fosso Wamba, S., Queiroz, M. M., & Trinchera, L. (2020). Dynamics between blockchain adoption determinants and supply chain performance: An empirical investigation. *International Journal of Production Economics, 229*, 107791. https://doi.org/10.1016/j.ijpe.2020.107791
13. Sheel, A., & Nath, V. (2019). Effect of blockchain technology adoption on supply chain adaptability, agility, alignment and performance. *Management Research Review, 42*(12), 1353–1374. https://doi.org/10.1108/MRR-12-2018-0490
14. Saberi, S., Kouhizadeh, M., Sarkis, J., & Shen, L. (2019). Blockchain technology and its relationships to sustainable supply chain management. *International Journal of Production Research, 57*(7), 2117–2135. https://doi.org/10.1080/00207543.2018.1533261
15. Wong, L.-W., Tan, G. W.-H., Lee, V.-H., Ooi, K.-B., & Sohal, A. (2020). Unearthing the determinants of Blockchain adoption in supply chain management. *International Journal of Production Research, 58*(7), 2100–2123. https://doi.org/10.1080/00207543.2020.1730463
16. Treiblmaier, H. (2018). The impact of the blockchain on the supply chain: A theory-based research framework and a call for action. *Supply Chain Management, 23*(6), 545–559. https://doi.org/10.1108/SCM-01-2018-0029

17. Queiroz, M. M., Telles, R., & Bonilla, S. H. (2019). Blockchain and supply chain management integration: a systematic review of the literature. *Supply Chain Management, 25*(2), 241–254. https://doi.org/10.1108/SCM-03-2018-0143
18. Yusof, H., et al.. (2018). Behavioral intention to adopt blockchain technology: Viewpoint of the banking institutions in Malaysia. *International Journal of Advanced Scientific Research and Management, 3*. Accessed 06 Mar 2021. [Online]. Available: www.ijasrm.com.
19. Gokalp, E., Coban, S., & Gokalp, M. O. (2019). Acceptance of blockchain based supply chain management system: Research model proposal, https://doi.org/10.1109/UBMYK48245.2019.8965502.
20. Chang, J., Katehakis. M. N., Melamed, B., & Shi, J. (Junmin). (2018). Blockchain design for supply chain management. *SSRN Electronic Journal.*https://doi.org/10.2139/ssrn.3295440.
21. Gökalp, E., Gökalp, M. O., & Çoban, S. (2020). Blockchain-based supply chain management: Understanding the determinants of adoption in the context of organizations. *Information Systems Management*, 1–22. https://doi.org/10.1080/10580530.2020.1812014
22. Makhdoom, I., Abolhasan, M., Abbas, H., & Ni, W. (2019). Blockchain's adoption in IoT: The challenges, and a way forward. *Journal of Network and Computer Applications, 125*, 251–279. https://doi.org/10.1016/j.jnca.2018.10.019
23. Kouhizadeh, M., Saberi, S., & Sarkis, J. (2021). Blockchain technology and the sustainable supply chain: Theoretically exploring adoption barriers. *International Journal of Production Economics, 231*, 107831. https://doi.org/10.1016/j.ijpe.2020.107831
24. Perboli, G., Musso, S., & Rosano, M. (2018). Blockchain in logistics and supply chain: A lean approach for designing real-world use cases. *IEEE Access, 6*, 62018–62028. https://doi.org/10.1109/ACCESS.2018.2875782
25. Hughes, L., Dwivedi, Y. K., Misra, S. K., Rana, N. P., Raghavan, V., & Akella, V. (2019). Blockchain research, practice and policy: Applications, benefits, limitations, emerging research themes and research agenda. *International Journal of Information Management, 49*, 114–129. https://doi.org/10.1016/j.ijinfomgt.2019.02.005
26. Fosso Wamba, S., Kala Kamdjoug, J. R., Epie Bawack, R., & Keogh, J. G. (2020). Bitcoin, Blockchain and Fintech: A systematic review and case studies in the supply chain. *Production Planning and Control, 31*(2–3), 115–142. https://doi.org/10.1080/09537287.2019.1631460
27. Berdik, D., Otoum, S., Schmidt, N., Porter, D., & Jararweh, Y. (2021). A survey on blockchain for information systems management and security. *Information Processing and Management, 58*(1), 102397. https://doi.org/10.1016/j.ipm.2020.102397
28. Banerjee, A. (2018). Blockchain technology: Supply chain insights from ERP. *Advances in Computers, 111*, 69–98.
29. Chang, Y., Iakovou, E., & Shi, W. (2020). Blockchain in global supply chains and cross border trade: A critical synthesis of the state-of-the-art, challenges and opportunities. *International Journal of Production Research, 58*(7), 2082–2099. https://doi.org/10.1080/00207543.2019.1651946
30. Macrinici, D., Cartofeanu, C., & Gao, S. (2018). Smart contract applications within blockchain technology: A systematic mapping study. *Telematics and Informatics, 35*(8), 2337–2354. https://doi.org/10.1016/j.tele.2018.10.004
31. Casino, F., Dasaklis, T. K., & Patsakis, C. (2019). A systematic literature review of blockchain-based applications: Current status, classification and open issues. *Telematics and Informatics, 36*, 55–81. https://doi.org/10.1016/j.tele.2018.11.006
32. Kshetri, N. (2018). 1 Blockchain's roles in meeting key supply chain management objectives. *International Journal of Information Management, 39*, 80–89. https://doi.org/10.1016/j.ijinfomgt.2017.12.005
33. Wang, Y., Han, J. H., & Beynon-Davies, P. (2019). Understanding blockchain technology for future supply chains: a systematic literature review and research agenda. *Supply Chain Management, 24*(1), 62–84. https://doi.org/10.1108/SCM-03-2018-0148
34. Venkatesh, V., Morris, M. G., Davis, G. B., & Davis, F. D. (2003). User acceptance of information technology: Toward a unified view. *MIS Quarterly: Management Information Systems, 27*(3), 425–478. https://doi.org/10.2307/30036540

35. Venkatesh, V., & Zhang, X. (2010). Unified theory of acceptance and use of technology: US vs. China. *Journal of Global Information Technology Management, 13*(1), 5–27. https://doi.org/10.1080/1097198X.2010.10856507
36. Venkatesh, V., Thong, J. Y. L., Chan, F. K. Y., & Hu, P. J. H. (2016). Managing citizens' uncertainty in e-government services: The mediating and moderating roles of transparency and trust. *Information Systems Research, 27*(1), 87–111. https://doi.org/10.1287/ISRE.2015.0612
37. Dwivedi, Y. K., Rana, N. P., Jeyaraj, A., Clement, M., & Williams, M. D. (2019). Re-examining the unified theory of acceptance and use of technology (UTAUT): Towards a revised theoretical model. *Information Systems Frontiers, 21*(3), 719–734. https://doi.org/10.1007/s10796-017-9774-y
38. Dwivedi, Y. K., Rana, N. P., Janssen, M., Lal, B., Williams, M. D., & Clement, M. (2017). An empirical validation of a unified model of electronic government adoption (UMEGA). *Government Information Quarterly, 34*(2), 211–230. https://doi.org/10.1016/j.giq.2017.03.001
39. Wong, L. W., Leong, L. Y., Hew, J. J., Tan, G. W. H., & Ooi, K. B. (2020). Time to seize the digital evolution: Adoption of blockchain in operations and supply chain management among Malaysian SMEs. *International Journal of Information Management, 52*, 101997. https://doi.org/10.1016/j.ijinfomgt.2019.08.005
40. Francisco, K., & Swanson, D. (2018). The supply chain has no clothes: Technology adoption of blockchain for supply chain transparency. *Logistics, 2*(1), 2. https://doi.org/10.3390/logistics2010002
41. Low, C., Chen, Y., & Wu, M. (2011). Understanding the determinants of cloud computing adoption. *Industrial Management & Data Systems, 111*(7), 1006.
42. Puklavec, B., Oliveira, T., & Popovič, A. (2018). Understanding the determinants of business intelligence system adoption stages an empirical study of SMEs. *Industrial Management & Data Systems, 118*(1), 236–261. https://doi.org/10.1108/IMDS-05-2017-0170
43. Shahzad, F., Xiu, G. Y., Khan, I., Shahbaz, M., Riaz, M. U., & Abbas, A. (2020). The moderating role of intrinsic motivation in cloud computing adoption in online education in a developing country: A structural equation model. *Asia Pacific Education Review, 21*(1), 121–141. https://doi.org/10.1007/s12564-019-09611-2
44. Badr, F., Nasser, A.-A., & Jawad, M. S. (2019). Factors of cloud computing adoption by small and medium size enterprises (SMEs). *International Journal of Innovative Research in Electrical, Electronics, Instrumentation and Control Engineering, 7*(1), 2321–5526.
45. Shee, H., Miah, S. J., Fairfield, L., & Pujawan, N. (2018). The impact of cloud-enabled process integration on supply chain performance and firm sustainability: The moderating role of top management. *Supply Chain Management, 23*(6), 500–517. https://doi.org/10.1108/SCM-09-2017-0309
46. Senyo, P. K., Effah, J., & Addae, E. (2016). Preliminary insight into cloud computing adoption in a developing country. *Journal of Enterprise Information Management, 29*(4), 505–524. https://doi.org/10.1108/JEIM-09-2014-0094
47. Wamba, S. F., & Queiroz, M. M. (2020). Blockchain in the operations and supply chain management: Benefits, challenges and future research opportunities. *International Journal of Information Management, 52*, 102064. https://doi.org/10.1016/j.ijinfomgt.2019.102064
48. Alshamaila, Y., et al. (2013). The usage and adoption of cloud computing by small and medium businesses. *International Journal of Information Management, 33*(5), 861–874. https://doi.org/10.7753/ijcatr0205.1003
49. Alharbi, F., Atkins, A., & Stanier, C. (2016). Understanding the determinants of cloud computing adoption in Saudi healthcare organisations. *Complex & Intelligent Systems, 2*(3), 155–171. https://doi.org/10.1007/s40747-016-0021-9
50. Kumar, A., & Krishnamoorthy, B. (2020). Business analytics adoption in firms: A qualitative study elaborating TOE framework in India. *International Journal of Global Business and Competitiveness, 15*(2), 80–93. https://doi.org/10.1007/s42943-020-00013-5
51. Ramaswamy, H. G. H. D. R. (2015). Understanding determinants of cloud computing adoption using an integrated TAM-TOE model. *Journal of Enterprise Information Management, 28*(1), 107–130.

52. Nam, K., Dutt, C. S., Chathoth, P., Daghfous, A., & Khan, M. S. (2020). The adoption of artificial intelligence and robotics in the hotel industry: Prospects and challenges. *Electronic Markets, 31*, 553. https://doi.org/10.1007/s12525-020-00442-3
53. Amini, M., & Bakri, A. (2015). Cloud computing adoption by SMEs in the Malaysia: A multi-perspective framework based on DOI theory and TOE framework. *Journal of Information Technology & Information Systems Research, 9*(2), 121–135.
54. Mrhaouarh, I., Okar, C., Namir, A., & Chafiq, N. (2018). Cloud computing adoption in developing countries: A systematic literature review. *2018 IEEE International Conference on Technology Management, Operations and Decisions, 2018*, 73–79. https://doi.org/10.1109/ITMC.2018.8691295
55. Hair, J. F., Sarstedt, M., Hopkins, L., & Kuppelwieser, V. G. (2014). Partial least squares structural equation modeling (PLS-SEM): An emerging tool in business research. *European Business Review, 26*(2), 106–121. https://doi.org/10.1108/EBR-10-2013-0128
56. Podsakoff, N. P. (2003). Common method biases in behavioral research: a critical review of the literature and recommended remedies. *Journal of Applied Psychology, 885*(879), 10–1037.
57. Byrne, B. M. (2013). *Structural equation modeling with Mplus*. https://doi.org/10.4324/9780203807644.
58. Hair, J. F., Sarstedt, M., Pieper, T. M., & Ringle, C. M. (2012). The use of partial least squares structural equation modeling in strategic management research: A review of past practices and recommendations for future applications. *Long Range Planning, 45*(5–6), 320–340. https://doi.org/10.1016/j.lrp.2012.09.008
59. Kline, R. B. (2015). *Principles and practice of structural equation modeling*. Guilford Publications.
60. Nunnally, J. C. (1994). *Psychometric theory 3E*. Tata McGraw-Hill Education.
61. Hair, J. F., Black, W. C., Babin, B. J., Anderson, R. E., & Tatham, R. L. (2010). *Multivariate data analysis* (7th ed.). Prentice Hall.
62. Moerdyk, A. (2009). *The principles and practice of psychological assessment*. Van Schaik.
63. Henseler, J., Ringle, C. M., & Sinkovics, R. R. (2009). The use of partial least squares path modeling in international marketing. *Advances in International Marketing, 20*, 277–319.
64. Hair, J. F., Sarstedt, M., Ringle, C. M., & Mena, J. A. (2012). An assessment of the use of partial least squares structural equation modeling in marketing research. *Journal of the Academy of Marketing Science, 40*(3), 414–433. https://doi.org/10.1007/s11747-011-0261-6
65. Fornell, C., & Larcker, D. F. (1981). Evaluating structural equation models with unobservable variables and measurement error. *Journal of Marketing Research, 18*(1), 39–50. https://doi.org/10.1177/002224378101800104
66. Cable, D. M., & DeRue, D. S. (2002). The convergent and discriminant validity of subjective fit perceptions. *The Journal of Applied Psychology, 87*(5), 875–884. https://doi.org/10.1037/0021-9010.87.5.875
67. Byrne, B. M. (2001). Structural equation modeling with AMOS, EQS, and LISREL: Comparative approaches to testing for the factorial validity of a measuring instrument. *International Journal of Testing, 1*(1), 55–86. https://doi.org/10.1207/s15327574ijt0101_4
68. Alkhater, N., Walters, R., & Wills, G. (2018). An empirical study of factors influencing cloud adoption among private sector organisations. *Telematics and Informatics, 35*(1), 38–54. https://doi.org/10.1016/j.tele.2017.09.017
69. Maroufkhani, P., Wan Ismail, W. K., & Ghobakhloo, M. (2020). Big data analytics adoption model for small and medium enterprises. *Journal of Science and Technology Policy Management, 11*(2), 171–201. https://doi.org/10.1108/JSTPM-02-2020-0018
70. Tashkandi, A. A., & Al-Jabri, I. (2015). Cloud computing adoption by higher education institutions in Saudi Arabia: Analysis based on TOE. *International Conference on Cloud Computing, 2015*, 1–8. https://doi.org/10.1109/CLOUDCOMP.2015.7149634
71. Yadav, V. S., Singh, A. R., Raut, R. D., & Govindarajan, U. H. (2020). Blockchain technology adoption barriers in the Indian agricultural supply chain: An integrated approach. *Resources, Conservation and Recycling, 161*, 104877. https://doi.org/10.1016/j.resconrec.2020.104877

72. Saurabh, S., & Dey, K. (2021). Blockchain technology adoption, architecture, and sustainable agri-food supply chains. *Journal of Cleaner Production, 284*, 124731. https://doi.org/10.1016/j.jclepro.2020.124731
73. Di Vaio, A., & Varriale, L. (2020). Blockchain technology in supply chain management for sustainable performance: Evidence from the airport industry. *International Journal of Information Management, 52*, 102014. https://doi.org/10.1016/j.ijinfomgt.2019.09.010
74. Queiroz, M. M., Fosso Wamba, S., De Bourmont, M., & Telles, R. (2020). Blockchain adoption in operations and supply chain management: Empirical evidence from an emerging economy. *International Journal of Production Research*. https://doi.org/10.1080/00207543.2020.1803511
75. Durach, C. F., Blesik, T., Düring, M., & Bick, M. (2020). Blockchain applications in supply chain transactions. *Journal of Business Logistics, 42*, 12238. https://doi.org/10.1111/jbl.12238
76. Wu, H., et al. (2019). Data management in supply chain using blockchain: Challenges and a case study. In *Proceedings - International Conference on Computer Communications and Networks, ICCCN*, 2019. https://doi.org/10.1109/ICCCN.2019.8846964.
77. Dwivedi, S. K., Amin, R., & Vollala, S. (2020). Blockchain based secured information sharing protocol in supply chain management system with key distribution mechanism. *Journal of Information Security and Applications, 54*, 102554. https://doi.org/10.1016/j.jisa.2020.102554
78. Tönnissen, S., & Teuteberg, F. (2018). Using blockchain technology for business processes in purchasing – Concept and case study-based evidence. *Lecture Notes in Business Information Processing, 320*, 253–264. https://doi.org/10.1007/978-3-319-93931-5_18
79. Bai, C., & Sarkis, J. (2020). A supply chain transparency and sustainability technology appraisal model for blockchain technology. *International Journal of Production Research, 58*(7), 2142–2162. https://doi.org/10.1080/00207543.2019.1708989
80. Holotiuk, F., & Moormann, J. (2018). Organizational adoption of digital innovation: The case of blockchain technology. *Research Paper.* Accessed 06 Mar 2021. [Online]. Available: https://aisel.aisnet.org/ecis2018_rp/202.
81. Wang, Z., Wang, T., Hu, H., Gong, J., Ren, X., & Xiao, Q. (2020). Blockchain-based framework for improving supply chain traceability and information sharing in precast construction. *Automation in Construction, 111*, 103063. https://doi.org/10.1016/j.autcon.2019.103063
82. Hwang, Y., Lin, H., & Shin, D. (2018). Knowledge system commitment and knowledge sharing intention: The role of personal information management motivation. *International Journal of Information Management, 39*, 220–227. https://doi.org/10.1016/J.IJINFOMGT.2017.12.009
83. Martins, R., Oliveira, T., & Thomas, M. A. (2016). An empirical analysis to assess the determinants of SaaS diffusion in firms. *Computers in Human Behavior, 62*, 19–33. https://doi.org/10.1016/j.chb.2016.03.049
84. Risius, M., & Spohrer, K. (2017). A blockchain research framework: What we (don't) know, where we go from here, and how we will get there. *Business and Information Systems Engineering, 59*(6), 385–409. https://doi.org/10.1007/s12599-017-0506-0

Revisiting Trust in Supply Chains: How Does Blockchain Redefine Trust?

Warwick Powell, Shoufeng Cao, Marcus Foth, Shan He, Charles Turner-Morris, and Ming Li

1 Introduction

> To give a name to a thing is as gratifying as giving a name to an island, but it is also dangerous: the danger consists in one's becoming convinced that all is taken care of and that once named, the phenomenon has also been explained. – Primo Levi

> What is needed is an electronic payment system based on cryptography instead of trust ... – Satoshi Nakamoto

The idea of trust is often emphasised in the competitive business environment where information asymmetry is a common issue. The emergence and adoption of new technologies, such as blockchain, has seen an often unreflective and uncritical emphasis on the idea of trust in business landscapes. Yet, the invocation of the idea

W. Powell
QUT Design Lab, Queensland University of Technology, Brisbane, QLD, Australia

BeefLedger Ltd, Brisbane, QLD, Australia

S. Cao (✉) · M Foth
QUT Design Lab, Queensland University of Technology, Brisbane, QLD, Australia
e-mail: shoufeng.cao@qut.edu.au

S. He
School of Chemistry and Chemical Engineering, Guangzhou University, Guangzhou, China

College of Science and Engineering, Flinders University, Adelaide, SA, Australia

C. Turner-Morris
BeefLedger Ltd, Brisbane, QLD, Australia

M. Li
Shanghai Key Laboratory of Intelligent Information Processing, School of Computer Science, Fudan University, Shanghai, China

China Electronics Standardization Institute, Beijing, China

A. Bouras et al. (eds.), *Blockchain Driven Supply Chains and Enterprise Information Systems*, https://doi.org/10.1007/978-3-030-96154-1_2

of trust creates the need to conceptually revisit it and critically explore its effects on transactions so as to (i) better redefine trust, (ii) when it does and does not matter and (iii) how this relates to the core properties of blockchain technologies in the context of supply chains. Our reading of the academic literature, industry whitepapers and the mainstream press suggests that trust and blockchain technology are concepts that are often used almost interchangeably. Following the definition of blockchain as a 'trust machine' by *The Economist* magazine in 2016, blockchain is widely taken as a trust solution in many areas, including pharmaceuticals [1, 2], food [3–7], gemstones [8], intellectual property and other digital artefacts [9–11], identity registries [12] and financial applications [13–15]. Yet, it has an implicit 'taken for granted' character when it comes to the trust affordances of blockchain technologies.

Despite the prevalence of the trust trope in blockchain discourse, and its frequent invocation in the application case of supply chains, there is little by way of explicit investigation of what is really meant by trust, and whether in fact it matters at all, and if it does matter, under what conditions. The quotes at the beginning of this chapter go to these two points, which underpin this chapter's argument. In the first quote, Primo Levi warns that naming something is gratifying but dangerous, because we run the risk that the act of naming is confused with understanding. The ad hominem invocation of 'trust' whenever blockchain technology and its (claimed) virtues in supply chains are discussed is symptomatic of this move. The second quote is from the original Satoshi Nakamoto Bitcoin white paper [16]. Nakamoto proposed a solution to the double-spending problem in decentralised digital payment systems, which at their heart, sought to obviate the need for a trusted party (understood as an intermediating role between parties to a transaction or exchange) while protecting the system from double-spending. As the quote makes clear, the design of the Bitcoin blockchain architecture – a combination of cryptography and economics – was to replace trust with cryptography. Nakamoto's intervention was not about a 'trust machine' at all; it was about how to enable the exchange of digital value to function reliably without trust presuppositions. Nakamoto concluded the white paper by saying:

> We have proposed a system for electronic transactions without relying on trust. We started with the usual framework of coins made from digital signatures, which provides strong control of ownership, but is incomplete without a way to prevent double spending. To solve this, we proposed a peer-to-peer network using proof-of-work to record a public history of transactions that quickly becomes computationally impractical for an attacker to change if honest nodes control a majority of CPU power. [Emphasis added]

It seems that in much of the discourse since Nakamoto, the word 'instead', in the first quote above, has all but been forgotten. As for the explicit conclusion that the Bitcoin blockchain enables electronic transactions without relying on trust, this too has largely been ignored in the burgeoning supply chain and blockchain literature.

While many studies argued that blockchain creates trust between supply chain partners by ensuring information sharing in an immutable and secure manner [4], others claimed that trust is a necessary precondition for information sharing between companies [17]. This chapter focuses the discussion of trust and blockchain on the food supply chain that is mostly operated with trust-based relationships [18–20].

Batwa and Norrman [21] argue that 'a lack of agreement remains regarding what constitutes trust, and there is no generally accepted definition' (p. 205). In response, this chapter follows on from Levi's cautionary note and aims to recapture some conceptual clarity around the trust concept associated with blockchain technologies and supply chains. The contribution of this chapter is threefold: (i) we discuss what is trust from both the perspective of human relationships and business transactions and posit that blockchain cannot guarantee absolute trust, although it is widely perceived as a trust mechanism; (ii) we present how blockchain can contribute to supply chains beyond the trust assumption based on our learnings from a blockchain use case in food supply chains; and (iii) we reflect how blockchain technology-mediated features can redefine supply chain trust in a broad sense by comparing the rise of technology-enabled social commerce in China.

Section 2 offers a critical review of the blockchain-trust trope in the literature, which develops an approach to understanding trust as distinct from other types of relationships that people are involved in. This is followed by a discussion of the role of blockchain in supply chains in Sect. 3. After presenting our real-life learnings and reflections from an applied use case of blockchain in the beef supply chain in Sect. 4, we reflect on these general themes and their relevance to trust in supply chain environments in Sect. 5. Finally, Sect. 6 concludes this chapter with synthesised results and implications.

2 Trust and Blockchain

The blockchain literature is replete with references to trust. Yet, there is little reflection on what is meant by the idea. Indeed, the various ways in which 'trust' is enlisted in discussions about blockchains lead to less clarity and more confusion. This section explores how we can understand trust from both a human relationship and a business context. On this basis, the blockchain-trust trope is discussed.

2.1 What Is Trust?

Despite the frequent invocation of trust in the blockchain literature, there is little explicit contemplation of trust *tout court*. The same cannot be said for the wider philosophical, psychological and to some extent, the economic literature. Much of the literature presupposes trust to be some form of attribute, either a subjective one, which resides in the minds of actors, often thought of as a stance or an attitude (I trust so-and-so, suggesting that trust is an attribute of my consciousness), or – *pace* Simmel – a social property that exists and operates as a form of invisible social glue that inheres in things (institutions) or other people (so-and-so is trustworthy).

As a cognitive or affective attribute, as generally conceived, trust either connotes a rationalised frame concerned with probabilistic calculus, knowledge and identification [22] or as little more than a set of non-cognitive beliefs or set of affective attitudes. In the latter sense, it is reduced to a set of warm feelings and not much more. Abstractly, these approaches posit trust as either a set of necessary conditions or as static properties. If the former conflates trust with something else, and at best reduces the way we understand trust to be 'calculated distrusting', and the latter sees trust as an affective residue, it is hard to see what is so special about trust at all. Yet, all through the literature – whether it is sociological, psychological or economic – the idea of trust is pivotal and warrants more than this confused treatment.

Seeking to have an understanding of human activity, there is the tendency to elide the richness of the interactions and background practices and knowledge involved in trust and trust building. The richness is about how we understand trust and trusting as an ongoing process, a mutual or reciprocal dynamic relationship, which is formed through trusting between two parties. If trust's distinctiveness is its dynamic richness embedded in the complexities of human-to-human relationships, we are thus better able to grasp what it is that goes towards the formation of trust and why it is always a work in progress. Trust is built through interactions. These interactions between people involve promises, commitments and frustrations. Everyday encounters anchor the ways in which promises, commitments and frustrations play out and shape the thickness or thinness of trust in a relationship. They also, through time, impact the extent to which one could consider the relationship to be one imbued with trustworthiness. Frequent failure, for example, to live up to promises can erode trust as the other party feels let down. This could be as simple as consistent lack of punctuality, as a sign of disrespect, which eventually corrodes the trustworthiness of the relationship. Yet, corrective action – in response to direct or indirect suggestions – can contribute to the revitalisation of trust.

For relationships between people, as Robert Solomon argues in the book edited by Wrathall and Malpas [23], 'trusting is the product of participation and mutual communication in relationships. Trust is not a matter of reliance, and it is not just a matter of expectations (which presume a certain amount of risk . . . '. The idea here at the heart of trust *qua* trust is that it is a post hoc shorthand way of describing a lived and dynamic experience. Through these exchanges, the parties themselves are transformed, as is the relationship itself. Research on trust formation in clinical care contexts sheds light on the importance of interpersonal communications in the cultivation of trust. Brown [24], for instance, explores the phenomenology of trust in the context of gynae-oncology care, and shows that interpersonal communication is primary to trust because of the concreteness of intersubjective experience. This is what Bredlau [25] has described in terms of the collaborative endeavour of cultivating shared worlds, which embed in our relationships with others and with the world. She argues in the context of relations between infants and adults that collaboration (i.e. acting together) is the basis of perception and that this entails the cultivation of trust. In other words, trust is not simply a feeling that people perceive; it is an embodied way of perceiving that involves people living their trust in each other through the shared perceptions of the world around them and cultivating these shared worlds in ways that protect rather than damage them.

However, authentic trust is not pure; rather, it is the opposite of this kind of trust that manifests as doubts and uncertainty. Trust cannot be read as separate from the lived state of courage-anxiety as a unity, wherein these states – according to Merleau-Ponty's phenomenology – are conditions of the existence of being:

> As a matter of principle, humanity is precarious: each person can only believe what he recognises to be true internally and, at the same time, nobody thinks or makes up his mind without already being caught up in certain relationships with others, which leads him to opt for a particular set of opinions. Everyone is alone and yet nobody can do without other people ... It is understandable that our species ... should find this situation both cause for anxiety and a spur to courage [26, 27].

The inescapable sociability of human existence is the gist of trust understood as the dynamics that leads a person to go for a set of opinions. This is because no-one's mind is made up in isolation of how people enter certain relationships with others. In other words, opinions are formed together, however provisional they often are. Trust is thus emblematic of the perpetual precariousness of existence and our relation to an enigmatic world [26]. According to Utley [27], trust is when subjects experience an equilibrium between anxiety and courage, which enables a person to get on with life. In this balance, the operation of trust is hidden from view. When confronted with circumstances that call into question the balance, when anxiety emerges as the dominant affective state, subjects are called upon to be courageous. But people are never alone. Acknowledging the presence of doubt and uncertainty gives actors the possibility to overcome them, and in doing so, strengthens trust in their relationship.

In the context of business practice transformation, Fernando Flores and colleagues [23, 28, 29] explore these general themes, and argue that the destruction of trust in a corporate context most readily takes place in environments of change. Change threatens livelihoods and accustomed ways of living and working, and therefore undermines trust. This is because such change impacts any sense of security that may have existed between firms, whatever the anchors of that have been. Such senses of security are vulnerable because they presuppose 'an underlying feeling that our identities are fixed, fragile, and constantly under threat of attack' [30]. In contexts where actors' security is threatened, distrust emerges. Introducing change in this environment can be highly destructive. So, any changes in corporate strategy must align with trust-building activities [30].

Trust and commitment are historically company-specific and are shaped by organisational values and culture [31]; these trust-building exercises are the corporate 'putting into practice' of the general idea of focal events, as discussed before. Trust building involves changes to organisational design and process, new forms of commitment making and role formation. Therefore, there is a need for parties involved to evaluate each other's sincerity, competency and her own care for their own identity. Care for identity here means cultivating practices focused on forming and fulfilling commitments and sustaining credibility as someone who makes and fulfils important offers. For Flores [30], therefore, a critical trust-building focal event is 'regular and honest assessments of managers and employees' in open settings. Regularity is necessary to mitigate the early-stage risk of participants gaming the processes (i.e. acting out an expected role to enhance their own positions within the organisation). Conducting such evaluations publicly also mitigates the risk of sustained power plays, as exposure to peers makes it less likely. Public focal events also enable people to see how what they say and do can affect others, leading to change in others as well as in themselves. Such events open up participants in their fullness, not just through speech acts that are verbalised, but through embodied interactions. Through these kinds of focal events, participants come to disclose to themselves and others new ways of being and discover that they do not have to be fragile. These new styles of engagement and interaction enable people to progressively transform themselves through collaborative action into trusting colleagues. Trust colleagues as roles are founded in interactive declaratives via the speech act. Speech acts are commitments that are not discharged until those to whom they are made declared satisfaction. Speech acts are events and processes involving others, in which those making the commitments have responsibility for the ways they are with others in the world. It is through focal events, in which participants can live out requests, offers, promises, orders and declarations that enable new trusting relationships to be formed and tested.

2.2 Blockchain-Trust Trope

If, as Salomon and Flores [29] and others discussed above indicate, trust is an embodied phenomenon resulting from interactive human engagement, phenomenologically experienced as the unified transcendence of courage-anxiety, then it follows that strictly speaking it is not something that inheres in machines. Machines do not have trusting relationships with other machines, and people do not have trusting relationships with machines. Without the risk of feedback and rejection from others, courage-anxiety does not define the state of engagement. Furthermore, that people do not have trusting relationships with machines is because trust is an interactive phenomenon wherein those involved in the creation of trust atmospheres have done so through shared attunements in focal events. Through involvement in these events, participants contribute to the ongoing formation of themselves as well as to change in others. Machines are not changed through these encounters.

Understanding trust in its distinctiveness enables us to critically reflect on how the blockchain literature has approached the question. Consider this discussion by Mougayar [32]:

> If blockchains are a new way to implement trusted transactions without trusted intermediaries, soon we'll end up with intermediary-free trust. ... Intermediary-controlled trust came with some friction, but now, with the blockchain, we can have frictionless trust. (p. xxiii)

So, this raises a question of what needs to be done next when trust is 'free'. Mougayar [32] asked: 'what does a trusted blockchain enable'? Inter alia, he argues that the blockchain offers 'programmable trust'. He describes: 'By inserting rules that represent trust inside transactions, the blockchain becomes a new way to validate these transactions via logic in the network, not via a database entry or central authority. Therefore, a new "trust factor" is created that is part of the transaction itself' (p. 46).

Mougayar's [32] discussion exhibits several conflations. Firstly, he confuses the issue of trust with the presence or absence of trusted intermediaries. As we discuss below, the presence of third parties in transactions is better understood not as a question of trust but rather, as an institutional cost necessary to deal with the state of non-trust. Third parties are necessarily interposed to mediate transactions when the transacting parties are not in trust-based relations. Third parties do not need to be trusted per se to fulfil the functions demanded of them by economic agents involved in transactions but gain their authority from their ability to exact punishment on non-performing parties. This leads to the idea of 'frictionless trust', though we are none the wiser as to what trust means or entails. Secondly, Mougayar [32] presupposes trust to be a tangible *something*, which, akin to a flow of energy or water, seeks out the path of least resistance. In this schema, trust is something that exists somewhere; it is simply a question of where. The idea of trust being something tangible finds its final form by way of programmed rules. For Mougayar [32], such rules 'represent trust inside transactions' so that something called a 'trust factor' is created. These are non sequitur*s*: non-code trust is replaced by rules (in code), which in turn creates a 'trust factor'; and yet, there is no discussion as to what trust actually is, without which it is impossible to contemplate the idea that 'it' can be codified or represented, or more generally, that it merely takes different forms.

The *non sequitur* of the general argument is also clear in Williams' discussion about blockchain and trust [33]. For Williams, blockchains enable the production of immutable records that are visible to all, but where one can remain anonymous. He says, 'You can remain anonymous, but your transaction cannot. Thus, blockchain serves as a robotic generator of unconditional trust between humans. Unconditional, *because no trust is necessary*. Everything is guaranteed by algorithm. With guaranteed trust, there is no fear of fraud' (p. 78). In other places, he invokes the idea of 'mechanical trust' (p. 79). He concludes:

> We each have our own definition of trust ... Trust and trustless are two sides of the same coin. Most of us probably don't have a definition for trustless. At first, it sounds sinister, as in untrustworthy. However, in terms of blockchain, trustless is the trustworthiest possible state. *Trustless means no trust necessary*. It's built in. (p. 82)

Williams [33] concedes that there is no generally accepted idea of trust ('we each have our own definition'). He proceeds to presume that its meaning can be gleaned by counterpositioning it with trustlessness ('two sides of the same coin'). Yet, this is hardly any clearer if for no other reason than that the idea of trust is also inseparable from mistrust and distrust and untrustworthiness. The absence of trust (i.e. a state of trustlessness), we would suggest, is just that; it also implies an absence of mistrust, distrust and untrustworthiness. Trust is not counterposed to trustlessness. Rather, trust is counterposed to mistrust, distrust and untrustworthiness. Trustless, on the other hand, is the absence of the entire rubric altogether. The absence of trust shifts *the register* to something altogether different. Williams [33] in the end concedes this when he says that 'trustless means no trust necessary'. Had he ended it there, we would have a useful place to begin. Unfortunately, because of the failure to think beyond the trust-mistrust-distrust register, Williams is compelled to add that trust is not necessary, because it is 'built in'. Why say that 'no trust is necessary' only to later assert that there is 'guaranteed trust' or 'mechanical trust'? Trust is re-invoked just as we show the possibility of understanding economic transactions in the absence of trust *tout court*.

The discursive trope seems to boil down to this: pre-blockchain, trust has been inherited in third-party institutions that straddled transactions between two parties. Blockchain seemingly replaces these institutions with codes, and many programmers tend to operate under a positivist epistemological stance rather than a constructivist one [cf. 34]. Ergo, so the argument goes, code has replaced third-party institutional trust and embedded trust into the algorithmic architecture itself [cf. 35]. Trust has doppelgänger-like qualities in that whatever 'it' is, it can assume different forms: third-party institutions or algorithmic code. Yet, this begs the question, what is the essence of trust? That is, what makes trust *trust*, and not something else?

These conceptions show that trust is ultimately substantivised with distinct properties, which inheres either in minds or in persons (and possibly things). In some conceptions, such as Hardin [36], both these approaches are pulled together via a game theoretic rubric, which treats trust as a function of human self-interestedness and attitudes of suspicion towards others, where the mediating calculus is one of probability. The technicist blockchain 'take' on trust tends to be of the latter variety, focusing on trust as a property of non-technological institutions, which can be substituted by some idea of 'programmable trust' wherein trust is rendered as a measure of probabilities associated with the actions of others. Ethereum founder's, Vitalik Buterin, recent discussion on trust is along these lines [37]. Within a technicist game theoretic frame, it is possible to dissect so-called devices for commitment that make trustworthiness possible. In the presence of such devices, of probability calculus, behavioural game strategy and ideas of rational expectations, an index of trustworthiness is therefore calculable.

The ability to render the idea of trust calculable within a mathematical frame is no doubt appealing in the context of the possibilities of smart contracts as 'self-executing' code. Here, rendering interactions calculable via a calculus of inputs-outputs, 'if this, then that', introduces a level of certitude about outcomes conditional on prescribed informational circumstances being satisfied, which is claimed to be representative of trust. This is where we demur. To speak of trust in the context of calculus of conditional certitude conflates trust with something else; this something else is more akin and better understood in terms of *reliability*. Calculative reliability is not reducible to trust *tout court*, which as we have argued, is quite a deal fuzzier and ambiguous, and dynamic than the certitude of self-executing code. The certitude that can be 'baked in' to the transactional back-office is not without value, however, as we show when we consider blockchain applications in the context of supply chains below. But, if it does have value, it is in its ability to deliver algorithmic certitude as a kind of what Solomon calls 'calculating distrusting' [23].

We thus make the distinction between trust and reliability. We can add to this distinction some related ones such as dependability, confidence and predictability [29]. Reliability, dependability, confidence and predictability are important aspects of human interactions and social relationships to the world, but aside from being purely metaphoric, the invocation of trust by rights should be preserved for thinking about and describing relationships between and amongst human beings. Machines (including computers) cannot literally be trusted. We rely upon them as we find them dependable and predictable. 'To equate trust with predictability is a mistake because we are dealing with people in dynamic, reciprocal relationships rather than with recurrent phenomena governed by (more or less) clear, lawlike regularity' [29]. It is also not merely a question of likelihood or probability that the other will fulfil our expectations. Trusting is a two-way relationship which affects the parties involved, and the relationship itself. Even if we say we trust a machine, the extent to which we trust it does not affect the extent to which it is likely to perform as expected.

3 Blockchain and Supply Chains

The literature posits that the introduction of blockchain technologies into supply chains contributes to the creation of trust and enhances supply chain performance. This section explores this claim from a supply chain functionality perspective and how blockchain can meaningfully contribute to supply chains.

3.1 Supply Chain Functionality and Trust Issues

Supply chains typically involve economic agents interacting across time and space to transform and create products and services, ultimately for end consumption. These agents are connected at a material level in terms of the movement of products from one to the other as the processes of transformation take place. Agents are also connected in a non-material sense via the movement of money in exchange for the movement of goods. The movement of money is governed by the flow of information about the things as money does not flow unless certain informational conditions are satisfied. Financial relations between agents are characterised by credit-and-debt relationships. This usually involves a financial third party to mediate payments through the provision of securitised credit [38–40].

Functional supply chains can be understood as a circulation system with three interconnected flows: the product flow, the money flow and the information flow. Talk of such flows draws on the conceptual imagery of Marx's discussion about the circulation of capital in *Capital* Volume 2. There, he describes an integrated system where capital assumes three forms – industrial, commodity and finance – and the processes of reproduction and circulation are about how these metamorphose one into another and interact with each other, as constraints and conditions of possibility, through time and space. Figure 1 depicts the supply chain flows in a financialised system, in which money (M) is exchanged for a commodity (C) which is then transformed through a production process (P) to become a new commodity (C^1). This new commodity C^1 is then exchanged for money (M^1), and so on.

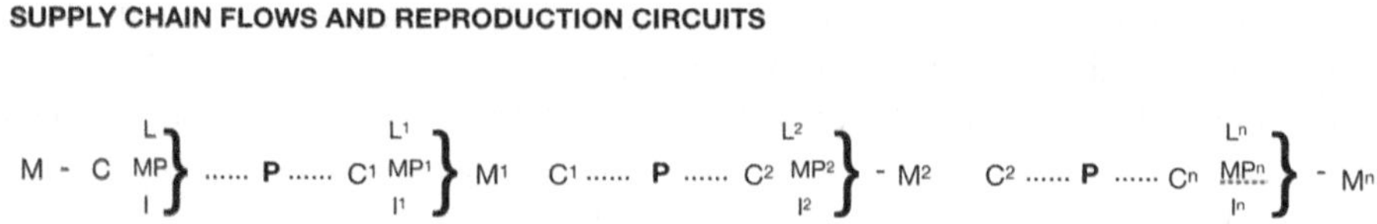

Fig. 1 Financialised supply chain schematic. Note: M money, C commodity, L labour, MP means of production, I information, P production

A full, complete circuit takes place when the original money (M) is realised as M^n after going through the phases of production and sales. A successfully completed circuit is tantamount to the supply chain reproducing itself. The processes of valorisation and transformation take place through time and place, where the work of each phase of transformation – production and then realisation through sales and consumption – has concrete temporal dimensions. The transformation of commodities through processes of production into new commodities takes time, just as the sale of the commodity post-production to either the next phase of transformation or for final consumption. Disruptions to the processes of transformation can, if sustained, have deleterious effects on the processes of supply chain reproduction. Disturbances to the flow of the supply chain circuits of transformation hamper the repetitive metonymy of industrial production and its associated credit finance circuits; and the greater the disturbances, the greater the quantum of money that must be held by each node in the supply chain to ride out the periods of disturbance. In plain terms, the greater the delays in transforming the circuits of production and sale (realisation), the larger volumes of money capital needed to sustain the reproduction of the supply chain's activities. This money capital is sourced from accumulated profits or from credit providers.

Accordingly, reducing the time of circulation of capital (i.e. the completion of a full circuit) is a key dynamic in financialised supply chains, as the shorter the duration of circulation, the less money capital is required to be held in reserve and, typically, the less credit needed. Holding money reserves and incurring costs of credit are both suboptimal utilisations of a given quantum of capital. Assuming that a given return on capital can be realised through the completion of a full circuit, it follows that the faster the circuit can be completed in a given period of time (e.g. 1 year), the greater the return that can be achieved for a given unit of initial capital.

In the sphere of production, mechanisation and automation are the key drivers in reducing the total time of circulation. *Information* plays a contributing role in driving effective mechanisation and automation. It speeds up production converting C to C^1. If information contributes to productivity growth, we can also note the role of information *about the commodities* in the transaction M-C itself as well as its end-of-circuit realisation C^1-M^1. In this formulation, we could say that the hyphen denotes the flow of information. Delays in realisation (i.e. in conversion of commodity capital to money capital form) take place if, for instance, the commodity is unsaleable or where there is insufficient demand. The speed of information flow through enhanced communication technologies also impacts the period of circulation. Advances in communications address information synchrony, but do not necessarily address the issue of information inadequacy and asymmetry. The existence of inadequate and asymmetric information between transactional members results in the trust issues between supply chain partners and, on the other hand, highlights the importance of building trust relationships to mitigate those risks. Early research [17] suggested that trust relationships support information sharing between supply chain partners. However, inter-firm trust relationships are fragile as a firm may take advantage of the other's trust for their own interests. This makes firms cautious of sharing information and communicating risks with their supply chain partners [41, 42], which hinders inter-firm trust building. The introduction of blockchain technology that has immutable and tamper-proof characteristics could be an answer to this paradox.

3.2 How Can Blockchain Meaningfully Contribute to Supply Chains?

The sustainable operations of a supply chain rely on profit accumulation above and beyond reproduction costs. The financial flows within a supply chain effectively distribute the aggregate revenue to the various actors, wherein above-cost surpluses are incrementally captured along the way. Such supply chain activities largely do not rely on trust to function. This is because most transactions associated with products, services and financial flows are finalised by 'strangers' and institutional functionaries [43]. In other words, the condition of functional supply chains is *transactional dependability* in conditions of zero trust.

However, much discussion in the literature claims that there is a significant social cost to establishing trust for commerce, via mechanisms and institutions such as 'the rule of law', and various associated arbitration and court systems and such like [44]. We suggest that these are better understood not as the costs of establishing trust but as the costs of dealing with the consequential uncertainty of outcomes of non-trust, and the costs exacted upon parties due to counterparty non-performance or change of circumstances. The reality is that these institutions are not trust-based but depend entirely upon some capacity to exact punishment [45]. The existence of legally enforceable contracts, governing supply chain transactions, which include punishments in the event of non-performance, is symptomatic of a zero-trust environment.[1] If parties trusted each other, there would be no reason for such contracts and their associated institutional buttresses. The presence of contracts and other institutional desiderata indicates a need for any forms of protection in an absence of trust.

With this understanding, we argue that the deployment of blockchain technologies in supply chain ecosystems is not about instituting trust. Rather, we claim that

[1] There are some similarities in this argument to that advanced by Williamson [46].

blockchain technologies can contribute meaningfully to supply chains in several ways, without the trust predicates so often claimed by blockchain advocates. This can be explained in that the deployment of blockchain is about increasing reliability, and from that dependability, in conditions of zero trust (at best), and distrust/mistrust at worst. In this context, the extent of reliability and then dependability refers to the presence or otherwise of information asymmetry between and amongst participants as the basis of actor decision-making and conduct and the likelihood of actor behaviours and behavioural outcomes to meet required conditions. Should trust emerge at all via these dynamics and interactions, it is a by-product.[2] Additionally, information asymmetry can be understood as an embedded property of supply chains involving multiple parties of varying configurations of power relations, which is a precondition for capricious or opportunistic action. Industry structure is a key institutional and market condition of existence of real supply chains, wherein capriciousness is always present-in-potential.

As an innovative technology with such fundamental features as explicit data validation rules, transparent processes, irreversible record and fraud proofs [37], blockchain has the potential to address the reliance on trust building in addressing these uncertainties and reduce risks of capricious actions in supply chains. In short, blockchain has the potential to reduce information asymmetry and the space for capricious conduct, thereby increasing information reliability. More effective flow of information contributes to increased velocity or circulation of commodities, reducing the amount of capital required to be held in reserve and reducing the presence of uncertainty and the cost of finance.

4 Learning from a Blockchain Use Case in Supply Chains

Supply chain collaboration is a traditional solution to reduce supply chain costs and to improve reliability [49] and become more strategically important in a contemporary business environment exposed to various interdependent risks and disruptions [50]. On this score, the supply chain literature stresses the importance of trust building and maintenance. Unfortunately, trust-based relationships are costly to build and can be easily challenged by opportunistic behaviours and/or changing circumstances [51].

In seeking solutions to tackle trust challenges, BeefLedger has been pioneering the development and commercialisation of an integrated blockchain-enabled beef provenance platform and smart contracting payments regime [19, 20]. Figure 2 shows a snapshot of BeefLedger's blockchain-based beef provenance and smart

[2] Not unrelated is the idea that trustworthiness is a result of safety and dependability, as articulated by Roth [47]. Market design, therefore, must be about safety and dependability for participants. Trustworthiness is a residual consequence. Sabel [48] introduces the idea of 'learning by monitoring' as an explanation of successful collaboration. In this case, trust is the consequence of learning embodied in ongoing monitoring.

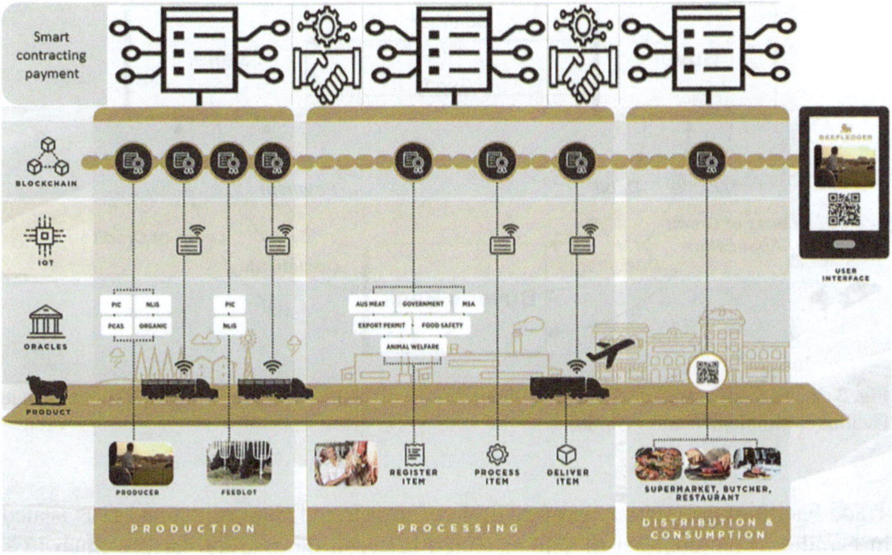

Fig. 2 The architecture for beef provenance and smart contracting payments. (Source: Adapted from Powell et al. [19])

contracting payment architecture. It is a universal digital platform project using blockchain technology with a view to use product provenance data as a basis for increasing the confidence of supply chain participants and streamlining payments. It offers supply chain agents, including consumers, a platform to verify the certification information of the products they purchase and improve the efficiency of the supply chain by reducing information asymmetry amongst transaction parties. BeefLedger makes use of blockchain as a strong validator of transaction records and the power of token economics to optimise the supply chain operations with decentralised models.

Our learnings from the ongoing work with the BeefLedger project offer empirical evidence to revisit the question of trust in supply chains. A beef supply chain generates a wealth of information about cattle breeds, sex, age, feed, weight and locations. It also involves information about meat quality, weight and storage and transport conditions. Verification of this information in compliance with procurement requirements is the condition precedent of the exchange of products for money. Information adequacy and symmetry are pivotal to the provision of credit and the completion of the commodity-money circuit, where payment is in effect the release of funds by the credit provider. The provision of trade credit has been used to facilitate cross-border trade for many centuries [52]. Trade credit has historically taken the form of a promissory note, such as a letter of credit (LC), issued by the credit provider for the purchaser. Figure 3 summarises the procedures defined by the

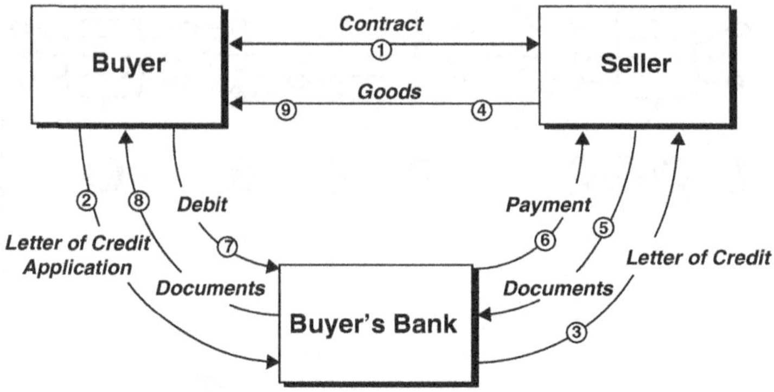

Fig. 3 Transactions and documentary flow, letters of credit. (Source: United Nations, Trade Facilitation Implementation Guide)

Trade Facilitation Implementation Guide of the United Nations.[3] The LC is issued in parallel to the contract of sale executed between the trading parties. Such LCs continue to dominate cross-border trade payments, even today. LCs are issued by the buy-side financier to the sell-side; upon the sell-side satisfying the conditions of the LC, the funds are released. Satisfaction of the conditions of the LC takes *documentary* form. To activate the LC, the sell-side is required to prepare or collate and provide the necessary documents as set out in the LC, to the LC issuer. Upon confirmation of the authenticity and satisfactory nature of the documents, the LC issuer completes the settlement.

In the transaction of beef exports, a typical LC requires the provision of a pile of documents to satisfy documentary conditions and cause the LC to be executed. These documents are provided at times digitally and in most cases in analogue form. This is confirmed by a leading bank agribusiness finance executive who was interviewed by the authors in April 2020. The finance executive stated that the processing of LCs for cross-border transactions still requires the provisioning of copies or originals of documents 'delivered in an envelope to the branch headquarters' whereupon the documents are viewed by a team of (human) evaluators. In the case of beef trade from Australia, the documents are typically (1) commercial invoice (issued by the seller/manufacturer), (2) load out summary report (signed by an Aus-Meat-certified inspector), (3) quarantine or non-wood declaration for containers (issued by the seller), (4) certificate with respect to meat (issued by the Department of Agriculture, Fisheries and Forestry), (5) packing list (issued by the manufacturer), (6) a certificate of origin (issued by the Australian Chamber of Commerce and Industry) and (7) the bill of lading (issued by the shipping agent).

Information about the product is key to the exchange, and accordingly a focus of capricious conduct risk. Capriciousness is characterised by sudden, unaccountable

[3] Accessed here: http://tfig.unece.org/contents/letters-of-credit.htm. 02 October 2020

and/or unpredictable actions on the part of one of the parties involved in the exchange. Letter of credit fraud is a widely acknowledged risk in cross-border commerce as it is warned by the FBI.[4] As a result, the presence of documentary fraud in the performance of letters of credit in cross-border trade is evidence of such informational malfeasance [53–55]. Asymmetrical relationship between different actors involved in a transaction, coupled with siloed data creation and storage systems, is the condition of existence of informationally driven caprice. When information asymmetry enables capricious conduct, supply chain sub-optimality is an almost inevitable outcome. Actions that can impact the timely realisation of commodities to money, such as those associated with informational caprice leading to either hidden action or hidden information, adversely impact upstream actors in the immediate term, and can increase overall supply chain instability by hampering the liquidity and viability of essential producers and service providers. Additionally, the growing need for credit increases the overall cost of the operations of the supply chain.

To address information asymmetry and associated financial losses, our BeefLedger team developed a blockchain-enabled multi-sig consensus mechanism. This multi-sig consensus mechanism not only enables the secure updating of a data state in accordance with specific state change rules but also allocates distributed rights to perform the state update amongst some set of agents. As information is formed or collected and recorded via a set of processes involving more than one party, involving the application of transparent rules, the opportunity for information caprice is significantly diminished. As such, blockchain technologies can provide supply chain agents with an informational base that – through the processes of collective responsibility in their production and subsequent management – they can each rely upon to go about their respective activities and transactions with each other. In other words, blockchain technologies in supply chain contexts remove the fundamental basis for hidden action and hidden knowledge. Without either, markets can be made safer, so that participants can go about their business focused on their interests without strong incentives to game the system [47, 56].

5 Reflections on Technology-Mediated Trust

This section presents our reflections on how blockchain can redefine trust and technology-mediated trust in a broad sense with social commerce in China leveraged by new technologies, such as WeChat – a Chinese social networking app with over one billion users.

[4] https://www.fbi.gov/scams-and-safety/common-scams-and-crimes/letter-of-credit-fraud

5.1 *Blockchain Cannot Guarantee Absolute Truths*

When considering blockchain as a digital, decentralised and distributed ledger to record transactional information in a chronological order for permanent and tamper-proof records, blockchain-based supply chains can be viewed as a 'tamper-proof system which will stand against any cheating or fraud attempts' [21]. While public (permissionless) blockchains facilitate the 'perfect' situation for absolute truths, the concern about privacy and confidentiality issues reduces its applicability in supply chains. According to Batwa and Norrman [21], 'private blockchains allow only a preselected and limited number of participants to be authorised to use the ledger', where data entries are observed by a small group of witnesses. Blockchains for supply chains cannot deliver absolute truths due to opportunistic behaviours and collusion risks between supply chain actors, and consequently result in trust issues. The trust issue also emerges in a private blockchain-based supply chain where a dominant manufacturer or retailers are a central authority and may manipulate their partners for their own interests.

In addition to the trust issues between supply chain partners, there is an issue with trust in the technology (blockchain) or in the infrastructure. Although the potential has been raised by academia and industry, blockchain infrastructure has yet to evolve as a 'general purpose technology' [57]. Current blockchain consensus mechanisms and data architecture that were developed for cryptocurrency help mitigate malicious data manipulation when data is stored in the blockchain system. However, the 'garbage in garbage out' issue is yet eliminated if fraudulent data is registered onto the blockchain system [19]. Blockchain's inability to ensure data authenticity at the entry points can further reduce the level of trust in the blockchain-based supply chain. The development of fit-for purpose consensus mechanisms and/or sensor-enabled data architecture could be a potential solution to guarantee the reliability and integrity of original data.

5.2 *Blockchain Is More Than a Trust Machine*

Since blockchain cannot guarantee absolute truths of the information, it is not a synonym for trust. To suggest so is a result of a failure to examine what it is that makes trust to be trust and not something else, and conflates trust with other kinds of relationships, particularly reliability. On the contrary, blockchains enable functional economic relationships to be established in the absence of trust and can achieve this at lower cost than other techniques. The technology delivers what Batwa and Norrman [21] describe as 'a trust-free environment based on the reliability and security of the information stored on the blockchain' – by reducing capriciousness in relation to information. Blockchain can be taken as a transparency machine in which anyone (i.e. supply chain members, authorities and consumers) can join the network and view/census the data on that network. In a supply chain context, such transparency breeds accountability, which can nudge supply chain partners to work more responsibly because they are accountable for their actions.

Trust is an embodied relationship between people, and their interactions involving mutual commitments through time, which is not something that machines (including blockchain and the Internet) do. Trust is neither something that describes the relationships that can form between people and machines, but a by-product of reliability and integrity in an environment exposed by uncertainties and risks. Nakamoto knew this when the Bitcoin white paper explicitly sought to enable digital transactions between people – erstwhile strangers, as identities did not need to be explicitly disclosed – without reliance on trust. This could be done because algorithms, deployed across a decentralised network of computers, could be relied upon to perform without caprice under specific operating conditions. Machines mediated the interaction of strangers (who could not form trust between each other and did not need to in any case) by providing sufficient conditions of reliability and accountability for the exchange to proceed and for the recorded exchange.

We displaced the centrality of trust in supply chain relationships with our real-life use case, showing that reliability is a sufficient condition of existence of supply chain functionality and transparency can breed accountability. This then raises a question of where trust sits, if at all, in a technology-mediated supply chain environment.

5.3 Technology-Mediated Trust in China's Social Commerce

We now reflect on the place for trust and how trust combined with machine-enabled reliability and relationships of extended trust via a technologically mediated 'economy of acquaintances' that has the potential to radically transform supply chain relationships and dynamics in a broad sense. The recent emergence of social commerce in China that combines first-generation e-commerce functionalities (platform-based sales and buying) with social communication features is a good example to illustrate this general point. With social commerce, consumers have access to products through the recommendations from their social acquaintances who share their shopping and consumption experience on their social media, like WeChat. This is a trust-based purchase or what has been called the economy of acquaintances as consumers view information about products and services received from friends more valuable and credible than information from other sources, including the anonymous information from strangers that was the norm in conventional e-commerce models [58].

Webs of interpersonal networks are amplified in China through the affordances of new technologies. In particular, the functionality offered by the WeChat app recasts the ways in which social networks are established, maintained and cultivated. WeChat has now morphed into a social commerce tool, with seamless payment capabilities, as part of China's burgeoning mobile economy [59]. A number of studies have indicated and explored how WeChat has now become increasingly important in the formation of relationship/guanxi networks in China, ranging from peer-to-peer relationships between professional peers [60] and more generally across the community at large.[5] WeChat works for guanxi development because it features low anonymity, high privacy and closed community [61]. As Shao and Pan [62] have shown, 'platform interactivity and media richness are significant technology affordances that promote users' guanxi networks, and their influences are mediated by social interaction and shared understanding'.

WeChat indeed offers a technical environment that revivifies sharing, with the additional dimension of speed and scalability efficiency, and which emulates the intimate relationships that underpin the production of trust. Crary [63] paints a somewhat dystopian picture when it comes to the effects of social technologies: 'One inhabits a world in which long-standing notions of shared experience atrophy, and yet one never actually attains the gratifications or rewards promised by the most recent technological options' (p. 31). The experience of WeChat as a guanxi-related capability suggests that the dynamics and effects are more ambiguous.

This example shows that when people do not have trusting relationships with technology, it does not mean that technology has no place in the lived dynamics of trust. This is a provisional observation that requires further explorations; but some exploratory empirics seem to support this statement [64]. If it is right, we can envisage a world where WeChat social commerce-enabled capabilities can be mobilised to activate networked cohorts of consumers. This is not only happening with 'group buying' models such as Pinduoduo (拼多多) [65] but also with the more recent 'community group buying' (社区团购) [66, 67].

6 Conclusions

This chapter explores what it is to trust and what makes trust distinctive and, on this basis, presents the empirical learning of how blockchains can enable supply chain transactions to take place between strangers and corporations in a zero-trust environment, without a traditional enforcement intermediary. To take a step forwards, this chapter reflects how technology, including blockchain, can redefine trust in a broad sense with primary and secondary evidence available. Our investigation of the question of what makes trust trust and not something else offers a space to revisit trust in supply chains with the mediation of new technologies, such as blockchain.

Blockchain technologies fulfil to a greater extent the claims of calculative algorithms insofar as enhancing predictability and dependability are concerned. This is in place of trust. Even so, trust is not without place in the supply chains of today and the future, but not in the ways that blockchain advocates have

[5] See China Internet Network Information Center (2015) Chinese User Behaviour in Social Media 2015 Research Report (2015年中国社交应用用户行为研究报告)

so far suggested. A reimagined supply chain anchored through trusting relationships amongst consumers (viz. group buying dynamics embedded into trust-based WeChat-mediated guanxi networks) on one hand, with emergent intimacy-at-a-distance with producers, could transform supply chain dynamics considerably. Promises and commitments made to each other, by consumer groups and producers, give rise to demands on blockchain technologies to deliver reliable functions. What we can, therefore, imagine is a blockchain-enabled reliability architecture that enables the bridging of consumer and producer communities that can separately work on trusting, safe in the knowledge that their intentional commitments to each other are backed up by reliable information systems that mitigate gaming risks otherwise made possible by asymmetric information. In the end, blockchain technology may not be about trust directly, but it is not entirely irrelevant when it comes to trust in supply chains.

Acknowledgement This study was supported by funding from QUT, BeefLedger Ltd. as well as the Food Agility CRC Ltd., funded under the Commonwealth Government CRC Program. The CRC Program supports industry-led collaborations between industry, researchers and the community.

References

1. Satwik, P. M., Geluvaraj, B., & Ashok Kumar, T. A. (2018). A study on applications of AI, ML, DL and blockchain in healthcare and pharmaceuticals and its future. *International Journal of Computer Sciences and Engineering, 6*, 765–770. https://doi.org/10.26438/ijcse/v6i8.765770
2. Omar, A. S., & Basir, O. (2020). Secure anti-counterfeiting pharmaceuticals supply chain system using composable non-fungible tokens. https://doi.org/10.1201/9780429324932-14
3. Tian, F. (2017). A supply chain traceability system for food safety based on HACCP, blockchain Internet of things. In *2017 international conference on service systems and service management* (pp. 1–6).
4. Creydt, M., & Fischer, M. (2019). Blockchain and more - algorithm driven food traceability. *Food Control, 105*, 45–51. https://doi.org/10.1016/j.foodcont.2019.05.019
5. Kamilaris, A., Fonts, A., & Prenafeta-Boldύ, F. X. (2019). The rise of blockchain technology in agriculture and food supply chains. *Trends in Food Science and Technology, 91*, 640–652. https://doi.org/10.1016/j.tifs.2019.07.034
6. Kamath, R. (2018). Food traceability on blockchain: Walmart's pork and mango pilots with IBM. *The Journal of the British Blockchain Association, 1*, 3712.
7. Lin, J., Shen, Z., Zhang, A., & Chai, Y. (2018). Blockchain and IoT based food traceability for smart agriculture. In *Proceedings of the 3rd international conference on crowd science and engineering (ICCSE'18)* (pp. 1–6). ACM.
8. Cartier, L. E., Ali, S. H., & Krzemnicki, M. S. (2018). Blockchain, chain of custody and trace elements: An overview of tracking and traceability opportunities in the gem industry. *Journal of Gemmology, 36*, 212–227. https://doi.org/10.15506/JoG.2018.36.3.212
9. Gürkaynak, G., Yılmaz, İ., Yeşilaltay, B., & Bengi, B. (2018). Intellectual property law and practice in the blockchain realm. *Computer Law & Security Review, 34*, 847–862. https://doi.org/10.1016/j.clsr.2018.05.027
10. Malaurie-Vignal, M. (2020). Blockchain, intellectual property and fashion. *Journal of Intellectual Property Law & Practice, 15*, 92–97. https://doi.org/10.1093/jiplp/jpaa009

11. Foth, M. (2017). The promise of blockchain technology for interaction design. In A. Soro, D. Vyas, J. Waycott, B. Ploderer, A. Morrison, & M. Brereton (Eds.), *Proceedings of the 29th Australian computer-human interaction conference (OzCHI 2017)* (pp. 513–517). Association for Computing Machinery.
12. Dunphy, P., & Petitcolas, F. A. P. (2018). A first look at identity management schemes on the blockchain. *IEEE Security Privacy, 16*, 20–29. https://doi.org/10.1109/MSP.2018.3111247
13. Mori, T. (2016). Financial technology: Blockchain and securities settlement. *Journal of Securities Operations & Custody, 8*, 208–227.
14. Oh, J., & Shong, I. (2017). A case study on business model innovations using Blockchain: Focusing on financial institutions. *Asia Pacific Journal of Innovation and Entrepreneurship, 11*, 335–344. https://doi.org/10.1108/APJIE-12-2017-038
15. Fosso Wamba, S., Kala Kamdjoug, J. R., Epie Bawack, R., & Keogh, J. G. (2020). Bitcoin, Blockchain and Fintech: A systematic review and case studies in the supply chain. null, *31*, 115–142. https://doi.org/10.1080/09537287.2019.1631460
16. Nakamoto, S. (2009). Satoshi Nakamoto. Bitcoin: A peer-to-peer electronic cash system. See: https://bitcoin.org/bitcoin.pdf
17. Ghosh, A., & Fedorowicz, J. (2008). The role of trust in supply chain governance. *Business Process Management Journal, 14*, 453–470. https://doi.org/10.1108/14637150810888019
18. Hearn, G., Collie, N., Lyle, P., Choi, J., & Foth, M. (2014). Using communicative ecology theory to scope the emerging role of social media in the evolution of urban food systems. *Futures, 62*, 202–212. https://doi.org/10.1016/j.futures.2014.04.010
19. Powell, W., Foth, M., Cao, S., & Natanelov, V. (2021). Garbage in garbage out: The precarious link between IoT and blockchain in food supply chains. *Journal of Industrial Information Integration, 100261*. https://doi.org/10.1016/j.jii.2021.100261
20. Cao, S., Powell, W., Foth, M., Natanelov, V., Miller, T., & Dulleck, U. (2021). Strengthening consumer trust in beef supply chain traceability with a blockchain-based human-machine reconcile mechanism. *Computers and Electronics in Agriculture, 180*, 105886. https://doi.org/10.1016/j.compag.2020.105886
21. Batwa, A., & Norrman, A. (2021). Blockchain technology and trust in supply chain management: A literature review and research agenda. *Operations and Supply Chain Management: An International Journal, 14*, 203–220. https://doi.org/10.31387/oscm0450297
22. Exon, S. N. (2011). Maximizing technology to establish trust in an online, non-visual mediation setting. U. La Verne L. Rev, *33*(1), 27–41
23. Wrathall, M., & Malpas, J. (Eds.). (2000). *Heidegger, coping, and cognitive science: Essays in honor of Hubert L. Dreyfus* (Vol. 2. 2, 415).
24. Brown, P. R. (2009). The phenomenology of trust: A Schutzian analysis of the social construction of knowledge by gynae-oncology patients. *Health, Risk & Society, 11*, 391–407. https://doi.org/10.1080/13698570903180455
25. Bredlau, S. (2019). On perception and trust: Merleau-Ponty and the emotional significance of our relations with others. *Continental Philosophy Review, 52*, 1–14. https://doi.org/10.1007/s11007-016-9367-3
26. Merleau-Ponty, M. (2004). *The world of perception*. Routledge.
27. Utley, F. (2014). Considerations towards a phenomenology of trust. *Symposium, 18*, 194–214. https://doi.org/10.5840/symposium201418111
28. Spinosa, C., Flores, F., & Dreyfus, H. L. (1997). *Disclosing new worlds: Entrepreneurship, democratic action, and the cultivation of solidarity*. MIT Press.
29. Solomon, R. C., & Flores, F. (2003). *Building trust: In business, politics, relationships, and life*. Oxford University Press.
30. Flores, F. (2000). Heideggerian thinking and the transformation of business practice. In *Heidegger, coping and cognitive science: Essays in honour of Herbert L. Dreyfus* (Vol. 2, pp. 271–291). The MIT Press: Cambridge, Massachusetts, United States.
31. Yuan, Y., Feng, B., Lai, F., & Collins, B. J. (2018). The role of trust, commitment, and learning orientation on logistic service effectiveness. *Journal of Business Research, 93*, 37–50. https://doi.org/10.1016/j.jbusres.2018.08.020

32. Mougayar, W. (2016). *The business blockchain: Promise, practice, and application of the next internet technology*. John Wiley & Sons.
33. Williams, S. P. (2019). *Blockchain: The next everything*. Simon and Schuster.
34. Foth, M., Odendaal, N., & Hearn, G. (2007). The view from everywhere: Towards an epistemology for urbanites. In D. Remenyi (Ed.), *Proceedings ICICKM 2007: 4th international conference on intellectual capital, knowledge management and organisational learning* (pp. 127–134). Academic Conferences Limited.
35. Dourish, P. (2016). Algorithms and their others: Algorithmic culture in context. *Big Data & Society, 3*, 2053951716665128. https://doi.org/10.1177/2053951716665128
36. Hardin, R. (1985). Game theory & the nuclear standoff. *Worldview, 28*, 20–24. https://doi.org/10.1017/S0084255900046660
37. Buterin, V.: Vitalik buterin: On public and private blockchains, (2015).
38. Cutler, T., Hindess, B., Hussain, A., & Hirst, P. Q. (2013). *Marx's capital and capitalism today*. Routledge.
39. Fu, J., Matous, P., & Todō, Y. (2018). *Trade credit in global supply chains*. RIETI.
40. Giovannetti, A. (2016). *Trade credit, bank credit and formation of supply chains: Can banks amplify contagion risk?*https://doi.org/10.2139/ssrn.3301348
41. Singh, A., & Teng, J. T. C. (2016). Enhancing supply chain outcomes through Information Technology and Trust. *Computers in Human Behavior, 54*, 290–300. https://doi.org/10.1016/j.chb.2015.07.051
42. Cao, S., Bryceson, K., & Hine, D. (2020). Improving supply chain risk visibility and communication with a multi-view risk ontology. *Supply Chain Forum: An International Journal, 21*, 1–15. https://doi.org/10.1080/16258312.2020.1717990
43. Murphy, P. (2015). The stranger society: The case of economic and social development in the tropics. *Budhi: A Journal of Ideas and Culture, 19*, 107–134.
44. Davidson, S., Novak, M., & Potts, J. (2018). The cost of trust: A pilot study. The Journal of The British Blockchain Association, *1*(2). https://doi.org/10.31585/jbba-1-2-(5)2018.
45. Foucault, M., Davidson, A. I., & Burchell, G. (2008). *The birth of biopolitics: Lectures at the Collège de France, 1978–1979*. Springer.
46. Williamson, O. E. (1993). Calculativeness, trust, and economic organization. *The Journal of Law and Economics, 36*, 453–486. https://doi.org/10.1086/467284
47. Roth, A. E. (2015). *Who gets what – and why: The new economics of matchmaking and market design*. Houghton Mifflin Harcourt.
48. Sabel, C. F. (1993). Studied trust: Building new forms of cooperation in a volatile economy. *Human Relations; Studies Towards the Integration of the Social Sciences, 46*, 1133–1170. https://doi.org/10.1177/001872679304600907
49. McLaren, T., Head, M., & Yuan, Y. (2002). Supply chain collaboration alternatives: Understanding the expected costs and benefits. *Internet Research, 12*, 348–364. https://doi.org/10.1108/10662240210438416
50. Cao, S., Bryceson, K., & Hine, D. (2019). An ontology-based Bayesian network modelling for supply chain risk propagation. *Industrial Management & Data Systems, 119*, 1691–1711. https://doi.org/10.1108/IMDS-01-2019-0032
51. Dyer, J. H., & Singh, H. (1998). The relational view: Cooperative strategy and sources of interorganizational competitive advantage. *AMRO, 23*, 660–679. https://doi.org/10.5465/amr.1998.1255632
52. Mooney, J. L., & Blodgett, M. S. (1995). Letters of credit in the global economy: Implications for international trade. *Journal of International Accounting, Auditing and Taxation, 4*, 175–183. https://doi.org/10.1016/1061-9518(95)90016-0
53. Alavi, H. (2016). Mitigating the risk of fraud in documentary letters of credit. *TalTech Journal of European Studies, 6*, 139–156. https://doi.org/10.1515/bjes-2016-0006
54. Zhang, Y. (2012). Documentary letter of credit fraud risk management. *Journal of Financial Crime, 19*, 343–354. https://doi.org/10.1108/13590791211266340
55. Letter of Credit Fraud. https://www.fbi.gov/scams-and-safety/common-scams-and-crimes/letter-of-credit-fraud

56. Vulkan, N., Roth, A. E., & Neeman, Z. (2013). *The handbook of market design*. Oxford University Press.
57. Ozcan, S., & Unalan, S. (2020). Blockchain as a general-purpose technology: Patentometric evidence of science, technologies, and actors. *IEEE Transactions on Engineering Management, 1–18*. https://doi.org/10.1109/TEM.2020.3008859
58. Lin, J., Luo, Z., Cheng, X., & Li, L. (2019). Understanding the interplay of social commerce affordances and swift guanxi: An empirical study. *Information & Management, 56*, 213–224. https://doi.org/10.1016/j.im.2018.05.009
59. Ma, W. (2016). *China's mobile economy: Opportunities in the largest and fastest information consumption boom*. Wiley.
60. Niedermeier, K. E., Wang, E., & Zhang, X. (2016). The use of social media among business-to-business sales professionals in China. *Journal of Research in Interactive Marketing, 10*, 33–49. https://doi.org/10.1108/JRIM-08-2015-0054
61. Wang, X. (2016). *Social media in industrial China*. UCL Press.
62. Shao, Z., & Pan, Z. (2019). Building Guanxi network in the mobile social platform: A social capital perspective. *International Journal of Information Management, 44*, 109–120. https://doi.org/10.1016/j.ijinfomgt.2018.10.002
63. Crary, J. (2014). *24/7: Schlaflos im Spätkapitalismus*. Verlag Klaus Wagenbach.
64. Zhang, Z., & Gu, C. (2015). Effects of consumer social interaction on trust in online group-buying contexts: An empirical study in China. *Journal of Electronic Commerce Research, 16*, 1–21.
65. Ye, Q., Feng, Y., Yang, P., Yang, C., & Yang, L. (2019). The influence of gamification mechanics on online group-buying participation, presented at the 25th Americas Conference on Information Systems, AMCIS 2019, Mexico: Cancun.
66. Sigley, G., Powell, W., & Cao, S. (2020). Community group buying, vulnerable communities and COVID-19 in China. In N. Georgeou & C. Hawksley (Eds.), *State responses to COVID-19: A global snapshot at 1 June 2020* (pp. 50–51). Western Sydney University.
67. Zhang, J. J., & Tsai, W.-H. S. (2015). United we shop! Chinese consumers' online group buying. *Journal of International Consumer Marketing, 27*, 54–68. https://doi.org/10.1080/08961530.2014.967902

The Blockchain-Based Digital Certificate for the Transport of Dangerous Goods

Adnan Imeri, Christophe Feltus, Nazim Agoulmine, and Djamel Khadraoui

1 Introduction

The transport of dangerous goods (TDG), also named hazardous goods (e.g., oils, gas, chemical products, radioactive substances, corrosive products, explosives, medical waste), consists in the carriage of goods presenting potential important risks to the people, to material, and/or to the environment, and which necessitates dedicated and specially reinforced security measures therefore. This transport of dangerous goods (TDG) represents an excessively important activity for the countries of the European Union and worldwide, as most member states increase in transport of dangerous goods in the recent years. The highest increase, in EU, was recorded in 2018 and concern Belgium (77.3%), Slovenia (46.7%), Croatia (42.3%), and Finland (36.7%).[1] According to global statistics [1], dangerous goods may constitute about fifty percent of the global transportation in the next years, should it be by road, railway, air, or seas. Compared to traditional transportation e.g., general supply chains, the TDG is a particular class of transportation that is subject to specific requirements among which the human and environmental safety.

[1] https://ec.europa.eu/eurostat/statistics-explained

A. Imeri (✉)
Luxembourg Institute of Science and Technology, Esch-sur-Alzette, Luxembourg

Université of Evry Val d'Essonne, Evry, France
e-mail: adnan.imeri@list.lu

C. Feltus · D. Khadraoui
Luxembourg Institute of Science and Technology, Esch-sur-Alzette, Luxembourg

N. Agoulmine
Université of Evry Val d'Essonne, Evry, France

A. Bouras et al. (eds.), *Blockchain Driven Supply Chains and Enterprise Information Systems*, https://doi.org/10.1007/978-3-030-96154-1_3

It also incorporates rigorous information immutability and the traceability of the DG movement [2], as indicated in the "Agreement concerning the International Carriage of Dangerous Goods by Road" [3] applicable since 1 January 2021.

In this context, this chapter aims to propose a platform to support the verification of the identity, of the history of transportation, and of the location over time of the dangerous goods by means of blockchain-based digital certificate acting as a method for documented recorded identification. The principle of the blockchain is that a specific data is recorded as a series of "blocks" which is distributed over the network and is accessible by users possessing private keys that they use to identify themselves and electronically sign transactions. This "block" also contains (1) hash values that allow verifying the data and (2) a piece of the hash value from the previous block that guarantee traceability and integrity of the information. When users create more data, new blocks are successively added to this block chain and are recorded with ledger-based technology to track transactions but also to ensure accountability.

In parallel, a digital certificate is a credential which allows an organization to identify and share information in a secure way over Internet or other private network by means of a pair of public/private key. Using jointly **blockchain technology** and **digital certificate** in the paper aims to ensure transaction *transparency* thanks to an unalterable record distributed among many users, *easy access* thanks to the collaborative environment that makes it easier for all agents to rapidly access on the transportation information, less *paperwork* thanks to the electronic distribution of data, and especially, *strong users identification* thanks to the digital certificates' credentials. This signifies, by the way, greater gains in efficiency, more streamlined approach at the management level, more reactivity in the treatment of information, and less risks of treatment-based errors.

Besides proposing a blockchain-based digital certificate for the TDG, our approach also analyzes to what extent the blockchain may be specified to integrate and be compatible with the **Internet of Things** (IoT) technology and specifications. IoT for the TDG has been considered as an important technology to move toward the digital society and is capable of supporting intelligent applications such as container information forecasting, container gate-in and gate-out management, fire control, and environmental parameters monitoring [4]. Our platform is fully compatible with the IoT technology and allows leveraging the benefits generated so far.

1.1 Supply Chain Management

The extraordinarily growing globalization of production and the megabit of data generated by the manufacturing and transportation processes have forced industries to set up supply chain management sufficiently autonomous and efficient to support the integration of key business processes from the original suppliers through the end-users [5]. According to [6], nowadays the commonly accepted paradigms of supply chain management are no more appropriate for operating in *data-driven smart manufacturing* and goods transportation, provided the cost and effectiveness impact engendered by the imposed unnecessary constraints on the system. For Li et al. [6], the origin of this problem lies with the lack of structural limitations of the current paradigms, that is., to deal with the massive volume of data emerging at the various stages of production and transportation. This statement is especially relevant for the sector of the TDG, as explained in Sub Section 1.2, provided the overload of information legally required by the governments (e.g., Directive 2008/68/CE, "TMD" decree, Regulation 84-810 and 2003-699, Article L. 5331-2).

1.2 Supply Chain for Dangerous Goods

In this section, we present a study concerning the supply chain of dangerous goods (DGs). Initially, we present the definition of DG, then details of the supply chain of DG highlighting the complexity in the TDG, including the main stakeholders involved in TDG.

Dangerous goods (DGs) are considered as any material or substance or a mixture of substances (gases, liquid, or solids), which exposes potential risks (identified as hazardous) for harming humans, animals, property, and the environment [3]. DGs are classified based on their physical and chemical effects ADR2021. ADR classifies DG in categories such as "Explosives," "Gases," "Flammable liquid," "Flammable solids," "Oxidizing substances and organic peroxides," "Toxic and infectious substances," "Radioactive material," "Corrosive substances," and "Miscellaneous dangerous substances and articles" [3, 7].

The supply chain of DG is complex and belongs to the regulated domains. The complexity originates from the involvement of many regulatory frameworks at the national and international levels. The regulatory framework governs TDG entirely [8]. Table 1 shows the main regulatory frameworks applied in the TDG. In the context of our study, we are mainly focused on road transport of DG as one of the most used transport modes in the supply chain of DG [13].

The TDG requires strict procedures for preparing transportation and its specificity, documentation, and DG treatment. The DG storage, treatment, and reuse or processing (for industrial purposes) refer to the management part of DG. Figure 1, presents the general supply chain for DG. For operation with the DG, various participants are involved, such are "Consignors," "Transporter," "Driver and vehicle crew," "Filler," "Loader," "Unloader," "Consignee," "Tank-operator/portable tank operator," and "DG Safety Advisor." Section 4 of ADR specifies roles (participants) and legal responsibilities for each involved party in TDG [3].

1.3 Research Method

At a methodological level, the research that we tackle concerns the improvement of the traceability in the field of the transport of dangerous goods. Accordingly,

Table 1 International regulatory framework and agreements for TDG, specific to the mode of transport

Mode of transport	Regulatory framework	International organization	Abbrev.
Road (Land)	European Agreement on the International Carriage of Dangerous Goods [3]	UNECE	ADR
Inland Waterway	European Agreement on the international carriage of Dangerous Goods by Inland Waterway Navigation [9]	UNECE	ADN
Rail	Regulation for the International carriage of Dangerous Goods by Rail [10]	OTIF	RID
Sea	International Maritime Dangerous Goods Code [11]	IOM/CCC	IMDG Code
Air	Dangerous Goods Regulations; Technical Instructions For The Safe Transport of Dangerous Goods by Air [12]	ICAO	DGR IACI IT

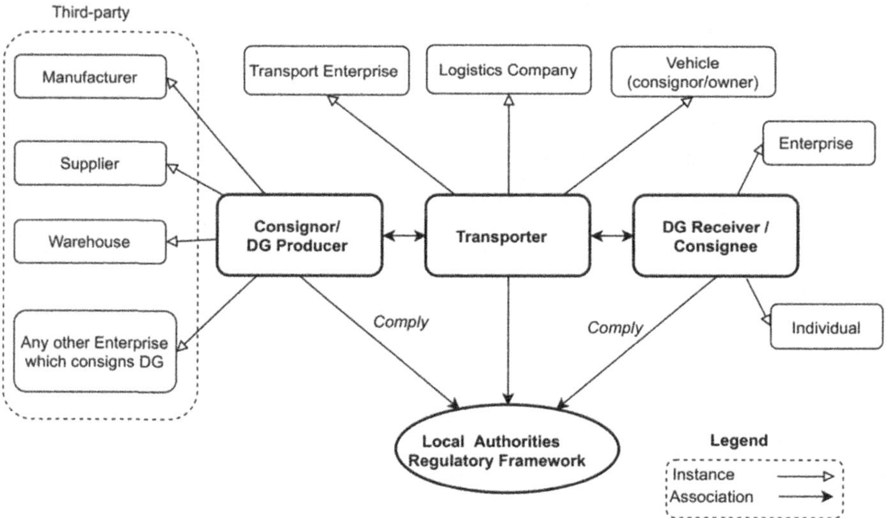

Fig. 1 The involved stakeholders and basic organization of the supply chain for TDG. Inspired from [3]

we have defined and conceptualized a blockchain-based solution that aims to enable following the DG life cycle from its origin (depart point) to destination (processing of DG). Through this research, we strengthen the stakeholders' trust in the TDG chain by raising up the transparency level through the information system which sustains this chain. Accordingly [14], explains that the **Design Science Research (DSR)** paradigm seeks to extend the boundaries of human and organization capability by creating new and innovative artefacts. Practically, provided that we aim to design a new artifact (the BC-based solution) to allow the stakeholder to trust the DG transportation with IT enablers, we acknowledge that this research may plainly be considered in the scope of DSR [15]. As advocated by the DSR theory [14, 15], the method that we use to design this solution is an iterative approach consisting first of analyzing the problem under scope and in defining the requirement for a solution, second of defining and validating the relevant concepts, and third of designing the blockchain-based solution.

Given that our artifact is motivated by real problems and relies on the knowledge of the field, we need to involve practitioners and end-users all along with the artifact-building activities. Therefore, we have applied the design research method proposed by [16]: the Action Design Research method which objective is to strengthen the connections between the end-users (TDG companies) and the researchers by combining the building, intervention, and evaluation (BIE) activities. Given that the elaboration of our artifact strongly relates to the information system, we apply an **IT-Dominant BIE** Generic Schema (Fig. 2). When applied to our research, at step 1, we (researchers) have first performed a workshop to identify the problem of transparency and traceability of DG, in cooperation with the practitioner, that is, The Ministry of Transportation in Luxembourg. The output from this workshop significantly highlights the need to have a platform (solution) that allows "managing" the life cycle of DG in an end-to-end manner. In step 2, we have proposed a conceptual solution for information sharing and traceability related to TDG. The general conceptual solution has been validated by the scientific practitioners in [2, 17]. At step 3, we proposed a BC-based solution (beta version), and at step 4, the proposed solution was presented to the involved stakeholders and end-users and was accepted and supported as the main solution to highlight the transparency in TDG. The components of the solution were published in [7], which proposes blockchain and IoT integration. Finally, at step 5, we plan to extend the solution by integrating it on the main TDG BC-based platform. Finally, according to [18], the evaluation

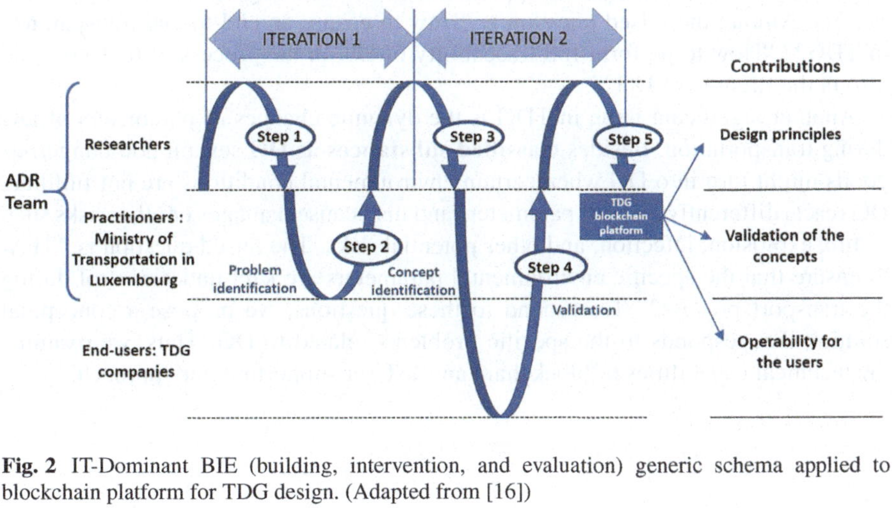

Fig. 2 IT-Dominant BIE (building, intervention, and evaluation) generic schema applied to blockchain platform for TDG design. (Adapted from [16])

of a designed artifact must use precise evaluation criteria. Provided that the goal of our research is to support end-users with an innovative TDG blockchain-based platform, the validation criteria is the operability of this platform, defined in ISO 25010 (SquaRE [19]), that is, the *ability* of the blockchain-based platform to be easily operated by a given user in a given environment. In our context, this given environment consists of the TDG infrastructure operated during the daily activities of the TDG companies. This ultimate validation should be achieved in future works.

The outline of this chapter is organized as follows. Section 2 shows the research motivation and general problem definition. Section 3 presents the main characteristics of blockchain technology. In Sect. 4, we show related works studies. Section 5 shows the conceptual approach for a digital certificate. The proof of concept (PoC) implementation is shown in Sect. 6. Finally, in Sect. 7, we conclude and present our future works.

2 Motivation and Problem Definition

DGs are sensitive and require strict supervision works in order to maintain safety and security. Entirely, the TDG process requires end-to-end transparency and to comply with the regulatory framework (as shown in Fig. 1). Authorities and the involved stakeholders require to know the life cycle of DG, starting from the preparation of DG for transport, the information during the transport, and the definitive treatment of DG. For being able to monitor the TDG, it requires adopting an approach that enhances transparency. This will be achieved with the help of technological means which ensure information immutability, availability, and security [20]. The existing systems, which are largely centralized databases [13], do not have enough technical capabilities to support data immutability and lack of availability since the centralized approach is prone to a single point of failure [7, 8, 13, 21]. Among the raised question is "How to ensure an end-to-end transparency in TDG?" "How to perform full traceability of DG in the process of transport and also in the lifetime of DG?"

Another significant issue in TDG is the dynamic changes of parameters of DG during transportation. Besides **classified substances as DG** several non-dangerous goods might turn into DG when certain environmental conditions are not fulfilled. DG reacts differently on such parameters and may cause damages or other risks such as fire, explosion, infection, and other potential risks. The raised question is, "How to ensure that the specific environmental parameters are kept under control during the transport process?" To respond to these questions, we propose a conceptual solution that responds to the specific problems related to DG. Thus, we examine the technical capabilities of blockchain and IoT for supporting our approach.

3 Background: Blockchain Technology and Its Main Characteristics

Blockchain is a distributed decentralized database that allows storing append-only transaction data. The blockchain network comprises several decentralized nodes that communicate with each other in a peer-to-peer mode. All the nodes included in the blockchain network contain the same ledger, and they rely on communication in distributed nodes, thus avoiding any central authority [22]. The blockchain nodes gather transactions into "blocks." The transactions are initially validated by performing cryptographic checks (public-private key cryptography). The process of adding a new block into blockchain is called "mining," and the nodes that perform this mining are called miners [23]. The miner[2] proposes a new block after performing specific computing power condition [24] or being delegated by other nodes to perform mining [25]. After proposing the new block, it is added to the main ledger chained with the previous block, thus achieving consensus over the transaction state by the majority of involved nodes according to the consensus protocol used, for example, Proof of Work and Proof of Stake [23]. The block of transactions that are stored into the blockchain is immutable, and cryptography tools ensure data integrity [26]. Among the main blockchain fundamental characteristics is that the block of data is linked together, so block N contains the hash address of the previous block N-1 [26, 27]. The tendency to change the information stored into blockchain is denied by consensus protocol which verifies the state of data [22].

The smart contract (SC) is an autonomous computer code encoded to react and support a specific problem [26]. It is deployed on the blockchain and executed based on its specifications to perform a specific task. SC implements a certain level of business logic and, in combination with blockchain technological capabilities, constitutes a powerful tool to solve information-related issues such as transparency, traceability, immutability, availability, and interoperability [17, 26].

4 Related Works Studies

In this section, we present some related works studies toward transparency and traceability in SCM with the help of blockchain and smart contracts.

The research from [28] shows the possible advancements of blockchain technology in operations and supply chain management. It includes enhancing product safety and security, reducing supply chain costs, improving supply chain sustainability, reducing third-party dependencies, and reducing illegal counterfeiting. The research highlights the need for further studying the blockchain technology opportunities for further adaption to supply chain operations. The research in [29]

[2] Different terms are associated with the miner, for example, full node, validator, and backer.

shows a traceability mechanism for the medicine supply chain. The approach intends to trace information from manufacturing to end consumer, which will be retrieved by scanning QR code of medical products. The authorized parties, which are authorized by the regulatory authorities of the medical supply chain, can retrieve this information. This solution, that is, "Medical supply chain" uses permissioned blockchain [30] and has a transaction data structure similar to Bitcoin [31], with a slight difference in encryption of QR code. The research from [32] explores a blockchain-based solution as a proposal to enforce sustainability in supply chain management in terms of worker protection and a safe work environment. The solution intends to respond to the consumer inquiries for social sustainability requested by consumers. It uses blockchain, IoT, and big data analytics to perform traceability from sellers and respond to consumers. The research from [33] shows an approach for digitizing and sharing the vehicles. It intends to solve the issues of vehicle odometer fraud by proposing a blockchain-based solution for storing, managing, and sharing vehicle life cycle information with several stakeholders. Similarly, in [34] a proof of concept is shown for the trading of cars in the "market of lemons[3]". It uses the principal blockchain technology features, and it organizes the research works based on design science research to provide a trustfree platform. In case of any possible error, the research includes the safeguard mechanism in transaction correction for trading in "market of lemons" [17]. The research from [35] presets a product life cycle (PLM) management. It intends to collect and manage information and knowledge to achieve competitiveness. The raised issues are sharing this information among the involved stakeholders, highlighting concerns in inseparability, openness, and decentralization since PLM is mainly implemented in a centralized way. To overcome the mentioned issues, this research proposes a blockchain-based solution integrated with IoT and M2M. In [36], the certificate of provenance for goods is proposed by using blockchain. The research in [37] presents an independent online shipment tracking framework, which intends to complement the current SCM enterprise-based solutions. The research is related to the transportation of goods from supplier to customer, known as the physical distribution phase. The current online shipment solution is considered restricted to all stakeholders, information is provided by a carrier, the sharing of information is done on a needed basis, and it remains a single source of information. The research from [38] presents *originChain*, a traceability system based on BC and smart contracts. This system intends to provide transparent, tamper-proof traceability data, data availability, and also it considers regulatory-compliance aspects by automatically checking them. It is mainly applied to companies that import products to China. It considers the traceability perspectives of the suppliers and retailers. The supplier's traceability perspective is to prove the product origin and quality and regulatory compliance, while the retailer's perspective is on product origin and quality. The *originChain* works as traceability providers, and the stakeholder that needs such a system applies for traceability services. The architecture of *originChain* indicates that the nodes are

[3] Market of Lemons: https://www.investopedia.com/terms/l/lemons-problem.asp

geographically distributed over three different premises and supported by private BC. Data storage aspects in the BC manage several data sources off-chain while storing the hash address of such data on-chain. However, this solution is limited to service providers, and its traceability services are provided following a "contract" signed between parties for the offered traceability services. The research from [39] treats the problem of determining the provenance for the goods in the supply chain. In an inter-organizational and complex supply chain, the physical provenance of goods, for example, pharmaceutic or authentic luxury goods, is not always possible because of technological limitations and the complexity of the supply chain. For solving such issues, this research highlights the potential of BC technology. In combination with IoT and using the ontologies that represent knowledge about provenance and traceability, provenance issues are answered. This research aims to develop an ontology-based BC approach for responding to provenance problems in the supply chain. Using the ontologies is for better data standards and formal specification for automated interfaces, which helps develop a better supply chain. In this context, the TOVE Ontology[4] for fundamental concepts of traceability is used to provide the provenance of goods in SC. Proof of concepts is developed, which uses a "traceable resource unit," an object to be traced from one part to another part of SC [40].

Beyond the current research, our approach presents a dynamic digital certificate for transparency and traceability improvements in the supply chain of DG. It considers dynamic environment parameters retrieved during transportation and warehousing of DG. In the context of our study, the concept of digital certification does not indicate any static issued statement, but indeed it signifies the end-to-end life cycle of specific DG, including all involved stakeholders, processes, and information. We present a concept of a digital certificate associated with a specific TDG process and dynamically maintain changes at the administrative, static (physical level), and dynamic level (environmental data retrieved from the DG surrounding environment). The proposed blockchain-based digital certificate continuously maintains the DG state and remains active until the end of the DG life cycle.

5 Blockchain-Based Digital Certificate for Transparency and Management of TDG

This section shows the conceptual approach for a digital certificate for improving the transparency in transport of DG.

[4] http://www.eil.utoronto.ca/theory/enterprise-modelling/tove/

5.1 Conceptual Approach for Blockchain-Based Digital Certificate

In a single DG lifecycle, the process of transport and management[5] of DG imposes at last three operation phases. The first phase is the "preparation for TDG," the second phase is the "process of transport of DG," and the last phase is the "treatment of DG" which certainly finishes the life cycle of a DG. With the concept of "digital certificate," we intend to maintain traceable information for any DG operational phase. Figure 3 shows the concept of formulation of digital certificate.

At the first phase, that is, "process of transport of DG," the specification and set of information about "authorization" to transport DG are required. Further, the identification of the involved stakeholders and DG physical characteristics need to be provided. That immediately establishes the core of the *digital certificate* which indicates that a specific set of parameters is established (stored) in distributed ledger with the help of SC. In the subsequent phases of the process of TDG, the "same" digital certificate (specific to DG) is continuously "up-dated" (addind a new parameter to the ledger). Following in the second phase, that is, "process of transport of DG" the information about the transport process is continuously captured and immutably stored in the blockchain. The eventual update on DG characteristics, for example, quantities or physical parameters, is evidenced and reported immediately to the responsible stakeholders. Finally, the third stage, that is, "treatment of DG" gathers all the details about the final treatment of DG, which also indicates the end of the DG life cycle.

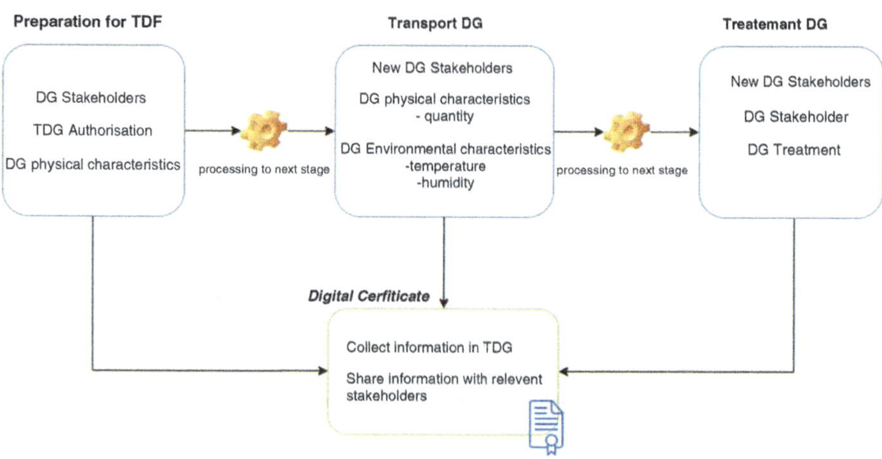

Fig. 3 The concept of the digital certificate from a different process perspective

[5] The term "management" describes storing, maintaining, and processing the DG.

5.2 *Digital Certificate as for the DG*

This section presents the conceptual design of the digital certificate.

The TDG stakeholders, particularly the competent authorities, require surveillance of DG movement across the geographic area under their jurisdiction in and cross-border context. The stakeholders and even the end customers require information for the physical flow of goods from the departure point to the destination point. To have access to a such information, the establishment of a traceability mechanism is required. Traceability is the possibility to track and trace the history, administration, or location of the DG located in the warehouse or during transportation [2]. Tracking and tracing the information of the active and passive processes in the TDG enhances monitoring and auditing aspects. The active traceability makes it possible to know the exact location of the DG that is in transit. The passive traceability enables the inquiry of any possible information regarding the completed process in TDG.

To manage the traceability aspects, we present the concept of *digital certificate.* The *digital certificate* is established at an early TDG planning phase, before transport starts, by gathering the necessary information, as shown in Sect. 3. The *digital certificate* remains valid during and after the transport process. It contains significant information articles for the TDG. Instances of such information includes "ID_DG_Process," "ID_DG_Provider," "ID_DG_Receiver," "ID_DG_Transporter (Sub_Contractors_ID)," "ID_DG_Good," "loading, quantity at departure (or arrival)," "risk level (sensitivity)," "Truck _ID," "Container_ID," "ID_IoT_Devices," and "Timestamp."

Additionally, we introduce the article "ID_IoT_Devices" representing the set of all IoT devices that are part of our TDG control system. The IoT device allows for capturing digital information from physical objects (truck, containers), provides real-time information for the geographic location of DG, and measures the DG state inside the truck. In [7], we presented an extensive study on the integration of blockchain and IoT. Furthermore, the "Container_ID" identifies any container (or other types of the load of DG), while "Truck_ID" presents the identification of the truck that transports the DG. In a single transport process, there might be several trucks involved. The "timestamp" identifies the date and time of any activity involving the DG. The aforementioned information articles remain available and are updated during the process flow. New values are captured and appended in the *digital certificate* articles based on "local information push" and "real-time" information flow. At any time, the authorized stakeholders may retrieve the *digital certificate* with all the information during an end-to-end process. The information retrieval is further shown in the Merkle-tree style (BC data structure). At a high-level view, the *digital certificate* concept presents a virtual *sub-ledger* formed from the global ledger. It presents an interactive component that allows new information articles to be added based on the need for that information. We propose using SC to gather and store this information as a segregated sub-ledger, maintaining the transaction history for an end-to-end process.

Figure 4 illustrates the concepts of a *digital certificate* in an end-to-end transport. As shown here, the certificate is established with significant information articles

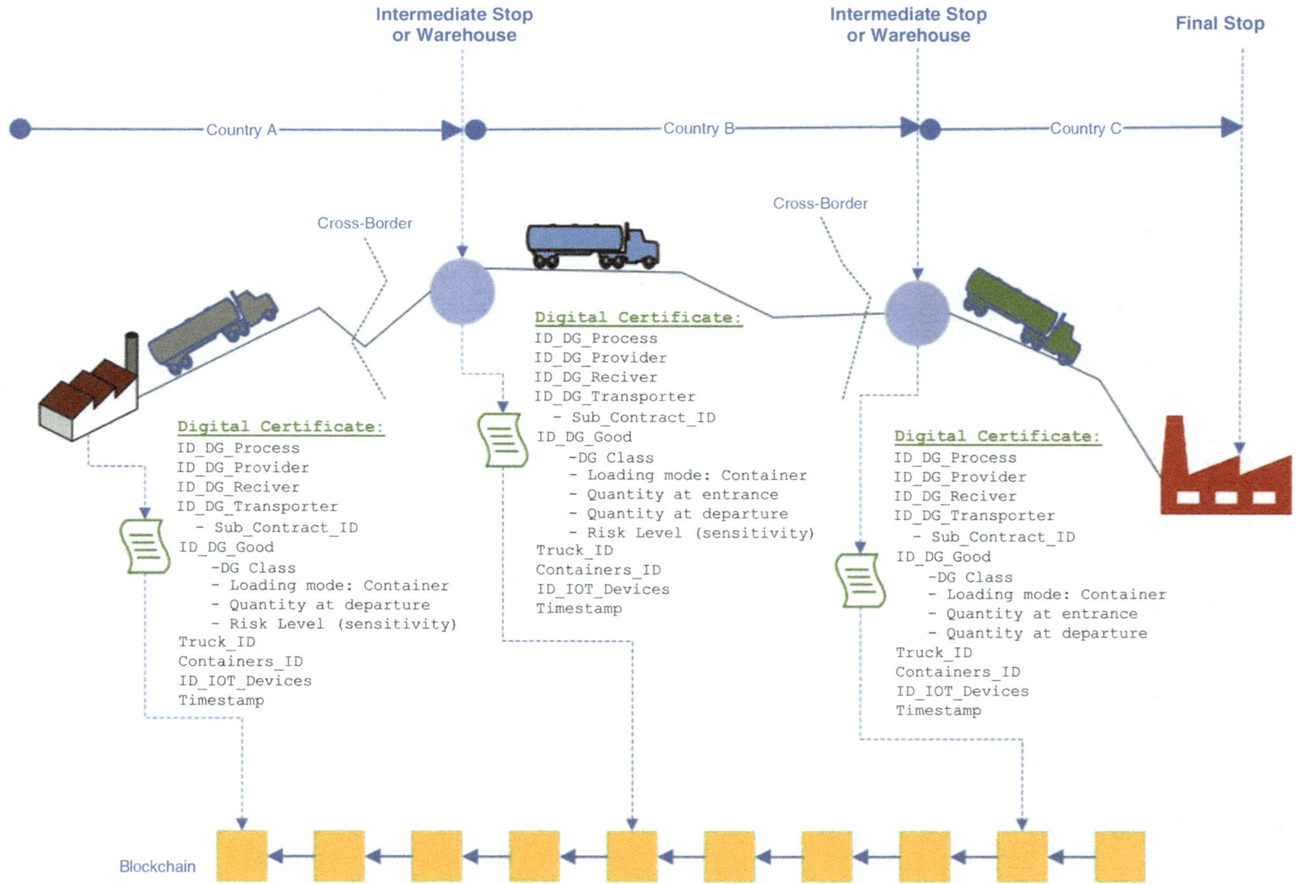

Fig. 4 The concept of digital certificate for digital traceability and management of DG

at the departing point in the transport process. It gathers previous information known from the certification of the stakeholder process and authorization and combines additional detailed information for the transport process. There might be intermediate stops[6] during the transport process in different countries (e.g., from country A to country B). At any entry on the intermediate stop, the *digital certificate* is updated with the last (on the push and real-time) information. The intermediate stop might play the role of warehousing the DG, meaning that the transport will not continue immediately, and the DG received remains stored there for a certain time. The *digital certificate* remains open for this process, identified by articles "ID DG Process." After a certain time, the same DG may be moved to another warehouse or directly to the destination point. It uses the same *digital certificate* to continue the process and update it accordingly.

We formally present some parameters, that is, quantity that we consider continuously in the *digital certificate* with the help of SC.

Consider we have the set of DG noted D.

$$(\forall d \in D)\,(\exists\, quantity\,(d) = \epsilon) \xrightarrow{transportation} (\forall d \in D)\,\big(\exists\, quantity\,(d) = \big(\epsilon' \vee \epsilon\big) \wedge \big(\epsilon \neq \epsilon'\big)\big) \tag{1}$$

In the Eq. (1), the ϵ signifies DG quantity (ϵ' - different quantity). After transporting and warehousing DG, the quantity may differ from its initial measure. This signifies that either the DG is separate in other quantities or used partially (if the warehouse is the destination point). The *digital certificate* calculates these quantities and keeps the ledger updated. Even in the situation in which the separated part is transported to other stakeholders (may be located in other countries), which might be repeated several times (by subcontracting other certified transporters), it still keeps that information until the end of the life cycle of the DG. That highlights aspects of monitoring and control for DG, even if they are separated into smaller quantities. The final step on the digital certificate counts k-parts as the sum of entire quantity of DG ($\epsilon = \epsilon_1, \epsilon_2, \ldots, \epsilon_k$, thus $\epsilon = \sum_i^k \epsilon_i$) from its departure until its treatment. Formally and empirically, that is the first indication that the DG is treated according to the regulatory framework and not misused (thrown in open land or sea).

The digital representation of DG and its characteristics through *digital certificate* enhance the management aspect in TDG. We refer to the ability to manage some characteristics of DG digitally as *digital management*. The *digital management* aspects provide stakeholders with extensive information for the current capacity, type, and related storage information for the DG in the warehouse. Based on that information, they might decide if they possibly host additional quantities of the DG or not. Furthermore, the digital information for the DG distributed in several warehouses allows stakeholders to have the most relevant information about their DG capacities circulation under their ownership. In the context of *digital*

[6] Contrary to the warehouse where DG is stored for a longer time, the intermediate stop is used for driver exchange or rest, and in terms of time, it takes several minutes until to H hours.

management, the information is received digitally. Unlike paper-based approaches, we measure the temperature (or humidity) of the arriving DG and write it on paper. In the paper-based approach, after a certain time, there is not only the disadvantage of one-time temperature measures on arrival, but also there is no mechanism to prove that the temperature was as it is written on the paper. Moreover, there is no way to return on that particular day (or hour) and verify the process flow with empirical data. The *digital management* provides digital information in the end-to-end process. Monitoring the state of DG is during the entire end-to-end process enhances quality control aspects and improves the management aspects of the process, and in addition, it can be verified at any time. Awareness of the current location of the DG and its condition is managed through the TDG control system. This tracking and tracing feature allows quick response in case of emergencies identified autonomously by the IoT devices or by manual alerting (by information push). In both cases, the system provides information to the involved authorities and the emergency response teams.

6 Proof of Concept (PoC): Smart Contract for Digital Certificate

This section aims to show details of the initial proof of concept (PoC) implementation for blockchain-based *digital certificate.*

To evaluate our approach, we used Hyperledger Fabric (HF) Go Lang SDK [41] for implementing the PoC. Our approach proposes a collaborative architecture that allows different stakeholders to join the network and share information based on their operations in TDG. This architecture enables future prospective stakeholders to join the network continuously. To achieve that, we deploy HF-based architecture, which further allows us to develop TDG system components. In this solution, we assume that all the involved stakeholders are allowed to access all information. Thus, we share all this information in a single channel, named *"Global Channel TDG."* Figure 5 shows the architectural organization of the proposed solution. The network is composed at last of four blockchain nodes (knows as *peers* in HF jargon), that is, "DG Receiver," "DG Transporter," "DG Provider," and "Authorities." These nodes use the *"Global Channel TDG"* as a communication channel to exchange information for TDG.

To draw attention to the business logic of the *digital certificate*, we developed SC called *SC_Digital_Certificate.* It is installed (deployed) in the *"Global Channel TDG,"* operates actively on the shared channel, and collects information according to the TDG process stage. Collecting and sharing a particular set of information, the *SC_Digital_Certificate* formalizes a mini-ledger for each DG, thus composing the *digital certificate.* Listing 1.1 presents a small code partition of the *SC_Digital_Certificate,* while the complete code is shown in [42].

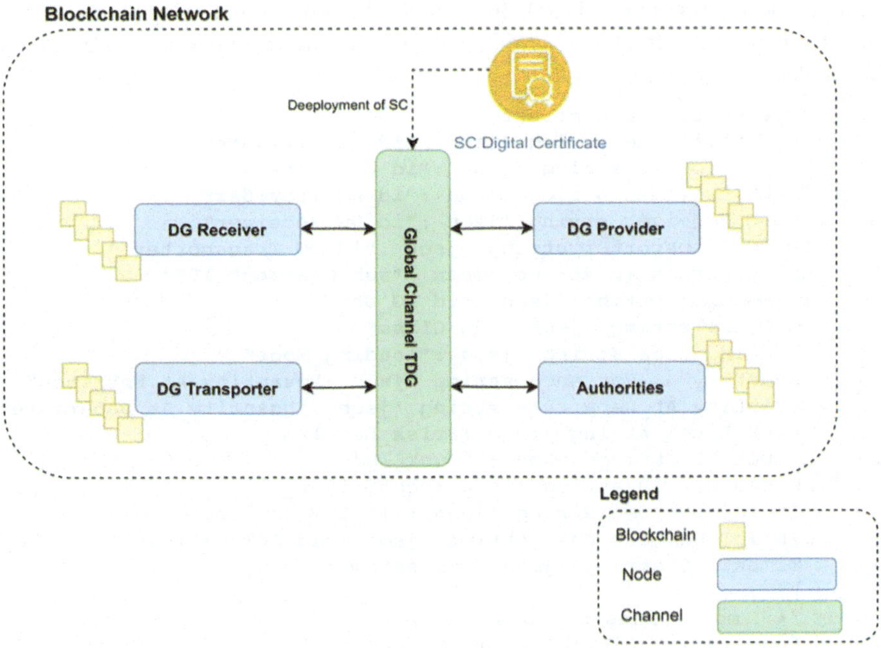

Fig. 5 The network of BC-based stakeholders in TDG

For accessing and testing the digital certificate SC, we have specified an API[7] which enables us to interact with the *digital certificate.* This interaction allows us to retrieve the information that is listed in the *digital certificate.* Listing 1.2 shows the information retrieved from the *digital certificate* in JSON format. The components "id_Certificate":ID_0006101 identifies uniquely the *digital certificate* for curtain DG (or process, identified "id_DG_Process":ID_DG_0011658. In an end-to-end process, the information received is continuously added in the *digital certificate* parameters, thus forming a completed ledger of transaction related to a specific DG associated with a specific process, that is, "id_DG_Process":ID_DG_0011658. The information stored in the digital certificate also serves as a referential point for the other SCs, which are complementarily implemented to support the TDG system. For example, by receiving the information from IoT devices, in case of the temperature, for example, "id IoT Temp Data": +33.11 °C passes the risk level "risk-Level":T + 31 °C, then another SC is triggered to notify the relevant stakeholders for a possibly disastrous situation. Similarly, it maintains trace on the quantity of DG in the departure point, that is, "quantity_At_Departure":6.5 liters/ton, then it checks the quantity at "quantity_At_Entrance" in the warehouse

[7] Application programming interface for GO: https://github.com/hyperledger/fabric-contract-api-go

of at the destination point. That helps to audit the process and being aware of how the DG are distributed among several stakeholders for treatment or are treated at a single destination point.

```
type Certificate struct {
ID_Certificate string 'json :"id_Certificate"'
ID_DG_Process string 'json :"id_DG_Process"'
ID_DG_Provider string 'json :"id_DG_Provider"'
ID_DG_Receiver string 'json :"id_DG_Receiver"'
ID_DG_Transporter string 'json :"id_DG_Transporter"'
Sub_Contract_ID string 'json :"sub_Contract_ID"'
ID_DG_Good string 'json :"id_DG_Good"'
DG_Class string 'json :"dg_Class"'
 Loading_Mode string 'json :"loading_Mode"'
 Quantity_At_Entrance string 'json :"quantity_At_Entrance"'
 Quantity_At_Departure string 'json :"quantity_At_Departure"'
 Risk_Level string 'json :"risk_Level"'
 Truck_ID string 'json :"truck_ID"'
 Container_ID string 'json :"container_ID"'
 ID_IoT_Devices string 'json :"id_IoT_Devices"'
 ID_IoT_Devices_Data string 'json :"id_IoT_Devices"'
 Timestamp string 'json :"timestamp"'
 }
 /*...more lines of code ... */
 func (s *SC_CERTIFICATE) CreateCertificate(ctx contractapi.
  TransactionContextInterface, certificate string) (string,
 error){

 var dg_process_certificate Certificate

 /*...more lines of code ... */

 if process_certificate != nil {
 fmt.Printf("the certificate already exist with ID %s",
 dg_process_certificate.ID_Certificate)
 return "The certificate already exists", err
 }
 /*...more lines of code ...*/

 func (s *SC_CERTIFICATE) UpdateCertificate(ctx contractapi.
TransactionContextInterface ,certificate_updated string) error {

 /*... more lines of code ... */
```

Listing 1.1 The short representation of code for SC Digital Certificate


```
{"id_Certificate":"ID_0006101",
"id_DG_Process":"ID_DG_0011658",
"id_DG_Provider":"Esch Hospital",
"id_DG_Receiver":"EcoGroup Swiss",
"id_DG_Transporter":"AGI Transport Group",
"sub_Contract_ID":"--",
"id_DG_Good":"DG611768",
"dg_Class":"6.1",
"loading_Mode":"container",
```

```
    "quantity_At_Departure":"6.5 liters/ton",
    "quantity_At_Entrance":"6.5 liters/ton",
    "risk_Level":"T+31C",
    "truck_ID":"TR006987",
    "container_ID":"CO698774",
    "id_IoT_Temp":"TempIoT:DHT11DG",
    "id_IoT_Temp_Data":"+20.17C",
    "id_IoT_Location":"EM-506RE"
    "id_IoT_Location_Data":"49.497509, 5.982500"
    "timestamp":"14/05/2021 17:01:12"}
```

Listing 1.2 The representation of the digital certificate in JSON format

7 Conclusion and Future Works

Transparency and traceability are critical properties in numerous supply chains. Similarly, in TDG, transparency is highly required from the involved stakeholders, particularly from the authorities as the responsible party to govern this process. In this work, we present the concept of the digital certificate, which enables storing and maintain information for an end-to-end TDG. The digital certificate proposes an active and dynamic mini-ledger that allows continuous monitoring of the DG state. In TDG, there are specific parameters (temperature, humidity) that need to be kept under control to avoid adverse situations. We propose a blockchain-based digital certificate to maintain the TDG process and actively update its state according to the information received from IoT devices or stakeholders. The proposed digital certificate is dynamic, and it is associated with a specific DG, thus enabling the digital management of DG. The dynamicity remains on selection, sharing, and triggering other events with the help of different SC. At the TDG process run-time, collecting this information in real-time enables monitoring the TDG process by responsible stakeholders. The digital certificate enables TDG process audit, thus at any time, the relevant (authorized) stakeholders in TDG can request specific information to verify the correctness of the process.

In the actual pandemic of COVID-19 [43], safe transportation of vaccine is crucial. The issue with the COVID-19 vaccine transportation is the maintenance of low-rate temperature degree, which may expose several risks if the temperature is not maintained in the range of "normality." In such a situation, to improve transparency, it must have real-time information that remains immutable during the end-to-end process. Thus, the digital certificate would add value to improving transparency since the received real-time information remains immutable.

We consider the proposed approach a contribution to the transparency in supply chain by storing almost dynamically information on the blockchain. In future works, we intend to extend the operation scale of our approach by extending the number of involved stakeholders and providing large-scale IoT devices.

References

1. Lukasik, Z., Kúsmińska-Fija'lkowska, A., & Kozyra, J. (2017). Transport of dangerous goods by road from a European aspect. *Zeszyty Naukowe. Transport/Politechnika Slaska.*
2. Imeri, A., & Khadraoui, D. (2018). The security and traceability of shared information in the process of transportation of dangerous goods. In *2018 9th IFIP International Conference on New Technologies, Mobility and Security (NTMS)*, 1–5. IEEE.
3. U. N. E. C. for Europe (UNECE). (2020, Nov 19). Agreement concerning the international carriage of dangerous goods by road (ADR 2021). In *European Agreement Concerning the International Carriage of Dangerous Goods by Road (ADR).*
4. Ding, L., Chen, Y., & Li, J. (2016). Monitoring dangerous goods in container yard using the internet of things. *Scientific Programming*, 1–25.
5. Mentzer, J. T., et al. (2001). Defining supply chain management. *Journal of Business Logistics, 22*(2), 1–25.
6. Li, Q., & Liu, A. (2019). Big data driven supply chain management. *Procedia CIRP, 81*, 1089–1094.
7. Imcri, A., Agoulminc, N., & Khadraoui, D. (2020). Blockchain and IoT integrated approach for a trusted and secured process to manage the transportation of dangerous goods. *Revista de Sistemas e Computaç ão-RSC, 10*(1), 26–41.
8. Imeri, A., Khadraoui, A., & Khadraoui, D. (2017). A conceptual and technical approach for transportation of dangerous goods in compliance with regulatory framework. *JSW, 12*(9), 708–721.
9. European agreement concerning the international carriage of dangerous goods by inland waterways: (ADN) including the annexed regulations, applicable as from 1 January 2017. volume 1: OCLC: 992936978.
10. RID. Intergovernmental organisation for international carriage by rail (RID). (2019, Jan). https://otif.org/en/?pageid=1105. Accessed on 02/15/2020.
11. OTIF. International martime organization (imdg) code. (2019, Jan). https://www.iata.org/en/publications/dgr/. Accessed on 02/15/2020.
12. IATA. (2017, Jan). Dangerous goods regulations. https://www.iata.org/en/publications/dgr/. Accessed on 02/15/2020.
13. Torretta, V., Rada, E. C., Schiavon, M., & Viotti, P. (2017). Decision support systems for assessing risks involved in transporting hazardous materials: A review. *Safety Science, 92*, 1–9.
14. Hevner, A. R., March, S. T., Park, J., & Ram, S. (2004). Design science in information systems research. *MIS Quarterly*, 75–105.
15. Peffers, K., Tuunanen, T., Rothenberger, M. A., & Chatterjee, S. (2007). A design science research methodology for information systems research. *Journal of Management Information Systems, 24*(3), 45–77.
16. Sein, M. K., Henfridsson, O., Purao, S., Rossi, M., & Lindgren, R. (2011). Action design research. *MIS quarterly,* 37–56.
17. Imeri, A., Agoulmine, N., Feltus, C., & Khadraoui, D. (2019). Blockchain: Analysis of the new technological components as opportunity to solve the trust issues in supply chain management. In *Intelligent Computing-Proceedings of the Computing Conference* (pp. 474–493). Springer.
18. March, S. T., & Smith, G. F. (1995). Design and natural science research on information technology. *Decision Support Systems, 15*(4), 251–266.
19. de Noimalizacio'n, O. I. (2011). ISO-IEC 25010: 2011 systems and software engineering systems and software quality requirements and evaluation (SQuaRE)-system and software quality models. *ISO.*
20. Feltus, C., Khadraoui, D., De Remont, B., & Rifaut, A. (2007). Business governance based policy regulation for security incident response. *Crisis, 7.*
21. Imeri, A., Agoulmine, N., & Khadraoui, D. (2019). A secure and smart environment for the transportation of dangerous goods by using blockchain and IOT devices. In *7th International Workshop on ADVANCEs in ICT Infrastructures and Services (ADVANCE 2019),* 1–8.

22. Zheng, Z., Xie, S., Dai, H.-N., Chen, X., & Wang, H. (2018). Blockchain challenges and opportunities: A survey. *International Journal of Web and Grid Services, 14*(4), 352–375.
23. Antonopoulos, A. M. (2014). *Mastering bitcoin: Unlocking digital cryptocurrencies*. O'Reilly Media, Inc.
24. Nguyen, G.-T., & Kim, K. (2018). A survey about consensus algorithms used in blockchain. *Journal of Information Processing Systems, 14*(1), 101–128.
25. Bouraga, S. (2021). A taxonomy of blockchain consensus protocols: A survey and classification framework. *Expert Systems with Applications, 168*, 114384.
26. Xu, X., Weber, I., Staples, M., Zhu, L., Bosch, J., Bass, L., Pautasso, C., & Rimba, P. (2017). A taxonomy of blockchain-based systems for architecture design. In *2017 IEEE international conference on software architecture (ICSA)*, 243–252. IEEE.
27. Nofer, M., Gomber, P., Hinz, O., & Schiereck, D. (2017). Blockchain. *Business & Information Systems Engineering, 59*(3), 183–187.
28. Cole, R., Stevenson, M., & Aitken, J. (2019). Blockchain technology: Implications for operations and supply chain management. *Supply Chain Management: An International Journal*, 469–483. https://eprints.lancs.ac.uk/id/eprint/131605/
29. Kumar, R. & Tripathi, R. (2019). Traceability of counterfeit medicine supply chain through blockchain. In *2019 11th International Conference on Communication Systems & Networks (COMSNETS)*, 568–570. IEEE.
30. Helliar, C. V., Crawford, L., Rocca, L., Teodori, C., & Veneziani, M. (2020). Permissionless and permissioned blockchain diffusion. *International Journal of Information Management, 54*, 102136.
31. Nakamoto, S. (2019). Bitcoin: A peer-to-peer electronic cash system. Technical report, Manubot.
32. Venkatesh, V., Kang, K., Wang, B., Zhong, R. Y., & Zhang, A. (2020). System architecture for blockchain based transparency of supply chain social sustainability. *Robotics and Computer-Integrated Manufacturing, 63*, 101896.
33. Brousmiche, K. L., Heno, T., Poulain, C., Dalmieres, A., & Hamida, E. B. (2018). Digitizing, securing and sharing vehicles life-cycle over a consortium blockchain: Lessons learned. In *2018 9th IFIP international conference on new technologies, mobility and security (NTMS)*, 1–5. IEEE.
34. Notheisen, B., Cholewa, J. B., & Shanmugam, A. P. (2017). Trading real-world assets on blockchain. *Business & Information Systems Engineering, 59*(6), 425–440.
35. Liu, X., Wang, W., Guo, H., Barenji, A. V., Li, Z., & Huang, G. Q. (2020). Industrial blockchain based framework for product lifecycle management in industry 4.0. *Robotics and Computer-Integrated Manufacturing, 63*, 101897.
36. Martin, M. First ever European certificate of origin through blockchain — business west. https://www.businesswest.co.uk/blog/first-ever-european-certificate-origin-through-blockchain, 06 2018. Accessed on 05/08/2021.
37. Wu, H., Li, Z., King, B., Ben Miled, Z., Wassick, J., & Tazelaar, J. (2017). A distributed ledger for supply chain physical distribution visibility. *Information, 8*(4), 137.
38. Lu, Q., & Xu, X. (2017). Adaptable blockchain-based systems: A case study for product traceability. *IEEE Software, 34*(6), 21–27.
39. Kim, H. M., & Laskowski, M. (2018). Toward an ontology-driven blockchain design for supply-chain provenance. *Intelligent Systems in Accounting, Finance and Management, 25*(1), 18–27.
40. Imeri, A., Khadraoui, D., & Agoulmine, N. (2019). Blockchain technology for the improvement of SCM and logistics services: A survey. In *Industrial engineering in the big data era* (pp. 349–361). Springer.
41. Fabric, H. Introduction — hyperledger-fabricdocs main documentation. https://hyperledger-fabric.readthedocs.io/en/latest/blockchain.html. Accessed on 05/09/2021.
42. Imeri, A. Smart contract codes. https://git.list.lu/adnan_imeri/thesisaimeri/-/blob/master/SmartContractCodes/SC_Digital_Certificate_DG. Accessed on 05/14/2021.
43. County-Level COVID-19 Vaccination coverage and social vulnerability — united states, December 14, 2020–March 1, 2021. https://www.ncbi.nlm.nih.gov/pmc/articles/PMC7993557/. Accessed on 05/15/2021.

An ERP and Planning System Enabled Decentralized Supply Chain Using Blockchain Technology

Arnab Banerjee

1 Introduction

Supply chain is the vital link in any organization that controls the relationship of demand and supply through the coordination of manufacturer, supplier, logistics provider, and customer. The goal of any supply chain is to deliver greater value to end customer, most economically in the shortest possible time with the best possible quality. Supply chain is an established and essential business process that connects a customer's requirement with a supplier through a channel of manufacturer or distributor. There is a tremendous focus to rationalize and improve supply chain processes in the current pandemic situation. To better serve a customer and meet their service level expectations, the supply chain needs to be extremely agile and adaptable, while to be economical, it must be lean. To balance this regime of being agile while being lean has led to many supply chain strategies. Some of the renowned strategies are postponement strategy, adoption of information technology, manufacturing focused strategies, building resiliency and redundancy, adoption of many optimization techniques, and geography-specific strategy like where to manufacture and where to stock or distribute. Due to all these, the supply chain has become increasingly global in the last 20 years. The focus of manufacturing has moved to low-cost economies of Asia, while consumer market and distribution are closer to customers in North America and Europe. This has resulted in a skewed supply chain with a global appeal and complex decision-making process. Today, the supply chain is distributed with an intricate network and lot of dependencies. The time for decision making is becoming an increasing important factor to effectively serve customer at right time with right cost.

A. Banerjee (✉)
Global Supply Chain, Micron Technology, Hyderabad, Telangana, India

A. Bouras et al. (eds.), *Blockchain Driven Supply Chains and Enterprise Information Systems*, https://doi.org/10.1007/978-3-030-96154-1_4

As per the United Nations Conference on Trade and Development (UNCTAD), there are more than 80,000 active multinational companies (*this is as per UNCTAD report of 2006*) [1]. UNCTAD defines a company as multinational if 10% of its revenue is generated outside of the home country. So, the multinational has businesses globally and is generally large corporates. Large corporations have many divisions, product lines, and geography of business, and most of the time, they are all interrelated. Simply stated, these business divisions working independently lead to a decentralized supply chain (DSC), while a central team or division deciding for the entire chain is a centralized supply chain.

Among the various strategies adopted in supply chain, there has been a lot of research on the centralization and decentralization of supply chain. Though there are certain advantages of centralization as well as for decentralization, there is no clear winner. Some well-known companies like HP decided to decentralize the supply chain structure, while Office Depot decided to centralize a previously decentralized supply chain organization [2]. This chapter relooks at the business processes in decentralized supply chain and the challenges it faces in its processes with the adoption of ERP and planning systems. Further, it examines the use and adoption of technology to solve and improve the decentralized supply chain operations.

2 Centralized and Decentralized Global Supply Chain

The supply chain construct began with the centralization as the default realm. The authority and decision-making power lied with few in the entire organization. The centralized decision making is entitled to take decision for all supply chain partners [3]. The centralized supply chain is global in nature, product-wise it could be highly diversified with multiple zones and hubs but the operation is centrally controlled. For example, consider a globalized company that has multiple subassembly plants and a final assembly plant before product is shipped to end customer. The subassembly plants will have their own supply chain with its distribution network, manufacturing operations, customer management, and suppliers. Similarly, final assembly plant will have its own supply chain with its distribution network, manufacturing operations, customer management, and suppliers, or there may be contract manufacturer as well in the network of the supply chain. But all decisions are driven by one central supply chain team which in most cases is based on the final assembly plant or corporate head office.

There are certain forces, market needs, and business reasons for decentralization of supply chain. The market demands for product variety and product mix, the low human labor costs in specific locations, the need for speed to react to customer, the constant eroding of margins, need for specific talents, evolution of Information and Communication Technologies enabling information exchange, and political forces are the principal reasons toward globalization and decentralization.

In a decentralized supply chain, the decision making is housed in the entity facing the immediate customer and managing its supply chain. In a way, it independently

Table 1 Comparison of centralized and decentralized supply chain

Centralized supply chain		Decentralized supply chain	
Pros	Cons	Pros	Cons
Standardized systems and processes	Limited to geographic talent	Better service to customer. Better service level	Lesser bargaining power and economy of scale
Company culture is consistent	Cost ineffective (no cost advantage)	Extremely agile	Reduced control on culture
Better and consistent visibility	Agility and nimbleness is a challenge	Reduced cost operations due to localized effort	Visibility challenges
Leaner supply chain compared to decentralized	Reduced service levels	Better ability to handle market-specific product	Lesser control on operations
Lower logistics spend	Lesser ability to handle market-specific product	Better customer trust and customer relevance	Increased logistics spend
Better control on operations	Reduced supply chain velocity	Increased supply chain velocity	

manages the demand, supply, and resources. The decision making is localized for each area or entity. In the previous quoted example of the globalized company with multiple subassembly plans and a final assembly plant, the decision making is at individual plant managing the supply chain. In a way in the entire supply chain of subassembly plants, final assembly plant, contract manufacturer, and distributors, every entity owns plans and manages it themselves. Based on experience and study, the author has prepared a comparison of centralized and decentralized supply chain. Table 1 shows the comparison with pros and cons.

Centralized global supply chain is an ideal scenario. In today's world with globally spread supply chain where sourcing of products is from all over the world, manufacturing being very Asia centric and distribution being closer to end customer an ideal centralized supply chain is far from being reality. Today, almost all multinational companies with global operations follow a decentralized supply chain.

2.1 Challenges in Decentralized Global Supply Chain

There are numerous challenges facing a decentralized supply chain today. It can range from taking an appropriate and informed decision, local optimized performance, attaining global optimal performance, and serving the best to end customer to name a few. In this section, we study such challenges.

The challenges are studied in two folds. The first step is to review the published literatures and identify the problems discussed therein which are still not appropriately solved. A further synthesis and analysis of these challenges are provided with practical examples. Then (second) the author shares the challenges he came across in his experience related to this area which are not having appropriate published literature. The literature review was carried out to understand, analyze, and prepare taxonomy of the issues as per the researchers in decentralized supply chain across the world. Table 2 shows the taxonomy of the challenges in decentralized global supply chain.

In the published problems in Table 2, there are certain aspects which are not clearly highlighted. Ψ1For example, in forecast-related problems, readers will assume that there are techniques available like CPFR or customer forecast generation which should solve the problem of forecasting. But with pandemic hitting the world, the dependency of people became an equal factor. With the aspect of digital information, independence from human effort became immensely important. With most of the transactions going online, the real-time availability of transparent data, which can be trusted and transaction being non-repudiated, became very important. These cannot be solved by traditional CPFR techniques or EDI mechanisms. Due to the introduction of e-commerce and hypersonic fast supply chains, the demand shaping methodology is changing. The supply feed is turning in daily and which is being changed in to an everyday demand sensing and demand shaping process. This is leading to extreme agile and customer savvy supply chain owing to the digital age of buying and selling. This needs an unprecedented level of demand and supply transparency which is not possible with traditional techniques of CPFR. The need for data is far more real time, accurate, and trustworthy. These are some of the aspects not possible with CPFR. Ψ2Similarly, inventory remains a key focus area for every company. No one wants to store unwanted inventory, neither do they want to lock their capital. Every company wants to hedge its risk but want the availability when required. That's why concepts of bonded inventory, vendor managed inventory, and supplier consigned are very popular. Most of these use EDI as the technique of communication apart from emails. The need of the hour is to establish a continuous, trustworthy, transparent system which is not highlighted by these researches.

Review of the published literature brings out a very strong similarity among the problems discussed in the listed papers. All the published research papers build a mathematical model to solve a specific problem which is noteworthy, achievable, very appropriate and helps optimize the supply chain. But in all the cases, it leaves out the softer aspects like that of trust among the entities, information sharing risk, human aspects of information, real-time visibility of information, trust of data, availability of data, standardization of data, variability in data and allied challenges related to these. In some cases, it is noted as an assumption and asked to be treated separately. Another aspect which came up very clearly in these paper reviews is that in many of the cases, there are assumptions that decisions made are completely rational, informed, and devoid of any human behavioral impacts. Realistically, there is not much research done which touches on these aspects, namely:

Table 2 Taxonomic analysis of challenges in decentralized supply chain

Decentralized supply chain challenges		
Groupings	Description	References
Information delays and synchronization issues	Cases of information delay and information loss due to decentralization. Information synchronization and distortion is a known issue in decentralized supply chain	[4, 5]
Organizational barriers, collaboration issues, and decision making	Collaboration challenges among partners due to lack of transparency and visibility. Managerial decisions get challenged from one partner organization to another. Decision making is slow and gets challenged Organizational barriers of material control and cash flow are a significant challenge in decentralized global supply chain	[6, 7]
Challenges in manufacturing and material flow	Collaborative production network Risk in global transportation Coordinating manufacturing complexity Controlling cost Optimizing or trade-off between cost, quality, and flexibility	[8]
Challenges in supplier development	Geography-specific supplier development Development of competing suppliers in different geographies Supplier trust to discourage any chance of opportunistic expropriation	[9]
Challenges in forecasting Ψ1	Sharing of information among various entities which is required to generate an accurate forecast Challenges in confidential policies Challenges in data reliability and standardization Lack of information system's compatibility Increased risk of demand uncertainty	[10]
Supply planning challenges	Local optimization vis-à-vis a global optimization Sharing unreliable/inflated numbers Local constraints playing a role Sharing partial information about things and entities which determine a good supply plan	[11]
Challenges in inventory management Ψ2	Inventory synchronization Optimizing the inventory holding cost across entities for a global supply chain optimization (not driven by individual entity optimization/profit) Replenishment order synchronization Time coordination of decisions and information sharing	[12]
Supply chain risk	Misalignment of incentives between suppliers and buyers Competition among suppliers Competition among buyers Asymmetric information among supply chain parties	[13]
Bullwhip effects	Amplification or stock out of inventory Negative impact on customer service Huge variance in inventory holdings	[14]

(continued)

Table 2 (continued)

Decentralized supply chain challenges		
Groupings	Description	References
Challenges in profit sharing and intercompany accounting	The idea of profit sharing for the global optimization of supply chain is not widely practiced The intercompany accountings are generally not shared and transparency in those is missing	Author's experience
Trust and decision-making issues	The element of trust is highly sensitive in decentralized supply chain	Author's experience
Information transparency issues	Entities with companies or entities across companies though being supply chain partners are not open to share facts, information, and data	Author's experience
Inventory visibility issues	Providing visibility of entity's own inventory is highly sensitive and most of the organizations are not open to this concept	Author's experience

1. How will information be made available seamlessly across supply chain entities?
2. How do we factor in the element of trust in information availability?
3. How to bring the aspect of rationality in information availability and how can these be tied back to decisions made?
4. How to remove the information misalignment to facilitate a sound and rational decision?
5. What are the means and measure of information synchronization?

The subsequent sections of this chapter deal with the options on how to solve these problems. It analyzes and proposes mechanisms on how appropriate and matured technology can solve these problems. It relooks at the fundamental way of structuring and using technology for decentralized supply chain. It identifies pillars and drivers of decentralized supply chain and how technology can improve them to achieve a better supply chain.

3 Supply Chain Enabled with ERP and Planning System: Capabilities and Limitations

Over the years, the supply chain management, and its processes and practices, has undergone a significant improvement. In the last three to four decades, technology has evolved from material requirement planning (MRP) to manufacturing resource planning (MRP II) to enterprise resource planning (ERP) to advanced supply chain planning and optimization (APS/APO), and today it is moving toward integrated business planning, network optimizations, and sales and operations planning. With technology adoption, the supply chain processes improved and brought significant business benefits. Almost all leading global companies run enterprise resource planning (ERP) and demand/ supply planning software [15].

Over the past two decades, ERP has had the most significant impact on supply chain processes and its improvements. However, despite these improvements and enabling of digital processes with enterprise grade digital infrastructure, most companies struggle with visibility into demand, operations, and supply. Bringing the decentralization aspect into it, the challenge becomes murkier and intruding. ERP is a system that integrates the departments of an organization and its resources to maximize utilization and performance. ERP transforms how the organization interacts intrinsically and extrinsically. It provides a platform for all the departments like production planning, material planning, operations, inventory, warehousing, design, sales, distribution, accounting, and customer service to act in unison. ERP marries the information flow to material flow creating a homogeneous environment for business processes and decision making. It removes physical boundaries and strengthens centralized processes but all within an organization or enterprise. It doesn't have the ability to cut across enterprises.

The architecture and topology of ERP fails to bridge the gap across enterprise collaborations [16]. So, data sharing across enterprises is complex and is dependent on many third-party applications. Order tracking and product traceability are currently managed through EDI and messaging systems. Reports and RFID scans are also used at various checkpoints to track the movement of goods. Most of the time across enterprises, transfer of information like that of demand, supply, inventory, and/or master data is exchanged using middleware like Boomi, MuleSoft (*to give an example*), etc. This indicates that the future system must provide real-time data from anywhere and from any system. Removing the dependency of system is one of the major improvements needed. In all these, there are few critical missing pieces which are not addressed by the ERP system. These are, namely, trust and authenticity of data, non-repudiable capability, transparency, and security of data, and above all ability to track changes with no one entity owning all the data. So, a smoother and robust interorganizational data sharing system with capabilities as discussed before is missing. This acts as a major hindrance to serve the customer more effectively.

As in ERP, planning systems have also evolved over the last two decades. They have built in optimization capabilities apart from generating a companywide supply plan for execution. The planning systems have been enhanced to provide budget plans, long-range plans/strategic plans, execution plans, network optimizing plans, sales and operations plan, and rapid plans, to name a few. Capabilities like attribute-based planning, rapid planning, and collaborative planning are developed to cater to specific industry or process needs. The planning software of today has the capability to plan not only for the current organizations but for its partners as well. Today's planning systems support vendor managed inventory and collaborative planning, forecasting, and replenishment (CPFR). But the challenge lies in having the unified master and transactional data to plan. Sharing such sensitive data by partners brings in the element of trust, which is beyond the scope of these planning systems.

4 Pillars and Drivers of Decentralized Supply Chain

Decentralized supply chain will always need to work on an overarching strategic plan across the entities to be successful. The plan will hold all partners of supply chain together with a common objective. Individual entities can drive their own decisions to meet their own local objectives. There are key aspects impacting the decentralized team in supply chain; these are:

- Ability to respond rapidly to supply chain needs
- Sudden demand shifts from customer
- Supply chain breakdown and disruptions impacting supply
- Shortages in upstream supply chain
- Localized disruption in services as happening in pandemics
- Need to cooperate and synchronize in geographically spread teams

These aspects need to be maturely handled by each team. These are possible with empowered decision team and collaborative decision making. The teams should be driven by strong relationships and customer objective in mind and not individual goals of each entity. It must be driven and supported by strategic plans. The plans have to clearly identify the supply chain pillars and drivers. The pillars and drivers must enable a trustable and cohesive decentralized supply chain.

4.1 *Pillars of Decentralized Supply Chain*

Figure 1 shows the pillars of the decentralized supply chain. The pillars form the founding principles on which the decentralized supply chain can operate. Based on experience and analysis, six founding principles of decentralized supply chain are

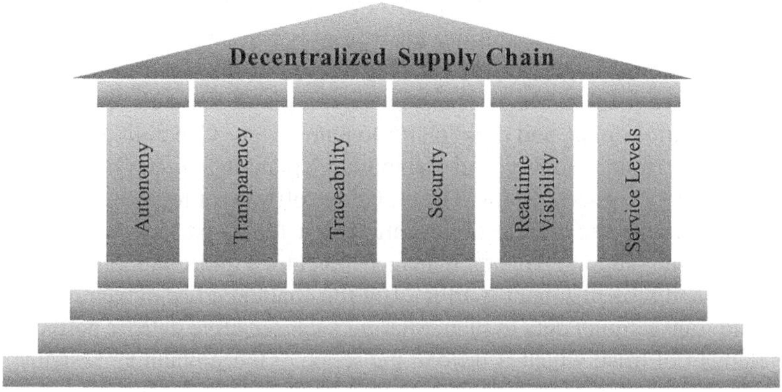

Fig. 1 Pillars of decentralized supply chain

proposed. Each of them has its own function and reason why it ought to be one of the pillars of decentralized supply chain and how it brings all the entities of the supply chain together. Each of the pillars is explained henceforth:

Autonomy This pillar is one of the guiding principles of decentralized supply chain (DSC). This provides the autonomy or independence of each entity to take its decision. But it must align with the overall structure of decentralized supply chain. The autonomy provides the ability to voice concerns and be independent in its decision and action and overall helps to grow and sustain.

Transparency This pillar drives the trust and transparency among the members of the decentralized supply chain. This is a critical element without which the decentralized supply chain cannot exist. Transparency drives alignment and orientation among many other factors.

Traceability Another aspect of decentralized supply chain that can help bring members together as well as make them responsible is the traceability. The data, decision, and information traceability form a key element of membership and reliability.

Security In a decentralized supply chain, there are several entities with numerous transactions among them. Some of these transactions are sensitive like related to design elements which can be highly confidential information or can be process related which are controlled through IP. In such transactions, there are sensitive information like formulae, demand picture, supply scenarios, customer lists, and inventory information which are confidential but are shared. The security and confidence on the security of these information sharing is of paramount importance for the success of the decentralized supply chain.

Real-time Visibility Supply chain is all about synchronizing the material flow with the information flow to meet customer demands. This becomes crucial when there are entities across enterprises. Visibility is an aspect engrained in this act of synchronization. The visibility to some of the key aspects of supply chain is very key for its uninterrupted success. These are, namely, visibility to demand, supply, inventory, in transits, fluctuations, disruptions in production, etc. These can severely impair the supply chain in a decentralized environment. So, getting a proper visibility into these critical aspects of supply chain is key to the success of decentralized supply chain.

Service Levels In a decentralized supply chain setup, the dependency among the entities is high. Service level becomes critical among them to add trust and dependency. So, matching up to the desired service levels and improving upon it calls for the smoother functioning of decentralized supply chain.

4.2 Drivers of Decentralized Supply Chain

Figure 2 shows the drivers of the decentralized supply chain. These drivers are the fusing force which keeps the partners engaged and drive them toward mutual cohesiveness. If any of these drivers are broken, then the mutual coordination among the entities are at risk, and the idea of decentralized but coordinated supply chain leads to a fragmented supply chain. It is very important to have technology, people, and process to enable and support these drivers to have a seamless and coordinated decentralized supply chain.

Based on experience and analysis, these six drivers of decentralized supply chain are proposed. Each of them has its own purpose to drive the cohesion and coordination among the entities for a unified strategic goal of the supply chain. Each of the drivers is explained henceforth:

Economics of Supply Chain Companies move toward a decentralized supply chain for many reasons. But the most important reason is the economics of the supply chain. It should always be in favor of the overall benefit of all partners. It is the economics of making things available to customer on time, in budget, and in right quantity that will drive the decentralization.

Swiftness in Decision Making Decentralized supply chain brings entities across the enterprises together. But bringing new partners in the chain brings the risk of delayed reaction or decision making. Hence, the speed of reaction or swiftness in decision making becomes a critical driver in holding the decentralized entities together toward a common goal. The swifter, smoother, and steadier the decision-

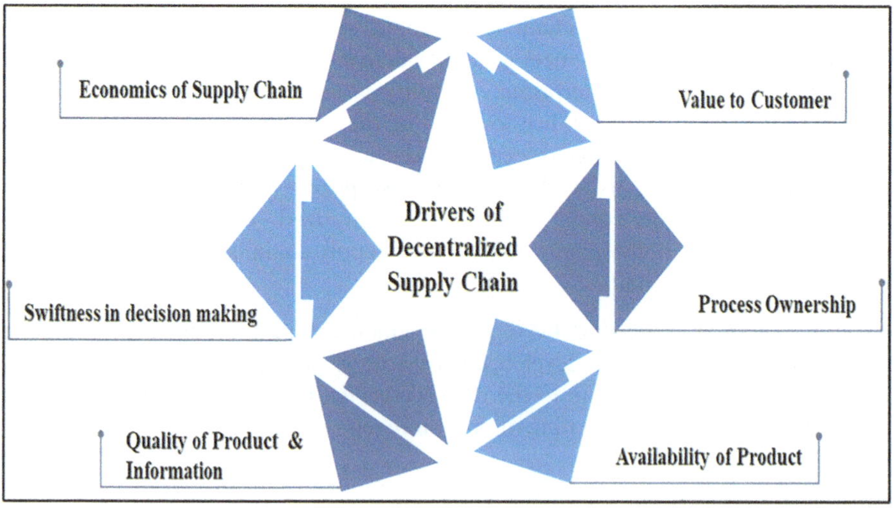

Fig. 2 Drivers of decentralized supply chain

making mechanism is, it will lead to a better performing supply chain among the partners.

Quality of Product and Information There is no denying of the fact that quality of product is the most important factor to win and retain business from customers. But in supply chain, it is the information and flow of information which makes products move. Thus, the quality of information and product helps reduce overhead among the entities and their team. The reduction in overheads reduces friction among teams leading to a well-oiled supply chain. This makes information and product flow smoother and synchronized and improve overall supply chain efficiency. So, these two aspects go together in a decentralized supply chain and drive the performance of all the entities together. This has a dominant impact on supply chain performance and sustenance in the long run.

Availability of Product Classically, supply chain brings product to customer based on their demand from supplier or manufactures it. There are numerous entities in between, and in a decentralized supply chain, the decision making is independently done by each entity. As products move through the supply chain getting transformed/manufactured or distributed toward its customer, the predictable and reliable availability of the product at each logic step at the required time holds the entities together. This predictability and reliability for making the product available decides the credibility of the entity. Superior on time availability marks a worthier credibility and reliability. This improves the supply chain performance.

Process Ownership Supply chain transactions are highly complex processes involving numerous teams, people, and technology. It involves high volume transactions and at times things go wrong or there can be disruptions. It is at these testing time the entities in a decentralized supply chain need to own up the process and solve the problem at hand. Also, they need to proactively change or improve the process to mitigate such risk or problem in the future. Having such confidence building measures and process improvements among the entities brings healthy competition (among entities/partner) and enhances supply chain performance.

Value to Customer For any supply chain, the goal is to serve the customer well. With decentralization of the decision making and processes, this becomes challenging. But the entire chain must be driven by the goal to serve immediate partner and bring value to the end customer. This value can drive the entities to serve each other and in the best interest and best way.

As we understand the pillars and drivers of supply chain, let us now look and understand the technology that can greatly help the decentralized supply chain.

5 Blockchain: A Powerful Technology to Improve Harmonization

Blockchain is a distributed ledger which records transaction data as blocks. The data in the blocks are immutable, secure and chronologically maintains transaction data. Blockchain can also be described as a network where members are a node in the chain. Blockchain uses distributed ledger technology (DLT) and using it the records created are indelible. In simple terms, blockchain acts as a platform (democratized with equal rights) and removes the dependency on a single centralized authority for any transactional data. At the same time, it is secure and transparent. Blockchain securely transfers data and centrally shares information with its members with trust playing an underlying and important role. Blockchain is a powerful mechanism to capture, store, and securely make the data available to all its members. As blockchain brings together several entities without the need for a centralized authority, it improves the coordination, trust, transparency, and harmonization among the entities/ node. The most important aspect of blockchain is it has the capability to bring together independent systems from multiple stakeholders and act as a platform. In a simple representation, Fig. 3 represents how blockchain can be a central element to several stakeholders spread across multiple systems. These stakeholders can use ERP along with any other allied/satellite systems. The data from these stakeholders will flow into blockchain, thus centralizing the transactional data in the blockchain platform. Figure 3 also shows that blockchain is independent of the integrating system and data, and thus it can bring in any new entity easily.

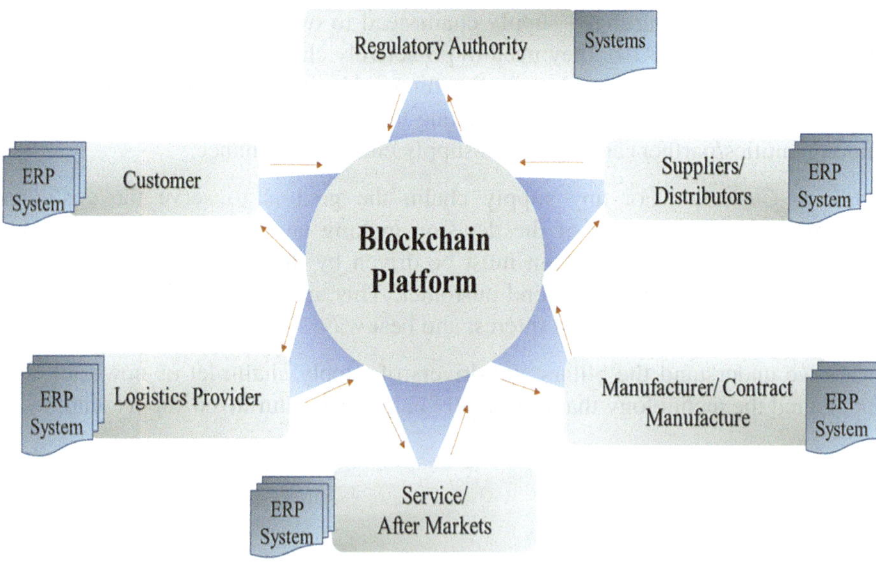

Fig. 3 Blockchain platform for multiple stakeholders

5.1 Types of Blockchain

We can see that blockchain system is a network of members (nodes) connected through a distributed ledger technology. These data are shared among several computers/ nodes rather than being stored on a central server. One of the powerful features of blockchain is on the controlled data access to certain members and the ability to write business logics through smart contracts. In blockchain, the transaction data can be verified by rules (smart contracts) applicable to all unlike a single centralized authority. The biggest benefit of blockchain is the ability to share data seamlessly and securely with partners. There are three types of blockchain as being used today. They offer different types of architecture to operate and integrate. These are as follows:

Open or Permission-less Blockchain These are also known as public blockchain. In this type of blockchain, anyone can join the blockchain network. There is no one partner or node owning or managing the rules of blockchain membership. Here, all the partners together own it and everyone is equal in the network. Bitcoin and Ethereum networks are examples of open blockchain architecture. The open blockchain network is not recommended if the blockchain is for a specific purpose. This blockchain architecture works on the consensus mechanism. The consensus mechanisms are drawn through the proof of work. The proof of work drives the need for authenticators or miners. These play a crucial role as they are the gatekeepers to verify transactions and calculate credits. This architecture requires significant computational power to maintain a large-scale distributed ledger and standardize calculations among numerous participants and authenticators. Due to this challenge, open blockchain architecture is not so readily accepted to work. Though Bitcoin network is one of the earliest known blockchain systems, there are not many like it.

Permissioned or Private Blockchain Network This architecture is more suitable if it's for a specific purpose. In this architecture, there is a particular organization or a single defined owner of the network. The owner of the network defines the specific business rules based on which members are qualified and added. Smart contracts are business rules defined to engage the members and qualify/filter the data to get into blocks. These standardized and well-defined criteria are the cornerstone of the permissioned blockchain. In the permissioned network, participant entry is decided by founding members (node) or a group of existing member (nodes), as decided by founding member. One example of private blockchain networks is Oracle Blockchain Cloud Services developed on Hyperledger Fabric.

Consortium Blockchain Network Consensus network is like a semiprivate blockchain architecture which is owned and controlled by a preselected group of members. It is not necessarily controlled by the founding member or there may be no one founding member. This group of members decides on future memberships, rules, etc. The right to read the blockchain may be public or restricted to the participants. For example, one might imagine a consortium of 15 financial institutions, each of which operates a node and of which 10 must approve every block of data for the block to be valid. A consortium blockchain provides many of the same benefits affiliated with private blockchain like efficiency and transaction privacy. R3 and BiTA are examples of consortium blockchain.

Any kind of blockchain network can be connected to multiple applications or systems. The capability of connecting blockchain networks to enterprise resource planning (ERP) system has been the most beneficial of them all [16, 17]. This has opened the opportunity to connect and transmit the transacting system data securely to partners for seamless data sharing, decision making, and transparency. As rightly stated by Litan et al. (2019), blockchain networks have emerged as a promising innovation to affirm the integrity of data shared among constituents in multiparty process collaboration. This also sets the pitch for the fitment of blockchain in a decentralized supply chain. With blockchain technology, the real-time collaboration, analytical reporting, data-driven decision making, and efficiency of transactions look very promising. This was definitely not possible few years back with the traditional systems. Blockchain has paved the way to devise process and system for making more efficient decentralized supply chain.

6 Decentralized Supply Chain Enabled by ERP, Planning System, and Blockchain

Today, most of the global companies already have ERP as their backbone execution system, while the supply chain is driven by some specialized advanced planning system. ERP enables all business transactions from manufacturing, procurement, and order management to accounting and transactional reporting. Companies collaborate with their suppliers/customer through EDI, XML, or some point-to-point messaging system. Though these specialized systems are very modern and poised for the future, they exhibit the limitations when it comes to across enterprise transactions, coordination, and collaboration. A decentralized supply chain is about the partner entities which makes the product move and meet customer demands based on information shared. It is all about the coordination among the customer, supplier, manufacturer, contact manufacturer, and service providers, etc. that enables the supply chain. Some of the key issues which are a sore point among the partners are trust, security of data, data access among partners, seamless and device-independent data capture, real-time and reliable availability of data, data synchronization, and visibility of data. These and similar points are an outcome of research of many publications as mentioned in Table 2. Apart from it, as the data, process, and complexity proliferate with time in these ERP and planning systems, the visibility, security, scalability, and reliability of process and data diminish leading to inefficiency. This is where the adoption of blockchain along with ERP and planning system enables and powers the decentralized supply chain.

6.1 A Complex and Intriguing System of Systems in Supply Chain

ERP – enterprise resource planning – is a system which uses all the resources of an enterprise and drives coordination and automation among them. It brings procurement, manufacturing, inventory, engineering, order management, warehouse management, accounting, ledger reporting, cash management, e-commerce, and human resource under one single system, driving coordination, automation and scalability.

Planning system –The planning system is an algorithm-driven process of coordinating resources to balance demand and supply based on information signals for ultimately helping delivery of goods to customers. It considers every aspects of supply chain right from manufacturing, inventory, distribution, and procurement to order management. The demand planning aspects have demand forecasting, S and OP Process, and deriving consensus forecast, while the supply planning has plans to meet demands, inventory norms, sourcing decisions, production, and procurement plans.

The global standard today is a system of system for supply chain which combines ERP and planning system for the best possible outcome to drive business process and decisions.

The combination of ERP and planning system together brings with it its own challenges like:

- Across enterprise opaqueness: ERP brings visibility and automation in data and process within an enterprise. But across the enterprises (across systems of ERPs), the visibility to process and data is opaque. It is dependent on reports or EDI messages only.
- Modularity: ERP system is designed and developed in a highly modular way so that it remains flexible. At time due to this modularity, the data availability across enterprise becomes one of its weaknesses.
- Its functionalities are restrictive when it needs to coordinate with other partners and systems.
- Security: The data security threat is a reality in ERP. ERP is definitely not the most secure of the system specially as it has to provide access to outside of the organization where then it has to rely more on the network control rather than ERP system control.
- Transparency and accessibility: With the data stored in different ERP systems, the transparency of process and data is very challenging to achieve among partners. With security access and data access, the process is not only slow and cumbersome but also rudimentary and inefficient.
- Reporting: With data in different systems of ERP the single view of supply chain and its status is difficult to achieve.

To overcome these challenges, the author proposes the use of blockchain along with ERP and planning system for an efficient supply chain which will weave all the entities together. This will be particularly very helpful for decentralized supply chain.

6.2 *Decentralized Supply Chain with ERP, Planning, and Blockchain*

Bringing the distributed ledger technology (blockchain) into the decentralized supply chain is a game changer. It overcomes most of the process, system, and data challenges as posed by the decentralization. The issues faced in decentralized supply chain as emphasized in Table 2 can be overcome. The author has drawn Fig. 4 to depict how blockchain can help overcome the shortcoming in a decentralized supply chain which is already enabled with ERP and planning system. In Fig. 4, a supplier, customer, manufacturer, and distributors are all independent companies, but each of them becomes a node in the blockchain network. Thus, the blockchain network acts as a unified platform bridging the gaps of data visibility, communication gap, transparency, and traceability, to name a few. Figure 4 can also be explained as

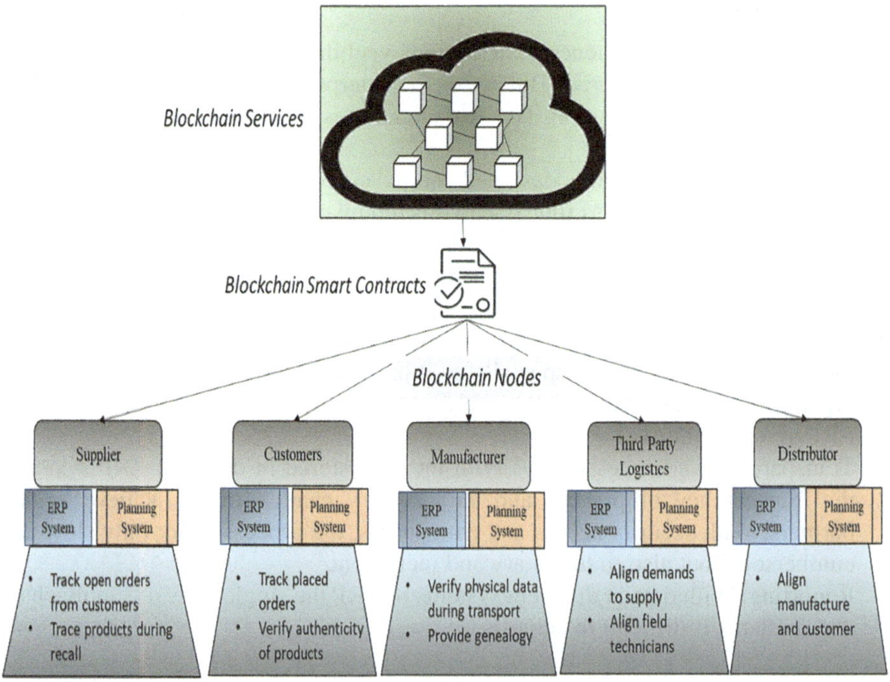

Fig. 4 Blockchain platform for a decentralized supply chain

the transaction data (as required and agreed) from each of the supply chain entity will flow into blockchain. It can be seen in Fig. 4 that each of the entity has its own ERP and planning system representing all independent companies. For the various supply chain challenges discussed in previous sections, the blockchain system of networks is a credible option to solve the problem. With the backdrop of a decentralized supply chain, blockchain offers new ways to automate business processes among the partners without setting up complex and expensive centralized IT infrastructure. In a decentralized supply chain, a blockchain provides capability to have a distributed ledger in a peer-to-peer network where members can interact with each other without a trusted intermediary, in a verifiable manner.

Figure 5 provides another view of a global supply chain where the entities are globally spread. In the figure, each entity is an independent company and has its own processes to run their business for their enterprise. Various ERP and planning systems will be a part of each of the entity. At the same time, it is a part of the blockchain network also. Data from the various ERP/planning system will flow into the blockchain network, and thus the blockchain network will act as a unified structure bringing in the transparency, security, and ownership. The figure shows that various partner entities are involved in transfer of goods and information while they carry on their own supply chain transactions. The data from these entities helps in transparency, financial traceability, accountability and improvises in processes with governmental agencies. There are many industries which are highly regulated, for example, pharma, nuclear components, chemicals, food, mining, and aerospace components, to name a few. In such industries, the onus of providing the right data at the right time for regulatory compliance lies with the

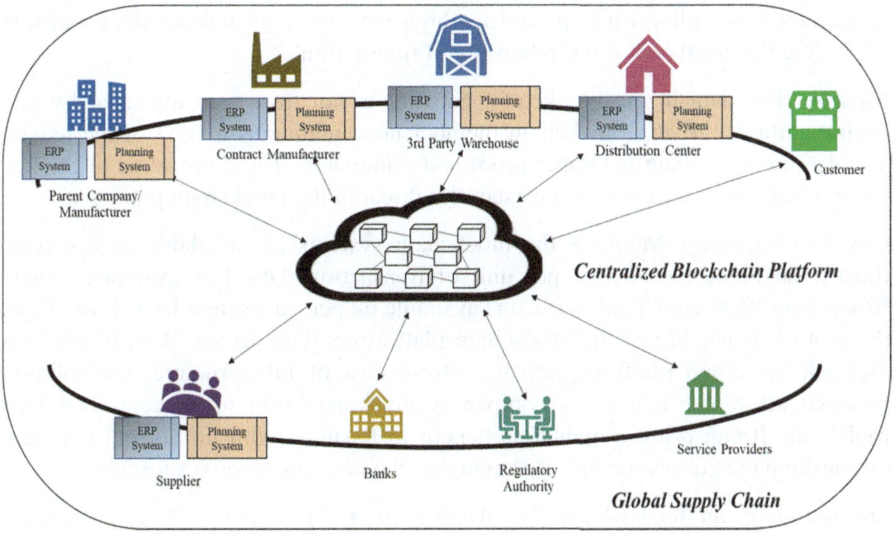

Fig. 5 Blockchain with ERP and planning system for a decentralized global supply chain

manufacturer. In such a case, blockchain is a matured and best fit solution. Bringing in the government regulator into the blockchain network brings in the required transparency as desired and required by regulators. The data being transparent and immutable adds to the worthiness of the cause and is a game changer. Due to this, there are many blockchain-related solutions to comply with US Drug Supply Chain Security Act (DSCSA) and Europe's Falsified Medicines Directive. This has resulted in blockchain solutions like MediLedger project from Chronicled, Akiri, and Medicalchain. But this approach does have a drawback that it needs interoperability among blockchain which is still not very generically available among the blockchain networks and continues to be a major hurdle.

The blockchain platform seamlessly brings the physical world data into cyber computing environment and stores it in a distributed ledger. This is the game changing attribute for the decentralized supply chain which bridges most of the gaps and challenges in a multipartner scenario. There are various ways and means by which blockchain along with ERP and planning systems will solve the supply chain challenges. Some of the key aspects are described in subsequent section:

Scalability The data from multiple entities originating from numerous transactions can be feed into the blockchain network. The blockchain network will act as the platform. Enterprise grade blockchain designed by Oracle, Microsoft, and SAP based on Ethereum or Hyperledger can handle big data in the distributed ledgers efficiently. Thus, a scalable data-driven supply chain organization is built cutting across partners. This in a way acts as a platform and removes other barriers as well.

Reliability Some of the key features of blockchain are being non-repudiable and immutable. These two features in supply chain (especially when data transfers across entities) improve the reliability of the transactions. With ERP and blockchain combination, the platform is poised for high velocity, high volume data transfers improving the consistency and reliability of transactions.

Security The data in the blockchain network is not owned or managed by any central authority. Every blockchain member node maintains a copy of the ledger. The data in blockchain is tamper-proof and immutable. These are some of the key capabilities which remove the data security threat in the blockchain platform.

Cost of Ownership Many of the blockchain systems are available as a service (hosted on cloud), costed at per unit of transaction data. For example, Oracle Blockchain Platform Cloud Service is available on per transaction basis [18]. Thus, the cost of ownership of the blockchain platform is data driven. With blockchain available on cloud platform and no upfront cost of infrastructure, the solution becomes affordable and many companies are doing Proof of concept (POC) on trial basis. It can bring tremendous benefit to business with no upfront cost and diminishing cost of ownership. It also makes the investment very affordable.

Transparency and Accessibility The data stored in blockchain platform is the same in every node/member and that can be accessed over web, applications, mobile, or desktop. This greatly improves the transparency of data and its access across all the entities of the supply chain. With the inbuilt security of blockchain and blockchain being the cardinal system of data storage cutting across the entities and enterprises, the data access and usage is seamless and transparent.

The blockchain platform brings benefits to all the supply chain partners in a decentralized operation. But every partner has a different aspect of benefit in the management of its supply chain owing to blockchain. There are certain needs and expectations which will be the same for every entity, while there will be few unique to a particular entity. The following sections detail out how blockchain platform will improve all the entities' coordination and cohesiveness and at the same time bring in more value to customer, saving money and simplifying processes. All the entities are picked up from Fig. 5 as it represents almost all the entities in a global decentralized supply chain:

Parent Company/OEM This is the external customer facing entity which receives end customer orders to be fulfilled. It can have mechanism to share order details in the blockchain network which can in turn help contract manufacturer (and suppliers) with transparency in demand (components). Based on the information shared or willingness to share, it can derive the following:

- Real-time order tracking based on blockchain data (component tracking from supplier, services tracing, logistics tracking, and manufacturing tracking), in short across partners.
- Traceability of product from contract manufacturer or OEM to customer, as it can trace back to customer or Tier N supplier.
- Easier product recall.
- Better root cause analysis of problems in products and supply chain. Better fault-finding capability in main product or components based on data available in blockchain.
- With shared information and visibility to inventory, the demand and supply planning can be more effective and agile.
- Customer order promising, customer order information and tracking can be more accurate and real time. Customers will have more real-time information on their fulfillment of their orders.

Contract Manufacturer Today, most of the manufacturing hubs are in the low-cost economies of Asia. Real-time data availability from trading partners in the blockchain platform (especially subassembly or contract manufacturers) can help all supply chain partners with better visibility and informed decision making. Some of the benefits of the data availability to and from contract manufacturer are:

- Product serialization reporting for authentication and traceability
- Real-time reporting of manufacturing status and quality
- Minute level details of manufacturing/storage conditions for traceability/fault analysis and recall purposes. It also can help know the manufacturing status.
- Real-time information of shipment schedules and status from contract manufacturers

- Confirmation on arrival of subassembly from feeder plants to main plant (progress in supply chain goods movement)
- Suppliers' material shipment schedules and confirmations to contract manufacturers
- Breakdown information/potential supply chain disruptions at contract manufacturer's facility

Third-Party Warehouses Insight into the movement of goods in-transit is always helpful in supply chain. With blockchain, the real-time tamper-proof data of arrivals and departures from warehouse can help all supply chain partners. This insight will provide the following benefits:

- Synchronized logistics with manufacturer and customer support team through the blockchain platform.
- This can help in real-time scheduling of technicians for services of new installations.
- Minute level details of product storage conditions for traceability/fault analysis and recall purposes when the product is moved directly to customer via third-party warehouse from contract manufacturers.
- Real-time monitoring of shipments across geography and on oceans.

Distribution Centers/Warehouses In many of the supply chains, this is the last storage point before product goes to customers or retail chains. The real-time data insights of arrivals/departures, pilferages, losses, and damages will help drive analytics or control tower decisions or insights for reporting into upcoming delivery delays (or problems), exact schedules of arrival, etc. Benefits are listed below:

- Synchronized field service and product delivery with blockchain smart contracts
- Advanced alerts/ASN from manufacturer to customer for preparation and housekeeping
- Minute level details of product storage conditions for traceability/fault analysis and recall purpose
- Synchronized warehouse staffing as per schedules, thereby reducing unnecessary staffing
- Extending the goods movement visibility to all stakeholders including end customers (where possible) for better planning

Banks Many a time banks lack the visibility in supply chain leading to delays in clearances, issuances of legal letter (required for port clearances or border transfers), or payments. It is envisaged that adding banks to the blockchain platform with the required necessary access to data may solve many of the delays faced by companies today in global supply chain. The main shortcoming is the trust due to which layers of proofs and data are required to be submitted to get the clearances (facilitating the delay). Having banks in the blockchain platform with suppliers, manufacturers, and customer can truly change the way commercials are run today. It can completely change the way payments and controls are built in systems to overcome trust deficits.

Service Providers Service providers provide services for installation or repair. The service must be synchronized with the availability of products from contract manufacturer or OEM and needs customer's consents for availability, time, and duration. In today's world, this coordination is completely manual, time consuming, and effort intensive. Many a times availability of product and schedule of technicians are completely out of synch due to visibility to each other's schedule. Having the three key entities (service provider, manufacturer, and customer) in the same blockchain platform with the required data access can completely transform the way the business is carried out today. It can bring in the following benefits:

- The effort in coordination can be transformed to automatic except some manual intervention due to exceptions. Smart contracts will play a big role in this.
- The synchronization of availability of product and service technicians can save time for customers and scheduling effort for manufacturer and service provider.

Regulatory Authority There are many products which undergo regulatory authority testing before they become eligible for sale to customers. These include (but not limited to) medicines, healthcare products, medical devices, etc. Also, there are products which need to undergo some special screening or certifications from authorities for their fitness before being shipped to customers. These are products used in sensitive places like nuclear reactors, boilers, furnaces, or gas chambers. For such certification or fitness of use approval, authorities need a plethora of information and test results to meet its procedures and purpose. Making all the data available to authority makes the process cumbersome and time consuming. It is also marred with corruption, mistrust, and cost escalations. Bringing the entities like manufacturer, customer, and governmental/regulatory authority into the blockchain platform and having the required data access can help transform it into a transparent process. It can bring in the following benefits:

- Authorities can access the required information or data from manufacturer, thereby reducing time of approval.
- The immutability and transparency of data by manufacturer to regulatory authority and customer can herald a new chapter in transparency and trust.
- The sharing of design, ingredients, and process to required parties can help protect the IP. Blockchain will protect the digital assets by regulating the access on the intended information. Blockchain can have smart contracts to verify NDA before providing access to sensitive IP assets. This will avoid data leaks and access by unauthorized parties. Blockchain can enable evidence of creatorship and provenance authentication. Blockchain can control and track distribution of IP products, digital rights management (e.g., online music sites), establishing and enforcing IP agreements, licenses, or exclusive distribution networks through smart contracts. All these can lead to robust IP management.

End Customer Customers today have very limited opportunity to verify the authenticity of a product and to know its provenance. Similarly, end customer's information is almost off limits for most of the manufacturers which makes it very difficult in case of a recall. Blockchain platform can provide the capability to hold this information in the platform cutting across enterprises and making the information available to multiple stakeholders:

- Parent company's ability to know the end customer
- Customer's ability to check product provenance based on smart contracts from blockchain
- Product serialization and end customer information for recall
- Possibility of product feedback from end customer to manufacturer, in a more seamless way.

Blockchain platform can cut across industries and systems enabling partners to adapt to a highly collaborative process of sharing and transacting. The blockchain will be able to provide transparency and security of data at the same time. The enterprise blockchain platform will disrupt the typical way the business of collaboration among partners happens today. Today, it is predominantly reports driven and with blockchain it will be more real time and data driven. Blockchain will completely change the way the entities collaborate today among enterprises for real-time decision making. With these let us now look at the pillars and enablers of supply chain how they are influenced by blockchain.

In many of the global corporations, it is not uncommon to have multiple ERP systems, MES, or WMS. It is generally found that the planning systems, reporting mechanism, and master data systems are centralized in an enterprise, while the execution systems like MES, ERP, and WMS are multiple. The multiplicity comes due to geography/business divisions or even product lines. So blockchain is useful where data needs to be centralized and transparent across the company's boundaries. It is also equally useful in global corporations where systems are disparate and unharmonized/asynchronized within the company's boundaries. In such cases, blockchain can act as the chosen centralized system which may hold data from multiple ERP systems/MES/WMS/TMS and becomes the key source of control towers and analytics. For example, many of the large multinational corporations have geography-based ERP system like Oracle ERP in North America, while Europe and Asia are on SAP. There are also cases where the manufacturing execution systems (MES) are divided by operations like say in semiconductor the front-end operations (wafer manufacturing) are on one MES, while the assembly and test is on a different MES. In such cases, blockchain can act as the chosen platform of centralization. Relevant MES data is collected using IOT system and brought over to the centralized blockchain platform which are shared with multiple stakeholders/nodes and used for various analytics, root cause analysis, and reporting purpose.

6.2.1 ERP and Blockchain Enabling the Pillars of Decentralized Supply Chain

The pillars are the building blocks of a decentralized supply chain. The pillars together make sure the activity of each entity is supported by the others for an

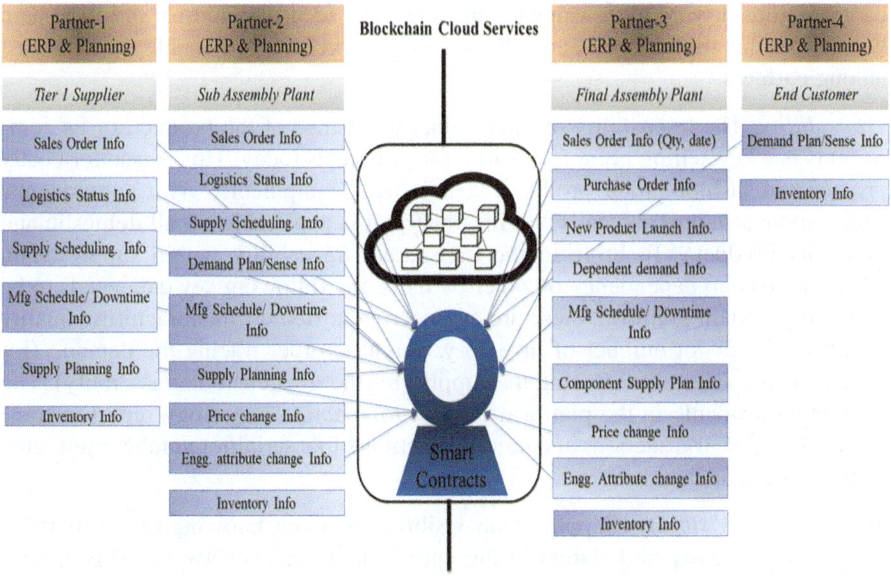

Fig. 6 Supply chain transaction among partners – data centralized in blockchain platform

identified end goal. The entities together make up a smooth supply chain delivering value-added goods to the end customer. Though individual entity profits are important, the end goals of the end-to-end supply chain are paramount. To achieve the goals, these pillars are identified. The blockchain platform together strengthens these pillars in multiple ways. These are further explained through a simplified four-level supply chain which is represented in Fig. 6. Through the figure, it is explained how supply chain transactions across entities undergo a transformative change with the blockchain platform and thus reinforcing the pillars in the decentralized supply chain.

Figure 6 shows there are four supply chain partners, namely, a tier 1 supplier, subassembly plant, a final assembly plant, and a customer. The supply chain transactions are selectively exposed to blockchain platform so that it can drive the desired benefits for end customer.

Transparency There are multitudes of transactions which take places in a supply chain. Some of the key information from a partner is selectively exposed to blockchain platform. Some of the examples as shown in Fig. 6 are price changes/ net prices from final assembly/subassembly plants, demand scenarios from customers and final assembly plants, manufacturing scheduling and downtimes of the manufacturing units, and engineering attribute info from design partners, just to name a few. Availability of this information with the required partners brings in a lot of supply chain transparency and removes the need to build up inventory or lead time in the supply chain to cope with the uncertainty. This transparency will lead to lead time reduction to final customer and reduction in cost of product due to lesser inventory carrying, thus driving more value to customer. The security and trust of blockchain will enable this transparency, and attributes of blockchain will enable the data trust among partners.

Traceability The traceability of the origin, provenance of the product, or its components is a key selling point for many of the products today. This is true for costly products in fashion, food products, and critical equipments. With components/ subcomponent failures/ recalls and insurances, it is applicable for all domestic and industrial products. To bring in the transparent traceability within supply chain where there is no dependency on other partners, the following key data needs to be on the blockchain platform, these are engineering attributes, manufacturing quality results, serial or lot number of inventory, purchase order tracing the demand (for supplier), and sales order tracing the supply (for the final customer/assembly). The data being available in the platform enables to generate genealogy report to trace origins based on transactions and unique identifiers like serial/lot number transacted over purchase or sales orders.

Supply Chain Visibility Supply chain visibility is about knowing the availability of product (quantity and status) in the entire supply chain network. This applies to products from suppliers, logistics providers, manufacturers, third-party service providers, and/or even with customers. During the pandemic of COVID-19, every aspect of supply chain like procurement, sourcing, manufacturing, planning, and logistics struggled. The supply chain shock indicated the need, importance, and focus on supply chain visibility in the business scenario. The research of Alice et al. (2020) and Lian and Fan (2020) signals the need and importance of supply chain visibility. The pandemic exposed the vulnerability or lack of it and brought it to the forefront. It is the supply chain complexity, deficit of trust, or system limitation which binds or limits the visibility. The blockchain platform brings all the supply chain transaction information from each of the partners and makes it centrally available. The following are some of the key tenants of the supply chain visibility:

- Demand picture from customers
- Shipment and logistics insight from 3PL
- Supply picture from supplier and contract manufacturer
- Tentative dates of fulfillment from suppliers
- New Product Introduction (NPI) information from supplier or manufacturer
- Promotions or demand changes from supplier or manufacturer
- Real-time manufacturing status from manufacturer or contract manufacturer

This improves the supply chain performance, opportunity to reduce human dependency, and preparedness for disruption. This also improves fulfillment and brings in transparency with customer, thus improving credibility and trust.

Autonomy In a decentralized supply chain, the partners operate in tandem with each other to serve end customers. But like in any business, the best comes when the operations have the flexibility to have their own decisions and ability to switch or change to meet the tactical plan or attend the most pressing need. This autonomy of business operations for every entity is critical to survive, thrive, and improve. As the blockchain platform brings in the transparency, traceability of transactions, and visibility in supply chain, it also brings in the autonomy for the entities. It empowers them to make changes as per the current plan or scenario and blockchain enables it to share it to other entities. Validations built in the smart contracts will enable a transaction or raise flags if the changes brought over are not meeting any designed criteria or process. There are possibilities to build alerts based on the situation or data received from a partner entity with the help of smart contracts. All these will build in autonomy of the supply chain partners all the while preserving the transparency, traceability, and visibility of transactions.

Service Levels In simple terms, service levels are a function of demand, lead time, information flow, and availability of products. Blockchain enables a seamless and transparent information flow among the trading partners in real time and in synch with the actual product flow. The service levels among the partners will improve as the transparency and supply chain visibility improves. This will be enabled through inventory holding and reduced supply uncertainty. The inventory will be better utilized to meet higher priority demands. Strained supply scenario from suppliers (for components) will help build alternates to keep pace for production. The smart contracts on engineering attribute changes or scheduled engineering change orders can help inventory managers plan and rationalize inventory. This will help in avoiding stock out situation or stockpiles.

On average, it is considered that there are 28 parties involved in transporting one sea container, and all have their own record-keeping systems. If we expand it further to the products coming from suppliers and subassemblies, the number of parties in the decentralized supply chain explodes multiple times. Blockchain, which is a trustworthy digital database at its core, stores the digital records of transactions among all the parties. Thus, blockchain platform not only enhances these pillars but also digitizes the entire decentralized supply chain.

Smart Contracts: A View of Applications in Real World

It is very important that we understand how smart contracts are designed, used, and implemented. The best way to describe and explain this is through examples in real world. Smart contracts are versatile and are used in every aspect of business and supply chain. Smart contracts as described above are business rules written as code into blockchain application layer. The rules are applied to everybody in the network. Smart contracts are thus an automated, secured, trustless, cost-effective, fast, and accurate means of bringing business login in blockchain network. Table 3 provides a curated list of real-life smart contract application in various industries and in various spheres of supply chain.

The smart contracts ingest complex information, convert them into business application logic, and execute it on blockchain network. The data may be coming

Table 3 List of smart contract from various industries

Industry	Smart contract example
Manufacturing supply chain	Change in engineering attribute in master data to trigger notification Planned downtimes to be communicated to high impact customers New product launch info into system can trigger notification to customers
Agri-supply chain	Smart contract to verify the origin of product. Based on which the product is accepted and is delivered Smart contract to verify the date of harvest to accept or reject a lot
Distribution industry supply chain	For a price change from manufacturer, distributor can trigger a notification to customer For ship and debit settlement, smart contracts may be designed to verify rules of authorizations like quantity, date, customer, etc.
Pharma supply chain	Validate origin of ingredients before receiving for drug manufacturing Validation of patient records for drug approval by FDA For Drug Supply Chain Security Act validation of medicines before selling to customers
Insurance industry	Validation of insurer records, vehicle details, and other information before processing claims Real-time data verification from insurer for reinsurance cases

into blockchain from ERP/MES/ planning or any other transactional system. . The source of data or type of data is not a factor, what matters is the data and the applicable logic in it.

6.2.2 ERP and Blockchain Powering the Enablers of Decentralized Supply Chain

As discussed in previous sections, there are various aspects of supply chain like its data, transactions, and setups which can be shared on the blockchain platform. The blockchain platform thus becomes an ubiquitous system available to different partners driving multitudes of supply chain benefits. Figure 7 expands the role of blockchain platform for driving the enablers of the decentralization. The key enablers of decentralization are studied further, and a detailed analysis is carried out as to how the blockchain platform influences and impacts them. The blockchain platform positively affects different aspects of supply chain and drives it to improve the enabler for a more efficient and value-driven decentralized supply chain.

The following are the impacts of blockchain platform on each of the enablers:

Economics of Supply Chain The decentralization should be working in every partner's favor, economically! It is the single biggest factor to enable the decentralization and drive it perpetually. This is possible when the decision making is collaborative. So, having inventory holding transparency, manufacturing downtime transparency, and supply situation transparency drives better efficiency and cost

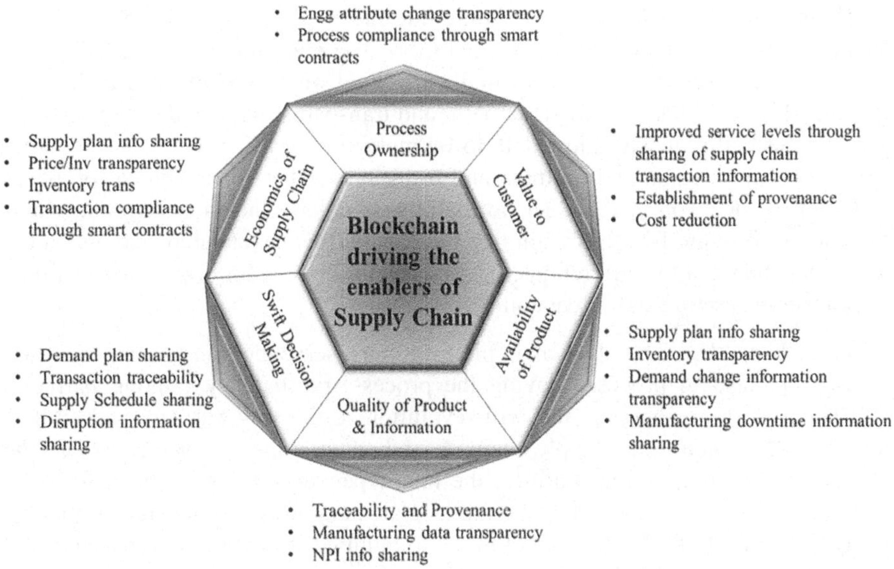

Fig. 7 Blockchain platform impacting the decentralized supply chain enablers

savings, reduces supply chain shock, and removes unwanted inventory. These are possible only with the blockchain platform. Another aspect which greatly influences the profitability and cost is the transparency in demand and supply plans. The sharing of forecasts or potential/expected demands and vis-à-vis the projected supply situation can enable a highly collaborative supply chain driving profitability and reducing cost. Last but not the least, the supply chain transactions' compliance (like purchase order, sales order, inventory transfer, and internal transfers) among the partners can greatly reduce burden, effective use of people, purpose-driven reporting, productive use of workforce, and less of non-value adding work. These are possible only with a blockchain platform which cuts across enterprises and makes data available independent of any single authority owning it. Thus, blockchain platform can enable the decentralization of the supply chain and help the economics of supply chain.

Swiftness in Decision Making The entities forming the decentralized environment bring with them hosts of disparate systems driving their backend supply chain transaction processing (ERP), reporting, demand, and supply planning as well as the manufacturing execution system (MES). The flow of data among the system is driven by EDI, B2B messaging, XML, and middleware technologies. Sometimes the data from one system moves to another system through batch processes with approvals. This builds latency (lack of swiftness) in the data flow which gets evident in the material flow impacting the customer deliverables. This is the symptom which needs to be solved, and one of the most prominent ways of solving this problem is through the centralized data system.

There will be an API-driven real-time interface built from the MES, ERP, and supply chain systems into blockchain platform. The real-time data availability will drive two purposes. Firstly, it will make any kind of data available for decision making. This will enable a swift, smooth, and transparent tactical decision-making process. Secondly, it will allow data to be merged, cubed, or segregated together from different streams and partners and bring it together for analytical purposes and strategic decision making. The availability of data in such a system underlines the features brought by blockchain like the data is true, dependable, and authentic. These capabilities thus differentiate the blockchain-driven platform from other data warehousing systems and its capabilities.

Process Ownership The blockchain platform must serve the transparency not only in data but also in process. Having the process transparency (among partners) will bring in the ownership and will revolutionize the way partners and entities interact in a decentralized supply chain. As the material moves forward toward the end customer along various entities, the interdependence of the entities for data, material, information, and process comes up as a key factor to manage. Typically, today the sharing of information is limited to required information of material, and there is no sharing of process information. In general, in a steady-state condition, this is not required, but if there is a recall or a product issue, then this information becomes important. In reverse logistics scenario, this information is key to return, repair, reprocess, or dispose. With the subscription-based economy picking up and its impact on supply chain, the process information among partners is playing a crucial role. Due to these factors and requirements, the ownership of the process becomes a problem. It's a challenge which needs to be sorted out. Blockchain platform can solve this problem in the following ways:

- Sharing of engineering information and its change thereof can greatly help eliminate or reduce rework, return, and noncompliance. Thus, sharing of the process information securely through blockchain will be made available only for eligible candidates.
- Compliance of transaction processes and proof thereof helps in identifying the process dispersion and root cause of the problem. Blockchain platform will help build the compliances with smart contracts.
- There can be smart contracts built in different processes of manufacturing, logistics, and inspection which can help raise attention from different partners based on the type and nature of nonconformance/issue. It will be purely data driven.
- Sharing of design can be enabled among partners on the blockchain network. This will reduce the traditional sharing mechanism over emails and other mechanism. This can bring in process transparency as well as security.
- Blockchain platform can securely and immutably record the transfer of ownership of the product with accurate time and history. This can be useful for insurance claims and root cause identification issues.
- Built-in security measures can protect fraud transactions thus retaining the ownership of the product and IP.

Quality of Product and Information As discussed in earlier sections, the quality and reliability of the information in the supply chain reduce burden of coordination among partners. This also improve the material flow and supply chain efficiency. Blockchain platform can significantly improve the quality and information aspect of an end-to-end supply chain cutting across multiple partners. One of the key usages of blockchain is to provide product provenance and traceability. It's not that without blockchain it is not possible to have product provenance or traceability, but blockchain's mature technology makes it simple and scalable. Blockchain can enable sharing of manufacturing data and physical environmental data during manufacturing among other things with partner. This will improve product quality and transparency as well as bring in trust. The sharing of supplier problems, specifications, partnering in designs, and improvements thereof are things which can be easily and securely adopted through the blockchain platform and which will immensely improve the quality of product and the information getting shared.

Availability of Product Product availability in supply chain is one of the most used parameters to measure the supply chain health and functioning. In a decentralized scenario, it is the interdependence of product availability among the partners which plays a deciding role in its success or problems. Blockchain platform can eliminate some of the issues and/or it can alleviate some of the problems. The following are some of the nuances through which blockchain can significantly help the decentralized supply chains in managing their enablers:

- Most of the supply chain partners will have their own ERP system. As data traverses through multiple systems, it increases latency, reduces information transparency, and builds information silos. This leads to data redundancy and ultimately impacts the availability of product for its customers or partners. Blockchain's repository of data at every node will reduce data silos and greatly improve the latency and transparency.
- Product quality issues can be sorted out with the platform. Inventory transparency can be built with blockchain and this will improve the product availability across partners.
- Sharing of nonavailability of manufacturing lines due to maintenance or problems, supplier product quality issues, or supplier product availability information helps in achieving transparency. This also facilitates expectation management (of end customers) and positively impacts availability. Sharing of nettable/ good/ shippable inventory available to partners has been found to greatly help partners. This is widely used by distributors to know the manufacturers' availability.
- To improve the collaboration among the customer-supplier, customers can share the build plans using blockchain. Blockchain will seamlessly and transparently allow the supplying entity to know of their products' demand in the future (both near and long term). These will be highly reliable as these will be customer forecasts. Customer using smart contract in blockchain will selectively expose the items' demands to supplier as per the sourcing of the item. Today (without blockchain), supplier forecasts are shared and commitments received but are based on a cadence (frequency) and many a times offline. Blockchain will bring

in the traceability of change and provide room for discussion or agreement on this while being real time, transparent, and secure.

Value to Customer In a decentralized supply chain, there are internal and external customers. Bringing value to customer is always an enriching goal for any supply chain and its partners. The following are the way, means, and mechanism by which blockchain platform can bring this value to customers:

- Cost reduction – Blockchain platform removes dependency on third-party systems and third-party information. Thus, it provides the possibility to decommission legacy systems and infrastructure and significantly reduce IT costs. Partners will have the possibility to reduce the need for manual intervention in aggregation, amending, and sharing supply chain data. The regulatory reporting, compliance reports, and audit documents will become easier and require less manual effort. As a result, employees of every partner will focus exclusively on core supply chain activities. This will result in effort saving and man power rationalization leading to cost reduction/savings.
- Provenance – The establishment of product provenance and traceability will bring in a lot of value to the supply chain and customer. It will also bring in credibility and can help charge premiums for its products. In cases of recall, it can help a seamless recall mechanism, thereby reducing cost of ownership. This will provide an enriching experience to customer and more power to manufacturer.
- Service Levels – In a decentralized supply chain, there are internal and external customers. Having an improved service levels and product availability among the partners brings in a lot of value to customer.

The discussion above portrays the different aspects of the blockchain platform and how it can help drive the enablers of the decentralized supply chain. So, adoption of blockchain for driving these enablers is key for improvement of decentralized supply chain.

6.2.3 Challenges in Integrating Blockchain with ERP

Though there are innumerable benefits in integrating blockchain with ERP for a decentralized supply chain, there are challenges as well. It is prudent to understand and know the challenges of integration beforehand so that it can be prepared accordingly.

Technology acceptance challenge – With an existing ERP, investing in blockchain needs a lot of concrete reason for organizations and leaderships to get convinced. Lack of understanding of blockchain technology among leaders, looking at competitors at what they are doing, lack of standards, and lack of skilled resources are some of the major challenges in acceptance of the technology.

Data-related challenge – Data in blockchain has to be correct and reliable. An incorrect data in blockchain doesn't serve any purpose and is detrimental to the investments. As data in blockchain is immutable, so it makes the wrong data all the more problematic. With an unreliable data, the supply chain partners with which the blockchain will connect to various ERPs will become incoherent and misaligned. Such a step can have catastrophic effect. So having correct data is very important and key to blockchain's integration with ERP. Data standardization is equally important when blockchain and multiple ERP are coming together. The data has to be consistent when it gets referred by multiple partners/ERPs. As an example, let's say an item with code A in one company needs to be referred with a common name or id across multiple partners, mix up in this will lead to complete failure. So, data standardization across partners is key to this success.

Trust and Partnership Challenges – When supply chain collaborates, then it is not only its system but also its people and processes that collaborate. This collaboration needs immense trust to share data and open up the processes with your partners. Once these barriers are overcome, then only a true transparent supply chain can be established cutting across the barriers of systems and processes.

Scalability and Interoperability – Adopting blockchain is additional cost on top of other systems which are already in place. Blockchain integrating with ERP is primarily done to establish transparency across companies and breaking the data siloes. This leads to data getting replicated across nodes. Also, companies have a single ERP system connecting to multiple blockchain systems, and thus interoperability of blockchain becomes important from long-term sustainable systems perspective.

These are some of the challenges in integrating blockchain with ERP, and companies need to be aware of these challenges when they move toward such an integration.

7 Discussion: Future of Decentralized Supply Chain with Blockchain and ERP

Digital revolution is characterized by the convergence of different technologies for the betterment of product, benefit to customers and business processes. The future of supply chain with blockchain application will also converge people and process, blurring the lines of digital and physical world. It will increasingly use machine learning algorithms, and data from blockchain for the purpose of improving processes, providing visibility and transparency, and continuously aiding in faster and accurate decision making. Blockchain will increasingly become the centralized data repository cutting across systems, enterprises, and partners. It will be blockchain and not individual ERPs which will be hooked to various analytics platforms and reporting mechanisms like Tableau/Power BI, etc. Blockchain will drive the centralized reporting, providing analytical views and driving the decentralized supply chains' efficiency and performance for global corporations.

As the blockchain platform matures, it will be able to bring in more partners and their trustworthy data for decision making which will greatly improve the supply chain and its operations. The systems of ERP, supply chain planning and MES will continue to evolve adding more functions, and technologically it is moving and continue to move to cloud architecture. Moving forward API (application programming interface) will be the mechanism to hook up any external system. This can be facilitated with some middleware applications like Boomi, MuleSoft, or Fusion. This will enable easier adoption of blockchain as also its integration with MES or ERP and planning systems. With this, the data from different applications will democratize in blockchain. Blockchain will drive most of the compliance reporting, partner reporting/information, analytics reporting, KPIs for partners, and supplier negotiation, and this will move to a more centralized and capability-driven operations on the platform while having all the flexibility of decentralization.

There will be more advancement in the interoperability of MES and ERP and blockchain systems. Today, IBM, Oracle, SAP, and Microsoft are building capabilities of interoperability of blockchain services among themselves (Hyperledger and Ethereum) [19]. In the future, the interoperability of blockchain will expand to all big and small ERP vendors. Availability of API in ERP system for integration with leading blockchain vendors will become a selling point and a necessity. These will get smoother with more advancement in technology and will have wider reach adding in the satellite systems apart from ERP. The supply chain partners will come together to form blockchain-driven consortiums which can be industry based, product based, or partner based, and those consortiums will drive the process landscape. These consortiums can even have leading ERP vendors also as a partner to the consortium and can help provide industry standard processes, KPIs, and other services. The blockchain platform will be mostly built as enterprise grade that is designed, developed, and poised to handle huge volume of data. The load of data warehousing and reporting from ERP/planning system/MES will move to blockchain platform. This will have a corresponding impact on the need for skilled resources for underlying technology.

With the blockchain platform, the decentralized supply chain will be transforming from the way it operates today. It will continue to provide the flexibility of decentralized decision making, and at the same time, the platform will provide the benefits of centralization driving efficiency, performance, trust, and service levels.

7.1 Conclusion

Decentralization of supply chain is inevitable and will continue to evolve. The supply chain is increasingly going to be global, decentralized, and geographically spread. Blockchain based on the distributed ledger technology will greatly help improve decentralized supply chain operations and performance. An integrated blockchain with ERP, planning system and MES will be the lynchpin of success for a decentralized supply chain. It can derive significant benefit in supply chain execution as well as in reporting.

The combined architecture of these systems will enable the pillars and enablers of decentralized supply chain. Blockchain platform will enhance the pillars of decentralized supply chain, namely, transparency, traceability, visibility, autonomy, and service levels and at the same time digitizing the supply chain driving performance and execution superiority. The blockchain platform will enhance the decentralization processes and positively impact the economics of supply chain, swift decision making, quality and reliability of product, availability of product, and value to customer. It will transform the supply chain into a digital, connected, and efficient decentralized supply chain.

The architecture presented in this chapter is generic and can help any type of supply chain orchestration. Overall this digital adoption in decentralized supply chain is poised to transform business and serve human mankind for its betterment!

References

1. Cheung, B. (2020). What countries are most multinational corporations based in? *Investopedia.* https://www.investopedia.com/ask/answers/021715/why-are-most-multinational-corporations-either-us-europe-or-japan.asp. Last accessed 2021/4/21.
2. Rangavittal, G., & Sohn, T. (2008). The impact and dynamics of centralization in supply chain decision making. Thesis Project. https://dspace.mit.edu/handle/1721.1/45243. Last accessed on 2021/3/22.
3. MH&L Staff. (2003) Centralized Vs. decentralized decision-making. https://www.mhlnews.com/archive/article/22036969/centralized-vs-decentralized-decisionmaking. Last accessed on 2021/4/24.
4. Chen, F. (1999). Decentralized supply chains subject to information delays. *Management Science, 45*(8), 1076–1090.
5. Saxena, A., Ganesh, K., Saxena, A., & Page, T. (2009). Partially centralised decisions and information synchronisation in supply chain. *International Journal of Enterprise Network Management, 3*(3), 246–267.
6. Fu, H., & Ma, Y. (2019). Optimization and coordination of decentralized supply chains with vertical cross-shareholding. *Computers & Industrial Engineering, 132*, 23–35.
7. Lu, S. Y. P., Lau, H. Y. K., & Yiu, C. K. F. (2012). A hybrid solution to collaborative decision-making in a decentralized supply-chain. *Journal of Engineering and Technology Management, 29*(1), 95–111.
8. Mourtzis, D., & Doukas, M. (2013). Decentralized manufacturing systems review: Challenges and outlook. In K. Windt (Ed.), *Robust manufacturing control* (Lecture notes in production engineering). Springer.
9. Proch, M., Worthmann, K., & Schlüchtermann, J. (2017). A negotiation-based algorithm to coordinate supplier development in decentralized supply chains. *European Journal of Operational Research, 256*(2), 412–429.
10. Tliche, Y., Taghipour, A., & Canel-Depitre, B. (2020). An improved forecasting approach to reduce inventory levels in decentralized supply chains. *European Journal of Operational Research, 287*(2), 511–527.
11. Prasad, T. V. S. R. K., Srinivas, K., & Srinivas, C. (2017). Decentralized production–distribution planning in multi-echelon supply chain network using intelligent agents. *Opsearch, 54*, 217–232.
12. Wang, Q., Chay, Y., & Wu, Z. (2011). Streamlining inventory flows with time discounts to improve the profits of a decentralized supply chain. *International Journal of Production Economics, 132*(2), 230–239.
13. Schmitt, A. J., Sun, S. A., Snyder, L. V., & Shen, Z. M. (2015). Centralization versus decentralization: Risk pooling, risk diversification, and supply chain disruptions. *Omega, 52*, 201–212.

14. Hassanzadeh, A., Jafarian, A., & Amiri, M. (2014). Modeling and analysis of the causes of bullwhip effect in centralized and decentralized supply chain using response surface method. *Applied Mathematical Modelling, 38*(9–10), 2353–2365.
15. Banerjee, A. (2018). Blockchain technology: Supply chain insights from ERP. In P. Raj & G. C. Deka (Eds.), *Advances in computers* (Vol. 111, pp. 69–98).
16. Banerjee, A. (2018). Integrating blockchain with ERP for a transparent supply chain. Infosys White Paper. https://www.infosys.com/Oracle/white-papers/Documents/integrating-blockchain-erp.pdf. Last accessed 2021/3/12.
17. Banerjee, A. (2019). Blockchain with IOT: Applications and use cases for a new paradigm of supply chain driving efficiency and cost. In S. Kim, G. C. Deka, & P. Zhang (Eds.), *Advances in computer* (Vol. 115, pp. 259–292). *Elsevier*. https://doi.org/10.1016/bs.adcom.2019.07.007
18. Oracle. (2018). Blockchain Platform pricing options. https://www.oracle.com/in/application-development/cloud-services/blockchain-platform/. Last accessed 2021/5/8.
19. Owen, P. (2019). Microsoft, SAP announce interoperability of azure blockchain service and SAP cloud platform blockchain service. SAP TechEd 2019. https://www.sapinsideronline.com/blogs/microsoft-sap-announce-interoperability-of-azure-blockchain-service-and-sap-cloud-platform-blockchain-service/. Last accessed 2021/4/5.

Toward the Application of Blockchain Technology to Enhance Traceability and Information Sharing in the Supply Chain of Textile Supply Chain: Application to the Order-to-Cash Process

Manal Hader, Abderrahman El Mhamedi, David Tchoffa, and Abdellah Abouabdellah

1 Introduction

Supply chain transparency has drawn great interest from researchers and practitioners, and with the increase in counterfeit products and unethical labors, supply chain transparency has become an urgent matter [11]. Textile supply chain is among the supply chains that require transparency due to its complexity and its large geographical extensibility of actors which make it very opaque and vulnerable [12]. The participants in the textile supply chain are connected by a network, but they do not have enough visibility about important information related to their work. Furthermore, some of the associated parties utilize unethical methods to create and distribute their products which have led to dramatic issues in the past. This has caught the government's attention to the problems of textile industry and pushed them to put pressure on decision-makers in this sector to remedy it under penalty of sanctions and amends [14]. Other major issues of textile supply chain are counterfeits and security [18]. Counterfeiting issues in the textile industry aren't only confined to final products but also touch semifinished products unlike other sectors [18]. These counterfeit products do not just have an economic impact but can sometimes harm the health of customers given the poor quality of the raw material used (Ekwall, 2009). Traceability is a vital element to all sorts of sectors and supply chains [19] which will enable us to track supply chain process and trace products [8]). In fight against the growth of textile traceability issues, many Internet of things (IoT)-based systems are used to keep track of the items and processes at different

M. Hader (✉)
Paris 8 University, The National School of Applied Sciences, Paris, France
e-mail: manal.hader@etud.univ-paris8.fr

A. El Mhamedi · D. Tchoffa · A. Abouabdellah
Paris 8 University, Kenitra, Morocco
e-mail: a.elmhamedi@iut.univ-paris8.fr; d.tchoffa@iut.univ-paris8.fr

A. Bouras et al. (eds.), *Blockchain Driven Supply Chains and Enterprise Information Systems*, https://doi.org/10.1007/978-3-030-96154-1_5

levels of the supply chain. But up to now, almost all of these technologies are monopolistic, unbalanced, and obscure, which leads to confidence problems such as tampering, manipulation, corruption, and faking information. Furthermore, those monopolistic technologies are subject to breakdown because a simple failure will lead the whole system to crash [15], which leads to a crucial question that has yet to be addressed: whether or not the information supplied by textile supply chain participants in the traceability system can be trusted. As a result, the textile market is unsafe which may expose the customers to serious security concerns. We feel that implementing blockchain technology might be a solution to the mentioned issues that can eliminate dependency on a single entity. Rather than saving information in an obscure environment with the blockchain technology, for every actor in the supply chain, all data about textile goods may be stored in a common and transparent system. This might be a valuable addition to the textile supply chain. The following is a breakdown of the paper's structure. The available reviews on the applicability of blockchain technology and centralized systems in textile supply chains are presented in Sect. 2. Then, in Sect. 3, a typical textile supply chain flow is given, followed by the use of the BigchainDB platform in Sect. 4. Section 5 offers the use case, while Sect. 6 delves more into the benefits and drawbacks of the suggested model for this study.

2 Literature Review

In accordance with ISO 9000:2015, traceability is described as the ability to identify and track the history, distribution, location of products, parts, materials, and services. A traceability system monitors and records the flow of processes, products, and services from vendors, manufactured and ultimately distributed as final products. It provides a number of advantages, including increased visibility throughout the supply chain, improved quality, and greater process control [17]. Traceability also makes it possible to overcome obstacles in a retail network and reduce the risks that come with them in supply chain by determining real-time upstream source and downstream recipients. It also assists with decision-making, remanufacturing, recycling, and product recalls. Previously, investigations were carried out to create various technologies and techniques for tracking products in a supply chain and prevent related risks [5]. Regarding textile industry, Shuchih Ernest Chang et al. [21] argued that the lack of information sharing represents a major obstacle in the supply chain of textile sector in Hong Kong and demonstrated that the lack of standards or a uniform platform for sharing information consists of a direct reason of this. Gobbi and Massa have proposed a model to analyze the traceability system in the Italian textile industry which they named Traceability and Fashion (TF). Their model was adopted by the Union of Italian Chambers of Commerce [7]. Furthermore, with the arrival of IoT, many surveys have recommended the use of relevant technologies for textile supply chain traceability systems. Track and trace systems are used to track items as they move through the supply chain's tiers. It entails assigning a unique code to each product or set of items, such as RFID, and then using that code as a tracking element. Keung and Wu in their research suggested a RFID-based supply chain in the apparel sector. They described how their proposition improves the efficiency of a supply chain by facilitating coordination in processes; however, they concluded that despite the multiple benefits of this technology, security issues in information exchange are still a major concern in this industry, demonstrating the inadequacy of such technologies [9]. Agrawal et al. proposed a method to implement a traceability system centered on products for monitoring and controlling production operations and supply chain transactions. In their study, they provided secured tags that aid in the security of the clothing supply chain at the item level and limit unauthorized entry to the item information. However, they recommended that future studies can be conducted to ensure that the traceability system is secure at the enterprise level to avoid an incident on the information exchanging means [2]. All the studies listed above emphasized the use of a centralized system as one of the most successful approaches to promote data transparency in supply chains to date. Currently, a new disruptive technology known as blockchain has arisen as a major issue with a completely different approach. In their work, Casey and Wong demonstrated the potential benefits of blockchain technology in the manufacturing supply chain [4]. They suggested that the inherited benefits of the blockchain could build trust through visibility and transparency within any operation and transaction in the supply chain. They also offer a use case to demonstrate how blockchain technology can be applied to transform supply chains. Moreover, prior literature has demonstrated that there are multiple advantages of blockchain technology which can be applied in the supply chain to stock and exchange information with other actors such as vendors, customers, etc. Among these researches, some researchers showed that blockchain technology can also be used to decrease intermediaries' use, enabling decreased expenses and increased performance [10]. Based on the literature review, IoT has been used by multiple actors for supply chain traceability. However, these are still centralized systems, and no decentralized systems for product tracking have been deployed in the textile supply chain. In this study, a decentralized information system for textile supply chain monitoring and traceability is built using blockchain and IoT. Compared to centralized systems, this new approach would be a game-changing innovation, providing a secure, transparent, and open information system for all supply chain stakeholders. We feel that our proposal represents a fresh approach to supply chain traceability and substantially improve textile supply chain's performance.

3 Textile Supply Chain (TSC) Management

3.1 The Typical Model of the Textile Supply Chain

Supply chain management (SCM) is described as the connection of the core business processes from final user through first vendors that offer raw materials, services, and information to customers and other players, therefore adding value [3].

The textile supply chain represents an illustration of an integrated supply chain, according to Abernathy et al. [1], who said that the textile industry is a worldwide system. Fibers may be manufactured in one nation, spun into yarns, woven into textiles, and stitched into garments in another country, before being marketed elsewhere in the world [1].

The textile supply chain, in general, entails a number of procedures, a variety of raw materials, and a number of intermediary products. The majority partners of the TSC network are raw material vendors (spinning factories and accessory suppliers), manufacturers (knitting factories), trading firm's holders, retailers, or the end customers. A structure of a textile supply chain is presented in Fig. 1.

The flow of TSC is shown in Fig. 1. The general working steps of traditions of textile supply chain management (TSCM) are as follows:

- In the first step: the textile producers gather their raw materials from several vendors to knit the clothes as clothes produced contain the processes of spinning and knitting. Knitting is a process of building fabric by meshing a sequence of loops of one or more yarns. Spinning is the conversion of fibers into yarn. The finest fashionable clothes require a significant amount of study and patience.
- In the second step: after product manufacture, they send it to the trading firms.
- In the third step: the retailers get the final products which they usually order according to their needs and order forecast.
- In the final step: the retailers sell the clothes directly to the end users.

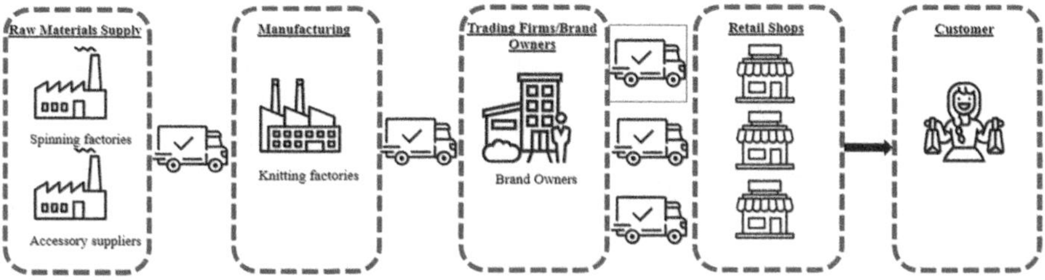

Fig. 1 Working mechanisms of a typical textile supply chain without blockchain

3.2 *Major Shortcoming of Existing Supply Chain Management System*

With the fast growth of Internet technologies and centralized mechanism, such as an EDI, ERP, and RFID system, a lot of emerging technologies have been used in trace- ability systems of the textile industry's supply chain for the validation and coordination of up-to-date process status information [20].

As previously stated, virtually all of these systems are centralized (as presented in Fig. 2). Moreover, enterprises with small resources still rely heavily on manual operations or phone calls, e-mail correspondence, and web-based service to achieve minimum efficiency which remains ineffective to attend synchronization among supply chain partners.

In addition, the intervention of centralized middlemen, who are expected to enhance confidence between stakeholders, leads to confusion when they experience system dysfunction caused by manipulation or fraudulent attacks.

Because of these issues, the adoption of a coordinated system based on the various assets is not widespread among existing textile companies, which reduces the overall efficiency of the supply chain.

Figure 3 illustrates the framework of the supply chain traceability mechanism that is widely used in business today.

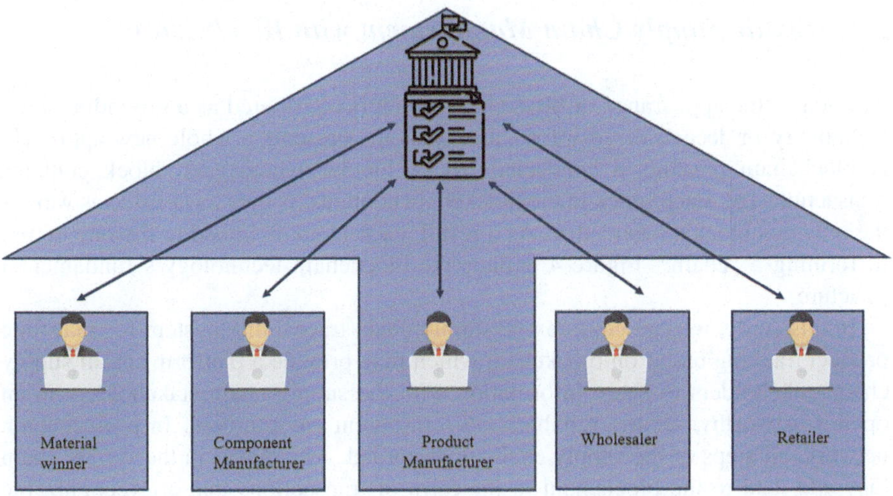

Fig. 2 Supply chain management by centralized entity. (Source: Martin Verwijmeren [22])

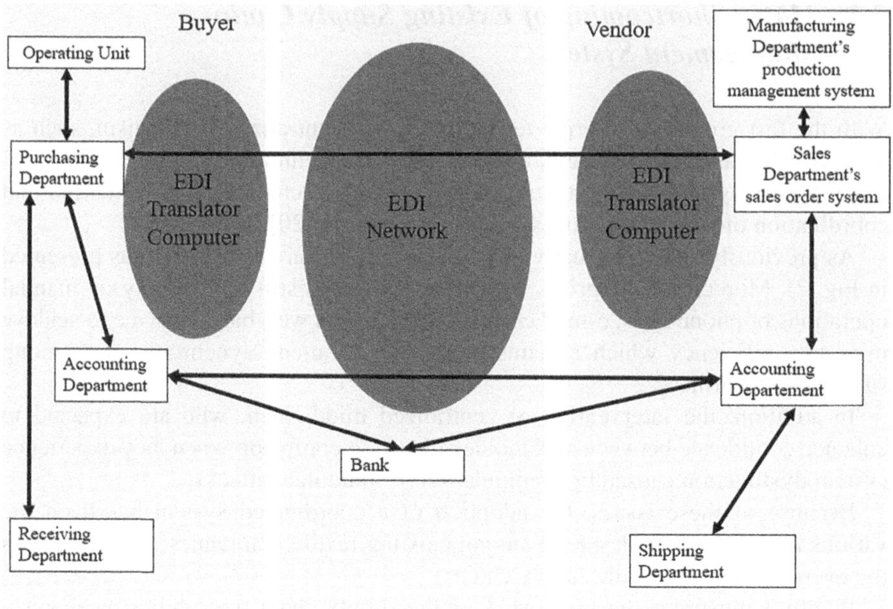

Fig. 3 Traditional method of supply chain traceability (EDI and VAN). (Source: Schneider [20])

3.3 Textile Supply Chain Management with Blockchain

Nowadays, the appearance of blockchain which is considered as a groundbreaking technology in decentralized information systems presents a whole new approach. A blockchain presents a connected list of blocks, where each block contains transactions [6]. Each block in the blockchain contains its own hash value as well as the previous block's hash value. As a result, each block is linked to the one before it, forming a "chain." Figure 4 depicts the blockchain technology's fundamental structure.

In this study, we present a textile supply chain traceability system for real-time product tracking based on blockchain which may provide a platform for all supply chain stakeholders to share information with the supply chain stakeholders in an open, trustworthy, secure, reliable, and transparent environment. In a blockchain network, all steps of the supply chain are recorded. Any player in the supply chain may add data to the blockchain in the form of transactions that are recognizable in the system, and all of the data in the blockchain is accessible. Every new transaction in the network is recorded in an immutable block that is time-stamped to maintain track of the specific product in the end-to-end chain and to ensure that the information included in the block is not tampered with. As shown in Fig. 5, our proposed system is a typical decentralized distributed system which integrates Internet of things such as RFID and WSN to collect data. A tag (RFID) is applied

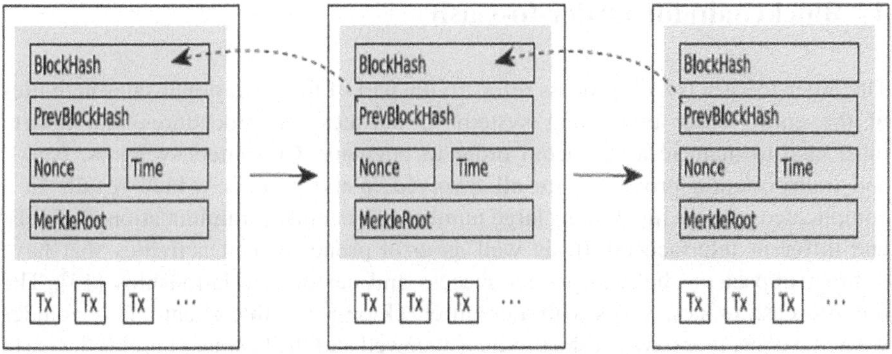

Fig. 4 A basic block diagram of blockchain [6]

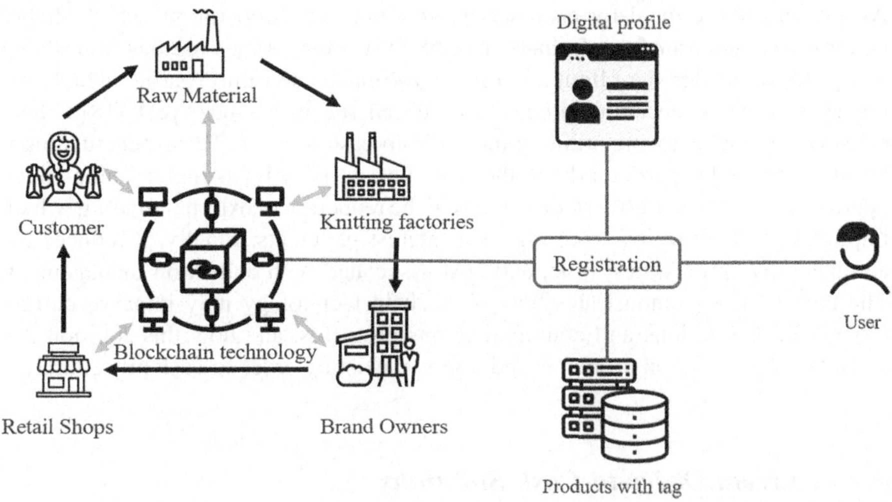

Fig. 5 Overview of textile supply chain management system with blockchain technology

to each product, which has a unique code that connects the physical items to their digital identities in the system. This digital depiction might be used to create a product profile. Users have their own virtual representation, which comprises important associated data. A blockchain-based system eliminates the need for a centralized trust authority; instead, all system users may log in and check the authenticity and history of any product. Security and immutability are guaranteed via a "mining process" which build trust among stakeholders. The general diagram of TSCM with blockchain is shown in Fig. 5.

4 Blockchain for Order-to-Cash

The order-to-cash (O2C) process refers to the part of the operational sales activities of the entire order processing system. It outlines the procedures that a firm must take to manage a sale from order to payment. Customers, vendors, banks, and transportation providers are all involved in the process, which results in a complicated process involving a large number of systems, communication channels, and different interface effort, as well as error-prone manual activities that have a direct impact on the enterprise's success and customer relationships [13]. The order-to-cash process starts with a credit check on a possible client and concludes when the consumer pays for the products received and the business applies the cash. Customers, Customer Service, Operations, Distribution, Sales and Marketing, and Finance and Accounting are the six departments engaged in the order-to-cash cycle. As a result, it is critical for each service to complete its operation, which should be error-free and transfer information correctly via the various regions. Improving this process enables the elimination of inefficiencies and third parties which can impact positively the entire process as we can see in the next part [18]. There are several benefits to streamlining the order-to-cash process. These benefits might be quite valuable, particularly if the firm invests heavily in higher-value-added operations and so on. Furthermore, it aids in the reduction of external funding, which improves profitability by lowering loan interest payments. Finally, it reduces the administrative procedures, time, and cost associated with collection management. The next section demonstrates how blockchain technology may improve current order-to-cash solutions and communications protocols, and how this solution can assist to solve common problems and improve existing order-to-cash procedures.

4.1 Current Order-to-Cash Solutions

Enterprise resource planning (ERP) solutions, which include SAP, Oracle, and PeopleSoft, enable automated data transfer across functional departments in the O2C pipeline. Nonetheless, ERP systems do not handle the management of customer risk, address potential order processing errors, or deal with cash flow following a customer invoicing. ERP systems are now used to manage business operations in most companies. These systems are used for a variety of purposes, including human resources, purchasing, finance, and sales procedures such as the O2C process. ERP systems need to be tailored to the requirements of each organization due to the uniqueness of business operations. The ERP system has a crucial part to play in changing the processes of a company [16]. However, these ERP solutions do not interact with other organizations' systems because each company uses a different ERP solution. Moreover, supply chains are ecosystems with multiple stakeholders and companies, which makes it complicated to have a holistic view of the supply chain and leads most of the time to inefficient processes and poor cross-functional integration. In the case of the (O2C) process, this can lead to inefficient receivables management and the occurrence of process failures, for example, a high error rate in order taking, customers who are unable or unwilling to pay on time, poor collection methods, and inadequate customer inquiry management systems are all factors that contribute to high error rates in order fulfillment. Blockchain technology has the potential to dramatically change this. This technology has the potential to serve as a missing link between many technologies. Additionally, it is difficult to make significant modifications to ERP systems once implemented. For this reason, when incorporating blockchains into legacy ERP systems, it is necessary to be mindful that there should be minimal modifications to existing ERP and minimal disruption to normal business processes.

4.2 *The BigchainDB for O2C Process*

To overcome the technological limitations of blockchain technologies, which include restricted scalability, low transaction rate, and high-power consumption, we chose to use the BigchainDB platform, which is with high data rate, low response time, strong query features, distributed monitoring, immutable data storing, and embedded support for assets. BigchainDB, in fact, is like a blockchain database [15], as it is defined on the official BigchainDB website. This platform was chosen because it is open source and can run a single node on any virtual machine. BigchainDB transactions are defined by three different elements which are as follows:

1. *The asset*: it represents physical to digital objects that we want to represent, for example, a dress with flowers or a cotton. It is impossible to modify or alter the information inside the asset.
2. *The metadata*: it allows the user to add details and information to the transactions, like origins, characteristics, transporter, etc. And this metadata can be updated for each transaction.
3. *The transaction ID*: it refers to the id of the transaction represented with a hash function over the entire information of the transaction. Figure 6 shows an example, from BigchainDB official site, of these elements.

This platform allows the definition of two main transactions. The first one is the CREATE transaction and the second one is the TRANSFER transaction. The first one allows users to create a new record in the database and the second one enables the user to transfer the ownership of defined record to another user.

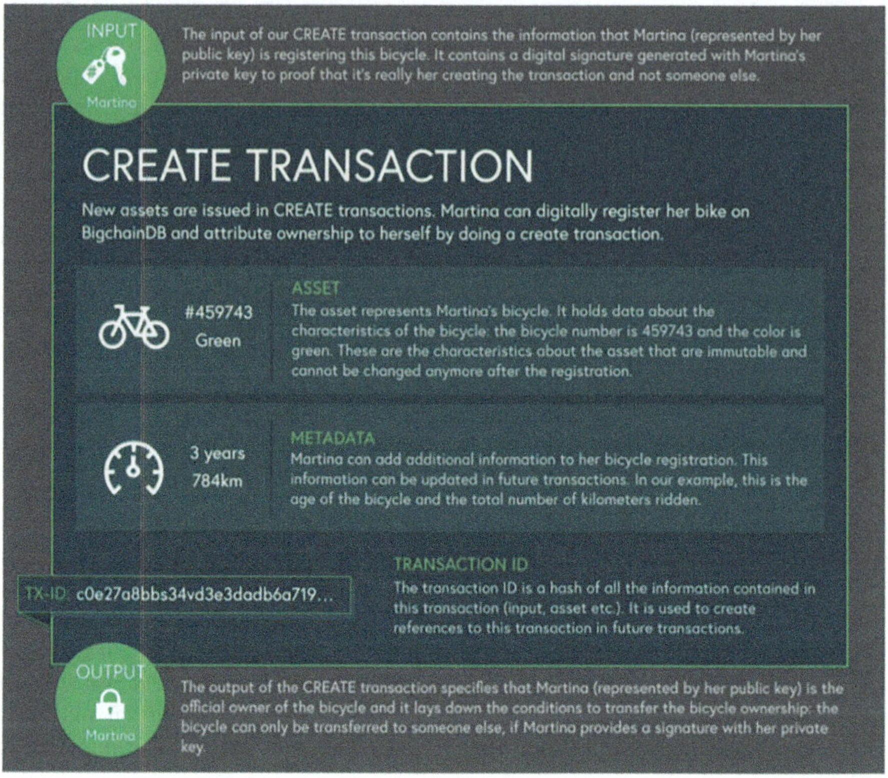

Fig. 6 Example of bicycle transaction using BigchainDB. (Source: BigchainDB official site)

5 Use Case

In this section, a use case of BigchainDB is presented that is integrated into the order-to-cash process. Through the example of the international commerce, it is illustrated exactly the way BigchainDB can streamline, automate, and reduce the complexity of the order-to-cash flow and remove the middleman from the process. As way of illustration, traditional method is illustrated in Fig. 7, while the BigchainDB is illustrated in Fig. 8.

The technological functionalities of the adoption are presented below: Supplier sells goods to a retailer that are delivered by a transportation service provider.

- *Step 1:* the retailer places a sales order with the supplier – When a supplier gets a retailer's order, which includes products, configuration, pricing, and delivery choices, the cycle begins.

  The merchant then requests a letter of credit from its financial institution, which is then issued to the supplier's financial institution.

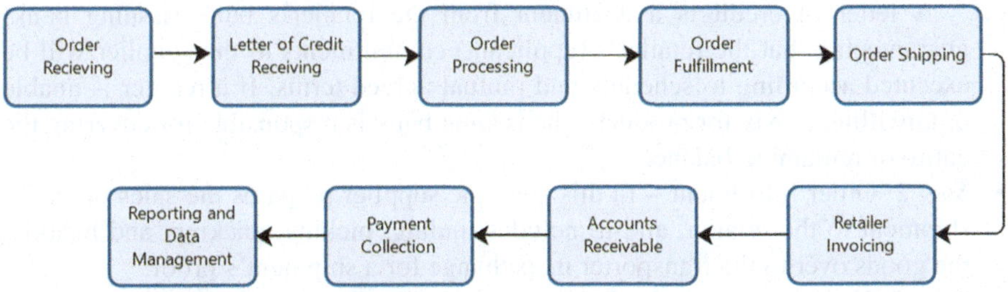

Fig. 7 Conventional order-to-cash process

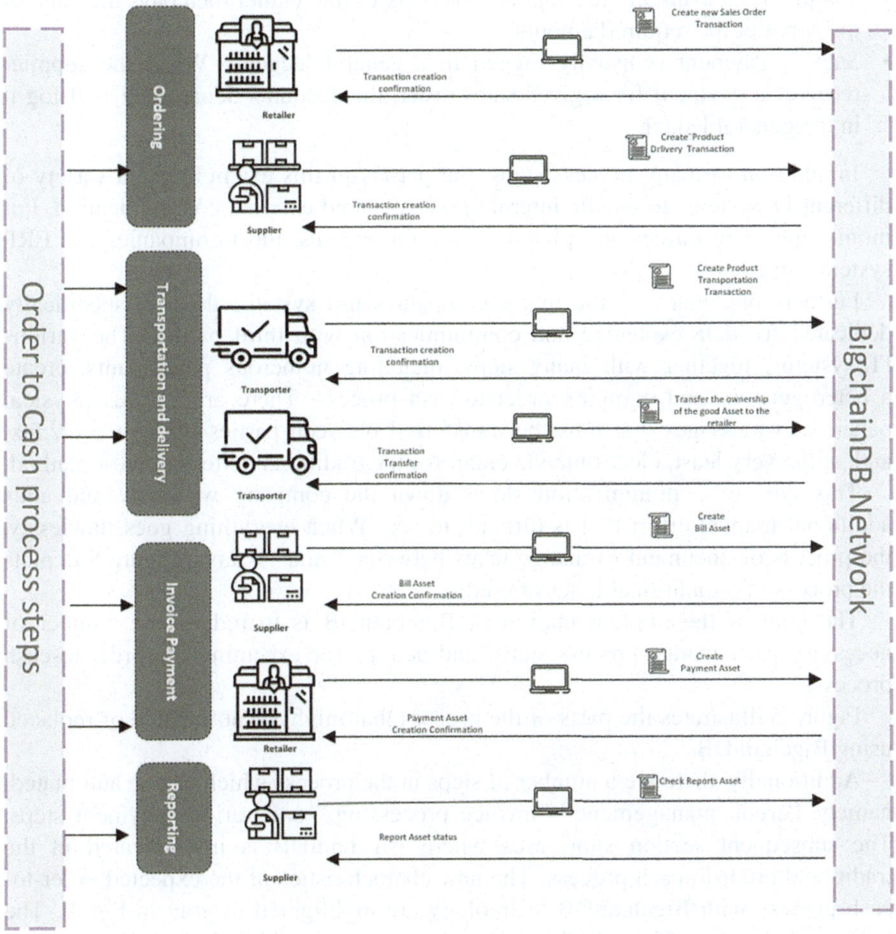

Fig. 8 Proposed procure-to-pay process with smart contract technology

A letter of credit is a document from the retailer's bank (issuing bank) guaranteeing that the retailer's (applicant) commitments to the supplier will be executed according to schedule and mutual agreed terms. If a retailer is unable or unwilling to pay for products, the issuing bank is responsible for covering the entire or remaining balance.

- *Step 2*: Order fulfillment – In this step, the supplier prepares the sales order for shipment to the retailer, and it includes finding, picking, packing, and handing the goods over to the transporter in exchange for a shipment's proof.
- *Step 3*: The invoice is created and sent to the retailer or an invoice is generated and sent to the retailer.
- *Step 4*: Payment – At this stage, the retailer orders its bank to pay the required amount to the bank of the supplier. The bank of the retailer then pays the bank of the supplier the required amount.
- *Step 5*: Payment is usually logged in a general ledger – When the supplier receives a payment for a given sales order, the accounts department will log it in the general ledger.

In addition to many process steps, the parties in this example use a variety of different IT systems to handle internal processes and external communication. For monitoring of resources and planning of requirements, most companies use ERP systems, like.

Furthermore, many of the major companies use systems that are specifically dedicated for data exchange and communication with third parties. The various IT systems, together with many steps, including numerous participants, create a heterogeneous and complex order-to-cash process. There are various physical papers and messages that must be transferred between parties through post, fax, and, at the very least, electronic via email for the traditional letter of credit method.

This type of communication slows down the company workflow and adds additional manual effort that is difficult to see. When everything goes flawlessly, the process of document exchange takes between 7 and 10 days. Figure 8 depicts the process of a traditional letter of credit.

The goal of the implementation of BigchainDB is to reduce the number of necessary participants, process steps, and actions for executing the order-to-cash process.

Figure 6 illustrates the parts of the process that might be automated or replaced using BigchainDB.

Additionally, there are a number of steps in the process which can be automated, namely, "credit management," "invoice processing," and various payment steps. The subsequent section showcases where BigchainDB is implemented in the traditional order-to-cash process. The new characteristics of the expected order-to-cash process with BigchainDB technology are highlighted in gray in Fig. 9. The banks are substituted by a BigchainDB platform upon which the requirements are implemented. The BigchainDB serves as a sort of distributed ledger to which all the involved parties can access, and the terms are integrated into the blockchain network

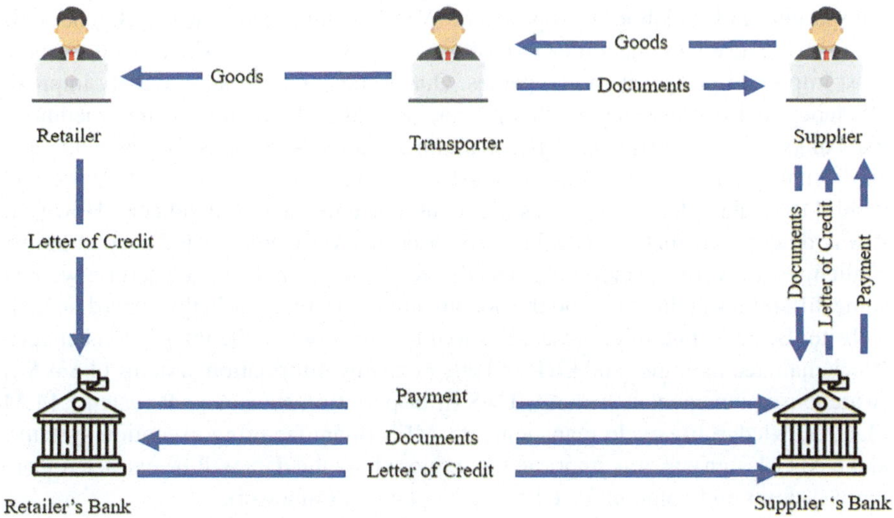

Fig. 9 Conventional credit of letter management

and enabled for "sales and demand matching," "automatic invoice processing and payment," as well as "leaving an audit trace."

To get things started, the retailer issues a sales order on the blockchain to the provider, which is then paired by a terms check implemented in BigchainDB beforehand. The contractual terms are determined by the BigchainDB platform, which ensures that the contractual terms are respected. The retailer checks the order with the delivery after having received the purchased items, and the data of the invoice will be processed automatically after its acknowledgment. The confirmation on accuracy of the transaction automatically initiates the operation of transferring the committed amount to the supplier's account while maintaining a seamless audit trail that is available to all involved parties for further reporting. It is worth mentioning here that for starters, banks are no longer needed. Blockchain brings the required security and trust among the two contractual parties. In addition, unneeded process steps are dropped by using self-executing smart contracts (letter of credit), and several of the remaining processes can be automated (e.g., credit management, invoice processing, and payment).

6 Conclusion

In this paper, we suggest a new strategy for a traceability system in the textile industry's supply chain based on decentralized technology. This system will offer real-time information about apparel products to all supply chain partners, reducing the danger of centralized information systems and providing a more secure, distributed, transparent, and collaborative approach. We also suggested that the BigchainDB platform be used in the order-to-cash process which is considered one of the most important processes in companies. Our proposition can significantly improve efficiency and transparency of this process with the elimination of intermediaries like banks in our use case and can also automate some operations like invoicing and credit management, which will obviously improve supply chain performance and rebuild the stakeholders' and investors' confidence in the textile industry. However, it was determined that for BigchainDB to be market-ready for industry, multiple challenges are yet to overcome especially for creating multi-node servers; we had some difficulties in this case and the documentation is not clear in this regard on their website. Besides that, future research should focus more on the integration between Blockchain technologies and ERP and other existing information systems like WMS (warehouse management system), TMS (transportation management system), PLM (data/knowledge life cycle management), MES (manufacturing execution system), and CAD (design), as it is important to explore how the data will be extracted from these systems and communicated to the blockchain framework.

References

1. Abernathy, F. H., Volpe, A., & Weil, D. (2004). *Previewing the apparel and textile industries after 2005: Prospects and choices*. The Harvard Center for Textile and Apparel Research. http://www.hctar.org
2. Agrawal, T. K., Koehl, L., & Campagne, C. (2018). A secured tag for implementation of traceability in textile and clothing supply chain. *International Journal of Advanced Manufacturing Technology, 99*, 2563–2577. https://doi.org/10.1007/s00170-018-2638-x
3. Håkansson, A., Nguyen, N. T.,Hartung, R. L., Howlett, R. J., & Jain, L. C. (2009) Agent and multi-agent systems: *Technologies and applications third KES international symposium, KES-AMSTA 2009, Uppsala, Sweden, June 3–5, 2009.* Proceedings Bigchaindb-Whitepaper. 2016.
4. Casey, M. J., & Wong, P. (2017). Global supply chains are about to get better, thanks to blockchain. *Harvard Business Review Digital Articles, 13, 1–6.*
5. Cheung, H. H., & Choi, S. H. (2011). Implementation issues in RFID-based anti-counterfeiting systems. *Computers in Industry, 62*, 708718. https://doi.org/10.1016/j.compind.2011.04.001
6. Tian, F. (2016). An agri-food supply chain traceability system for China based on RFID & blockchain technology, *Proceedings of 2016 IEEE 13th International Conference on Service Systems and Service Management (ICSSSM)*, pp. 1–6. https://doi.org/10.1109/icsssm.2016.7538424.
7. Gobbi, L., & Massa, I. (2015). Supply chain management in textile sector: The case of the Italian T-fashion traceability system. *International Journal of Environment and Health, 7*, 359–370. https://www.bigchaindb.com/whitepaper/bigchaindb-whitepaper.pdf
8. Ilie-Zudor, E., Kemény, Z., Ekárt, A., et al. (2014). A solution for information management in logistics operations of modern manufacturing chains. *Procedia CIRP, 25*, 337–344. https://doi.org/10.1016/j.procir.2014.10.047
9. Keung Kwok, S., & Wu, K. K. W. (2009). RFID-based intra-supply chain in textile industry. *Industrial Management & Data Systems, 109*(9), 1166–1178.
10. Koetsier, J. (2017). *Blockchain beyond bitcoin: How Blockchain will transform business in 3–5 years*. Accessed 29 Mar 2019.
11. Kumar, V., Agrawal, T. K., Wang, L., & Chen, Y. (2017). Contribution of traceability towards attaining sustainability in the textile sector. *Text Cloth Sustain, 3*, 5.

12. Kumar, V., Koehl, L., & Zeng, X. (2016). A fully yarn integrated tag for tracking the international textile supply chain. *Journal of Manufacturing System, 40, 76–86*. https://doi.org/10.1016/j.jmsy.2016.06.007
13. Zhang, L., Allam, A., & Gonzales, C. A.. (2006). Service-oriented order-to-cash solution with business RSS information exchange framework. *2006 IEEE International Conference on Web Services (ICWS'06)*, pp. 841–848. https://doi.org/10.1109/ICWS.2006.121.
14. Lee, S.-Y. (2008). Drivers for the participation of small and medium sized suppliers in green supply chain initiatives. *Supply Chain Management: An International Journal, 13*, 185–198.
15. McConaghy, T., Marques, R., Müller, A., De Jonghe, D., McConaghy, T., McMullen, G., Henderson, R., Bellemare, S., & Granzotto, A. (2016). *BigchainDB: A scalable blockchain database*. White paper, BigChainDB.
16. Müller-Jentsch, D. (2005). *Deeper integration and trade in Services in the Euro-Mediterranean Region: Southern dimensions of the European neighborhood policy*. World Bank.World Bank. https://openknowledge.worldbank.org/handle/10986/733
17. Pigni, F., Crave, S., & Ravaini, A. (2007). Traceability in the textile and clothing industry: Issues and implications for RFId adoption: *The 2nd Mediterranean conference on information systems, MCIS*. Venice, Italy, p 2007.
18. Corbellini, S., Ferraris, F., & Parvis, M. (2006). A cryptographic system for brand authentication and material traceability in the textile industry. 2006 IEEE *Instrumentation and Measurement Technology Conference Proceedings, Sorrento,* pp. 1331–1335.
19. Saak, A. E. (2016). Traceability and reputation in supply chains. *Int J Prod, 177*, 149.
20. Schneider, G. P. (2017). *Electronic commerce* (12th ed.). Cengage Learning.
21. Chang, S. E., Chen, Y.-C., & Ming-Fang, L. (2019). Supply chain re-engineering using blockchain technology: A case of smart contract based tracking process. *Technological Forecasting and Social Change, 144*, 1–11.
22. Verwijmeren, M. (2004). Software component architecture in supply chain management. *Computers in Industry, 53*(2), 165–178.

Exploiting Cost-Effective IoT Devices for Trustless Agri-Food Supply Chain Management: A Practical Case Study

Miguel Pincheira, Massimo Vechio, and Raffaele Giaffreda

1 Introduction

Today, the vast majority of traditional logistic information systems in Agriculture and Food (Agri-Food) supply chains merely tracks and stores orders and deliveries without providing features such as transparency, traceability, and auditability. These features surely improve food quality and safety; therefore, they are increasingly being requested by consumers [24]. However, the supply chain in Agriculture and Food is a highly complex process due to the disparity of stages and actors involved. Each stage has particular characteristics, and each actor has different requirements. Thus, achieving transparency, traceability, and auditability along this complex process is not a simple task and requires collaboration between all the involved actors [8]. Collaboration requires overcoming several barriers such as the lack of willingness to share information, skepticisms for security and reliability, limitations of actual contractual relations, and mostly the uncertainty about the impact of the information sharing [25].

Thus, several Research & Development communities are concentrating efforts on adopting some specific digital technologies to realize them in the Agri-Food supply chain management. The Internet of Things (IoT) has contributed to this development, with technologies such as RFIDs and Wireless Sensor Networks. An increasing number of cost-effective connected devices enabled remote monitoring of food transportation scenarios with fine granularity. The devices contribute along the whole Agro-Food supply chain, e.g., from production to consumption [22] creating a more detailed and accurate description of the entire process.

M. Pincheira (✉) · M. Vechio · R. Giaffreda
OpenIoT Research Unit, Fondazione Bruno Kessler, Trento, Italy
e-mail: mpincheiracaro@fbk.eu; mvecchio@fbk.eu; rgiaffreda@fbk.eu

A. Bouras et al. (eds.), *Blockchain Driven Supply Chains and Enterprise Information Systems*, https://doi.org/10.1007/978-3-030-96154-1_6

Centralized cloud-based architectures are the current choice for IoT systems, where a validating third party provides services such as authentication, authorization, and data handling for both sensing devices and end users [4]. These architectures simplify the design and the deployment of IoT systems and applications; however, they introduce additional concerns regarding privacy and data management [5, 27]. Moreover, centralized cloud infrastructures typically lack transparency and auditability [3] and present a single point of failure for the entire system. These challenges are vital issues on an Agri-Food supply chain system, requiring radically new approaches for the architectures behind such systems and applications.

In recent years, there has been a growing interest in integrating blockchain technologies into IoT [2] for enabling trustless architectures. Blockchain uses a unique combination of cryptography, data structures, and incentive mechanisms to maintain a particular type of distributed database (i.e., a *ledger*) in a peer-to-peer network. The distributed ledger is immutable by design and offers an auditable and transparent source of information. Blockchain provides a trusted repository of information for IoT systems, where data is secure and traceable, and the data source can be precisely identified [16]. For an Agri-Food supply chain system, blockchain directly benefits the entire process by enabling the seamless inclusion of several actors [23] and making their interactions leaner, faster, and more transparent [2]. Thus, blockchain is attracting increasing interest for security and transparency in various steps in the Agri-Food supply chain process [11, 21]. However, previous work has only focused on the conceptual application of blockchain in Agri-Food supply chains or has failed to address the role of cost-effective IoT devices.

In this chapter, we present a fully decentralized traceability system for Agri-Food supply chain management. The proposed solution is blockchain-agnostic and considers cost-effective IoT sensor devices. The devices produce and consume valuable information along the whole supply chain and directly interact with the underlying blockchain. To assess the feasibility of the proposed solution, we engineered and deployed a prototype for a *from-farm-to-fork* use case: a classical food traceability scenario fostering certified traceability of food along the whole supply chain, e.g., from agricultural production (the farm side) to consumption (the fork side). Then, we focus on evaluating the impact that the blockchain integration process has at the IoT device level in terms of memory, program size, communications, and power consumption, using two different blockchain implementations.

The remaining of this chapter is organized as follows: Sect. 2 summarizes the current state of the art in the adoption of blockchains as an enabling technology for the traceability in Agri-Food supply chains; Sect. 3 describes the proposed system architecture; Sect. 4 contains details about our implementation; Sect. 5 describes our experimental setup; Sect. 6 presents our preliminary results; Sect. 7 concludes the chapter.

2 Related Work

The last few years have witnessed an explosion of research and development activity around the Blockchain technology, mainly within the financial technology (FinTech) industry. Indeed, its intrinsic capability of providing immutable and tamper-proof records, together with its potential of enabling trust and reliability among untrusted peers, represents too attractive features, preventing this technology to stay relegated into a single vertical sector. For this reason, several industries beyond the FinTech sector have already identified the Blockchain technology as a driver for a paradigm shift. For data reliability, ProvChain [9] explored the use of the Blockchain technology in a cloud storage scenario to verify three levels of data provenance: collection, storage, and validation. In this chapter, the use of blockchains showed good results in terms of tamper-proof records and user privacy, with very low overhead for the storage itself. In a similar context, the authors on [15] explored the use of blockchains with smart contracts to achieve secure data provenance, using the Open Provenance Model (OPM) with an access control-based privacy-preserving solution.

Also the adoption of some IoT devices and technologies in the supply chain management sector has attracted a lot of research interest in the last few years. From the impact of autonomous identification system [12] to the application of RFID technologies in logistics [19], the technological maturity of the devices and of the sensors is literally revolutionizing each step of the process. Specifically for the Agri-Food domain, the authors of [18] presented an inventory transparency use case, also adopting some IoT devices. There, the goal was to explore the use of RFID and NFC-based devices to achieve transparency and real-time information production directly on the field, enabling persistence by means of a centralized, cloud-based database. This is indeed the classical paradigm adopted by far the majority of the current IoT-based solutions.

However, the use of both the Blockchain and the IoT technologies in the Agri-Food domain is still an underexplored, yet worth-to-explore, research field. A traceability system based on the blockchain and the RFID technology was proposed in [20], with a sharp focus on Chinese food markets. The work considered fresh food asset tracking as fruits, vegetables, and meat, by means of RFID-based devices for the data acquisition and blockchains for data persistence. The authors of [21] presented a supply chain traceability system for food safety, based on HACCP (Hazard Analysis and Critical Control Points), and focus on transparency. There, they described the process of crop plants in different phases, from harvesting to retailing, without going into the details of a performance analysis. The authors on [11] explore the use of smart contracts for a credit evaluation blockchain-based system to food supply chain management. The authors on [10] present case study applied to Shandong province in China where blockchain-based system, based on a consortium blockchain implementation, is used to optimize trading portfolio of buyers in the food supply chain. With a more practical approach, the authors on [17] present a blockchain-based traceability system, for the soybean. The work presents a detailed description of an implementation using Ethereum network and focused on the smart contracts supporting the system.

Overall, to the best of our knowledge, the current literature lacks a detailed analysis of the impact that a blockchain may have on the traditional IoT-based system and in particular on the more constrained sensing IoT devices. If sensing devices become direct actors on the blockchain system, they can provide a *"root of trust"* for the sense data. Moreover, a trusted source of information not only benefits IoT systems but also other types of blockchain-based applications, with sensing IoT devices acting as trusted oracles [7].

3 Blockchain-Based Traceability

In this section, we describe our proposal of a blockchain-based traceability system for the Agri-Food supply chain. In our proposal, cost-effective sensing devices measure several parameters along the entire process. In order to define the requirements for our proposed architecture, we must first formalize the requirements of a traceability system and then identify the key elements of each stage that provides transparency and trust to the entire process.

3.1 Supply Chain Process

The authors on [1] addressed the issue of a food supply chain from an operation's perspective, identifying several activities and process, as well as actors and items. In order to integrate the IoT environment, they simplify the process into 5 generic stages: Agricultural/Production, Distribution/Transport, Storage, Consumption, Waste/Disposal. On the other hand, the authors in [25] propose a virtualization of the food supply chain, which is represented by an architecture where the real objects are mapped to a virtual object. The authors simplified the supply chain process into four actors: Farmer, Food Processor, Transporter/Trader, and Retailer. For the particular case of Extra Virgin Olive Oil traceability, the author at [26] defined 4 steps for the process: Harvesting, Milling, Storage, and Packing.

Based on these previous works, and similarly to [6], we simplified the process into 3 stages: Farming, Transportation, and Market as shown in Fig. 1. Each of these stages is composed of several activities, with specifics actors, which are important to the traceability and are briefly introduced in the following:

(a) **Provider:** Providers of raw materials, such as seeds and nutrients, but also pesticides, chemicals, etc.
(b) **Producer:** Usually, the farmer, e.g., the responsible of the actions from seeding/planting to harvesting.

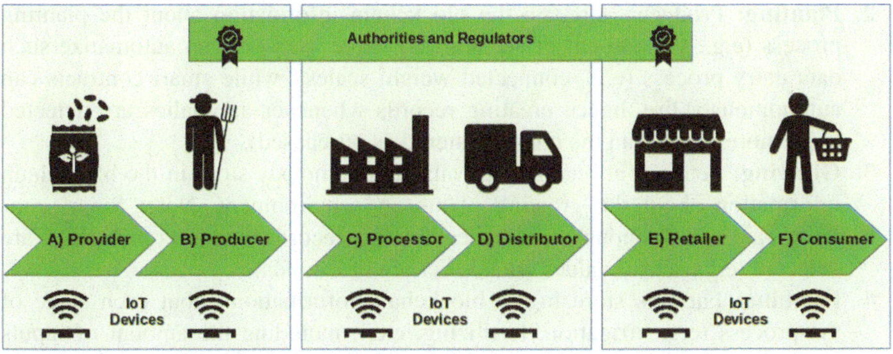

Fig. 1 Simplified version of the Agri-Food supply chain management process [6]

(c) **Processor:** This actor may perform various actions, from simple packaging to more complex processes (e.g., pressing of the olives).
(d) **Distributor:** This actor is responsible of moving the output of the processor (e.g., the product) from processor's site to retailers.
(e) **Retailer:** This actor is responsible of selling the products, representing it either small local stores or big supermarkets.
(f) **Consumer:** The final element of the chain.

Along the whole process, authorities provide standards, regulations, laws, rules, and policies that the involved actors have to comply with.

3.2 Functionalities

To coherently define the high-level functionality of our architecture, we had a bottom-up approach through which we extracted the set of requirements starting from a complete use case, namely, *from-farm-to-fork*. The latter is, indeed, a classical food traceability use case that fosters certified traceability of food along the whole supply chain, from agricultural production to consumption. Our proposed solution shall provide consumers with a complete history of the food he is buying. The only pre-condition is that all the participants (so including the IoT devices) are registered users of the underlying blockchain, meaning that they have the correct public/private key pairs to digitally sign each operation on the distributed ledger. In the following, we summarize the list of extracted requirements:

1. **Raw Materials Purchasing:** Producers and providers store in the blockchain the details of sales and purchases of raw materials, including technical information of products and amounts. Note: Smart tags (e.g., barcode, QR codes) can be used to automatize this process.

2. **Planting:** Producers store in the blockchain information about the planting process (e.g., the amount of seeds used). Note: Sensors can automatize such data entry process (e.g., connected weight scales), while smart contracts can autonomously fire, hence creating records whenever anomalies are detected (e.g., more seeds than the ones registered as purchased).
3. **Growing:** Sensors, at regular intervals, autonomously store in the blockchain information about the growing plants and environment. Note: Smart contracts can asynchronously fire, hence creating records whenever anomalies are detected (e.g., sensor values outside certain thresholds).
4. **Farming:** Farmers store in the blockchain information about each stage of the process (e.g., irrigation, fertilizing, etc.), including the amount of inputs applied. Note: Sensors can automatize such data entry process (e.g., chemical sensors and multisensory systems), while smart contracts can autonomously fire, hence creating records whenever anomalies are detected (e.g., sensor values outside certain thresholds).
5. **Harvesting:** Farmers store in the blockchain details about the harvesting. Note: Sensors can automatize such data entry process (e.g., connected weight scales), while smart contracts can autonomously fire, hence certifying that the process from seeding to harvesting is compliant with certain regulations (e.g., organic, fair trade, etc.).
6. **Delivery to processor:** Farmers transfer the ownership of the products to distributors, directly through the blockchain. Note: Sensors (e.g., GPS sensors) and smart contracts can automatize this process or create records whenever anomalies are detected during the delivery phase (e.g., sensor values outside certain thresholds).
7. **Processing:** Considering the simplest case of a packaging processor, the latter store in the blockchain details about the received amount of product from distributors, the packaged amount, and, eventually, the amount of product lost during the processing phase. Note: Sensors can automatize such data entry process (e.g., connected weight scales), while smart contracts can autonomously fire, hence creating records whenever anomalies are detected (e.g., the packaged amount is larger than the received amount).
8. **Delivery to retailers:** Processors transfer the ownership of the processed product to distributors, directly through the blockchain. Note: Sensors (e.g., GPS sensors) and smart contracts can automatize this process or create records whenever anomalies are detected during the delivery phase (e.g., sensor values outside certain thresholds).
9. **Retailing:** Retailers store in the blockchain details about the received amount of product from distributors. Then, at regular intervals, sensors autonomously store in the blockchain information about the status of the retail environment. Note: Smart contracts can asynchronously fire, hence creating records whenever anomalies are detected (e.g., sensor values outside certain thresholds).

10. **Consuming:** Retailers store in the blockchain details about the sold products, while consumers are able to transparently verify the whole history of a product before buying it. Note: Smart tags can be associated to each package, so that consumers can easily retrieve the whole history of the product.

3.3 Proposed Architecture

We propose an architecture able to rely on the Blockchain and the IoT technologies to achieve transparency, auditability, and immutability of the stored records in a *trustless* environment. In our architecture, sensing devices have a unique blockchain identity and act as trustworthy datasources for smart contracts [7]. Our architecture uses smart contract to implement the business logic of the traceability process. For instance, once basic contract could agree the transport of the raw material to the processing factory. The contract could hold the payment in escrow and based on the information provided by the sensors during the transportation. Sensors could automatically cancel the payment, if, for instance, the temperature or humidity during transportation exceeds the agreed thresholds. Moreover, our architecture allows to seamlessly integrate additional actors that can provide the rewards or certifications, using the transparent and immutable register of all the information captured by the sensor across the entire supply chain process [14]. The architecture is shown in Fig. 2.

To obtain fine-grained information across the entire process, we rely on low-cost, energy-efficient sensing devices. To fully exploit the potential of the combination of the IoT with blockchains, these monitoring devices are considered proper actors of the underlying blockchain [13].

In our architecture, each device manages its own blockchain identity, hence autonomously issuing and signing its own transactions in the blockchain when needed. Thus, each monitoring node can transmit the value it measures directly toward a blockchain node. The transactions are directly fed purposely designed

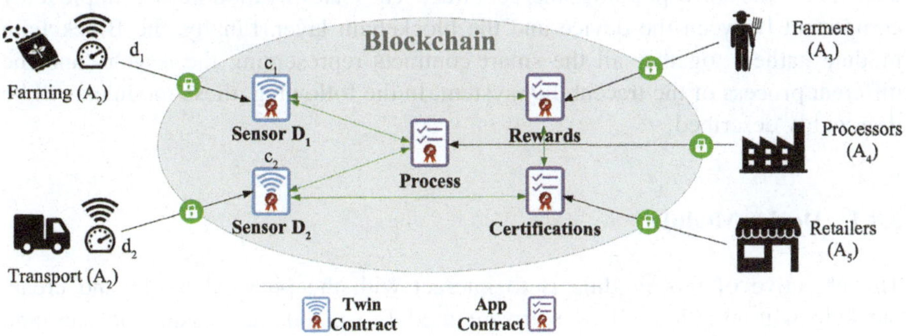

Fig. 2 High-level architecture for blockchain-based traceability

smart contracts deployed in the blockchain network. This process guarantees the integrity of the data by creating immutable, auditable, and non-repudiable records that are easily verifiable by other users.

To keep low the transaction rate of the sensing nodes, we allow for aggregating multiple readings at the sensor side. This means that a sensor node can transact aggregated values to the blockchain (for instance, hourly or daily values depending on the requirements of the application), while the individual data points can be stored in more traditional IoT platforms/services. In this way, the users (or the service provider) can set the frequency of the reports, based on the trade-offs in terms of energy budget of the sensor nodes, transaction cost in the public blockchain, and maximum delay tolerable by the application/business processes.

In our system, each device is represented by a unique smart contract deployed in the blockchain. More formally, if an IoT deployment D is composed of n sensor devices d_i (with $i = 1, \ldots, n$) such that $D = [d_1, \ldots, d_n]$, then we assume that $\forall\, d \in D \quad \exists!\, c \in C$, where $C = [c_1, \ldots, c_n]$ represents the group of smart contracts c_i mapping the i-th device in the blockchain. Therefore, each smart contract can be seen as the device's "digital-twin" in the blockchain (for analogy, we refer to it as the device's "smart-twin"). This contract has a template interface, including both public and private methods. Private methods update the state of the twin in the blockchain and can be invoked only by the device owning the blockchain identity, while public methods simply provide a standardized interface for other smart contracts. Thus, a billing contract or a transportation contract can use device's smart contracts as transparent sources of information in a trustless way.

3.4 *Software Framework*

We conceptualized our architecture into a layered software framework similar to current IoT layered architectures. The software framework, shown in Fig. 3, is divided into three modules, namely the Device, Gateway, and Blockchain modules. The Device module converts the sensed values into blockchain transactions that are later sent to the corresponding smart contract. The Gateway module is a simple relay component between the device and the blockchain layer. Finally, the Blockchain module gathers together all the smart contracts representing the sensors and the different process of the traceability system. In the following, these modules will be thoroughly described.

3.4.1 Device Module

The objective of this module is to interact with the physical world and create blockchain transactions. This software module run on the sensing devices and has three components: Sensing, Blockchain Integration, and Communications. The sensing components interface with the sensor, and its output is a sensed value from

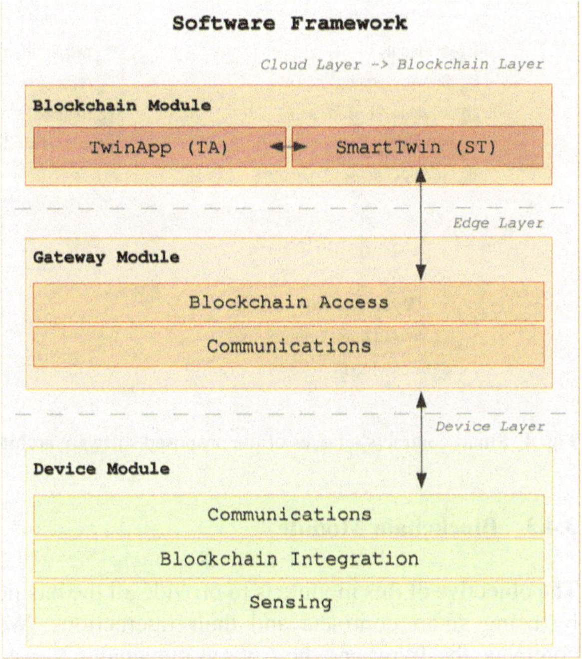

Fig. 3 Layered software framework

the physical world. The Blockchain integration component converts the sensed value into a blockchain transaction, making the device direct actor in the blockchain system. The communications components send the transactions to the blockchain. Typically, this is done using a constrained communication protocol to reach a gateway (on the next layer), which later forwards the transaction to blockchain. The complexity of this component will depend on the blockchain implementation used (to create a transaction) and in the communications protocol selected.

3.4.2 Gateway Module

The objective of this module is to receive the transactions from the lower layer and then forward to the next layer, making the appropriate protocol conversions. The gateway module has two components: Communications and Blockchain access. Communications handles the restricted communication protocol with the lower layer to receive the transaction. Blockchain Access simply forwards the transaction to a peer on the blockchain, typically using the standard TCP access to the Internet. Despite the protocols used, the transaction is digital signed and the device, and it cannot be modified in this layer. The complexity of the module will depend on the communications protocols used.

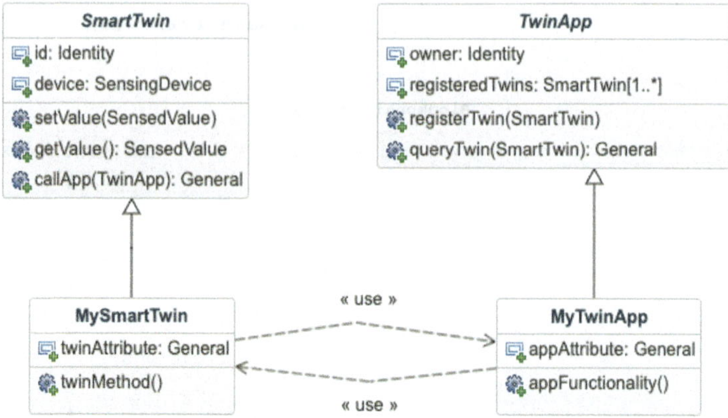

Fig. 4 Smart contracts' classes of the proposed software architecture

3.4.3 Blockchain Module

The objective of this module is to provide all the business logic using the application by using smart contracts and their interactions. We define two types of smart contracts: the Twins and the Apps as depicted in Fig. 4. From a software perspective, these contracts are high-level abstract classes with a series of primitives that can be extended to fulfill the requirements of each application.

The SmartTwins are simplified representations of the IoT devices in the shape of "*smart twins*." As an interface, the SmartTwin implements three methods, namely `getValue()`, `setValue()`, and `callApp()`. `getValue()` is used by the sensing device to update the twin. `getValue()` is used by TwinApp contracts to interact with the SmartTwin. `callApp()` is used by the SmartTwin to interact with the TwinApp. The SmartTwin has two basic properties, a unique identification, and the identity of the sensing device that it represents. It is important to notice that the method `setValue()` is restricted only to the sensing device.

The TwinApps are the types of applications that can interact with SmartTwin and provide two basic methods, namely, `registerTwin()` and `queryTwin()`. In our architecture, SmartTwins are required to first register with a particular application, by using the `registerTwin()` method. After registration, the TwinApp can interact with the SmartTwin using the `queryTwin()` method. The TwinApp maintains two properties, the identity of the owner of the app and a list of all registered SmartTwins that can interact with the application.

This module also provides a REST Application Programming Interface exposing the capabilities of the architecture to other applications. It relies on the API provided by the underlying blockchain network and should allow and easy integration with the existing software systems and other software components (e.g., user graphical interface).

4 Implementation

To better describe and quantitatively assess the benefits of the proposed technology architecture, we implemented it as a fully working prototype. In particular, we focused on the *Delivery to processor* functionality described in Sect. 3.2 as shown in Fig. 5. Our architecture is blockchain-agnostic; therefore, for our evaluation, we tailored our architecture to two different blockchain implementations: Ethereum and Hyperledger Sawtooth. Nonetheless, migrating the architecture to other implementations should not present a major issue. The reasons of choosing these implementations are two-folds. First, we have references for both public and private blockchain networks. Second, the selected blockchains provide different levels of customization for the records included on the ledger (transactions). Ethereum works with a single transaction structure, while Hyperledger Sawtooth allows the definition of a custom transaction structure.

4.1 Device Module Implementation

The values acquired by the sensing devices need to be converted into a blockchain transaction. For Ethereum and Sawtooth, there is no official implementation that can be used in constrained IoT devices, and, to the best of our knowledge, no third-party libraries providing cross-platform compatibility exist. For this reason, we decided to implement our own software library, based on open-source initiatives and favoring cross-platform compatibility over code optimization. We opted for the C language within the Arduino development framework.

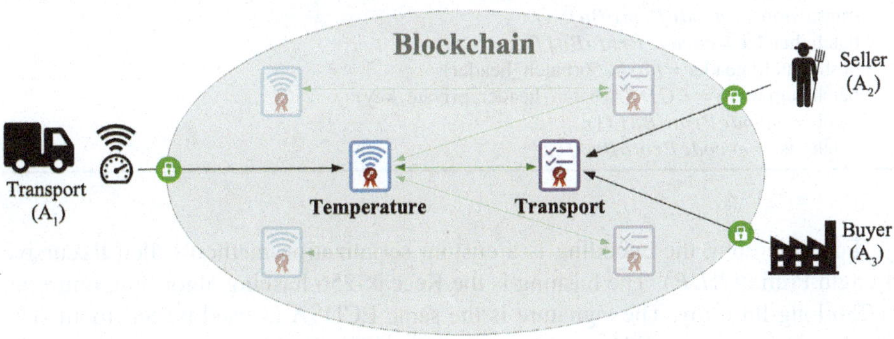

Fig. 5 Implementation of Delivery to Processor functionality of the proposed architecture

4.1.1 Sensing Component

For our prototype, we implemented a sensing stage using a DHT11 temperature and humidity sensor. The sensing stage includes an open-source library to read the values from the sensor that, in this case, is only temperature as an integer.

4.1.2 Blockchain Integration Component

The values acquired by the sensing devices need to be converted into a blockchain transaction, as the minimal unit of information inside the blockchain network. The process of creating a transaction for a particular payload (i.e., the sensed value) varies between implementations; however, the process typically includes 3 steps: encoding for serialization of the data, hashing for integrity of the payload, and digital signing for identity.

For Sawtooth, the encoding uses ProtoBuff, a serialization scheme proposed by google. The hashing of the payload uses the SHA512 algorithm. To sign the transactions, Sawtooth uses the Elliptic Curve Digital Signature Algorithm (ECDSA), with the sepk256 parameters, and the SHA256 hashing. Algorithm 1 shows the process, and while the transaction itself is created half-way the algorithm, the final result is a batch list that might include several transactions.

Algorithm 1: Creating a sawtooth transaction

Result: Sawtooth Transaction (Batch list)
hash_payload = $hash512$(payload);
tx_header = $encodeProtoBuff()$;
hash_tx_header = $hash256$(tx_header);
header_signature = $ECDSA$(hash_tx_header, private_key);
transaction = $encodeProtoBuff()$;
batch_header = $encodeProtoBuff()$;
hash_batch_header = $hash256$(batch_header);
batch_signature = $ECDSA$(batch_header, private_key);
batch = $encodeProtoBuff()$;
batch_list = $encodeProtoBuff()$;

For Ethereum, the encoding is a custom serialization method called Recursive Length Prefix (RLP). The hashing is the Keccak-256 hashing algorithm, returning a 256-long-bit array. The signature is the same ECDSA as used by Sawtooth. The process of creating an Ethereum transaction is shown in Algorithm 2.

Algorithm 2: Creating an Ethereum transaction

Result: Ethereum Transaction
tx_body = $encodeRLP()$;
hash_tx_body = $hash256$(tx_header);
tx_signature = $ECDSA$(hash_tx_header, private_key);
transaction = $encodeRLP()$;

4.1.3 Communications Components

For a reference, we used serial communications at 115200 bps between the device and the gateway using a USB connection.

4.2 Gateway Module Implementation

The transaction sent by the device is received by this module and forwarded to the next layer. We implemented this module in Python 3.6.

4.2.1 Communications

In our prototype, this module interfaces with the serial port at 115200 and receives the transactions as a byte array.

4.2.2 Blockchain Access

The transaction, received on the serial port, is sent to a blockchain node using a network connection. In this prototype, the nodes (both for Ethereum and Sawtooth) are hosted on a physically different computer server and can be accessed by a REST API.

4.3 The Blockchain Module

For our prototype, we implemented a SmartTwin for temperature sensor and TwinApp for the transportation process. For Ethereum, the smart contracts were implemented using solidity language and compiled for version 0.6.2. For Sawtooth, the contracts were implemented using Python 3.6.

5 Experimental Setup

To evaluate our solution, we tested our cross-platform prototype on different microcontroller (MCU) boards. To address truly constrained devices, we set a maximum clock speed of 100 MHz and selected seven different boards from the AVR, ARM, and ESP32 architectures. While a comprehensive evaluation of all possible IoT boards is far beyond the scope of this chapter, the selected pool should provide a reference for other scenarios. Table 1 presents all the boards, detailing clock speed, program space, memory size, model, and a reference price (updated to May of 2021).

5.1 Hardware and Software Setup

For Ethereum, we used the official Geth client (version 1.10.1-stable) to run two independent nodes: one node for the Ropsten network, working with Proof-of-Work consensus (PoW), and the other node for the Goerli network, working with Proof-of-Authority (PoA). Each node runs on a virtual machine with 4 GB of Ram, 20 GB of SSD, and 4 vCPU on an OpenStack server using a clean Linux Ubuntu installation (version 18.04). For Sawtooth, we used the official client (version 1.2.6) to run a private network using the dev-mode engine as a test network. The scripts that deploy and interact with the smart contracts were implemented using Python (version 3.6) and ran on a Lenovo T490s notebook, with 16 GB of Ram 256 SSD disk, and an Intel i-7 processor at 1.90 GHz over a clean Linux Ubuntu (version 18.04). The notebook and the nodes shared the same LAN connection.

Table 1 The hardware platforms used during our performance evaluation

Device	Model	MCU	Architecture	Clock (MHZ)	Prog. mem. (KB)	SRAM (KB)	Price (EUR)
UNO	Arduino Uno	ATMega328P	8-bit AVR	16	32	2	18
EVERY	Arduino nano every	ATMega4809	8-bit AVR	20	48	6	12
L031	STM32L031	Cortex M0+	32-bit ARM	32	32	8	10
F303	STM32F303	Cortex M4	32-bit ARM	72	64	12	10
L452	STM32L452	Cortex M4	32-bit ARM	80	512	96	12
ESP32	ESP DevKit	WRover-E	32-bit ESP32	80	1024	320	10

6 Evaluation

6.1 Device Module Footprint

Using the statistics provided by the compilers, we estimated the footprint of each component of the device module. The results, in terms of disk usage (flash memory usage), are shown by means of Table 2 (absolute values) and Fig. 6a (normalized to the total available flash memory). The same approach was taken for the memory usage, by means of Table 3 and Fig. 6b. Sensing (Sens) and Communications (Comms) are the same for both implementations. The footprint of Blockchain Integration for Ethereum is represented by Eth, and the Blockchain Integration for Sawtooth is represented by Saw. From these results, we can see that the Sawtooth implementation has a bigger footprint on the device, and only 4 of the 6 boards are capable of running the entire module.

6.2 Device Module Processing Times and Power Consumption

We measured the processing time and power consumption of each board when creating 100 transactions. We used a Otii device[1] cable to provide current measurements with an accuracy of $\pm(1\% + 0.5\,\mu A)$ at 5V with a rate of 1000 samples/s. As a

Table 2 Disk usage of the device module (expressed in bytes)

Device	Available	Sens.	Eth	Saw	Comms.
UNO	32,256	2014	26,840	35,214	2202
EVERY	49,152	1956	27,428	35,735	3105
F303	65,536	3040	29,940	33,404	14,240
L031	32,768	6168	30,796	34,432	14,724
L452	524,288	3032	33,120	36,568	17,336
ESP32	1,310,720	1496	289,318	293,674	267,270

Table 3 Memory usage of the device module (expressed in bytes)

Device	Available	Sens.	Eth	Saw	Comms.
UNO	2048	207	1158	3214	188
EVERY	6144	196	611	2435	177
F303	12288	928	1540	3124	908
L031	8192	896	1508	3102	876
L452	163,840	936	1560	3144	916
ESP32	327,680	13,660	14,996	16,292	13,612

[1] https://www.qoitech.com/.

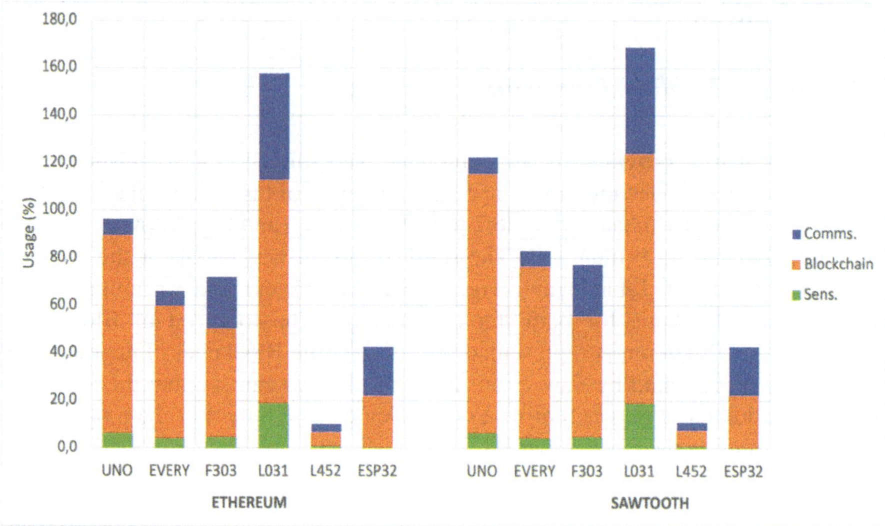

(a)

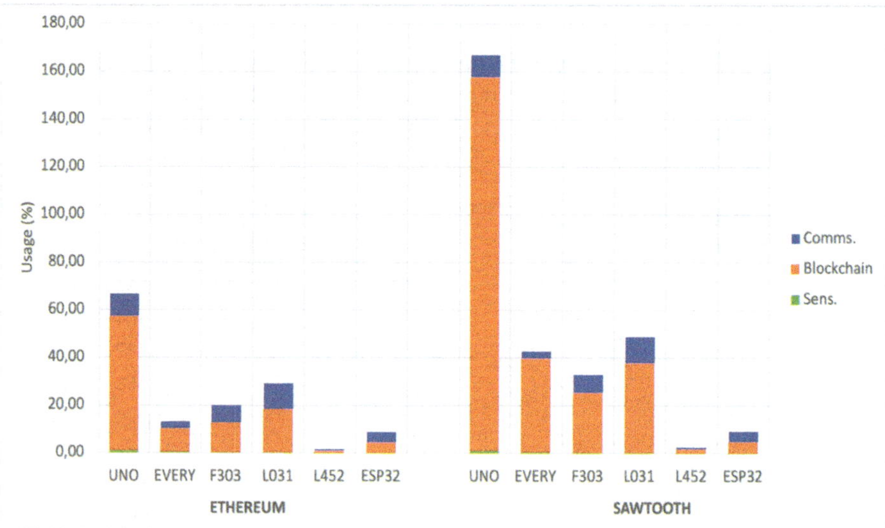

(b)

Fig. 6 Footprint of the device module in reference to the total available in each board. (**a**) Disk usage. (**b**) Memory usage

reference, we used an idle state for 5s before each working state (i.e., sensing, blockchain integration, and communications). It is important to notice that now low-power mode was used for the idle state. The average of all the experiments is depicted in Table 4 and Fig. 7a for the Ethereum implementation and in Table 5 and

Table 4 Power requirements (at 5v) during working and idle states on the device module with the Ethereum implementation

Device	State	Current (mA)	Current (var)	Energy (J)	Time (s)
UNO	Idle	34.38	2.85	0.86	5.01s
UNO	Work	34.36	2.37	0.73	4.26s
EVERY	Idle	29.46	0.17	0.73	4.98s
EVERY	Work	30.02	0.23	0.63	4.17s
F303	Idle	65.0	0.12	1.63	5.01s
F303	Work	67.93	1.0	0.08	0.23s
L031	Idle	47.43	0.0	1.18	4.98s
L031	Work	47.39	0.04	0.17	0.7s
L452	Idle	48.79	0.0	1.27	5.0s
L452	Work	50.15	0.08	0.04	0.16s
ESP32	Idle	42.26	0.03	1.06	5.0s
ESP32	Work	61.98	55.23	0.03	0.11s

Table 5 Power requirements (at 5v) during working and idle states on the device module with the Sawtooth implementation

Device	State	Current (mA)	Current (var)	Energy (J)	Time (s)
EVERY	Idle	29.4	0.44	0.73	4.98s
EVERY	Work	29.99	0.58	1.28	8.53s
F303	Idle	64.67	0.27	1.62	5.01s
F303	Work	67.86	1.76	0.2	0.58s
L452	Idle	51.87	0.0	1.35	5.0s
L452	Work	52.95	0.06	0.12	0.44s
ESP32	Idle	42.23	0.02	1.06	5.0s
ESP32	Work	59.93	43.35	0.09	0.31s

Fig. 7b for the Sawtooth implementation. As shown by the results, the processing times for creating a Sawtooth are longer and thus have higher power requirements on the IoT device.

6.3 *Transaction Cost*

We considered a price of ETH of 307 USD based on the year average price in 2020, as reported by Etherscan.[2] According to the information provided by the *Geth* client, we obtained the gas needed for each type of transaction in our architecture. In a public network, this gas translates into monetary cost by setting a gas price in reference to ETH typically using a $gwei$ where 1 $gwei = 0.000000001\ ETH$.

[2] https://etherscan.io/chart/etherprice.

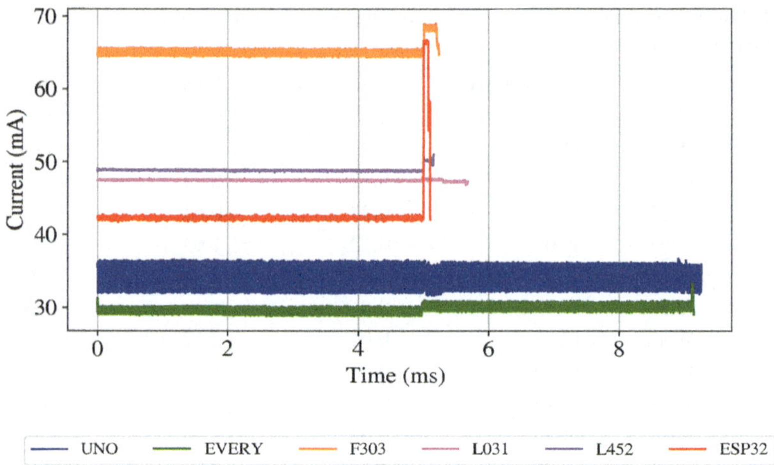

(a)

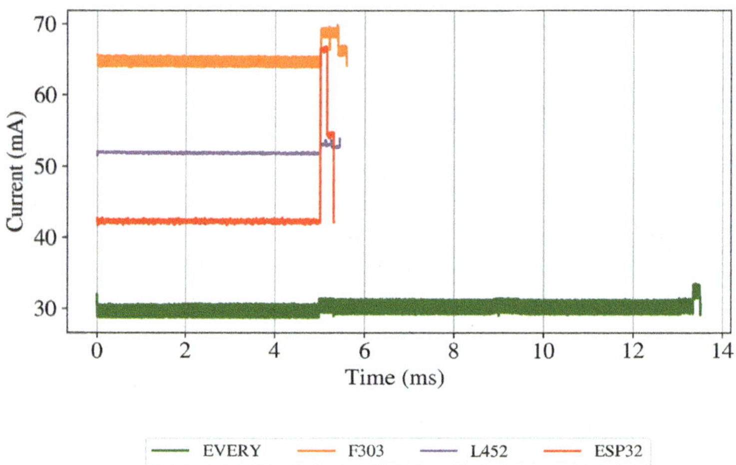

(b)

Fig. 7 Power consumption of the device module. (**a**) Ethereum implementation. (**b**) Sawtooth implementation

Higher *gas* values should translate into faster processing times; however, estimating the behavior of a blockchain network is a task beyond the scope of this work. Table 6 translates the gas of the four main transactions into USD using the average price and 3 different *gas* values. In contrast, Hyperledger Sawtooth, as most of private blockchain implementations, does not require the payment of a transaction fee. As we can see in the results, costs of the application on a public network range from a few cents to less than 8 USD.

Table 6 Transaction cost with 1 Ether equal to 307 USD

Transaction	Gas	80 gwei	100 gwei	120 gwei
Create TwinApp	2.071.380	5.09 USD	6.36 USD	7.36 USD
Create SmartTwin	988.000	2.43 USD	3.03 USD	3.64 USD
setValue() on SmartTwin	107.284	0.26 USD	0.33 USD	0.40 USD
queryTwin() on TwinApp	143.947	0.35 USD	0.44 USD	0.53 USD

6.4 *Transaction Processing Times*

We evaluated the real transaction processing time for executing the `setValue` operation on a SmartTwin contract. We tested this operation, as it is the most frequent transaction in the architecture. We sent one transaction approximately each 30 min over a period of one week on two different networks, namely Ropsten and Goerli. Table 7 shows the processing time for each network, and Figure 8 shows the frequency distributions of these times. The average blockchain processing time was 39 s on the Ropsten and 15 on Goerli using different gas prices. In Sawtooth, the average processing time for the transaction was less than 1 s.

7 Conclusions

Our proposed architecture enables the integration of IoT and Blockchain technologies, creating transparent, fault tolerant, immutable, and auditable records that can be used for an Agri-Food traceability system. Regarding our practical evaluation: even if the Hyperledger Sawtooth-based implementation had better time response in terms of measured metrics with respect to the Ethereum one, both implementations have different properties and capabilities that need to be considered before choosing one over the other. In some cases, it may be convenient to trade off the high latency of Ethereum with its scalability and reliability, since it enables larger numbers of participants and its software maturity is far higher than Hyperledger Sawtooth. Moreover, from an economic perspective, recall that the monetary cost of using the Ethereum network can be avoided, simply by using private networks. From an application perspective, Ethereum imposes the limitation of having a single language for implementing smart contracts, as well as a fixed structure for the records, which may represent a drawback when developing more sophisticated business logic. However, Hyperledger Sawtooth is still far for being considered a mature implementation at the level of Ethereum.

These differences are also noticeable when integrating constrained sensing devices. In our proposed architecture, constrained IoT devices are direct actors of a public blockchain network, directly feeding smart contracts without interposing third-party intermediaries. Using our prototype, we quantitatively assessed the impact both implementations have in terms of memory, program size, commu-

Table 7 Transaction processing times in terms of minimum, maximum, average, and variation on Ropsten and Goerli networks

Gas price	Ropsten network				Goerli network			
	Min	Max	Avg	Std	Min	Max	Avg	Std
80 gwei	04	116	25.05	21.21	02	32	16.26	6.49
100 gwei	02	116	26.16	17.87	02	32	16.30	6.11
120 gwei	02	487	39.45	56.62	02	32	16.09	5.69

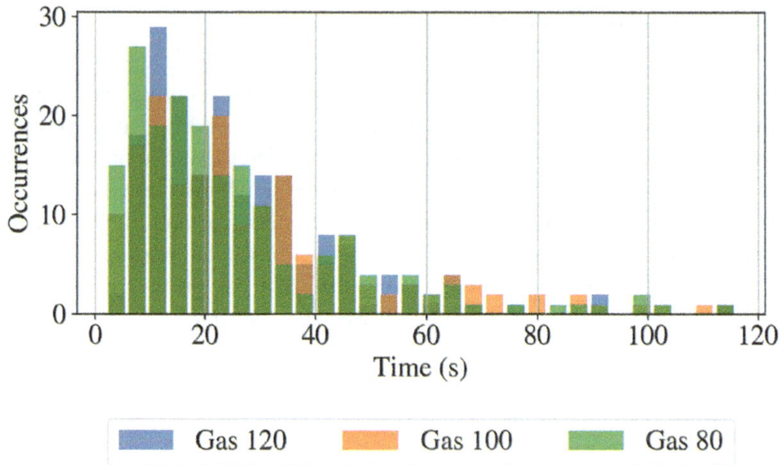

(a)

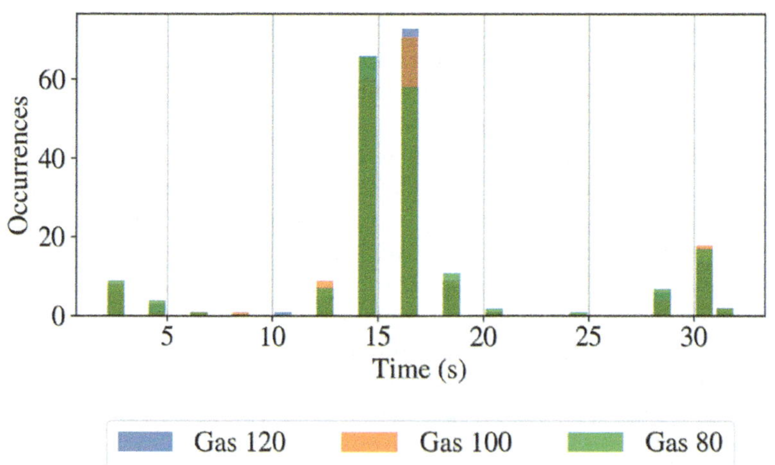

(b)

Fig. 8 Processing times with different gas prices. (**a**) Ropsten network. (**b**) Goerli network

nications, and power consumption at sensing node. Our results have shown that affordable, constrained devices can interact directly with the blockchain. A tiny 8-bit microcontroller, with only 32 KB of program space and 2KB of memory, can transform a sensed value into an Ethereum transaction. However, the program space used for these blockchain operations limits further functionalities on the board, such as more complex communications schemes. In contrast, creating a Sawtooth transaction requires more disk and space on the microcontroller, and less constrained devices are needed. Moreover, the processing time and thus the energy requirements of the devices are also higher than those needed by the Ethereum client.

Future works will revolve around the design and the development of the smart contracts supporting the entire proposition. Once the smart contracts are defined, we will evaluate our architecture from an economical point of view. In particular, we will assess the trade-off between transaction fees and processing time on public blockchains, also evaluating the cost of storing the sensed values in the blockchain. This will set the foundation for establishing realistic thresholds of the proposed architecture in a real-world deployment.

References

1. Accorsi, R., Bortolini, M., Baruffaldi, G., Pilati, F., & Ferrari, E. (2017). Internet-of-things paradigm in food supply chains control and management. *Procedia Manufacturing, 11*, 889–895.
2. Ali, M. S., Vecchio, M., Pincheira, M., Dolui, K., Antonelli, F., & Rehmani, M. H. (2018). Applications of blockchains in the Internet of Things: A comprehensive survey. *IEEE Communications Surveys Tutorials, 21*(2), 1676–1717.
3. Armbrust, M., Fox, A., Griffith, R., Joseph, A. D., Katz, R., Konwinski, A., Lee, G., Patterson, D., Rabkin, A., Stoica, I., et al. (2010). A view of cloud computing. *Communications of the ACM, 53*(4), 50–58.
4. Biswas, A. R., & Giaffreda, R. (2014). Iot and cloud convergence: Opportunities and challenges. In *2014 IEEE World Forum on Internet of Things (WF-IoT)* (pp. 375–376). IEEE.
5. Botta, A., De Donato, W., Persico, V., & Pescapé, A. (2016). Integration of cloud computing and Internet of Things: A survey. *Future Generation Computer Systems, 56*, 684–700.
6. Caro, M. P., Ali, M. S., Vecchio, M., & Giaffreda, R. (2018). Blockchain-based traceability in agri-food supply chain management: A practical implementation. In *2018 IoT Vertical and Topical Summit on Agriculture-Tuscany (IOT Tuscany)* (pp. 1–4). IEEE.
7. Heiss, J., Eberhardt, & J., Tai, S. (2019). From oracles to trustworthy data on-chaining systems. In *Proc. of the IEEE International Conference on Blockchain.*
8. Kassahun, A., Hartog, R., Sadowski, T., Scholten, H., Bartram, T., Wolfert, S., & Beulens, A. (2014). Enabling chain-wide transparency in meat supply chains based on the EPCIS global standard and cloud-based services. *Computers and Electronics in Agriculture, 109*, 179–190.
9. Liang, X., Shetty, S., Tosh, D., Kamhoua, C., Kwiat, K., & Njilla, L. (2017). ProvChain: A blockchain-based data provenance architecture in cloud environment with enhanced privacy and availability. In *Proc. of the CCGRID* (pp. 468–477).
10. Mao, D., Hao, Z., Wang, F., & Li, H. (2018). Innovative blockchain-based approach for sustainable and credible environment in food trade: A case study in Shandong province, China. *Sustainability, 10*(9), 3149.

11. Mao, D., Wang, F., Hao, Z., & Li, H. (2018). Credit evaluation system based on blockchain for multiple stakeholders in the food supply chain. *International Journal of Environmental Research and Public Health, 15*(8), 1627.
12. McFarlane, D., & Sheffi, Y. (2003). The impact of automatic identification on supply chain operations. *The International Journal of Logistics Management, 14*(1), 1–17.
13. Pincheira, M., & Vecchio, M. (2020). Towards trusted data on decentralized IoT applications: Integrating blockchain in constrained devices. In *2020 IEEE International Conference on Communications Workshops (ICC Workshops)* (pp. 1–6). https://doi.org/10.1109/ICCWorkshops49005.2020.9145328
14. Pincheira, M., Vecchio, M., Giaffreda, R., & Kanhere, S. S. (2021). Cost-effective IoT devices as trustworthy data sources for a blockchain-based water management system in precision agriculture. *Computers and Electronics in Agriculture, 180*, 105889.
15. Ramachandran, A., & Murat, K. (2017). Using blockchain and smart contracts for secure data provenance management. arXiv preprint arXiv:1709.10000.
16. Reyna, A., Martín, C., Chen, J., Soler, E., & Díaz, M. (2018). On blockchain and its integration with IoT. Challenges and opportunities. *Future Generation Computer Systems, 88*, 173–190.
17. Salah, K., Nizamuddin, N., Jayaraman, R., & Omar, M. (2019). Blockchain-based soybean traceability in agricultural supply chain. *IEEE Access, 7*, 73295–73305. https://doi.org/10.1109/ACCESS.2019.2918000
18. Srinivasan, S., Shanthi, D., & Anand, A. (2017). Inventory transparency for agricultural produce through IoT. *IOP Conference Series: Materials Science and Engineering, 211*(1), 012009.
19. Sun, C. (2012). Application of RFID technology for logistics on Internet of Things. *AASRI Procedia, 1*, 106–111.
20. Tian, F. (2016). An agri-food supply chain traceability system for China based on RFID and blockchain technology. In *Proc. of the ICSSSM* (pp. 1–6). IEEE.
21. Tian, F. (2017). A supply chain traceability system for food safety based on HACCP, blockchain and Internet of Things. In *Proc. of the ICSSSM* (pp. 1–6).
22. TongKe, F. (2013). Smart agriculture based on cloud computing and IoT. *Journal of Convergence Information Technology, 8*(2), 210–216.
23. Tschorsch, F., & Scheuermann, B. (2016). Bitcoin and beyond: A technical survey on decentralized digital currencies. *IEEE Communications Surveys & Tutorials, 18*(3), 2084–2123.
24. Verdouw, C., Sundmaeker, H., Meyer, F., Wolfert, J., & Verhoosel, J. (2013). Smart agri-food logistics: requirements for the future internet. In *Dynamics in logistics* (pp. 247–257). Springer.
25. Verdouw, C. N., Wolfert, J., Beulens, A., & Rialland, A. (2016). Virtualization of food supply chains with the Internet of Things. *Journal of Food Engineering, 176*, 128–136.
26. Zanoni, B. (2014). Extra-virgin olive oil traceability. In *The extra-virgin olive oil handbook* (pp. 245–250).
27. Zissis, D., & Lekkas, D. (2012). Addressing cloud computing security issues. *Future Generation Computer Systems, 28*(3), 583–592.

Configuring Blockchain Architectures and Consensus Mechanisms: The Healthcare Supply Chain as a Use Case

Ghassan Al-Sumaidaee, Rami Alkhudary, Zeljko Zilic, and Pierre Féniès

1 Introduction

Blockchain technology brings to fruition extensive research on distributed ledger technologies, cryptography and consensus algorithms that had been conducted in computer science for decades [1]. Blockchain was presented for the first time in the white paper of Nakamoto [2]. This mysterious person or group of anonymous developers, we still do not know the real identity of Nakamoto, presented Bitcoin, the first application of blockchain. The most comprehensive and straightforward definition of blockchain can be formulated as a distributed ledger or database of non-erasable blocks of digital assets, information or transactions that are registered by following a precise consensus mechanism where there is no need for a central party to manage the network or maintain its integrity [2–5].

Blockchain applications and unique characteristics attracted wide attention in academia and industry [6–9]. Beyond the financial industry, blockchain can bring many benefits to operations, logistics and supply chain management, such as traceability [10, 11], transparency [12, 13] and security [14, 15]. Several organisations have already deployed blockchain to revolutionise their supply chain networks to improve service quality and ensure a better flow of the financial and physical flows [16–18].

However, the literature on blockchain in supply chains falls short to distinguish between different blockchain architectures. The most sophisticated literature sheds light on three blockchain systems: public, private and consortium [19, 20]. In these

G. Al-Sumaidaee (✉) · Z. Zilic
McGill University, Montreal, QC, Canada
e-mail: ghassan.al-sumaidaee@mail.mcgill.ca

R. Alkhudary · P. Féniès
LARGEPA, Université Paris-Panthéon-Assas, Paris, France

A. Bouras et al. (eds.), *Blockchain Driven Supply Chains and Enterprise Information Systems*, https://doi.org/10.1007/978-3-030-96154-1_7

three systems, transactions are visible to all or some users (referred to as nodes). Also, any user can trace the registered information in real time. However, these systems differ according to access, consensus mechanisms and where data are recorded or stored.

Public blockchains are open networks with no restrictions on participation. Associated addresses publicly identify the network's users. Trust in this system is derived from cryptographic techniques to reach a consensus and validate transactions. Given Bitcoin as an example, the Proof of Work (PoW) algorithm is used as a consensus mechanism. Each user can have an identical copy of the transactions' hashes. Private blockchains extend the technology applications beyond the financial sector. Several organisations have incorporated blockchain's features into their scope of work, albeit with some modifications to suit their needs. Users are not allowed to join the private blockchain network freely. They must obtain permission from the organisation or group of organisations that control the network. Different consensus mechanisms are used in private blockchains, such as the Proof of Authority (PoA) algorithm. Consequently, there is no need for mining to validate transactions. Each entity can have the hash of the registered information. However, there is a need to have servers or use cloud services to stock the source of information. Consortium blockchains are very similar to the private blockchain, except that they have a small number of equally powerful nodes as validators.

This paper offers an insight to supply chains by explaining several consensus mechanisms of blockchain architectures. This is vital because the literature addresses blockchain in a very general way. We illustrate that blockchain systems are not limited to private, public and consortium. We demonstrate that a new supply chain configuration can emerge each time we change the consensus mechanism of blockchain. We focus on the healthcare supply chain, as it adds an extra layer of risk and complexity given its direct impact on patients and public health. In doing so, we outline some of the most state-of-the-art blockchain systems underpinned by the consensus algorithms that we present in this paper, namely, Proof of Work (PoW), Proof of Stake (PoS), Delegated Proof of Stake (DPoS), Proof of Authority (PoA) and Practical Byzantine Fault Tolerance (PBFT).

The remainder of this paper is structured as follows: Sect. 2 outlines the methodology that we employed to collect and analyze the pertinent literature. Section 3 elaborates on the reported consensus mechanisms and their applications in the healthcare supply chain. Finally, Sect. 4 concludes and provides future research directions.

2 Methodology Used to Collect the Literature

We conducted a systematic literature review (SLR) to collect the pertinent literature on blockchain technology in operations and supply chain management [21–24]. This is to articulate the most well-known consensus mechanisms used today to reach a consensus within blockchain systems and outline their applications in the healthcare industry.

We used two academic search engines: Scopus and Business Source Ultimate. Then, the following search string was employed: (blockchain OR blockchains OR "block chain") AND (Health OR Healthcare OR EHealth OR Medical OR Telemedicine). To control quality [25, 26], we limited the review to English language journals classified in Thomson Reuters (listing of 2018). The search was conducted in October 2020, producing 277 academic papers. The authors' read each paper title, abstract and more text needed to include the review only papers that proposed healthcare supply chain systems underpinned by blockchain. This procedure minimised the number of articles to 66 articles. This number is consistent with academic reviews published in peer-reviewed journals [9, 27, 28].

3 Blockchain Architectures and Consensus Mechanisms

This section presents the most known consensus algorithms deployed today to reach a consensus within blockchain systems. We introduce the PoW, PoS, DPoS, PoA and PBFT (see Table 1). We focus on the healthcare supply chain, one of the most appealing industries to use blockchain, to outline some of the most state-of-the-art blockchain systems.

3.1 Proof of Work

Proof of Work (PoW) is the best-known consensus algorithm used in most cryptocurrencies in circulation today. It was mainly developed to solve the problem of double-spending in the literature of computer science. This problem represents fraudulent behaviour that includes spending the same coin multiple times on the Internet. PoW allows users (any node within the blockchain system) to validate and register transactions on the blockchain ledger [19, 29].

Table 1 Consensus mechanism attributes

Consensus mechanism	Power consumption	Centralisation level	Blockchain system	Healthcare adoption	References
PoW	High	Low	Public	Low	[29, 55–57]
PoS	Low	Moderate	Public	Low	[38, 58–60]
DPoS	Low	Moderate	Public	Low	[56, 61–63]
PoA	Low	High	Private/consortium	High	[29, 38, 55, 61]
PBFT	Low	Moderate	Private/consortium	High	[58, 63–65]

This is done through mining, where all nodes on the network use specific machines with considerable computation power to solve a challenging puzzle [30]. Through mining, the validating nodes must find an arbitrary number called a "nonce". The time to find the new hash (every 10 minutes on average on the Bitcoin network) is controlled by the difficulty level adjusted by the network's protocol [31]. The validating nodes or miners are rewarded when they successfully verify a group of transactions (a block) and register it on the blockchain ledger.

Yazdinejad et al. [32] proposed a blockchain architecture underpinned by the PoW algorithm for a decentralised hospital network. The new system connects the hospital's Internet of things (IoT) devices through a peer-to-peer network. The designed system limits the mining process only to nursing stations to reduce the computational power required. Nursing stations are particular nodes authorised to validate and register medical information according to predefined conditions with the help of remote monitoring devices.

In the same vein, Akkaoui et al. [33] proposed a secure system, EdgeMediChain, for efficient health data management. Both blockchain and edge computing were combined to meet the healthcare supply chain needs. EdgeMediChain consists of four layers, all of which are decentralised and own independent computation power. The system was designed to achieve better performance and facilitate data sharing among the healthcare supply chain entities. Five virtual machines were implemented to test the system. The PoW algorithm was used in one of the virtual machines for global blockchain emulation. The initial results showed that the system accelerated and secured medical data exchange and gained higher throughput.

Figure 1 depicts the proposed model.

3.2 *Proof of Stake*

Proof of Stake (PoS) is another consensus algorithm introduced to reach a consensus within blockchain systems and solve the extensive energy consumption caused by PoW. The PoS algorithm selects nodes randomly with a high coinage to validate

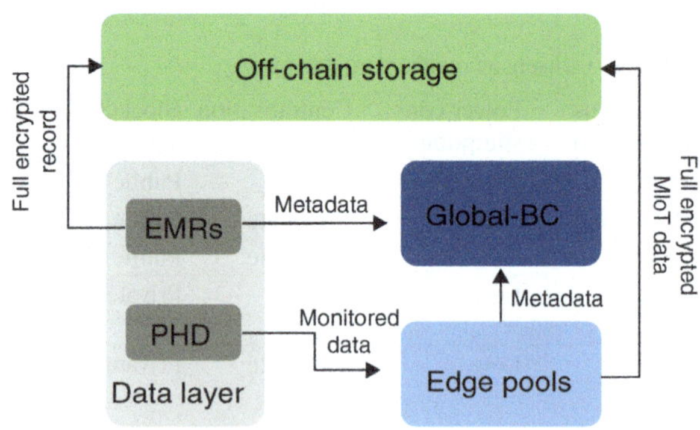

Fig. 1 EdgeMediChain configuration [33]

and register new blocks of transactions on the blockchain ledger [34]. Miners are determined based on their coin share (stake-based system), where any node trying to cheat loses its entire stake (a considerable amount of coins). This ensures an acceptable level of security compared to PoW [35].

The PoS algorithm improves the blockchain network's effectiveness because the mining process is limited to a certain number of nodes. This considerably reduces the extensive energy consumption caused by PoW. In addition, PoS is much more efficient in addressing the scalability problem confronted with blockchain systems underpinned by PoW. The scalability problem is embedded in the limited capability to handle many transactions in a short time [34]. This is a real problem within public blockchains that use PoW.

Malamas et al. [36] proposed a blockchain system to ensure secure access to medical data between different healthcare supply chain entities. The authors claim that the proposed system offers several advantages for patients, doctors, technicians and insurance companies, including fast transaction processing and temporal access roles. In the designed system, the hash of medical data is stored on the blockchain ledger, while the primary data can be still stored on servers. The system was tested in two Ethereum-based blockchains, where PoS was used as the underlying consensus mechanism. PoS accelerated adding new blocks: 1000 transactions per second and a new block added every 12 seconds on average.

Similarly, Yang et al. [37] designed a medical data sharing system based on blockchain. As shown in Fig. 2, the developed system stores the encrypted medical data on the cloud, where the hash associated is stored on the blockchain ledger. This maintains the confidentiality and privacy of the medical data. The systems used the PoS algorithm and included several healthcare supply chain entities such as hospitals, cloud services providers, medical facilities, patients, etc. The authors advocated that the system achieved its objectives to secure data exchange and facilitate real-time communication among healthcare entities.

3.3 Delegated Proof of Stake

Delegated Proof of Stake (DPoS) is a modified version of the PoS algorithm, founded as another alternative to solve the extensive energy consumption caused by PoW. The DPoS algorithm has a different mechanism to reach a consensus within the blockchain system. More precisely, blocks are validated by particular nodes "witnesses" chosen by the other nodes in the network "voters". Voters authorise witnesses (validating nodes) to maintain the blockchain and add new blocks of transactions [38]. Both PoS and DPoS share the exact staking mechanism. In other words, nodes are asked to deposit some coins if they want to be involved in mining. Witnesses are replaced continuously over time. If previous witnesses wished to keep their roles, they should be recognised as honest nodes. This consensus mechanism supports the decentralised approach of blockchain systems more than the PoS

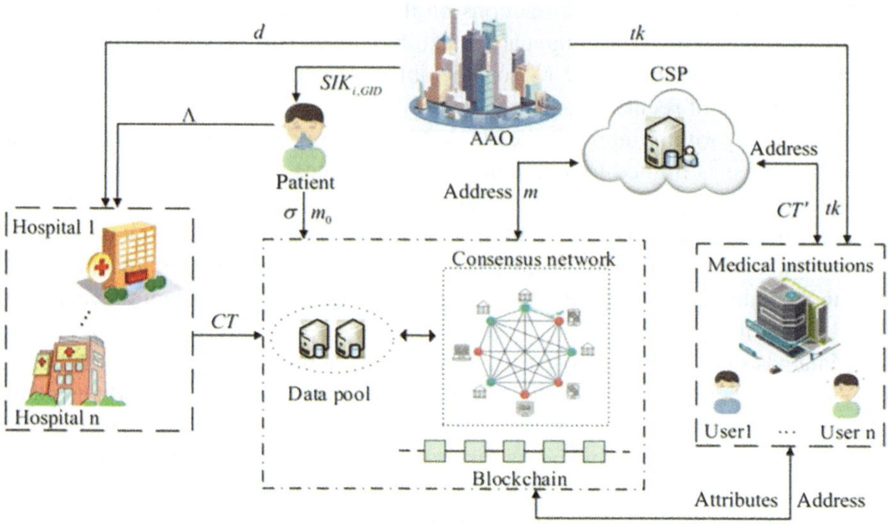

Fig. 2 Medical data sharing model [37]

algorithm, which is almost centralised, where dominant nodes with significant stakes could manipulate the mining process [39].

In contrast to the PoS mechanism, witnesses do not need to own a significant amount of stakes to be selected, as each vote is weighted according to its holder's stake [40]. However, the security level of a blockchain system underpinned by the DPoS algorithm is questioned with a small number of users. In other words, if there are only a small number of users, the entire network is threatened. This is because if 51% of the delegated nodes had agreed to be malicious, the whole network would be compromised.

Abdellatif et al. [41] presented a decentralised and secure healthcare supply chain based on blockchain and edge computing. The system aims to instantly share large amounts of secure medical data among the healthcare supply chain entities. The designed system is underpinned by DPoS and has many components (nodes) such as medical IoT devices that monitor and update patient health status information. Other nodes are allowed to conduct analysis and make sense of the data generated to be after that shared on the blockchain ledger. Official healthcare representatives could join the network and supervise its activities. The designed system entitles the healthcare stakeholders to access and trace all related information in real time.

In a similar vein, Wang et al. [42] proposed a smart healthcare supply chain based on blockchain, GuardHealth, to improve privacy and protect patient's personal information. The authors advocated that GuardHealth is the first system that introduced the graph neural network (GNN) to detect malicious nodes in the healthcare supply chain. The designed system uses the DPoS algorithm to leverage the chain's efficiency and security. The volume of health data represented the delegated stakes on the network. Each entity along the chain encrypts its data and

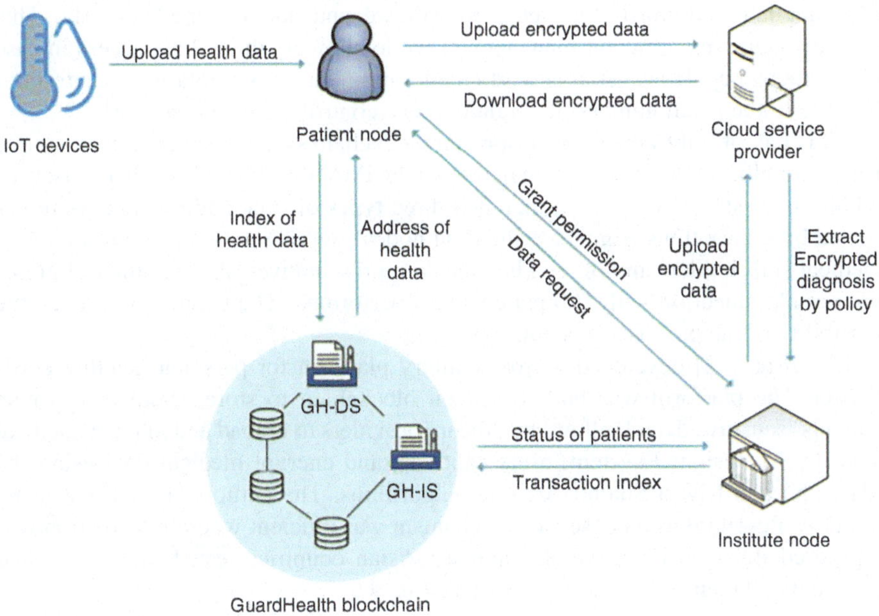

Fig. 3 GuardHealth model [42]

stores it on the cloud. Each entity can choose with whom to share the private key to decrypt the registered information. The system proposed double chains hosted on the cloud—one with the hash of the information and another with the original information. The GuardHealth model is illustrated in Fig. 3.

3.4 *Proof of Authority*

Proof of Authority (PoA) was introduced in March 2017 by Gavin Wood, the Ethereum co-founder, to solve spam attacks that severely affected the Ethereum Ropsten network [43]. The PoA algorithm is a reputation-based consensus mechanism. In other words, the nodes with a good reputation are considered trusted to add new blocks of transactions [44]. This mechanism is often used within private blockchain systems since users are known, and the validating nodes are limited to a certain number [45]. Some examples of industries where PoA could see successes are financial banking and supply chains. Regarding the healthcare supply chain, the validating nodes must be authentic. This is evident given the high level of data sensitivity which directly affects people's lives.

It would also be pointless for hospitals to build up extensive computational resources to mine new blocks [46]. This is what makes the PoA algorithm much appealing in this industry. The PoA algorithm allows trusted healthcare stakeholders (doctors, labs, administrators, etc.) to validate and add the medical data. This ensures secure and efficient management while allowing immediate access in case of an emergency. However, it is worth mentioning that PoA is relatively centralised because of the small number of validators who control the whole network.

Zhu et al. [47] introduced a consortium blockchain system using the open-source Ethereum blockchain. The system deployed the PoA algorithm to reach a consensus within the system. The system included three types of users: administrators represented by transactions' signers (validating nodes), service providers represented by medical stakeholders and official healthcare representatives. A case study of breast tumour classification with 100 patients was performed. The simulation proved the feasibility of the proposed system.

Lee et al. [48] developed a cross-country platform for personal health records (PHR). The platform was built based on blockchain to store, share and protect patients' sensitive data. It allows healthcare providers to upload and manage medical data. In the designed system, users can hash and encrypt medical data using the SHA-256 and Rivest-Shamir-Adleman algorithms. The authors argued that using the PoA algorithm as a consensus mechanism was efficient where information was registered much faster. Several Southeast Asian countries tested the system and proved its efficiency for sharing PHR (see Fig. 4).

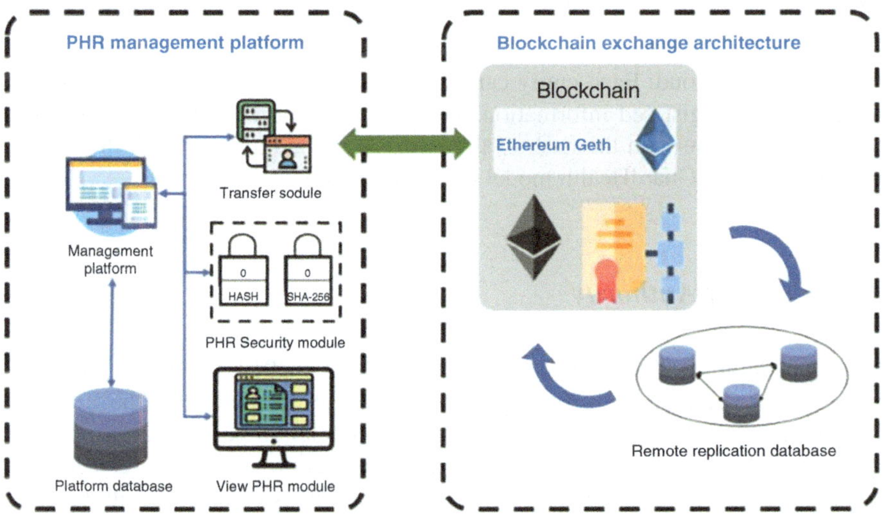

Fig. 4 PHR management platform [48]

3.5 Practical Byzantine Fault Tolerance

Practical Byzantine Fault Tolerance (PBFT) was introduced in 1999 by Miguel and Barbara [49] as a solution to several problems of the original Byzantine Fault Tolerance (BFT) systems [50]. The original BFT algorithm incurs high operational costs compared to other non-BFT systems, as it requires $3f + 1$ replicas to tolerate f fault replicas. If the network has some nodes equal to $3f + 1$, then the number of honest nodes must be greater than $2f + 1$, which means that the dishonest nodes should be less than f [51]. The PBFT algorithm is designed to work properly even if there are some dishonest nodes in the network. The PBFT algorithm is an excellent alternative to PoW and PoS because it does not require considerable computational resources or stakes to reach a consensus. PBFT is often used in consortium blockchain systems [52].

Here, we give an example to explain how PBFT reaches a consensus within a decentralised blockchain system. Suppose four nodes in the network: A, B, C and D. A is the primary node, while B, C and D are backup nodes. Assume that A, B and C are honest nodes, and D is the dishonest node. To start the process, a user creates a request and sends it to node A to forward the request to the backup nodes. If all the backup nodes accepted the message, they move to the prepare phase, and if not, they send a reject message back to the user. If the pre-prepared message is successfully received by more than $2f$ nodes, then the preparation phase is realised, and they will move to the next phase (commit phase). The commit information now will be broadcasted to other nodes. If more than 2f nodes successfully receive the commit message, the final consensus is achieved [50]. It is worth mentioning that there is a specific time for the primary node to send the request, and if it failed, this node is replaced.

Zghaibeh et al. [53] proposed a multilayer and smart health management system based on blockchain. The designed system was managed by three main groups: nodes, users and medical IoT devices. The nodes represent the government layer responsible for managing and controlling the blockchain model (centralised approach). Users are people who share their medical and personal data with the nodes. Finally, the medical IoT devices feed the blockchain ledger with real-time data regarding the patients' medical status. As a perfect fit for the system, PBFT was adopted as a consensus mechanism.

For another example, Pournaghi et al. [54] suggested a system, MedSBA, for a medical data record based on blockchain and attribute encryption algorithm. The attribute encryption algorithm allowed patients to control their medical records. Blockchain was used to guarantee that the data shared is reliable by following a precise consensus mechanism. As shown in Fig. 5, two blockchain systems were implemented: permissioned (private), where the original data is recorded, and permissionless (public), where the hash of data is registered. The designed system represents a typical healthcare supply chain with five entities. The first entity starts with hospitals and health insurance companies. The second is embedded in the cloud services that store the patients' encrypted data. The third is the blockchain

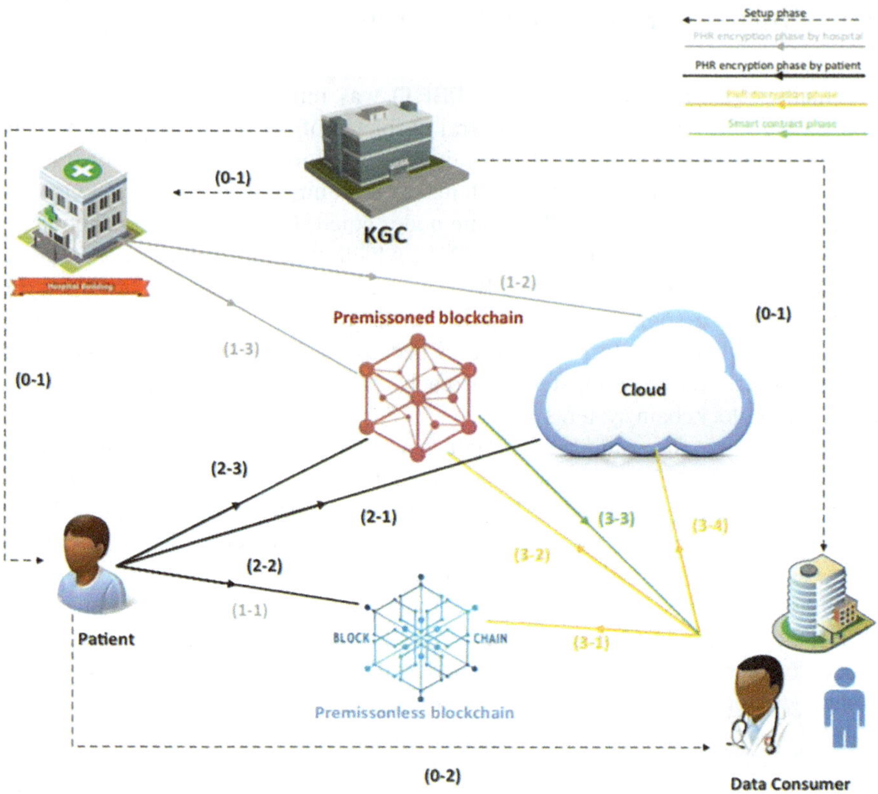

Fig. 5 MedSBA architecture [54]

architecture, including its double chains (private and public). The fourth is other stakeholders that benefit from the registered data. Stakeholders can be legal entities that represent official institutions or other healthcare services. The last entity represents patients that are responsible for their data. In other words, they decide to share their data by giving access to the original data, not merely access to the hash.

To conclude, Fig. 6 demonstrates the mechanisms of the consensus algorithms elaborated in this paper.

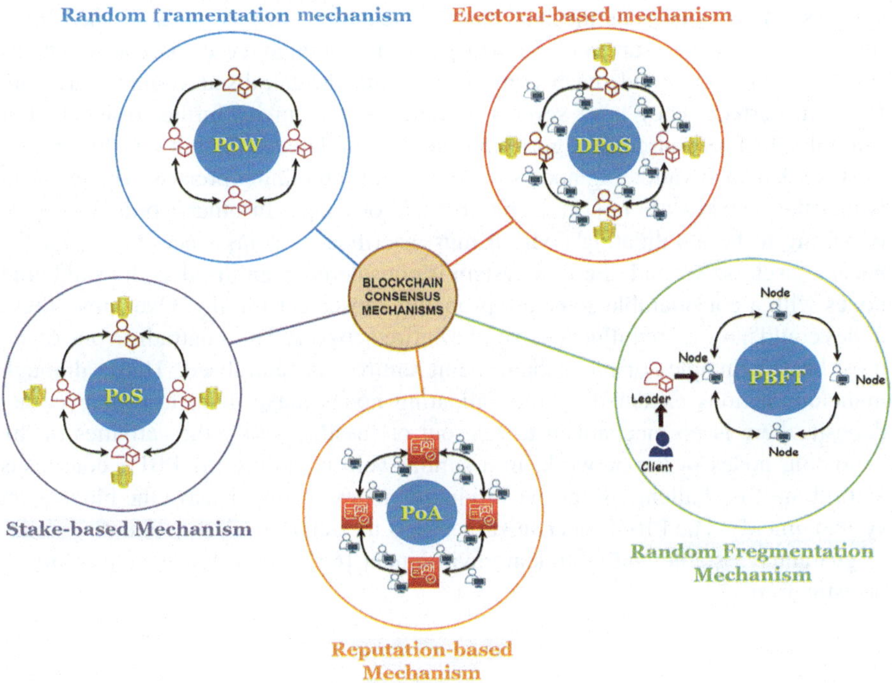

Fig. 6 Blockchain consensus mechanisms

4 Conclusions and Future Research Directions

Blockchain is a central technology that will revolutionise operations and supply chain management across different industries. It represents a paradigm shift towards fully decentralised supply chains. Since 2015, research focusing on using this cutting-edge technology is growing in all directions. The healthcare supply chain is not an exception. Several medical systems have been developed based on blockchain.

This paper presented the most well-known consensus algorithms (PoW, PoS, DPoS, PoA and PBFT) to reach a consensus within decentralised systems. We demonstrated that blockchain architectures and supply chain configurations could change radically each time we change the blockchain system's consensus mechanism. This is important as the literature on blockchain technology in operations and supply chain management falls short to distinguish between different blockchain architectures, let alone analysing the technology's benefits for each system. Additionally, we focused on the healthcare supply chain as a use case to outline the most state-of-the-art applications of the presented consensus mechanisms.

Here, we suggest some important research directions. Consensus algorithms, for example, are an essential element for reaching consensus within blockchain systems. Many consensus mechanisms were explored in this paper to shed more light on their usage in supply chain management. Although these consensus systems solve real problems and reach consensus within decentralised systems, they are far from perfect. They have several weaknesses that invite further research. For example, the PoS consensus algorithm is not free of defects. First, it sets the amount of stake that each validating node should own for the mining process. The problem is that these stakes are not amenable to trade or usage. In other words, if a node is willing to be a validating node, it must sacrifice its coins since these deposits became useless. Second, the PoS system is considered centralised as the validating nodes with a considerable stake are probably chosen for mining. Over time, these nodes could have more influence over the entire network. This contradicts one of the most basic principles of blockchain, being entirely decentralised. Third, although malicious actions executed by the validating nodes make them lose their coins' deposit, there is no mechanism to rule out or feasibly verify the activities of the validating nodes in the network. In a similar vein regarding the PBFT consensus algorithm, it is challenging for the validating nodes to join or leave the blockchain system quickly. The PBFT mechanism restricts the activities of the validating nodes to guarantee a stable and confident environment [66]. These issues solicit further investigation.

References

1. Alkhudary, R., Brusset, X., & Fenies, P. (2020). Blockchain in general management and economics: A systematic literature review. *EBR., 32*, 765–783. https://doi.org/10.1108/EBR-11-2019-0297
2. Nakamoto, S. (2008). *Bitcoin: A peer-to-peer electronic cash system.* https://bitcoin.org/bitcoin.pdf
3. Alkhudary, R. (2020). Blockchain technology between Nakamoto and supply chain management: Insights from academia and practice. *SSRN Journal.* https://doi.org/10.2139/ssrn.3660342
4. Kshetri, N. (2017). Blockchain's roles in strengthening cybersecurity and protecting privacy. *Telecommunications Policy, 41*, 1027–1038. https://doi.org/10.1016/j.telpol.2017.09.003
5. Queiroz, M. M., & Fosso Wamba, S. (2019). Blockchain adoption challenges in supply chain: An empirical investigation of the main drivers in India and the USA. *International Journal of Information Management, 46*, 70–82. https://doi.org/10.1016/j.ijinfomgt.2018.11.021
6. Cai, Y., Choi, T., & Zhang, J. (2020). Platform supported supply chain operations in the blockchain Era: Supply contracting and moral hazards*. *Decision Sciences, deci.12475*. https://doi.org/10.1111/deci.12475
7. Hald, K. S., & Kinra, A. (2019). How the blockchain enables and constrains supply chain performance. *IJPDLM, 49*, 376–397. https://doi.org/10.1108/IJPDLM-02-2019-0063
8. Kamble, S., Gunasekaran, A., & Arha, H. (2019). Understanding the blockchain technology adoption in supply chains-Indian context. *International Journal of Production Research, 57*, 2009–2033. https://doi.org/10.1080/00207543.2018.1518610
9. Queiroz, M. M., Telles, R., & Bonilla, S. H. (2019). Blockchain and supply chain management integration: A systematic review of the literature. *SCM, 25*, 241–254. https://doi.org/10.1108/SCM-03-2018-0143

10. Agrawal, T. K., Sharma, A., & Kumar, V. (2018). Blockchain-based secured traceability system for textile and clothing supply chain. In S. Thomassey & X. Zeng (Eds.), *Artificial intelligence for fashion industry in the big data era* (pp. 197–208). Springer Singapore.
11. Behnke, K., & Janssen, M. F. W. H. A. (2020). Boundary conditions for traceability in food supply chains using blockchain technology. *International Journal of Information Management, 52*, 101969. https://doi.org/10.1016/j.ijinfomgt.2019.05.025
12. Sander, F., Semeijn, J., & Mahr, D. (2018). The acceptance of blockchain technology in meat traceability and transparency. *British Food Journal, 120*, 2066–2079. https://doi.org/10.1108/BFJ-07-2017-0365
13. Chod, J., Trichakis, N., Tsoukalas, G., Aspegren, H., & Weber, M. (2020). On the financing benefits of supply chain transparency and blockchain adoption. *Management Science, 66*, 4378–4396. https://doi.org/10.1287/mnsc.2019.3434
14. Kshetri, N. (2018). 1 Blockchain's roles in meeting key supply chain management objectives. *International Journal of Information Management, 39*, 80–89. https://doi.org/10.1016/j.ijinfomgt.2017.12.005
15. Wang, R., Liu, H., Wang, H., Yang, Q., & Wu, D. (2019). Distributed security architecture based on blockchain for connected health: Architecture, challenges, and approaches. *IEEE Wireless Communications, 26*, 30–36. https://doi.org/10.1109/MWC.001.1900108
16. Chang, S. E., Chen, Y.-C., & Lu, M.-F. (2019). Supply chain re-engineering using blockchain technology: A case of smart contract based tracking process. *Technological Forecasting and Social Change, 144*, 1–11. https://doi.org/10.1016/j.techfore.2019.03.015
17. Lacity, M. (2018). Addressing key challenges to making enterprise blockchain applications a reality. *MIS Quarterly Executive., 17*.
18. Lu, Q., & Xu, X. (2017). Adaptable blockchain-based systems: A case study for product traceability. *IEEE Software, 34*, 21–27. https://doi.org/10.1109/MS.2017.4121227
19. O'Leary, D. E. (2017). Configuring blockchain architectures for transaction information in blockchain consortiums: The case of accounting and supply chain systems. *Intelligent Systems in Accounting, Finance and Management, 24*, 138–147. https://doi.org/10.1002/isaf.1417
20. Zheng, Z., Xie, S., Dai, H., Chen, X., & Wang, H. (2017). An overview of blockchain technology: Architecture, consensus, and future trends. In *2017 IEEE international congress on big data (BigData Congress)* (pp. 557–564). IEEE.
21. Durach, C. F., Kembro, J., & Wieland, A. (2017). A new paradigm for systematic literature reviews in supply chain management. *Journal of Supply Chain Management, 53*, 67–85. https://doi.org/10.1111/jscm.12145
22. Thomé, A. M. T., Scavarda, L. F., & Scavarda, A. J. (2016). Conducting systematic literature review in operations management. *Production Planning & Control, 27*, 408–420. https://doi.org/10.1080/09537287.2015.1129464
23. Tranfield, D., Denyer, D., & Smart, P. (2003). Towards a methodology for developing evidence-informed management knowledge by means of systematic review. *British Journal of Management, 14*, 207–222. https://doi.org/10.1111/1467-8551.00375
24. Webster, J., & Watson, R. T. (2002). Analysing the past to prepare for the future: writing a literature review. *MIS Quarterly, 26*, xiii–xxiii. https://doi.org/10.2307/4132319
25. vom Brocke, J., Simons, A., Riemer, K., Niehaves, B., Plattfaut, R., & Cleven, A. (2015). Standing on the shoulders of giants: challenges and recommendations of literature search in information systems research. *CAIS, 37*. https://doi.org/10.17705/1CAIS.03709
26. Okoli, C. (2015). A guide to conducting a standalone systematic literature review. *CAIS, 37*. https://doi.org/10.17705/1CAIS.03743
27. Alkhudary, R., & Gardiner, P. (2021). Stages in project managers' careers: Learning and growth opportunities. *International Journal of Project Management*. https://doi.org/10.1016/j.ijproman.2021.03.006
28. Mysen, T. (2013). Towards a framework for controls as determinants of export performance: A review and analysis of empirical literature 1995-2011. *European Business Review, 25*, 224–242. https://doi.org/10.1108/09555341311314807

29. Monrat, A. A., Schelen, O., & Andersson, K. (2019). A survey of blockchain from the perspectives of applications, challenges, and opportunities. *IEEE Access, 7*, 117134–117151. https://doi.org/10.1109/ACCESS.2019.2936094
30. Bano, S., Sonnino, A., Al-Bassam, M., Azouvi, S., McCorry, P., Meiklejohn, S., & Danezis, G. (2019). SoK: Consensus in the age of blockchains. In *Proceedings of the 1st ACM conference on advances in financial technologies* (pp. 183–198). ACM.
31. Bozic, N., Pujolle, G., & Secci, S. (2016). A tutorial on blockchain and applications to secure network control-planes. In *2016 3rd Smart Cloud Networks & Systems (SCNS)* (pp. 1–8). IEEE.
32. Yazdinejad, A., Srivastava, G., Parizi, R. M., Dehghantanha, A., Choo, K.-K. R., & Aledhari, M. (2020). Decentralised authentication of distributed patients in hospital networks using blockchain. *IEEE Journal of Biomedical and Health Informatics, 24*, 2146–2156. https://doi.org/10.1109/JBHI.2020.2969648
33. Akkaoui, R., Hei, X., & Cheng, W. (2020). EdgeMediChain: A hybrid edge blockchain-based framework for health data exchange. *IEEE Access., 8*, 113467–113486. https://doi.org/10.1109/ACCESS.2020.3003575
34. Nguyen, C. T., Hoang, D. T., Nguyen, D. N., Niyato, D., Nguyen, H. T., & Dutkiewicz, E. (2019). Proof-of-stake consensus mechanisms for future blockchain networks: Fundamentals. *Applications and Opportunities. IEEE Access., 7*, 85727–85745. https://doi.org/10.1109/ACCESS.2019.2925010
35. Mingxiao, D., Xiaofeng, M., Zhe, Z., Xiangwei, W., & Qijun, C. (2017). A review on consensus algorithm of blockchain. In *2017 IEEE international conference on systems, man, and cybernetics (SMC)* (pp. 2567–2572). IEEE.
36. Malamas, V., Kotzanikolaou, P., Dasaklis, T. K., & Burmester, M. (2020). A hierarchical multi blockchain for fine grained access to medical data. *IEEE Access., 8*, 134393–134412. https://doi.org/10.1109/ACCESS.2020.3011201
37. Yang, X., Li, T., Pei, X., Wen, L., & Wang, C. (2020). Medical data sharing scheme based on attribute cryptosystem and blockchain technology. *IEEE Access., 8*, 45468–45476. https://doi.org/10.1109/ACCESS.2020.2976894
38. He, Q., Guan, N., Lv, M., & Yi, W. (2018). On the consensus mechanisms of blockchain/DLT for internet of things. In *2018 IEEE 13th international symposium on industrial embedded systems (SIES)* (pp. 1–10). IEEE.
39. Yadav, A. K., & Singh, K. (2020). Comparative analysis of consensus algorithms of blockchain technology. In Y.-C. Hu, S. Tiwari, M. C. Trivedi, & K. K. Mishra (Eds.), *Ambient communications and computer systems* (pp. 205–218). Springer Singapore.
40. Carrara, G. R., Burle, L. M., Medeiros, D. S. V., de Albuquerque, C. V. N., & Mattos, D. M. F. (2020). Consistency, availability, and partition tolerance in blockchain: A survey on the consensus mechanism over peer-to-peer networking. *Annales des Telecommunications, 75*, 163–174. https://doi.org/10.1007/s12243-020-00751-w
41. Abdellatif, A. A., Al-Marridi, A. Z., Mohamed, A., Erbad, A., Chiasserini, C. F., & Refaey, A. (2020). ssHealth: Toward secure, blockchain-enabled healthcare systems. *IEEE Network, 34*, 312–319. https://doi.org/10.1109/MNET.011.1900553
42. Wang, Z., Luo, N., & Zhou, P. (2020). GuardHealth: Blockchain empowered secure data management and Graph Convolutional Network enabled anomaly detection in smart healthcare. *Journal of Parallel and Distributed Computing, 142*, 1–12. https://doi.org/10.1016/j.jpdc.2020.03.004
43. Curran, B. (2018). *What is proof of authority consensus? Staking your identity on the blockchain*. https://blockonomi.com/proof-of-authority/
44. Cong An, A., Thi Xuan Diem, P., Thi Thu Lan, L., Van Toi, T., & Duong Quoc Binh, L. (2019). Building a product origins tracking system based on blockchain and PoA consensus protocol. In *2019 international conference on advanced computing and applications (ACOMP)* (pp. 27–33). IEEE.

45. Singh, P. K., Singh, R., Nandi, S. K., & Nandi, S. (2019). Managing Smart home appliances with proof of authority and blockchain. In K.-H. Lüke, G. Eichler, C. Erfurth, & G. Fahrnberger (Eds.), *Innovations for community services* (pp. 221–232). Springer International Publishing.
46. Hölbl, M., Kompara, M., Kamišalić, A., & Nemec Zlatolas, L. (2018). A systematic review of the use of blockchain in healthcare. *Symmetry., 10*, 470. https://doi.org/10.3390/sym10100470
47. Zhu, X., Shi, J., & Lu, C. (2019). Cloud health resource sharing based on consensus-oriented blockchain technology: Case study on a breast tumor diagnosis service. *Journal of Medical Internet Research, 21*, e13767. https://doi.org/10.2196/13767
48. Lee, H.-A., Kung, H.-H., Udayasankaran, J. G., Kijsanayotin, B. B., Marcelo, A., Chao, L. R., & Hsu, C.-Y. (2020). An architecture and management platform for blockchain-based personal health record exchange: Development and usability study. *Journal of Medical Internet Research, 22*, e16748. https://doi.org/10.2196/16748
49. Miguel, C., & Barbara, L. (1999). *Practical byzantine fault tolerance*.
50. Wu, Y., Song, P., & Wang, F. (2020). Hybrid consensus algorithm optimization: A mathematical method based on POS and PBFT and its application in blockchain. *Mathematical Problems in Engineering, 2020*, 1–13. https://doi.org/10.1155/2020/7270624
51. Zhang, L., & Li, Q. (2018). Research on consensus efficiency based on practical byzantine fault tolerance. In *2018 10th international conference on modelling, identification and control (ICMIC)* (pp. 1–6). IEEE.
52. Zheng, X., & Feng, W. (2021). Research on practical byzantine fault tolerant consensus algorithm based on blockchain. *Journal of Physics: Conference Series, 1802*, 032022. https://doi.org/10.1088/1742-6596/1802/3/032022
53. Zghaibeh, M., Farooq, U., Hasan, N. U., & Baig, I. (2020). SHealth: A blockchain-based health system with smart contracts capabilities. *IEEE Access, 8*, 70030–70043. https://doi.org/10.1109/ACCESS.2020.2986789
54. Pournaghi, S. M., Bayat, M., & Farjami, Y. (2020). MedSBA: A novel and secure scheme to share medical data based on blockchain technology and attribute-based encryption. *Journal of Ambient Intelligence Humanized Computing, 11*, 4613–4641. https://doi.org/10.1007/s12652-020-01710-y
55. Pandey, P., & Litoriya, R. (2020). Implementing healthcare services on a large scale: Challenges and remedies based on blockchain technology. *Health Policy and Technology, 9*, 69–78. https://doi.org/10.1016/j.hlpt.2020.01.004
56. Praveen, G., Anand, M., Singh, P. K., & Ranjan, P. (2021). An overview of blockchain consensus and vulnerability. In T. Senjyu, P. N. Mahalle, T. Perumal, & A. Joshi (Eds.), *Information and communication technology for intelligent systems* (pp. 459–468). Springer Singapore.
57. Kaur, S., Chaturvedi, S., Sharma, A., & Kar, J. (2021). A research survey on applications of consensus protocols in blockchain. *Security and Communication Networks, 2021*, 1–22. https://doi.org/10.1155/2021/6693731
58. Bodkhe, U., Mehta, D., Tanwar, S., Bhattacharya, P., Singh, P. K., & Hong, W.-C. (2020). A survey on decentralized consensus mechanisms for cyber physical systems. *IEEE Access, 8*, 54371–54401. https://doi.org/10.1109/ACCESS.2020.2981415
59. Kaur, M., Khan, M. Z., Gupta, S., Noorwali, A., Chakraborty, C., & Pani, S. K. (2021). MBCP: Performance analysis of large scale mainstream blockchain consensus protocols. *IEEE Access., 9*, 80931–80944. https://doi.org/10.1109/ACCESS.2021.3085187
60. Bamakan, S. M. H., Motavali, A., & Babaei Bondarti, A. (2020). A survey of blockchain consensus algorithms performance evaluation criteria. *Expert Systems with Applications, 154*(113385). https://doi.org/10.1016/j.eswa.2020.113385
61. Azbeg, K., Ouchetto, O., Jai Andaloussi, S., & Fetjah, L. (2021). An overview of blockchain consensus algorithms: Comparison, challenges and future directions. In F. Saeed, T. Al-Hadhrami, F. Mohammed, & E. Mohammed (Eds.), *Advances on smart and soft computing* (pp. 357–369). Springer Singapore.
62. Wan, S., Li, M., Liu, G., & Wang, C. (2020). Recent advances in consensus protocols for blockchain: A survey. *Wireless Networks, 26*, 5579–5593. https://doi.org/10.1007/s11276-019-02195-0

63. Lao, L., Li, Z., Hou, S., Xiao, B., Guo, S., & Yang, Y. (2020). A survey of IoT applications in blockchain systems: Architecture, consensus, and traffic modeling. *ACM Computing Surveys, 53*, 1–32. https://doi.org/10.1145/3372136
64. Khan, D., Jung, L. T., Ahmed Hashmani, M., & Waqas, A. (2020). A critical review of blockchain consensus model. In *2020 3rd international conference on computing, mathematics and engineering technologies (iCoMET)* (pp. 1–6). IEEE.
65. Alam Khan, F., Asif, M., Ahmad, A., Alharbi, M., & Aljuaid, H. (2020). Blockchain technology, improvement suggestions, security challenges on smart grid and its application in healthcare for sustainable development. *Sustainable Cities and Society, 55*, 102018. https://doi.org/10.1016/j.scs.2020.102018
66. Tang, H., Sun, Y., & Ouyang, J. (2020). Excellent practical byzantine fault tolerance. *Journal of Cyber Security, 2*, 167–182. https://doi.org/10.32604/jcs.2020.011341

Blockchain-Based Supply Chain System in Automotive Industry for Small- and Medium-Sized Manufacturing

Yuqiuge Hao, Petri Helo, Nikolaos Tsoniotis, and Rayko Toshev

1 Introduction

With the rapid development of various technologies, the automotive market will be completely different from today. We expect more integrated, personalised, shared and connected cars in the automotive industry [3]. It is believed that the impact of blockchain in the automotive industry is so significant. Therefore, it is vital to be aware of the potential for this disruptive technology and understand how it changes the complex automotive industry.

Blockchain is known as a technology that supports bitcoin and other similar currencies but is also much more than that. In the automotive industry, using blockchain technology can transform products, services and processes. Heutger and Kuckelhaus [4] illustrate several interesting industrial examples of using blockchain technology to managing physical assets in the automotive and its manufacturing industry, for instance, Groupe Renault storing the digital assets of its vehicles on the blockchain, Microsoft and VISEO connecting maintenance events by blockchain and Bosch and local certification authority using blockchain to prevent illegal odometer manipulation [4]. Various cases demonstrate how automotive companies have moved fast to seize the potential of using. There is a lot of research addressing the usage and implementation of blockchain in the automotive industry [1]. From previous research and practical cases, three different use case categories of blockchain application in the automotive industry are summarised, namely, (1) verification and authentication for process improvements, (2) vehicle (assets)

Y. Hao (✉) · P. Helo · R. Toshev
University of Vaasa, School of Technology and Innovations, Vaasa, Finland

N. Tsoniotis
Ideas Forward P.C, Thessaloniki, Greece

A. Bouras et al. (eds.), *Blockchain Driven Supply Chains and Enterprise Information Systems*, https://doi.org/10.1007/978-3-030-96154-1_8

management in transfer and distribution and (3) transparent finance, payments and insurance to increase the security [1, 3, 8, 10].

Although blockchain has many advantages and brings many benefits to the automotive industry, different stakeholders in the industry confront other challenges [10]. It always lacks a clear roadmap when it comes to adopting blockchain. To the best of our knowledge, most researchers focused on the particular phase of the life cycle in the automotive industry. There is a need to design a complete framework to provide on-demand, customised blockchain-based services meeting all critical requirements for the automotive industry. Besides, more and more SMEs join the automotive industry to improve efficiency, optimise investments and processes and increase flexibility [21]. The automotive industry is not only for big players.

Small and medium enterprises (SMEs) have low product volumes and relatively a large number of partners. As a result, these limitations constitute bottleneck problems and restrict SMEs' access to different advanced technologies and business models [17], which, in turn, prevents them from quickly penetrating new markets. Based on Vatankhah Barenji et al. [17], it's crucial to provide a solution for SMEs to solve (1) centralisation management problem, (2) security and trust issues and (3) heterogeneous data challenges. Therefore, using emergent blockchain technology can solve the above barriers and provide a distributed solution for SMEs [19].

This study aims to study blockchain technology and its impact on the automotive industry and SMEs. Subsequently, we will examine the case for a blockchain-based supply chain and elaborate on implementing it in the automotive industry. This paper is based on an ongoing EU Horizon 2020 project AVANGARD (advanced manufacturing solutions tightly aligned with business needs), started in 2019. The project's goal is to design a concept of microfactory for the production of urban electric vehicles and addresses its associated challenges. This project aims to apply Industry 4.0 solutions and minimise the footprint of both the production and use phases of the vehicles. The whole manufacturing and supply chain process are digitalised. From an electronic device, the client will be able to configure the vehicle, make the purchase order and follow the vehicle manufacturing, assembly and delivery evolution. At the same time, the manufacturing system can receive the order and decide the most suitable microfactory of the system to manufacture this vehicle attending to location, workload, availability of goods and environmental impact.

To address our goal of this research, the rest of this paper is organised as follows: an overview of blockchain technology and analyses of blockchain technology's implications for the supply chain are provided in Sect. 2. Section 3 will present an in-depth analysis of using blockchain in a cloud-based automotive supply chain system. In Sect. 4, we will discuss blockchain's growth opportunities and challenges in the automotive industry and how companies can act to the changes. We will also conclude this research in this section.

2 Literature Review

In this section, literature related to the blockchain is discussed. The collected literature is analysed from four levels. The first level is about blockchain technology and its main characteristics. The second level is about its impact on supply chain management. The third level is its impact on the automotive industry, and the fourth level, progressive level, is its impact on SMEs. This will serve as a ground for designing a blockchain-based supply chain system for automotive industry.

2.1 Blockchain Technology and Its Impact on Supply Chain Management

Bitcoin is a hot topic nowadays in this digital currency era. However, the blockchain technology behind it could prove much more significant [6]. Blockchain is a digital, decentralised, distributed ledger technology that provides a way for information to be recorded, shared and maintained by a community. Here are three critical characteristics of blockchain:

- Transparent: The transactions are recorded near real time to the blockchain and also synchronised on multiple computer systems. At the same time, it is visible to all participants with identical copies maintained. This principle can remove disputes, reduce uncertainty and, at the same time, increase trustworthiness [3, 5, 12, 13].
- Decentralised: From the business point of view, it is a peer-to-peer network that is entirely organised and managed by its associated members, without relying on a single middle authority or unified infrastructure that built trust [7]. From the technical point of view, decentralisation indicates a design of distributed system structure to deal with the data processing from verification, storage, maintenance and transmission. In this structure, the trust between distributing nodes is built through mathematical methods rather than centralised organisations [5].
- Immutable: One or more transactions are grouped to form a new block. All members of the network can verify the transactions in the block. If no consensus on the validity of the new block is reached, the block is rejected. Likewise, if consensus exists that the transactions in the block are valid, the block is added to the chain [7]. It is nearly impossible to tamper information to a blockchain without been detected. Blockchain can increase the trustworthiness of data and decrease the chances of fraud [3].

From the time it was developed, blockchain has been described as an efficient and permanent ledger to record events, transactions and information. The various unique features of blockchain technology have seen it considered for applications in many areas to improve the scope of the business areas and operational performance, including commerce, judiciary, finance, banking, healthcare, military and defence, equity crowdfunding, securities issuance, trading and settlement, insurance, notary public, music industry, Internet of Things and other non-financial applications [2].

Today, blockchain is being deployed in many forms. Still, blockchain technology has the potential to open new business models. This is mainly related to the complete public trust that is a unique characteristic of this technology. According to Piscini et al. [31], blockchain technology is a gatekeeper in the emerging trust economy of different parties on the supply chain.

The blockchain can create value for the industry through three main points: (a) unlocking business efficiencies, (b) disintermediating suppliers and (c) enabling new business and customer offerings [9]. In logistics, blockchain technology introduced the digital distributed ledger for shipment management. Similarly, blockchain can be implemented in the supply chain with practical benefits, such as efficient, timely and transparent transactions [2].

According to the Council of Supply Chain Management Professionals (CSCMP), SCM is based on two fundamental approaches: (i) planning, implementing and controlling the primary activities and delivering value for the ultimate customers and (ii) the centralised management and coordination of corresponding business processes within as well as across the companies. Pain points of the supply chain are:

- Weak control by the core enterprise
- Lack of supervision and hard to trace and match
- Information isolation
- Lack of trust

The integration of the supply chain can be considered a force that is trying to uplift the relationships between all the segments in the supply chain to enable better decision-making by providing visibility and highlighting the bottlenecks. Blockchain for supply chain management is a digital innovation and emergent allowing technology. It offers distinctive features such as real-time information sharing, improved security, transparency, reliability, traceability and visibility which improve the efficiency of the supply chain.

2.2 *Challenges and Opportunities of Blockchain in Automotive Industry*

The industrial sector (including the automotive ones) is considered a primary target of blockchain technology. The first application of blockchain in the automotive industry is digital currency bitcoin and digital payments. However, same as in other industries, the main features of blockchain could be beneficial for applications more than digital currency and digital payment in the automotive industry. Since 2017, at the Frankfurt auto show, auto suppliers ZF and IBM announced they were jointly developing a blockchain-based vehicle services payment platform. Another example is a blockchain-based platform called "Dubbed Car eWallet". It provides different services to change the vehicle business model more simply and securely, from the car-sharing pool, shopping in the car, dealership maintenance and payments processing. Furthermore, French carmaker Renault is also researching applications for blockchain technology. Blockchain is used to certify information about repair and maintenance when it is resold [30].

The automotive industry has its unique importance, considering its ranges from government regulatory parties, manufacturers, suppliers and vendors to spare parts suppliers [8], and covers many sectors across the entire supply chain from upstream to downstream. The automotive industry becomes a complex and wide-ranging ecosystem [8].

Some of the most typical applications of blockchain technologies are their use in the transfer of assets and digital applications and distributed information records created using smart contracts, considered an ideal way to program logical business and operations. It impacts all industry sectors, and it is not surprising that the automotive industry has also been influenced by this revolution [8].

The integration of the automotive industry and blockchain technology offers exciting solutions to some of the most pressing automotive problems, especially those related to the connected automotive industry. The power of this technology can drive innovation and solutions across the entire automotive ecosystem. To this day, there have been made several efforts to use blockchain for improving the automotive industry. This study identifies various automotive critical functional areas that can be leveraged using blockchain technology and their growth potential.

It is well noticed that blockchain technology is becoming more vital and crucial in the automotive industry. It influences the industry in the same way as other prominent technologies such as artificial intelligence, machine learning, 3D printing and IoT [29].

It has been widely realised that primary automotive industries have started to use blockchain technology in various scenarios over the last 2 years, such as vehicle supply chain, security, car service, autonomous vehicles, manufacturing process, insurance, etc. For example, General Motors (GM), Porsche, BMW have partnered with blockchain start-ups like XAIN, Spring Labs and VeChainThor to address complex issues (Table 1).

Moreover, SME companies are considered the backbone of most of the economies [32], and their survival is vital for a healthy economy. In Europe alone, there are approximately 21 million companies belonging to the SME sector. These 21 million companies provide a source of income for approximately 90 million people on the African continent. SMEs have to be strengthened to overcome the economic challenges surrounding them [20]. Despite their status as the essential part of any economy, SMEs find it difficult to:

- Find investors/finance
- Scale their operations
- Process payments
- Hire additional services

Table 1 Examples of blockchain applications in automotive industry

Key functional areas	Example	References
Smart manufacturing	Identification Blockchain can be used with digital twins, and can monitor and track digital asset information more effectively than traditional manufacturing. Through RFID tags, the authenticity of each material and asset can be verified. In addition, the blockchain can also protect data sharing between machines and prevent counterfeiting problems. This also helps to issue a safe and direct recall and improve quality control	Fraga-Lamas and Fernández-Caramés [10], Li et al. [14]
Supply chain and logistics monitoring	Visibility and traceability of supply chain and logistics. The automotive supply chain is considered to be very complex because it contains many types of assets, stakeholders and parties. A complete supply chain needs to manage the transfer of products and related transactions and the exchange of knowledge between organisations. Blockchain provides visibility, transparency and optimisation of logistics whilst providing seamless integration of transaction, payment and logistics information. For supply chain stakeholders, it is always clear to exchange knowledge and obtain constant details about who performs what, when and where	Kshetri [15], Saberi et al. [16], Sharma et al. [8], Stenholm et al. [24], Supranee and Rotchanakitumnuai [25]
Autonomous vehicles	Car-as-a-Service Blockchain technology contributes to the development of autonomous vehicles. Blockchain solutions can interconnect autonomous vehicles and realise car-sharing services. Data about autonomous vehicles will be exchanged in a safe, reliable and seamless manner. Blockchain can protect user privacy whilst protecting data security. In addition, the platform can process all payments after the trip, and update user records with the history of the trips performed	Sharma et al. [8], Fraga-Lamas and Fernández-Caramés [10], Singh and Kim [26], Pedrosa and Pau [27]
Aftersales services	Ownership transfer Blockchain technology increases the transparency of transactions and simplifies the process of car ownership changes. Buyers and sellers can execute goods transactions by using smart contracts without the need for an intermediary Automated services Most cars have error records. Once this information is shared on the blockchain, service professionals can easily access this information, diagnose problems quickly and repair the car in a shorter time. When the car needs maintenance, the service request can be triggered automatically. This will enable condition-based maintenance services. In addition, maintenance status can be easily tracked without visiting the mechanical station	Sund et al. [28], Sharma et al. [8]

(continued)

Table 1 (continued)

Key functional areas	Example	References
Insurance and security	Insurance Most insurance claims are fraudulent, and covert methods are used when issuing insurance policies and managing stocks, leading to increased operating costs and inefficiency. Blockchain solves this problem by implementing transparent recording of vehicle sensor data in a decentralised network. Blockchain provides new additional services for remote communication, providing insurance companies with driver location, driving duration, acceleration and braking behaviour, vehicle speed and other information. Blockchain can also incorporate insurance into other carriers, such as user files; this process can be called car sharing Security Vehicles are becoming more and more autonomous, which makes them more closely connected and more vulnerable to deadly cyberattacks. This is why the blockchain uses a robust encryption root that cannot be reverse engineered. The distributed ledger feature of the blockchain facilitates data storage and provides immutability	Sharma et al. [8], Fraga-Lamas and Fernández-Caramés [10]

With all the emerging technologies, SMEs must find ways to collaborate and share competency in a trustable manner to seize more business opportunities in a turbulent market environment. The new digitalisation trends and automation can form a significant challenge for SMEs [18]. In many current solutions and research, SMEs have encountered some bottleneck problems. Blockchain technology has been introduced recently for the manufacturing industry as peer-to-peer network which improves the system's security and where third party can be omitted [17].

3 Design of Blockchain-Based Supply Chain System for Automotive Industry

The automotive industry is one of the most promising applications of blockchain. In the previous section, we have evaluated the opportunities of using blockchain across the automotive industry to improve the supply chain. We also analysed the characteristics of blockchain in resolving business issues for SMEs. In this section, we will discuss the scenario in the electric vehicles sector.

Particularly in the electric vehicles (EVs) sector, the reality is that more and more SMEs are capable of developing EVs, and this will reshape the automotive value chain [11]. In most of the automotive industry, a centralised manufacturing model is a primary choice. Many giga-factories are operating in Europe, China and the USA. The current status of automotive factories consists of the production plant in which the final products are stored in the inventory (stock). Afterwards, the distributor collects a specific high volume for its region and each of the retailers' request from the distributor for the needs of the user/market. However, manufacturing plants across Europe seek into reduced wasted materials, energy consumptions and carbon footprint. Therefore, more and more SMEs are involved in manufacturer EVs locally based on local/regional needs. This manufacturing model only consists of modular production and the retailers in the broader region. Therefore, the supply chain is simplified and only consists of suppliers, regional factories, dealers and customers. Here in this demand-driven electric vehicles manufacturing, there are many use cases that need to be improved and verified through blockchain technology.

3.1 Functional Requirement

This paper is based on the ongoing EU Horizon 2020 project AVANGARD (advanced manufacturing solutions tightly aligned with business needs) started in 2019. The goal of the project is to design a concept of microfactory for the production of urban electric vehicles and address its associated challenges. This project aims to apply Industry 4.0 solutions and minimise the footprint of both the production and use phase of the vehicles. The whole manufacturing and supply chain process is digitalised. From an electronic device, the client will be able to configure the vehicle, make the purchase order and follow the evolution of the vehicle manufacturing, assembly and delivery. At the same time, the manufacturing system is able to receive the order and decide the most suitable microfactory of the system to manufacture this vehicle attending to location, work load, availability of goods and environmental impact.

Within this project, the blockchain technology is used to secure the whole process, and also to fulfil the track and trace functionalities of the supply chain and recording transactions amongst stakeholders and machines/software under its immutable and verifiable framework. The proposed blockchain component needs to be able to satisfy the following parameters:

- F1: Support the required decentralisation, which will ensure trust and immutability, whilst unconstructive facilitation of business level processes is guaranteed.
- F2: Record key transactional activities either organically recorded by value chain actors or programmatically sourced by key IoT devices and software components.
- F3: Facilitate granular access to key data points by participating actors based on defined stratification, supported by smart contract functionality.

According to the market demands, the following information needs to be secured by blockchain:

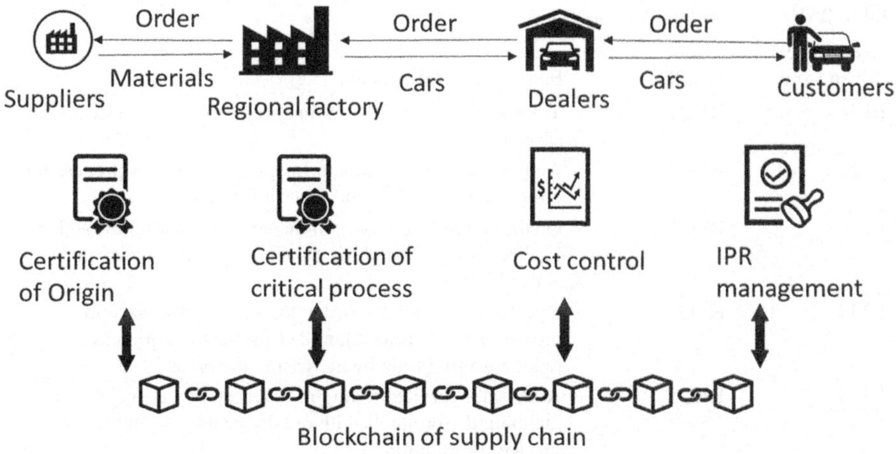

Fig. 1 A scenario of how blockchain technology can support certification and verification in regional demand-driven factory

- I1: Certification of origin – Customers who order the car will receive a certification of origin of all the materials which will be stored on a blockchain network. From suppliers to end consumer, the certifications are accessible and placed on a blockchain to be shared in a secure environment, i.e. made in Italy, Poland, Greece and Portugal.
- I2: Certification of critical process – Besides verifying virtual information of the product, it is also essential to warrant the physical movements of products in the supply chain.
- I3: Cost control – From extraction to end-of-life management and governing supply chain activities and its financial flow with smart contracts, for instance, in areas of financial transitions between participants in the entire ecosystem. For example, EV may use a windshield wiper which comes from a supplier, and to calculate the carbon footprint of whole car, the amount of carbon emission during the production should be shared by the supplier.
- I4: IPR management – Blockchain enabled IPR management system is secure, immutable and traceable. The provided IPR is easily checked by customers and any other participants in the supply chain. The IPR saved in blockchain can also be used when customers want to sell the electric car in the future (Fig. 1).

Based on the business requirements and information requirements, the basic functional requirements of designing a blockchain-based supply chain system in demand-driven electric vehicles factory are as follows (Table 2):

- Customer/user registration. Customers or other users from the participating stakeholders will have to be able to register to the system whilst creating their unique identity in the process. This will allow for logging activities under a unique identification schema.

Table 2 Functional requirements

Requirement driven from	Req ID	Functional requirements
F1,I1	REQ1	Track and trace: materials and products provided by all the suppliers
F2,I2	REQ2	Activity record: manufacturing process, such as processing craft, time, operators and other information
F2,I2	REQ3	Quality control: connect all the key information through IoT technologies, and trace the process and quality in the entire life cycle
F2,I3	REQ4	Sale-service: track the order and supply process, and provide flexible price plan to customers. Customer can reduce waiting time by increasing the price
F3,I4	REQ5	After-sales service: failing product tracing, to recall and maintain the products with quality problems, and record service information

- Stakeholder managed software/hardware registration. Manufacturing value chain stakeholders are expected to register their software (e.g. ERP, MES) or hardware (e.g. 3D printer, etc.) to the blockchain network. This will allow to attest ownership to participating actors, create a unique ID for the software/hardware components and facilitate logging of manufacturing processes, for example, information about production start and end time resulting from MES planning and execution, energy consumed resulting from IoT monitoring, material consumed, logging CO_2 production data, etc.
- Customer order requests. The necessary rules and REST APIs will be coded to support the implementation of front-end elements in the web applications that allow the logging of a customer's order including metadata, hashing of design files, etc. This transaction and textual metadata will be logged, files will be hashed and all state changes along with the actual files will also be forwarded to the relevant external databases via the ledger-sync subscriber. In the case of a design, the file upload hash will be compared against prior uploads. If a match is found under a different ID, and not under a suitable Creative Commons license, then the customers will be warned of infringing IP rights. If there is no match, then they will be asked to indicate if they produced the design or not and choose a Creative Commons license. This can be further extrapolated in future iterations to support an open marketplace of designs.
- Quotation, acceptance and payment. The system and/or system users will propose a quote for the order, which will either be rejected or accepted, lead to an order adaptation or proceed with payment. All these transactions will be foreseen, coded in the Transaction Processors for handling and logging, supported by the required REST APIs and logged accordingly. The metadata will similarly be forwarded to the external database via the ledger-sync subscriber.
- With the various software and hardware components registered, the smart contract functionality of the Transaction Processors' code can log agreed upon

activities during the production process, from order finalisation to asset dispatched to the customer. This will be facilitated per case, logged in the blockchain as well as forwarded to the external databases. Furthermore, logged transactions could be accessed granularly by the participating stakeholders, creating a vehicle passport that holds the overall history of the produced vehicle, yet with subsets of metadata and transactional logs accessible depending on defined access rights. As such the blockchain component will facilitate admin roles that can manage access rights for registered users, and potentially system components. Thus, a vehicle passport is envisioned as a complete historical record, yet fostering restricted access based on user roles, thus not exposing sensitive manufacturing information but facilitating the expected transparency to customers and stakeholders alike.

3.2 Technical Architecture

To facilitate the functional requirement described in Sect. 3.1, a block-based supply chain system, namely, BSS, is proposed as an integrated solution to organise and manage all related activities and operations. This subsection will discuss the technical architecture of BSS.

In this BSS platform, it is possible that the system/user can audit and certify some processes and data across the entire supply chain of EV, from suppliers, manufacturer and dealers to customers. As blockchain is a vertical enabler, several functionalities can be facilitated and audited accordingly by employing blockchain-based user identities, transactional activity logging at various levels of abstractions depending on the business modelling of the final solution or the various components to be employed. Subsequently, blockchain logging and transactional activity can be deployed as either privately accessible by some or all of the manufacturing partners or publicly accessible by other stakeholders participating in the manufacturing value chains from collaborators to consumers.

The technical implementation framework of this proposed BSS depicted with a cross-layered structure in Fig. 2. The supply chain consists of suppliers, regional factories, dealers and customers. Therefore, the record for all the generated data whilst EV transfer between each party are store in the form of a distributed leger. In this framework, it consists of five main layers, from top to bottom, namely, user layer, application layer, cloud layer, blockchain services layer and storage layer:

- *User layer:* Different stakeholders in the manufacturing value chains, such as customers, dealers, shop floor operators, manufacturing managers and suppliers, have different access to the cloud and blockchain services. The manager is the head of the supply chain system and initiates system changes based on conditions set in the smart contract.

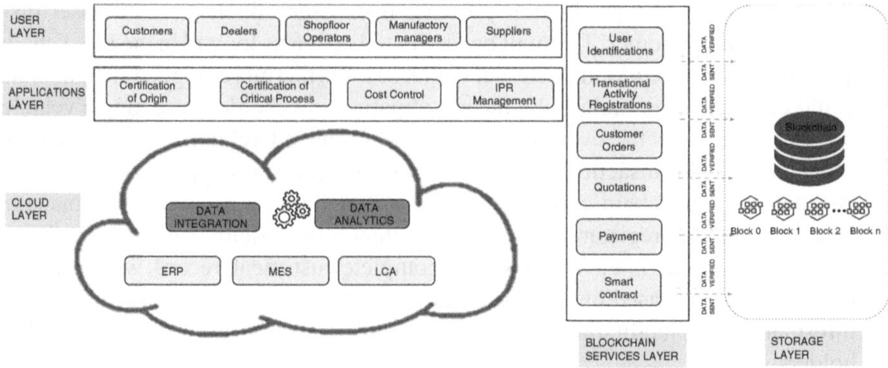

Fig. 2 Blockchain-based supply chain system (BSS) implementation framework

- *Application layer:* This layer defines various typical application scenarios and instances of blockchain-based supply chain. As described in Sect. 3.1, the blockchain can be applied to secure information: certification of origin, certification of critical process, cost control and IPR management.
- *Cloud layer:* The cloud layer is providing a cloud-based infrastructure to connect different tools, such as ERP, MES and LCA, and also integrate different data sets.
- *Blockchain services layer:* The blockchain services layer is responsible for synthesizing all related information from three other layers in vertical position. It consists of six components: user identifications, transactional activity registrations, customer orders, quotations, payment and smart contract.
- *Storage layer*: All the data blocks are generated in this layer. It is not only acting as a data storage but also operating encryption method, managing chain structure and adding timestamp to data block. The chain structure defines block header, block body and address.

3.3 Implementation

In this project, a hybrid blockchain is implemented in order to facilitate value chains of disparate partners, allow access to transactional data under a stratified model from completely private up to and including public access and support ease of integration with various setups such as software tools, IoT devices and stakeholders themselves, all the above without sacrificing decentralisation, immutability and eventually trust amongst participating actors.

By considering the overall technical architecture of BSS and comparing different blockchain framework, Hyperledger Sawtooth was chosen to support BSS. The reasons are as follows:

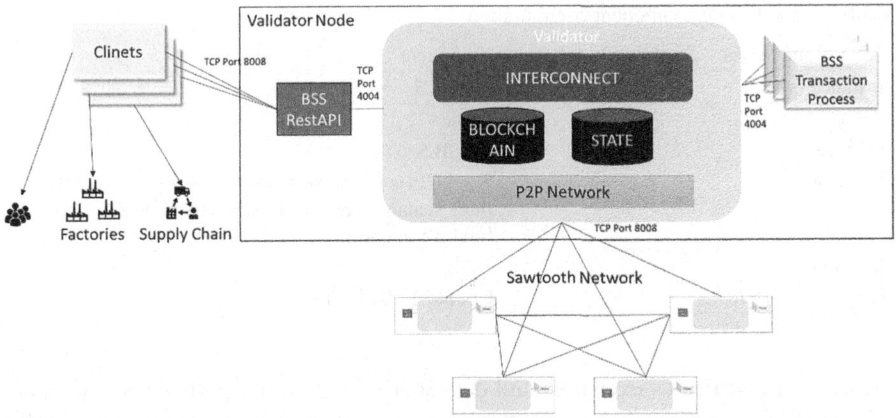

Fig. 3 Sawtooth Validator Node

- Sawtooth can be configured to support both private permission and public permissionless network configurations out of the box.
- Sawtooth's architecture is based on pluggable components that allow for flexibility and scalability.
- Sawtooth requires no transaction costs.

The Sawtooth blockchain node will be set up as per Fig. 3, with the Validator Nodes constructed as a multi-container Docker environment. A Docker within the frame of Sawtooth supports encapsulation, isolation, portability and control over the external communication of each Docker image, supporting scalability, efficient use of system resources, faster software delivery cycles and instant rollout. This approach is considered ideal for supporting the upcoming cloud services integration activities.

Each Validator Node will include the Validator, the Transaction Processors, the Consensus Engine and the required REST APIs and Clients. The *Clients* could interface with any system, software, device or any stakeholder interacting with BSS interfaces. The *BSS RestAPI* receives requests from the front-end implantation and facilities communication with the Validator. The *BSS Transaction Processor* holds application-specific code equivalent to smart contract functionality. Implementation will be undertaken in the Python programming language.

The multi-container Docker environment will clone the pilot implementation setup, based on the following configuration (Table 3):

3.4 Blockchain Demonstrator

This subsection presents a blockchain-based demonstrator for the proposed blockchain-based supply chain system (BSS). In the demonstration, we described a

Table 3 Blockchain component configuration

AWS cloud server – Sawtooth blockchain component	
Instance type	1 × EC2
Server type	Large
Storage	64 GB SSD
Processor	2 × vCPUs (Intel Xeon Processor, up to 3.0 GHz Intel Scalable Processor, each vCPU thread of an Intel Xeon core)
Memory	8 GB
Operating system	Ubuntu 18.04.5 LTS

use case of certificates exchange and data sharing with other partners by members of a manufacturing supply chain in the EV market. The implementation has to fulfil the following requirements:

- Allow members to create their own network of partners.
- Allow members to create, upload and manage a certificate with fixed and variable properties.
- Allow members to share the certificate with other members either a certificate or its metadata.
- All members can verify the authenticity of a certificate if it has been uploaded by a member of the supply chain.
- Allow members to handle custodianship and ownership separately taking under consideration one of the main complexities of any value chain.
- Support policies to facilitate transfer of custodianship and/or ownership to members of a partner network.
- Visualise at least one set of variable parameters and allow for manual update of their values.

Figures 4, 5, 6, and 7 present the screenshot of the dashboard of proposed BSS.

Figure 4 demonstrates the dashboard which holds an overview of Number of assets users' own across facilities and those that users don't own but are currently in users' facilities. Users can create asset categories, and check assets in transit, Sent/Received shipment requests, and also check number of partners in users' network. Other data are also included, along with a map for visualising the shipments in transit or already delivered.

Figure 5 demonstrates how to add a new partner. A partner can be either a colleague from user's company or a driver from a logistics company in the case of this demo. Colleagues can be co-owners of any assets that the user has, just by adding them to assets. To add a partner, user needs to know their Blockchain or Partner Key which acts as a unique identifier. By pressing Add, a request is sent to partners which they §can accept or decline. Conversely, user can delete it if it was sent by mistake. By pressing the eye icon, user can see more details about this partner.

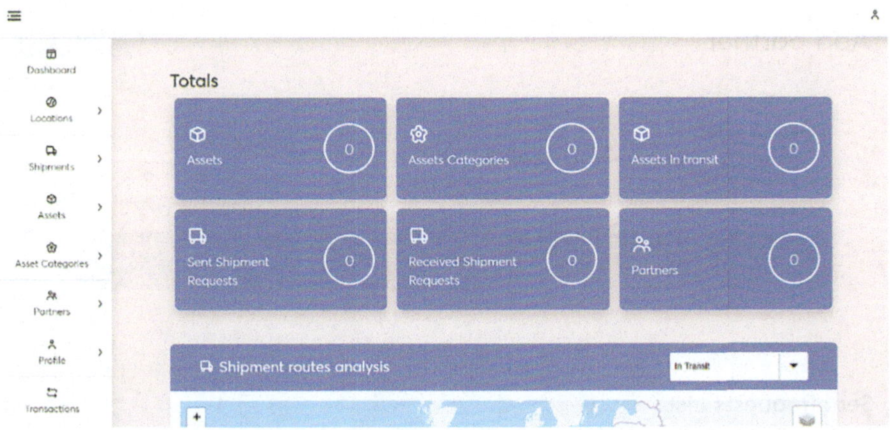

Fig. 4 The main page of BSS

Figure 6 shows thee shipment routs. Once the shipment requests have been sent, user can go to Locations > Map and see shipments in Transit or Delivered. Upcoming features will include a filter to customise the time span user wants to check out. In Transit shipments are depicted in a dashed line. Delivered shipments are depicted with a solid line. Now that shipments are sent and delivered, user can go to Locations > Assets by location and monitor how many of user's assets are where. In this list, user can see how many of the common assets amongst user and partners are located to which location and how many of the assets users don't own but are currently in user's location.

Figure 7 depicts the transaction records. This is a blockchain-powered supply chain pilot system. All relevant transactions are logged in the blockchain and can be accessed by participants, as depicted in Fig. 7. Participants are restricted to access only those transactions that derive from their own network of partners. Measures are in place to avoid data spillovers between networks. Finally, as transactions increase in numbers, the user is facilitated to filter them for quick identification per:

- Transaction type
- Partner transactions
- Asset-oriented transactions

4 Discussions and Conclusions

Blockchain technology is a revolutionary innovation that can transform lots of existing traditional systems into more secure, distributed, transparent, collaborative systems whilst empowering its users. Blockchain-driven solutions can seamlessly aggregate all information, provide important services and add value to industrial

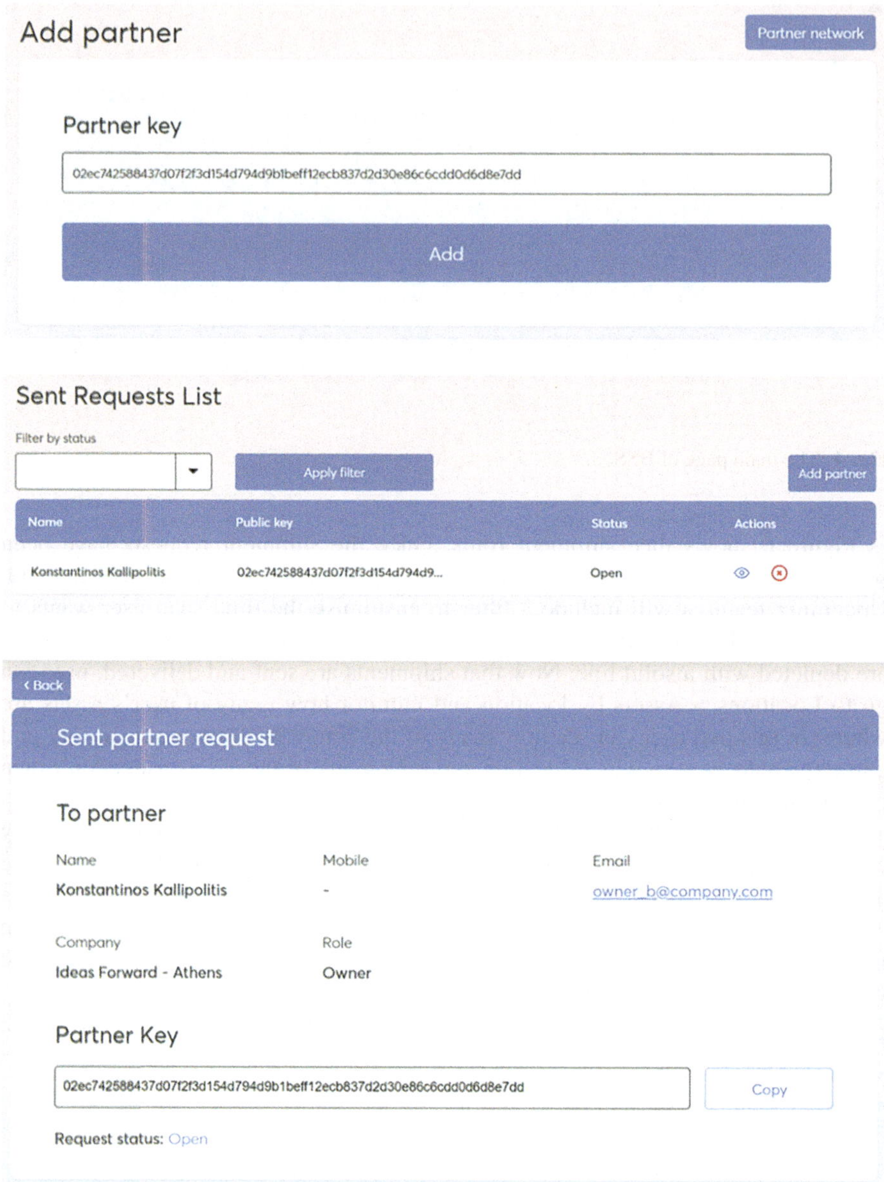

Fig. 5 Add new partner information pages

companies. The most important capability of blockchain is that it helps to unlock the full potential of other advent technologies, such as cloud, augmented reality, IoT and 3D printing. With the development and growth of maturity, blockchain technology will allow manufacturers to fully deploy other advanced technologies

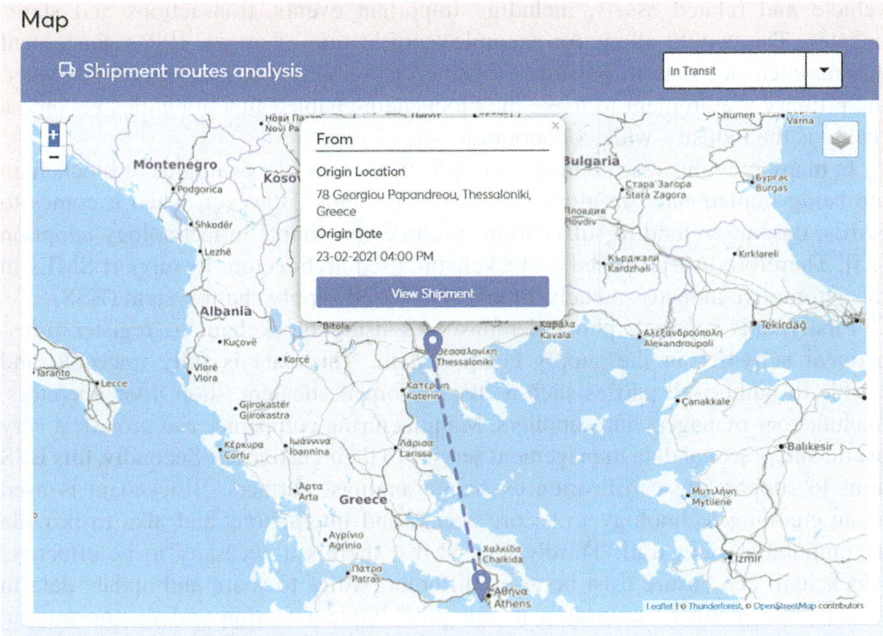

Fig. 6 The shipment routs analysis shown on map

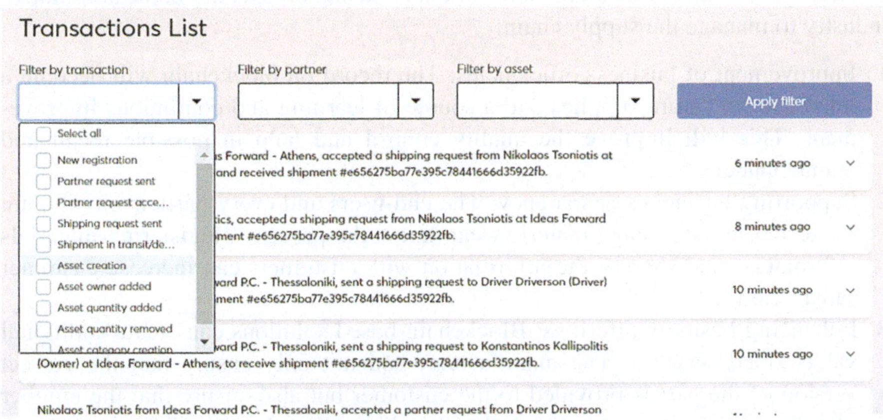

Fig. 7 The transaction is listed in the blockchain

and innovative business models. Therefore, more efficient factory operations that require data sharing and collaboration between complex companies and machine networks will be created and become the new norm for the entire industry [22].

This research demonstrates integration of blockchain and supply chain in automotive industry. In the future, the entire automotive industry could collaborate on a single trustable blockchain-based platform to store the information of every vehicle and related assets, including important events, transactions and status updates. This would allow, for example, certification of origin, IPR management and maintenance data to be stored together as a comprehensive record. However, the primary requirement to make the blockchain-enabled functionalities become a reality is the industry-wide collaboration [4].

In many previous research papers or practical cases, the examples of blockchain are being implemented in global international giants. However, when it comes to SMEs, they often tend to suffer from resource constraints in technology adoption [23]. Therefore, we proposed a blockchain-based architecture to support SMEs in the automotive industry, namely, blockchain-based supply chain system (BSS).

Firstly, this research paper demonstrates using blockchain to register transactional activities in the supply chain system. This data is fully traceable and visible to authorised parties such as the customers, dealers, shop floor operators, manufactory managers and suppliers. Manufacturing companies can provide a very useful and practical data management service to their customers. Secondly, this BSS aims to support the certification exchange amongst partners. Blockchain is used as an enabling technology to secure access and interactions and also to provide an immutable audit trail. Thirdly, For SMEs, there's a necessity to be effective. Blockchain can ensure trust between different parties to share and update data in an effective manner. According to our pilot implementation and demonstration, it is proved that blockchain technologies will build a trustful ecosystem for the automotive market.

Hereby, we summarise three main benefits of using blockchain in the automotive industry to manage the supply chain:

1. Improvement of business efficiencies: The record on blockchain will become a reference for future supplies and a source of learning and continuous improvement. This will improve the quality control and help in possible recall and maintenance.
2. Supporting business transparency: The end-users and every participant who are interested in early-stage materials can know the process. Registering materials information and sharing the information with customers can increase customer satisfaction.
3. Enhancing business offerings: Blockchain-based solutions can create additional value-added services. The manufacturer can not only ensure that the correct version of the part is provided to the customer but also ensure that the number of authorised copies is provided, thereby eliminating the risk of version control errors.

Nevertheless, it is very challenging to implement blockchain to support supply chain system, especially in SMEs. It is challenging to collect data from machines and processes employed in production activities whilst ensuring data immutability and ownership is respected throughout. It is even more challenging to gather data from stakeholders' activities and interactions within a value chain. Although blockchain solutions can create value for industrial organisations in several different ways, this does not mean that it is an equally viable solution for all companies or industrial manufacturing. Furthermore, regulators worldwide are still examining the potential responses to the ever-increasing influence of blockchain-led solutions. Based on many previous cases, regulatory concerns are the number one barrier to blockchain adoption [22].

Most companies have seen the benefits of blockchain. However, since blockchain is a foundational technology that is adopted gradually instead of sudden, it might take years until it profoundly changes the supply chain management landscape.

Acknowledgements This work is under the framework of EU project AVANGARD. This project has received funding from the European Union's Horizon 2020 research and innovation program under grant agreement No 869986. The dissemination of results herein reflects only the authors' view, and the commission is not responsible for any use that may be made of the information it contains.

References

1. Rabah, K. (2018). Convergence of AI, IoT, big data and blockchain: A review. *The Lake Institute Journal, 1*(1), 1–18.
2. Aslam, J., Saleem, A., Khan, N. T., & Kim, Y. B. (2021). Factors influencing blockchain adoption in supply chain management practices: A study based on the oil industry. *Journal of Innovation & Knowledge, 6*(2), 124–134.
3. Lawson, T. (2018). *Accelerating technology disruption in the automotive market: Blockchain in the automotive industry*. Deloitte. Accessed by: https://www2.deloitte.com/cn/en/pages/consumer-business/articles/blockchain-in-the-automotive-industry.html
4. Heutger, M., & Kuckelhaus, M. (2018). *Blockchain in logistics*. DHL. Accessed by: https://www.dhl.com/content/dam/dhl/global/core/documents/pdf/glo-core-blockchain-trend-report.pdf
5. Chen, G., Xu, B., Lu, M., & Chen, N. S. (2018). Exploring blockchain technology and its potential applications for education. *Smart Learning Environments, 5*(1), 1–10.
6. Swan, M. (2015). *Blockchain: Blueprint for a new economy*. O'Reilly Media, Inc..
7. Hackius, N., & Petersen, M. (2017). Blockchain in logistics and supply chain: Trick or treat? In *Digitalization in supply chain management and logistics: Smart and digital solutions for an industry 4.0 environment. Proceedings of the Hamburg international conference of logistics (HICL)* (Vol. 23, pp. 3–18). epubli GmbH.
8. Sharma, P. K., Kumar, N., & Park, J. H. (2019). Blockchain-based distributed framework for automotive industry in a smart city. *IEEE Transactions on Industrial Informatics, 15*(7), 4197–4205.
9. Sánchez Pérez, A. M., Tarifa Fernández, J., & Cruz Rambaud, S. (2020). Assessing blockchain investments through the learning option: An application to the automotive and aerospace industry. *Mathematics, 8*(12), 2213.
10. Fraga-Lamas, P., & Fernández-Caramés, T. M. (2019). A review on blockchain technologies for an advanced and cyber-resilient automotive industry. *IEEE Access, 7*, 17578–17598.
11. Özel, F. M., Davies, H. C., Ernst, C. S., & Nieuwenhuis, P. (2014). How to strategically position European SMEs as part of an electric vehicle technology value chain. *International Journal of Electric and Hybrid Vehicles, 6*(3), 227–254.

12. Ko, T., Lee, J., & Ryu, D. (2018). Blockchain technology and manufacturing industry: Real-time transparency and cost savings. *Sustainability, 10*(11), 4274. English, M., Auer, S., & Domingue, J. (2016). Block chain technologies & the semantic web: A framework for symbiotic development. In *Computer science conference for University of Bonn Students*, J. Lehmann, H. Thakkar, L. Halilaj, and R. Asmat, Eds (pp. 47–61). sn.
13. Sundarakani, B., Ajaykumar, A., & Gunasekaran, A. (2021). Big data driven supply chain design and applications for blockchain: An action research using case study approach. *Omega, 102*, 102452.
14. Li, Z., Barenji, A. V., & Huang, G. Q. (2018). Toward a blockchain cloud manufacturing system as a peer to peer distributed network platform. *Robotics and Computer-integrated Manufacturing, 54*, 133–144.C.
15. Kshetri, N. (2018). 1 Blockchain's roles in meeting key supply chain management objectives. *International Journal of Information Management, 39*, 80–89.
16. Saberi, S., Kouhizadeh, M., & Sarkis, J. (2018). Blockchain technology: A panacea or pariah for resources conservation and recycling? *Resources, Conservation and Recycling, 130*, 80–81.
17. Vatankhah Barenji, A., Li, Z., Wang, W. M., Huang, G. Q., & Guerra-Zubiaga, D. A. (2020). Blockchain-based ubiquitous manufacturing: A secure and reliable cyber-physical system. *International Journal of Production Research, 58*(7), 2200–2221.
18. Paardenkooper, K. (2019). Creating value for small and medium enterprises with the logistic applications of blockchain. In *International conference on digital technologies in logistics and infrastructure (ICDTLI 2019)* (pp. 269–274). Atlantis Press.
19. Wu, H., Li, Z., King, B., Ben Miled, Z., Wassick, J., & Tazelaar, J. (2017). A distributed ledger for supply chain physical distribution visibility. *Information, 8*(4), 137.
20. Ilbiz, E., & Durst, S. (2019). The appropriation of blockchain for small and medium-sized enterprises. *Journal of Innovation Management, 7*(1), 26–45.
21. Calabrese, G. (2001). Small-medium suppliers and the new car industry. *International Journal of Automotive Technology and Management, 1*(4), 471–489.
22. Galea-Pace, S. (2020). *The role of blockchain in manufacturing*. Manufacturing Global. Com, https://www.manufacturingglobal.com/smart-manufacturing/role-blockchain-manufacturing. Last accessed: 2021/05/01.
23. Gupta, N. (2019). *Should small and medium-sized enterprises adopt blockchain?*. Medium.com Last access: https://medium.com/akeo-tech/should-small-and-medium-sized-enterprises-adopt-blockchain-ff6c1cca784f. Last accessed: 2021/05/01.
24. Stenholm, D., Stylidis, K., Bergsjö, D., & Söderberg, R. (2017). Towards robust inter-organizational synergy: Perceived quality knowledge transfer in the automotive industry. In *DS 87-6 proceedings of the 21st international conference on engineering design (ICED 17) Vol 6: Design information and knowledge, Vancouver, Canada, 21-25.08. 2017* (pp. 011–020).
25. Supranee, S., & Rotchanakitumnuai, S. (2017). The acceptance of the application of blockchain technology in the supply chain process of the Thai automotive industry. In *Proceedings of the international conference on electronic business (ICEB)* (Vol. 2017, pp. 252–257).
26. Singh, M., & Kim, S. (2017). Blockchain based intelligent vehicle data sharing framework. *arXiv preprint* arXiv:1708.09721. D.
27. Pedrosa, A. R., & Pau, G. (2018). ChargeltUp: On blockchain-based technologies for autonomous vehicles. In *Proceedings of the 1st workshop on cryptocurrencies and blockchains for distributed systems* (pp. 87–92).
28. Sund, T., Lööf, C., Nadjm-Tehrani, S., & Asplund, M. (2020). Blockchain-based event processing in supply chains—A case study at IKEA. *Robotics and Computer-Integrated Manufacturing, 65*, 101971.
29. Zoria, S. (2019). *How is blockchain technology impacting the automotive industry*. Medium.com. https://medium.datadriveninvestor.com/how-is-blockchain-technology-impacting-the-automotive-industry-728875a7c940. Last assessed: 2021/05/01.

30. Boucher, N. (2020). *The blockchain, transformation vector for the future of the automotive industry*. Renault Group. https://www.renaultgroup.com/en/news-on-air/news/the-blockchain-transformation-vector-for-the-future-of-the-automotive-industry/. Last assessed: 2021/07/28.
31. Piscini, E., Hyman, G., & Henry, W. (2017). Blockchain: Trust economy tech trends 2017. *Deloitte Insights*. https://www2.deloitte.com/insights/us/en/focus/tech-trends/2017/blockchain-trust-economy.html
32. Kumar, R., Singh, R. K., & Dwivedi, Y. K. (2020). Application of industry 4.0 technologies in SMEs for ethical and sustainable operations: Analysis of challenges. *Journal of Cleaner Production, 275*, 124063.

Designing an Efficient Consensus Protocol for Supply Chain

Mohammad Saidur Rahman, Ibrahim Khalil, and Abdelaziz Bouras

1 Introduction

Supply chain is a complex ecosystem with multiple participants with different roles and responsibilities. For example, *retailers*, *distributors*, *manufacturers*, *suppliers*, and *customers* are a few key participants in a typical supply chain system (see Fig. 1). Traditional supply chain management systems are designed based on cloud computing technology to ensure scalability and accessibility of supply chain data from anywhere at any time [30, 19]. However, the cloud computing platform cannot be fully trusted [6, 23, 24]. Giving an example from the supply chain point of view, supply chain data stored in the cloud can be altered or false data can be injected by the dishonest cloud service provider to give financial advantage to dishonest participants during the supply chain operations. Data in the supply chain system can be altered by an internal and external attacker to give benefits to one or more supply chain stakeholders or hamper the supply chain process [2]. Therefore, a trustworthy platform is required to prevent data modification attack.

Blockchain technology is getting increased attention by the researchers from the industries and academia to design trustworthy systems in different sectors such as healthcare [31], manufacturing [1], agriculture [7] including supply chain systems [25, 10, 18]. Blockchain is a distributed ledger that is distributed among all nodes

M. S. Rahman (✉)
RMIT University, Melbourne, VIC, Australia
e-mail: mohammadsaidur.rahman@rmit.edu.au

I. Khalil
School of Computing Technologies, RMIT University, Melbourne, VIC, Australia
e-mail: ibrahim.khalil@rmit.edu.au

A. Bouras
Qatar University, Doha, Qatar
e-mail: abdelaziz.bouras@qu.edu.qa

A. Bouras et al. (eds.), *Blockchain Driven Supply Chains and Enterprise Information Systems*, https://doi.org/10.1007/978-3-030-96154-1_9

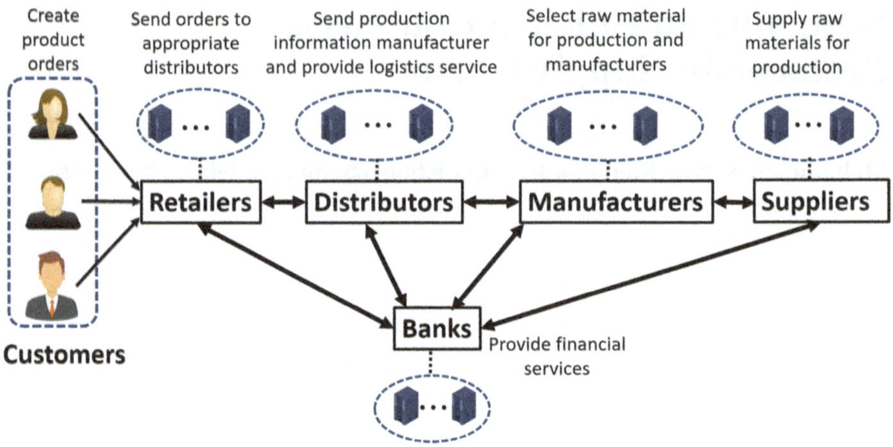

Fig. 1 An overview of a supply chain system

that are connected in a peer-to-peer fashion. The distributed ledger is created using a special type of data structure that stores data as blocks, and blocks are logically linked together via cryptographic hash algorithm [26]. As the data are replicated among all nodes in the network, it is extremely difficult to modify any data or insert fake data. Thus, blockchain provides security of stored data and can build trust among stakeholders of a supply chain system. A consensus mechanism [17] is one of the key mechanisms in blockchain-based system that will ensure the consistency and integrity of supply chain data.

Several researches have been conducted that show the prospects of blockchain-based supply chain system [16, 25, 1]. Nevertheless, a little attention is given to the consensus mechanisms that would fit well in the supply chain system. The existing blockchain-based supply chain systems apply consensus mechanisms that are mainly designed for cryptocurrency such as Bitcoin [28]. The cryptocurrency is fundamentally different from supply chain systems. The supply chain system involves transactions from stakeholders with different types of roles and responsibilities. It is extremely important to select a consensus mechanism that is suitable for supply chain. Especially, the transactions in supply chain require fast consensus for avoiding any delay in the operations. Hence, our method employs a novel consortium consensus mechanism for supply chain systems by leveraging multisignature technology. Multisignatures [15] enable multiple signers to create a compact signature for a message block. The multisignature can be considered useful for verifying a block before adding it to the blockchain [9]. The proposed consensus mechanism that leverages the multisignature schemes for block verification offers a less complicated implementation of the distributed ledger and ensures higher efficiency and scalability for achieving consensus. Overall, this chapter has the following focus:

1. Designing a consensus mechanism is developed to focus on supply chain systems. The consensus mechanism has two parts: *leader selection* and *block*

mining. The proposed consensus mechanism adopts a leader selection method similar to RAFT [21].
2. Developing a multisignature-based block mining process is introduced for higher efficiency and scalability. The proposed consensus uses the identity-based multisignature [13] for proposing a block and verification process.

2 Background

In this section, we give a brief introduction of the consensus mechanism and identity-based multisignature schemes that are the bases of our proposed consensus mechanism.

2.1 Consensus Mechanism in Blockchain

In general, the *consensus mechanism* in a blockchain network is a part that makes the nodes agree on a single piece of data [17]. In other words, the mechanism decides whether a block is going to be added in the blockchain or not. The process of adding blocks to the linked list is a significant factor to security and scalability. This can be achieved with a state machine replication (SMR) algorithm. The SMR algorithm makes a network agrees on a unique, constantly growing, ordered set of transactions. The terms consensus mechanism and SMR algorithm are closely related. Hence, they are often used interchangeably.

In order to achieve consensus, an algorithm has to provide two properties: *safety* and *liveness*. The safety in the consensus mechanism means that a new entry to the transaction log cannot be changed later once nodes confirmed it. The liveness represents that a transaction submitted by an honest user gets accepted if the user has sufficient connectivity. As consensus mechanisms are Byzantine Fault Tolerant (BFT), blockchains are deemed to be trustless. In a blockchain network, other nodes may behave in malicious ways. Therefore, blockchain users do not need to trust others. In general, consensus algorithms cannot tolerate more than a third of the nodes being malicious [22]. A blockchain may allow more byzantine faults. There are several consensus mechanisms that are widely used in blockchain such as *Practical Byzantine Fault Tolerance (PBFT)*, *Proof of Elapsed Time (PoET)*, *Steller Consensus Protocol (SCP)*, *Hashgraph*, *Raft*, and *Tendermint* [5].

The consensus mechanism depends on the architecture of the blockchain network. Blockchain networks can be classified as *public*, *consortium*, or *private* blockchain in order of decreasing degrees of openness available for participation by nodes [27]. The *public blockchain* is also referred to as a permissionless blockchain since any node can freely enter and exit the network. The public chain is the earliest and most widely used blockchain architecture. Bitcoin [20] is the most widely known example of the public blockchain. The *private blockchain* is also known as the permissioned blockchain and is only used in private organizations or institutions

[3]. Unlike public blockchains, private blockchains are generally not open to the outside world and are only open to individual individuals or institutions.

The consortium blockchain is a hybrid architecture comprising features from both public and private blockchains. A consortium blockchain is also a permissioned blockchain, in which participation is limited to a consortium of members to participate; each node might refer to a single organization or institution in the consortium. The number of nodes in a consortium blockchain is determined by the size of the pre-selected participants in the blockchain. For example, a supply chain blockchain is designed for a consortium of twenty participants. In that case, the maximum number of nodes in this consortium blockchain is twenty, and the number of nodes required to reach the consensus depends on which consensus algorithm the consortium blockchain uses. The consortium chain accesses the network through the gateways of member institutions. The consortium chain platform generally provides members' information authentication, data read and write permission authorization, network transaction monitoring, member management, and other functions. Each member can have permissions assigned by the consortium to access the ledger and validate the generation of blocks. The well-known Hyperledger project is an example of a consortium blockchain [8]. Since there are relatively few nodes participating in the consensus process, the consortium blockchain generally does not use the PoW mining mechanism as the consensus algorithm. Consortium chains' requirements for transaction confirmation time and transaction throughput are very different from those of public chains.

2.1.1 Raft Protocol

Raft [21] or the Raft Consensus Algorithm is developed to facilitate practical implementation for industry applications. The main idea of RAFT is that each node in the blockchain starts from the identical initial state and executes a series of instructions in the same sequence. The primary objective of the Raft consensus mechanism is achieving a consistent state. As a result, the Raft uses a consistent algorithm log method to synchronize instructions and manage replicated logs.

In Raft algorithm, nodes are divided into three roles that are mutually convertible. Roles include: *leader*, *follower*, and *candidate*. Only one node can act as a leader in the whole cluster of nodes. The number of nodes in a cluster must not be less than five. The leader is designated to receive user requests, maintain replication logs, and communicate with followers.

At the start of the time, all nodes are followers that passively respond to requests from the leader. Follower nodes do not exchange any message with each other, while they are acting as passive nodes. A follower node responds to log replication requests received from the leader node and responds to election requests that are sent from candidate nodes. The follower node passes the election request directly to the leader node once a follower receives a request from the user.

A candidate node initiates the election process. In the absence of a leader node, due to a crash or network failure, one or more blockchain nodes propose them as

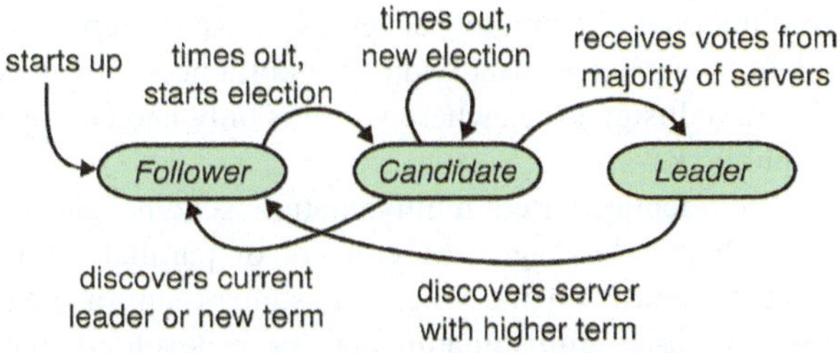

Fig. 2 An overview of server states of RAFT protocol [21]

candidate nodes and initiate an election process for electing a new leader node. After the successful execution of the election process, a candidate node is selected as the leader node, and the status of the candidate node is changed to leader. Figure 2 shows how the three roles change states. Each round of an election process is called a *term* that elects only one leader. Term is represented by a continuously increasing number.

The Raft algorithm consensus has two phases: *leader election* and *log replication*. The leader election phase is activated by a mechanism called *heartbeat mechanism* where a leader node broadcasts a message to all follower nodes periodically and maintains its authority. Otherwise, any of the follower nodes switches its role to candidate role and initiates a leader election mechanism assuming that the leader has failed [21]. Next, the new candidate node increases its current term and asks votes for itself. In addition, the new candidate node broadcasts a message called *RequestVoteRPC* to other blockchain nodes and waits for any of the following situations [21]:

- A candidate node that wins the election with more than half of the server votes becomes a leader node.
- A candidate loses the election as another candidate node has got more than half of the votes. The loosing candidate node receives the corresponding heartbeat from the winner and becomes a follower node.
- No winner is found, and the election process is re-instantiated after a random timeout period. The term increases.

The log replication phase is the second phase where the leader node accepts the user request. Based on the request, it updates the log information and broadcasts a heartbeat message to all follower nodes. All follower nodes synchronize the leader node's log once the heartbeat message is received.

2.2 *Identity-Based Multisignature Scheme*

A multisignature includes a group of participants for signing the same message and generates an output known as multisignature [4]. The multisignature can be verified with the set of public keys of the participants that sign the message. The verification of standard multisignature schemes needs the public keys of all signers. Therefore in applications where bandwidth is a bottleneck, it can be useful to consider identity-based multisignatures where verifiers only need unique identifiers of signers instead of public keys.

The identity-based multisignature scheme can be *serial*[11] or *parallel*[13]. This chapter leverages the concept of parallel multisignature scheme: a parallel multisignature scheme where all signers sign a data or file in parallel [11]. The identity-based multisignature scheme is developed based on the concept of identity (ID)-based cryptosystems. In ID-based cryptosystem, a user's public key is derived from their identity, and private key is computed by a trusted third party known as private-key generator (PKG). ID-based cryptosystems provide better flexibility of the key management over the traditional public-key cryptosystems (PKCs), and signature can be verified with signer's identity [12].

3 Multisignature-Based Consensus Mechanism

In this section, we discuss our proposed consensus mechanism for supply chain systems. We develop a consensus mechanism that consists of two parts. In the first part, an election process determines a *leader node* among the blockchain nodes. The leader node selection process is inspired by the RAFT Consensus algorithm [21]. We assume that we have b number of participants in a supply chain management system that forms a consortium of participants. Each participant takes part in the consensus mechanism. However, our version of the RAFT inspired leader node election algorithm divides blockchain nodes into two groups—a single *leader node* and the rest of the nodes are *proposer nodes* (see Fig. 3).

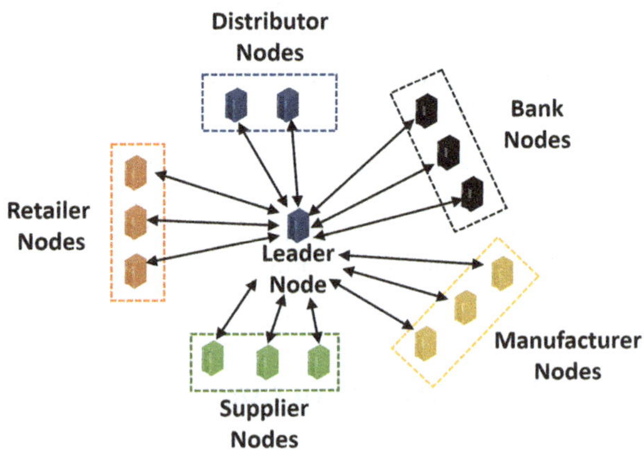

Fig. 3 Overview of the consortium of the proposed RAFT-based consensus

3.1 Leader Node Selection

Initially, all nodes are proposers and receive transactions from users. A node is randomly selected as the leader node to mine the first block. As a result, nodes are divided into two groups. The leader node periodically sends a request to all proposer nodes. A proposer node passively responds to the requests from the leader. If a proposer does not receive any request from the leader node, it initiates the leader election process by claiming itself a candidate. It is possible that multiple nodes have declared themselves as candidate. Nodes that have failed to declare them as candidate will be considered as voters and vote their suitable candidate. If a candidate gets a maximum number of votes, the node declares itself as the leader node and starts sending messages to the proposer.

3.2 Block Mining

The second part involves the block mining process that is developed by leveraging an identity-based multisignature scheme [13]. The block mining process involves two phases: *proposal phase* and *verification phase*. In the proposal phase, blockchain nodes use the multisignature scheme for initiating the mining phase and certify a proposed block. The certified block can be verified by the leader node in the verification phase. An overview of the block mining process is illustrated in Fig. 4. The steps are as follows:

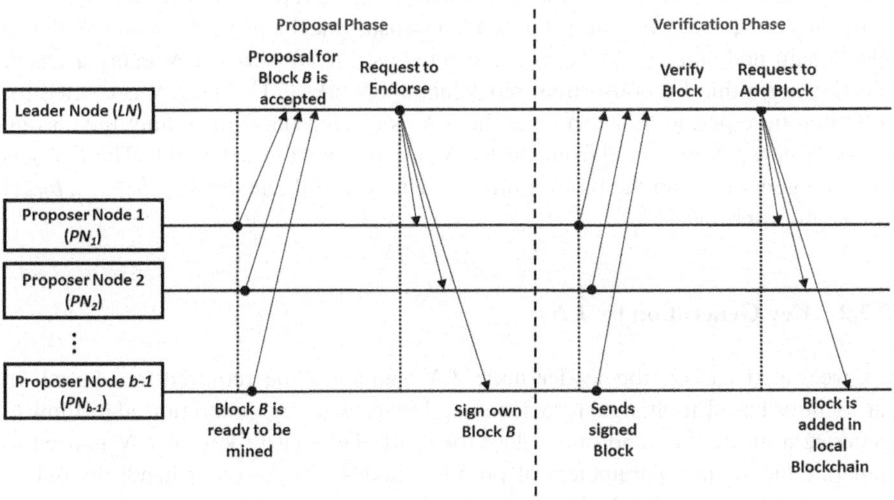

Fig. 4 Overview of the block mining process

1. A *leader node* (LN) is elected by the nodes of the blockchain network for a short period of time according to the leader selection mechanism of RAFT protocol. For example, only for mining the current block. Other nodes become *proposer nodes*. LN generates required keys for proposer nodes. Keys include a public key (PK), a master key (MK), and private key s_i for each proposer node (i.e., miner). LN sends PK and the respective private key s_i to each proposer node.
2. In a blockchain network, each proposer node or miner contains *a proposed block* $\mathcal{B}$ that needs to be added in the blockchain. Each miner signs their respective proposed block $\mathcal{B}$.
3. Once $\mathcal{B}$ is signed, each miner generates their own signature verification parameter and shares their signature verification parameters to each other to produce a combined signature verification parameter. Finally, each miner sends the signed $\mathcal{B}$ and the combined signature verification parameter to LN.
4. LN uses verification parameters to verify all received signed blocks $\mathcal{B}$. If all blocks are verified correctly, LN asks proposer nodes to add the proposed block in the blockchain.

The aforementioned tasks can be divided into four parts: (1) public-key generation by LN, (2) private-key generation by LN for all miners, (3) signing proposed block by miners, and (4) block verification by LN. Detailed discussion of each part is provided below.

3.2.1 Preliminaries

Assume that there are b number of blockchain nodes in the blockchain network BCN. The set BCN_{nodes} of blockchain nodes can be represented as: $BCN_{nodes} = \{bn_1, bn_2, \ldots, bn_b\}$. In our proposed consensus mechanism, we assume that a blockchain node $bn_i' \in BCN_{nodes}$ is elected as a *leader node* LN using a leader election algorithm for consortium blockchain networks [21]. The LN is elected for a limited time period. For example, the LN is elected only for mining the current block. A new LN is elected from the BCN_{nodes} to mine the next block. The LN acts as a key generator and the block validator. The rest of the nodes $\{b_1, b_2, \ldots, b_{b-1}\}$ act as proposer nodes.

3.2.2 Key Generation by LN

As we stated earlier, the leader node LN generates the required key based on an identity-based multisignature scheme. LN runs a key generation algorithm to generate a master key and public key for itself. The master key of LN is used to generate the signing parameters of proposer nodes. On the other hand, the public key is used for verifying the block proposed by proposer nodes.

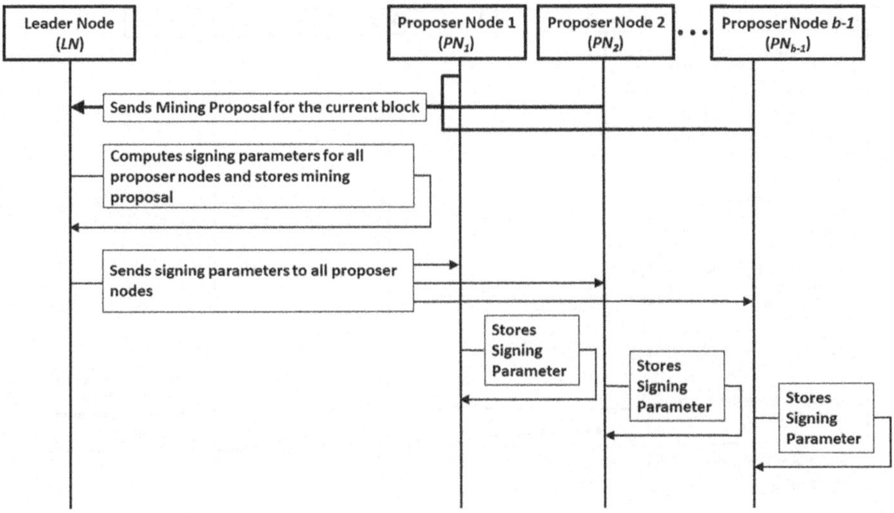

Fig. 5 Overview of the proposal for mining

3.2.3 Blockchain Node's Mining Proposal Generation

A proposer node generates its *signing key* sk_i in collaboration with LN. The signing key is generated in a way so that it can be used to sign only the current block (i.e., the block to be mined), and the key cannot be used for signing any previous block. Hence, sk_i includes the *proposer node ID*, *current block number*, and *timestamp*. As a result, corrupted proposer blockchain nodes cannot use their private keys for creating fork (i.e., two different but equally valid versions of the blockchain) [29]. An overview of the mining proposal generation is presented in Fig. 5. The generation of PR_i has the following steps:

1. A proposer node bn_i sends its identification number (ID_i), the sequence number of the block to be mined ($\mathcal{B}$), and timestamp $\mathcal{T}_i$ to LN.
2. If $\mathcal{B}$ is the current block number and $\mathcal{T}_i$ is greater than the timestamp when the last block mined, LN generates a *mining proposal* by hashing ID_i, $\mathcal{B}$, and $\mathcal{T}_i$ using a hash function.
3. LN signs the ID_i, $\mathcal{B}$, and $\mathcal{T}_i$ using LN's master key and generates a miner's signing key sk_i. The signing key sk_i is sent to the proposer node.
4. The LN stores the mining proposals from all blockchain nodes as a collection: $J = \{J_1, J_2, \ldots, J_{b-1}\}$.

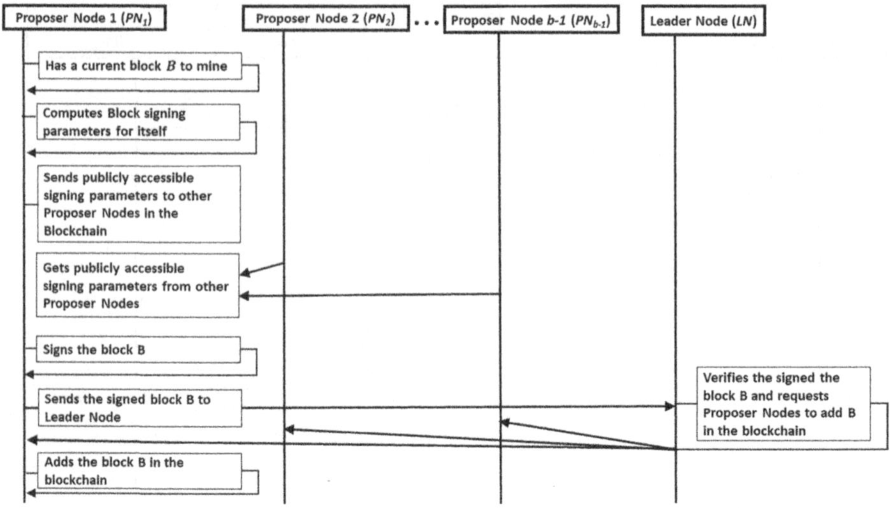

Fig. 6 Overview of the block signing process

3.2.4 Signing Proposed Block by Proposer Nodes

In the signing process of a proposed block $\mathcal{B}$, all of the proposer nodes sign in a combined manner by leveraging an identity-based multisignature scheme. All proposer nodes use their respective signing key and the leader node's public key. An overview of the block signing process is shown in Fig. 6. The signing process involves the following steps:

1. Using the identity-based multisignature scheme, every proposer node computes their own *publicly accessible signing parameters* to sign the current block in a manner so that the signed block can be verified by the leader node.
2. Each proposer node broadcasts its parameter to other proposer nodes.
3. Upon receiving other proposer nodes' publicly accessible signing parameters, each proposer node combines them to compute a parameter that is the same for all proposer nodes.
4. Each blockchain node signs their current block $\mathcal{B}$ with the combined parameter and the signing key received from the leader node to generate the signed block. The signed block is sent to leader node LN.
5. LN verifies signed blocks, sent by proposer nodes, with its master key. The verification is successful if all signed blocks have the same state. Once the blocks are verified, LN recommends all blocks to add their proposed block to the current blockchain and announces the mining process as complete.

4 Performance Analysis

In this section, the performance of the proposed RAFT and multisignature-based consensus algorithm for supply chain is discussed. The analysis is performed in terms of security and efficiency from the perspectives of both RAFT protocol and identity-based multisignature.

4.1 Security Analysis

As it is stated earlier, the proposed consensus mechanism involves two parts. The first part is the *leader selection* that is built on the RAFT protocol. Hence, the security of the leader node selection process depends on the security of the RAFT protocol. In our proposed consensus mechanism, there is only one leader node and $(b - 1)$ proposer nodes. The leader node is responsible for the key generation of all other proposer nodes, and it is selected based on the votes of the majority of the proposer nodes. Thus, the leader node is assumed to be trusted. Moreover, the life span of a leader node is limited [14]. The second part of the proposed consensus mechanism is designed based on multisignature scheme where all signers must sign the same block to add the block in the blockchain. Also, the identity-based multisignature scheme forces each proposer node to add their identity in the mining process, which helps the leader node to generate individual signing keys. At the time of signing a block, the proposer nodes involve each other's secret parameters, which makes the signing process secured. Finally, the leader can influence the mining process if only if all proposer nodes are corrupted. From that point of view, the proposed consensus mechanism is secured.

4.2 Efficiency

Unlike the existing consensus mechanism, our proposed consensus mechanism does not involve high-computational resources. As multisignature scheme requires fewer steps and keys for the verification of the signed entity, it itself is an efficient process. Hence, signing and verification of the proposed block with multisignature scheme are efficient. Nevertheless, the actual time for the mining process involving multisignature scheme may vary depending on the multisignature scheme that is used.

5 Conclusion

In this chapter, we present a novel consensus mechanism for the supply chain management system. The proposed consensus mechanism is designed considering a consortium blockchain network involving all supply chain stakeholders. Blockchain nodes select a leader node to mine a block using RAFT protocol that allows changing the leader node for each mining task to ensure trust and security mining process. The identity-based multisignature scheme makes the consensus process lightweight and practical. Nevertheless, the proposed consensus mechanism creates an avenue of further investigation to find the suitability of this consensus mechanism in diverse supply chain scenarios. Different types of leader node selection processes and multisignature schemes should be investigated to find a consensus mechanism that would fit all supply chain scenarios.

Acknowledgments This chapter was made possible by NPRP grant NPRP11S-1227-170135 from the Qatar National Research Fund (a member of Qatar Foundation). The statements made herein are solely the responsibility of the authors.

References

1. Abeyratne, S. A., & Monfared, R. P. (2016). Blockchain ready manufacturing supply chain using distributed ledger. *International Journal of Research in Engineering and Technology, 5*(9), 1–10.
2. Akinrolabu, O., New, S., & Martin, A. (2018). Cyber supply chain risks in cloud computing-bridging the risk assessment gap. *Open Journal of Cloud Computing, 5*(1), 1–19.
3. Aras, S. T., & Kulkarni, V. (2017). Blockchain and its applications—a detailed survey. *International Journal of Computer Applications, 180*(3), 29–35.
4. Bagherzandi, A., & Jarecki, S. (2010). Identity-based aggregate and multi-signature schemes based on RSA. In *International workshop on public key cryptography* (pp. 480–498). Springer.
5. Baliga, A. (2017). Understanding blockchain consensus models. In *Persistent.*
6. Baumann, A., Peinado, M., & Hunt, G. (2015). Shielding applications from an untrusted cloud with Haven. *ACM Transactions on Computer Systems, 33*(3), 1–26.
7. Bermeo-Almeida, O., Cardenas-Rodriguez, M., Samaniego-Cobo, T., Ferruzola-Gómez, E., Cabezas-Cabezas, R., & Bazán-Vera, W. (2018). Blockchain in agriculture: A systematic literature review. In *International Conference on Technologies and Innovation* (pp. 44–56). Springer.
8. Cachin, C., et al. (2016). Architecture of the Hyperledger blockchain fabric. In *Workshop on distributed cryptocurrencies and consensus ledgers* (Vol. 310). Chicago, IL.
9. Drijvers, M., Gorbunov, S., Neven, G., & Wee, H. (2020). Pixel: Multi-signatures for consensus. In *29th USENIX Security Symposium (USENIX Security 20)* (pp. 2093–2110).
10. Francisco, K., & Swanson, D. (2018). The supply chain has no clothes: Technology adoption of blockchain for supply chain transparency. *Logistics, 2*(1), 2.
11. Gangishetti, R., Gorantla, M. C., Das, M. L., & Saxena, A. (2006). Identity based multisignatures. *Informatica, 17*(2), 177–186.
12. Gorantla, M. C., Gangishetti, R., & Saxena, A. (2005). A survey on ID-based cryptographic primitives. *IACR Cryptology ePrint Archive, 2005*, 94.

13. Harn, L., Ren, J., & Lin, C. (2009). Efficient identity-based GQ multisignatures. *International Journal of Information Security, 8*(3), 205–210.
14. Huang, D., Ma, X., & Zhang, S. (2019). Performance analysis of the Raft consensus algorithm for private blockchains. *IEEE Transactions on Systems, Man, and Cybernetics: Systems, 50*(1), 172–181.
15. Itakura, K., & Nakamura, K. (1983). A public-key cryptosystem suitable for digital multisignatures. *NEC Research & Development* (71), 1–8.
16. Korpela, K., Hallikas, J., & Dahlberg, T. (2017). Digital supply chain transformation toward blockchain integration. In *Proceedings of the 50th Hawaii International Conference on System Sciences*.
17. Lamport, L., Shostak, R., & Pease, M. (1982). The byzantine generals problem. *ACM Transactions on Programming Languages and Systems, 4*(3), 382–401.
18. Longo, F., Nicoletti, L., Padovano, A., d'Atri, G., & Forte, M. (2019). Blockchain-enabled supply chain: An experimental study. *Computers & Industrial Engineering, 136*, 57–69.
19. Manuel Maqueira, J., Moyano-Fuentes, J., & Bruque, S. (2019). Drivers and consequences of an innovative technology assimilation in the supply chain: cloud computing and supply chain integration. *International Journal of Production Research, 57*(7), 2083–2103.
20. Nakamoto, S. Bitcoin whitepaper (2008). https://bitcoin.org/bitcoin.pdf (17.07.2019)
21. Ongaro, D., & Ousterhout, J. (2014). In search of an understandable consensus algorithm. In *2014 {USENIX} Annual Technical Conference (USENIX ATC 14)* (pp. 305–319).
22. Pease, M., Shostak, R., & Lamport, L. (1980). Reaching agreement in the presence of faults. *Journal of the ACM, 27*(2), 228–234.
23. Rahman, M. S., Khalil, I., Alabdulatif, A., & Yi, X. (2019). Privacy preserving service selection using fully homomorphic encryption scheme on untrusted cloud service platform. *Knowledge-Based Systems, 180*, 104–115.
24. Rahman, M. S., Khalil, I., Atiquzzaman, M., & Yi, X. (2020). Towards privacy preserving AI based composition framework in edge networks using fully homomorphic encryption. *Engineering Applications of Artificial Intelligence, 94*, 103737.
25. Saberi, S., Kouhizadeh, M., Sarkis, J., & Shen, L. (2019). Blockchain technology and its relationships to sustainable supply chain management. *International Journal of Production Research, 57*(7), 2117–2135.
26. Sun, H., Wang, X., & Wang, X. (2018). Application of blockchain technology in online education. *International Journal of Emerging Technologies in Learning, 13*(10).
27. Tasca, P., & Tessone, C. J. (2017). Taxonomy of blockchain technologies. Principles of identification and classification. arXiv preprint arXiv:1708.04872.
28. Urquhart, A. (2016). The inefficiency of bitcoin. *Economics Letters, 148*, 80–82.
29. Webb, N. (2018). A fork in the blockchain: Income tax and the bitcoin/bitcoin cash hard fork. *North Carolina Journal of Law & Technology, 19*(4), 283.
30. Wu, Y., Cegielski, C. G., Hazen, B. T., & Hall, D. J. (2013). Cloud computing in support of supply chain information system infrastructure: understanding when to go to the cloud. *Journal of Supply Chain Management, 49*(3), 25–41.
31. Zhang, P., Schmidt, D. C., White, J., & Lenz, G. (2018). Blockchain technology use cases in healthcare (Vol. 111, pp. 1–41).

Blockchain Technology Regulation: Time for Standardized Frameworks

Assam Hammi, Anjaneyulu Jinugu, Malike Bouaoud, Ahmed Hefnawy, and Abdelaziz Bouras

1 Introduction

Blockchain is an innovative technology consenting new distributed software architectures, where the data structure is a list of blocks. The operation's principle with regard to this data is to securely record and combine transactions that have happened within the blockchain network in order to transfer the ownership of digital assets [1]. Blockchain technology compromises an encouraging substitute where a centralized management system is not desirable or possible. Blockchain and its distributed ledger technology (DLT) promises unchangeability and truthfulness of data without the necessity of a third party. Thus, blockchain, as disruptive technology, is revolutionizing the existing systems of trust. It also carries self-execution processes; this can be achieved with its smart contract functionality. However, when we start implementing blockchain technology in real projects, and after passing the demonstration phase of feasibility, we face many constraints with regard to the lack of common terminology, legal status of contracts, and individual privacy and data protection. The establishment of international blockchain standards

A. Hammi (✉) · A. Bouras
Qatar University, Doha, Qatar
e-mail: assam.hammi@qu.edu.qa; abdelaziz.bouras@qu.edu.qa

A. Jinugu
Ministry of Transport and Communications (MoTC), Doha, Qatar
e-mail: ajinugu@motc.gov.qa

M. Bouaoud
Qatar Central Bank, Doha, Qatar

A. Hefnawy
Delos Delta, Australia

A. Bouras et al. (eds.), *Blockchain Driven Supply Chains and Enterprise Information Systems*, https://doi.org/10.1007/978-3-030-96154-1_10

might appear necessary. This would influence blockchain future development, as this technological paradigm is still at an infancy-innovative phase.

2 Background

Unlike other existing systems, the specificity and strength of blockchain technology is no longer to require the use of a trusted third party to validate the transfer of ownership but to be able to share, through consensus, the responsibility for this validation on a community (through "mining" machines). Such move from centralized registers technology to distributed ledger technology needs consensus and mature standardization. Such standards start as technical applications which need to be harmonized, converged, and matured into international standards. Blockchain technology is expected to respect alike sequence [2]. Many standards development organizations (SDOs) have initiated efforts in order to normalize blockchain and DLT in terms of interoperability and identify what sectors could benefit most from this nascent technology by delivering a common and clear shared technical foundation for industry [3]. This will accelerate adoption's degree of the blockchain technology among digital economies of services and goods. As per the British Standards Institution (BSI) report prepared by RAND Europe [4], the priority areas proposed about the potential role of standards in supporting the development and adoption of the blockchain and DLT are illustrated as timeline in relation to these areas (see Fig. 1). This timeline includes three terms; the short term where terminology and vocabulary are highlighted, then from the medium term to the long term, where other areas must be focused on such as interoperability, security, privacy, and data governance without forgetting end-user identity and provenance tracking as well as the technical aspects.

As mentioned previously, many SDOs made initiatives to standardize the blockchain technology [3], i.e., ISO, IEEE, NIST, etc. A timeline summarizing those efforts is depicted in Fig. 2.

- The ISO has formed with Standards Australia (SA), a technical committee (ISO/TC 307), to address blockchain and DLT standardization concern.
- The International Securities Association for Institutional Trade Communication (ISITC) has formed with the Organization for the Advancement of Structured Information Standards (OASIS) the blockchain and DLT working group to define a technical standard in terms of safety and security.
- The World Wide Web Consortium (W3C) has initiated a blockchain community group to produce message format standards for blockchain, guidelines for usage of storage, etc.
- The Institute of Electrical and Electronics Engineering (IEEE) has launched a standard program of blockchain among other "the Standard for the Framework of Blockchain Use in IoT4."

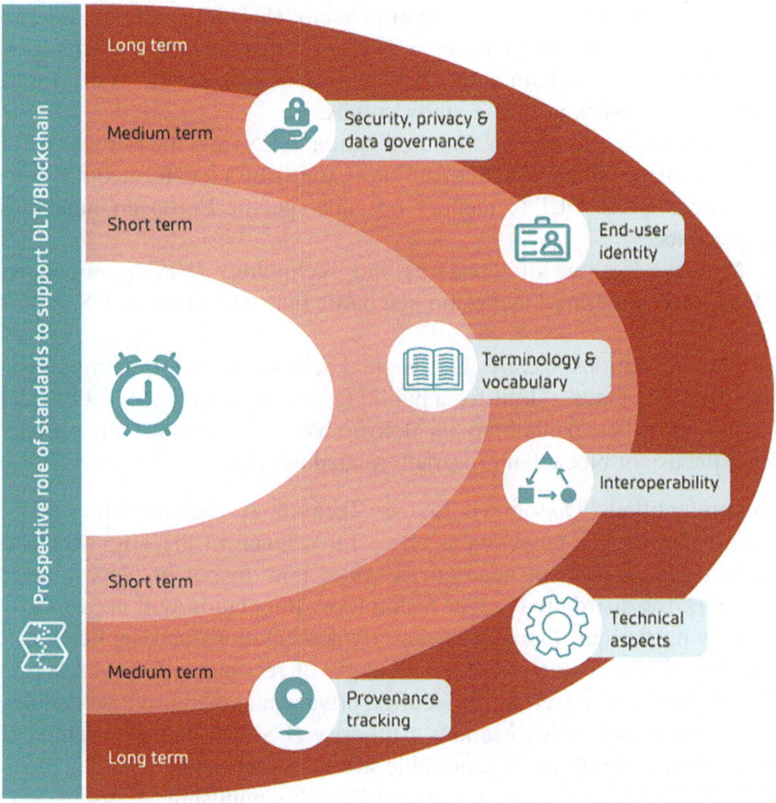

Fig. 1 Areas where standards could potentially play a role in supporting DLT/blockchain. (Source: RAND Europe [4])

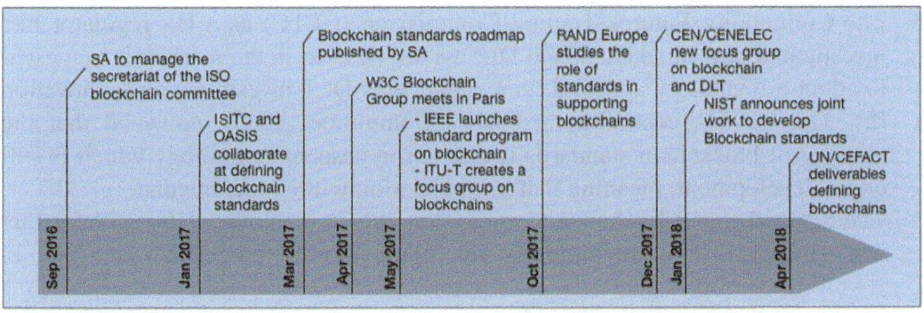

Fig. 2 Various organizations have started devoting efforts to standardize blockchains and DLT (enhanced by the authors)

- The Telecommunication Standardization Sector (ITU-T), under the International Telecommunication Union (United Nations), has formed a focus group on application of blockchain and DLT to propose a way forward for related standardization work in ITU-T study groups.
- The European Committee for Standardization (CEN) and the European Committee for Electrotechnical Standardization (CENELEC) has formed a focus group on blockchain and DLT to identify possible specific European standardization requirements.
- The National Institute of Standards and Technology (NIST) cooperated with ISO in order to define blockchain standards that will improve US government services.
- The United Nations Centre for Trade Facilitation and Electronic Business (UN/CEFACT) made a draft for a public review of white paper on the technical applications of blockchain to its deliverables[1]; the blockchain project team sought the use of blockchain for trade-related use cases.
- A report entitled "Distributed Ledger Technology: beyond blockchain" was disseminated by the government office for science in the UK[2] which clearly stated that "Government needs to consider how to put in place a regulatory framework for distributed ledger technology. Regulation will need to evolve in parallel with the development of new implementations and applications of the technology." The report presented a couple of recommendations related to the global perspective, governance, security, privacy and disruptive potential, etc.
- The European Securities Markets Authority (ESMA) had highlighted from a public policy point of view the possible strengths and weaknesses that blockchain and DLT would have on securities markets. By publishing a discussion paper entitled "The Distributed Ledger Technology Applied to Securities Markets,"[3] ESMA has attempted to have feedback from the industry to be taken into consideration when promulgating policies and regulations; however, ESMA did not explicit any reaction on that time.
- The Commodity Futures Trading Commission (CFTC) as a US regulator had investigated how blockchain and DLT would be used in the market. It suggested to adopt a regulatory approach that encourages DLT investment and innovation [5]. The CFTC Technology Advisory Committee (TAC) renowned that the absence of blockchain standards is due to the nascent technology which is still under development, meaning that its application will be incremental.
- The Securities and Exchange Commission (SEC) is another US regulator that was dynamically investigating possible application of blockchain and DLT in

---

[1] https://uncefact.unece.org/display/uncefactpublicreview/Public+Review%3A+Blockchain+Whitepaper

[2] https://assets.publishing.service.gov.uk/government/uploads/system/uploads/attachment_data/file/492972/gs-16-1-distributed-ledger-technology.pdf

[3] https://www.esma.europa.eu/sites/default/files/library/2016-773_dp_dlt.pdf

the public securities market; one of the SEC commissioners alerted that "as the market holds Blockchain technology, regulators need to be in a position to lead"[4].

- Since 2013, China started promulgating a series of policies, laws, and regulations related to blockchain in order to promote the healthy development of this technology and to reduce investment risks. One of the recent policies issued by the State Internet Information Office is called "Regulations on blockchain information service management" [6].
- For the moment, there are no specific regulations dealing with blockchain and DLT in Australia.[5] Despite that, the Australian Securities and Investments Commission (ASIC) released an information sheet called "INFO 219 Evaluating distributed ledger technology"[6] that highlights the approach to the regulatory issues with regard to blockchain adoption and DLT solution.

3 Blockchain Applications Through Regulation Perspective

3.1 Financial Sector

To properly define the scope of regulation for the use of blockchain in the financial sector, it is important to understand the various use cases with blockchain. Indeed, the multiple use cases are supported by different levels of acceptance or adoption. The first and foremost use case is related to the forms of payments and mainly the use of blockchain for currencies. People around the world have discovered the development of new form of currencies that bear no legal tender. However, they gained a large interest from the public due to their decentralized nature as well as the confidentiality that these currencies are holding against a central regulator with a sense of freedom. The rise in popularity of the cryptocurrencies has pushed national governments to act upon it. Nowadays, central banks, the main financial sector regulator and guarantor of national currencies, are working at issuing central bank-issued digital currencies (CBDCs) that also changes the role of the regulators with regard to currency notes. Indeed, this implies multiple changes in the way the currency is disseminated as well as raise questions on the necessity to develop the wholesale market, i.e., the roles of the private banks may not hold any currency in the future. The other use of blockchain still relates largely to the domain of payment transactions and specifically the transfer of money to end users. The electronic transfer from account to account for decades relies on a heavy infrastructure. The

[4] https://www.sec.gov/news/speech/surfing-wave-technology-innovation-and-competition-remarks-harvard-law-schools-fidelity

[5] https://www.globallegalinsights.com/practice-areas/blockchain-laws-and-regulations/australia

[6] https://asic.gov.au/regulatory-resources/digital-transformation/evaluating-distributed-ledger-technology/

use of blockchain for payment transfer allows for increase speed of operations for near instant transaction which clearly competes with traditional payment methods.

It has to be noted that both use cases can leverage both centralized (CLT) and decentralized ledger-based technologies (DLT) as the transfer of digital assets' ownerships can be validated by both old and new ledger techniques. However, for the latter, and in terms of regulations, there is currently no precise way to trace those transfers[7]unlike the centralized ledger where a manner to securely achieve that goal (transfers of digital assets' ownerships) is applied via trusted third parties under the supervision of a control authority (regulator). Regulations still have to fill the gap with every major development of technology such as blockchain, whether by completing existing legal text related to old technology or by finding a common denominator between the old and new technology of a kind that market integrity and stockholders' security. The traditional approach in regulating the financial sector is often based on the principles of "whitelisting" as an analogy to the term used in cybersecurity. Indeed, the only authorized systems would become eventually those that are defined by a central regulator, bearing a legal tender and excluding de facto any other form of development.

3.2 Logistics Sector

Blockchain-based applications for logistics sector intend whether to alternate the existing practices and current logistics procedures in a digitized form or to fully eliminate them [6]. For example, Wave, which is a blockchain application, eradicates completely what's called bill of lading (the well-known document delivered by shipper to acknowledge receiving cargo for shipment) and directly connects the producer and the purchaser by a blockchain solution where the two parties involved can access to the shipment data with full transparency. Nevertheless, the blockchain application from Chain of Things (CoT) lab which is called Chain of Shipping[8] focuses on how to alleviate fraud and inefficiencies in the shipping and logistics industry by the use of IoT to digitize bill of lading. Modum.io AG company [7] combined blockchain technology and IoT sensors in the pharmaceutical logistics sector. During the process of medical products transportation, smart contract guarantees the record of data and the accessibility of all parties by providing a code representing a contract that is self-executing to ensure temperature category compliance as per EU regulation (GDP 2013/C 343/01) Good Distribution Practice of medicinal products for human use.[9] Once again, no clear regulations are yet in

[7] http://www.revue-banque.fr/banque-investissement-marches-gestion-actifs/article/reglementation-blockchain-defi-neutralite-techn#restricted_content

[8] https://www.chainofthings.com/news/2016/12/10/chain-of-shipping-conference-a-review

[9] https://eur-lex.europa.eu/LexUriServ/LexUriServ.do?uri=OJ:C:2013:343:0001:0014:EN:PDF

force in this area, and the adoption of the blockchain-based applications for logistics sector may confront by barriers in terms of legal rules.

3.3 Healthcare Sector

Blockchain technology offers a holistic potential as well in terms of decentralization, security, immutability, and privacy in the healthcare area by storing and sharing electronic medical records, personal healthcare data, etc. Different blockchain-based applications deal with healthcare information exchange such as BlocHIE [8] which is designed for sharing and storage of data among medical institutions and patients. The platform is composed of blockchain network where the collected healthcare is stored, hospitals and clinics where patients' diagnostic records are shared with other medical institutions through the blockchain network, and IoT devices that share the daily healthcare data of individuals in an automatic manner to the blockchain network. However, there are concerns with regard to protection of privacy laws when it comes to personal data. The fact that immutability is one of the strong data integrity features of blockchain ensures that once the data record is saved, it cannot be changed or erased. This is contradictory with legal obligation such as GDPR regulation in the EU [9] (General Data Protection Regulation) that reinforced the rights of individuals to request personal data to be deleted.

3.4 Architecture, Engineering, and Construction Sector

Several public organizations from various sectors are supporting blockchain initiatives and following approaches that keep them up with the novelty of this technology [10]. Among others, the Architecture, Engineering, and Construction (AEC) sector is investigating on how blockchain technology could present benefit to the field, and how to integrate this technology with the adopted ones such as Building Information Modeling (BIM) and Digital Twins (DT) [11]. Bimchain.io,[10] which is a French start-up, has developed a proof of principle to integrate blockchain within BIM in order to accelerate BIM process and workflow. The aim is to make fast transition from dual process to distributed BIM process by using smart contracts. Thus, PoC (proofs of contributions) are linked to the BIM 3D model with automated payments ensuring that all participants are devoted to reach a certain quality level. There is mutual relationship between BIM and blockchain; data either can be incorporated from blockchain and its DLT to BIM model or can be sent from BIM model to blockchain itself informing about changes and updates that must be considered for use later by smart contract to execute automatic payments, for example [12]. The

[10] https://bimchain.io/technology/

fact that there is only one source of true information related to all aspects of the process gives to the integration of blockchain technology within BIM process an important role step for the whole sector's development. Xiong, Feng et al. designed a blockchain-based Construction Supply Chain (CSC) framework to tackle challenges facing the old approaches, i.e., postponements, waste of data, and transmission costs. By eliminating intermediaries, reduction of limitations would be possible as they also introduced a private key distribution method in blockchain to help recover lost private keys [13]. The Centre for Digital Built Britain (CDBB) made necessary the investment in research linked to blockchain regulations in the AEC sector, and required the transformations of developed business models to provide a good demonstrator for the AEC sector [14].

4 Challenges

Most of the countries in the world are open to freedom of speech, and it is being safeguarded by their constitution. On the other hand, assets are owned by people with the governed laws and regulations, and these laws are developed to keep them closed. Similarly, blockchain or cryptocurrencies should be regulated with right laws and regulations as these are digital assets. So, there is the need of the hour for the regulators to understand the regulations and challenges of blockchain technology.

Deloitte [15] conducted a global survey on blockchain technology in 2020; the top two greater barriers to adopt blockchain technology among the organizations are (1) replacing or adapting existing legal systems and (2) potential security threat. Haitham [16] said that definition of some regulatory terms such as legality of transaction ownership and trade finality needs to be updated or changed in the blockchain technology arena. Moreover, confidentiality of transactions and data privacy are the two major concerns of the regulators while implementing the blockchain technology. Sakho et al. [17] mentioned that recently a lot of people invested in blockchain or cryptocurrencies, and they revealed that this environment is tremendously volatile due to enormous cases of financial thefts, scams, and stock market manipulations. These scenarios are increasing nowadays and the authors concluded that the lack of regulation is a major concern.

The European Union (EU) understood salient potential benefits of blockchain technology and distributed ledger technology (DLT). EU proactively planned to develop laws and regulations to update the potential of these technologies. Unfortunately, a lot of European institutions felt that these technologies should be adopted by more institutions, that more innovation is needed, and that proof of concepts should be developed. Based on all these factors, regulators of EU may have to wait some more time to regulate these emerging technologies [18]. The USA and EU embraced smart regulatory hands-off approach in financial and related sectors for future innovation in blockchains [19]. In addition, blockchain technology is not limited to a particular country's jurisdiction, and thus many legislations should be rewritten or be changed when the blockchain technology takes off fully in collaboration with other nations [20]. Blockchain technology-related services should be regulated by multiple government agencies, and it is very sensitive and difficult to draft laws for the blockchain technology [21]. So, regulators should not undervalue these challenges while developing regulations of blockchain technology.

Cermeño [22] stated that in principle technology cannot be regulated, but its events can be regulated including the blockchain technologies, and he has discovered 11 blockchain regulatory challenges in the financial sectors:

- Reduction of anonymity of transaction through Anti Money Laundering (AML) directives Know Your Customer (KYC)
- Legal nature of blockchains including territoriality and liability
- Recognition of blockchains as immutable, tamper-proof sources of truth
- Conciliation of "right to be forgotten" and blockchain's immutability
- Legal validity of documents stored in blockchain as a proof of possession or existence
- Legal validity of financial instruments issued on the blockchains
- Real-world enforceability, territoriality, and liability of smart contracts
- Treatment of shared information in blockchains from the perspective of cross-border flow of data and data protection
- Use of the blockchain as a valid ruling register for the IoT
- Regulatory reporting information standards definition on the blockchain
- Definition of a regulatory sandboxes approach to test blockchains

In the contemporary digital world, financial system across the globe is governed by combination of technical and legal codes. Therefore, to introduce the blockchain technology into the financial system, regulators have certain questions to be answered [23]:

- Do regulators make rules?
- Are the rules fixed or changeable?
- In case of fraud, can regulators access the data to investigate it?
- Blockchain technology is garbage-in and garbage-out, who will maintain quality of data?

Garcia-Teruel [24] highlighted that in real estate sector, the following legal challenges need to be addressed for an efficient implementation of blockchain technology:

- Verification of identity of the parties: most of the blockchains does not require any personally identifiable information (PII) to create new wallet, and thus if any financial transaction is complete without proper identification, that transaction is illegal.
- Control of legality and effectiveness of the contract: in a mortgage loan, obligation of detecting and informing parties with regard to possible unfair terms before it got approved. Blockchain technology is a distributed system that does not need any legal checks before approving the loan.

Table 1 DLT features and regulatory challenges [26]

Feature	Samples of regulatory challenges
Distribution, shared ledger	Applicable law with respect to nodes set up in different states Legal subjects in multiple jurisdictions Distributed storage solutions to meet the requirements of production environments Interoperability requirements New civil or commercial law forms, organizations, and contracting Protection of secrecy in open environments
Autonomy and responsibility	Legal smart contract definition and enforceability (valid source code execution) Boundaries of anonymity Applicable law Liability of smart contract managers (SC layer governance) Intellectual property of code
Tamper evidence and resistance	Regulation that needs the correction or removal of data in the ledger: Data protection laws/right to be forgotten Content that infringes on third parties' rights (e.g., copyright, trademark, etc.) Illegal content
Incentive mechanism and digital assets	Coin, token, tokenization legal common (UNCITRAL) definition ICO definition and minimal requirements for investor protection Crypto asset/token financial system: legal concept and boundaries Supervisory policies and procedures by applicable rules
Openness and transparency/anonymity	AML issues, secrecy leaks, personal security Anonymization (no name/encrypted users vs KYC) and pseudonymization

- Co-ownership and other rights in rem: in EU governments should agree for particular properties to change ownership, and it is not possible in smart contract.
- Amendment of the ledger: human errors may happen during registration of any property, and this type of cases cannot be handled in blockchain technology.

One of the approaches to overcome the challenges and regulate the blockchain technology is to develop blockchain standards in alignment with the prevailing regulatory standards for cybersecurity, risk management, cloud computing, and financial services [25].

ITU-T focus group on application of blockchain and DLT has analyzed selected features of DLT and their regulatory challenges. More details about the DLT features and regulatory challenges are mentioned in Table 1.

ITU proposed recommendations for each challenge for the users as well as the regulators, and these are not discussed in detail in this manuscript. The selected DLT properties are:

- Distribution and ledger sharing
- Autonomy and responsibility
- Tamper evidence and resistance
- Incentive mechanism and digital assets

- Openness, transparency, and anonymity

The regulatory challenges for the DLT attribute distribution and ledger sharing are:

- Suitability of laws to nodes developed in different states
- Responsible subjects in various jurisdictions
- Production servers' storage locations
- Heterogeneity of operating systems, programming languages, and nodes' management at various locations
- Digital civil or commercial law agreements like multilateral association agreements
- Various countries' data protection rules
- Data collection, management of data, and analysis of data outside the country boundaries

The regulatory challenges for the DLT attribute autonomy and responsibility are:

- Legalization and enforcement of smart contract
- Automatic decision-making (ADM) as it is very complex and less transparent
- Limitations of legal liability for actors who play the key role in information system operation

The regulatory challenges for the DLT attribute tamper evidence and resistance are:

- Managing technological changes
- Correction or removal of personal and nonpersonal data in the ledger

The regulatory challenges for the DLT attribute incentive mechanism and digital asset are:

- Legal definition of the terms coin, token, and tokenization
- Definition for initial coin offerings (ICO) and set minimal requirements to protect investors
- Boundaries for the crypto asset/token financial system
- Supervisory policies and procedures by applicable rules

The regulatory challenges for the DLT attribute openness, transparency, and anonymity are [26]:

- Auditing issues due to high levels of privacy
- Competition challenge due to complete transparency

Across the globe, some countries are already working on overcoming the abovementioned challenges of blockchain technology in collaboration with industry leaders, academicians, legislators, regulators, and governments. Similarly, as there are no stipulated standards and policies in Qatar on the blockchain technology,

Qatari regulators should develop policies and standards to be one of the top leaders in the arena of emerging technologies.

5 Discussion

Blockchain and its DLT present a lot of advantages and benefits such as safety, traceability, and cost-effectiveness, which are considered as key elements in the supply chains sector, where many players are committed from the early production's stage to the market handover. Those players are mainly producers, suppliers, consumers, and policy makers who are brought together via blockchain technology such as DLT and smart contracts to improve the overall effectiveness of their sector [27]. However, the role of regulators remains far away due perhaps to their affiliation to different organizations that are using different programs and applications [28]. Kamilaris et al. stated in their study [29] that any kind of digital assets (cryptocurrencies) cannot be trusted in food supply chains without a form of policies that make it a complete solution; hence, the absence of common regulation on how blockchain technology should be used is still persisting.

According to MarketsandMarkets, the global blockchain market size is projected to grow from USD 258 million in 2020 to USD 2409 million by 2026, at a compound annual growth rate (CAGR) of 45.1% during the forecast period [30]. In the same vein, the blockchain market size in Qatar was projected at USD 0.8 million in 2018 and is estimated to grow by 120% annually and will reach USD 19.4 million in 2022.[11] To capture Qatar's blockchain market, several public and private organizations have started several projects to work on blockchain technologies. Some of the initiatives in Qatar are made through Qatar National Research Fund agency (a member of Qatar Foundation) in different sectors such as finance and FinTech, logistics and supply chains, energy, and smart grids. Such developments are made in collaboration with several higher education institutions such as Qatar University and Hamad Bin Khalifa University. The latest QNRF ROS[12] seminar highlighted some of these initiatives. Some of them are made in partnership with local stakeholders, such as ministries and local industries. For instance, Qatar University and the Royal Melbourne Institute of Technology (RMIT) of Melbourne are currently implementing the SupplyLedger on efficient blockchain-based supply chain systems, involving MOTC and Qatar Railways Company as stakeholders. MOTC as government authority responsible for land transport, maritime transport, information technology, digital society development, and cybersecurity is looking to the outcome of the project toward issuance of new policies and regulations related to the adoption of blockchain technology for the supply chain in Qatar. Qatar Rail which is the responsible authority for the country's new rail network, including

[11] https://tdv.motc.gov.qa/Investment-Catalogue/Blockchain

[12] https://www.qnrf.org/en-us/Newsroom/Press-Releases/fintech21-research-outcome-seminar

Doha Metro and Lusail smart city Tram, is collaborating as technical partner for the proof of concept related to the logistics sector. Hamad Bin Khalifa University team has developed a smart contract-based energy trading platform, using a specialized Ethereum blockchain network. This platform supports energy providers to directly trade their energy surplus with electric vehicle owners in a peer-to-peer manner. A last example is related to MEEZA, a local IT services and solutions provider, which partnered with the CWallet to power the blockchain-based digital wallet platform services. This platform ensures that personal data of MEEZA users is protected at all costs with highest standards.[13]

6 Conclusion

The increasing evolution's pace of the emerging technologies, such as blockchain and its DLT, rises a critical need to revise and/or enforce many of today's regulations, especially those related to new network-based technologies. Indeed, the existing rules' obsoleteness does not frame these emerging technologies. Decision-makers and governments across the globe should consider making ready an adequate regulatory environment in order to facilitate the adoption/implementation of such technologies. This should incorporate a set of standardized frameworks and best practices to take up the full benefit of these new technologies. We have described in this paper the existing regulation landscape related to blockchain and its DLT highlighting some challenges and ways to overcome them.

Acknowledgments This publication was made possible by NPRP grant NPRP11S-1227-170135 from the Qatar National Research Fund (a member of Qatar Foundation). The statements made herein are solely the responsibility of the authors.

References

1. Marsal-Llacuna, M.-L., & Oliver-Riera, M. The standards revolution: Who will first put this new kid on the blockchain? In *2017 ITU kaleidoscope: Challenges for a data-driven society (ITU K)* (Vol. 2017). IEEE.
2. Hyland-Wood, D., & Khatchadourian, S. (2018). A future history of international blockchain standards. *The Journal of the British Blockchain Association, 1*(1), 3724.
3. Gramoli, V., & Staples, M. (2018). Blockchain standard: Can we reach consensus? *IEEE Communications Standards Magazine, 2*(3), 16–21.
4. Deshpande, A., et al. (2017). Distributed Ledger Technologies/Blockchain: Challenges, opportunities and the prospects for standards. In *Overview report* (p. 40). The British Standards Institution (BSI).

[13] https://www.meeza.net/?s=CWallet&lang=en

5. Kakavand, Hossein, Nicolette Kost De Sevres, and Bart Chilton. "The blockchain revolution: an analysis of regulation and technology related to distributed ledger technologies." Available at SSRN 2849251 (2017).
6. Wang, Q., Min, S., & Li, R. (2020). Is China the world's blockchain leader? Evidence, evolution and outlook of China's blockchain research. *Journal of Cleaner Production*, 121742. Weernink, Marissa Oude, et al. "The blockchain potential for port logistics." (2017).
7. Bocek, T., et al. (2017). Blockchains everywhere-a use-case of blockchains in the pharma supply-chain. In *2017 IFIP/IEEE symposium on integrated network and service management (IM)*. IEEE.
8. Jiang, S., et al. (2018). Blochie: a blockchain-based platform for healthcare information exchange. In *2018 IEEE international conference on smart computing (smartcomp)*. IEEE.
9. Esposito, C., et al. (2018). Blockchain: A panacea for healthcare cloud-based data security and privacy? *IEEE Cloud Computing, 5*(1), 31–37.
10. Carson, B., et al. (2018). *Blockchain beyond the hype: What is the strategic business value* (pp. 1–13). McKinsey & Company.
11. Mason, J. (2017). Intelligent contracts and the construction industry. *Journal of Legal Affairs and Dispute Resolution in Engineering and Construction, 9*(3), 04517012.
12. Giuda, D., Martino, G., et al. (2020). The construction contract execution through the integration of blockchain technology. In *Digital transformation of the design, construction and management processes of the built environment* (pp. 27–36). Springer.
13. Xiong, F., et al. (2019). A key protection scheme based on secret sharing for blockchain-based construction supply chain system. *IEEE Access, 7*, 126773–126786.
14. Lamb, K. "Blockchain and smart contracts: What the AEC sector needs to know, 2018."
15. Deloitte. (2020). *Deloitte's 2020 global blockchain survey from promise to reality*. Deloitte Insights.
16. Al Salmi, H. (2020). Blockchain in post-trade: Blocked by regulations and legal challenges. *Journal of Securities Operations & Custody, 12*(1), 21–28.
17. Sakho, S., Jianbiao, Z., Essaf, F., & Mbyamm Kiki, M. J. (2019). Blockchain: Perspectives and issues. *Journal of Intelligent & Fuzzy Systems, 37*(6), 8029–8052.
18. Jurgita, M. (2018). Blockchain and virtual currency regulation in the EU. *Journal of Investment Compliance, 19*(3), 33–38.
19. Yeoh, P. (2017). Regulatory issues in blockchain technology. *Journal of Financial Regulation and Compliance, 25*(2), 196–208.
20. Harwood-Jones, M. (2016). *Blockchain and T2S: A potential disruptor*. Standard Chartered Bank.
21. De Filippi, P., & Hassan, S. (2018). *Blockchain technology as a regulatory technology: From code is law to law is code*. University of Illinois at Chicago Library.
22. Cermeño, J. S. (2016). Blockchain in financial services: Regulatory landscape and future challenges for its commercial application. *BBVA Research Paper, 16*(20), 1–33.
23. Ozili, P. K. (2019). Blockchain finance: Questions regulators ask. In *Disruptive innovation in business and finance in the digital world* (pp. 123–129). Emerald Publishing Limited.
24. Garcia-Teruel, R. M. (2020). Legal challenges and opportunities of blockchain technology in the real estate sector. *Journal of Property, Planning and Environmental Law., 12*(2), 129–145.
25. Meguerditchian, V. (2017). *Roadmap for blockchain standards report*. Standards Australia.
26. ITU-T Focus Group on Application of Distributed Ledger Technology (FG DLT). (2019). *Technical Report FG DLT D4.1 Distributed ledger technology regulatory framework*.
27. Li, Zhi, et al. (2018). Toward open manufacturing. *Industrial Management & Data Systems*.
28. Lee, Hau L., et al. (2017). *Technology in agribusiness: Opportunities to drive value*. White paper.
29. Kamilaris, A., Fonts, A., & Prenafeta-Boldΰ, F. X. (2019). The rise of blockchain technology in agriculture and food supply chains. *Trends in Food Science & Technology, 91*, 640–652.
30. MarketsandMarkets. (2020). *Blockchain IoT Market by Component (Hardware (IoT Sensors & Crypto-Wallets), Software and Platform, and Services), Application (Smart Contract, Security, and Asset Tracking and Management), Organization Size, Vertical, and Region – Global Forecast to 2026*. MarketsandMarkets.

TMSLedger: A Transactions Management System Through Integrated Odoo Hyperledger Smart Contracts

Abdelhak Belhi, Houssem Gasmi, Assam Hammi, Abdelaziz Bouras, Belaid Aouni, and Ibrahim Khalil

1 Introduction

In the design and manufacturing of products, many actors in a supply chain scenario interact with each other to manufacture a product. These communication channels are intended to be used for the exchange of goods and services between these actors. However, the complexity often increases exponentially with new actors, and effectively managing the good communication between these actors and securing their transactions becomes quite a complicated task. Issues related to traceability, transparency, sustainability, reliability, and efficiency often arise in highly collaborative scenarios involving many stakeholders.

Proven in the financial sector and logistics industries, blockchain technology is a collaborative platform that guarantees the security of transactions by design with advanced consensus and cryptography mechanisms. It has the particularity of allowing trust between collaborators without being dependent on a third party or a regulatory authority. There are many types of blockchains as one can find fully public blockchains, widely used with cryptocurrencies, and licensed blockchains (private or consortium) which are used in commercial and industrial applications.

A. Belhi (✉)
Joaan Bin Jassim Academy for Defense Studies, Doha, Qatar

H. Gasmi · A. Hammi · A. Bouras
Computer Science and Engineering, College of Engineering, Qatar University, Doha, Qatar
e-mail: houssem.gasmi@qu.edu.qa; assam.hammi@qu.edu.qa; abdelaziz.bouras@qu.edu.qa

B. Aouni
College of Business and Economics, Qatar University, Doha, Qatar
e-mail: belaid.aouni@qu.edu.qa

I. Khalil
School of Computing Technologies, RMIT University, Melbourne, VIC, Australia
e-mail: ibrahim.khalil@rmit.edu.au

A. Bouras et al. (eds.), *Blockchain Driven Supply Chains and Enterprise Information Systems*, https://doi.org/10.1007/978-3-030-96154-1_11

What is unique about these supply chains is that they often include many participants who interact with each other to make a product. Problems such as intellectual property, deadlines, product quality, etc. are directly linked to the effectiveness of cooperation with these actors. In traditional systems, it is often extremely difficult to track and identify communication problems. However, blockchain has proven to be an architecture that solves such challenges through design.

Blockchain technology has many advantages, but unfortunately does not have the ability to easily adapt to existing collaborative platforms, especially in the industrial sector despite the fact that it is considered disruptive and has a lot of potential [1–3].

Blockchain is now being integrated into many applications in domains related to manufacturing, supply chains, etc. However, due to the complexity and nature of the established platforms, blockchain integration is far from being a straightforward task due to the difference in architecture and the way transactions are executed.

Through this chapter, we study the integration of blockchain with industrial information systems focusing on a simple manufacturing supply chain case study. We propose a proof of concept of blockchain integration through a popular open-source blockchain platform and an enterprise information system. For this task, we selected the Odoo framework which is an open-source platform for developing a wide variety of enterprise information systems. The processing of transactions and their critical data storage will then be offloaded from the Odoo framework to be handled by blockchain smart contracts as well. For this task, we selected the Hyperledger Fabric blockchain development platform. Hyperledger Fabric allows the creation of blockchain smart contracts. The two platforms (Odoo and Hyperledger) were selected as they are open-source, which facilitates the development of our integration approach. As per the architecture, we mostly focus on a broker-based integration consisting of a software component that is integrated with Odoo and communicates with the blockchain network to manage Odoo workflow processes using customized smart contracts. We present our proof of concept which is based on an exemplar small-scale manufacturing supply chain and demonstrate how can blockchain be integrated into this scenario (see Fig. 1).

The remainder of this chapter is organized as follows. In Sect. 2, we present a state-of-the-art overview of related works on blockchain integration in the context of industrial applications. In Sect. 3, we present our integration method for integrating blockchain through Hyperledger smart contracts with the open-source supply chain/PLM platform Odoo. The choice of this platform was mainly due to its openness and the availability of its documentation. However, such integration should also be possible with platforms allowing API integration. In Sect. 4, we present the implementation of our approach. Finally, we draw our conclusion in Sect. 4 and highlight a set of future challenges.

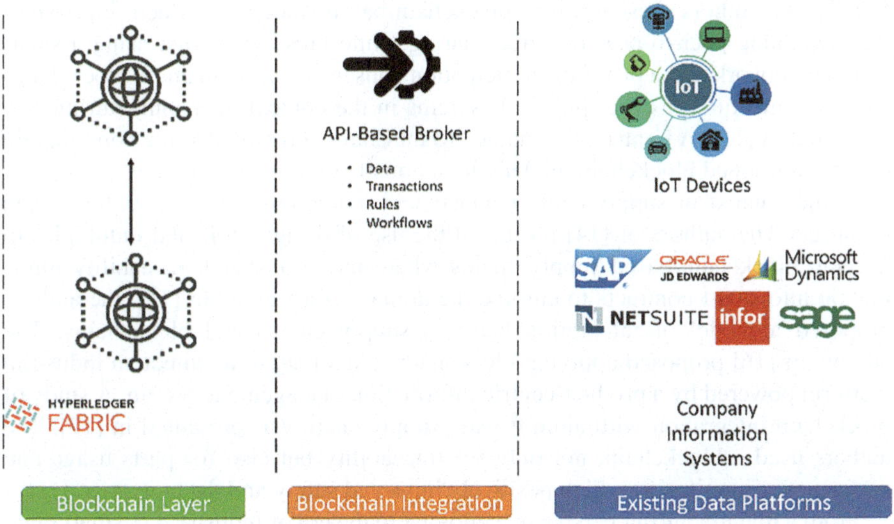

Fig. 1 Integration of industrial information systems highlight

2 Related Work

Since its financial success, blockchain is deemed a disruptive technology in several sectors due to its concept of securing transactions by design. In modern industrial applications, IoT device management is one of its great uses as it ensures the security of sensor and device data from end to end [4, 5]. Blockchain is now considered as an enabling technology for the effective implementation of decentralized applications and was found to enforce the United Nation's sustainable development goals in modern companies [6]. It had been the subject of many contributions related to smart manufacturing and Industry 4.0.

Numerous contributions investigated blockchain integration with different facets of supply chain management. A review of recent applications involving blockchain in the context of supply chain management was presented in [7]. In [8], the authors perform an empirical study involving blockchain integration on operation management and manufacturing and present a detailed analysis of potential drawbacks and obstacles that prevent its effective integration. The authors of [5] study the integration of blockchain, the Internet of Things (IoT), and machine learning for enhancing quality control in smart manufacturing. The authors of [9] study the impact of blockchain integration with supply chains in the context of additive manufacturing. In [10], the authors present a novel blockchain-based application to maintain productivity in the context of automotive spare parts manufacturing. From a more practical point of view, the authors of [11] present a novel blockchain-based service composition model called Block-SC in the context of cloud manufacturing (CM) aiming at providing an efficient collaboration platform of service composition.

In [12], the authors present a new blockchain-based shared manufacturing framework enabling peer-to-peer resource sharing while preserving trust using a smart contract network and a proof-of-participation consensus mechanism. A blockchain-based architecture of cyber-physical systems in the context of manufacturing was presented in [13]. A contribution name "ManuChain" investigated the combination of a permissioned blockchain model with a holistic optimization model.

In the context of supply chain management, numerous applications have been proposed. The authors of [14] presented the use of design tools and ontologies to develop blockchain-based supply chains where they translated traceability information into smart contracts to enforce the domain constraints. In [15], the authors proposed a model of integration between supply chains and blockchains. The authors of [16] proposed applying blockchain technology to architect an industrial platform powered by a product-centric information management system. A study of blockchain integration with aircraft parts supply chain was presented in [17]. The authors used a blockchain, not only for traceability but also for parts usage and performance monitoring which positively impacted safety and data integrity.

From a manufacturing perspective, moving to the era of Industry 4.0, smart manufacturing is becoming a reality through emerging technologies such as blockchains, Internet of Things (IoT), cloud manufacturing (CM), and artificial intelligence (AI). Manufacturing giants such as BMW and Ford are adopting blockchain technology to improve the efficiency of their supply chains and attain business innovation. Leading technology companies and innovative start-ups collaborated to create the Trusted IoT Alliance which aims to develop the necessary standards to integrate blockchains and IoT. The main goal of the standard is to develop smart contract interfaces that enable the exchange of data between blockchain-enabled systems. The alliance efforts are focused on using blockchains for the trusted identification of hardware and documentation immutability.

To encourage the adoption of blockchains by the industry, the cloud-based blockchain as a service (BaaS) was proposed by various vendors. Businesses can use this cloud-based solution to develop, host, and use their blockchain applications which include their smart contracts through a blockchain infrastructure that is developed by a vendor. It provides tools that simplify the management and deployment at scale. Similar to the increasing trend of software as a service (SaaS) where access to the software is granted on a subscription-basis, BaaS enables businesses to tap into a blockchain network using its configuration without having to invest in developing their blockchain infrastructure and without requiring in-house expertise in the subject especially for resource-constrained enterprises [18].

The Mobility Open Blockchain Initiative (MOBI) is an initiative formed by giant automotive companies such as General Motors (GM), Ford, and BMW to help in making automobiles safer, more affordable, and accessible using blockchain technology. To give new cars a digital entity, MOBI specified the first blockchain-based car identity standard. This enables the tracking of significant events during the lifetime of the car. The blockchain digital identity can also be used to exchange information between cars such as location, speed, travel direction, driver behavior, and even driver intention predictions [19].

Blockchains are very resilient platforms that have multiple advantages in collaborative applications. Unfortunately, a lot of work has to be undertaken in order to achieve a smooth and seamless integration. There seems also a lot of interest to integrate this technology in manufacturing and supply chains as it enables a whole wider spectrum of applications and opens the way for peer-to-peer trust.

3 Broker-Based Manufacturing Workflow Management Through Smart Contracts

In this section, we present our proposed architecture as well as a proof-of-concept integration between an established small-scale manufacturing supply chain and a permissioned blockchain. As it is known, most industrial information systems are based on a client/server architecture where information and processing are centralized. This has some advantages but presents various risks related to security, availability, and trust. Indeed, systems such as ERP, PLM, WMS, and TMS are some of the highly collaborative industrial applications, and yet their information is somehow centralized [20, 21]. Blockchain, since its revolution in the financial sector, was considered a disruptive technology as it renews or redefines the concept of trust between peers and introduces new mechanisms for establishing peer-to-peer transactions while ensuring security among other benefits through concepts such as consensus, etc. Our solution shifts the management of business workflows from a centralized ERP platform (Odoo) to a distributed blockchain platform (Hyperledger). This means that the tracking of a transaction is more robust and also all transactions are final (see Fig. 2). In the following, we present details of our solution by presenting its design principle, architecture, studied proof of concept, as well as some tests and evaluations.

3.1 Case Study Scenario

The scenario of the case study (highlighted in Fig. 3) consists of the following actors:

- *Customer:* a food factory that needs a new machine to improve its efficiency and increase its production
- *Designer:* a design firm specialized in industrial machines design
- *Manufacturer:* bespoke machine manufacturing company
- *Supplier:* raw materials supplier
- *Transporter:* goods transportation company

The supply chain starts with a customer which wants to get a design for a machine. He formulates his requirements in a document and sends it to a designer

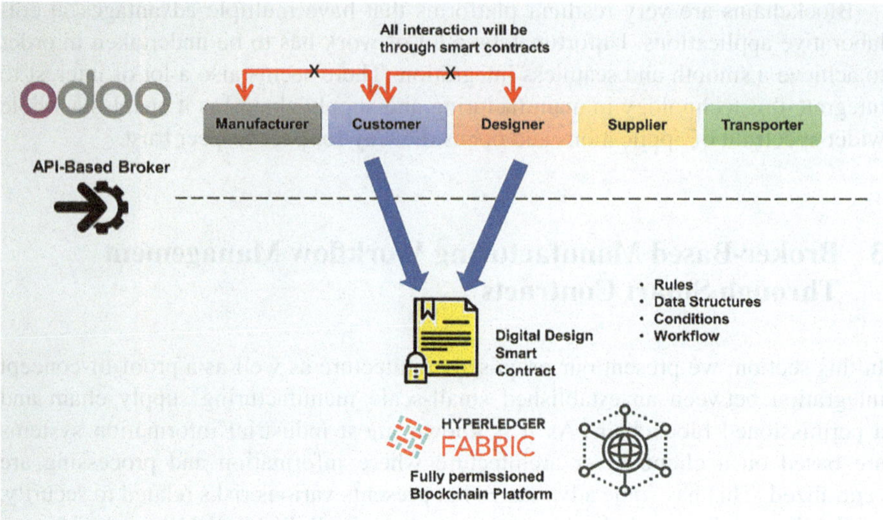

Fig. 2 Integration higher-level architecture

for quotations. The designer then evaluates the financial standing of the customer and upon satisfying a certain rating, prepares the design and sends it to the customer. If the customer accepts a design, the typical transactions between him and the designer take place (quotation, invoice, etc.). Once the design is finished, it is delivered to the customer who will, in turn, send it to a manufacturer with the same interaction patterns. The presentation of the case study focused mainly on the interaction between the customer and the designer where the following aspects are highlighted:

- The smart contracts representing the different actors in the blockchain such as the customer, designer, and manufacturer
- The smart contracts representing the transactions between actors such as the one representing the relation between the customer and designer
- The representation of the domain entities such as design and quotation
- Asset transfer in the blockchain, for instance, transferring the ownership of the design from the designer to the customer and vice versa.
- Create and transfer fungible tokens using an account-based model for payment aspects
- Establishing private channels between groups of actors in the blockchain

The system has been implemented using the Hyperledger Fabric platform as it is the most suitable platform allowing a permissioned access to the blockchain besides other features that will be highlighted in the next sections.

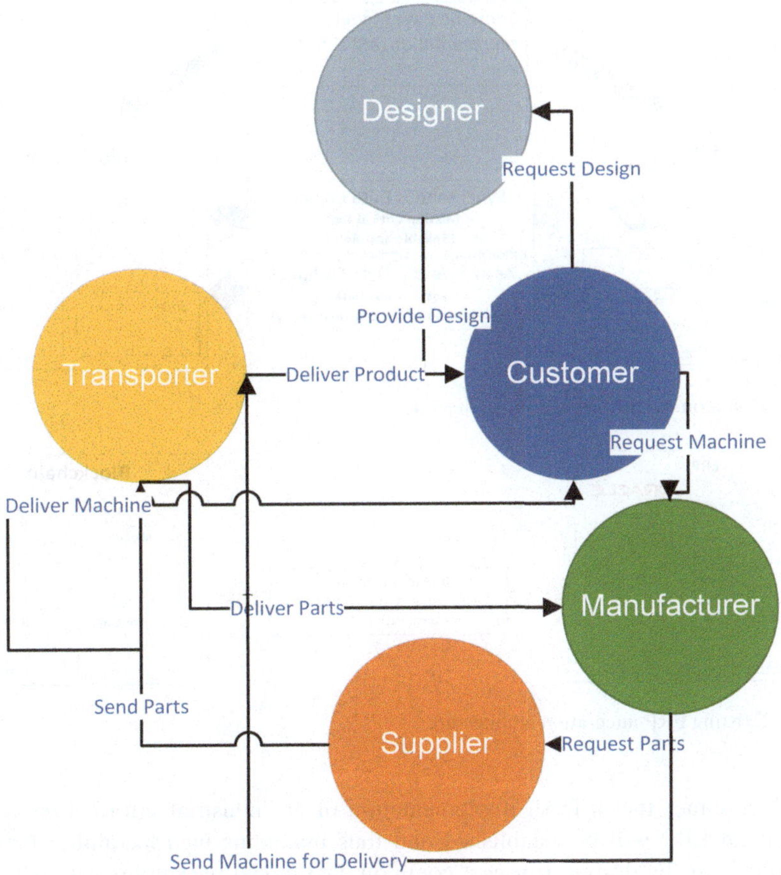

Fig. 3 Proof-of-concept supply chain

3.2 *Architecture and Design*

When analyzing blockchain frameworks such as Ethereum and Hyperledger, it turned out that these frameworks, in addition to providing core blockchain transaction concepts and data storage, provide a rich and well-established programming interface allowing to run the decentralized transactions through smart contracts performing changes to blockchain data.

Our goal through this chapter is to manage the supply chain workflows as well as the transaction in the Odoo ERP/PLM framework using Hyperledger Fabric smart contracts. However, to ensure the soundness of the system and to guarantee the integrity of data when combining both platforms, there needs to be a one-to-one mapping between the data and the business logic in both platforms. This can be achieved using one of our proposed integration strategies. The first strategy (see

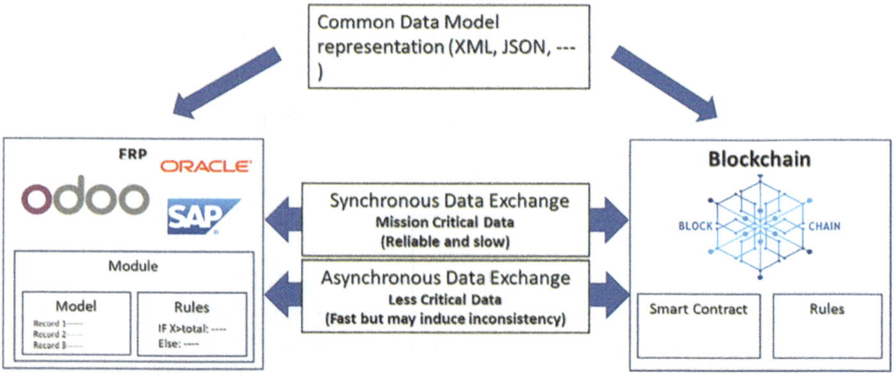

Fig. 4 Common model integration architecture

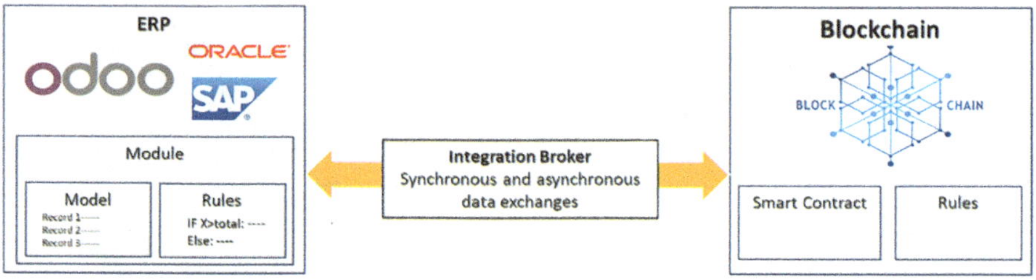

Fig. 5 Existing ERP integration architecture

Fig. 4) assumes that a fresh implementation of an industrial information system such as an ERP will be established and thus maintains interoperability between both platforms by design. It uses a common data model regrouping rules and data structures written in a markup language such as XML or JSON. A translation module is implemented in each platform, and a library written in Python is used in our example with the Odoo ERP platform, and another one written in JavaScript for Hyperledger.

The second strategy (see Fig. 5) assumes that both platforms are independent from each other, and a software component called an "Integration Broker" acts as a messaging platform between both systems. This broker can be compared to an API but it implements advanced functionality and does not perform actions by itself. Instead, it connects to the blockchain via the Hyperledger JavaScript SDK and provides a RESTful API which is used by Odoo to interact with the Hyperledger smart contracts.

In our proof of concept, we only included our second integration strategy based on the Integration Broker. The first strategy is currently under development and will be subject to our future work.

As per the workflow management, we concluded that managing workflows in both platforms can be risky and might induce errors due to communication issues and trust challenges. In our integration, all critical workflow management

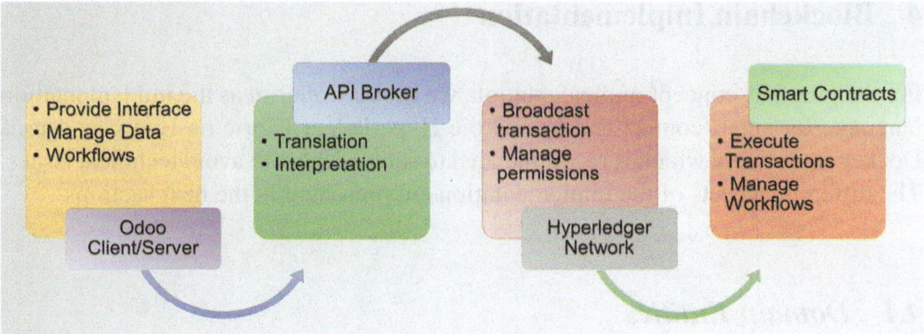

Fig. 6 Integration data flow

happens through the blockchain using smart contracts. For each workflow, a smart contract involving the collaborating actors and making all necessary data controls is established and instantiated following the steps highlighted below:

1. Assuming that transaction or workflow processes have been already established and coded in a smart contract template (JavaScript used in our experiments with Hyperledger), the smart contract is instantiated between the collaborating actors.
2. Following instantiation, the information is naturally broadcasted to all blockchain nodes (by design). All participating nodes have the same blockchain data (data + smart contracts). A strong consensus mechanism manages the consensus of the data. No further modifications are possible to the structure of the contract other than the ones defined before the instantiation.
3. The workflow process is managed using the methods and procedures defined in the smart contract template. These methods, when triggered, are executed in all nodes, and the consensus is preserved by design.
4. When the workflow is completed, the contract will be still instantiated in the blockchain. No further action can be performed including the deletion of the contract or the data, as all blockchain transactions and data are final.

The following figure (Fig. 6) summarizes the data flow between the integration framework components.

Following the definition of the design principle and the establishment of a small supply chain to develop our proof of concept, we established the integration using the broker-based solution as it is more suitable for existing ERP installations and is more straightforward in terms of implementation. Although we already started working on the common meta-model solution, it turned out to be much harder than the broker-based one in terms of implementation and will be subject to our future contributions.

4 Blockchain Implementation

For the proof-of-concept implementation, we used JavaScript as the implementation language for smart contact and hosted the Hyperledger Fabric on Linux as it uses Docker extensively which is recommended to run on Linux to avoid technical issues. The different aspects of the implementation are presented in the next sections.

4.1 Domain Entities

The use case consists of the domain concepts such as design, design request, quotation, invoice, receipt, etc. So how are these concepts created in the blockchain? All concepts in the blockchain are inherited from a class called *State* predefined in Hyperledger Fabric (Fig. 7). It has a unique key and a life cycle current state of the concept where the key and current state are determined by the specific subclass. The class has also helper functionality to convert to and from the JSON format. An example domain concept in the system is the *IndustrialDesign* concept. To define it, we inherit from the *State* class and add the entity-specific properties. The *currentState* and *currentFeeState* are defined as enumerated values. The *createInstance* method is used to generate instances of the entity.

Domain entities are typically initiated in smart contracts either to create a new instance such as a new Invoice or retrieved as an existing instance from the database for further processing. The definition of entities can be nested, for instance, the *Invoice* is composed of a list of *LineItems* which is also defined in the same manner by extending the *State* class.

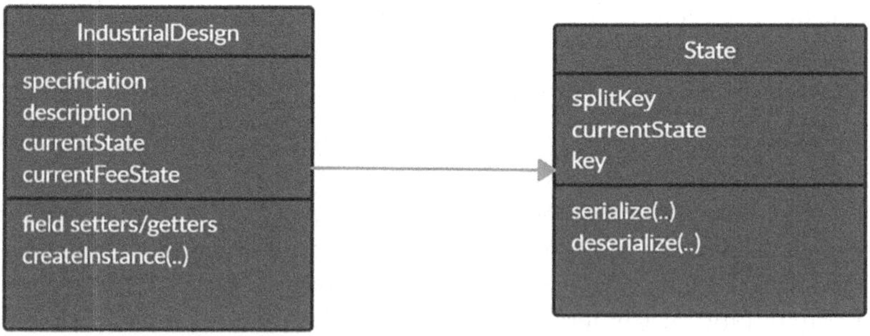

Fig. 7 Concept representation in Fabric

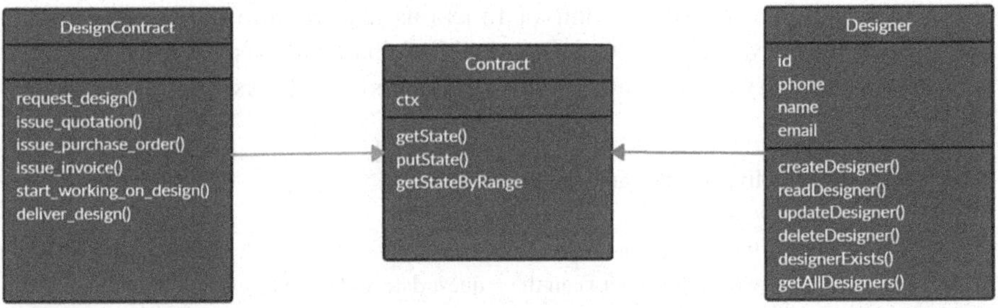

Fig. 8 Smart contracts in Fabric

4.2 *Smart Contracts*

Smart contracts in the blockchain are used in our case study to represent two concepts: the actors in the system such as the customer and the relation between actors such as the relation between the customer and the designer. All smart contracts inherit from the *Contract* class as shown in (Fig. 8). The smart contracts for the actors in the system contain mainly the Create, Read, Update, Delete (CRUD) operations.

All the *Designer* methods take as a first argument a *ctx* variable that represents the blockchain context. This variable is used to manipulate the entity in the blockchain, for instance, to store a *Designer* in the blockchain, we invoke the *ctx.putState()* method. The relation between actors of the system is governed by smart contracts which are defined in Fabric as a regular class where the methods of the class represent the contract clauses that should be honored (Fig. 8). For instance, the relation between the *Customer* and the *Design* is defined in the *DesignContract* class as follows:

Smart contract 1: Request an IndustrialDesign from a designer

Input:*ctx, requester, designer, design_code, spec, description, requestDate*
Retrieve the customer(*requester*)
Create design request(*requester, designer, design_code, spec, de-scription, requestDate*)
If*customer_credit_rating > 3***then**
    Set design state(*ACCEPTED*)
end
else
    Set design state(*REJECTED*)
end
Store the design(*contract_id, design*)

As with entities, the smart contract functions also require the passing of the blockchain context variable *ctx* to access the blockchain database. Another example is the *design delivery* smart contract which is defined as follows:

Smart contract 2: Deliver the design to the customer

Input:*ctx, contract_id*
design ← retrieve the design contract(*contract_id*)
job_days ← get the difference between the request date and today(*contract_id*)
fees_reduction = Update fees based on delay(*contract_id, job_days*);
design.fees = *fees* + *fees_reduction*
store_the_design(*contract_id, design*)

This design delivery smart contract calculates the delay in the delivery of the design and based on that update the agreed-upon fees. If there is no delay, the *Designer* will be paid full fees; otherwise, his fee will be deducted according to the length of the delay.

4.3 Asset Transfer

Transferring assets between supply chain members in the blockchain is just a matter of changing an attribute in an entity to represent the owner. The *pay design fees* smart contract changes the owner of the design from the designer to the customer after settling the payment as follows:

Smart contract 3: Pay design fees

Input:*ctx, contract_id, customer_id*
financial transaction logic [Details in Smart Contract 4]
design ← retrieve the design contract(*contract_id*)
design.owner = *customer_id*
store_the_design(*contract_id, design*)

4.4 Financial Transactions

The financial transactions between supply chain members are implemented using the ERC-20 account-based model [22]. A smart contract can either create or transfer fungible tokens using an account-based model. In this model, there is an account for each participant that holds a balance of tokens. A *mint* transaction creates tokens in an account, while a *transfer* transaction debits the caller's account and credits another account. To test the model, we allowed all the participants to call the *mint* function to create a certain limited amount in their account. The smart contract *mint* function takes the client certificate as the client identity through an API and credits their account with the requested number of tokens. To transfer money to another account, a *transfer* function is called to transfer the requested tokens to the account of the recipient. The recipient should provide their client ID to the sender to complete the transfer. The following is an example of a financial interaction between the *Customer* and the *Designer* where the customer calls the *mint* function to generate 7000 tokens and then transfer 300 to the *Designer*:

	Smart contract 4: Transfer money
1	**Input:***ctx, designer_id, customer_id*
	mint(*customer_id*, 7000)
2	*customer_balance* ← get available mints (*customer_id*) // *output*: 7000
3	*designer_balance* ← get available mints (*designer_id*) // *output*: 0
4	*accountId* = get account id(*designer_id*)
	transfer from customer to designer(*customer_id, accountId, 300);*
5	*customer_balance* ← get available mints (*customer_id*) // *output*: 6700
6	*designer_balance* ← get available mints (*designer_id*) // *output*: 300

4.5 Private Channel Transactions

Hyperledger Fabric uses an immutable ledger for each channel in addition to the chaincode that manipulates the state of assets. This ledger either can be visible to all the network participants or can be limited to a specific subset of participants. In the latter case, participants will have their segregated transactions and ledger. To balance between total transparency in the network and the needed privacy between subgroups of participants, we created dedicated channels for subsets of participants and authorized them to use their private data. We further obfuscated the data by encrypting the values in the chaincode using the AES cryptographic algorithm before sending it to the ordering service which will append it to a block in the ledger. The encrypted data in the ledger can only be decrypted using the user key that was used to encrypt the data.

4.6 Blockchain Integration

As discussed before, we selected the Odoo open-source platform as an industrial information system and the Hyperledger Fabric as the blockchain platform. We established a small manufacturing supply chain scenario involving five actors being customer, manufacturer, designer, transporter, and supplier. These actors are collaborating in order to make a product. Figure 3 represents a diagram of this supply chain.

All actor interfaces are implemented in Odoo. However, the transactions that are undertaken between actors, which traditionally should be undertaken in Odoo, are performed in the blockchain using smart contracts. Odoo only interacts with the blockchain and triggers critical transactions. All communication between Odoo and Hyperledger is performed using a broker component implemented in Node.JS which conveys all the transactions that will be executed in the blockchain using smart contracts from Odoo. The broker relies on the Hyperledger JavaScript SDK for connecting the broker to the blockchain network. A RESTful API was established to allow secure and reliable communication between Odoo and Hyperledger Fabric. This API implements all the necessary security tools to allow communication between both platforms.

All client interfaces for workflow management were adapted to get use of the API broker. Figure 9 shows the Odoo interface for the design contract between the customer and the designer. The interface implements all the usual UI elements such as lists, etc. The transaction state is the most obvious data field that only gets changed following an invocation of the smart contract associated with the task.

As depicted in Fig. 9, we can see the interface allowing interaction with the design workflow. The current state of the design is a value that is controlled by the smart contract deployed in the blockchain. The colored buttons control the state of the design contract. Switching from a state to another is conditioned by business logic rules that are enforced in both Odoo and the smart contract to ensure the soundness of the system. As an example, the design cannot be moved to the delivered state unless a file is attached. This is enforced in Odoo to notify the user before the action is sent to the blockchain, and if by any chance the restriction in Odoo is not enforced due to an issue or due a tampering attempt, the smart contract will not shift to the delivered state if a file is not attached. Additionally, as can be seen in Fig. 9, it is worth noting the UI element displaying the PDF file of the design was customized by us. Figure 10 shows the Kanban view of the designs organized by their status.

4.7 Tests and Evaluations

To test and evaluate our proof of concept, we implemented the complete workflow of the interaction between the customer and the designer in our small-scale supply chain. In the following, we present the typical workflow of providing a design between the designer and the customer following a request to issue a design coming from the customer. The actor performing these actions is the designer. The contract which is named "Design contract" has six states, three of which are highlighted in this example (2, Initiated; 4, Started working on the design; 6, Delivered). The other

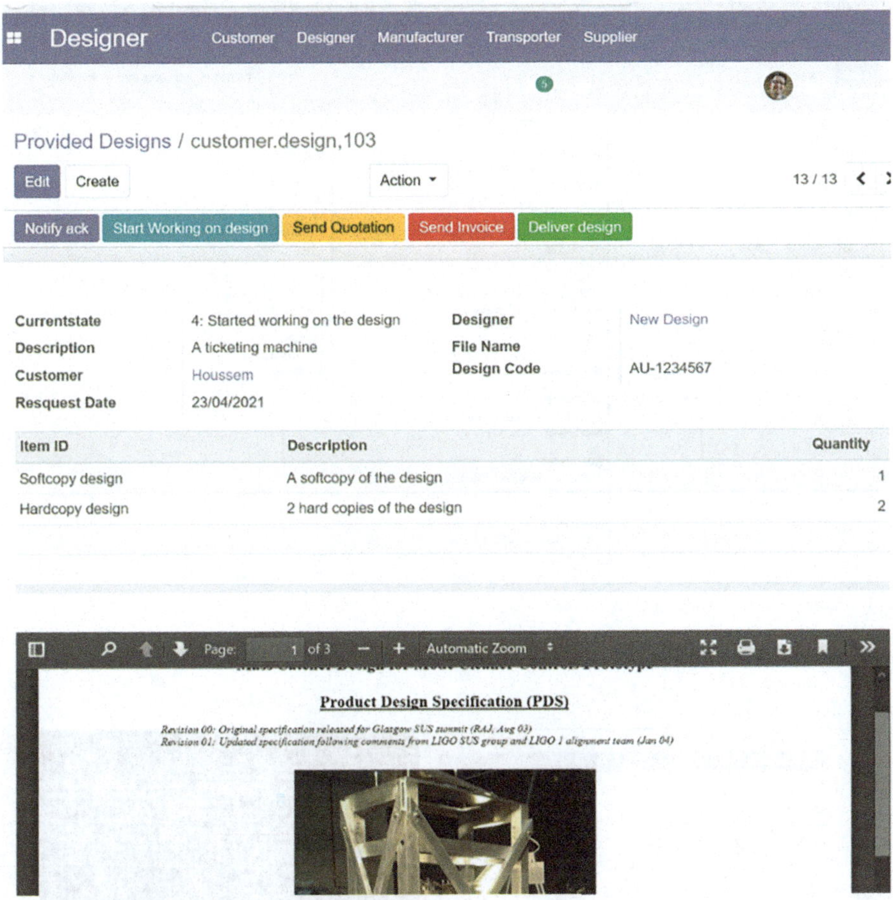

Fig. 9 Odoo interface

states are intermediate states or exceptions. A rule stating that the contract cannot move to the final state (6) unless the design includes a file is included in the smart contract.

1. The **first** step highlighted in Fig. 11 is the initiation of the contract by the customer.
2. The **second** step highlighted in Fig. 12 is the contract state from the perspective of the designer after he acknowledges it and clicks "Start working on the design" button.
3. The **third** step highlighted in Fig. 13 is the design edition interface where all the information, as well as the file, are added.

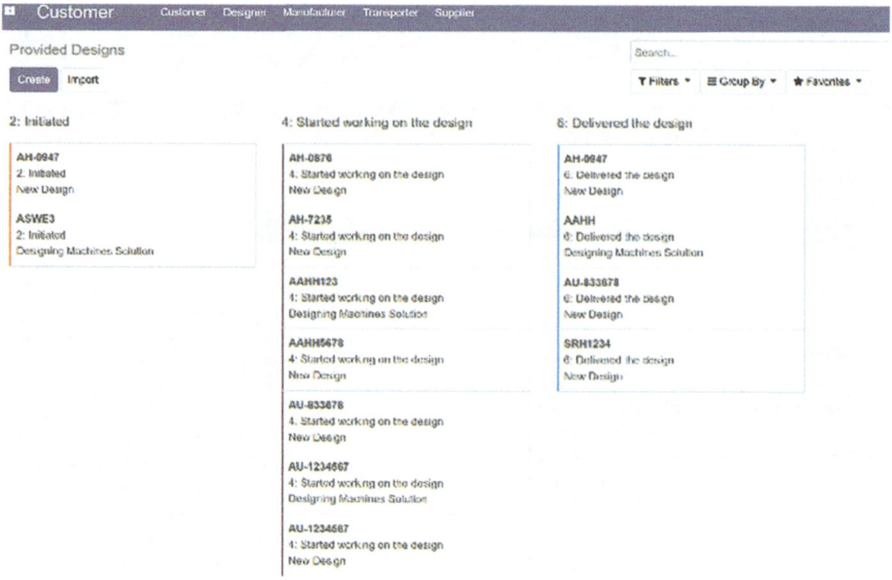

Fig. 10 Designs *Kanban* view (status from the blockchain)

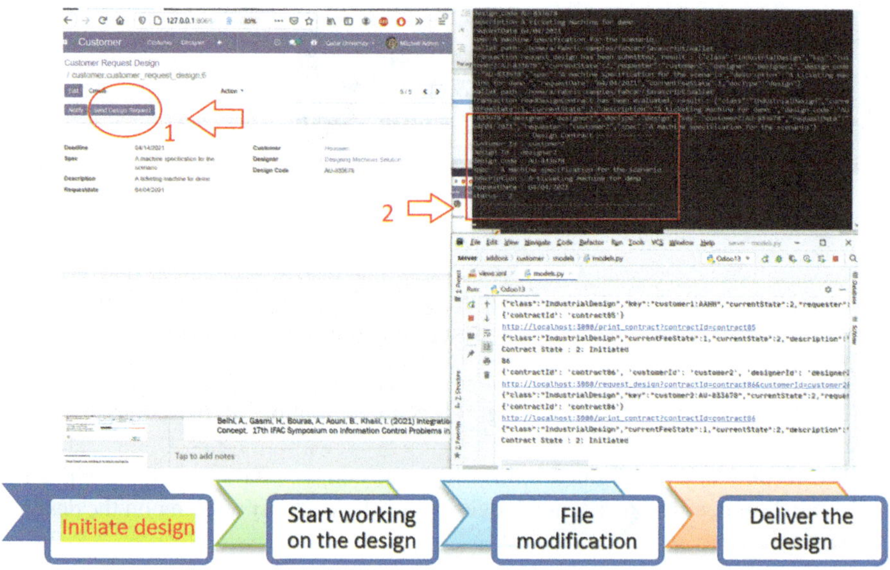

Fig. 11 Customer initiates the design

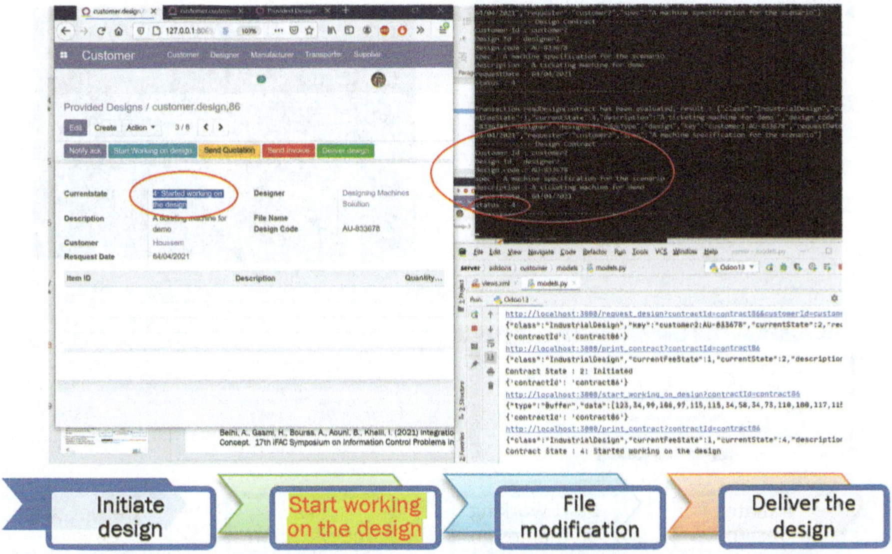

Fig. 12 The designer starts working on the design

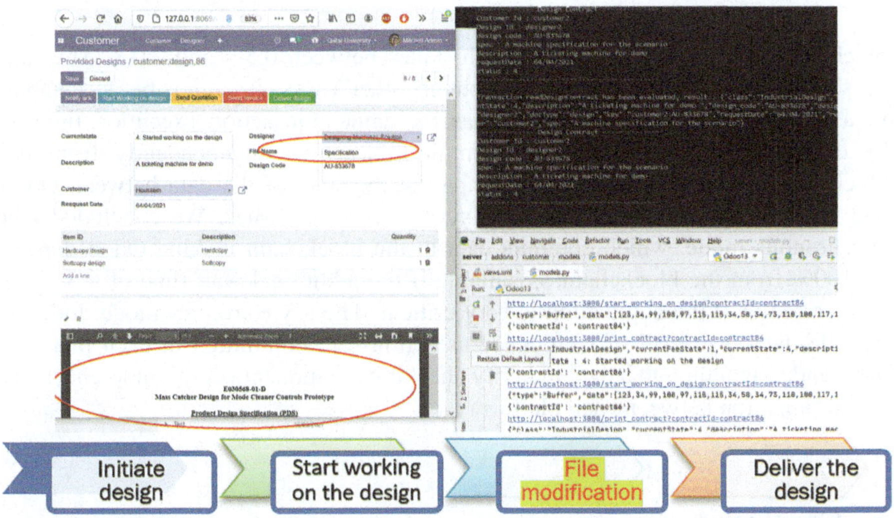

Fig. 13 The designer edits the design and adds the file

4. The **final** step which is highlighted in Fig. 14 is the final step where the designer delivers the design.

As per the evaluation in terms of time. Adding an extra software component indeed adds more complexity. In the synchronous mode and depending on the integration strategy in the API broker, the average delay to get a commit from the

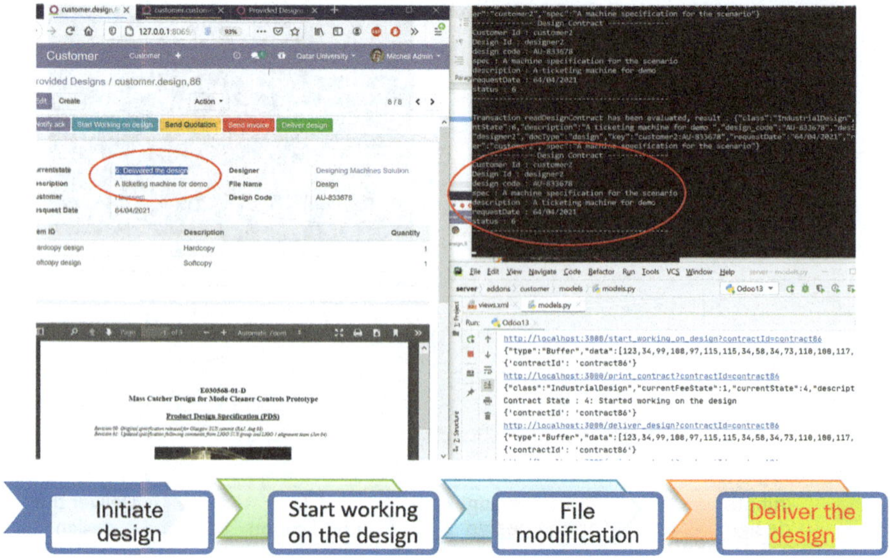

Fig. 14 The designer delivers the design

blockchain in Odoo (bidirectional path) takes between 0.5 s and 2.0 s. This can be seen as tolerable in some cases, but in other cases, it cannot be acceptable. In asynchronous mode, the system has the same transaction execution time as by default. However, Odoo will commit transactions independently from the blockchain. Data integrity checks comparing the state of the data between Odoo and blockchain are used to spot any synchronization issues. We concluded that synchronous mode, which commits data in the blockchain making Odoo depend on 100% from the blockchain, is suitable if the additional wait time of 0.5–2.0 s is tolerable or if the application is very critical. The asynchronous mode does not provide the same level of confidence as actions are committed in each platform independently although a data integrity checking component is present to check the synchronization between each platform.

5 Conclusion

Blockchain's impact on manufacturing and industrial applications was compared by some people to the wheel invention. This disruptive technology showed its potential in revolutionizing product design and manufacturing in many ways. In this chapter, we were interested in ways to integrate this technology with industrial information systems such as PLM, ERP, WMS, etc. We presented a broker-based integration of blockchain smart contracts with industrial workflows. We used Hyperledger Fabric as a permissioned blockchain platform to store the transaction data and manage the life cycle of smart contracts. Hyperledger Fabric was mainly selected as it is an open-source platform used extensively in the enterprise environment. As for the information system, we used Odoo which is an open-source framework written in Python. We presented our proof-of-concept integration with a scenario of a small-scale manufacturing supply chain involving a limited number of actors and demonstrated that the Odoo workflows can easily be adapted to be fully managed using smart contracts, thus increasing the security and enhancing the traceability and trust of critical business transactions. We highlighted the fact that we have two main integration strategies although we only presented a broker-based one. The integration based on the common meta-model (interoperability) will be subject to our future works.

Acknowledgments This publication was made possible by NPRP grant NPRP11S-1227-170135 from the Qatar National Research Fund (a member of Qatar Foundation). The statements made herein are solely the responsibility of the authors (www.supplyledger.qa).

References

1. Thiraviya Suyambu, G., Anand, M., & Janakirani, M. (2020). Blockchain – A most disruptive technology on the spotlight of world engineering education paradigm. In *Procedia computer science* (pp. 152–158). Elsevier B.V. https://doi.org/10.1016/j.procs.2020.05.023
2. Belhi, A., Bouras, A., Patel, M. K., & Aouni, B. (2020). Blockchains: A conceptual assessment from a product lifecycle implementation perspective. In *IFIP international conference on product lifecycle management* (pp. 576–589).
3. Rahman, M. S., Khalil, I., & Bouras, A. (2021). A framework for modelling blockchain based supply chain management system to ensure soundness of smart contract workflow. In *BT – 54th Hawaii International Conference on System Sciences, HICSS 2021, Kauai, Hawaii, USA, January 5, 2021.*, http://hdl.handle.net/10125/71295
4. Pal, K., & Yasar, A. U. H. (2020). Internet of things and blockchain technology in apparel manufacturing supply chain data management. In *Procedia computer science* (pp. 450–457). Elsevier B.V. https://doi.org/10.1016/j.procs.2020.03.088
5. Shahbazi, Z., & Byun, Y.-C. (2021). Integration of blockchain, IoT and machine learning for multistage quality control and enhancing security in smart manufacturing. *Sensors, 21*, 1467. https://doi.org/10.3390/s21041467
6. Leng, J., Ruan, G., Jiang, P., Xu, K., Liu, Q., Zhou, X., & Liu, C. (2020). Blockchain-empowered sustainable manufacturing and product lifecycle management in industry 4.0: A survey. *Renewable and Sustainable Energy Reviews, 132*, 110112. ISSN 1364-0321. https://doi.org/10.1016/j.rser.2020.110112
7. Dietrich, F., Ge, Y., Turgut, A., Louw, L., & Palm, D. (2021). Review and analysis of blockchain projects in supply chain management. In *Procedia computer science* (pp. 724–733). Elsevier B.V. https://doi.org/10.1016/j.procs.2021.01.295
8. Lohmer, J., & Lasch, R. (2020). Blockchain in operations management and manufacturing: Potential and barriers. *Computers and Industrial Engineering, 149*, 106789. https://doi.org/10.1016/j.cie.2020.106789
9. Kurpjuweit, S., Schmidt, C. G., Klöckner, M., & Wagner, S. M. (2021). Blockchain in additive manufacturing and its impact on supply chains. *Journal of Business Logistics, 42*, 46–70. https://doi.org/10.1111/jbl.12231

10. Hasan, H. R., Salah, K., Jayaraman, R., Ahmad, R. W., Yaqoob, I., & Omar, M. (2020). Blockchain-based solution for the traceability of spare parts in manufacturing. *IEEE Access, 8*, 100308–100322. https://doi.org/10.1109/ACCESS.2020.2998159
11. Aghamohammadzadeh, E., & Fatahi Valilai, O. (2020). A novel cloud manufacturing service composition platform enabled by blockchain technology. *International Journal of Production Research, 58*, 5280–5298. https://doi.org/10.1080/00207543.2020.1715507
12. Yu, C., Jiang, X., Yu, S., & Yang, C. (2020). Blockchain-based shared manufacturing in support of cyber physical systems: Concept, framework, and operation. *Robotics and Computer-Integrated Manufacturing, 64*, 101931. https://doi.org/10.1016/j.rcim.2019.101931
13. Lee, J., Azamfar, M., & Singh, J. (2019). A blockchain enabled cyber-physical system architecture for industry 4.0 manufacturing systems. *Manufacturing Letters, 20*, 34–39. https:/ /doi.org/10.1016/j.mfglet.2019.05.003
14. Kim, H. M., & Laskowski, M. (2018). Toward an ontology-driven blockchain design for supply-chain provenance. *Intelligent Systems in Accounting, Finance and Management, 25*, 18–27.
15. Francisco, K., & Swanson, D. (2018). The supply chain has no clothes: Technology adoption of blockchain for supply chain transparency. *Logistics, 2*, 2.
16. Mattila, J., Seppälä, T., Holmström, J.: Product-centric information management: A case study of a shared platform with blockchain technology. (2016).
17. Madhwal, Y., & Panfilov, P. B. (2017). Blockchain and supply chain management: Aircrafts'parts'business case. *Annals of DAAAM Proceedings, 28*.
18. Singh, J., & Michels, J. D. (2018). Blockchain as a service (BaaS): Providers and trust. *Proceedings – 3rd IEEE European Symposium on Security and Privacy Workshop EURO S PW 2018*, 67–74. https://doi.org/10.1109/EUROSPW.2018.00015
19. Powell, L. M., Schwartz, J., & Hendon, M. (2021). The mobility open blockchain initiative: Identity, members, technologies, and future trends. In *Revolutionary applications of blockchain-enabled privacy and access control* (pp. 99–118). IGI Global.
20. Sureephong, P., Chakpitak, N., Buzon, L., Bouras, A.: Cluster development and knowledge exchange in supply chain., http://arxiv.org/abs/0806.0519, (2008).
21. Khedher, A. B., Henry, S., & Bouras, A. (2011). Integration between MES and product lifecycle management. In *ETFA2011* (pp. 1–8). https://doi.org/10.1109/ETFA.2011.6058993
22. Zahnentferner, J. (2018). Chimeric ledgers: Translating and unifying UTXO-based and account-based cryptocurrencies. *IACR Cryptology ePrint Archive, 2018*, 262.

Index

A. Bouras et al. (eds.), *Blockchain Driven Supply Chains and Enterprise Information Systems*, https://doi.org/10.1007/978-3-030-96154-1

R

S

T

The manufacturer's authorised representative in the EU is Springer Nature Customer Service Centre GmbH, Europaplatz 3, 69115 Heidelberg, Germany. If you have any concerns regarding our products, please contact ProductSafety@springernature.com

Printed and bound by CPI Group (UK) Ltd, Croydon, CR0 4YY
28/09/2026
02224091-0007